HAIL THE KING

A Verse-by-Verse Journey Through
the Book of Revelation

JEFF THOMPSON

LUCIDBOOKS

Hail the King
A Verse-by-Verse Journey Through the Book of Revelation

Copyright © 2024 by Jeff Thompson

Published by Lucid Books in Houston, TX
www.LucidBooks.com

All rights reserved. No part of this publication may be reproduced, stored in a retrieval system, or transmitted in any form by any means, electronic, mechanical, photocopy, recording, or otherwise, without the prior permission of the publisher, except as provided for by USA copyright law.

Scripture quotations marked (KJV) are taken from the King James Version (KJV): King James Version, public domain.

Scripture quotations marked (NKJV) are taken from the New King James Version®. Copyright © 1982 by Thomas Nelson. Used by permission. All rights reserved.

Scripture quotations marked (YLT) are taken from the 1898 Young's Literal Translation Of The Holy Bible by J.N. Young, (Author of the Young's Analytical Concordance), public domain.

ISBN: 978-1-63296-702-2 (Paperback)
ISBN: 978-1-63296-658-2 (Hardback)
eISBN: 978-1-63296-659-9

Special Sales: Most Lucid Books titles are available in special quantity discounts. Custom imprinting or excerpting can also be done to fit special needs. Contact Lucid Books at Info@LucidBooks.com

This book is dedicated to the men of God who faithfully preached the Book of Revelation before me in churches large and small, believing the Word of God even when it seemed impossible.

Special Thanks

Charlene, for your love, encouragement, and kindness . . .

CONTENTS

Preface xvii

Introduction 1
   The Basics Of Eschatology..1
   The Main Eschatological Views 3
   Problems With Post-Millennialism And Amillennialism................7
   The Rapture According To Premillennialism.................................8
   Why Take A Literal Approach To The Biblical Text? 10
   Is The Book Of Revelation For Academics Only? 15
   Testing Your Eschatology..16
   Closing Thoughts 18

Preview Of The Book Of Revelation 20
   Outline Of Revelation..22

Revelation 1 26
   Greeting The Seven Churches..30
   Vision Of The Son Of Man..34
   No Words Can Contain His Glory..37
   What Happened To John At The Sight Of Jesus? 39
   Jesus' Titles 40
   Closing Thoughts 41

Revelation 2:1–7 43
- Introduction To The Seven Churches 43
- Map of the Seven Churches..43
- Textually Common Traits Among The Churches........................46
- The Church In Ephesus 47
- History And Culture Of Ephesus 47
- Into The Text...50
- Closing Thoughts 68

Revelation 2:8–11 69
- The Church In Smyrna..69
- History And Culture Of Smyrna 70
- Into The Text...74
- Application To All Churches 89
- Application To All Believers..92
- Closing Thoughts 93

Revelation 2:12–17 95
- The Church In Pergamos...95
- History And Culture Of Pergamos 96
- Into The Text...104
- Application To All Churches 117
- Application To All Believers..118

Revelation 2:18–29 121
- The Church In Thyatira..121
- History And Culture Of Thyatira 123
- Into The Text...125
- Application To All Churches 144
- Application To All Believers..145
- Closing Thoughts 146

CONTENTS

Revelation 3:1–6 .... **148**
    The Church In Sardis 148
    History And Culture Of Sardis 149
    Into The Text 159
    Application To All Churches 174
    Application To All Believers 174

Revelation 3:7–13 .... **176**
    The Church In Philadelphia 176
    History And Culture Of Philadelphia 177
    Into The Text 184
    Application To All Churches 200
    Application To Individual Believers 200
    Closing Thoughts And An Assignment 201

Revelation 3:14–22 .... **202**
    The Church In Laodicea 202
    History And Culture Of Laodicea 204
    Into The Text 212
    Application To All Churches 234
    Application To All Believers 234
    Closing Thoughts On The Seven Churches –
    The End Is Approaching 236

The Rapture **239**
    Reflecting On The Letters To The Seven Churches 239
    Into The Text (Revelation 4:1–2) 241
    Jesus On The Rapture 247
    Pattern Is Prophecy: The Traditional Jewish Wedding 248
    The Righteous Are Spared From God's Wrath 251
    The Second Coming Of Christ 253
    What The Time Of The Rapture Will Look Like 255

Birth Pangs	256
The Days Of Noah And Lot	260
The Rapture Will Be A Global Event	262
1 Thessalonians 4:13–18	263
Harpazo	265
Back To 1 Thessalonians 4	267
Closing Thoughts	268

Revelation 4 270

The Church In Heaven	270
The Throne Room Of Heaven	271
The 24 Elders	274
A Storm Brewing	278
Sea Of Glass	279
The Four Living Creatures	280
Crowns As Rewards	283
Jesus, The Creator	287
Jesus Seated At The Right Hand Of The Father	288
Closing Thoughts	290

Revelation 5 292

The Title Deed	292
The Scroll	293
History Of The Typical Title Deed Scroll	293
The Title Deed To The Earth	294
"Worthy Is The Lamb"	311
The Divine Council	313
Closing Thoughts	315

Revelation 6 318

The First Six Seals	318
Isaiah 61 And The Day Of Vengeance	318
The Purpose Of The Tribulation	320

CONTENTS

Understanding God's Wrath 321
The Coming "Day Of The Lord" 324
The First Horseman/Seal: Antichrist 325
The Significance Of The Bow 329
A Sidenote On Timing 333
The Second Horseman/Seal: War 334
The Third Horseman/Seal: Famine 334
The Fourth Horseman/Seal: Widespread Death On Earth 336
The Fifth Seal: The Cry Of The Martyrs 339
The Sixth Seal: Cosmic Disturbances 341
Looking Ahead 344
Chart of the Judgments of Revelation 345
Closing Thoughts 345

Revelation 7 .... **347**
The 144,000 And The Great Revival 347
A Renewed Focus On Israel 347
Who Can Stand? 350
The Sealed Servants 351
Sealing In The Old Testament 356
Is Pure Tribal Dna Possible? 357
The "Missing" Tribes 357
The Saved Servants 358
Palm Branches 359
Three Distinct Groups 364
Palm Sunday 367
Closing Thoughts 369

Revelation 8 .... **370**
The First Four Trumpets 370
Prelude To The Seventh Seal: Silence In Heaven 370
First Trumpet: Vegetation Is Struck 376

Second Trumpet: The Seas Are Struck 378
   Third Trumpet: The Waters Are Struck 379
   Wormwood 381
   Fourth Trumpet: The Heavens Are Struck 382
   Woe To Earth's Inhabitants 384
   Closing Thoughts 385

Revelation 9 .... **389**
   Trumpets Five And Six 389
   Fifth Trumpet: Locusts From The Bottomless Pit 389
   The Abyss 390
   Sixth Trumpet: Angels From The Euphrates 400
   Closing Thoughts 410

Revelation 10–11:2 .... **412**
   The Mighty Angel With The Little Book 413
   John Eats The Little Book 419
   The New Temple In Jerusalem 423
   The Temple Mount And A Peace Plan 428
   3.5 Years 430
   Closing Thoughts 434

Revelation 11:3–19 .... **435**
   The Two Witnesses 435
   The Identity Of The Two Witnesses 440
   The Deaths Of Elijah And Moses 442
   Elijah And Fire From Heaven 444
   Other Powers Of The Two Witnesses 446
   The Two Witnesses Killed 447
   The Two Witnesses Resurrected 449
   The Seventh Trumpet Begins 452
   Closing Thoughts 458

CONTENTS

Revelation 12:1–6 462
    The Enigma Of Israel 462
    The Woman, The Child, And The Dragon 463
    Lucifer's Fall 466
    Why Satan Tries To Destroy Israel 467
    Israel Flees 472
    Where Does Israel Go? 475
    Israel's Preservation In Isaiah 479
    Closing Thoughts 480

Revelation 12:7–17 482
    How To Overcome 482
    Into The Text 483
    Satan's Tactics 486
    More Of Satan's Tactics 488
    How To Overcome Satan 491
    Satan On Borrowed Time 495
    The Woman/Israel Is Persecuted 496
    Closing Thoughts 499

Revelation 13:1–10 501
    The Antichrist's Regime (Part 1) 501
    The Beast From The Sea 502
    Daniel 7 Unlocks V.2 504
    The Roman Empire 509
    The Source Of Antichrist's Power 511
    Antichrist's "Resurrection" 511
    Closing Thoughts 520

Revelation 13:11–18 522
    The Antichrist's Regime (Part 2) 522
    The Image Of Antichrist And Daniel 3 529

What Is The Image?..530
The Mark Of The Beast...531
The Number Of The Beast 535
What Scripture Says About The Mark And
Number Of The Beast 536
Closing Thoughts 539

Revelation 14 .... **543**
The Lamb And The 144,000 543
Three Angels Speak From The Sky...................................553
Comfort For Tribulation Saints 560
The Fullness Of The Gentiles 562
The Grapes Of Wrath 563
Closing Thoughts 566

Revelation 15–16 .... **569**
The Seven Bowl Judgments 569
Setting Up The Bowl Judgments......................................570
First Bowl: Sores..575
Second Bowl: The Sea Of Blood 577
Third Bowl: Other Waters Turned To Blood 578
Fourth Bowl: Heat Wave 579
Fifth Bowl: A Preview Of The Outer Darkness 580
Sixth Bowl: Euphrates Dried Up 582
Seventh Bowl: The Earth Utterly Shaken.........................586
Closing Thoughts 589

Revelation 17 .... **591**
The Woman Of Highly Questionable Character..............591
The Mystery (Vv.1–6) 592
Who Is The Harlot?...593
The Explanation (Vv.7–18) 595
More On Nimrod 596

CONTENTS

Back To The Text 600
Why The Woman Is Not The Roman Catholic Church 607
Back To The Scarlet Woman And The Scarlet Beast 611
Closing Thoughts 613

Revelation 18 .... **614**
The Fall Of Economic Babylon 614
Into The Text 617
Conspiracies And Comparisons 628
"Babylonians" Compared To Laodiceans 630
What James Says About The Coming Destruction
Of Babylon 633
Closing Thoughts 635

Revelation 19:1–10 .... **637**
The Second Coming (Part 1) 637
Heaven Rejoices Over The Death Of Babylon 638
The Marriage Supper Of The Lamb Is Announced 641
Parallels Between A Traditional Jewish Wedding
And The Church's Destiny 645
Closing Thoughts 651

Revelation 19:11–21 .... **652**
The Second Coming (Part 2) 652
The Beast And His Armies Defeated 659
More Scriptures On The Second Coming 667
Israel's Destiny 669
Closing Thoughts 671

Revelation 20:1–6 .... **673**
The Millennial Kingdom 673
Exploring Millennial Views 673
Satan Bound 1,000 Years 676

Who Goes Into The Millennium?...680
The Millennium 686
We Crave Life In The Millennium 689
The Millennium In Isaiah 65...690
Closing Thoughts 692

Revelation 20:7–15 .... **694**
The Final Judgment...694
Satanic Rebellion Crushed...694
The Great White Throne Judgment 699
The Second Resurrection 701
A Logical Problem With Annihilationism..................................704
Back To The Text...704
Accountability For Revelation Received......................................707
Refuting Partial Annihilationism Regarding Time 708
Back To The Books..709
Closing Thoughts 711

Revelation 21:1–5 .... **716**
The Hope Of Heaven 716
A New Reality 719
Our Good Passions Still Intact 725
Knowing People In Heaven 726
Loving The Lord More Than Those We've Lost 728
All Things New 732
Closing Thoughts 735

Revelation 21:6–27 .... **737**
The New Jerusalem..737
Our Inheritance 741
A Warning..743
The New Jerusalem..746
12 Gates – 12 Apostles 747

CONTENTS

The Glory Of The New Jerusalem 752
Closing Thoughts 754

Revelation 22 .... **757**
Amen 757
The River Of Life 757
From Genesis To Revelation 761
Resurrected Bodies 762
The Time Is Near 769
Jesus Testifies To The Churches 776
A Final Warning 779
"I Am Coming Quickly" 781
Closing Thoughts 781

Appendix A: End-Times Review **784**

Appendix B: How Do We Know The Tribulation Will Last Seven Years? **790**
Key Phases Of Daniel's Prophecy 798
Events Between The 69th Week And The 70th Week 798
The 70th Week 801
The Church Age 803

Appendix C: The Theology Of Supersessionism **805**

Appendix D: Differences Between Gog And Magog In Ezekiel And Revelation **807**

Notes **810**

PREFACE

You've likely heard the saying, *"Jack of all trades, master of none."* But did you know that it's a misquote? Benjamin Franklin coined the original phrase, and his exact words were, *"Jack of all trades, master of ONE."* It encapsulated Franklin's belief that everyone should know something about everything and everything about something.

Every person should become an expert in something, and I suggest that every Christian's area of expertise should be the Bible. We shouldn't know more about politics or Pokémon or conspiracy theories or sports than we do about the Scriptures. Growing in our knowledge of God's Word should be the lifelong pursuit of everyone who follows Jesus.

If you're not a Christian or if you're a skeptic of Bible prophecy, I believe the best way I could prove the Bible's integrity to you would be to present multiple prophecies that have already been fulfilled. After all, if the Bible has a track record of perfectly predicting events, then it would be reasonable for us to take seriously those prophecies within its pages that are yet to be fulfilled. And when we reach **Revelation 2–3**, that's exactly what we'll find as we encounter some mind-blowing examples of fulfilled Bible prophecies.

Whether you are a believer or not, I'm glad you're reading this. And if you'll approach this study with an open mind and a desire for the truth, I believe you will be *astounded* by what will be revealed in the pages of this book.

My desire to know more about Bible prophecy started early. I recall a time when I was 16 and riding in a Chevy Suburban packed with friends from my church's youth group. We were talking about crazy things in the Bible, and it wasn't long before someone said,

> *"Dude, have you read Revelation? There are dragons and beasts coming out of the sea, angels of death, and all kinds of crazy stuff in there!"*

We all laughed at one of Christianity's classic inside jokes—that pretty much nobody really knows what's going on in the Book of Revelation. And for most believers, that inside joke holds true for the rest of their lives—and for good reason. While you can jump into almost any other book in the Bible and figure out what's going on relatively quickly, Revelation can feel like you're dropping in on someone else's apocalyptic LSD trip.

In the rare instances when I encountered a church or pastor teaching from Revelation over the years, they would very selectively focus on the few verses they understood and sweep away the rest of the book with a comment like, *"Jesus wins in the end, and that's all that matters."*

Over the years, I gleaned a few snippets of information from books, low-budget end-times movies, and the odd sermon. After walking with Jesus for years, my understanding of Revelation still sounded something like this:

> *"I'm pretty sure Jesus comes back at some point . . . and there might be a Rapture . . . there's an antichrist . . . a Battle of Armageddon . . . something with 666 . . . and lots of bad stuff that's going to happen."*

My knowledge of what the Bible teaches about the end-times was scattered and lacked any semblance of a cohesive understanding. I felt like I had seven pieces of a 100-piece puzzle. I couldn't see the big picture, and I had no idea how the pieces I had fit with the rest of the puzzle. Perhaps you can relate.

Then at the age of 23, I took a position at a church where the pastor was halfway through a message series on the Book of Revelation. I was surprised and asked someone, *"You mean the parts we can understand?"* I was even more surprised when they replied, *"No, the whole thing. We're going through the book verse by verse."* As an employee of the church, I didn't want to look completely confused, so I nodded politely while thinking, *"How is that possible?"*

I listened attentively to the rest of the series and then went back and listened to the recordings of the messages I had missed. By the time I had listened to the full series, I was surprised to find that I actually *understood it*. I *understood* the Book of Revelation! I understood every chapter and practically every verse, and it changed my life.

My prayer is that you would have a similar experience, and I've written this book believing in faith that you will because as we shall see in Chapter 1, God *wants* you to understand the Book of Revelation. So, let's get to it!

INTRODUCTION

THE BASICS OF ESCHATOLOGY

The first word we need to learn on this journey is "eschatology." It's the term used for the theological study of Bible prophecies related to the end of the world, "the end-times" or "the last days." If you're studying eschatology, you're studying end-times Bible prophecies, which is what we'll be doing in this journey through Revelation.

Within Christendom, there is a frequently repeated critique of those who love to dig into eschatology, and it goes something like this: *"If you're too Heavenly minded, you'll be no earthly good."* I remember opening a prominent Christian music magazine and reading their review of a concept album that a well-known artist had just released. All the songs were focused on Heaven and Jesus' coming for His Church. It was a brilliant album. But the reviewer accused the album of *"suffering from 'I'll Fly Away' syndrome."*

Both critiques are rooted in the belief that Christians too focused on the coming of Jesus and eternity in Heaven will neglect the things they should be doing for Jesus on the earth, here and now. The assumption is that they'll live useless lives as they waste their days gazing longingly toward the heavens instead of sharing the Gospel and occupying themselves with the work of the Kingdom.

My testimony and that of countless others is that eschatology has the completely opposite effect on a person. Because the reality is that you won't be any earthly good *until* you're Heavenly minded!

Most Christians are familiar with the importance of storing up treasure in Heaven and living for eternity rather than placing too much value on the temporal nature of our earthly lives. What Revelation does is move that knowledge from the head to the heart. Instead of having a blurry and vague concept of the end-times, Revelation shifts your understanding into gloriously detailed high-definition to such a degree that the *reality* of what is to come overwhelms you in the best possible way.

Imagine if I told you that if you worked hard and sacrificially saved money for 50 years, you'd have a nice retirement. That would motivate you to a certain degree. Now imagine I told you the same thing, except this time I gave you a special pair of glasses that you could put on whenever you wanted, and they would allow you to *see* your future in detail. Imagine putting those glasses on and seeing yourself smiling and laughing with your spouse, surrounded by your adult children and your grandchildren, in a wonderful house, in a beautiful setting. Imagine *seeing* your comfort and how good things will be. You would become significantly more motivated to save for your retirement. And anytime you were feeling uninspired or tired of the work, sacrifice, and discipline, you could simply put on the glasses, take one more look at that glorious future, and find fresh motivation.

That's what Revelation does for the person who reads and understands it. It makes the *reality* of Heaven and eternity so vivid that it inspires a deeper level of wholehearted, sacrificial living for Jesus during one's earthly life.

That's why the time you take to study this book will be one of the most profitable investments you will ever make.

THE MAIN ESCHATOLOGICAL VIEWS

I feel a responsibility to inform you upfront that eschatology is *not* a salvation issue. Our beliefs regarding the Rapture, Tribulation, antichrist, etc., have no bearing on our eternal destination. We are saved by placing our faith in the substitutionary life, death, and resurrection of Jesus—not by perfecting our end-times theology. There are many reasons to study what the Bible says about eschatology, as we shall see, but salvation is not one of them. So, please relax and know that if you don't hold my views on the Book of Revelation, but you do love Jesus, we're still part of the same spiritual family on the same journey, seeking to know and understand more about our Lord.

I encourage you to not believe anything I say simply because you read it in this book. Do your own research. Dig into the Scriptures for yourself. Our goal is to be like the Bereans, who, when visited by the Apostle Paul,[1] did not take anything he said at face value but instead searched the Scriptures for themselves to see if what Paul was teaching was the truth. And Paul *commended* them for doing so.

If you don't hold my views on eschatology, I'm honored that you're reading this, and I applaud your desire to know God's Word more deeply. I believe that it's always good to familiarize oneself

---

[1] Cf. Acts 17:10–11.

with other theological perspectives, as the truth can stand up to whatever scrutiny we place it under.

And speaking of different views, I thought it might be helpful to provide a brief overview of the three most popular eschatological views. One of the positions has three sub-positions, but we'll explain that when we get there. These will be broad, generalized descriptions because they would take up this whole book if they weren't. So, regardless of your current view, please know that I'm doing my best to represent each perspective *accurately* but *briefly*. And while this might all sound a bit technical, hang with me—this Introduction is as technical as we'll get in this book.

When it comes to how Christians view the end-times, the first divergence of views takes place around the issue of the *Millennium*. The Millennium is spoken of in many places in Scripture, but perhaps most famously in **Revelation 20:4–6**, where we read:

> **. . . I saw thrones, and they sat on them, and judgment was committed to them. Then *I saw* the souls of those who had been beheaded for their witness to Jesus and for the word of God, who had not worshiped the beast or his image, and had not received *his* mark on their foreheads or on their hands. And they lived and reigned with Christ for <u>a thousand years</u>. But the rest of the dead did not live again until <u>the thousand years</u> were finished. This *is* the first resurrection. Blessed and holy *is* he who has part in the first resurrection. Over such the second death has no power, but they shall be priests of God and of Christ, and shall reign with Him <u>a thousand years</u>.**

I know there's a whole bunch of stuff in that passage you may not understand yet, and I promise we'll explain it later (when we

INTRODUCTION 5

reach **Revelation 20**). What I want you to notice for now is all the references to a specific period of 1,000 years. This is the Millennium we're talking about. And when it comes to *this* Millennium, all Christians agree that it's *something*, but we have significant disagreements over *what* exactly it is.

The three main views on eschatology derive from how we view the *relationship* between the Millennium of **Revelation 20** and the future earthly return of Jesus. This will become clear as we go through each position.

How you interpret the Millennium of **Revelation 20** will inform your overall interpretation of the Book of Revelation. If you believe it to be *figurative*, you will interpret most of Revelation *figuratively*. If you believe it to be *literal*, you will interpret most of Revelation *literally*.

With that in mind, let me try to briefly lay out the three main views on the Millennium:

1. **Premillennial** – "Pre" means "before." This view holds that Jesus will physically return to the earth *before* the Millennium begins. Jesus will return with His Church and reign with them from His throne in Jerusalem for the *literal* thousand years of the Millennium. During this time, the earth will be redeemed to an Eden-like state, and Satan will be bound. At the end of the thousand years, Satan will be released to offer a final choice to humanity, which will result in the rebellion of some, a final judgment of those who rejected Jesus, and the eternal damnation of Satan and his legions. The universe will then be destroyed, and new heavens and a new earth will be created.

2. **Post-Millennial** – "Post" means "after." This view holds that the Gospel will spread across the earth with increasing success to such a degree that eventually, almost all people will turn to Jesus. This Gospel movement will culminate in a golden age[2] in which Christian ethics and character will rule humanity through the Church. *After* this, Jesus will physically return to the Christianized earth to conduct a final resurrection and judgment.

   The Post-Millennial view, which holds that the Church's influence is destined to steadily increase, is a significant factor in the rising popularity of movements such as Christian Nationalism and Theonomy.

3. **Amillennial** – "A" means "no" or "none." This view holds that the Millennium of **Revelation 20** is *figurative* or *mystical* rather than literal (in length and detail). According to this view, the Millennium refers to the Church Age, which began on Pentecost in **Acts 2** around AD 32 and continues to the present day. Jesus' reign during this "Millennium" is *spiritual*, and as the Gospel spreads across the earth, all things are being redeemed. The crescendo of this redemptive movement will be the physical return of Jesus to oversee a final judgment and rule over the restored heavens and earth.

4. **Preterism** is the view that the events described in Revelation all took place around the fall of Israel and Jerusalem (~AD 70) in the first century AD. Technically, Preterism falls under the Amillennial view.

---

[2] Generally not viewed as a literal thousand years.

INTRODUCTION

While each position has more detail and nuances, that's the *broad* overview.

PROBLEMS WITH POST-MILLENNIALISM AND AMILLENNIALISM

When we conclude our study through Revelation, I believe you'll understand why I hold the views I do. But while we're here, I want to share a few thoughts about Post-Millennialism and Amillennialism and why I don't hold those positions.

As I just mentioned, Amillennialism is the view that there is *no* literal Millennium. It's entirely figurative, mystical, and/or spiritual in nature. In this view, the Gospel is spreading across the earth, all things are being made new, and the Church is called to partner with Jesus in that work here and now. Things are trending up and will continue to do so until practically the whole earth is redeemed, at which time Jesus will return to the earth.

Post-Millennialism has similar views, except it holds that there will be a literal thousand years of the Church reigning on the earth before Christ's return.

As respectfully as I can say this, I feel like the past 2,000 years of human history disprove the notion that we're *trending up* here on planet earth. And I think that anyone paying attention to the world around them would be inclined to agree. All you have to do is look out your window, walk the streets, watch the news, get on the Internet, and it's obvious—things are *not* getting better. We are *not* trending up. Even nonbelievers overwhelmingly feel like things are getting worse, and the world is increasingly spiraling out of control. In summation, I believe that *observable reality* disproves Post-Millennialism and Amillennialism.

THE RAPTURE ACCORDING TO PREMILLENNIALISM

Another divergence among the eschatological views is centered on the Rapture of the Church.

"The Rapture" is the term given to a literal future event when Jesus will remove all those who are His (known collectively as "the Church") from the earth, meet them **"in the clouds,"**[3] and take them to be with Him in Heaven. The most well-known verses on the Rapture are found in **1 Thessalonians 4:16–17**, where Paul writes:

> **...the Lord Himself will descend from heaven with a shout, with the voice of an archangel, and with the trumpet of God. And the dead in Christ will rise first. Then we who are alive *and* remain shall be caught up together with them in the clouds to meet the Lord in the air. And thus we shall always be with the Lord.**

Note: Amillennialists and Post-Millennialists do not believe in any type of Rapture.

Under the Premillennial view, there are three main sub-views about the Rapture that have to do with its *timing*. These views differ specifically with where the Rapture occurs in relation to the seven-year Tribulation period described in **Revelation 6–19** (all your questions will be answered in later chapters of this book). For now, let's be content to understand the Tribulation as "the bad stuff that happens to those on the earth in the Book of Revelation."

---

[3] 1 Thessalonians 4:17.

In the graphic below, the three sub-views are shown on the second level of the chart:

1. **Post-Tribulation ("Post-Trib")** – The Church will be raptured *after* the Tribulation period (seven years).

2. **Mid-Tribulation ("Mid-Trib")** – The Church will be raptured at the *halfway point* of the Tribulation (three and a half years in).

3. **Pre-Tribulation ("Pre-Trib")** – The Church will be raptured *before* the Tribulation begins.

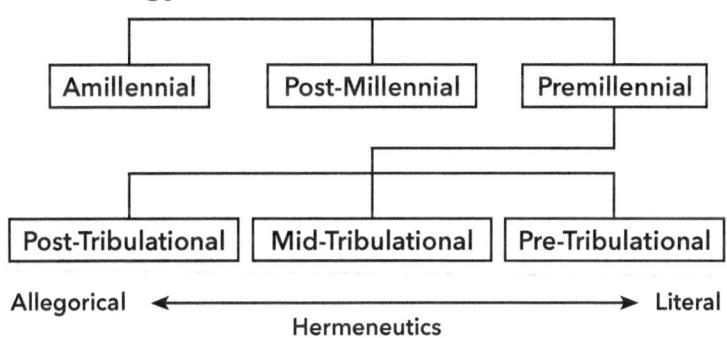

Regarding the word at the very bottom of the chart, "Hermeneutics" is the technical term for how we approach the task of interpreting the Bible.

- Generally, a *soft* hermeneutic approaches the Scriptures with a bent toward interpreting things *figuratively*, especially unfulfilled prophecies and miracles. From the chart, you can see that if you favor a *figurative* approach to Bible prophecy, you'll likely hold to an Amillennial eschatology and won't believe in any form of Rapture.

- Conversely, a *firm* hermeneutic approaches the Bible with the assumption that it is speaking *literally* unless there is a compelling reason to assume otherwise. If you favor **a** *literal* **approach** to God's Word, you'll probably hold a Premillennial eschatology and believe in a Rapture.

A person's hermeneutics have a significant impact on their theology—especially their eschatology. Let me be upfront with you about the view I take in this study: I employ a *firm* hermeneutic, which will lead us to affirm a *Premillennial, Pre-Trib* eschatology.

And if that's not your view, let me encourage you to stick with me to see *how* I reached that view. Then, once you've heard and seen the evidence, you can evaluate whether you think my conclusion is reasonable.

WHY TAKE A LITERAL APPROACH TO THE BIBLICAL TEXT?

Why start with a *firm* hermeneutic—a *literal* approach to the text? First, because conveying specific, literal meaning is the primary reason words and languages exist! We created words to communicate specific things.

If you think about it, we start by taking *all* text and conversation literally unless there is a compelling reason not to. If you say to me, *"Jeff, do you know where I can get a cup of coffee?"* it would be crazy for me to begin with the assumption that by *"cup of coffee,"* you meant *"the meaning of life."* Any reasonable person would start with the assumption that you were speaking literally instead of figuratively.

It only makes sense to approach the Word of God with the same rationale. We begin by assuming the Scriptures are speaking literally unless there is a good reason to suggest the text is speaking figuratively. For example, when Jesus tells His audience something that is described as a "parable," we know it is a fabricated story. We know that because the Bible *tells us* it's a parable. That's a good reason not to take Jesus' words literally in that instance. And there are many other good reasons not to take a text literally. But beginning with an assumption of literalism until contrary evidence appears is always the most logical approach to any text or conversation.

Second, we know that in the Old Testament, there are over 300 prophecies that speak of Jesus' First Coming (the Incarnation). The overwhelming majority of those are *literal*. We know this because Jesus has already fulfilled them.

The Bible contains significantly more prophecies relating to Jesus' *Second* Coming. If the prophecies concerning His First Coming were primarily fulfilled literally, why wouldn't we expect the prophecies that speak of His *Second* Coming to likewise be primarily fulfilled literally? What justification would we have for completely changing our hermeneutical approach to prophecy?

Or is the reality that we have no justification, and we simply find the Bible's end-times prophecies too fantastic, offensive, embarrassing, or hard to understand?

Some will say, *"Well, John's writings bear similarities to other apocalyptic secular writings of the time, and those writings were figurative, so Revelation must be part of that same genre."*

Really? Are we to believe there weren't savior or divine hero prophecies and mythologies in other cultures in the centuries before Jesus' First Coming, when the prophets were writing about the coming Messiah? Are we to believe that the surrounding cultures in Isaiah's time didn't have "prophecies" about a leader who would rise and deliver them? Of course, they did. We know this from archaeology. Did that mean the prophecies about Jesus being the Messiah *weren't* true or literal? Of course not. We know they were.

So, the question remains: How can we justify holding to a primarily *figurative* view of end-times prophecies in light of the *literal* nature of the prophecies concerning Jesus' *First* Coming?

Of course, there *are* many good reasons to not take a text literally. But the problem in the Church is that many approach the subject of Bible prophecy figuratively when there is *not* a good reason to do so. Here are some *bad* reasons to approach a biblical text allegorically:

1. "It's too hard to believe."

Many people struggle to accept some of the things written in the Bible because they seem impossible. They say, *"It's too fantastic. It's too 'out there.' It's too supernatural."* Perhaps the events violate the natural order or the rules of physics, creating an *intellectual* obstacle for the reader.

A person who finds the supernatural hard to believe does not just have a problem with Revelation or Bible prophecy. That person has a problem with *the Bible*. Because the pages of Scripture are *packed* with supernatural miracles, that person will have to allegorize the creation account, the global flood, the plagues of Egypt, the supernatural ministry of Jesus, the miracles of the Early Church, and on and on and on. Where does it end? It's a path that, if followed to its conclusion, will

INTRODUCTION

force that person to allegorize even the Resurrection—the central event of the Bible and Christianity.

The Bible *begins* with an overwhelming miracle:

In the beginning God created the heavens and the earth.

It has been rightly observed that if you can believe **Genesis 1:1**, you'll have no problem with the rest of the Bible. If you can believe that God made the entire universe—everything that exists—out of nothing, then you'll have no problem believing when you read about God working other miracles because the One who established and created the laws of nature must, rationally, be able to transcend them.

If you can accept that God *created* the universe out of nothing ("*ex nihilo*" in Latin), precisely the way He wanted to, does it not logically follow that He is equally capable of *ending* it exactly as He wants to? The beginning of the universe was astonishing, and its end shall be no less so.

From a Christian perspective, it doesn't make sense to reject a view of the end-times solely because it seems too fantastic. By that logic, one would also have to reject divine creation, the Resurrection, and countless other miracles recorded in the Bible.

And even from a purely scientific perspective, no view should be rejected simply because it seems unbelievable. At one time, the idea of the earth orbiting the sun seemed unbelievable. Every proposed view must be evaluated based on the *evidence*.

2. "It offends me . . . it's embarrassing."

I'll keep this one brief: Our feelings are irrelevant. God is *God*. He's not looking for suggestions on how the end of the world should go down, and He's certainly not concerned about whether His plans meet with our approval.

Furthermore, our feelings have no bearing on what is and is not true. The truth does not bend to our will. To pursue the truth in any field, we must check our feelings at the door.

3. "I don't understand it."

To allegorize a biblical text simply because we don't understand it is pure hubris. It is absolute arrogance. Because it means we have esteemed ourselves so highly that we are willing to claim, *"If I can't understand it, there's only one possible explanation: it cannot be understood."* Therefore, it must be allegorical, or something like that.

This approach leaves no room for the simple explanation that *we might not know everything*. There might be knowledge we have yet to acquire that would unlock our understanding of the text without reducing it to a vague metaphor.

There are good reasons not to interpret a text literally. But the three reasons I just mentioned are *not* good reasons. Unfortunately, they're probably the most popular reasons for not taking biblical prophecy literally.

INTRODUCTION

IS THE BOOK OF REVELATION FOR ACADEMICS ONLY?

Some take the stance that Revelation is impossible for a lay person to comprehend. They say, *"Revelation is allegorical, and to understand John's allegories, you must be well-versed in the apocalyptic literature of John's day. If you're not, you're wasting your time trying to make sense of it."*

Such reasoning implies that God has withheld the ability to understand the Book of Revelation from 99% of believers over the past 2,000 years because all those first-century Christians who weren't highly schooled or blessed with an academically elite pastor had *no hope* of understanding Revelation. But does that square with reality? When we read the Bible, do we see Jesus conducting His ministry or the Holy Spirit empowering the Church based on intellectual ability? No, we don't.

This view implies that when missionaries plant churches and when we share the Gospel with unbelievers, we might as well be handing out Bibles with all the texts related to the end-times removed because they won't be able to understand them anyway!

Because I don't want to give it all away, I'll just tell you that this view is *incompatible* with the first three verses of Revelation.

Familiarity with relevant historical literature, archaeology, and other subjects can add richness and new layers to our understanding of Scripture. But the truth remains that the Bible includes prophecy, and it was written for *all* believers. It was written for believers in places where all they have is a Bible. And if Jesus' selection of His disciples tells us anything, it's that He doesn't need highly educated men to get His message across. Praise God, you and I don't need to be highly educated to understand the message of the Scriptures—*including* end-times prophecies.

TESTING YOUR ESCHATOLOGY

While percentages vary wildly, every view of end-times Bible prophecy takes *some* of the text literally and *some* of the text figuratively. And whatever your current view, you need to be able to explain *why* you interpret certain parts of the Bible literally and other parts figuratively. As we've discussed, when it comes to the parts you take figuratively, the reasons should not be: *"It's too hard to believe," "It offends me,"* or *"I don't understand it."*

As we journey through Revelation, you will see *why* I take some parts literally and others figuratively. Why would anyone take the Second Coming of Christ *literally* but hold the Millennium to be *mystical*—especially when both events appear in the same chapter?[4] Why allegorize the Rapture but cling to a belief that the heavens and earth will be restored literally?

Whatever your view, it's important that you know how to *evaluate* your current eschatology. You can use two tests to determine the validity of your eschatology. First, can you explain *why* you take some biblical texts figuratively and others literally?

If the answer is, *"I don't know!"* I think that's a good thing. Because all of us need to be willing to recognize where we do and do not have a solid understanding or position in different areas of theology. I am 100% sure of my belief in the essentials of Christianity: that Jesus lived a perfect life, died on the Cross, and rose from the grave in my place; that the security of my salvation is by faith in Christ alone; and so on. But there are nonessential areas in which I'm not 100% sure yet. In some areas, I'm 50% sure; in others, I'm 60%, 70%, 80%, or 90% sure. I'm still working

---

[4] Revelation 20.

some stuff out. I'm not fully satisfied with some of my own answers yet.

I'm not trying to pick a fight with anybody. I'm simply trying to provoke us into asking good questions about our current eschatological beliefs.

Second, does your approach work everywhere in the Bible? I believe that this test will allow you to conclude for yourself which view of the end-times is most accurate. In fact, this is a test that will help you in *any* area of theological study. If, for example, you're evaluating different views on soteriology (the theology of salvation), pneumatology (the theology of the Holy Spirit), or in this instance, eschatology, this test will help you assess the different theological systems that exist within Christianity.

One's eschatology must be *affirmed*, not contradicted, by the rest of Scripture. In other words, if a doctrine is true, it will work and make sense *everywhere* it appears in the Bible. It won't work in the New Testament but not in the Old Testament. It won't work well with Paul but not so well with Jesus. If it's true, it'll work well *everywhere* in the Bible.

And I emphasize the word "well." Because sometimes, there's not a *direct* contradiction, but there are what I call "textual contortions." That is, some explanations and interpretations are clearly weak and stretch reason. When evaluating two or more theological views, ask questions such as these:

Which view works better across the whole text of the Bible?

Which view allows for the plainest reading of the text?

Which view requires the least "textual contortions"?

While there are end-times prophecies all over the Bible, I believe there are four "super texts" that any serious student of Bible prophecy must study:

- The Book of Revelation
- 1 and 2 Thessalonians
- The Olivet Discourse by Jesus in Matthew 24 and 25, Mark 13, and Luke 21
- The second half of the Book of Daniel

The most accurate eschatological view is the one that best harmonizes *all* these texts.

I'm delighted that you're still with me, and hopefully, we can agree that beginning with a literal approach to the text is the most logical approach because that's what we're going to do. We'll start with a literal approach, depart from it when there is a good reason to do so, and see where that leads us.

CLOSING THOUGHTS

I have a simple homework assignment for you before you dive into the rest of this book: Get yourself a journal or notebook and write down your questions about the end-times. Write down what you would love to understand more clearly and then begin to pray regularly over that list. Ask the Lord to give you insight and understanding.

If you'll do that, I believe the Lord will begin to answer your questions over the coming weeks, months, and years. And every time He gives you an answer, cross off that question and write down the date you came to the place of understanding. I think you'll find your faith built up as you begin to see God faithfully answer your questions and give you understanding.

As we get ready to undertake this study of the Book of Revelation, the one thing I would say to you is that however good you think God's plans are for those who love Him, the truth is *even better than you could imagine*. Treasure these precious words from Jesus to His disciples:

> *Let not your heart be troubled; you believe in God, believe also in Me. In My Father's house are many mansions; if it were not so, I would have told you. I go to prepare a place for you. And if I go and prepare a place for you, I will come again and receive you to Myself; that where I am, there you may be also. And where I go you know, and the way you know.*
>
> **Thomas said to Him,** *"Lord, we do not know where You are going, and how can we know the way?"*
>
> **Jesus said to him,** *"I am the way, the truth, and the life."*
>
> —John 14:1–6a

Note: This book was created from my sermon notes, which means it won't feel like a typical commentary. When there's an opportunity for life application, we'll follow that trail. When there's a sidebar topic we need to pursue, we'll do that too. Our journey will take more of a scenic route through Revelation, and I believe we'll be richer for it.

PREVIEW OF THE BOOK OF REVELATION

By the simple act of starting this book, you are taking on a challenge that many Christians seem to think is *impossible*—understanding the Book of Revelation.

And the good news is that your hopes are not misplaced! "Revelation" is the Greek word "apokalupsis," which means *"an uncovering, a revealing, a revelation."* This book's name tells us it is a reveal-ing, not a conceal-ing.

A *revelation* occurs when something previously obscured or hidden is suddenly made clear. One of the primary purposes of the Book of Revelation is to tackle subjects that had been hidden, obscured, or confusing and make them clear by bringing *revelation* to the reader (that's you!).

In fact, the first words of this amazing book tell us it is, **"The Revelation of Jesus Christ."** And it gets better. Because God also promises a *special blessing* to anyone who reads and responds to the contents of Revelation—something He does in no other book of the Bible. Why? Because the Lord wants us to understand that this book is *special,* and He really wants us to read it. We find this promise in **Revelation 1:3:**

Blessed *is* he who reads and those who hear[5] the words of this prophecy, and keep those things which are written in it; for the time *is* near.

Think about this for a moment:

- The book is titled "Revelation," referring to something obscure being made clear.
- The book opens by telling us it is a **"revelation."**
- God promises a special blessing to those who read and respond to the contents of Revelation.

With those facts established, it wouldn't make any sense to believe that God then made the rest of the book impossible to understand—merely an indecipherable collection of codes and metaphors. What *would* make sense is that if God wanted us to understand this book, He would have made it *understandable*.

If the church you attend has ever studied through Revelation, it is the exception. Most churches avoid Revelation as they avoid Leviticus or the second half of the Book of Daniel. Revelation consistently ranks among the least-taught books of the Bible and is avoided like the plague by most pastors. Why? Perhaps you've heard some of the reasons:

"It's all about things that are coming in the distant future. We need to focus on things that are happening here and now."

"It's scary, and we don't want to scare people in Church."

---

[5] "Hear" can also be translated "understand."

"There's so much weird stuff in there, and we don't want first-time guests to think our church is weird."

"There are so many interpretations of Revelation; who knows which one is right?"

And yet the Lord promises to *bless us* if we read it. He desires that we *respond* to it. And that's because foremost, this is not a book about the end of the world: Revelation is a book about **"Jesus Christ"** and is therefore intended for *all* believers.

Whether we realize it or not, when we ignore the Book of Revelation in our churches, we withhold a special blessing and revelation of Jesus from our brothers and sisters. That's why I am so glad that you are reading this. I *know* you're going to be blessed. Not because of me but because *God* has promised it.

OUTLINE OF REVELATION

Revelation has another unique feature. To help make this book easier to understand, God included a simple and straightforward *outline* that helps us to follow the sequence of events. We find this outline in **Revelation 1:19**, where Jesus instructs John to:

> ***Write the things which you have seen, and the things which are, and the things which will take place after this.***

This outline reveals the three "acts" of Revelation:

1. The things which John *has seen* (Chapter 1)
2. The things which *are* (Chapters 2–3)
3. The things which will take place *after this* (Chapters 4–22)

Act 1 – Chapter 1

The first act, *"the things which you have seen,"* refers to what John has seen up to this point. Namely, the resurrected Jesus.

Act 2 – Chapters 2–3

The second act, *"the things which are,"* refers to **Revelation 2–3**, in which Jesus dictates letters to seven churches. Those churches, in their order, prophesy the roughly 2,000 years of Church history (known as the Church Age), from AD 32 to the present, with incredible detail and precision. Yes, you read that right, and it will be mind-blowing when we get into it!

Revelation 2–3, which describes the Church Age, ends with Jesus saying:

> *Behold, I stand at the door and knock. If anyone hears My voice and opens the door, I will come in to him and dine with him, and he with Me.*
>
> —Revelation 3:20

Act 3 – Chapters 4–22

And then Jesus tells John to write about *"the things which will take place after this."* After what? After the events of **Revelation 2–3**, which is the Church Age. When we reach that point in our study, we'll learn that a supernatural global event will occur at the end of the Church Age and kick off this third act.

Jesus described the third act to John as *"the things which will take place after this."* The original Greek words behind the phrase *"after this"* are "meta tauta." And here's the neat thing: the next place that same Greek phrase appears is in the opening of **Revelation 4**, which begins with the words, *"After these things."*

In the **Revelation 1:19** outline, Jesus identified the third act of Revelation with the phrase "meta tauta." And to ensure we could easily locate that third act, God had it begin at the next place where that same phrase appears, which is **Revelation 4:1**.

Let's take a quick look at that whole verse:

> **After these things [meta tauta] I looked, and behold, a door** *standing* **open in heaven. And the first voice which I heard** *was* **like a trumpet speaking with me, saying,** *"Come up here, and I will show you things which must take place . . .*

Note the phrase that comes next:

> *. . . after this* [meta tauta].

We find that when the Bible employs a phrase or word repetitively, it usually means the Holy Spirit wants us to notice something.

Revelation 4:1 *begins* with "meta tauta" and *ends* with "meta tauta." Apparently, the Holy Spirit wants us to understand where the Church Age *ends* and where the next "act" *begins*. So, He marked that exact place in Scripture with "meta tauta" to serve as a giant "X."

"The things which are" (the Church Age) is the *second* act. As the Church Age ends with Jesus knocking on the door,[6] **Revelation 4** opens with John seeing a door open in Heaven, hearing the voice of Jesus (which sounds like a trumpet), and that voice calling him to, *"Come up here."* When we reach that point in our study, we'll learn

---

[6] Cf. Revelation 3:20.

that this is when the Church leaves the earth and heads up to the presence of Jesus.

It's interesting that although the word **"church"** appears over 20 times in the first three chapters of Revelation, it will not appear again (in the narrative) after **Revelation 4:1**. We'll find that's because the Church will be *removed* from the earth at that point.

So, what have we learned so far? This book is a revelation. It's in the business of revealing, not concealing. There is a special blessing that comes with reading and responding to it. And God has even given us an easy-to-understand outline for the whole book.[7]

---

[7] Appendix A contains a helpful overview of the end-times, which can be used as a reference as you work through this study or as a review at the end of it.

REVELATION 1

Our story begins around AD 96, more than 60 years after the resurrection and ascension of Jesus. John the Apostle has been exiled to the island of Patmos and has been there for around a decade at this point. He was sent there as punishment for refusing to acknowledge Caesar Domitian as divine.

Patmos is essentially a big rock that rises out of the ocean. It's 6 miles wide, and 10 miles long. It had a small native population and a Roman garrison, and it's where the resurrected and glorified Jesus visits John while he's praying, to give him this revelation. John writes it down, and the book finds its way back to the Church and eventually to us. He gives the book title in the very first verse of Chapter 1:

> ¹ **The Revelation of Jesus Christ, which God gave Him to show His servants—** . . .

The Father shared this revelation with Jesus so that Jesus could share it with those who love and serve Him:

> **. . . things which must shortly take place. And He sent and signified** *it* **by His angel to His servant John,** . . .

As you study Bible prophecy, you'll discover that one of the ways God shows affection is by sharing His plans. That's what we see here in **V.1**, where God tells us that He is sharing this revelation because He wants those who serve Jesus to know what He has planned.

And the more we see of God's plans, the more we understand His character—the more of Him is *revealed* to us. That's why, even though this book seems to be mainly about future events, the Lord describes it as **"The Revelation of Jesus Christ."**

I must point out that it is a rookie mistake to refer to this book as "Revelations" (plural). If you're guilty, it's time to repent and change or risk one day hearing my voice shout around a corner, *"REVELATION! SINGULAR!"*

I promise I'm not just crazy. It matters because this book is a single, cohesive revelation. It consists primarily of an extensive, flowing timeline that works together. It's a *revelation*, not multiple, unrelated revelations.

There are just a few more things you need to know about **V.1**, and then I promise the rest of this chapter will go faster.

In the phrase **"things which must shortly take place,"** the original Greek words translated **"shortly"** are "en tachos." They are the root of our word, "tachometer"—that gauge in our vehicles that displays the RPMs (revs per minute) of an engine. The idea behind "en tachos" is not something that is getting closer in a linear or consistent manner, but something that is approaching with *increasing* speed.

If you've ever driven a vehicle with a standard (or "stick shift") transmission, then you've experienced "en tachos" when you floor the gas pedal. The needle on the tachometer moves up with increasing speed and then *takes off* as you get close to the red line, and your vehicle begins *rapidly* accelerating.

The best example of "en tachos" was given by Jesus, who likened the signs of the end-times to a woman in labor: *"all these things are merely the beginning of birth pangs."*[8] When a woman having her first child has her first contractions, it's alarming. It's intense. And then a pattern emerges, prompting the woman to call the hospital and say:

> *"I'm having contractions! My baby is coming!"*

> The nurse asks, *"How far apart are the contractions?"*

> The woman replies, *"15 minutes!"*

> And the nurse, who has been down this road before, says, *"I got news for you. You're just getting started. Things are going to get much more intense before your baby is born."*

And they *do*. That last hour before the baby is born is not the same as the first hour! It's an entirely different level of intensity. That's the idea behind "en tachos" and what we're meant to have in mind when John refers to **"things which must shortly take place."** Notice that this revelation will also be given in *signs*. Let's look at **V.1** again:

> [1] **The Revelation of Jesus Christ, which God gave Him to show His servants—things which must shortly take place. And He sent and signified it by His angel to His servant John, . . .**

In the original Greek, **"signified"** literally means *"sign-ified."* It's the word "sēmainō," which means *"a sign, to give a sign, communicated."* There are a few possible explanations for why God would choose to communicate much of this revelation in *signs*:

---

[8] Matthew 24:8 NASB.

1. **The Safety of Believers:**

    If you're unfamiliar with the Old Testament and read Revelation on your own, many things would be impossible to understand. But by opening the Old Testament, these things can be *decoded* relatively easily.

    Did you know that Revelation contains more references to the Old Testament than any other New Testament book (over 800)? And none of them are quotations; they're all *allusions*.

    Many things in Revelation would have been offensive to Roman emperors who believed themselves to be gods (e.g., Jesus coming to rule over the earth). But if soldiers searched your house and found a copy, they could read it, but they wouldn't be able to understand it because they wouldn't have the *key* to unlock the *code*. We do. And we will do just that as we study through the text.

2. **Visual Language Changes Far Less Than Textual Language**

    The word **"awful"** used to mean "full of awe" and was used to describe reverential wonder. But if you came up to me after the church service this Sunday and shared that you found the service to be awful, I wouldn't appreciate it! The word means something completely different today because *textual language* changes.

    However, when things are described *visually*, we have a much greater chance of grasping what is being described and can apply our current vocabulary to the subject.

In summary, Jesus tells us that these signs, like birth pains, will *accelerate* and increase in *intensity* as the end of the Church Age approaches.

Back to the Text

In **V.2**, Jesus shared this revelation with John:

> ...**² who bore witness to the word of God, and to the testimony of Jesus Christ, to all things that he saw.**

That means God got everything He wanted to say into this book and nothing that He didn't.

> **³ Blessed is he who reads and those who hear the words of this prophecy, and keep those things which are written in it; for the time is near.**

There's that beautiful promise we talked about earlier. As you study Revelation, let me encourage you always to pray before you begin and thank the Lord, in faith, for the blessing you're going to receive:

> *"Thank You, Father, that as I take this time to read the revelation of Your Son, Jesus, You have promised that I will be blessed."*

GREETING THE SEVEN CHURCHES

In **VV.4–5**, we're going to see the whole Trinity at work:

> **⁴ John, to the seven churches which are in Asia:**
>
> **Grace to you and peace from Him who is and who was and who is to come, and from the seven Spirits who are before**

His throne, ⁵ and from Jesus Christ, the faithful witness, the firstborn from the dead, and the ruler over the kings of the earth.

First, we see God the Father, who is described as *eternal:* **"from Him who is and who was and who is to come."** Then, in **V.5**, we see the Son, **"Jesus Christ."** And in between them, in **V.4**, we see **"the seven Spirits who are before His throne."** This refers to the Holy Spirit.

Unlike the Jews of John's day, most of us don't come from a solid Old Testament background. They had been raised in the Old Testament scriptures and it wouldn't be unusual to know one or more Jews who had memorized most of them. Among the congregations and leaders of the Early Church, there were many converts who had a sound background in the Hebrew Scriptures. When they heard the phrase **"the seven Spirits,"** they would have immediately recognized the reference, and their minds would have gone to **Isaiah 11:1–2**.

To help us understand why, let's count the Spirits as we read through them (I've underlined them):

> **There shall come forth a Rod** [a shoot] **from the stem of Jesse,**
> **And a Branch shall grow out of his roots** [that's Jesus].
> **The <u>Spirit of the Lord</u> shall rest upon Him,**
> **The Spirit of <u>wisdom</u> and <u>understanding</u>,**
> **The Spirit of <u>counsel</u> and <u>might</u>,**
> **The Spirit of <u>knowledge</u> and of <u>the fear of the Lord</u>.**

The Jews believed Isaiah was referring to the *complete* spirit of God (seven being the number of completion/perfection in biblical numerology)—the One we know as the *Holy Spirit*.

I struggle to read the following few verses aloud without being overcome with emotion, and if you realize how hopeless you are without Jesus, you will too. Continuing in **V.5**, John lays out what Jesus has done for us, drawing the obvious conclusion that Jesus deserves all glory:

> **To Him who loved us and washed us from our sins in His own blood,** [6] **and has made us kings and priests to His God and Father, to Him** *be* **glory and dominion forever and ever. Amen.**
>
> [7] **Behold, He is coming with clouds, and every eye will see Him, even they who pierced Him. And all the tribes of the earth will mourn because of Him. Even so, Amen.**
>
> [8] *"I am the Alpha and the Omega, the Beginning and the End,"* **says the Lord,** *"who is and who was and who is to come, the Almighty."*

We're not reading someone's opinion; we're reading the very Word of God. We're hearing the plans of the One who *holds* the future. These are not plans in the sense that we think of plans—things we would *like* to see or *hope* to see. When God makes a plan, it is a future event as certain as the events of yesterday. May we study God's Word with the appropriate reverence and awe.

Where **V.7** reads, **"Behold, He is coming with clouds,"** John is referring to the Second Coming. We'll talk more about that when we get to **Revelation 19**.

Then **V.7** goes on to say, **"and every eye will see Him, even they who pierced Him."** In the minds of Early Church Jews, this would have sounded very similar to the words of the prophet Zechariah, who, more than 500 years before Jesus was born, wrote of an end-times event when *"they"* would look upon Him *"whom they pierced."* Prophesying from the perspective of the Messiah (Jesus), we read:

> *... I will pour on the house of David [the people] and on the inhabitants of Jerusalem [the location] the Spirit of grace and supplication; then they will look on Me whom they pierced. Yes, they will mourn for Him as one mourns for his only son, and grieve for Him as one grieves for a firstborn.*
>
> —Zechariah 12:10

Jesus promises that on the day He returns to the earth, He will pour out *"the Spirit of grace and supplication"* on the nation of Israel *("the house of David")* and the city of *"Jerusalem,"* and they will finally *get it*. The Jewish people will understand that Jesus was and is Messiah, and a beautiful reunion will take place. But it will begin with weeping and mourning, as they realize that despite all the prophecies of the Old Testament, their ancestors missed their Messiah and even arranged His murder.

What's so fascinating is that this prophecy about an *end-times* event was recorded over 500 years before Jesus was even *born*. It's over 2,500 years old!

Additionally, Jesus prophesies the *method* of His execution, declaring He will be *"pierced."* When Zechariah recorded this, the Law mandated *stoning* as the method of capital punishment in Israel. Crucifixion wasn't even invented until a couple of hundred years later. The crucifixion part of this prophecy has already been fulfilled. Therefore, we can trust the rest will be too.

Some believe that Revelation is about historical events in Israel beginning around AD 70 (i.e., the fall of Jerusalem and the destruction of the Temple). But look at **V.7** one more time:

> **... He is coming with clouds, and every eye will see Him, even they who pierced Him. And all the tribes of the earth will mourn because of Him.**

Have all these things happened? Has Jesus returned to the earth with the clouds, in view of everyone on earth? Surely, we can all agree the answer is a resounding "*No*." In just this one verse, we can already see that Jesus and Revelation cannot be referring solely to historical events.

VISION OF THE SON OF MAN

> **⁹ I, John, both your brother and companion in the tribulation and kingdom and patience of Jesus Christ, was on the island that is called Patmos for the word of God and for the testimony of Jesus Christ.**

John was exiled to Patmos because he refused to cease preaching the Gospel. We can see God's hand at work in this because when He desires to speak with someone on a profound level, He often leads them to a place of isolation (for a season).

John the Baptist went to the school of the *wilderness*, where the Lord spoke into his life and prepared him for ministry.

Paul didn't begin planting churches immediately following his Damascus Road conversion. He spent around three years in the wilderness area of Arabia, receiving direct revelation from Jesus.

And sometimes, the Lord works similarly in *our* lives. Sometimes,

REVELATION 1

we find ourselves in a season of isolation, relationally or emotionally, because God wants to do significant work in us and give revelation that will alter the course of our lives.

Now, John begins to receive *revelation*:

> ¹⁰ *I was in the Spirit on the Lord's Day, . . .*

John is not referring to the Sabbath or Sunday. He is using the word **"Day"** about a *season* of time (e.g., *"In his day, they didn't have the Internet"*). Specifically, the season of time covering the events of **Revelation 4:1** onward, but we'll get into that in later chapters.

As we read through this description of Jesus, which begins in **VV.10–13**, I want you to notice every appearance of the words **"like"** and **"as"**...

> *...and I heard behind me a loud voice, <u>as of</u> a trumpet,* ¹¹ *saying, "I am the Alpha and the Omega, the First and the Last," and, "What you see, write in a book and send it to the seven churches which are in Asia: to Ephesus, to Smyrna, to Pergamos, to Thyatira, to Sardis, to Philadelphia, and to Laodicea."*

> ¹² **Then I turned to see the voice that spoke with me. And having turned I saw seven golden lampstands** [menorahs], ¹³ **and in the midst** [in the middle] **of the seven lampstands One <u>like</u> the Son of Man** [a title for Jesus]**, clothed with a garment down to the feet and girded about the chest with a golden band.**

Readers with a Jewish background would have noticed the references to menorahs and a golden band (i.e., sash) and associated this **"Son of Man"** with the work environment[9] and attire[10] of a *high priest*. The description continues in **VV.14–16**:

> **¹⁴ His head and hair *were* white <u>like</u> wool, as white <u>as</u> snow, and His eyes <u>like</u> a flame of fire; ¹⁵ His feet *were* <u>like</u> fine brass, as if refined in a furnace, and His voice <u>as</u> the sound of many waters; ¹⁶ He had in His right hand seven stars, out of His mouth went a sharp two-edged sword, and His countenance *was* <u>like</u> the sun shining in its strength.**

We see Jesus dressed and ministering as a high priest, but we also notice that He is in the **"midst"** of these menorahs and is holding **"seven stars"** in His hand. This is where believers usually throw their hands up in frustration and say, *"Well, Book of Revelation... I tried. I really did."*

Take heart. Let me show you just how easy Revelation will be to understand. Hang with me and skip down to **V.20** for a moment:

> *The mystery of the seven stars which you saw in My right hand, and the seven golden lampstands: The seven stars are the angels of the seven churches, and the seven lampstands which you saw are the seven churches.*

The original Greek word used there for *"angels"*[11] means messengers—divine or human. To this day, there is disagreement over whether the term should be viewed as referring to individual *angels* assigned to these churches or the *pastors* of these churches. I'll share which way I lean and why a bit later.

---

[9] Cf. Exodus 25:31–40.

[10] Cf. Exodus 28:39; 39:29.

[11] Aggelos.

So, the mystery is solved! The mysterious **"stars"** are either angels or pastors, and the menorahs (the **"lampstands"**) represent seven churches. That's it. You don't have to be a mystic or a scholar. And these details will become even clearer in **Revelation 2**.

NO WORDS CAN CONTAIN HIS GLORY

I asked you to notice all the times the words **"like"** and **"as"** were used in **VV.10–16**, and I'll tell you why—John is seeing things for which there are no words. His language and every language are simply inadequate for describing the glory of the resurrected Jesus. So, John must use words and descriptions that are as close as he can get using his earthly vocabulary. And he uses words such as "like" and "as" to let us know that he is *not* being literal; he's simply doing the best he can with the words he has at his disposal.

In **V.14**, John does *not* say, "His head and hair WERE made of white wool and snow." He says, **"His head and hair were white LIKE wool, as white AS snow."** It's the best John can do to describe the brightness of Jesus' face and hair.

If you ignore the presence of **"like"** and **"as"** in John's description and take it literally, you'll end up with one of those crazy artists' renderings of Jesus where He's got fire coming out of His eyes, brass sneakers on his feet, and the sun for a face. Those images are awkward to give to the kids in Sunday School to color, and it's not what John saw.

If he were here today, I have no doubt John would tell us that whatever image his description conjured in our minds, the real thing was infinitely more glorious.

Did you notice that while all the other descriptive phrases are qualified with the words **"like"** or **"as"** or **"as of,"** none of those qualifiers are present where it says, **"out of His mouth went a sharp two-edged sword"**? This would seem to imply that John saw a sword *literally* coming out of the mouth of Jesus.

Now, we know from verses like **Hebrews 4:12** and **Ephesians 6:17** that this **"sword"** is a metaphor for the *Word of God*. Did John know that when he wrote this? We don't know. What's important is that Jesus wanted *us* to understand that God's Word comes from our Lord's mouth.

I want to highlight something back in **V.13**, where we find Jesus ministering as a high priest. Scripture tells us that unlike all other high priests, who had to offer ongoing sacrifices for sin, Jesus offered Himself, **"once for all,"** as the sacrifice to end all sacrifices.[12]

But in **V.13**, we see Jesus also taking on *another* priestly duty—keeping the menorahs burning by ensuring they had enough fuel (i.e., oil). Think through the imagery with me: What do the seven lampstands/menorahs represent? **V.18** tells us they represent the seven churches, which together represent *the* Church. So, who is the One who keeps the light of the Church shining? It's not us. It's our great high priest, *Jesus*.

Don't get caught up in fear when you hear some Christian sociologists announce that their latest study proves that Christianity is dying and that the Church is only one generation from extinction. *Jesus* has taken on the responsibility of keeping the Church shining. The reason I have hope for the future of the Church is not because of you or me or even my children. It's because *Jesus* is the One who established and sustains the Church. If it all depended on us, then we'd have a real problem. But praise God, it doesn't.

Instead, let's devote our energies and efforts to being the kinds

---

[12] Hebrews 7:23–28.

of churches that bless Jesus to the degree that He is moved to say, *"I need to keep that lamp shining."*

WHAT HAPPENED TO JOHN AT THE SIGHT OF JESUS?

After describing the Jesus he saw, John explains what happened to him at that moment:

> ¹⁷ **And when I saw Him, I fell at His feet as dead.**

Wow. Two thoughts come to mind.

First, we live in a time when there is little to no reverence for God—His name or His Word. He is mocked. He is the butt of jokes in the media. We hear people say things like this:

> *"If God is real, He's got some explaining to do. He's going to have to tell me why He let tragedies happen and didn't heal kids with cancer. And then He'll need to explain why I went through the difficulties I experienced in my life. You better believe I'm going to have some questions for God!"*

John is a good guy. He's an apostle. He's been persecuted for serving Jesus and exiled to Patmos. In His Gospel, he's called **"the disciple whom Jesus loved."** Jesus *likes* John. And yet, when John encounters Jesus in the fullness of His glory, John can't handle it, and all he can do is fall on his face **"as dead."** When you one day find yourself in the presence of God, I can guarantee you will not be sticking a finger in His chest and saying, *"I've got some questions for You!"*

Second, you're probably aware that an entire segment of Christianity holds to a form of Pentecostal theology that espouses things like uncontrollably falling over or rolling around on the ground (i.e., being "slain in the Spirit"). They claim these manifestations are evidence of God's Spirit tangibly blessing and interacting with His people.

However, when we find people falling in the presence of God in the Bible, it's always described as a *near-death experience* and never a *desirable* experience. They would tell you, *"I thought I was a goner! I thought I was about to be vaporized! I've never been more afraid in my life!"*

John was *terrified*. Just look at what Jesus has to tell him next. Imagine the scene in your mind. John thinks he is about to die, and then he records this in **VV.17–18**:

> ...But He [Jesus] **laid His right hand on me, saying to me,** *"Do not be afraid; I am the First and the Last.* [18] *I am He who lives, and was dead, and behold, I am alive forevermore. Amen. And I have the keys of Hades and of Death."*

Jesus reassures John that because of Him, John *belongs* here (in the presence of God). And again, I can barely read those verses aloud because they are so gloriously *weighty*. They make me love Jesus more and long for the moment when I get to see Him face-to-face.

JESUS' TITLES

"Jesus" is His *name*, and "Christ" is His *title* (Greek for "Messiah"). Another of His titles is *"the First and the Last."* This title only appears in a few places in Scripture, and when John's Jewish readers heard it, they likely would have recalled **Isaiah 44:6**, where God the Father is speaking and says:

> *Thus says the Lord, the King of Israel,*
> *And his Redeemer, the Lord of hosts:*

"I am the First and I am the Last;
Besides Me there is no God."

In the Old Testament, God declared, *"I am the First and I am the Last."* Here in the New Testament, Jesus declares, *"I am the First and I am the Last."* Jesus is using one of God's titles because He *is* God—the same God who spoke back in Isaiah. They are *one*.

¹⁹ Write the things which you have seen, . . .

What has John seen up to this point? The resurrected and glorified Jesus.

. . . and the things which are, . . .

We'll begin studying those things in the next chapter.

. . . and the things which will take place after this.

Recall that the Greek phrase for *"after this"* is "meta tauta." That starts in **Revelation 4:1.**

²⁰ The mystery of the seven stars which you saw in My right hand, and the seven golden lampstands: The seven stars are the angels of the seven churches, and the seven lampstands which you saw are the seven churches.

We explained these symbols back in **vv.12 and 16.**

CLOSING THOUGHTS

Congratulations! You survived a survey of **Revelation 1**. Was it overly complicated? Was it too hard to understand? *Not at all.* And **Revelation 1** is the most complex chapter in the entire book, and you made it through that. The rest will be *easy*.

I hope you're starting to overcome any nervousness you may have felt. Be encouraged—God is going to bless you as you study through Revelation. Jesus is saying to us:

[17] . . . Do not be afraid; I am the First and the Last. [18] I am He who lives, and was dead, and behold, I am alive forevermore. Amen. And I have the keys of Hades and of Death.

And we respond to Him by saying:

[5] . . . To Him who loved us and washed us from our sins in His own blood, [6] and has made us kings and priests to His God and Father, to Him *be* glory and dominion forever and ever. Amen.

REVELATION 2:1-7

INTRODUCTION TO THE SEVEN CHURCHES

In **Revelation 2** and **3**, Jesus dictates seven letters to John, each to a church in the region then known as Asia. The letters were addressed to the churches in Ephesus, Smyrna, Pergamos, Thyatira, Sardis, Philadelphia, and Laodicea. The seven churches were in the Roman province of Asia, which is today part of the country of Turkey. And thanks to the Roman Empire, they were all connected by well-built roads.

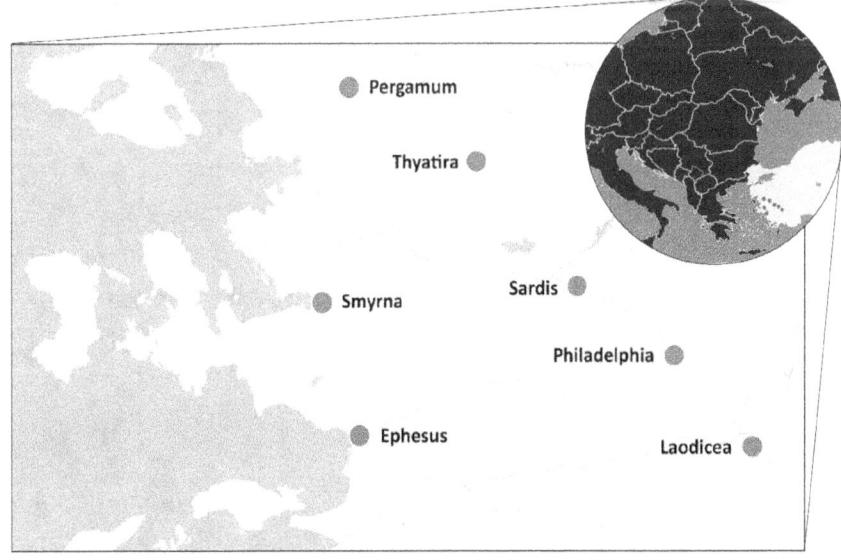

Each of the letters has four layers of application:

1. **The Local Church ~AD 96**

   Incredibly, the archaeological ruins of all seven churches have been discovered. In fact, they were only found because a group of archaeologists used the Bible as a guide in their search. These are all literal churches that existed when John recorded Revelation, and each letter speaks to issues they were dealing with at the time. John was an overseer of these churches and would have been awed to hear Jesus speak directly to these congregations he knew well and loved dearly.

2. **All Churches**

   You will notice that each letter ends with the phrase, ***"hear what the Spirit says to the churches."*** That tells us that these letters were also written for *anyone* who cares about the Church as a member or a leader. The main issues behind every problem, difficulty, and challenge churches face are addressed in these seven letters.

3. **All Believers**

   Toward the end of each letter, we find the phrase, *"**He who has an ear, let him hear.**"* It means, *"If you can hear this, you need to pay attention."*[13] We'll discover elements of *ourselves* in each of these churches. We'll be encouraged,

---

[13] Cf. Isaiah 6:9–10; Jeremiah 5:21; Ezekiel 3:27, 12:2; Matthew 13:9; Mark 4:9; Luke 8:8.

convicted, and like some of the original recipients, we may realize that God is calling us to make some changes.

4. **Prophecy**

   These seven letters lay out ~2,000 years of Church history (the Church Age) with mind-blowing precision and detail.

   One of the surprises is that the churches Jesus writes to are *not* all the obvious choices. There is no letter to the prominent and influential megachurches of Rome, Antioch, or Jerusalem. Why? Because the prophetic pattern that is going to emerge across these seven letters would only work with these specific churches in this specific order.

The Book of Acts covers the first 30 years of the Church. **Revelation 2–3** covers the next 2,000 years of the Church. This prophetic perspective is a relatively recent discovery, primarily because most of the Church Age had to pass for the pattern to emerge. We also needed to live in an age when historical knowledge is easily accessible so that the appropriate research can be done.

For us, the Church Age is almost entirely *history*, but John was recording it *prophetically* (likely unbeknownst to him), as he was living in the time of the first church of the Church Age.

TEXTUALLY COMMON TRAITS AMONG THE CHURCHES

We'll find a few common traits in all the letters:

- Each letter begins with the phrase, *"To the angel of the church of _____."* I believe the word *"angel"* is a reference to the *pastors* of these churches, rather than individual *angels* assigned to each church. I hold this view because I suspect Jesus did not communicate with His angels via the Roman postal system. Additionally, angels were not *leading* these churches. So, there wouldn't have been much point in Jesus telling them what changes needed to be made (as He will in the seven letters).

- The *name* of each church reveals something about its identity from God's perspective.

- Jesus introduces Himself with a *title* related to something each church needs to be reminded of.

- Each letter serves as a "report card" of sorts, and each church receives the appropriate feedback:
    - A commendation *("I love that you're doing this.")*
    - A criticism *("Stop doing this.")*
    - An exhortation *("Start/Keep doing this.")*

- Four churches have something missing from their report cards: two receive no *commendation* (Sardis and Laodicea), and two receive no *criticism* (Smyrna and Philadelphia).

- The churches that think they are doing well will find out they're not. The ones that think they aren't doing well will find that they're doing better than they think.

- Finally, each letter includes an exhortation to the reader (us) to be an *overcomer* of the issues Jesus raised in that letter.

THE CHURCH IN EPHESUS

"Ephesus" means "the desired one" or "desirable." It's a term of endearment, like "darling" or "sweetheart." This church was especially precious to Jesus, likely because it was led by some of those closest to Him during His earthly ministry.

HISTORY AND CULTURE OF EPHESUS

Ephesus was one of the largest, wealthiest, and most important cities in the Roman Empire; it was known as the "Supreme Metropolis of Asia." Founded around 1400 BC, Ephesus had a population of between 33,600 and 172,500 people,[14] which was significant at the time.

The city boasted a magnificent theater that seated 24,000 people; it had good road and river systems and a port. These traits made it a natural hub for commerce and business, with enormous quantities of goods moving through the city daily. As a result, it grew into a city of great *affluence*.

People from all over the known world traveled through Ephesus, bringing with them their ideas, philosophies, and belief systems. The Ephesian population was multicultural and considered themselves more enlightened than most. They had a *pluralistic* spirituality—the view that all spiritual concepts are true and valid in some form and

---

[14] Yes, estimates from contemporary historians really do vary this much.

ultimately all lead to "god." They were comfortable with almost any deity but extremely uncomfortable with the idea of one *supreme* God above all others (i.e., monotheism).

We know of at least 50 gods who were worshipped in Ephesus, including a wildly popular goddess whose Roman name was Artemis and whose Greek name was Diana. Her glorious temple was considered so spectacular that it appears in Antipater of Sidon's famous list of the Seven Wonders of the Ancient World.

Artemis was most famous for the specific *form* of worship she allegedly required. If you were an Ephesian man who wished to worship the city's "protective mother," you would enter Artemis' temple and meet in private with one of the women who served as a "sacred employee" and "worship" with her. You would pay the temple for her services, and that money would go into the temple coffers. If you were a woman who worshipped Artemis, sooner or later, you would be notified that it was your turn to volunteer in the temple as your act of "worship." As you can imagine, it was a stunningly effective form of fundraising and resulted in most of the city's men becoming highly devoted "worshipers" of Artemis.

We love to romanticize history, which often causes us to overlook cultural and religious abuses of men, women, and children. Just because this type of "worship" was normative in the culture does not mean that it wasn't horrifically traumatic for those who were *forced* to take part against their will. Understanding these brutal realities of the ancient world allows us to appreciate even more the radical model the Church presented for honoring personhood in marriage and society.

Thanks to Artemis, Ephesus rivaled Corinth as the "filth capital" of the Roman world. The Greek philosopher Heraclitus (535–475 BC) commented that the morality of animals exceeded that of the people of Ephesus, perhaps because the city's most popular religions were all rooted in the pursuit of pleasure known as *hedonism*.

The Apostle Paul and the Founding of the Church in Ephesus

You can read about the founding of the Church in Ephesus in the Book of Acts. It was the first of the seven churches in **Revelation 2–3** to be established in the Roman province of Asia Minor, and the other six were all planted out of Ephesus.

Around AD 64, Paul had a final meeting with the Ephesian elders.[15] He warned that after he was gone, Satan would send **"wolves"**—false teachers who would seek to lure believers away from the truth and divide the Church. To counter this, Paul recommended that they cling to God and His Word, and in the years that followed, the Ephesian elders did just that.

In light of that, the letter to the church in Ephesus is fascinating because it gives us insight into what happened over the 30 years following Paul's final visit with those elders.

Ephesus in Church History

Prophetically, Ephesus portrays the first church of the Church Age. We can call it "The Apostolic Church" because it was marked by the leadership of the apostles.

Shortly after Jesus' Ascension around AD 32, the eleven disciples were among a group of 120 believers praying in an upper room in Jerusalem.[16] The Holy Spirit came upon them, filling them with

---

[15] Cf. Acts 20:17–38.

[16] Cf. Acts 1–2.

boldness and power to preach the Gospel. Peter went outside and preached the greatest debut sermon of all time, resulting in 3,000 men responding by giving their lives to Jesus. The Church was born that day, and the Church Age began.

The Apostolic Age continued until around AD 100, by which time the apostles had all died.

INTO THE TEXT

As we journey through the text of each letter in Revelation, we'll draw out the different layers of application (the local church, all churches, all believers, and prophecy) as we go.

> ¹ *To the angel* [the pastor] *of the church of Ephesus write,*
>
> *"These things says He who holds the seven stars in His right hand, who walks in the midst of the seven golden lampstands: . . . "*

In **Revelation 1** we learned that the speaker is *Jesus*. And the title He gives Himself here is intended to remind the Church in Ephesus that He is *in their midst*.[17] We'll soon find out why they need this reminder.

Now we move on to the "report card" for the Church in Ephesus and, to be honest, it's pretty great! I would love to have Jesus commend me for these same things:

> ² *I know your works, your labor, your patience, and that you cannot bear those who are evil. And you have tested those who say they are apostles and are not, and have found them liars;* ³

---

[17] Cf. See our previous explanation of Revelation 1:20.

and you have persevered and have patience, and have labored for My name's sake and have not become weary.

- They actively served God with their lives *("I know your works, your labor")*.
- The Greek word used there for *"patience"*[18] means "durability, triumph, and fortitude that changes suffering into glory. It is a courageous acceptance of hardship, suffering, and loss."

Ephesus didn't want the Church in their city. Within a few years of Paul's planting this church, the trade guilds began trying to shut it down. Christians were persecuted and despised. But the Church in Ephesus understood and embodied the exhortation of Paul in **1 Corinthians 15:58**:

… my beloved brethren, be steadfast, immovable, always abounding in the work of the Lord, knowing that your labor is not in vain in the Lord.

- They had impeccable theology *("and that you cannot bear those who are evil. And you have tested those who say they are apostles and are not, and have found them liars")*.

Doctrine Must Be Measured by the Word of God

Remember that Paul had warned the Ephesian elders that false teachers and teachings would attempt to mislead their congregation from within and without. To protect against these

---

[18] Hupomone.

threats, Paul charged them to test everything against the Word of God—and they did. When someone would come in and attempt to distort the Scriptures, they were on top of it. They would expose that person and the falsity of their teaching and kick them to the curb if they would not repent. They were *doctrinally diligent*.

And I imagine their diligence would have made for some exciting church services. You can imagine someone asking, *"How was church today?"* The response might have been, *"It ended early. They threw out the guest preacher ten minutes into his sermon."* Such was the Ephesians' vigilance.

Jesus *loved* that they were taking His Word and the task of protecting the flock seriously. Concerning questionable teaching, Jesus didn't say, *"Don't worry about it. They just have a different interpretation. Different strokes for different folks!"* While there are many differences between denominations, the Church is made up of those who share a belief in the core tenets of the faith and Gospel. And when someone tried to mess with those core tenets, the Ephesian church tossed them out. And for doing so, Jesus commended them.

Psalm 138:2 declares, **"you have exalted above all things your name and your word"** (HCSB). Jesus cares deeply about the Bible because it directly reflects *Him*. When His *Word* is misrepresented, *He* is misrepresented. That's why Jesus has always expected His Church to take His word *seriously*.

Satan has been stirring up false teachers for as long as the Church has existed. What seems to be a recent phenomenon is the acceptance of false teachers in the name of "unity." There appears to be an increasing number of teachers and churches holding to beliefs *outside* orthodox Christianity. And yet, they find acceptance within the Church because of a misunderstanding of biblical unity.

When Jesus prayed that all believers would be unified,[19] He prayed that all *believers* would be unified. If someone does not hold to orthodox Christianity, they are *not* a believer, and Jesus does *not* want us to be unified with them. The Lord is not impressed when we give "grace" to false teachers and accept them as part of the Church. He expects us to have a zero-tolerance policy regarding false teaching.

And when we reach the letter to the Philadelphia church, we'll learn exactly what the fundamentals of orthodox Christianity are (i.e., the core beliefs that define a Christian).

After letting the Church in Ephesus know that He loves them and is proud of them, Jesus must share a *correction* with them.

Warnings Against Loving Theology More Than Jesus

⁴ Nevertheless I have this against you, that you have left your first love.

This is a critique that rips my heart out every time I read it. The original Greek word used here for *"love"* is "agape," the most profound, selfless, and sincere form of love and affection. Apparently, Ephesus *used* to have it, but somewhere along the line, they *lost* it. They were still living righteously—loving good, hating evil, and doing good works, but their affection and passion were gone.

They had become more passionate about the *things* of God than they were about *God Himself*. They loved their church, programs, and theology more than they loved Jesus.

---

[19] Cf. John 17:21.

Ouch.

It's as if Jesus is saying, *"I love all that stuff you're doing. It's great. But you're so into that stuff that you've forgotten about Me. You've forgotten about knowing Me and loving Me directly."*

This situation would be like me starting a fan club for my wife because I think she's so wonderful, but then becoming so busy running that fan club that I neglect to interact with my wife directly and personally, even though she's available to me. How foolish it would be for me to write article after article about how much I love my wife, without ever telling her directly to her face.

Such was the dynamic in the Church in Ephesus.

Reading the Bible reveals that specific characteristics define a Christian. But one characteristic stands above them all—a Christian *loves* God.

> **...one of them, a lawyer, asked *Him [Jesus]* a question, testing Him, and saying, *"Teacher, which is the great commandment in the law?"***
>
> **Jesus said to him, *"'You shall love the Lord your God with all your heart, with all your soul, and with all your mind.' This is the first and great commandment."***
>
> —Matthew 22:35–38

When Peter came face-to-face with the resurrected Jesus for the first time after denying all knowledge of Him three times, Jesus had only one question: *"do you love Me?"*[20]

Do you love Jesus *personally* and *directly*? I'm not asking if you

---

[20] Cf. John 21:15–19.

love the things of Jesus or the culture around Jesus or other people who love Jesus; I'm asking if you love Jesus *personally* and *directly*.

What cuts me so deeply about this is the realization that I can do all the Christian "stuff"—study the Bible, pray, serve at church, give sacrificially, evangelize, practice random acts of kindness—all without loving Jesus in the most meaningful sense of the phrase. My life can be full of "God stuff," and I can still miss *Jesus*.

To paint another picture of the dynamic we are discussing, imagine a husband who comes home from work with flowers for his wife. She gushes and says, *"Aw, I love that you were thinking about me today!"* But he replies, *"That's not really what happened. I put an appointment in my calendar to buy you flowers on the third Thursday of every month because flowers represent affection. Today is flower day, hence the flowers."*

The *action* is commendable. The *intention* and *discipline* are admirable. The problem is that this husband lost his passion for his wife somewhere along the line and is now just going through the motions as an emotionless ritual. He *loves* her, and if you asked him, he would tell you he *wants* her to feel loved, but he's not loving her *directly*. His heart is not fully present in his actions of devotion.

We're not talking about a *salvation* issue here. Nowhere in this letter does Jesus imply that the Ephesian believers are not saved. He wants them to know that they're missing the point of everything, which is loving and knowing *Him*. None of our good works or sacrifices bless Jesus if they're divorced from genuine affection for Him. The driving force in our lives is to be our love for *Jesus*—not our love for theology, the Church, or even the Bible.

I can sense some of you are uncomfortable with that last statement because you're like me in that you *love* the Bible. And if that's you, then you likely believe something like, *"As long as believers just keep studying the Word, everything else will work itself out."* The problem is that Jesus' letter to the Ephesians tells us that's not true.

The most glaring example is the religious leaders of Jesus' day. After almost 400 years of silence from God between the Old and New Testaments, the Pharisees called Israel to repent and return to the Scriptures—which was a great thing! But it wasn't long before they started loving the Scriptures more than the God they were written to reveal. And despite being men of the Word, immersed in the Scriptures daily, with the Old Testament memorized, they missed their Messiah, Jesus, when He was standing right in front of them.

Romans 1:25 declares the folly of those who worship the creature rather than the Creator they are intended to reveal. Similarly, the warning to the Church in Ephesus is to not worship the Scriptures above the Author they were written to reveal.

We must be cautious that the same thing doesn't happen to us. We must guard against slowly divorcing our emotions from our acts of devotion and falling into loving knowledge and legalism more than we love Jesus—blind to our regression because we're in the Word all the time.

I think about that a lot. It is so easy to mistake activity for affection. While it's true that affection will always lead to activity,[21] it is not true that affection is always present in our activity. The purpose of the Word is to reveal Jesus so that we might know Him more deeply, see Him more clearly, love Him more dearly, worship Him more rightly, and serve Him more devotedly.

Most of modern Christianity seems to have bought into a false

---

[21] Cf. James 2:14–26.

belief that external passion should *tone down* as spiritual maturity increases. Zeal should be replaced with temperance and seriousness, and passion is something for young people or a recovery church service. Just don't look for it among seasoned, mature people of the faith because they've *graduated* from all that.

May it never be so in my life. May it never be so in your life. May it never be so in our churches. May growing *old* never mean growing *cold*. May we be ever-increasing in our understanding and appreciation of Jesus and, therefore, ever-growing in our *passion* for Him.

I'm not proud of the number of times I've judgmentally looked at a passionately worshipping adult the same way I look at a passionately worshipping child. I've watched believers in other countries, recovering addicts, and recent converts expressively worship the Lord and condescendingly thought, *"That's so precious."* Jesus' letter to the Ephesians tells me I should instead be convicted and question why my worship expression lacks a similar level of passion.

How do I *know* if I'm loving Jesus personally and directly? As the adage goes, *"'Love' is spelled T.I.M.E."* When I'm truly loving Jesus, I *think* about Him and *want* to spend time with Him, talk to Him, and worship Him throughout my day.

I'm not talking about *legalism*; I'm talking about *intentionality*. We are intentional about the things that are important to us. So, if Jesus is important to us, we will *plan* time in our day to spend with Him. Jesus modeled this in His earthly ministry, getting up early in the morning to talk with His Heavenly Father as His custom. He *desired* that daily direct connection.

When you're truly loving Jesus, you look for those moments of connection throughout the day. Talking to Him becomes your first response when faced with a need or a burden. You naturally find yourself talking to the Lord when you're in a challenging situation. When you feel disconnected from Him, you take time during your commute to worship or listen to a Bible study. When something good happens, you instinctively thank Him.

Those are not things you *have* to do; they're things you *want* to do when you're truly loving Jesus.

Genuinely deep relationships are exceedingly rare. Most of our relationships are task-oriented—friendships we have because we're trying to accomplish the same *task*. Even within the Church, we share relationships partly because we're working together to build strong marriages, families, and churches.

In the intimacy of marriage, life can quickly become about the *tasks* of raising godly kids, building a business together, getting the kids through school, building a home, achieving financial goals, *task, task, task*. And the problem many couples face when their kids leave home is that a monumental *task* is finished. Suddenly, they realize that they haven't really been husband and wife—they've been coworkers. And the relationship between the two of them is, in reality, almost nonexistent.

Our relationship with Jesus is not to be based on working together toward a shared goal; knowing and enjoying Him *is* the goal. Everything else is secondary.

> **Now it happened as they went that He entered a certain village; and a certain woman named Martha welcomed Him into her house. And she had a sister called Mary, who also sat at Jesus' feet and heard His word. But Martha was distracted with much serving, and she approached Him and said,** *"Lord, do You not care that my sister has left me to serve alone? Therefore tell her to help me."*

And Jesus answered and said to her, *"Martha, Martha, you are worried and troubled about many things. But one thing is needed, and Mary has chosen that good part, which will not be taken away from her."*

—Luke 10:38–42

The Ephesians were like Martha—too busy with the work of the Kingdom to notice they were missing out on the opportunity to sit at the feet of the King. And to shake them out of it, Jesus says, *"you have left your first love."*

The same thing happens all too easily in our lives and churches. We find ourselves going through the motions of the Christian life. There's no fire or crisis, but there's no real *relationship*, and we only find ourselves close to Jesus when we need His help to accomplish a task or get through a difficult season. Our flesh draws us back, over and over, to a works-based and ritualistic faith. And that is not a real relationship.

Thankfully, Jesus gives us the remedy.

Love for Jesus Is Key

⁵ Remember therefore from where you have fallen; repent and do the first works . . .

The Lord asks the Ephesians to remember how they felt about Him when they first met Him and experienced the joy of salvation. And then He calls them to *"repent,"* which means embracing a change of mind (that inevitably leads to changed behaviors). Jesus is letting them know that being passionate about Him is not elementary; it's essential. Zeal is not something they're supposed to outgrow. They need to change their thinking and return to that simple love they had for Him when they first came to faith.

If you were radically saved or had a time in your life when your faith became *real*, what were you like? Did you crave His Word like an addict? Did you love to worship because you wanted to express your love for Christ? Would you talk to the Lord and think about Him throughout the day? Did you sing and lift your hands in worship and not care who saw you? Would you talk about your faith like a blubbering idiot to anyone who would listen because you were so excited about what Jesus had done in your life? Did you rise early in the morning because that was the only time you could set aside to have focused fellowship with Him?

Jesus tells the Ephesians and us that if we start doing those things again, we'll find the *passion* returning to our relationship with Him.

…or else I will come to you quickly and remove your lampstand from its place—unless you repent.

Remember that the *"lampstand"* represents the Ephesian church, not individual believers. The warning Jesus gives is that if this *church* continues going through the motions without any emotion, He'll shut it down. That's how seriously Jesus takes His relationship with His Church. She is His *bride*. His greatest desire is not nice, clean, well-organized churches that impress the outside world. He wants our *hearts*.

Ultimately, Jesus did shut down the Church in Ephesus. Some individuals repented and changed their ways, but collectively, they never really grasped that it's all about loving Jesus personally and directly. And their church died.

Fast-forward to our day, and think about the answers you often hear when you ask someone, *"What's your church all about?"*

"Loving the lost."
"Being the hands and feet of Jesus."
"Building strong marriages and families."
"Being a community of faith."

Those are all good things, but there is only one acceptable answer: *"Our church is all about loving Jesus."* The Church exists, first and foremost, to bless and honor *Jesus*. Everything else He wants His Church to be flows out of that focus. Having His Church be a blessing to Him matters more than anything else the Church can do.

After that incredibly challenging word, Jesus shares this encouragement with the Ephesians:

> **⁶ But this you have, that you hate the deeds of the Nicolaitans, which I also hate.**

It seems the Nicolaitans weren't an organized group called "The Nicolaitans." Rather, **"Nicolaitan"** was a term given to men who exhibited certain *behaviors*. And the Bible gives us some clues about what those behaviors were.

Many scholars believe the term **"Nicolaitan"** is itself a clue. It's a Greek compound word made up of the word "nicos," which means *"to conquest, utterly vanquish,"* and "laos," which means *"a people, the laity, the congregation/people of a church."* So, the word literally means *"to rule over the laity."*

This leads some to speculate that the Nicolaitans were men who claimed to be apostles but were teaching false doctrine, likely propagating the idea that they were somehow closer to God and more spiritually elite than ordinary Christians. This false teaching was used to divide the Church into two classes—leaders and everybody else.

Why would these Nicolaitans teach this? The motives are pretty obvious—financial gain, power, prestige, glory, and so on. All the usual temptations of the flesh.

This possible explanation seems to be confirmed by the appearance of the Nicolaitans in the third letter, written to the Church in Pergamos:

> [14] *... I have a few things against you, because you have there those who hold the doctrine of Balaam, who taught Balak to put a stumbling block before the children of Israel, to eat things sacrificed to idols, and to commit sexual immorality.* [15] *Thus you also have those who hold the doctrine of the Nicolaitans, which thing I hate.*

Jesus points out that the Church in Pergamos is *not* rejecting the Nicolaitans, as the Church in Ephesus did. Instead, they are accepting their false doctrine.

And then Jesus alludes to the Old Testament account of the prophet Balaam and his interaction with Balak that resulted in God's people *"stumbling"* because they became ensnared by sin. Specifically, they were eating things sacrificed to idols and committing sexual immorality.

You might be thinking, *"Wait a minute, Jeff. Didn't Paul write in 1 Corinthians 8 that eating meat sacrificed to idols doesn't matter because idols are nothing?"* Absolutely. In that instance, Paul was talking about buying meat in the public market, knowing it had come from an animal sacrificed to a pagan god. In that case, Paul said that *"an idol is nothing in the world,"* so it's just meat. But what Paul talks about in other places, and what Jesus is talking about here in **Revelation 2**, is *taking part* in that ritualistic sacrifice to a pagan god.

Jesus observed that Balaam caused Israel to stumble by becoming ensnared with sin, and the Nicolaitans were doing the same thing to the Church in Pergamos. For more insight, we'll need to take a closer look at the Old Testament account of Balaam and Balak, which we find in **Numbers 22–24**.

The Doctrine of Balaam

Balaam was a prophet for hire; I'll recap his story for you.

Israel is in the wilderness; they've come out of Egypt and are on their way to the Promised Land. God is blessing them as a people and causing them to flourish. Word is traveling fast that these Israelites serve an unstoppable God who works miracles and gives them victory in battle.

The king of the Moabites at the time is Balak. And the Moabites are *not* good people. Balak notices Israel getting closer and closer to his part of the world—there are 2 to 3 million of them—and he's *terrified*.

So, he calls for Balaam who has a legitimate prophetic gift, given to him by God. However, Balaam is not a man of great character, to say the least. Balak sends a delegation to Balaam offering to pay him to curse the Israelites for the Moabites. Balaam says that he can't do anything that the Lord won't let him do, so he promises to pray about this request.

They get together after Balaam prays about it, and he tells them that God says that he can't do it. Balak is disappointed, but he hasn't given up yet. Sometime later, he sends the entourage back to Balaam, saying that he is willing to pay him a lot of money if he will curse Israel for them.

This gets Balaam's attention, and he says that something feels different about Balak's request this time. So, he decides to ask the

Lord again whether he can curse Israel—just in case He's changed His mind.

By the way, if God ever says no and you press the issue until He says yes, just know you should *not* do that thing because it usually means God is about to teach you that you should've listened to Him the first time!

Balaam goes before the Lord again, and God reminds Balaam that He has already said no, but He tells Balaam that he can go with the Moabites if he really wants to, as long as he only says what God tells him to say. Balaam is thrilled. Dreaming of riches, he heads off with a smile to meet with King Balak.

Balak takes Balaam up on a hill where they can look over all the Israelites and tells him that it's time for him to earn his money. Balaam begins to speak, but all that comes out of his mouth are . . . *blessings!* He explains that he is unable to curse those whom God has blessed.

Balak is understandably displeased—he's not paying Balaam to *bless* Israel. He thinks that maybe the energy isn't right in the spot where they're standing, so he takes Balaam to another mountain and insists that he try again. Balaam begins to speak over Israel, and yet again, the only thing that comes out are *blessings*.

At this point, Balak is highly frustrated. Balaam wants to get paid, as opposed to being executed for scamming the king, so he comes up with a different plan. He tells Balak that he wants him to be satisfied with his services. And although *he* can't curse Israel, he can tell Balak how to make the Israelites bring curses upon *themselves.* Balaam tells Balak to send out all his good-looking women to seduce the men of Israel and invite the men to join their pagan sexual worship rituals. That way, they will bring a curse upon themselves because they're Yahweh's people, and if they get out of line, He will step in and discipline them because He loves them. And Balak can be the one to benefit when that happens.

Numbers 25:1–3 tells us what happened next:

> **Now Israel remained in Acacia Grove, and the people began to commit harlotry with the women of Moab. They invited the people to the sacrifices of their gods, and the people ate and bowed down to their gods. So Israel was joined to Baal of Peor, and the anger of the Lord was aroused against Israel.**

The pagans came to the people of God and enticed them to join them in their pagan worship rituals and sexual immorality.

Dangers of the Nicolaitan Spirit

What Balaam did is a *picture* of what the Nicolaitans were trying to do. The implication is that in Ephesus, the Nicolaitans were teaching that it was perfectly acceptable for Christians to join in the sexual rituals and pagan sacrifices at the Temple of Artemis. Perhaps they were arguing from the perspective of some sort of "hyper-grace" heresy, like those today who claim that you can live however you want, and God's grace will cover it. Or they may say that Christians can't sin because Jesus has already paid for all our sins.

Fortunately, the discerning Ephesian church knew the Scriptures, spotted the heresy a mile away, and were having none of it.

Please don't miss this point. Regarding the false teaching that says it is acceptable for the Church to compromise and join the world in her sins, Jesus is crystal clear: He *hates* it.

And regarding the teaching that church leaders are on a higher spiritual level than the congregation—that they are closer to God because of the position they hold—Jesus hates that too.

Sadly, we still see these perversions in modern churches, denominations, and movements wherever pastors or priests are considered to have a greater level of access to God than "normal" believers. Such perversions often lead to unhealthy manifestations of control over the laity, such as:

- Church leaders claiming that sins need to be confessed to *them* to be forgiven by God.
- Church leaders who demand congregants obtain their approval before making any major life decisions (e.g., *"We need to approve anyone you date."*)

The Nicolaitan "spirit" is at work in the church leader who says, *"We're not all equal under God. God wants church leaders to rule over their congregations like good kings."* That's heresy.

In **2 Corinthians 1:24**, the Apostle Paul writes:

> *. . . that does not mean we want to dominate you by telling you how to put your faith into practice. We want to work together with you so you will be full of joy, for it is by your own faith that you stand firm* (NLT).

Godly church leaders don't instruct out of a desire for power; they instruct out of a desire to help the saints grow in their faith and experience the fullness of life in Christ.

> **[7] He who has an ear, let him hear what the Spirit says to the churches.**

Jesus calls *individuals* reading this letter to take it to heart because this church, collectively, will not change.

V.1 told us the One writing this letter is, *"He who holds the seven stars in His right hand, who walks in the midst of the seven golden lampstands."* We know from **Revelation 1** that this is *Jesus*.

But here in **V.7**, who are we told is saying these things to the churches? *"The Spirit."*

I point that out because it's more evidence that the Trinity speaks with one voice, in perfect harmony, on all things. Who's saying these things to the Church in Ephesus? Is it Jesus? Is it the Holy Spirit? The answer is yes. **V.7** continues:

To him [the individual] **who overcomes . . .**

Who overcomes what? The temptation to live *religiously* rather than *relationally* with Jesus.

. . . I will give to eat from the tree of life, which is in the midst of the Paradise of God.

There was a tree of life in Eden, and **Genesis 3:22** tells us that anyone who ate from it would *"live forever."* The idea is that those who love Jesus will live forever in *"the Paradise of God."* They'll enjoy fellowship with God for eternity.

In this promise, I believe we are given a powerful reminder that being with Jesus forever is the eternal destiny of all who love Him. The Scriptures point to and reveal Jesus, but the end goal of our existence is not attaining perfect knowledge of the Scriptures—it's being with the one who *authored* the Scriptures.

As we study the Word, treasure it, and memorize it, may we never miss the forest for the trees—it's all about *Jesus*. And if we're growing in our *knowledge* of the Word but it's not resulting in greater *love* for the Lord, then we're missing the whole point.

Jesus *begins* this letter by reminding the Ephesians that He is in *their* midst, and then He *ends* this letter by telling them that one day they will be in *His* midst. *He* is where everything is headed. *He* is the point. And if we get so busy with the Jesus "stuff" that we miss Jesus, then we've missed *everything*.

CLOSING THOUGHTS

If you understand the Book of Revelation, but it doesn't make you love Jesus more, then it's meaningless. And I think it's timely that Jesus gives us this warning so close to the beginning of our study because we should not be doing this to feel more intelligent or sound more theologically educated. We should study this book because we want to know more about the Jesus we love so that we can love Him more faithfully, personally, and directly.

As the Shorter Westminster Catechism so perfectly renders it: *"Man's chief end is to glorify God and to enjoy Him forever."*

REVELATION 2:8-11

We're studying the second act of the Book of Revelation, which comprises **Revelation 2–3**. We learned that in these chapters, Jesus dictates letters to seven churches, and each letter has four layers of application: the local church ~AD 96, all churches, all believers, and prophecy.

The first letter was addressed to the Church in *Ephesus* and spoke prophetically of the period covering the birth of the Church ~AD 32 up to ~AD 100 (there will be some overlap in these periods). The second letter is addressed to the Church in Smyrna.

THE CHURCH IN SMYRNA

We know that the name of each church's location reveals a significant detail about them, and "Smyrna" means "myrrh." Myrrh was used in perfumes, for the religious purification of women, and as priestly anointing oil. But most famously, myrrh is an embalming spice that was (and is) used in wrapping bodies for burial because its beautifully fragrant aroma masks the stench of death.

It is made from the sap of small, thorny trees. To get it, you must repeatedly disfigure the tree by cutting through the bark to bleed the sapwood (yes, that's really how the process is described). When that sap dries and hardens, it becomes myrrh.

At this time in history, myrrh was worth more than its weight in gold, and its use here in **Revelation 2** is a perfect metaphor for the Church in Smyrna because its beautiful aroma can only be released when the hardened sap is crushed. During the first few centuries AD, the affection the Church had for the symbol of the Cross was puzzling to unbelievers, as crucifixion was the most excruciating death the Romans could conceive. And yet since the resurrection of Jesus, believers have loved the Cross because it's where Jesus loved us by being crushed in our place. Similarly, the beauty of Smyrna was revealed in her crushing.

HISTORY AND CULTURE OF SMYRNA

Smyrna was located around 40 miles north of Ephesus. After lying in ruin for centuries, Alexander the Great had the vision to rebuild it and create a glorious example of what a Greek city could be. His plans were carried out by two of his successors, who built a city nicknamed "The Beautiful" because of its picturesque architecture. By John's day, it had grown into a full-fledged metropolis and was the second-largest city in the Roman province of Asia. It was the first city in the province to build a temple to Roma, the *spirit* of Rome, and was known for being the regional headquarters of Caesar worship, the imperial cult.

The religious adoration of Rome and Caesar was central to the life of Smyrna's citizens. Failing to participate in the imperial cult would hamstring your chances of climbing the social or economic ladder and cause your neighbors to view you as *unpatriotic*.

In most parts of the Roman Empire around AD 96, you

could worship any god you wanted—including Jesus. However, in exchange for that religious freedom, you had to also acknowledge that Caesar was a god. Once a year, every person would have to visit their local Caesar temple or altar, profess Caesar as a god, sprinkle a pinch of incense on the altar, and speak these words: *"Kaiser Kurios" ("Caesar is Lord")*. In exchange for their compliance, the government would issue a certificate allowing them to freely worship the god(s) of their choice for the following year.

Things hadn't always been this way in the Empire. Caesar worship had been optional until the late first century when it became mandatory under Domitian.

Predictably, many religiously devout Jews refused to comply and were killed as a result. The Romans aspired to unify and rule over all the peoples of the earth, and soon realized that this narcissistic vision couldn't include Jews if they were all dead. So, they made a once-in-an-empire exception, making the Jews the only people *exempt* from the pinch offering to Caesar.

For several years, the Early Church was generally viewed by the Romans as a *sect* of Judaism—affording Christians the same exemption from pinch offerings enjoyed by the Jews. But it wasn't long before Jewish religious leaders who hated Christianity (because they considered it blasphemous) started going out of their way to inform Roman authorities that it was *not* a Jewish sect. This shift and the fact that new religions were not acceptable in the Empire exposed Christianity to a new wave of persecution. Many believers faced a life-or-death decision: should they make a seemingly *tiny* gesture—a proverbial *head nod* to Caesar—or hold firm to the truth that there is no God but Jesus?

The Church in Smyrna chose the latter. They decided to stand for Jesus and faced brutally intense persecution.

Smyrna in Church History

In light of what the Church in Smyrna was going through around AD 96 and the period of Church history it prophetically represents; we'll call the Church in Smyrna "The Suffering Church."

Prophetically, the back half of the period covered by Ephesus (the first church) coincides with the rise of Smyrna. As the age of the Apostolic Church was dying down, the age of the Suffering Church was coming to the fore, and the persecution experienced in Smyrna was being mirrored across the Empire.

In AD 54, Caesar Nero rose to power and unleashed a torrent of persecution that was characterized by an intense hatred of Christians and a demonic delight in causing them pain, suffering, and death.

Horrifically, Nero was just the first of ten successive Caesars who violently and passionately sought to erase all traces of Christianity from the Empire. Wave upon wave of persecution crashed down upon the Church until edicts from emperors Galerius[22] and Constantine/Licinius[23] brought it to an end. We're talking about unimaginable persecution that lasted for around *257 years*.

To put that in perspective:

- In AD 100, there were ~195 million people on earth. That number rose to ~200 million in AD 400.

- The 10 Caesars who persecuted the Church from AD 54 to AD 311 combined to martyr *5–7 million* Christians. That's around 3% of the earth's population during that time.

---

[22] The Edict of Serdica/The Edict of Toleration in AD 311.
[23] The Edict of Milan in AD 313.

- From those numbers, we can extrapolate to get an idea of the *scale* based on the current world population. In today's terms, we'd be looking at a campaign of persecution that claimed the lives of around *231 million* Christians over the past 257 years.

- Imagine a genocide of 900,000 Christians occurring every year for 257 years. Proportionately, that's what happened to the Suffering Church.

It's hard to fathom, and it happened to *the Church*.

Books such as *Church History in Plain Language*[24] and *Foxe's Book of Martyrs*[25] catalog the litany of horrors inflicted upon the Church, including being crucified, sown inside animal skins and torn to pieces by wild dogs or lions, dragged to death behind wild bulls, burned alive with one's family inside their home or at the stake, thrown into the sea with a heavy stone around the neck, poisoned, starved, stabbed, racked, scourged . . . and on and on the list goes.

Men were often forced to watch their families be tortured to death before receiving the same fate. The city of Phrygia was almost entirely Christian, so one day, the whole place was burned to the ground and its citizens were forced to remain in the flames.

Nero was famous for illuminating his palace gardens with Christians bound to stakes, covered in tar or wax, and lit on fire while he shouted, *"Now you truly are the light of the world!"* Anyone

---

[24] Bruce L. Shelley, *Church History in Plain Language*. 4th ed. (Nashville, Tennessee: Thomas Nelson, 2013).

[25] John Foxe and Harold J. Chadwick. *Foxe's Book of Martyrs* (Gainesville, Florida: Bridge-Logos, 2001).

who hated Christians was welcome to take in the sick spectacle for their entertainment.

Words cannot sufficiently capture the horrors inflicted upon those who loved Jesus in the years of the Suffering Church.

INTO THE TEXT

Jesus is writing to this church as they are experiencing unimaginable hardship. What is He going to say to them? What does He want them to know? What does He want them to remember? Let's find out:

> *⁸And to the angel* [the pastor] *of the Church in Smyrna write, "These things says the First and the Last, who was dead, and came to life: . . . "*

We know Jesus gives Himself a different *title* in each of the seven letters, and it's always related to something each church needs to be *reminded of*.

To a church enduring unspeakable persecution, Jesus introduces Himself as *"the First and the Last."* We talked about the Old Testament connections to that title in our study of **Revelation 1**. Jesus is drawing their attention to His eternal nature to encourage them that while their *suffering* is temporary, their *glory* will be eternal.

Jesus takes it a step further by reminding them that even earthly death is temporary for those who love Him. In calling Himself the One *"who was dead, and came to life,"* Jesus effectively puts an arm around these suffering saints and reminds them that He knows what they're going through. The suffering and death that He experienced were greater than anyone will ever experience. Everyone thought it was over when His dead body was laid in a tomb, but He's alive and glorified, and that will be their future too—no matter what happens to them on earth.

Now Jesus gives Smyrna their "report card," starting with a *commendation* (what they're doing well):

⁹ *I know your works, tribulation, and poverty . . .*

"Tribulation" is the Greek word *"thlipsis."* It means *"a pressing together"* or *"pressure."* It was used to describe the process in which grapes are crushed and pressed to produce wine, the method of torture where a man is slowly crushed to death by the weight of a large boulder, and the crushing of *myrrh* to release its fragrant aroma. When used to describe a time of trouble or distress, "thlipsis" is translated as "tribulation."[26]

Jesus commends this precious church for standing firm in the face of the crushing pressure of intense persecution. Their actions proved they genuinely valued the Kingdom of God more than their earthly lives.

The Lord specifically commends them for keeping the faith through *"poverty"*—a word meaning *"destitution."* It's a very different concept from what most of us know as poverty. In first-world countries, one can live below the poverty line while still (usually) having electricity, indoor plumbing, a cell phone, food, and more. "Destitution" is when poor people feel bad for you because you have *absolutely nothing*—no changes of clothes, no property, *nothing*.

---

[26] For the sake of clarity, I should mention that while the Church in Smyrna was enduring exceedingly difficult *"tribulation,"* they were not enduring *the* Tribulation. That's something completely different, which we'll get into in Revelation 6.

These faithful believers were viewed as *subhuman* because of their perceived animus toward the imperial cult and, therefore, the Empire. Much of the time, whatever property they had was confiscated by the authorities or plundered by their neighbors.

When imprisoned, they often had no food or clothing unless someone outside provided them. And if someone did, they risked ending up in that same prison themselves. The writer of the book of **Hebrews** speaks of believers who took such risks on his behalf:

> **. . . you had compassion on me in my chains, and joyfully accepted the plundering of your goods, knowing that you have a better and an enduring possession for yourselves in heaven.**
>
> —Hebrews 10:34

Our brothers and sisters in the Persecuted Church still face similar situations and difficult decisions today.

How devoted to Jesus was the Church in Smyrna? Remember, all they had to do to end their suffering was make a quick trip to the local Caesar temple, sprinkle a pinch of incense on the altar, and say, *"Caesar is god too."* And in an *instant*, they could have returned to hosting Bible studies and gathering for church services as free men and women, without fear of persecution.

But they didn't. They believed that Jesus, His name, and His glory were worth their *lives*. And they were right.

Polycarp: Bishop of Smyrna

I want to share an amazing story that embodies the courage and commitment of the Early Church during this season of persecution.

In Smyrna lived a man named *Polycarp*. He was a disciple of John the Apostle, who personally trained, ordained, and loved him as a brother. Polycarp became an elder in the Church and then, in AD 115, he became bishop of Smyrna. He was widely known, loved, and respected by the citizenry because he lived such an honorable life.

In AD 150, Polycarp was around 86 years old and still leading the Church in Smyrna. Eusebius, the great Christian historian, tells us that when the local authorities received an edict to clamp down on any locals refusing to participate in the imperial cult, they planned to have Polycarp do it first. It was a strategic decision they assumed would result in the prompt compliance of all other Christians in the city.

When the authorities approached Polycarp with their proposal, he declined. So, one Saturday evening, they seized him and brought him to the stadium (or theater), where Eusebius records:

> *He stepped forward and was asked by the proconsul if he was really Polycarp. When he said yes, the proconsul urged him to deny the charge. "Respect your years!" he exclaimed, adding similar appeals regularly made on such occasions: "Swear by Caesar's fortune; change your attitude."*

Polycarp responded:

> *"'For eighty-six years . . . I have been His servant, and He has never done me wrong: how can I blaspheme my King who saved me?'*
>
> *'I have wild beasts,' said the proconsul. 'I shall throw you to them, if you don't change your attitude.'*

'Call them,' replied the old man. 'We cannot change our attitude if it means a change from better to worse. But it is a splendid thing to change from cruelty to justice.'

'If you make light of the beasts,' retorted the governor, 'I'll have you destroyed by fire, unless you change your attitude.'

Polycarp answered: 'The fire you threaten burns for a time and is soon extinguished: there is a fire you know nothing about – the fire of the judgment to come and of eternal punishment, the fire reserved for the ungodly. But why do you hesitate? Do what you want.'

… the proconsul was amazed, and sent the crier to stand in the middle of the arena and announce three times: 'Polycarp has confessed that he is a Christian.'

Then a shout went up from every throat that Polycarp must be burnt alive.

The rest followed in less time than it takes to describe…"[27]

Polycarp was allowed to offer one final prayer. He used it to thank God for the privilege of dying for Him. The fires were lit, and he was soon gone.

That's what it meant to pastor the Church in Smyrna during a season of persecution. History records that Polycarp's death served as an even greater witness to the Church in Smyrna than his life.

It's incredible to consider the possibility that Polycarp had likely *read* the book of Revelation and that as he faced the end of his

---

[27] Eusebius. *The History of the Church* (London, England: The Folio Society, 2011), 108–109.

earthly life, he was encouraged and strengthened by Jesus' letter to the Church in Smyrna.

The Church in Smyrna Was Rich in Faith

After saying, *"I know your works, tribulation, and poverty,"* Jesus says,

> *... (but you are rich); ...*

These suffering believers needed to hear this because they were a lot like us in this regard: when things get difficult in our lives, we often assume we must be doing something wrong or that God is angry with us. Jesus lets them know they are *"rich"* from His perspective. They're doing great. He's proud of them and pleased with them.

If that's the case, then why are they going through all this suffering? It's because while we tend to be concerned with our *present* quality of life, Jesus is concerned with our *eternal* quality of life.

While He obviously cares about our current circumstances, Jesus also sees everything from an *eternal* perspective, which we can't yet—try as we might. The Lord knows that this life is **"a vapor,"**[28] a grain of sand compared to the beach of eternity. Therefore, trading earthly suffering for eternal reward is a truly profitable way to spend the currency of one's earthly life. It's the *best thing for us*—something every martyr in Heaven will attest to.

In 1956, Jim Elliot flew into the remote jungle of Ecuador with four other men. Their goal was to share the Gospel with a tribe

---

[28] James 4:14.

completely unreached by missionaries. Shortly after they landed, the tribe killed all five men.

While going through his belongings after his death, Jim's family found an old journal. In his entry dated October 28, 1949, Elliot had written:

> *"He is no fool who gives what he cannot keep, to gain that which he cannot lose."*[29]

The same passion for Jesus that consumed Jim Elliot consumed the Church in Smyrna and is still found in the hearts of all who genuinely love the Lord. (I encourage you to investigate the life of Jim Elliot further and discover what happened to that tribe in the years following his death.)

Jesus assures the believers in Smyrna that despite their poverty and persecution, they're rich in the only way that truly matters—*eternally*.

The heart of the Suffering Church was the *exact opposite* of the heart we'll find in the Last Days Church, Laodicea. When we reach **Revelation 3:17**, Jesus will tell them:

> **... *you say, "I am rich, have become wealthy, and have need of nothing" - and do not know that you are wretched, miserable, poor, blind, and naked ...***

The Suffering Church thought they were *poor*, but Jesus considered them *rich*. The Last Days Church will think they're *rich*, but Jesus will consider them *poor*.

---

[29] Elisabeth Elliot, *The Journals of Jim Elliot: Missionary, Martyr, Man of God.* (Grand Rapids, Michigan: Revell, 2023), 174.

A Synagogue of Satan

Let's continue with **V.9**:

> *... and I know the blasphemy of those who say they are Jews and are not, but are a synagogue of Satan.*

What a strange phrase: *"a synagogue of Satan."* The first persecution to come upon the Church was driven by Jewish religious leaders in Israel (not the people but the leaders)—the same leaders who rejected Jesus and helped arrange His execution at the hands of the Romans. Instead of simply barring Jewish Christians from their synagogues, these men were violating Torah[30] by betraying their ethnic brethren to the Romans, resulting in their imprisonment, torture, and even execution.

As mentioned earlier, while Jews were exempt from making the pinch offering to Caesar, many went out of their way to make sure the Romans were notified if a *Christian* didn't perform the ritual. It was a sad situation where those who should have welcomed Jesus as the long-awaited Messiah not only rejected Him but actively worked to persecute His Bride, the Church.

These are the leaders Jesus refers to as *"those who say they are Jews and are not, but are a synagogue of Satan."* The implication is that while they claimed to be serving God, their actions revealed they were serving Satan.

We observe this same dynamic in an exchange between Jesus and the religious leaders in **John 8:37–47**:

> *"I know that you are Abraham's descendants, but you seek to kill Me, because My word has no place in you. I speak what*

---

[30] Cf. Leviticus 19:18.

I have seen with My Father, and you do what you have seen with your father."

They answered and said to Him, *"Abraham is our father."*

Jesus said to them, *"If you were Abraham's children, you would do the works of Abraham. But now you seek to kill Me, a Man who has told you the truth which I heard from God. Abraham did not do this. You do the deeds of your father."*

Then they said to Him, *"We were not born of fornication; we have one Father—God."*

Jesus said to them, *"If God were your Father, you would love Me, for I proceeded forth and came from God; nor have I come of Myself, but He sent Me. Why do you not understand My speech? Because you are not able to listen to My word. You are of your father the devil, and the desires of your father you want to do. He was a murderer from the beginning, and does not stand in the truth, because there is no truth in him. When he speaks a lie, he speaks from his own resources, for he is a liar and the father of it. But because I tell the truth, you do not believe Me. Which of you convicts Me of sin? And if I tell the truth, why do you not believe Me? He who is of God hears God's words; therefore you do not hear, because you are not of God."*

Here's the idea: Jews who genuinely loved God recognized Jesus as Messiah and are considered by God to be *true* Jews—*true* sons of Abraham. In contrast, when it comes to Jews who not only reject Jesus but also persecute those Jews who *do* receive Him, Jesus doesn't mince words. He declared that Satan was their father. When Jesus refers to *"a synagogue of Satan,"* He's referring to Jewish religious leaders who persecute Jewish Christians, and by extension persecute *Him.*

Let me be clear—this is *not* an anti-Semitic statement. This is a *judgment* made by Jesus regarding Jewish religious leaders who were actively working to persecute Jewish Christians.

DON'T FEAR THE SUFFERING TO COME

¹⁰ *Do not fear any of those things which you are about to suffer* [note the future tense]. ***Indeed, the devil is about to throw some of you into prison, that you may be tested, and you will have tribulation ten days. Be faithful until death, and I will give you the crown of life.***

Much of this would have been difficult to hear because when you're in a trial, all you want is for it to be *over*. Instead, Jesus shares that this season of persecution is going to go on for a while—*"ten days,"* to be exact.

In the original Greek, the word *"days"* can mean *"a day"* but can also be used more broadly to refer to *a period, an age, a time, a while, years, times,* or even *waves.*

Prophetically, I believe that *"ten days"* likely refers to 10 waves of persecution driven by 10 successive Roman emperors from Nero to Diocletian—persecution that crashed down upon the Church for around 257 years.

Regarding its application to the literal Church in Smyrna around AD 96 and its application to all churches and all believers, I believe *"ten days"* is a reference to the first chapter of the Book of Daniel, where we read of four faithful Jewish men—Daniel,

Hananiah, Mishael, and Azariah[31]—who had been kidnapped and taken to Babylon, where they were to be trained as counselors to the king. The food and drink offered to them violated their religious convictions and commitments. So, Daniel requested they be given vegetables and water instead. The steward in charge of them was afraid that he would get into trouble if the king saw them looking gaunt and unhealthy. Daniel's solution was to propose a **"test"** for **"ten days."**[32] And in **Daniel 1:15**, we learn the outcome:

> **. . . at the end of ten days their features appeared better and fatter in flesh than all the young men who ate the portion of the king's delicacies.**

I believe Jesus wanted the Church in Smyrna to see themselves in Daniel and his Hebrew brethren. Like them, the Church in Smyrna was under tremendous pressure to give in to the demands of the culture and was surrounded by voices warning them that faithfulness to their God would cost them their lives.

At the end of the ten-day trial, Daniel and his brothers emerged looking **"better"** than those who had done things the world's way. And if the Church in Smyrna likewise remained faithful through their **"ten days"** of persecution, they too would emerge more glorious (in eternity) than those who did things the world's way.

And if you're not convinced of the connection yet, read the stories of those four men in the first half of the Book of Daniel. You'll find they all endure a *significant* trial for their faithfulness to

---

[31] The latter three being better known by their Babylonian names of Shadrach, Meshach, and Abed-Nego.

[32] Cf. Daniel 1:12.

God and, specifically, their refusal to participate in the imperial cult of Babylon.

Well, not only is Smyrna's persecution not going to end anytime soon, but Jesus tells them that it's going to get even *more* intense. And His exhortation is simply, *"Be faithful until death."*

In **Romans 12:19**, Paul refers to Old Testament passages[33] when he shares this instruction with believers:

Beloved, do not avenge yourselves, but *rather* give place to wrath; for it is written, *"Vengeance is Mine, I will repay,"* says the Lord.

When will the Lord repay those who love evil? In the Day of the Lord—the coming period which includes things like the Tribulation and the Great White Throne Judgment. If you love Jesus, justice for *your* sins and *your* wrongs was metered out upon Jesus at the Cross. Those who reject Jesus will receive justice for their sins in the coming Day of the Lord. And Revelation will detail that future time for us in the chapters ahead.

Notice that there is no talk of forming a militia to combat evil on the earth through military means. There is no talk of killing one's oppressors or plotting to overthrow the government. The message of the Bible is that vengeance belongs to the Lord, and Revelation confirms that He has a plan to ensure absolute justice is done.

The issue is *faith*. Will we trust God to be just and do what is right, in His timing rather than ours? Jesus' word to you and me is the same as it was to these precious Christians in Smyrna. There's no talk in this letter of *escaping* trials, only holding on and staying

---

[33] Cf. Deuteronomy 32:35; Psalm 94:1–2.

faithful. And history tells us they did. They *were* faithful until death, and that's why Jesus has no criticism for this church.

Really? They had *no* issues? How is that possible? Because persecution *purifies* the Church. There are no casual or half-hearted believers in a church when simply attending a service or Bible study might cost you and your family everything you have, including your lives. When that's the situation, the pastor doesn't ever have to preach on commitment.

In centuries past, gold would be purified manually. A goldsmith would heat a pot to incredible temperatures and then place raw gold inside, where it would begin to melt. As the gold liquified, the impurities would float to the surface, where the goldsmith would skim them off.

How did the goldsmith know when he finally had *pure* gold? Historians tell us the trade standard was the goldsmith being able to see his reflection in the liquid. That's what persecution does to the Church; it *purifies* us. Jesus uses it to "boil" distractions and impurities out of our lives so that we more clearly reflect *Him*.

The Church in Smyrna was purified by persecution, and that's why Jesus had no criticism for them.

Jesus promises *"the crown of life"* to those who stay faithful to Him, even to death. This is a *reward*, not a salvation issue. Salvation is **"the gift of God"**[34] and is never awarded based on our performance.

I find it beautiful that Jesus juxtaposes death with life in His exhortation, promising *"the crown of life"* to those who remain *"faithful until death."* He's letting them know that He can and will give them *life* to a degree they cannot even fathom.

What is *"the crown of life"*? The most likely explanation is that

---

[34] Ephesians 2:8.

it's a metaphor for eternal life. However, if these crowns are literal, we will learn their ultimate purpose in **Revelation 4**.

The Second Death

Following the structure employed in each letter, Jesus ends by reminding us there are things in here that *every* church and believer needs to hear:

> [11] *He who has an ear, let him hear what the Spirit says to the churches. He who overcomes shall not be hurt by the second death.*

What is *"the second death"*? Revelation tells us:

> **. . . Death and Hades were cast into the lake of fire. This is the second death.**
> —Revelation 20:14

> *. . . the cowardly, unbelieving, abominable, murderers, sexually immoral, sorcerers, idolaters, and all liars shall have their part in the lake which burns with fire and brimstone, which is the second death.*
> —Revelation 21:8

"The second death" is eternal death in the lake of fire. It is an eternity spent in complete separation from God, who is the only source of anything and everything good. It is an *eternity* apart from *goodness*.

To say it another way, He who is born *once* dies *twice*. He who is born *twice* dies *once*.[35] That is, almost everyone will experience the

---

[35] I heard Chuck Missler share this. It may have originated with D. L. Moody, but nobody seems to be sure.

first death, which is the end of our physical lives on this earth. But the Bible says the *essential* part of us, our spirit, will continue to live forever, one way or another.

That eternity will be spent in one of two conditions—eternal *life* or eternal *death*. Those who belong to Jesus will experience never-ending *life*. Those who do not belong to Jesus will experience never-ending *death*. Both states will be *active* and *ongoing* for all eternity.

When you place your faith in Jesus as your Savior and welcome Him into your life as Lord, He describes what takes place in your spirit as being *"born again."*[36] At that moment, His Spirit joins with your dead spirit, bringing it to life as a new creation.

A person who is only born *once* (physically) will die at the end of this earthly life and then again for *all eternity*. A person who is born *twice* (physically *and* spiritually) will die at the end of this earthly life but then *live* again for eternity.

Revelation 20:6 declares:

Blessed and holy *is* he who has part in the first resurrection. Over such the second death has no power . . .

Perhaps you read **V.11** and got nervous because it seems to say that only those who *overcome* persecution (i.e., stay faithful through it) will be saved *("**not be hurt by the second death**")*. In reality, those who are saved *will* overcome persecution, even to death.

Paul describes God's entire plan for us in **Romans 8:29–30**:

. . . whom He foreknew, He also predestined *to be* conformed to the image of His Son, that He might be

---

[36] John 3:3.

the firstborn among many brethren. Moreover whom He predestined, these He also called; whom He called, these He also justified; and whom He justified, these He also glorified.

Notice that throughout the entire process, no one is lost. No one falls through the cracks. The Lord knows those who love Him, and all who do are destined to be **"glorified,"** as Paul put it. Therefore, in the very next verse, Paul's conclusion is:

What then shall we say to these things? If God *is* for us, who *can be* against us?

Just as the Lord has always given His deliverers, prophets, and apostles the right words to say at the right time, for the past 2,000 years He has given special grace to believers facing death. If you are not sure you could handle intense persecution, but you know you love Jesus, then you can trust He will provide what you need when it's needed. Our Heavenly Father gives us *"our daily bread,"*[37] whether it's grace to manage stress at work, raise kids, get schoolwork done, or die for Him. If you love Jesus, then you are and will be an overcomer.

APPLICATION TO ALL CHURCHES

Sadly, the Church in Smyrna would not be the last church to experience persecution. Persecution has been the default state of the Church for 99% of the previous 2,000 years. Count your blessings if you are fortunate enough to live in a country where you are free

---

[37] Matthew 6:11.

to worship Jesus. Our brothers and sisters in places like Iraq, Syria, India, China, and Nigeria face persecution in forms no less evil and horrifying than what the Early Church faced.

The twentieth century saw an average of 150,000 Christians killed annually for their faith. In terms of total numbers, more Christians were killed in the 1900s for their faith than in any other period in the world's history. And that trend has only continued and increased in the twenty-first century.

What answer do you think you would get if you asked the average person on the street, *"Who do you think is the most persecuted people group in the world?"* Although mass media doesn't report the true picture of persecution, the correct answer is *"Christians,"* and it's not even close.

Throughout history, churches have needed and will continue to need the precious words of Jesus recorded in this letter for strength, peace, and comfort.

When we reach our study of the Church in Laodicea, we'll find it marked by a passion for a brand of Christianity that doesn't require sacrifice. They'll embrace pastors who say things like this: *"God's plan for your life is to make it amazing and wonderful because you're amazing and wonderful! And God wants to use His power to fulfill your dreams and agenda."* The problem is that this letter to the Church in Smyrna is in *all* our Bibles. And so, our theology must include room for the reality that sometimes suffering and death are part of God's plan for our lives. I know this is heavy, but it's the truth.

Jesus makes our lives wonderful, but He does not always define **"wonderful"** as we do. From Heaven's perspective, you and I being purified and made more like Jesus is *wonderful*. Trading earthly comfort for eternal reward is *wonderful*, and loving Jesus enough to share in His sufferings and death, being crushed like myrrh is *wonderful*. Does your theology of the Christian life and the goodness of God include room for suffering?

In **Romans 8:28**, Paul writes:

> **…we know that all things work together for good to those who love God, to those who are the called according to *His* purpose.**

The **"good"** God speaks of sometimes unfolds in eternity rather than in this life. Just ask Jesus. His earthly life ended in unimaginable pain and suffering. But then He rose to life, in glory that will last forever and never fade away.

God's promise to all believers—including those who died in Smyrna—is that He will do good in our lives. And the good that He does will last *forever*. We can take comfort in knowing we have that same promise. No matter how much it costs to stay faithful to Jesus in this life, it is nothing compared to the good He has prepared for us in eternity.

With that in mind, and with this precious church in mind, how do you think Jesus feels about preachers and churches who teach that:

- Suffering is the result of a lack of faith.
- Suffering is the result of a negative attitude or confession.
- Suffering is never God's plan.

We will see Jesus' answer when we reach the Church in Laodicea in **Revelation 3**. And when we do, you'll understand why I don't want to be that kind of preacher or be part of that kind of church.

APPLICATION TO ALL BELIEVERS

If you're a Christian, Scripture gives you two promises that don't usually end up on coffee mugs or bumper stickers. Jesus said:

> *These things I have spoken to you, that in Me you may have peace. In the world you will have tribulation; but be of good cheer, I have overcome the world.*
>
> —John 16:33

This is a promise Jesus gives His followers because He wants them to know they can have peace in Him, no matter what. And we need to know that because trials *will* come our way.

Satan (who currently runs the world system) becomes your enemy when you become a believer. And he sets all his wrath against *you*. He sets out to *destroy* you. If you've been a believer for more than a couple of years, I *know* you've had to walk through some trials.

We will have tribulation in our lives, but Jesus will still be with us. That's the first promise. The second is telling us the same thing, and it comes to us from Paul:

> **Yes, and all who desire to live godly in Christ Jesus will suffer persecution.**
>
> —2 Timothy 3:12

The Church in Smyrna and these two promises help me because they remind me that *this isn't Heaven.*

There's a problem when people get mad at God and say, *"Why would God allow this to happen in my life?"* Whether or not they're aware, they believe that following Jesus should result in a more comfortable, Heaven-like life here on earth. But *this is not Heaven.* We live in a fallen world. When the bottom falls out of my life (and it has), and everything looks hopeless, I have no reason to be mad at God. Instead, those moments should cause me to sigh deeply, remember where I am, and long for where I will one day be. Those moments should lead me to pray, *"Father, I am so looking forward to Heaven. I cannot wait to be in the place where Jesus rules and reigns and is fully revealed. It's going to be so good. Thank You that things will not always be like this."*

This is not Heaven. And when I truly grasp that, I realize it's OK if things don't all come together in this life because I will spend eternity enjoying a life where it *will* all come together around my glorious king, Jesus.

Our goal is not a perfect earthly life. Our goal is *Jesus*. And He has promised that those who desire Him more than this earthly life shall have Him.

CLOSING THOUGHTS

As an aside, I want to point out that this letter also applies especially to those who turn to Jesus *after* the Rapture—those who will be on the earth *during* the Tribulation. If you find yourself in that situation, I urge you to read the words of this letter slowly and repeatedly because they contain the path to eternal life.

Many of us *are* ready to die for Jesus. And the truth is that some days trading a bullet to the head for a fast pass to Heaven sounds pretty good! Because what's difficult for many of us is dying to *ourselves* and living for Jesus daily. How are you doing at dying to yourself every day in your relationships? In your marriage? In your family? At your place of work or school? In your finances?

I know we all fall short of the glory of God, and I'm not talking about perfection. Let's make it as simple as possible. Is there an area of your life where you know you're actively saying *"No"* to Jesus? If that's you, repent. Change. Say *"Yes"* to the Lord, die to yourself, and live for Him today. Because the phrase, *"No, Lord"* is an oxymoron. And while not every Christian will *die* a martyr, every Christian is called to *live* as one.

The world can change *fast*. The freedoms we enjoy cannot be assumed and are not guaranteed. Sooner or later, persecution is coming. And we would be wise to settle our commitment to Jesus long before it does.

This letter is in the Bible so that we might know what it means to **"Be faithful."** It means putting Jesus first and laying down your life for Him, even if it costs you *everything*.

REVELATION 2:12-17

THE CHURCH IN PERGAMOS

There are two primary interpretations of the name "Pergamos." I favor the one that best fits the big picture of the rest of Scripture and the pattern we see throughout the seven letters. "Pergamos" can mean "height" or "elevation," but the more compelling interpretation is found by noting that it is a compound word comprising the words "per" and "gamos."

"Per" means "mixed, objectionable, unacceptable, inappropriate." It's the root of the word "pervert," which we use to describe a person who engages in unacceptable and improper behavior. "Gamos" means "marriage." If somebody is monogamous, they are mono-gamos—married to one. If they are bigamous, they are simultaneously married to a second spouse (and are also an idiot). If they are polygamous, they are poly-gamos—married to more than one (usually several). That's the idea behind "gamos."

So, the compound word "Pergamos" means something like "unacceptable marriage." It refers to two things that do not belong together being joined. This church's name refers to its unholy marriage to the state, and that is why Pergamos is best described as "The Compromising Church."

HISTORY AND CULTURE OF PERGAMOS

When John recorded Revelation, Ephesus was the *intellectual* center of the province of Asia, and Smyrna was its most *beautiful* city. If you continued following the road system for about 100 miles, you would reach Pergamos (also known as Pergamon or Pergamum), Asia's most *important* city.

It was the capital of the province—the region's political and religious hub, famed for being the epicenter of Zeus worship. Zeus is the Greek version of Almighty God; he was considered the big dog in the pantheon of the gods. It was believed that Zeus was born in Pergamos, so the city boasted a grand altar and temple where sacrifices were offered to him. The structure was 115 feet wide, 110 feet deep, and 50 feet high. Surrounded by colonnades, it was the largest altar in the world.

Recall that at this time, you could worship any god you wanted in exchange for an annual offering of a pinch of incense and a two-word verbal acknowledgment of Caesar's deity. In Pergamos, you would do this at the temple of Zeus. The Caesars loved this because the pinch offering would look *spectacular* as a long line of people wound their way up the 60-foot-wide stairs of the massive structure. And wherever the emperor loved to hang out, the upper class would soon follow, which is why Pergamos became renowned for its wealth and fashion. It was the Paris or Milan of its day.

Like almost every other church in the region, the Church in Pergamos was under *intense persecution*. People were tortured, imprisoned, and executed for following Jesus. While the pinch offering created an annual flare-up of persecution, the continual presence of the imperial cult in Pergamos created a *daily* danger of persecution for believers. But as in Smyrna, faithful believers in Pergamos refused to acquiesce to the demands of Rome, and many were martyred for their stand.

Into this pressured environment came men preaching a seductive doctrine of *compromise*. They claimed to appeal to reason, assuring believers that God wanted them to live at peace with the authorities and didn't want them to suffer. Their message was: *"Give the pinch offering. God understands."* And when a person was facing the prospect of death by lions, this was an attractive message.

Pergamos in Church History

Prophetically speaking, the age of Smyrna ended around AD 313, and that's right about the time when Pergamos picked things up. Sadly, Pergamos is best known for the season of history when the Church married the state. We'll find that though it sounds wonderful, the reality is *catastrophic*. For this reason, Pergamos is known as the "The Compromising Church" and spans the years from ~AD 313 to ~AD 600.

But before we get into the story of Smyrna, we need to remember the big picture of Church history.

The Church was birthed around AD 32 in Jerusalem on the Day of Pentecost. It was amazing! But there was a little issue known as "The Great Commission." Jesus had commanded His disciples to *go* and make more disciples, but nobody was even thinking about leaving because fellowship in the newly birthed Church was so sweet!

Acts 8:1 tells us what happened when the first martyr of the Church, Stephen, was stoned to death:

> **…On that day a severe persecution broke out against the Church in Jerusalem, and all except the apostles were scattered throughout the land of Judea and Samaria.**

It took a wave of persecution to spread the Gospel from Jerusalem to Judea and Samaria. And throughout the centuries, God has often worked through persecution to spread the Gospel *"to the ends of the earth."*[38]

In AD 54 Caesar Nero began his horrific persecution of the Church. Guess what happened as a result? The Church was again forced to *scatter*. They fled across the Empire and the world, taking the Gospel with them. Consequently, the Church *exploded* in size over the next 250 years, despite Satan's best attempts to destroy it. As the Early Church writer Tertullian powerfully observed, *"the blood of Christians is . . . seed."*[39] The more Satan tried to kill the Church, the more it grew.

During this season of persecution, the Bishop of Carthage was forced to make an official statement, declaring that those who *intentionally pursued* martyrdom should not be revered as martyrs. Some believers were so focused on Heaven, so eager to be with the Lord, that they were doing everything they could to get themselves martyred! So, their bishop had to explain that they couldn't just knock on the door of the Coliseum—they had to at least make

---

[38] Acts 1:8.

[39] Tertullian, *The Complete Works of Tertullian: Apologeticus pro Christianis* (Hastings East Sussex, United Kingdom: Delphi Publishing Ltd), chap. 50, Kindle.

the soldiers come and get them if they wanted to be considered legitimate martyrs.

This widespread persecution continued until the early 300s when the most amazing thing happened in AD 312.

The Significance of Constantine in Church History

In AD 311, the Roman emperor Galerius issued the Edict of Serdica,[40] which legally ended the state's Great Persecution[41] of Christianity, granting Christians' beliefs legal status in the Empire.

Just a few months later, Galerius died, creating a power vacuum in the Empire. The fight for the throne came down to two contenders—Constantine and Maxentius. Having already secured Rome, Maxentius's victory was considered a formality. Constantine took a quarter of his troops, blitzed into Italy, and arrived just outside Rome in the fall of AD 312 at the Milvian Bridge, which spans the Tiber River.

Maxentius consulted books of occultic prophecies recorded over the years by various oracles and came across a prophecy about that very day. Even better, it prophesied that an enemy of Rome was destined to die! Assuming that enemy was Constantine, Maxentius was filled with the confidence of a man who believed the gods were on his side. And so, he left the security and fortifications of Rome to meet Constantine in battle.

The historical accounts of what happened to Constantine that same day are varied and possibly inflated by his storytelling in the years that followed. What seems certain is that he had a dream or

---

[40] Also called "The Edict of Toleration."

[41] Also known as the "Diocletianic Persecution."

vision in which he saw a *cross* and immediately understood it to be the symbol of Christianity. In front of the Cross were two letters from the Greek alphabet, "Chi" and "Rho," stacked on top of each other. Constantine understood these letters to be significant because they are the first two letters of the Greek word for "Christ" (Christos). You've probably seen this symbol in some type of religious setting. "Chi" is an "X," and "Rho" looks like a "P." Above this multi-layered symbol, Constantine saw the phrase, *"In this sign, conquer" ("in hoc signo vinces").*

The morning following his dream/vision, Constantine instructed his infantry to mark their shields with the symbol he had seen and likewise create standards under which they could march. Constantine informed his troops that he was now a Christian and proclaimed his dream/vision as undeniable evidence that God was on his side. He rallied his troops with the cry, *"We will conquer in the name of Christ!"*

On October 28, 312, with both Maxentius and Constantine convinced they were supernaturally favored to win, the Battle at the Milvian Bridge took place. Maxentius' forces were *routed*, and he met his death when his panicked and fleeing troops were forced into the Tiber and drowned. His body was recovered, and his head was placed on a spear for all to see as Constantine marched victoriously into Rome, where he would become one of the most famous emperors in history.

In AD 313, Constantine met with Emperor Licinius, who controlled the Balkans. Together, they issued the Edict of Milan, which committed the Empire to treat Christians benevolently and reaffirmed their legal religious status. It was a big deal because it sent the message that the Edict of Serdica (granted two years earlier) was not a temporary reprieve; it was to be the "new normal" in the Empire. Persecution was *over!*

As you can imagine, having an allegedly Christian emperor changed secular attitudes toward Christianity in a dramatic fashion. Being a Christian quickly became socially *advantageous,* and Christianity was soon considered *superior* to other religions. This upward social trend culminated in an astonishing moment in AD 380, when Emperor Theodosius I issued the Edict of Thessalonica, proclaiming Christianity the *state church* of the Roman Empire!

But let's get back to Constantine. In addition to leading the Empire from Rome, he declared the city the official center of Christianity. He created a new precedent in which the emperor was responsible for the well-being of the Church, including issues such as combating heresy and upholding theological positions. History tells us he considered himself the 13th disciple of Christ.

If you're not putting the pieces together yet, maybe this will help: Constantine anointed himself with a classic and blasphemous title used by the Caesars after him (and by Popes, to this day): *Pontifex Maximus*, meaning *"greatest priest."*

The Roman Catholic Church claims that Peter was the first Pope. The problem is that history tells a quite different story. For all intents and purposes, the first Pope was *Constantine*.

It's not hard to understand why many Christians thought these things to be positive changes at the time. But it was during this supposed golden age of Christianity—when it seemed like the Church's wildest dreams were coming true—that *corruption* began flooding into the Church.

Following Christianity's stratospheric rise in the Empire, pagan priests soon began migrating to the new state church, declaring themselves to now be "Christian" priests. They brought with them vestiges of their previous occupations—cultish pointy hats, red robes, censers for burning incense, and very quickly, "Christian" ministers began dressing like pagan priests and incorporating pagan practices into their worship rituals. Some examples of these practices and teachings, which appear *nowhere* in Scripture, include:

- Elevating Mary, the mother of Jesus, to divine status as a form of the feminine divine (which is present in practically all paganism)
- Praying to and for the dead
- Venerating and worshipping the dead
- Worshipping angels
- Worshipping relics
- Mass
- Priests and popes holding higher spiritual status with greater access to God than the laity (the regular folks)

The Bible declares that *all* believers are priests[42] because Jesus has fulfilled the Old Testament priesthood. That's why a leader in the Church is called an elder or a pastor, not a priest. Jesus' work on the Cross rent the curtain in the Temple, affirming Him as the only priest we need. But these pagan priests brought a human priesthood *back* into the Church.

What about their spectacular cathedrals? Jesus did away with those too. He prophesied the destruction of the Temple, which took place in AD 70, and He didn't promise to rebuild it. Instead, He spoke of a *different* Temple that would be raised again in three days, even if it were destroyed. Was He talking about a building? No. He was speaking of *Himself*.

And when Jesus ascended to Heaven, He promised the Holy Spirit would transform us into His Temple through His presence

---

[42] 1 Peter 2:5, 9.

indwelling us, just as it used to dwell in the Holy of Holies in the Jerusalem Temple. The Church Jesus established didn't need ornate, expensive, spectacular buildings. That was a *pagan* temple tradition. God's trophies are not buildings; they're you and me.[43]

If you've ever wondered why so many of our Christmas and Easter traditions seem to have nothing to do with Jesus (Rabbits? Eggs? Trees in our living rooms? Yule Logs?), it's because of the pagan symbolism that got mixed into the Church during the Pergamos age.

Churches had the Cross on one side of the stage and the flag of Rome on the other. They sang patriotic songs (essentially saying, *"I'm Proud to be a Roman"* and *"God Bless Rome"*) in church services. Very quickly, loving *Jesus* became inextricably linked to loving *the state*. A marriage of sorts took place as Christianity and paganism—the Church and the state—came together in an unholy union.

Can you imagine living in that time? One day, you're living under the constant threat of torture and death. Then suddenly, your prayers are answered! But you get even *more* than you ever dared to pray for because not only does persecution end, but suddenly the emperor is a *Christian!* Government and military leaders are being converted (allegedly)! Pagan places of worship are being transformed into churches! And then the state declares that Christianity is the official religion of the Empire!

When Constantine converted to Christianity in AD 312, around 10% of the Empire was Christian. By the end of the fourth century, that number had swelled to 95%. No wonder Augustine records that believers were so euphoric at this time that they believed they were living in the Millennium—the prophesied golden age of faith on

---

[43] Cf. Ephesians 2:4–8.

the earth (which we'll learn more about later). This was a *wonderful* season for the Church. Or was it?

Behind the scenes, Satan had changed tactics. He hadn't been able to kill the Church with persecution, so instead, he *joined* the Church and helped facilitate her marriage to the world system. He got on the inside, where it's always easier to commit sabotage.

INTO THE TEXT

What message will Jesus have for the Church in Pergamos? They had faithfully endured persecution and were now the toast of the town, enjoying all the societal benefits of being part of the religion that had become married to the state of Rome.

> ¹² ***And to the angel*** [the pastor] ***of the Church in Pergamos write,***

Jesus now uses a *title* for Himself that speaks specifically to something this church needs to be reminded of:

> ***These things says He who has the sharp two-edged sword:***

When a *"sharp two-edged sword"* or something similar appears in the Scriptures, it's pretty much always a reference to God's Word.[44] For example, in **Hebrews 4:12**, the author writes:

> **... the word of God *is* living and powerful, and sharper than any two-edged sword, piercing even to the division of soul and spirit, and of joints and marrow, and is a discerner of the thoughts and intents of the heart.**

---

[44] Cf. Ephesians 6:17.

Jesus feels that this church needs to be reminded that He always has His Word with Him because He and His Word are *one*. That means we cannot follow Jesus and simultaneously disregard His Word.

Around AD 96, the Church in Pergamos faced pressure from without (the Roman authorities) and within (false teachers) to compromise and give the pinch offering to Caesar. The only way to convince believers to do that was to *play down* the importance of the Word of God and get believers to trust their "teachers" to "interpret" the Scriptures on their behalf.

And as we get deeper into Church history, we're going to find that the Roman state church employed similar tactics, doing everything it could to keep congregants away from the Bible. The title Jesus uses for Himself is intended to warn believers on a compromising path to repent and return to the Word of God.

But Jesus is painting a second picture here. He presents Himself as the One **"who has the sharp two-edged sword."** This church was facing persecution from the state, which *literally* wielded the sword. Jesus reminds them that they need to have greater reverence and fear for the sword of their God than the sword of their government.

Recall how Polycarp responded when threatened with death by fire. He replied to the proconsul:

> *The fire you threaten burns for a time and is soon extinguished: there is a fire you know nothing about – the fire of the judgment to come and of eternal punishment, the fire reserved for the ungodly.*[45]

---

[45] Eusebius, 109.

Polycarp was saying that he was more concerned about avoiding the fire of eternal judgment than about avoiding the fire the government was threatening him with. That's the picture Jesus is painting here, presenting Himself as the One *"who has the sharp two-edged sword."*

Jesus taught this same perspective in **Matthew 10:28** (a verse I haven't heard mentioned in very many sermons), where He told His disciples:

> **. . . do not fear those who kill the body but cannot kill the soul. But rather fear Him who is able to destroy both soul and body in hell.**

Satan's Throne

> [13] **"I know your works, and where you dwell, where Satan's throne is.**

There are multiple plausible theories about the identity of **"Satan's throne"** in Pergamos. I'll share my opinion. As you dig into the Bible's stranger books, like Daniel, you'll find the Bible teaches that there are demonic entities over specific geographic regions. I think it's reasonable to assume that some of these demonic entities are the "gods" worshipped by various pagan religions.

I suspect that in declaring Pergamos city to be **"where Satan's throne is,"** Jesus revealed that the demonic force behind Zeus was *Satan himself.* If we could peek into the spiritual realm in AD 96, I believe we would have seen that the citizens of Pergamos were, in reality, worshipping *Satan.*

Unlike God, Satan is not omnipresent. And it seems that when Satan visited Pergamos, he found a city so perverted that he pulled up a chair and made himself at home. It was his favorite hangout spot at the time because it was where he felt most welcomed. The city was Satan's *spiritual* throne, and its famous giant altar to Zeus was *literally* his throne.

Regardless of your view, I'm confident we're on solid theological ground in assuming that Pergamos was a challenging spiritual environment in which to be a Christian.

Two different Greek words get translated into English as "dwell." One of them refers to a temporary state of dwelling *("paroikein")*, while the other refers to a permanent state of dwelling *("katoikein")*. Jesus uses the latter here; He is giving the persecuted believers in Pergamos this challenging instruction: **V.13** continues, making it clear that they are not to leave. They are to stay in Pergamos and be faithful to Him, whatever it costs them.

And you hold fast to My name, . . .

No matter what it cost, they held firm to the truth that Jesus alone was Lord, Savior, and God.

. . . and did not deny My faith (i.e., "your faith in Me") **even in the days in which Antipas was My faithful martyr, who was killed among you, where Satan dwells.**

All we know for sure about Antipas is what this verse tells us: He was martyred for being faithful to Jesus in Pergamos and was a well-known figure in the church there.

Church tradition is not always a reliable source, but it holds that Antipas was a disciple of John the Apostle, who ordained him Bishop of Pergamos during the reign of Caesar Nero. He was likely martyred around AD 68 for refusing to make the pinch offering in honor of Caesar Domitian.

According to Early Church tradition, Antipas was brought before the city's leader, who said, *"Antipas, everything is against you. If you don't do this, you will die!"* Antipas reportedly replied, *"Then, sir, I am against everything."* We miss the wordplay here unless we understand what the name "Antipas" means. "Anti" means "against" or "opposite," and "Pas" means "everything." When the town leader said, *"Everything is against you."* Antipas replied, *"Then, sir, I am Antipas" ("I am against everything")*.

In other words, Antipas was saying that it didn't matter what happened to him; he was committed to honoring Christ. According to Church tradition, Antipas was martyred by being roasted alive in a bronze cauldron shaped like a bull. It was a slow, agonizing, and painful death. And with his final breath, he refused to deny Jesus.

They killed Antipas in a horrific manner because they assumed it would terrify the rest of the Christians in Pergamos into submission. It didn't. They too, stood firm and faithful to the death.

If your Bible says "witness" instead of "martyr" in **V.13**, be aware that the accurate translation is "martyr" from the Greek word "martys." Antipas' *witness* was that he died being faithful to Jesus. And he is eulogized here with the highest of compliments—with Jesus referring to him by a title He used for Himself in **Revelation 1:5**: *"the faithful witness" ("pistos martys")*.

Jesus commends the local church in Pergamos around AD 96 for hanging in there through brutal persecution because they had already been experiencing it for around 40 years.

Regarding the *prophetic* application of this letter, the Church in AD 313 was finally experiencing the *end* of persecution after 257 brutal years. And Jesus commended them for standing firm.

Balaam, Balak, and the Nicolaitans

But Jesus needs to discuss some other things with the Church in Pergamos, and they're not as positive as His commendation:

> *¹⁴ But I have a few things against you, because you have there those who hold the doctrine of Balaam, who taught Balak to put a stumbling block before the children of Israel, to eat things sacrificed to idols, and to commit sexual immorality. ¹⁵ Thus you also have those who hold the doctrine of the Nicolaitans, which thing I hate.*

In our study of the letter to the Church in Ephesus (**Revelation 2:1–7**), we looked at these verses and talked about who Balaam and Balak were and how they related to the Nicolaitans. I will not go over all that again but suffice it to say that the Nicolaitans were false teachers trying to infiltrate the Church.

And these false teachers were teaching doctrines of *compromise*; they approved of believers *mixing* with the world and claimed that it was acceptable for them to participate in local pagan worship rituals, which included sexually immoral acts. It also seems these false teachers were trying to place themselves between the people and God, elevating their importance above the people of the Church. And the term for such teachers was "Nicolaitans."

Second Peter 2:15 warned that these kinds of false teachers would seek to infiltrate the Church:

> **They have forsaken the right way and gone astray, following the way of Balaam the** *son* **of Beor, who loved the wages of unrighteousness.**

As we study this letter to the Church in Pergamos and the next letter, remember this detail. Peter says these false teachers **"loved the**

wages of unrighteousness." There's a *financial* motivation behind their false teaching, just as there was with Balaam.

Jesus commended the Ephesians for not tolerating the Nicolaitans. But, sadly, the Church in Pergamos was tolerating them, and Jesus wanted them to know they were putting themselves in danger.

Many Christians in the Roman Empire understandably viewed the marriage of Church and state as a practical solution to the problem of persecution. But Jesus likened it to *adultery* because while they used to love Him wholeheartedly, now the Empire had half their heart. They used to identify themselves as citizens of Heaven, but now they identified foremost as citizens of *Rome*.

Here's how it all ties together—in referencing Balaam and Balak and the teaching of the Nicolaitans, Jesus implied that:

- Around AD 96, wolves were attempting to persuade the Church in Pergamos to compromise with their bodies—*"Give the pinch offering. Join in the pagan sexual worship rituals."*

- In the fourth century, wolves were attempting to persuade the Church to compromise with their hearts—*"You can serve both God and the Empire. To love one is to love the other."*

Both follow the pattern of Balaam, who instructed the Moabites to stir up God's wrath against Israel by getting them to take part in sexual worship rituals to pagan gods. Balaam's counsel was based on appealing to Israel's flesh to lead them into sin. Essentially, Balaam proved that if you get the world into the Church, and you'll soon get the Church to fall in love with the world. It worked with the children of Israel, and it worked with the Church in the fourth century.

The Church had been strong in the days of persecution when she had no political power or allegiance to Rome. But after marrying the state, she weakened significantly. Instead of being singularly devoted to Jesus, the Church's affections were now divided.

When you examine Church history in the early fourth century, you find men in the new Roman Church embodying the teachings of the Nicolaitans by presenting themselves as *mediators* between God and man, claiming that congregants had to go through *them* to get to God.

Want your sins forgiven? *You need to go through us.*

Want to pray to Jesus? *Only with our permission and only in our pre-approved formats.*

Want to gather to worship with other believers? *Only at an official service time and location.*

Want to know what the Bible says? *We'll tell you.*

Want to own a Bible you can read for yourself? *You can't. You're not a professional.*

First Timothy 2:5 says, "There is one God and one Mediator between God and men, the Man Christ Jesus."

From a prophetic perspective, Jesus criticized the Compromising Church for allowing *men* to occupy an office that belongs exclusively to *Jesus*.

From the perspective of Church history, this is an uncomfortably specific and strange picture being painted for us by Jesus:

- He describes a Church that has begun to embrace a pagan priesthood, where leaders rule over the people with abusive authority that they gained by presenting themselves as necessary mediators between God and man.

- Jesus describes a Church that has embraced compromise and joined itself to the world system and the state in a perverted and unnatural marriage.

- And He specifically points out they have forgotten what His *Word* says.

In my humble opinion, that's a description that overwhelmingly speaks to a particular part of Church history. It's a time that saw a host of heretical "firsts" hit the Church, such as leadership consisting of a state-sponsored priesthood, the Church exercising political authority, priests granting themselves special perks, and a near-total disregard for the Scriptures.

Jesus' reaction to this "new" Church is one of *strong* disapproval.

Was Constantine a Christian?

Before we go further, I would be remiss if I didn't at least acknowledge an infamous historical question raised by this study: Was Constantine a Christian? To this day, historians are split. He ended the persecution of the Church and replaced it with social and political favor, but he also ushered catastrophic spiritual corruption into the Church.

The likely answer is that there is no simple answer. Constantine doesn't have to be either a sincere and devoted Christian or the spawn of Satan. Perhaps he genuinely believed he was converted but wasn't. Maybe he was genuinely converted but also made some wicked decisions for political reasons. What's the truth? Only God knows, and we'll have to leave it at that.

The Exhortation to Pergamos

Now, here's the exhortation—what this church needs to do:

> *¹⁶ Repent, or else I will come to you quickly and will fight against <u>them</u> with the sword of My mouth.*

I underline the word *"them"* because when you read the whole letter, it's clear that Jesus is specifically threatening the Nicolaitans and those embracing their teachings. He's not threatening this entire church. You have the *church,* the institution, and then you have the *Church,* the people of God. Hopefully, we all understand that attending the institution of the church is not the same thing as being a Christian. Jesus is threatening those who are perverting the *institution* of the church. He's not threatening the *people* of the Church.

Notice *how* Jesus will wage war with those mixing paganism with the Church—*"with the sword of My mouth."* Think back to the title Jesus used for Himself in **V.12**. What is *"the sword of My mouth"* a reference to? The Word of God. The Bible.

Jesus says that if the Nicolaitans do not repent, He will attack their false teachings with *His Word.* Let me tell you why that's so fascinating from a historical perspective.

In the 1500s, a group of people began to be deeply troubled by the theological, spiritual, and moral corruption permeating the Church. Inspired and convicted by the Holy Spirit, they rose up and began to *protest*, earning themselves the name "Protestants" (literally *"those who protest"*).

They began to use the phrase "Sola Scriptura," Latin for "Scripture Alone," and their movement gained enough momentum to spark the historical revolution known as the Reformation. And it was just that—a movement whose goal was to *reform* the Church by returning her to what the Bible teaches. But the Reformation wasn't an *academic* battle. It was a literal *war*.

Jesus warned the church in Pergamos, *"I will come to you quickly and will fight against them with the sword of My mouth."* History tells us that *He did*. And we'll discuss that more when we study the letter to the Church in Sardis.

¹⁷ He who has an ear, let him hear what the Spirit says to the churches.

Remember, each of these letters has something to say to every *believer* and every *church*.

To him who overcomes . . .

Who resists compromise and clings to God's Word . . .

. . . I will give some of the hidden manna to eat.

As mentioned earlier, Revelation was written so that if a Roman soldier found it, they'd think it harmless apocalyptic fiction. But Jewish believers schooled in the Old Testament would understand precisely what was being discussed. There are two things we need to know to understand *"the hidden manna"* Jesus refers to:

1. Manna was the bread-like food God miraculously provided to feed and sustain the Israelites in the wilderness. In **Exodus 16:32**, God instructed Moses to put some of that manna inside the Ark of the Covenant to remind future generations of God's provision for His people. That was *literally* the *"hidden manna."*

2. In **John 6:32–35**, Jesus says:

> ... *"Most assuredly, I say to you, Moses did not give you the bread from heaven, but My Father gives you the true bread from heaven. For the bread of God is He who comes down from heaven and gives life to the world."*
>
> **Then they said to Him,** *"Lord, give us this bread always."*
>
> **And Jesus said to them,** *"I am the bread of life. He who comes to Me shall never hunger ... "*

So, when Jesus says, *"To him who overcomes I will give some of the hidden manna to eat,"* He is using Old Testament imagery to promise overcomers that if they look to Him instead of a human mediator, He will be everything they need—their food, their sustenance, and their provision (practically and spiritually). Jesus promises the overcomer *Himself*.

The ultimate fulfillment of this promise will be the Marriage Supper of the Lamb[46] when we feast with the Lord Jesus and toast Him as the King of kings. Those who decline the opportunity to feast as pagans on the earth will feast as saints at the table of the Lamb.

And I will give him a white stone, ...

We don't know exactly what this is referring to. I have encountered over 10 unique explanations in my research, and here's what I think is most important:

- In many legal settings (including Jewish), white stones were used to cast a vote of "innocent," as opposed to a black stone for "guilty."

---

[46] Cf. Revelation 19:9.

- As in the example above, white is repeatedly used in Revelation in association with righteousness.[47]

The overarching concept is that the one rejected for refusing to compromise with the world will be accepted, welcomed, and vindicated by Jesus in Heaven.

> *... and on the stone a new name written which no one knows except him who receives it.*

In the original Greek, the grammar clarifies that the *"new name"* spoken of here is *collective*. In other words, every overcomer will receive the *same "new name."*

This reference seems to be a shortened version of **Revelation 3:12**, where Jesus gives this promise to the overcomer:

> *I will write on him the name of My God and the name of the city of My God, the New Jerusalem, which comes down out of heaven from My God. And I will write on him My new name.*

In **Revelation 22:4**, we learn that in the eternal paradise of Heaven, those who belong to Jesus are promised:

> **They shall see His face, and His name** *shall be* **on their foreheads.**

These references seem to clarify that the *"new name"* we will receive is symbolic of the new eternal identity we will step into at the end of our earthly lives.

Yes, those who love Jesus are already born again and have the Spirit of God within them. But when we cross over from this life

---

[47] C.f. Revelation 3:4–5, 18; 4:4; 6:11; 7:9, 14; 19:11, 14; 20:11.

into eternity, we will be translated into our resurrected bodies and take on new roles as *"kings and priests."*[48] As John scandalously and gloriously wrote in his first epistle:

> **Beloved, now we are children of God; and it has not yet been revealed what we shall be, but we know that when He is revealed, we shall be like Him, for we shall see Him as He is.**
>
> —1 John 3:2

APPLICATION TO ALL CHURCHES

A quick note on Christians and politics. I'll keep it brief and controversial. When you look at the world political system, whose system is it? It's *Satan's*.[49] Whether you're a capitalist, communist, or socialist, they're all part of Satan's world system.

Jesus is a *king*. He's the *King* of kings. And God is not planning on redeeming the earth through political systems that ultimately originate from Satan. God's plan is to have Jesus return to the earth with His Church (us), *destroy* Satan's political systems, and reign as king. That's how God will correct the world's political systems—not by marrying the Church to the state or trying to "redeem" existing political systems.

While we should indeed pray for our politicians and work to accomplish as much good as possible through our political systems, we should never forget that our ultimate hope is in King Jesus—not politicians or elections or earthly halls of power.

---

[48] Cf. Revelation 1:6; 5:10.
[49] Cf. John 12:31; 2 Corinthians 4:4; 1 John 5:19.

In this letter, Jesus shares His desire that His Church remains focused on His Word. He knows that if we'll do that, we'll remember that we are citizens of *Heaven*, with **"one Mediator between God and men, *the* Man Christ Jesus."**

If we stay focused on His Word, we'll know Him for ourselves. *He* will be our *"manna,"* and we won't be deceived into thinking we can be married to both Jesus *and* the world.

APPLICATION TO ALL BELIEVERS

I encourage you to pray and reflect on what the Lord is saying to you through His letter to the Church in Pergamos. I can't escape the sense that *compromise* is this church's elephant in the room. They loved Jesus, but they also lived in a place where there were a lot of enjoyable distractions. Some indulged in a little compromise, and soon their faith was reduced to an easily managed ritualistic checklist that allowed them to orient their lives around selfish passions.

Around AD 96, a little compromise would have meant getting a pass on torture and death: *It's just a pinch offering*. Just listen to the preachers who were saying, *"God understands. He'll forgive you. He doesn't want you to suffer."* This letter confronts me with this question: *Where am I taking shortcuts, compromising what God's Word says, and ignoring certain parts of the Scriptures to make my faith a little less inconvenient?* Ask yourself:

- Am I in a place where I'm *craving* the things of this world more than the things of God?

- Am I in a place where I'm *praying* for the things of this world more than I'm praying for God to give me more of Himself?

When I was preparing to teach this sermon series to my church, the Lord directed my attention to **James 4:1–10**:

Where do wars and fights *come* from among you? Do *they* not *come* from your desires *for* pleasure that war in your members [your body/flesh]**? You lust and do not have. You murder and covet and cannot obtain. You fight and war. Yet you do not have because you do not ask.**

James knows this is where we'll say, *"But I have asked God for the things I want!"* So, he writes:

You ask and do not receive, because you ask amiss, that you may spend *it* on your pleasures.

In other words, the problem is that we're asking God to give us our *earthly* passions—the things our *flesh* craves.

Adulterers and adulteresses! Do you not know that friendship with the world is enmity with God? Whoever therefore wants to be a friend of the world makes himself an enemy of God.

Our choice is friendship with the world or fellowship with God. There is no "both" option.

Or do you think that the Scripture says in vain, *"The Spirit who dwells in us yearns jealously"*?

God wants *all* of us—our whole heart. He doesn't want half our devotion going to earthly things. He doesn't want our passion divided between Him and anything else. So, what do we do?

But He gives more grace. Therefore He says:

> *"God resists the proud,*
> *But gives grace to the humble."*

Therefore submit to God. Resist the devil and he will flee from you. Draw near to God and He will draw near to you. Cleanse *your* hands, *you* sinners; and purify *your* hearts, *you* double-minded. Lament and mourn and weep! Let your laughter be turned to mourning and *your* joy to gloom.

If you've been trying to satisfy yourself by pursuing the world instead of pursuing Jesus, *mourn* over that. Take it seriously. Because if you will, God gives us an incredible promise:

Humble yourselves in the sight of the Lord, and He will lift you up.

A little compromise, a few decisions here and there to make life a little bit easier . . . If you turn a blind eye to those things, you'll wake up one day and find yourself thinking, *"How did I get here?"*

Would you rather be *Smyrna* (living in difficulty but clinging to Jesus and beautiful to Him) or *Pergamos* (living the comfortable and compromised life but cheating on Jesus)? We're so good at justifying our compromises. That's why we need the Word of God to confront us with reality on a regular basis.

REVELATION 2:18-29

THE CHURCH IN THYATIRA

Thyatira was named by the conquering King Seleucus I Nicator in 290 BC, upon receiving the news that his wife had given birth to a baby girl. It comes from the Greek for "daughter" and means "a woman." As we shall see, this church will be defined by her obsession with a very specific woman.[50]

For this letter, we're going to focus primarily on the *prophetic* application, which covers a vast period in Church history. We'll see the natural progression of the things that began with Pergamos—compromise and paganism infecting the Church because of her marriage to the Roman state.

And if you felt a bit tense reading Jesus' letter to Pergamos, I should let you know it was *not* the most politically incorrect of the seven letters. That honor falls to *this* letter.

---

[50] Before being renamed Thyatira, the city was known as *Semiramis*. There are some intriguing connections between the prophetic identity of this church and a historical mythology that connects a woman bearing that name to ancient Babylonian paganism (as first discussed in Alexander Hislop's *The Two Babylons* in 1853). But after extensive research, I have not been able to confirm the veracity of those claims, so we won't be discussing them in this book.

If you come from a Roman Catholic background, some of this letter may be difficult to read and even more difficult to consider. Everything we're going to study will come straight from God's Word and the facts of history. I promise I don't have an impure agenda and, hopefully, my presentation of the information will show that.

If you disagree with my analysis and don't draw the same conclusions from the biblical text, that's OK. But do your homework. Be like the Bereans.[51] It's OK to be offended, but it's not OK to dismiss information simply *because* it's offensive. As followers of Jesus, we are called to be more concerned with the truth than our feelings.

Finally, I ask that you read everything I've written about this letter, even if you're deeply troubled by its contents. Because there's good news in here too, but you'll miss it if you quit early. Jesus will have some very *good* things to say about this church.

And if you've had nothing to do with the Roman Catholic Church, don't get too smug because in His next letter, Jesus will criticize Protestants, and He's going to have a hard time finding *anything* good to say about the mainline denominations!

Throughout these seven letters, Jesus will praise what is good, *wherever He finds it*, and call out what is bad, *wherever He finds it*. It's a safe assumption that whatever church background you're from, there will be something challenging to hear in at least one of these letters.

---

[51] Cf. Acts 17:11.

HISTORY AND CULTURE OF THYATIRA

When this letter was written, Thyatira was a blue-collar town. It didn't have the intellectual prestige of Ephesus, the beauty of Smyrna, or the political power of Pergamos.

Thyatira was the center of trade guilds (the precursor of what we call *unions*). Each guild would adopt a pagan deity as its *patron*, and many union meetings would involve acts of worship directed to that patron god. One can easily imagine the Catch-22 this would create for Christian tradesmen—they couldn't get jobs *unless* they were in a guild, but if they *were* in a guild, they would be expected to take part in pagan worship.

Sidenote (you probably guessed it): The concept of patron saints related to specific occupations goes back to these times and trade guilds.

One of Thyatira's primary industries was textiles (fabrics and clothing). They had developed world-leading techniques to produce purple dyes and cardinal fabrics, which were highly sought-after because their color evoked images of wealth and royalty. This was an old-school way of saying, *"I'm rich!"* This would be comparable to a Gucci belt or Louis Vuitton bag today.

You might remember Lydia,[52] who helped the Apostle Paul start the Church in Philippi. She was from Thyatira where she made her fortune in the trade of these kinds of fabrics, and she likely played a significant role in supporting the planting of the Church in Thyatira.

While we don't know much about the Church in Thyatira around AD 96, I believe the contents of this letter allow us to safely assume that this church had taken things a step further than the Church in

---

[52] Acts 16.

Pergamos. That is, they had allowed their church to be infiltrated by paganism and had *fully embraced* the unholy fusion.

Thyatira in Church History

Prophetically, this church covers the period from around AD 600 to the Present Day. And there's no getting around this; we'll refer to Thyatira as "The Roman Catholic Church." If that term is uncomfortable for you, this church can also be called "The Middle Ages Church."

This massive swath of history covers the rise of the Roman Catholic Church to its position as the most powerful church in the world. As I mentioned, it is simply the continuation of what began in Pergamos.

We don't have the real estate in this book to list the seemingly endless examples that would prove the point, but suffice it to say, this era is marked by incredible wickedness in the Church. Heresy, blasphemy, paganism, indulgences, simony (selling important positions in the Church, including the papacy), genocide, every sin imaginable—on and on it goes.

While it's true that the Church has almost *always* had people doing wicked things in its name, the Roman Catholic Church is unique because it has a clear, centralized, top-down hierarchy, and her historical wickedness was sanctioned from the highest levels.

My intention is not to bash the Roman Catholic Church for fun. And for that reason, I'm going to ask you to do your own research into the history of the Roman Catholic Church and her many *institutional* sins because they are well documented in the historical record.

As we learned, the Roman Catholic Church emerged from the marriage of the Church and state that began under Constantine around AD 312. The Church was flooded with professional pagan priests who migrated from their previous jobs to the new state religion. The leadership of this new "church" consisted of men who were, for the most part, not even Christians! And the inevitable result was rampant paganism, selfish ambition, greed, and hedonism in the Church.

Many fraudulent Christians have done wicked things over the centuries in the name of the Church. Sadly, this continues today in modern evangelical circles. But there is widespread understanding and acknowledgment within orthodox Christianity that those things were and still are *wicked*. Without getting into what would be a book's worth of material, I'll just point out that to this day the Roman Catholic Church remains by and large *unrepentant* for the litany of evils she has perpetrated across history.

INTO THE TEXT

> [18] *And to the angel of the Church in Thyatira write,*
> *"These things says the Son of God, who has eyes like a flame of fire, and His feet like fine brass: . . . "*

In choosing this title and description for Himself, Jesus reminds the Church in Thyatira that He is the Son of *God* and the only judge of truth. Let me explain.

Bronze is often associated with *judgment* in Scripture. We see an example of this in the bronze serpent raised on a standard by Moses while Israel was in the wilderness.[53] Everyone who looked

---

[53] Cf. Numbers 21:4–9.

upon it was healed of their sickness because the bronze represented that their sin had been *judged.*

While it might seem odd that a church would need to be reminded of such basic facts about Jesus, we're going to find that this church doesn't revere Him as the Son of *God* as much as they revere Him as the son of *someone else*—the queen of heaven.

This is the only letter where Jesus must *assert* His authority because this church is more focused on this woman than they are on Him, and as a result, they no longer view Him and His Word as authoritative.

Commendation of Thyatira

After that heavy start, let's talk about some good news and find out what *commendations* Jesus has for the Church in Thyatira on their report card:

> [19] ***I know your works, love, service, faith, and your patience; and as for your works, the last are more than the first.***

Jesus pays Thyatira a genuine compliment by pointing out that they're doing many *good* things, especially in areas such as serving the poor and meeting other social needs.

There was a time when the Roman Catholic Church had orphanages all over Europe. They were feeding the hungry, confronting justice issues, and making a huge difference for good in the world. No church in history has ever come close to the social impact this church had at various points in history.

Jesus says of their good works, **"the last are more than the first."** That is, they were getting *even better* at these things over time. Don't miss that. It's an incredible commendation. And regardless of your views of the Roman Catholic Church, they *are* a church.

They're here in the Book of Revelation, and we Protestants need to remember that.

In the next letter, we'll meet the Reformation Church, and Jesus won't have anything this good to say about them because their good deeds never came close to the social impact the Roman Catholic Church had during certain seasons of history.

I don't know about you, but I'm grateful Jesus included that commendation—even if only to break the tension in this letter! Soak it up, because next comes the *criticism*.

Criticism of Thyatira

²⁰ Nevertheless I have a few things against you, because you allow that woman Jezebel, who calls herself a prophetess, to teach and seduce My servants to commit sexual immorality and eat things sacrificed to idols.

As best we can discern from the data, it seems that around AD 96, the Church in Thyatira welcomed the heretical teachings of a female false prophet symbolically identified by Jesus as *"Jezebel."* She was teaching the Nicolaitan heresy that it was acceptable for Christians to take part in sexual immorality and worship other gods. Like the Gnostics, she likely taught that the spirit is the only thing that matters; therefore, what you do with your physical body is irrelevant.

Prophetically, the woman this church is named for and adores is viewed very differently by Jesus. We're told this *"Jezebel"* is *not* a prophetess but presents herself as one. In other words, she does *not* speak for God but claims she does.

Notice that Jesus refers to believers in this church as *"My servants."* They're supposed to be following *Him* but somehow, they've ended up serving *her* instead. All this is severe criticism. Let's keep digging.

Jezebel in the Old Testament

Jesus doesn't refer to *"that woman who is LIKE Jezebel."* He says, *"**you allow that woman Jezebel.**"* That's who she is. Jesus is very specific. Of all the examples in the Bible that Jesus could have used, He intentionally chose *Jezebel*.

You've probably never met a woman named Jezebel. That's because although most of us don't know *why* she's bad news, we know her name is associated with wickedness. In fact, Christians have been using her name as a substitute cuss word for centuries (e.g., *"She's a real Jezebel."*).

There are some things in the Old Testament we need to be aware of at this point in our study because the parallels to Church history are *astonishing*. As we mentioned in our study of **Revelation 1:1–20**, the Book of Revelation contains over 800 references to the Old Testament. So, let's go back and learn who Jezebel was and what she did.

During a dark time in Israel's history, she was ruled by a king named Ahab. He married Jezebel, daughter of Ethbaal, the king of the Sidonians, to seal a profitable trade alliance with Phoenicia. In **1 Kings 16:30–31**, we read:

> **Now Ahab the son of Omri did evil in the sight of the Lord, more than all who *were* before him. And it came to pass, as though it had been a trivial thing for him to walk in the sins of Jeroboam the son of Nebat, that he took as wife Jezebel the daughter of Ethbaal, king of the Sidonians; and he went and served Baal and worshiped him.**

The Word tells us that what Ahab did was worse than anything any king of Israel had done up to that point in history. What did he do? He engaged in a *Pergamos*—an unacceptable marriage—uniting himself and God's people with paganism and Jezebel.

Jezebel's father's name was *Ethbaal*, which means *"with Baal"*—the most prominent pagan god in the region. God hated Baal worship, and this Sidonian royal family was wholeheartedly committed to it.

As the story progresses, we see Jezebel lead God's people into paganism by engaging in Baal worship. She also leads them to worship the queen of heaven—the feminine divine; the central female goddess figure that appears in practically all expressions of paganism in various incarnations. Together Jezebel and Ahab usher in the worst period of pagan idolatry in Israel's history (up to that point).

Writing from God's perspective, the prophet Jeremiah documented the Israelites' participation in these pagan celebrations:

> *The children gather wood, the fathers kindle the fire, and the women knead dough, to make cakes for the queen of heaven; and they pour out drink offerings to other gods, that they may provoke Me to anger.*
>
> —Jeremiah 7:18

God was *appalled* by the behavior of His children during this time.

And if leading God's people into paganism wasn't bad enough, the Bible also tells us that Jezebel made it her mission to *kill* all the prophets of God.[54]

---

[54] Cf. 1 Kings 18:13; 19:14.

Let's recap what we've learned: Jezebel moved into the palace of Israel's king, who was supposed to lead the people to worship *God*. She became the first pagan queen of God's people, killed His prophets and true believers, and led the rest of the people into paganism. But the event Jezebel is *most* infamous for is found in the first fourteen verses of **1 Kings 21**:

> [1] **And it came to pass after these things** *that* **Naboth the Jezreelite had a vineyard which** *was* **in Jezreel, next to the palace of Ahab king of Samaria.** [2] **So Ahab spoke to Naboth, saying,** *"Give me your vineyard, that I may have it for a vegetable garden, because it is near, next to my house; and for it I will give you a vineyard better than it. Or, if it seems good to you, I will give you its worth in money."*
>
> [3] **But Naboth said to Ahab,** *"The Lord forbid that I should give the inheritance of my fathers to you!"*
>
> [4] **So Ahab went into his house sullen and displeased because of the word which Naboth the Jezreelite had spoken to him; for he had said,** *"I will not give you the inheritance of my fathers."* **And he lay down on his bed, and turned away his face, and would eat no food.** [5] **But Jezebel his wife came to him, and said to him,** *"Why is your spirit so sullen that you eat no food?"*
>
> [6] **He said to her,** *"Because I spoke to Naboth the Jezreelite, and said to him, 'Give me your vineyard for money; or else, if it pleases you, I will give you another vineyard for it.' And he answered, 'I will not give you my vineyard.'"*
>
> [7] **Then Jezebel his wife said to him,** *"You now exercise authority over Israel!"*

Naboth wasn't trying to be disrespectful toward his king; he was simply doing the right thing by honoring God above Ahab. Back when Israel conquered the Promised Land, it was divided among the twelve tribes. God then commanded them to never sell that land between tribes.[55] As a result, Naboth could not sell his land to Ahab without violating God's Word.

As Ahab sulks like a spoiled brat, I want us to notice some things:

- A corrupt and wicked man wants *property*.

- But the current owner of the property is a believer who is more concerned with honoring God's Word than pleasing the corrupt and wicked rulers.

- Jezebel comes along and reminds Ahab that he is the king. In other words, *"We don't have to take 'No' for an answer."*

Continuing with **V.7**, Jezebel says to Ahab,

"Arise, eat food, and let your heart be cheerful; I will give you the vineyard of Naboth the Jezreelite."

⁸ And she wrote letters in Ahab's name, sealed them with his seal, and sent the letters to the elders and the nobles who were dwelling in the city with Naboth. ⁹ She wrote in the letters, saying,

Proclaim a fast, and seat Naboth with high honor among the people; ¹⁰ and seat two men, scoundrels, before him to bear witness against him, saying, *"You have blasphemed*

---

[55] Cf. Numbers 36:7.

God and the king." Then take him out, and stone him, that he may die.

Note *how* Jezebel gets Ahab the property he wants: She claims to be doing something *legitimate* in the name of the *king*. She sends out instructions to the local authorities and tells them to announce a *religious ceremony* in which the locals will participate. At this event, the owner of the property is to be singled out and falsely accused by two men (other translations call them *"worthless men"*) of committing *blasphemy*.

There is to be *no trial* and *no investigation* to prove the validity of the charges or "witnesses." It's a rigged court and the sentence is to be served *immediately*. The innocent target of this operation never stood a chance.

¹¹ So the men of his city, the elders and nobles who were inhabitants of his city, did as Jezebel had sent to them, as it was written in the letters which she had sent to them. ¹² They proclaimed a fast, and seated Naboth with high honor among the people. ¹³ And two men, scoundrels, came in and sat before him; and the scoundrels witnessed against him, against Naboth, in the presence of the people, saying, *"Naboth has blasphemed God and the king!"* Then they took him outside the city and stoned him with stones, so that he died. ¹⁴ Then they sent to Jezebel, saying, *"Naboth has been stoned and is dead."*

With Naboth out of the way, Jezebel takes possession of the vineyard. *Mission accomplished.* **Second Kings 9:26** tells us they also killed all of Naboth's heirs, so there was nobody left alive who could claim the vineyard.

While King Ahab may have been wearing the crown, it's obvious Jezebel was the one calling the shots. She was the true power in the kingdom. Jesus' big issue with Thyatira is that they allow Jezebel to run the show instead of Him.

Why this whole sidebar to talk about Jezebel and Naboth's vineyard? Because of all the sins of Jezebel that the Bible could have told us about in detail, the one God chose documents her *acquiring property* through *false accusation* and killing Naboth for honoring God's Word. Jesus references this same Jezebel in His letter to Thyatira in **Revelation 2** because there are connections that He wants us to make. Let's go further down the rabbit hole.

The Roman Catholic Church's Thirst for Power

After centuries of unbelievably corrupt papal rule, the Roman Catholic Church developed an increasingly insatiable appetite for wealth and power, and its true nature was on full display in the historical regimen known as *the Inquisition*. It was perpetrated from around 1208 all the way up to the 1830s and was a means to accomplish two of the Vatican's highest priorities—eliminating those who opposed the church's rule and acquiring vast amounts of property and wealth.

How did they do it? While they didn't *technically* rule Europe, they did hold massive influence over the continent, and the Roman Catholic Church partnered with kings and sovereign powers in a campaign that worked something like this. If you were found to oppose the Roman Catholic Church (in word, deed, or thought), someone would be arranged/bribed to bring an accusation of heresy or blasphemy against you. To "get to the truth," you would be tortured until you "confessed." That confession would then be used in a *sham trial*, where additional false witnesses would testify against you. Your sentence would then be *immediately* applied—you could be jailed for the rest of your life or, more commonly, burned at the stake.

This tactic was not only employed against those who opposed the Vatican but also those who had the "misfortune" of owning wealth or property the Church wanted. The Roman Catholic Church would conduct the "investigation" and "trial" and render the verdict, but the *local authorities* would execute the sentence.

In exchange for their cooperation, the local rulers would split the person's wealth and/or property with the Church. As you can imagine, this created an insidious incentive for both the Church and local authorities to uncover "heretics" all over the place.

The Inquisition Horror Show

In the mid-1500s, a man named John Foxe fled England and settled in Germany to escape the Inquisition. There he wrote a book later commonly titled *Foxe's Book of Martyrs*, in which he chronicled the persecution of Christians across Europe. Here are just a few descriptions of the Inquisition from his writings:

> *At first The Inquisition was only concerned with charges of heresy, but it soon expanded its authority to include such charges of things such as sorcery, alchemy, blasphemy, sexual aberration, infanticide, reading the Bible in the common language . . .*
>
> *Regardless of the charges, the Inquisitors performed their examinations with the utmost severity, having little or no mercy on anyone no matter what their age, sex, race, high birth, distinguished rank or social standing, or physical or mental*

condition. And they were especially cruel to those who opposed Papal doctrine or authority, most particularly those who once were Roman Catholics and now were Protestants.[56]

It gets a little graphic here . . .

To do this, every method of physical torture known or that can be imagined was used—such as the stretching limbs on the rack; burning with live coals or heated metals; breaking fingers and toes; crushing feet and hands; pulling out teeth; squeezing flesh with pincers; inserting hooks into fleshy parts and pulling the hooks out through the flesh; cutting off small pieces of flesh; sticking pins into the flesh; inserting pins under fingernails or toenails; tightening ropes around flesh until they cut through to the bone, scourging with rods or various kinds of whips; beating with fists, rods, and clubs; twisting limbs and dislocating joints. The methods used by the sadistic Inquisitors are too numerous and horrendous to list.[57]

This was a dark, dark time in Church history. If you go back and read **1 Kings 21** again, you'll notice the Inquisition employed the *same tactics* Jezebel used against Naboth. The prophetic parallels are staggering, and I find any suggestion of coincidence much harder to believe than intentional design by the Bible's ultimate author.

As a result of the Inquisition and other campaigns of terror, the Roman Catholic Church became the largest landholder *in the world*. Today, they are the second largest landholder, surpassed only by

---

[56] Foxe and Chadwick, *Foxe's Book of Martyrs*, 61.

[57] Foxe and Chadwick, *Foxe's Book of Martyrs*, 61–62.

King Charles II. It's a matter of historical record that the Vatican has never even attempted to return any of the property or wealth acquired through the Inquisition (to families or countries).

The Inquisition also transformed the Vatican into what is believed to be the wealthiest country in the world, when you factor in debt load. The Vatican has *no debt*, while America is trillions of dollars in debt. The fact is, when you tally the church's impressive financial assets against its lack of liabilities, the Vatican is *easily* the wealthiest country in the world.

I feel I should acknowledge that there were Catholics then, as there are today, who saw these things happening and realized that this was not of God. As we're going to find out, sometimes there are godly people in very ungodly institutions.

While recent popes such as Benedict and Francis have publicly condemned these phases of Catholic history, they continue to allow the Vatican to operate in a similar vein. We know that both have personally been involved in burying sexual abuse and financial impropriety within the Church. Even though they recognize these things as evil, they cannot bring themselves to act to stop them. Could it be because the real power behind the Vatican is not the Pope but the woman Jezebel? I'll let you draw your own conclusions on that one.

Pagan Practices of the Church

Look back at **V.20** where Jesus says that this Jezebel leads His people *"to commit sexual immorality and eat things sacrificed to idols."* The *"sexual immorality"* is both literal and spiritual:

- It's *literal* because, around AD 96, pagan worship included sexually immoral rituals.

- It's *spiritual* because, in His Word, God repeatedly refers to His people worshipping false gods as fornication. He views it as *adultery*. This is what any individual believer or church is doing when they involve themselves with paganism.

In our study of the letter to the Church in Ephesus, we learned that in this context, the phrase *"eat things sacrificed to idols"* refers to participating in pagan worship ceremonies and rituals. We know that Jezebel did that in leading the Israelites to worship Baal. But there's a second meaning to the phrase *"eat things sacrificed to idols"* in the *prophetic* application.

The Roman Catholic Church teaches a doctrine called "transubstantiation," which declares that Communion (traditionally wine and bread) transforms into the *literal* body and blood of Jesus when it is consumed. Vatican Papal doctrine states that *". . . the Mass, the Lord's Supper, is ... A sacrifice in which the Sacrifice of the Cross is perpetuated."*[58]

The Vatican teaches that Communion, their Mass, is a *continuation* of the sacrifice of Jesus. Every time they observe the Lord's Supper, they believe that Jesus' body and blood are being sacrificed *again* to cover our sins. But what does the Bible say?

> **. . . such a High Priest** [Jesus, not the Pope] **was fitting for us,** *who is* **holy, harmless** [literally "innocent"], **undefiled, separate from sinners, and has become higher than the heavens; who does not need daily, as those high priests, to offer up sacrifices, first for His own sins and then for the**

---

[58] The Vatican, *Eucharisticum Mysterium—Instruction on Eucharistic Worship*, May 25, 1967. https://adoremus.org/1967/05/eucharisticum-mysterium.

people's, for this He did once for all when He offered up Himself.

—Hebrews 7:26–27

Jesus died *once* for our sins. It is the *finished* work of Jesus on the Cross that saves us, not Communion. Jesus wanted those at Thyatira to know that they were not taking Communion as *He* gave it to the Church. They were sacrificing to an idol, not worshipping Him.

It's important to recognize that Jesus doesn't say Jezebel is the problem. He says the Church *tolerating* and *approving* of her is the issue. The demonic entity behind Jezebel will exist and operate on the earth until Jesus comes back, and He knows that. But the Lord does not expect His people and His Church to *embrace* that spirit.

²¹ And I gave her time to repent of her sexual immorality, and she did not repent.

This is the longest of the seven letters, and the reason is likely because prophetically, this church exists for the longest *time* of the seven churches. But despite being around for over 1,600 years, this church refuses to repent.

²² Indeed I will cast her into a sickbed, . . .

"Sickbed" does not appear in the original Greek. It was the translators' best guess at a word that most likely means something like "death," "hell," or "Hades."

. . . and those who commit adultery with her into great tribulation, unless they repent of their deeds.

Remember, Jesus views those who should be worshipping Him but are instead practicing paganism as a wife sexually cheating on her husband. And if you don't believe that Jesus is going to ultimately deal *severely* with Jezebel and those who follow her, then you need to stop reading for a few minutes and go learn how her story ends in **2 Kings 9:30–37**.

Jesus doesn't say, *"You'll have trouble"* as He said to the Church in Smyrna when He told them their persecution would continue. Prophetically, Jesus refers here to the *Great* Tribulation[59]—the future time when the Church will be safely with Him in Heaven as He pours out His wrath on the earth. Let me be clear: Jesus is telling the Church in Thyatira that their *institution* and those who participate in their *institution's* spiritual immorality will be left on the earth for the Great Tribulation.

It's an incredibly serious warning that also implies believers who do *not* buy into the paganism of this institution *won't* be here for the Great Tribulation. There *are* real believers in this Church, but Jesus expects them to **"*repent*,"** meaning "turn away." Jesus expects that when true believers in this Church read His letter, they will recognize the paganism He points out and *turn away* from it.

If it's possible for those in this Church who follow Jezebel to be left on the earth *for* the Great Tribulation, then this Church must exist all the way *up to* the Great Tribulation. We'll soon see that each of the final four churches will exist up to the time of the Rapture, which means that they exist today.

Isn't it interesting that after "Jezebel" rose to power in this part of Church history, the Church began to emphasize the worship of Jesus' mother, Mary? Jesus makes it clear that the Mary of the Roman Catholic Church is *not* His mother, but *Jezebel*. It's a demonic entity. It's the feminine divine—the queen of heaven of paganism. And I

---

[59] Cf. Revelation 7:14.

believe the *real* Mary is dismayed by what this Church is doing in her name.

In **John 2:5**, we read her words for the last time in Scripture, and this is what the text says:

His mother said to the servants, *"Whatever He* [Jesus] *says to you, do it."*

Another time, a woman tried to venerate Jesus' mother by crying out:

"Blessed is the womb that bore You, and the breasts which nursed You!"

But He [Jesus] **said,** *"More than that, blessed are those who hear the word of God and keep it!"*

—Luke 11:27–28

If Mary were with us on the earth today, her message would be simple: Follow Jesus.

Let's shift our attention to **V.23**, which says:

²³ I will kill her children with death, . . .

The term *"children"* refers to *spiritual* children, not biological children. It refers to the generations that perpetuated the heresies that were first introduced into the Church in Thyatira.

If your Bible doesn't say ***"death"*** or something similar, then it's an inaccurate translation. I suggest it's referring to the *second* death. If those who are placing their faith in this Church to save them don't repent, their earthly, physical death will be followed by eternal death because no church has the power to save—only Jesus does.

History tells us the literal church in Thyatira failed to repent and ceased to exist by the end of the second century.

... and all the churches shall know that I am He ...

"He," not *"her."*

... who searches the minds and hearts. And I will give to each one of you according to your works.

Even though Jesus condemns the direction of this Church *institutionally*, He will judge each person in it *individually*. In Jeremiah, God says:

I, the Lord, search the heart,
I test the mind,
Even to give every man according to his ways,
According to the fruit of his doings.
—Jeremiah 17:10

Old Testament readers took the title *"Lord" ("Adonay" in Hebrew)* to be a reference to Almighty God. When Jesus says, *"I am He who searches the minds and hearts,"* He is linking Himself to this verse in Jeremiah and once again claiming to be the Almighty God of the Old Testament.

It feels like this letter is overdue for some good news, and here it is:

[24] Now to you I say, and to the rest in Thyatira, as many as do not have this doctrine, who have not known the depths of Satan, as they say, I will put on you no other burden. [25] But hold fast what you have till I come.

Remember that the few faithful believers in the Church in Thyatira didn't have other churches they could go to. Their church may have been corrupted, but it was the only church in town. The Church in Thyatira was *the* church in Thyatira. Jesus understood this; He knew that *some* of the people in this church were grieved by all the paganism and were not buying it. *Some of them* recognized Jezebel and refused to bow to her. So, Jesus urged *them* to hold on and stay faithful because He was coming for them soon.

In Church history, the next letter will reveal what happens when Jesus wages war against Thyatira with His Word.

When Jesus calls the things going on in this Church (institutionally), *"the depths of Satan,"* He's referring to how intimately associated this church is with the type of paganism that traces back to Jezebel and Baal.

> *[26] And he who overcomes, and keeps My works until the end, . . .*

Jesus wants those in this Church to do *His* works, not *her* works.

> *...to him I will give power over the nations—*
> *[27] "He shall rule them with a rod of iron;*
> *They shall be dashed to pieces like the potter's vessels"—*
> *as I also have received from My Father; . . .*

The *"rod of iron"* is a reference to **Psalm 2** and **V.9** specifically. It's a messianic Psalm that speaks prophetically of Jesus' future reign on the earth.[60] The Lord once again encourages believers with the incredible plans He has for us. In this instance, we will be ruling and

---

[60] It is worth studying Psalm 2 considering its connections to the Church in Thyatira.

reigning with Him in the Millennium (which we'll discuss when we reach **Revelation 19**).

Paul told believers:

> **Do you not know that the saints will judge the world? And if the world will be judged by you, are you unworthy to judge the smallest matters? Do you not know that we shall judge angels?...**
>
> —1 Corinthians 6:2–3a

The Vatican teaches that the Roman Catholic Church will reign on the earth at the end of all things. The only problem is that according to His Word, Jesus has other plans.

To the overcomer in Thyatira around AD 96, Jesus' message is this: If you'll reject the paganism that has invaded the Church and stay faithful to Me, you'll rule and reign with Me in a glorious future, when I crush all false gods under My feet.

To the overcomer in the historical age of the Catholic Church, Jesus' message is this: If you'll reject Jezebel and instead be faithful to Me, I'll give you what Jezebel craved most—power and authority. The Roman Catholic Church might call you a heretic. They might excommunicate you. They might burn you at the stake for blasphemy. But when I reign on the earth, you will reign beside Me. They won't.

> ...²⁸ *and I will give him the morning star.*
> ²⁹ *He who has an ear, let him hear what the Spirit says to the churches.*

Revelation 22:16 tells us exactly what *"the morning star"* is:

> *I, Jesus, have sent My angel to testify to you these things in the churches. I am the Root and the Offspring of David, the Bright and Morning Star.*

Jesus promises to give those in this Church who reject Jezebel and her paganism . . . *Himself*. And I think that's because this Church teaches that men cannot have direct access to God; they must go through a priest, a special service, or a ritual. But Jesus says that if they simply focus on His will and His Word, He'll give them Himself. And praise God, He has done just that. No matter who we are, we have been blessed with direct access to God through the sacrifice of our mediator and High Priest, Jesus Christ.

APPLICATION TO ALL CHURCHES

Jesus' message to all churches reading this letter is simply this: Don't tolerate Jezebel. Don't mix paganism with the Church. Stay in His Word and keep the focus on Him. This means we cannot dismiss the heresies of Catholicism in the name of "unity" or "different expressions of the faith."[61] We are not talking about secondary issues like election vs. free will or the gifts of the Spirit. We are talking about an institution that places *itself* as the mediator between men and God—claiming a position that belongs exclusively to Jesus.

Without a total abandonment of and repentance for such heresies (which this letter tells us there will never be), there cannot be unity between the Roman Catholic Church and the biblical Protestant Church. As Paul wrote concerning believers marrying unbelievers:

> **. . . what communion has light with darkness? . . . And what agreement has the temple of God with idols? For you are the temple of the living God . . . .**
>
> —2 Corinthians 6:14, 16

---

[61] "Ecumenism" is the theological term.

APPLICATION TO ALL BELIEVERS

Most of us live in places where we get to choose which church we belong to. And I don't see how a believer could be made aware of the things Jesus points out in this letter, genuinely repent ("turn away"), and continue to be part of the Roman Catholic Church. I'm not sure what kind of Catholic wouldn't participate in Mass, go to Confession, or believe in the authority of the Vatican!

Every former Catholic I've known worked through a progression along these lines: They began to see the things Jesus talks about, became troubled by them, researched them in the Bible for themselves, concluded that the Roman Catholic Church is heretically violating Scripture, worked through their Catholic guilt and their family's inevitable condemnation, and then eventually followed Jesus out of the Roman Catholic Church.

If you're a Catholic, I hope you'll take the words of Jesus to heart and begin following the truth, wherever it leads you and whatever it costs. Because Jesus is worth it.

For those of us who are not part of the Roman Catholic Church, we're generally all tempted by *legalism*. There's something about outsourcing our relationship with God that appeals to our flesh (perhaps because it's easier to indulge the flesh when God is kept at arm's length). A big part of us likes the idea of being saved by a list of dos and don'ts because it makes us our *own* saviors.

The Apostle Paul confronts this issue head-on in his letter to the Galatians. They had experienced the freedom of the Gospel and yet were choosing to go back to living under the Law of Moses. The insanity of this behavior prompted Paul to lament, **"O foolish Galatians! Who has bewitched you . . . "**[62]

---

[62] Galatians 3:1.

Paul explained that when Jesus went to the Cross, He took the punishment the Law assigned to each of us (because we are all guilty under the Law). From the Law's perspective, *we* died when *Jesus* died. Therefore, we are now **"dead to the Law."**[63]

Paul then took it a step further, explaining that living under the Law meant rejecting the grace God has offered us through Jesus. In other words, it meant *rejecting Jesus*. And that means living under the Law is, for all intents and purposes, no different from pagan idolatry. When we substitute a genuine relationship with Jesus for a list of dos and don'ts, we're drifting into legalism, the Law, and yes, even *paganism*.

The power of the Gospel is that it gives all of us *direct access* to God. As one of my favorite verses in all of Scripture exhorts us,

> **Let us therefore come boldly to the throne of grace, that we may obtain mercy and find grace to help in time of need.**
> —Hebrews 4:16

I believe Jesus would have every believer take this charge from His letter to Thyatira: Do not allow anybody in the Church to place themselves between you and Him or above His Word.

CLOSING THOUGHTS

It's worth pausing for a moment to marvel at the stunning *specificity* and *accuracy* of the prophetic layer in these seven letters. The level of detail in this letter is *astonishing* when you compare the story of Jezebel and Naboth's vineyard to the history of the Roman Catholic Church and the Inquisition.

---

[63] Romans 7:4.

And if you're still not convinced of the prophetic angle in the seven letters, just wait until we dig into the next letter. Remember, if any of these letters were in a different order, the chronology wouldn't line up with Church history. By the time we finish the final letter, it will be apparent there are only two possible explanations: genuine prophecy given by God, or coincidence beyond the point of absurdity (I think you'll end up on the prophecy side).

Finally, I want to encourage you with a question: How long has it been since you spent a few minutes thinking about how amazing it is that you have direct access to *God?*

If you've placed your faith in Jesus as your Savior, then His Spirit is in you right now. He is *with you.* Think about that. Think about it until you feel blessed. Because through Jesus, *you are.*

REVELATION 3:1-6

THE CHURCH IN SARDIS

Sardis is a semi-precious stone (also called "Sardius" or "Sardine Stone") that was sourced from the city bearing its name. Its present-day name is highly disputed (i.e., academics are divided on what exact stone this was), but tradition says it was blood red. We know from Scripture that it was used in the breastplate of the high priest in Old Testament times[64] and will feature in the New Jerusalem.[65]

Although Sardis stone was initially considered precious, it was later found to be extremely common. And while it has a once-great name, it's not identifiable today. We're going to discover that like the stone for which it is named, the Church in Sardis used to be special but now has only an empty name.

In the previous chapter, we studied the fourth church, Thyatira, which we learned was all about *a woman*. The Thyatirans adopted all kinds of pagan practices, including a pagan priesthood. They decided that Mary, the mother of Jesus, was really someone else—the feminine divine, the goddess known throughout history as "the

---

[64] Cf. Exodus 28:17, 39:10.

[65] Cf. Revelation 21:20.

queen of heaven." That church grew into what we know today as the *Roman Catholic Church*.

From ~AD 600 to ~AD 1450, the Roman Catholic Church was pretty much the only church on earth. And despite multiple and serious criticisms, Jesus still commends the Church in Sardis for the many good deeds she *has* done at various points in history (e.g., feeding the poor, taking a strong stand against abortion, etc.).

We also learned that the last four of the seven churches in **Revelation 2 and 3** exist today and will continue to exist up to the time of the Rapture.

As we deal with controversial topics in these letters, I think it's important to remember that Jesus tells *every* person and *every* church to pay attention to *every* letter. There is something He wants us to learn from *all* these churches. So, before we say, *"Man, those Catholics..."* or *"Man, those Protestants..."* we need to remember that we *all* need to guard against the mistakes these churches have made, and we are *all* capable of the good things these churches have done.

HISTORY AND CULTURE OF SARDIS

According to the Greek historian Herodotus, Sardis was founded in 1220 BC by the sons of Hercules (do with that what you will), the *Heraclides*, who later became known as *Lydians*, who made the city the capital of their mighty empire. Modern historians tell us it may have been established as early as 1400 BC.

Sardis was home to rich gold deposits—a phenomenon explained by the Greek myth of King Midas, who was rewarded by the god Dionysus with the power to change anything he touched to gold—and the city was located on the main route between the Anatolian highlands and the Aegean Sea.

For these reasons, Sardis quickly became a wealthy city. But things jumped to a whole 'nother level when it revolutionized commerce by introducing gold and silver coins to the world. By 560 BC, the final Lydian king, Croesus, was considered the wealthiest man in the world.

Sardis was an ideal location for an empire's capital as it sat atop cliffs 1,000–1,500 feet high and could only be accessed from one side (there were sheer cliffs in all other directions). This meant only the southern side of the city required defending, and it demanded a steep climb from the valley below. The consensus at the time of the Lydian Empire was that Sardis was *impenetrable*.

Around 547 BC, on the counsel of the Oracle of Delphi, Croesus attacked the Persian king Cyrus the Great in Cappadocia. It was a terrible military decision, and it led to a long, drawn-out battle, in which neither side emerged victorious. As winter approached, Croesus decided to return to Sardis to regroup and rally his allies before returning to battle in the Spring.

However, when the energetic Cyrus got word that the army of Croesus had dispersed, he quickly charged toward Sardis. Croesus retreated into the acropolis, confident in the belief that the city was impregnable. Cyrus besieged Sardis, but after 14 days, he could still find no way in. In desperation, he offered a handsome reward to any soldier who could.

One night, one of Cyrus' soldiers saw a Lydian soldier walking on the city wall accidentally drop his helmet outside the wall. Both men watched the helmet tumble down the cliffs. As the Persian soldier watched in amazement, his counterpart climbed over the wall and followed a hidden path down the cliffs, where he safely retrieved his helmet and then returned to Sardis by the same route.

The soldier relayed this information to Cyrus, and after noticing that nobody was guarding that side of the city's walls, the Persian army scaled the heights of Sardis and took the city, bringing an end to the Lydian Empire. History records the city was taken *as by a thief in the night*—a phrase that became a proverb used in association with Sardis, centuries before it appeared in the Scriptures.

Fast-forward to around 214 BC, and the same thing happened again when Antiochus III the Great successfully employed a skilled climber to find a route up the supposedly impregnable cliffs and walls, which were *completely unguarded*. Apparently, it's true that if history teaches us anything, it's that people learn nothing from history. Unbelievably, the citizens of Sardis didn't deal with the vulnerability that had led to their downfall centuries earlier, and as a result, were once again overtaken by failing to guard the side of the city they assumed was secure.

Due to this and several other successful assaults on the city, Sardis' legacy is defined by her failure to be vigilant. She became a real-life proverb—something that *appeared* impenetrable but ended up being overtaken as by a thief in the night. Sardis was a city of unjustified pretensions with defenses that flattered to deceive and pride that led to repeated downfalls.

Today, all that's left of the mighty acropolis of Sardis are a few Greek pillars. I share all that because Jesus alludes to that history in His letter to the Church in Sardis. The main thrust of His message will be: Sardis, you're not watching, and you should be, or you're going to get wiped out yet again.

Regarding the Church in literal Sardis ~AD 96, this letter implies they started well but failed to keep going in that same strength and were, at that time, all about *appearances* rather than *substance*. They had likely been a great church, but due to negligence, Sardis had become spiritually lifeless.

The story that unfolded prophetically in Church history was likely reflected in a condensed manner in the local church around AD 96.

Sardis in Church History

Prophetically, this letter speaks to the *Reformation Church*. We could also call this "The Denominational Church." This marks a period of Christian history that began with the Reformation around AD 1500 and continues to the present day. Remember, the Roman Catholic Church was the dominant church (pretty much the *only* church) on earth for ~900 years (AD 600 to AD 1500).

The years between Popes Sergius III (AD 904–AD 911) and John XIII (AD 965–AD 972) were so scandalous and depraved that they are sometimes referred to by historians as the "Pornocracy." They include the papacy of Octavian, a 16-year-old whose wealthy parents *bought* him the papacy (under the name John VII), which I guess answers the question, *"What do you buy the man who has everything?"*

The Birth of the Reformation Church

The Church had been in bad shape for centuries and would be for a few more until AD 1300 when various sincere Catholic priests were convicted by the Holy Spirit as they observed the state of the Church and its abject failure to represent Jesus.

One of those priests was John Wycliffe of Wycliffe Bible Translators fame. He held a Doctor of Theology degree and was a seminary professor and Oxford scholar. And in his church, he began to teach *against* some of the things happening in the Roman Catholic Church. He taught truths such as, *"It's wrong for the Church to steal peoples' property and have them burned at the stake. That is not of God."* He began to teach that Scripture is the highest authority, even above the Pope. He looked back at the history of the Early Church and observed that they had *venerated* the Scriptures, while in his day, people in the Church were not even *reading* the Scriptures.

And as he studied further, he learned that the Early Church had not believed the Eucharist to be the literal body and blood of Jesus (i.e., the Roman Catholic doctrine of transubstantiation). The Early Church believed the elements of Communion were simply *symbols*—reminders of Jesus' work on the Cross. And so, Wycliffe shared his discoveries publicly.

He also struck out at the sale of indulgences, the excessive veneration of the saints, the sorely lacking moral and intellectual standards of ordained priests, and various other issues. Wycliffe was a *bold* man.

But his greatest weapon, his greatest act of subterfuge, was translating the Bible from the Latin Vulgate into English in AD 1382, rendering Scripture accessible to the common man. This all went over so well with the Vatican that they issued an edict to have him burned at the stake. But Wycliffe was so respected by the local populace that when the edict reached his city's leaders, they delayed taking any action and intentionally never got around to executing him. And a short time later, Wycliffe passed away.

Thirty years later, a Czech priest named Jan Hus, a follower of Wycliffe's teachings, took up his mantle and began publicly raising the same issues. The Roman Catholic Church leaders heard about Hus, and burned him at the stake. And just to seal the deal, they dug up John Wycliffe's bones and burned those too—30 years after his death! I'm sure those looking on thought, *"We get it. You really, really didn't like John Wycliffe."*

Those who followed Hus' teaching became known as "Hussites." Following his death, they rebelled against their Roman Catholic rulers and defeated *five* consecutive papal military crusades intended to slaughter them. Those battles are known as "The Hussite Wars."

This sort of thing went on for a while, and more priests began to realize that something was seriously wrong with the Church. A groundswell of discontent within the Roman Catholic Church was stirring beneath the surface across Europe.

In 1455 in Germany, the Gutenberg Bible became the first mass publication produced on the famous Gutenberg press, which revolutionized publishing with its movable type.

Almost overnight, Bibles and books were being published in the common language for the common man, sparking a renaissance of learning as everyday men and women began expanding their knowledge through literature. These changes set the table for what happened next in the sixteenth century, and it's fascinating to see how God caused them to come together in the right place, at the right time.

Fast-forward to the 1500s, our focus remains on Germany—the greatest papal stronghold outside Italy at the time. The clergy was in a particularly bad state. They were uneducated and often impoverished—a combination sure to breed corruption when a position of power is added to the mix.

While the Vatican had long forbidden priests from taking wives, these men still had... um... *needs*. To get around that problem, local bishops would allow their clergy a live-in concubine in exchange for a moderate annual fine. But as people began to read the Bible for themselves and become more educated, they couldn't help but notice just how messed up this kind of behavior was. It was an increasingly combustible situation that only needed a spark, and God had plans to introduce just such a spark into the German church.

On November 10, 1483, in Saxony, Germany, Martin Luther was born. The son of a poor coal miner, he grew up observing his father's poverty, which motivated him to become a lawyer. In 1501, he entered the University of Erfurt. In 1504, near the end of his studies, Luther was caught in a lightning storm so severe that it caused him to rashly pray and promise God he would become a *monk* if he lived through the storm—which he did.

True to his word, Luther withdrew from law school, and in 1505 he entered St. Augustine's Monastery, where he obtained a bachelor's degree in theology. He continued to study and earned his doctorate in theology.

He began ministering in the city of Wittenberg and soon became a professor at the city's seminary. Despite all his accomplishments, Luther was unable to escape deep feelings of spiritual inadequacy and became obsessed with trying to *earn* God's favor and forgiveness.

He would whip himself until he bled, crawl for miles on his knees, spend hours in prayer, sleep outside in freezing weather with no blanket, fast for weeks at a time, make distant pilgrimages to supposedly sacred sites, and make frequent confessions—all in an attempt to show his devotion to God and thereby atone for his sins, perhaps even earning God's blessings. So frequent were Luther's visits to confession that his superior reportedly told him to stop *"calling every fart a sin."*[66]

And yet for Luther, nothing worked. He later described this period of his life this way:

---

[66] James M. Kittelson, *Luther the Reformer: The Story of the Man and His Career* (Minneapolis, MN: Fortress Press, 2016), 22. Kindle Edition.

"I lost hold of Christ the Savior and comforter and made of him a stock-master and hangman over my poor soul."[67]

In 1509, he made a pilgrimage to Rome, hoping to find the peace that had stubbornly eluded him. His journey on foot included crossing the Alps, which almost killed him. Forced to halt his journey and recover his health at a monastery at the foot of the mountains, he encountered a wise monk with whom he shared his existential angst. By God's design, that monk was well acquainted with the Scriptures and encouraged Luther to seek answers in the Book of Habakkuk.

As shocking as it sounds, the state of the Roman Catholic Church was such that despite Luther possessing a doctorate in theology, he had never even considered reading the Bible to connect with God. And when he did, it changed *everything*. Like Luther, Habakkuk had struggled with feeling that God was distant from his trials. And as he found himself in the words of Habakkuk, Luther came across Chapter 2, verse 4, which seared itself into his mind and changed the course of his life: **"the just shall live by faith."**

Luther eventually healed and made it to Rome, where he began to endure the rites of the Roman Catholic Church. But he continued to be haunted by **Habakkuk 2:4** as he watched men abuse themselves in various ways, such as climbing the Scala Sancta ("holy stairs") until their knees bled, in hopes of reducing their time in purgatory.

Luther left Rome with deep spiritual discontent. His soul was *troubled* by what he had witnessed. He didn't have things figured out

---

[67] Kittelson, *Luther the Reformer*, 40, Kindle Edition.

yet, but he knew that what was happening in the Church did not make any sense in light of Scripture.

Upon his return to Wittenberg, the seminary asked him to lecture on the Apostle Paul's letter to the Romans. Luther had never studied the epistle, and as he began to study, it became increasingly clear that what he was reading and what the Church was teaching were two *very different things*.

A light bulb turned on, and Luther saw the big picture. He recognized that the Christian's hope and life are found in what *Jesus* has done, not what *we* do or don't do.

On October 31, 1517, Martin Luther nailed his famous 95 Theses to the door of the Church in Wittenberg. They were 95 specific points of reform that he believed needed to take place in the Church. Out of respect for the leadership of the Church, Luther wrote in Latin, so the common people would not be able to read and gossip about his concerns. Luther raised issues such as these:

> *The selling of indulgences is wrong. How can giving the Church money serve as payment for your sins against God? That doesn't line up with the Scriptures. How does it make sense that you can buy somebody out of Purgatory? Why can't we have the Bible in common language, so that everyone can read it for themselves?*

Luther was naïve enough to believe that if the Church's leaders were shown their errors in the Scriptures, they would repent and change their ways. They didn't. And they still haven't. Almost immediately, Luther received a notice from the Church threatening him with ex-communication and giving him 60 days to retract his 95 theses or face death, likely by fire. In a moment of holy rebellion, Luther burned that notice.

Fortunately, the Roman Catholic Church was unable to assassinate Luther, as God had granted him favor with local princes and politicians. What followed shortly was the cultural and religious revolution known as the Reformation. And make no mistake about it, I would not have written this book, and you would not be studying the Book of Revelation for yourself, had the Reformation not taken place. It was *that important.*

Luther would go on to write hymns, including, "A Mighty Fortress Is Our God," as well as multiple commentaries (which are considered classics). And incredibly, he would translate the entire Bible into German.

The Reformation was a theological movement so dangerous to the Roman Catholic Church's grip on power that it sparked *centuries* of wars. The Vatican assigned every resource at its disposal to the task of stamping out Protestantism wherever it was gaining momentum, resulting in massacres across Europe. It was a *bloody* and *violent* revolution.

There was more war, persecution, and martyrdom than I have space to report, but I'll share one example—the St. Bartholomew's Day Massacre of 1572.

The Jesuits were (and are) an extremist arm of the Roman Catholic Church that formed around the value of absolute allegiance to the Pope. Their mission was (and is) to destroy all opposition to the Pope, by any means necessary. They organized and orchestrated the assassinations of several key French Huguenots (Calvinist Protestants) in Paris. Those murders incited citizens of the predominantly Catholic city, who quickly formed mobs and began killing every Huguenot they could find.

The violence soon spread to the countryside, and a few weeks later, when it was all said and done, around 70,000 Protestants had been slaughtered. The response in Rome, history records, was great rejoicing. The Vatican printed and sold a commemorative medal to mark the occasion, and the Pope sent a cardinal to Paris to extend his congratulations to the French king and queen mother.

It was *war*, waged by the Vatican against Protestants.

God wasn't only moving powerfully in Martin Luther's life during this time. He was doing something profound in the hearts of men across Europe. Men like John Calvin in Geneva, and Zwingli in Zurich, along with many Roman Catholic priests, were also recognizing the glaring conflicts between Scripture and the Roman Catholic Church.

People who followed Luther's specific teachings became known as "Lutherans," while those who followed the general movement of reform were referred to as "Protestants." The leaders of the Protestant movement agreed that the Church was desperately in need of reform. And so, they were called "Reformers," and their movement became known as "The Reformation."

The centuries that followed saw the emergence of great historical mainline denominations such as the Lutheran, Presbyterian, Methodist, and Anglican churches (and many more).

INTO THE TEXT

> *¹ And to the angel* [the pastor] *of the Church in Sardis write, "These things says He who has the seven Spirits of God and the seven stars: . . . "*

If you think back to **Revelation 1:1–20**, you'll recall that for Jewish believers, the phrase *"the seven Spirits of God"* brought to mind **Isaiah 11:2**, where the prophet Isaiah refers to seven characteristics of the complete Spirit of God. He was not talking about seven *different* spirits but the person we know today as *the Holy Spirit*.

In **Revelation 1:20**, Jesus told us the *"seven stars"* represent the messengers of each of the seven churches (likely the pastors). By introducing Himself with this title, Jesus is reminding the Church in Sardis that He is the One who holds the leadership of the Church in one hand and the Holy Spirit in the other.

The Holy Spirit has an *agenda* for the Church, and it's laid out across the pages of the New Testament. It's a tragedy when a church stops looking to Jesus and His Word and instead begins looking to the world for its mandate, vision, and methodology. When that happens, the Holy Spirit has left the building, and unless they repent, that church will soon be dead.

This can happen in any type of church or denomination, and it's what happened to the Church in Sardis and, prophetically, the Denominational Church.

In the countries where many of us live, we've witnessed this firsthand. We've seen the formerly great mainline denominations reduced to almost-entirely-secular community centers, increasingly departing from biblical orthodoxy in a desperate attempt to gain the approval of the culture.

Don't Be Ignorant of the Spiritual Gifts

In **1 Corinthians 12:1**, Paul wrote:

> **Now concerning spiritual *gifts*, brethren, I do not want you to be ignorant . . .**

In other words, we can be ignorant about a lot of things but as Christians, we cannot afford to be ignorant about spiritual gifts and how they work.

Sadly, the modern Church is *still* wrestling with much confusion regarding the Holy Spirit. Generally, there's a widespread lack of knowledge and understanding, and heresies and misrepresentations seem to abound. Here at the beginning of His letter to Sardis, Jesus reminds them that He and the Holy Spirit are a package deal.

Let's get into the church's report card, beginning with Jesus' commendation.

The "Non-Commendation" of Sardis

I know your works, that you have a name that you are alive, but you are dead.

No, you didn't miss something. There is *no commendation* for the Church in Sardis. Why? Jesus tells us it's because this church is **"dead."**

Let's not miss the gravity of what Jesus said. He didn't say they're sick or unhealthy; He said that they claim to be alive, but the truth is they're **"dead."**

In the original Greek, the word used for **"name"**[68] means *"to be covered by a name"* or to put it more simply, *"to have a label."* It's the root of our word "denomination," which was invented around the fifteenth century.

According to Jesus, the big problem with Sardis is that they think they're alive but they're dead. They're still proudly pointing to their great name (Lutheran, Presbyterian, Methodist, etc.), lineage, history, liturgies, buildings, social welfare programs, and founders (the Reformers), but Jesus says that they're dead. In effect, the Spirit has left the body. There's only a corpse left.

---

[68] Onoma.

There was a time in history (and sadly, this is still true in some places) when people would identify themselves by their denomination rather than as Christians. You'd ask someone, *"What religion are you?"* And they'd respond, *"I'm a Lutheran"* or *"I'm a Baptist"* instead of *"I'm a Christian"* or *"I follow Jesus"* because, to them, their denominational affiliation was of greater importance than even their allegiance to Jesus. Only the name of *Jesus* brings life. The Church in Sardis had forgotten that.

Along with the rise of denominations, the Roman Catholic Church spawned multiple state churches, such as the Church of England. And people baptized into those state churches would also point to the *name* as proof of their salvation (e.g., *"I've been baptized in the Church of England."*).

... you have a name that you are alive, but you are dead.

The Church in Sardis can be likened to Samson, the once mighty warrior who the Word tells us was blinded and placed in bondage by his sin, and tragically, Samson **"did not know that the Lord had departed from him."**[69]

² Be watchful, and strengthen the things which remain, that are ready to die, for I have not found your works perfect before God.

"Be watchful" is a reference to Sardis' history. Historically, they *weren't*. They were asleep at the wheel (so to speak), and it resulted in their destruction.

Apparently, this church *needs* to be watching out for certain

---

[69] Judges 16:20.

things, but they are not. We'll come back to that in a bit, so just tuck that away in your mind for now.

Perfect Works and the Reformation

Whatever this Church did was *good*, but Jesus says, **"I have not found your works perfect before God."** The idea is that He has not found their works *complete*. Part of the problem was that the Reformers didn't go *far enough*. The denominations that came out of the Reformation considered their theological work *finished* when, from the Lord's perspective, there was still much more to be done.

As you study Church history, you'll find that Calvin and Luther were still theologically off-base in several areas. Luther held to transubstantiation,[70] which is why he and Zwingli were unable to unite their Reformation movements. Luther declared that any lay pastors preaching publicly should be killed, as only professionals should preach. Calvin was, at a minimum, complicit in the murders of some of his theological opponents in Geneva.

The Reformers brought glorious clarity to soteriology, the theology of salvation. Despite some differences among them, those same Reformers dug into the Scriptures and did their best to bring the Church back to the Bible in other areas of the faith, such as Communion and Church leadership.

While commending them for their efforts, Jesus seems to be saying that the believers in Sardis and those who came after them needed to continue digging into other areas of theology with that

---

[70] It should be noted that contemporary Lutherans reject transubstantiation, instead affirming the presence of Jesus in Communion as a mystery.

same vigor. Areas of study such as eschatology (the end-times) and pneumatology (the Holy Spirit and His gifts) were pursued but with nowhere near the same level of devotion as the subjects pursued by the Reformers. In many of the denominations that emerged from the Reformation, there were still doctrines in place that relied on inaccurate interpretations. And Jesus clearly sees that as a big problem.

It appears that every Church revival, including the Reformation, follows a similar pattern:

1. It starts with a *man*.
2. That man is specially anointed by God and given a *ministry* for that specific time in history.
3. The man's *ministry* becomes a *movement*.
4. As it grows rapidly, the *movement* becomes a *machine*.

Man, ministry, movement, machine.

Eventually, the *men* who started the movement disappear, and all that's left are other men trying to keep the *machine* running. That's what has happened to many of the great denominations that emerged from the Reformation.

And when that happens, the *machine* becomes a *mausoleum*—a place to bury the *dead*.

Man, ministry, movement, machine, mausoleum.

That's the sad history and pattern of most denominations. They started with something rich, real, and powerful but over the centuries, they turned into a machine that was constantly pointing back to its history and great *name*, instead of pointing to Jesus.

Exhortation to the Church in Sardis

Now, Jesus tells the few true believers in Sardis what they need to *do*. This is their exhortation:

> ³ *Remember therefore how you have received and heard; hold fast . . .*

What has this church *"received and heard"* from the Lord, that they need to be reminded of? First, they received the doctrine "Sola Scriptura," which means "Scripture alone."

The Roman Catholic Church believes that the Bible is *one way* we get the truth. But they also believe that we can get truth from the traditions of the Church and the present leadership of the Church. That is, in their view, the Pope can *add* to what the Bible says, giving a more complete revelation of truth.

Sidenote: The Roman Catholic Church teaches (and still holds) that the Pope can declare he is speaking or writing *ex cathedra*, which imbues his statements with the same authority, standing, and sacred nature as Scripture (e.g., the doctrine of the assumption of Mary).

The Reformers looked at the Bible and they noticed it said things like:

> **All Scripture *is* given by inspiration of God, and *is* profitable for doctrine, for reproof, for correction, for instruction in righteousness, that the man of God may be complete, thoroughly equipped for every good work.**
>
> —2 Timothy 3:16–17

This caused them to wonder why they weren't teaching the Bible in their churches if it's inspired by God and designed to equip believers to live the Christian life. They began to ask themselves why they were following a church that taught traditions and the words of a man who sits on a throne as being on par with the Word of God. Finally, they began to declare, "Sola Scriptura" and started siding with the Word of God.

As they looked to the Bible for theological clarity, they noticed more and more Church doctrines in need of reform. This led to additional "Solas" like "Sola Fide," which means "Faith alone" and "Sola Gratia," which means "Grace alone."

They read verses like **Ephesians 2:8–9**:

> **. . . by grace you have been saved through faith, and that not of yourselves;** *it is* **the gift of God, not of works, lest anyone should boast.**

And they came to believe that no organization can grant salvation. It's not gained by going to Mass or being baptized as an infant. Salvation is by faith in the grace of Jesus. Faith alone—Sola Fide. Grace alone—Sola Gratia.

We're not saved because of anything we do—no amount of good works or charitable acts. We bring *nothing* to the table. God has saved us because He loves us. That's His heart. The Reformers realized that we don't need to earn our way to a right relationship with God. We can't. Jesus has done it all.

I get choked up thinking about the euphoria and joy that must have overwhelmed these men as they began to grasp these truths after a *lifetime* of trying to earn their salvation. The Reformers recognized that Christianity isn't about a religion or an institution. It's about *Jesus*, and what *He* has done for each of us. And out of that realization came "Sola Christo," meaning "Christ alone."

According to the Bible, we don't have to go through an intermediary to get to God. We don't have to have a priest, cardinal, or even a Pope go to God on our behalf. Remember, Scripture tells us there is **"one mediator between God and men, the man Christ Jesus."**[71] He is the One who has completed *all* the work on our behalf. Our salvation was secured and is *kept* secure by Jesus Christ and no one else. *Sola Christo.*

These four "Solas" logically culminated in "Soli Deo Gloria," meaning "Glory to God alone." He is the only One who must be elevated, praised, revered, and honored—the only One we must bow down before—the only One whose presence we anticipate with longing is *God*. Only God gets the glory, no man. As He declared,

I am the Lord, that is my name; And My glory I will not give to another, Nor My praise to carved images.
—Isaiah 42:8

God is not egotistical. He knows that we all worship something. And if He loves us, He will instruct us to worship the best thing for us. And there is nothing better for us than *Him*. If He loves us, He must command us to worship Him because allowing us to worship anything else would be to our detriment.

Hold Fast to the Truths of Scripture

³ Remember therefore how you have received and heard; hold fast...

At one time they said, *"If it's in the Bible, we believe it."* But tragically, over time, that changed. Jesus exhorts them to *"hold fast"* to the simple truths of Scripture about which they were once

---

[71] 1 Timothy 2:5.

so passionate. They are to stay away from new interpretations of Scripture that are motivated by a desire to harmonize the Bible with the values of the culture, as that path inevitably leads to heresies. In many sermons, Dr. H. A. Ironside wisely observed that when it comes to theology, *"If it's true, it's not new. And if it's new, it's not true."* The Bible counsels us to remember the former things[72] and walk in the old paths.[73] That's why Jesus told the Church in Ephesus to **"repent and do the first works."**[74]

Jesus doesn't tell Sardis, "*Move on to new things. You need to become a new Church for a new age. Adopt a slogan like, 'Open hearts, open doors, open minds'* (which I recently saw on a banner outside downtown Vancouver's oldest church building). He doesn't say that it's time to update His outdated views on sexuality or that churches should prioritize appeasing the values of the culture. Nor does He ask them to reinterpret the Bible as needed to avoid offending nonbelievers.

Jesus doesn't say *any* of that. What *does* He say?

. . . and repent.

Jesus tells them they need to change direction because they're on the wrong path. From His perspective, they're not *progressive*, they're *regressive*. They're broad-minded but only in the same way Jesus described the road that leads to destruction.[75]

If you reinterpret the Bible in such a way that anything offensive can be dismissed, why should a person believe any of it is true? And

---

[72] Cf. Isaiah 46:9.
[73] Cf. Jeremiah 6:16.
[74] Revelation 2:4.
[75] Cf. Matthew 7:13.

if a supposedly perfect God needs to change from day to day in response to the whims and opinions of *people*, then how can He be *God?* How can He even be *real?* Such a God would obviously be nothing more than a projection of the culture.

Jesus tells this Church that no longer holds to scriptural authority, *"repent."* Then Jesus explains what repentance *looks like* for them:

Therefore if you will not watch, ...

Did you catch that? He's being redundant on purpose. That's what He wants this Church to do that they are currently *not* doing; He wants them to *"watch."*

. . . I will come upon you as a thief, and you will not know what hour I will come upon you.

The use of the word *"thief"* is another allusion to the history of Sardis, which we discussed earlier. And when Jesus starts talking about the end-times, coming like a thief and people not knowing when He will be coming, I believe He's directing us to the only two places in Scripture that contain all three of those characteristics: **Matthew 24:42–43** and **1 Thessalonians 5:1–11**.

We don't have the space to go in-depth on those two passages, so I'll share a summary of the relevant aspects. In both passages of Scripture, Jesus comes to the earth for His Church. He's not talking about the *Second Coming*; He's talking about the *Rapture*. And in both cases, His coming is perceived differently by believers and nonbelievers. To believers, it's the greatest day of our lives. To nonbelievers, it's a *terrifying* event—like having your home broken into while you're sleeping. And that's because, for nonbelievers, the Rapture will be soon followed by the Tribulation when Jesus will pour out His judgment on the earth that has rejected Him.

In light of those Scriptures, I believe the warning Jesus is giving to the Church in Sardis means that if they don't repent, change course, and return to the truth of the Gospel, the majority of people in their church aren't going to be taken in the Rapture because the majority of people in their church are not saved.

It's a serious warning Jesus is giving because they think they're alive, they think they're saved, but they're dead. They don't have the Holy Spirit. They're *not saved*.

Revision of Biblical Truth

Four things the Bible specifically tells believers to watch for:

1. The coming of the Lord.
   Watch therefore, for you do not know what hour your Lord is coming. But know this, that if the master of the house had known what hour the thief would come, he would have watched… (Matthew 24:42–43)

2. Temptation.
   Watch and pray, lest you enter into temptation… (Matthew 26:41)

3. False teachers.
   …I know this, that after my departure savage wolves will come in among you, not sparing the flock. Also from among yourselves men will rise up, speaking perverse things, to draw away the disciples after themselves. Therefore watch, and remember that for three years I did not cease to warn everyone night and day with tears. (Acts 20:29–31)

4. Satan.
Be sober, be vigilant [be watchful]**; because your adversary the devil walks about like a roaring lion, seeking whom he may devour.** (1 Peter 5:8)

It's sobering to look at this list and then look at what's going on in mainline denominations (the institutions, not all their congregants) and many modern nondenominational churches. Unfortunately, you'll discover these four areas are increasingly neglected.

In the name of cultural relevance and palatability, many biblical truths have been (and are being) laid aside or "revised."

When it comes to Bible prophecies that are yet to be fulfilled or anything deemed too fantastical in the Scriptures (e.g., miracles), both are increasingly viewed the same way: figuratively. More and more churches are teaching that literal Bible interpretation is an antiquated and unenlightened approach.

Their eschatology doesn't include any level of urgency or immediacy that would give them a *reason* to be watching for the coming of the Lord. As a result, it's not something that's on their radar.

They can't be concerned with biblical personal righteousness and holiness because that would require holding to a standard of truth, which would inevitably result in certain actions being categorized as "sins." Such doctrine would be too judgmental for a modern "loving" church, so it's left up to the individual to do whatever they feel is right.

They can't be truly concerned about false teachers because who's to say what's false? Your truth is your truth. And if it makes you feel good, then it must be "life-giving," which is a higher priority than biblical truth.

And finally, they're not concerned with Satan because, after all, most of them are "enlightened" enough to know that neither Satan nor hell even *exists*, in any literal sense. The things Jesus instructs believers to watch for are the very things many churches today are willingly turning a blind eye to.

The Faithful in Sardis

[4] You have a few names even in Sardis who have not defiled their garments; and they shall walk with Me[76] in white, for they are worthy.

A segment of true believers in the Church in Sardis have not joined in their church's departure from biblical Christianity. Today, most of these faithful Christians have either left their denomination or participated in a schism within it over issues of biblical faithfulness. However, the majority in the Church in Sardis *have* compromised and now belong to congregations Jesus considers *dead*.

[5] He who overcomes shall be clothed in white garments, and I will not blot out his name from the Book of Life; but I will confess his name before My Father and before His angels. [6] "He who has an ear, let him hear what the Spirit says to the churches."

Luther and the Reformers deeply desired *"white garments"*—a clear reference to being forgiven and justified through Jesus and

---

[76] This implies a close relationship with God. Cf. Genesis 5:22–24; 6:9.

put in right relationship with God.[77] Jesus promises those in this church that He will give us white garments if we remember that it's Sola Fide (faith alone) and Sola Gratia (grace alone). If we will remember that it's faith in His grace that saves us, not our denomination, then we will be clothed in white and justified before Him. To state it plainly, the overcomer in Sardis is promised *salvation*.

The Doctrine of Eternal Security is the teaching often referred to as "once saved, always saved." It's the belief that once a person is saved, they cannot lose their salvation under any circumstances. Some who don't hold to this doctrine will point to the part of **V.5** where Jesus says:

> *... and I will not blot out his name from the Book of Life ...*

They say that means some names *can* be blotted out from the Book of Life. But that's not what it's saying. If you are a believer, you are an overcomer. And Jesus is simply assuring the believer that their name will *never* be blotted out of the Book of Life. It's a promise that if you're a believer, you don't have to worry about that ever happening.

Specifically, Jesus is assuring the true believers in the Church in Sardis they won't be lumped in with their dead church. Their salvation is secure because Jesus never allows the righteous to be collateral damage of His wrath simply because of their proximity to the unrighteousness.

---

[77] John is likely linking to Daniel 11:35; 12:1, 10.

APPLICATION TO ALL CHURCHES

Jesus wants all churches to remember that it's all about *Him*. It's all about His finished work on the Cross and simple faith in His grace, as revealed in His Word.

There's also a serious reminder for all churches to be diligent and *watchful*, especially for the coming of Jesus. He is coming and He is coming soon, and we are to encourage one another with this hope.

APPLICATION TO ALL BELIEVERS

This might seem like a question for children or teenagers at a youth group event, but it's just as meaningful, if not *more* meaningful, for us as adults: How would the way you live change if you knew Jesus was coming back in a year? Six months? A month? A week? *Tomorrow?* Because He really could!

If we believe that, let's live lives that reflect that belief. Let's prioritize the things of the Kingdom because all earthly things are destined to fade away. Let's take the opportunities to minister and share the Gospel that God gives us. Let's pray faithfully for the lost. And let's find hope in the reality that all of us, one way or another, will soon be in our true home, Heaven, where all wrongs will finally be made right.

Finally, do we know the Gospel? The Reformation was, at its core, a war over the Gospel because it's *that important*. I must have heard the Gospel thousands of times and yet I cannot get over it. Every year I grow in awe as I understand it just a little bit more or see it from another angle.

Do you know it? Can you share it, if asked? If there's one story we need to be able to tell, it's the story of how Jesus loves us so much that He died in our place that we might be brought into His Father's family as adopted sons and daughters.

> *"Therefore faithful Christian, seek the truth, listen to the truth, learn the truth, love the truth, speak the truth, adhere to truth and defend truth to the death."*[78]
>
> —Jan Hus

---

[78] Thomas A. Fudge, *Jan Hus: Religious Reform and Social Revolution in Bohemia* (London, England: I.B. Tauris, 2017), Chap. 3, Kindle.

REVELATION 3:7-13

THE CHURCH IN PHILADELPHIA

Philadelphia means, *"the city of him who loves his brother,"* and brotherly love gripped this church around AD 96 and in Church history, beginning around 1793.

This letter reveals a church that genuinely loved Jesus and cared about being faithful to Him above all else. And when you genuinely love Jesus, you can't help but catch His heart and love for your "brother." In both AD 96 and prophetically in Church history, Philadelphia loved Jesus and His Word, which drove them to love people near and far with the Gospel.

In the previous letter, we learned that the Church in Sardis prophetically represented the time of the Reformation and the many mainline denominations it birthed. Jesus told them that while they had a *name*—a famous history, great church founders, and a rich heritage—they were, in reality, *dead*. They had moved away from God's Word, and His Spirit (for the most part) had left the building.

We've learned about two of the four churches that exist today—Thyatira (the Roman Catholic Church) and Sardis (the Reformation Church). Let's dig into the third, *Philadelphia*.

HISTORY AND CULTURE OF PHILADELPHIA

Philadelphia was a beautiful and prosperous city built on the hillside of Mount Tmolus on a main road between Rome and Troas in the province of Asia Minor.

It was founded in 189 BC by the king of Pergamos, Eumenes II. His younger brother, Attalus II, traveled with him to establish the city, and Eumenes II so appreciated this that he named many of the new buildings and roadways after his sibling. They were so close that a coin was minted in Philadelphia bearing the image of Eumenes II on one side and his brother on the other. When Eumenes II died, he left the city to his brother, who responded by naming even more roads and buildings after his beloved brother than his brother had named after him. Their legendary kinship was why the city came to be known as Philadelphia, Greek for *"the city of him who loves his brother."*

The Romans used Philadelphia as a regional headquarters to promote Hellenism (Greek culture), including the Greek language, to the eastern part of the Empire. It was, for all intents and purposes, a *cultural* missionary city.

Today, Philadelphia is in Turkey and is named "Alasehir," which means *"The City of God"* in Arabic.

Philadelphia in Church History

Looking at Philadelphia on the prophetic level, we reach the time in history when the effects of the Reformation had run out of momentum. Sardis, representing the great mainline Protestant denominations, was spiritually dead. Philadelphia ushered in the next phase of Church history, beginning around 1793.

Prophetically, we can call Philadelphia "The Missionary Church," and we'll discover that it will *cease to exist* after the Rapture. Why? Keep reading.

Jesus told His disciples to take the Gospel into all the world,[79] and if we're honest, the Church has been wildly inconsistent in obeying Jesus' instruction.

As we discussed earlier, the Church was established around AD 32 and spread through persecuted saints being scattered across the Roman Empire. In AD 313, Constantine and Licinius issued the Edict of Milan, which officially ended the Empire's persecution of Christians. By the time AD 380 came around, Christianity had become the state religion. And by AD 600, the Church and state were so intimately "married" to one another that the work of spreading the Gospel was viewed as *complete* in the eyes of many.

And for the most part, that's how things stayed until the late 1700s when history records a great zeal for missionary work seized the Church:

> *At the beginning of the nineteenth century, Protestant Christianity scarcely existed outside Europe and America. Asia was almost untouched by the gospel, except for small traces in India and in the East Indies where the Dutch had taken over from the Portuguese.*[80]
>
> *For sheer magnitude the Christian mission in the nineteenth century is without parallel in human history.*[81]

---

[79] Cf. Mark 16:15.

[80] Shelley, *Church History in Plain Language*, 390.

[81] Shelley, 391.

In the late 1800s, churches and missionaries mobilized for the Gospel in a way not seen since:

> *By the end of the nineteenth century, almost every Christian body, from the Orthodox Church of Russia to the Salvation Army, and almost every country, from the Lutheran Church of Finland and the Waldensian Church of Italy to the newest denomination in the United States, had its share in the missionary enterprise overseas.*"[82]

Almost overnight, a door opened for the Gospel, and churches began sending missionaries to every corner of the earth. It was a move of God unparalleled in its global reach. At the same time, news was spreading of new lands being discovered, and the Holy Spirit stirred the heart of a man named William Carey to carry the Gospel to these unreached peoples.

Carey was the first modern-day missionary and went down in history as "The Father of Modern Missions." He was a shoemaker and Baptist preacher who took his exceptional gifts for languages and botany with him to India in the late 1700s, where he learned twelve languages and devoted his life to ministering the good news of the Gospel.

What is perhaps Carey's greatest quote perfectly captures his passion for the Gospel and the nations: *"Attempt great things for God; expect great things from God."*[83] His example inspired other legendary missionaries, including David Livingstone, who brought the Gospel

---

[82] Shelley, 398.

[83] Eustace Carey, *Memoir of William Carey* (London, England: Jackson and Walford, 1836), 75.

to South Africa in the mid-1800s, and Hudson Taylor, who founded the China Inland Mission in 1865.

This movement saw churches spring up worldwide, as men like D. L. Moody started initiatives such as the first Sunday School program for children. Prophetically, this season of Church history was marked by the rise of *evangelicalism*—a Christianity gripped by the Great Commission.

Rise of Christian Fundamentalism

You have to know Satan wasn't going to take all this sitting down. He watched as the Church returned to God's Word and was filled afresh with the power of God's Spirit, and he decided to do something about it.

His plan? Create *counterfeits* of Christianity that were *close* to biblical Christianity and yet just far enough away from it to not actually *be* biblical Christianity. They were similar enough to confuse, yet different enough to be void of any power to save. Movements and cults began to spring up at an unprecedented rate, such as:

- Mormonism in 1830
- Seventh Day Adventism (SDA) in 1863[84]
- Christian Science in 1875
- Jehovah's Witnesses in 1879
- The Unity School of Christianity in 1889

---

[84] While there is a broad spectrum of beliefs present in the modern SDA church, I would respectfully hold the founders' beliefs, teachings, and practices to clearly meet the reasonable definition of a cult, falling well outside the borders of historical orthodox Christianity.

As a result of this surge of cultish activity, a movement known as "fundamentalism" emerged within Christianity. What is "fundamentalism"? Let me explain by way of analogy.

I'm a huge basketball fan. I grew up watching Jordan and Olajuwon and still love the game. Like any sport, basketball has *fundamentals*. Specific characteristics define what basketball is and what it is not.

For example, if the Sacramento Kings decided to try out a new offense where their players tucked the ball under one arm and sprinted with it, using their free arm to push defenders out of the way, we know what would happen—the referee would blow his whistle, call a traveling violation, and likely eject the overly aggressive offender. If it were a rec game among friends, everyone would say, *"What are you doing?!"*

What if my teammates and I decided to try a new defensive scheme where we used giant foam gloves to stop the other team from getting off clean shots? We'd get a similar reaction, right? Why? Because *that's not basketball*.

What if I countered that argument by saying, *"Well, maybe what basketball means to me is different from what basketball means to you. Who are you to say what basketball is?"* Again, we know what would happen. Somebody would say something like, *"Jeff, it's not my opinion. Basketball is something that is defined by a specific set of rules. There's a rule book that lays out what makes basketball, basketball. If you play by some other set of rules, then what you're playing is no longer basketball; it's something else."*

We all understand this analogy regarding sports because we understand that the alternative to defined rules would be *chaos*. However, when it comes to Christians holding each other accountable to actually *live* like Christians, it's not unusual to hear a comment along the lines of, *"Who are you to say what is or is not Christian?"*

But just as basketball has a rule book that defines the game of basketball, Christianity has the Bible, which defines what is and is not Christian. And Christian fundamentalism is, in its truest sense, a movement rooted in remembering that Christianity is not open to each person's interpretation, desires, or opinions; it is *defined* by God's Word.

Evangelical Christians began to meet in 1905 to discuss all this because they recognized the need to clear up the confusion caused by all these "Christian" cults. Simultaneously, a new liberalism had infiltrated many Christian seminaries and college campuses. Professors and even some pastors were beginning to move away from biblical Christianity to such a degree that their teachings could no longer be considered orthodox.

In 1909 this group of concerned evangelicals came up with "The 5 Points of Fundamentalism," which defined the *fundamental* beliefs of Christianity, regardless of one's denominational affiliation or methodology (i.e., style of church). Here are the five fundamentals they came up with:

- The inerrancy of Scripture
- The literal nature of the biblical accounts (e.g., miracles, the Genesis creation account)
- The deity of Jesus (including the virgin birth)
- The bodily resurrection and physical return of Jesus
- The substitutionary atonement of Jesus on the Cross

The first point the fundamentalist group noted was that to be a Christian, one must agree that the Bible is God's Word, meaning it came from God, was given to men, and is without error in its original form. As Jesus said,

> **Heaven and earth will pass away, but My words will by no means pass away.**
> —Matthew 24:35

The second point was aimed mainly at liberal pastors and seminary professors. The fundamentalists felt the need to clarify that believing in the inerrancy of Scripture meant believing the Bible was *true*. When it says Jesus performed a miracle, it *actually happened*. When it says God made the world from nothing and Adam and Eve were the first humans, it means those things *actually happened*.

Third, they raised the necessity of belief that Jesus is *God*. Cults generally teach that Jesus is *not* God. It's one of the dividing lines between that which is Christian and that which is not. Building on the first and second points, they specifically included the virgin birth in this third point.

Fourth, Christians believe Jesus rose from the dead in a physical, glorified body, which He currently inhabits. And in the future, He will return to the earth in this same body to reign with His Church. Jesus' resurrection and future return are not intended to be understood as mystical or allegorical events but as literal events that have and will take place (respectively).

Finally, a Christian must believe that Jesus atoned (i.e., paid) for our sins by dying in our place on the Cross. Christians believe this is the *only way* for us to receive salvation.

"The 5 Point of Fundamentalism" was a needed and helpful document at the time and, sadly, such clarity is needed in much of the Church again today.

As you can see, true Christian fundamentalism as it was defined in years past is very different from how the term is perceived in popular culture, where a fundamentalist is considered to be something akin to a "crazy, uneducated, bigoted zealot." I think the truth is that we're in an age where whatever term we use for Bible-believing Christians, our culture will perceive it as a synonym for "crazy, uneducated, bigoted zealot" (as seems to be the fate of the more recent term, "evangelical").

INTO THE TEXT

> *[7] And to the angel of the Church in Philadelphia write, "These things says He who is holy, He who is true, "He who has the key of David, He who opens and no one shuts, and shuts and no one opens":*

The first part of Jesus' title is, *"He who is holy."* The word **"holy"** means *"set apart."* When we talk about God being *holy*, we are talking about the fact that He is on a completely different level to everyone and everything. He is the Almighty. He's always existed, and He predates everything because He is the source of everything. He's different from us in the most profound ways. He is perfect in power, knowledge, and righteousness. He is quite simply . . . *other*. To forget that He is holy is to forget who He is.

God's holiness should inspire awe, reverence, and yes, even fear. There's a reason God's Word tells us more than once that the fear of the Lord is the beginning of wisdom. A right view of God's holiness enables us to understand the seriousness of sin, the greatness of Jesus' work on the Cross, and just how blessed we are to be able to approach Him with confidence.[85]

---

[85] Cf. Hebrews 4:15–16.

Then Jesus refers to Himself as, *"He who is true."* The word *"true"* means *"absolute; real or genuine, in contrast to falsehood."* Jesus is absolute truth incarnate (we'll talk more about that in the next letter).

I think G. Campbell Morgan got it right when he succinctly explained that the holiness of Jesus' nature refers to His perfect *character*, while the truth of Jesus' nature refers to His perfect *conduct*.[86]

As we read the letter to the Church in Philadelphia, we'll realize that Jesus isn't reminding them of His holiness as a criticism. He doesn't think they've forgotten. Rather, He's saying it as an *encouragement*.

One of the things Revelation does (and I hope you're picking up on this) is drop little breadcrumbs intended to take your mind somewhere else in the Scriptures for an explanation or greater detail.

And when I was thinking about Jesus encouraging this Church by reminding them that He is *holy*, my mind went to **1 Peter 1**, where the Apostle Peter quotes the Old Testament and reminds his readers that God has commanded us, *"Be holy, for I am holy."*[87]

Jesus is holy in the sense that he is *other*. But He calls us to be holy in the sense that we are to be set apart, consecrated, and reserved for Him and His purposes. The life of every believer belongs to Jesus, and our call to holiness is a call to live in light of the truth that He is our master. We are not our own.

And that's how Jesus is encouraging this Church. He's urging

---

[86] Rod Mattoon, *Treasures from Revelation* (Springfield, IL: Rod Mattoon, 2003), 101.

[87] 1 Peter 1:16.

them to continue living set apart for Him, holding on to what is true.

The Key of David

Then Jesus calls Himself, *"He who has the key of David, who opens and no one shuts, and shuts and no one opens."* The *"key of David"* is an Old Testament reference we're not typically familiar with. It's from a part of the Book of Isaiah where a man named Eliakim is replacing a corrupt man named Shebna as governor (i.e., national treasurer) of the palace of King Hezekiah.

If you read **Isaiah 22**, starting around **V.15**, you'll find that even though the text speaks of Eliakim, it is *also* speaking prophetically of the Messiah.

As the king, Hezekiah sat and ruled from the *literal* throne of David (the second king in Israel's history). It was a real object, which the Bible referred to as "the throne of David."

The governor of the king's palace would be given an object called "the key of David." It too was a real, physical object that symbolized incredible power. While we don't know exactly what it was, we know it was a large enough to be worn over the shoulder.[88] Whatever it was, this "key" granted its bearer access to all the resources of the kingdom and the treasury. Additionally, it gave one the authority to grant others access to the king. If you wanted to get to King Hezekiah, you had to go through Shebna and then later Eliakim.

While that whole story is worth studying, all you need to know for now is that *"the key of David"* represents access to the king and the king's resources.

---

[88] Cf. Isaiah 22:22.

And here's how all that connects to this letter in **Revelation 3**: The titles Jesus gives Himself are intended to encourage believers to remain holy and focused on the truth of His Word, knowing they will be rewarded by Him.

Commendation Of Philadelphia

Here's the commendation Jesus writes in Philadelphia's report card:

⁸ I know your works.

If you're living for Jesus, His knowing your works is a good thing because He turns our earthly works for Him into eternal rewards that will be waiting for us in Heaven.

Jesus is the One who holds the keys to the Kingdom; when He opens something, nobody can shut it; when He closes something, nobody can open it. *That* Jesus tells this Church what He has done for them with those keys:

See, I have set before you an open door, and no one can shut it; for you have a little strength, have kept My word, and have not denied My name.

Compared to the other churches, Philadelphia is receiving an *exceptional* commendation from the Lord. Don't miss the connection that Jesus is making here between their *"works"* and this *"open door."* It's *because of* their righteous works that He has opened this door for them. When the Lord finds believers being faithful with what they have, He loves to give them more. As Jesus taught, ***"He who is faithful in what is least is faithful also in much."***[89]

---

[89] Luke 16:10.

We see this principle at work when Eliakim takes over from Shebna, and in **James 5:16**, where we are told that, *"The effective, fervent prayer of a righteous man avails much."* Even in the age of grace in which we live, there is still a connection between living righteously and having access to the King's resources. I would encourage you to meditate on and study that principle further.

Jesus says, *"I have set before you . . . "*—the Philadelphia church, specifically—*". . . an open door."* In **1 Corinthians 16:9**, the Apostle Paul wrote:

. . . a great and effective door has opened to me...

When you examine the context of that verse, it's obvious Paul is referring to an opportunity that had opened for Him to take the Gospel to a new region.

Because of how open doors are used in the Bible in relation to Christians on the earth, most scholars agree that **1 Corinthians 16:9** refers to opportunities to do missionary work—taking the Gospel to places and people that have not yet heard it.

Take a quick look ahead to the very last line of **V.9**. Jesus says, *"to know that I have loved you."* Whatever this Church is doing, Jesus *loves it*. And He declares that nobody will be able to shut the door that He has opened for them.

And yet, what we're currently seeing around the world seems to be the *closing* of that missionary door. It's increasingly difficult to send missionaries, as more and more countries refuse them entry. We're seeing incredible *indigenous* moves of God in places like Iran, Ethiopia, and China, but the missionary door for the Philadelphia church seems to be rapidly closing.

Jesus said, *"I have set before you an open door, and no one can shut it."* That means only Jesus can open or close this door. So, what's going on? Well, before Jesus closes *that* door, He's going to open *another* door in **Revelation 4:1**. He is going to come back for His Church. And He is coming soon.

... for you have a little strength, ...

The original Greek makes it clear that Jesus is saying, *"though you only have a little bit of strength..."* In other words, this means *"Even though there's not a lot of you and you don't hold significant sway over the culture..."*

Prophetically, this seems to imply that at the time of the Rapture, a small minority of churches will hold to a biblical standard of holiness and truth.

... have kept My word, ...

This Church emphasizes keeping God's Word—obeying, honoring, and loving the Scriptures. They keep the Bible central and honor it as authoritative over their lives. The New Testament lists the two identifying marks of a disciple of Christ. In other words, if you love God *internally*, these are the two *external* characteristics that will be evident in your life.

When Jesus was praying to His Father for His disciples, He said:

I have manifested Your name to the men whom You have given Me out of the world. They were Yours, You gave them to Me, and they have kept Your word.

—John 17:6

And then in **John 13:35**, Jesus famously said:

By this all will know that you are My disciples, if you have love for one another.

According to Jesus, the characteristics that mark us as His disciples are keeping His Word and loving one another. The Church in Philadelphia is actually doing what Jesus said to do, which is why He wants everybody to know that He *loves* this church. This is the church we should all want to be part of!

Not Denied My Name

Then Jesus says:

> *. . . and have not denied My name.*

The Church in Philadelphia, every church since, and you and I today, all need to hear this.

The third of the Ten Commandments is, **"You shall not take the name of the Lord your God in vain."** I agree with those who suggest this has nothing to do with cussing or bad language. The word **"vain"** in the original Hebrew means, *"emptiness, vanity, falsehood, nothingness, emptiness of speech, lying"* and—get this—*"worthlessness [of conduct]."* I believe that taking the name of the Lord in vain means identifying yourself as a Christian—a *"little Christ"*—while living in a way that grossly misrepresents Jesus. It means living as though it means nothing that you have been adopted into the family of God—that you are a child of the Father and a temple of the Holy Spirit.

Come to your own conclusion, but I believe Jesus is commending this church for living lives that prove they don't take His name *lightly*. They don't take His *honor* lightly. They understand they are **"ambassadors [representatives] for Christ."**[90]

---

[90] Cf. 2 Corinthians 5:20.

We live in a day and age when the word "God" is not offensive. Neither are the words "Allah" or "Buddha." But what name is offensive? *Jesus.*

Despite societal pressure, this Church is not confused or ashamed about who God is. His name is *Jesus*. His name means *"Jehovah is salvation"* because His is the only name under Heaven that has the power to save.[91] This Church *loves* the name of Jesus.

That's important because Peter told us that in the last days, there would be those who call themselves Christians but deny the name of Jesus in their teachings.[92] We saw that happen during this period of Church history when there was an explosion of new religious groups that professed to be Christian but were, in reality, *cults* that denied the Lord Jesus.

The good news for the Philadelphia church is that they've stayed focused on God's Word and haven't been deceived by or caught up in any false gospels, false teachers, or false religions. And Jesus commends them for that.

The Synagogue of Satan

Jesus continues in **V.9**:

> ⁹ *Indeed I will make those of the synagogue of Satan, who say they are Jews and are not, but lie—indeed I will make them come and worship before your feet, and to know that I have loved you.*

---

[91] Cf. Acts 4:12.

[92] Cf. 2 Peter 2:1.

We encountered *"the synagogue of Satan"* back in the letter to Smyrna,[93] where we learned it was likely a reference to Jews who were betraying their ethnic Christian brethren to the Romans to be imprisoned, tortured, or even executed. We can safely assume that around AD 96, a comparable situation existed in Philadelphia.

But what about the *prophetic* application of this warning? It's not as clear as the other letters, but I'll share my personal belief with you for your consideration.

The phrase *"the synagogue of Satan"* may refer to those who claimed to be doing *God's* bidding but were really doing *Satan's* bidding. When a church is loving and serving God faithfully, Satan will always stir up opposition. Generally, we know and expect this. But what still takes many Christians by surprise is when that opposition comes from those who claim to be serving Jesus.

I believe the past few decades have made it clear the Philadelphia Church will be attacked by not only the world system under Satan's rule but also another *church*—the Church in Laodicea, the Last Days Church, which we still study in the next and final letter.

The Philadelphia Church brought God's people back to the Word and the fundamentals of the faith. Unsurprisingly, Satan wasn't a big fan of that. But I don't believe the Church need be concerned by the world's ever-increasing hostility toward her. We know from our earlier studies of churches like Smyrna that persecution only purifies the Church and makes her more effective and beautiful.

We also learned how effectively Satan was able to undermine the power of the Church when he *joined* the Church and married her to the state,[94] the culture, and society at large. Similarly, I believe Satan

---

[93] Cf. Revelation 2:9.

[94] See the letters to the Churches in Pergamos and Thyatira.

is using the Laodicean Church to attack the Philadelphia Church. That is to say, he is attacking the Church that faithfully holds to the Word of God with the Church that elevates the culture above the Word of God.

Prophetically, *"the synagogue of Satan"* that biblically faithful churches are battling is the Laodicean Church—the church that is more concerned with the approval of the world than the approval of Jesus. It is the church that is falling over itself to publicly condemn biblically faithful churches in the hopes of scoring a few points with the culture.

And I believe Jesus is reminding us to stay faithful to Him and His Word. Because in the end, He will vindicate those who remain faithful, and the Laodicean Church will be exposed.

Obedience and Perseverance

¹⁰ Because you have kept My command to persevere, ...

Back in **V.8** Jesus commended this Church for keeping His Word, and then here in **V.10**, He commends them for keeping His *"command to persevere."* They're living in obedience to God's Word. They're reading it and heeding it. And that's why we want to be like them. They're staying faithful to Jesus.

The church in Philadelphia is all about God's Word, and God commends them because they have kept His *"command to persevere."* Here's what He's going to do for them:

> *... I also will keep you from the hour of trial which shall come upon the whole world, to test those who dwell on the earth.*

The original Greek is emphatic that *"the hour"* refers to a specific, appointed time (i.e., *"the hour of trial"*). Jesus is speaking of the

Tribulation. The Bible refers to it as a time of testing and trouble,[95] and according to Jesus, it's about to *"come upon the whole world."*

Also in the original Greek, *"hour"*[96] can refer to an hour, a day, or even a season. In this case, it refers to the hour of the Tribulation—a future period that will last seven years.

Some believe that Jesus is saying that He will sustain believers and give them the strength to endure the Tribulation. To support their position, they will often offer as evidence a line from Jesus' Great High Priestly Prayer in **John 17:15**, where He prays to His Heavenly Father regarding His disciples:

> *I do not pray that You should take them out of the world, but that You should keep them from the evil one.*

And they will say, *"See? Jesus wants His followers to be on the earth to endure suffering."*

The problem is that the original Greek makes it clear that is *not* what Jesus is saying in **Revelation 3:10**. The Greek phrase used to describe being kept from something consists of the verb *"tereo"* and the preposition *"ek."* The Greek word *"ek"* means *"out of, from, away from"* and when it's used with *"tereo"* it refers to a continuous existence outside of something.

There are different Greek prepositions one can use to communicate *endurance* rather than *removal* ("en" meaning "in," or "dia" meaning "through"). And here's the kicker—*"tereo"* and *"ek"* are only used together in one other place in the New Testament, and that is **John 17:15**.

In that verse, was Jesus praying that His disciples be kept *in*

---

[95] Cf. Jeremiah 30:7.

[96] Hora.

"the evil one" or *through "the evil one"*? Of course not. Jesus was praying that His disciples be kept *away from "the evil one,"* having *a continuous existence away from* Satan. Jesus asked His Heavenly Father to keep His disciples from Satan, and He promises the Church in Philadelphia they will be kept from the Tribulation.

I also want you to notice that this will not be a *local* event but a *worldwide* event:

> ***I also will keep you from the hour of trial which shall come upon…***

The Jews in Israel? Christians? The Church? *No.*

> ***…the whole world…***

It's going to be a worldwide event, meaning it clearly has not happened yet. But as we are discovering, it's coming soon. We're told that the *purpose* of this *"trial"* is *"to test those who dwell on the earth."*

Beginning in **Revelation 4**, we'll see terms such as *"those who dwell on the earth"* used to describe those on the earth who have rejected Jesus and will continue to do so throughout the seven years of the Tribulation, despite the evidence of the Rapture and overwhelming supernatural signs.

The Greek word for *"dwell"*[97] means *"to dwell permanently."* In contrast, the Bible calls believers **"sojourners and pilgrims"**[98] on the earth. We're just passing through a place that is not our home. But these people will consciously choose to align themselves with the world instead of Jesus, and the *"trial"* that is coming is for *them*, not for believers.

---

[97] Katoikeo.
[98] 1 Peter 2:11.

We'll find that after the Rapture, Revelation tells us there will be Gentiles (non-Jews) who become believers during the Tribulation, but most will be martyred at the hand of antichrist,[99] not supernaturally protected. The cost of their second chance will be their earthly lives.

There will, however, be a group of Jews who *are* supernaturally protected during the Tribulation, and they will evangelize an incredible number of people across the earth. When we reach that part of our study, we'll learn that everyone on earth will have to decide whether to take the infamous mark of the beast. Those Gentiles who become believers will obviously *not* take the mark, and for that decision, most will be executed.

So, it doesn't make a lick of sense to say that what Jesus is promising the Philadelphia Church is that He'll enable them to *endure* the Tribulation. Revelation doesn't describe believers empowered by God to *endure* the Tribulation; it describes nonbelievers who *turn to the Lord* in the Tribulation and are executed for it. Scripture also tells us those who are Gentile believers *before* the Tribulation will be *removed* before the Tribulation begins. And it's going to be fascinating when we study how God will accomplish that.

Read **V.10** again. I find it compelling that in the original Greek, the phrase *"the whole world"* means *"the whole world."* Even during the two World Wars, *"the whole world"* was not affected. Jesus uses that phrase intentionally because He wants us to understand that this coming *"hour of trial"* is going to be unlike anything the world has ever seen. Suffice it to say, Jesus *cannot* be referring to events that have already taken place in history.

---

[99] Cf. Revelation 6:9–11; 7:9–14.

You might recall Paul reassuring the Thessalonian believers by telling them:

> **...you, brethren are not in darkness, so that this Day should overtake you as a thief.**
> —1 Thessalonians 5:4

Believers are supposed to *recognize* the *"hour"* when these events are about to unfold. And just a few verses later, Paul reminds them:

> **...God did not appoint us to wrath, but to obtain salvation through our Lord Jesus Christ...**
> —1 Thessalonians 5:9

The *world* is going to enter the Tribulation. However, the *Church* (believers) is not. If you're a believer, you will *never* experience the wrath of God. Isn't that wonderful news?

What criticism does Jesus have for the Church in Philadelphia? *None.* They're keeping His Word and sharing the Gospel, and because they're doing that, Jesus has nothing critical to say—just as He had nothing critical to say about Smyrna, the Church that was dying for Him. Jesus has no criticism for the Church that is *suffering* for Him or the Church that is *proclaiming* Him.

Exhortation to the Church in Philadelphia

Regarding an exhortation, Jesus says:

> [11] *Behold, I am coming quickly! Hold fast what you have, that no one may take your crown.*

Just a quick reminder: Crowns speak of rewards, not salvation. The believer's salvation is a settled, finished issue.

Among the seven letters, crowns are only mentioned here and in the letter to Smyrna—the only two churches that also receive no criticism from Jesus.

Look at **V.11** again. When do we receive our crowns? The text implies believers have at least one crown *now* because no one can take something that's not already in your possession. That means even though believers may not know it or be able to sense it, many are walking around with crowns already. Jesus is *already* handing them out. And I can't help wondering how differently we would view each other, and our sufferings, if we could see those crowns presently.

Our future with Jesus is so certain that it's future history. It's as certain as the events of yesterday, that have already happened. We're already there, but not yet. This glorious, yet hard-to-fathom reality is what Paul was speaking of when he told us we've been seated with Christ in heavenly places[100]—*past tense*.

The exhortation is *"Hold fast."* Jesus assures them that they're doing great. He urges them to keep going and not let anyone take the crown He's already placed upon their heads.

That's encouraging because it reminds me to keep living in light of the ultimate reality of eternity and add to my treasure in Heaven.

Overcomers Are Pillars in the Kingdom

> [12] *He who overcomes, I will make him a pillar in the temple of My God, and he shall go out no more.*

The language Jesus uses here contrasts with the *unstable* reputation of the city of Philadelphia around AD 96. The city had

---

[100] Cf. Ephesians 2:6.

been destroyed by a catastrophic earthquake in AD 17 and despite being rebuilt, the city did not grow especially large because so many were terrified by the prospect of another disaster.

If we stay passionate about Jesus, if we keep the faith, God will establish us in His Kingdom like pillars in the Temple of the Old Testament. We'll be in our resurrected bodies, made like Jesus, impervious to our current highs and lows. We'll finally be truly stable. *Unshakable.* I can't wait. **V.12** continues:

> *I will write on him the name of My God and the name of the city of My God, the New Jerusalem, which comes down out of heaven from My God. And I will write on him My new name.*

This prophecy unfolds in **Revelation 21–22**, where we are told those who belong to Jesus **"shall see His face, and His name** *shall be* **on their foreheads."**[101]

In the previous letter, Sardis had a *name* they were so proud of, only to have Jesus tell them it was *empty*. And then here we see Jesus pointing to the *name* of *"my God,"* *"the city of my God,"* and the new name He's going to write on us. There's a lesson in there about the names and titles that we should be concerned with—the names and titles that *actually* matter.

In summary, Jesus promises the overcomer *citizenship* in His eternal Kingdom. As Christians, we are called to live our earthly lives as citizens of Heaven.

> [13] *He who has an ear, let him hear what the Spirit says to the churches.*

---

[101] Revelation 22:4.

APPLICATION TO ALL CHURCHES

Because the Church exists first and foremost for Jesus, we should all *lean in* when He tells us what He loves to see in His Church. And the letter to Philadelphia tells us that Jesus *loves it* when His Church catches His heart for the lost and His Word.

When we begin to love the lost with the heart of Jesus, this letter tells us He gets *actively involved* in opening doors for ministry.

It is impossible to be a church that *keeps* His Word without being a church that *teaches* His Word. I believe it's clear from His letter to Philadelphia that Jesus wants His Church to study His Word, take it to heart, and seek to keep it (i.e., live it out). As churches, we are called to join the Holy Spirit in reaching out to the lost and to *learn* God's Word so that we might *live* God's Word.

APPLICATION TO INDIVIDUAL BELIEVERS

If you're a believer, you *are* an ambassador for Christ. If you're a Christian, then you are a *"little Christ."* You represent the name of Jesus, and part of the responsibility that comes with that is understanding that the way you live can help people understand the reality of a God who loves them.

Jesus loves you. There is nothing you need to do to earn His favor or blessings. You can't earn your salvation; Jesus already did that for you. But if you're interested in being a blessing to the Lord, if you're interested in representing Him well to the world around you, then I would encourage you to spend some time praying, reflecting, and meditating on the four positive traits of the two churches for which Jesus had no criticism:

- Keep His Word as the authority over your life.

- Proclaim His Word by sharing the Gospel as you have opportunity.
- Be willing to suffer persecution for Him.
- Live ready to die for Him.

CLOSING THOUGHTS AND AN ASSIGNMENT

Earlier, I shared that Revelation takes your mind to other places in Scripture. As I contemplated Jesus introducing Himself by emphasizing His holiness, I found my mind taken to **1 Peter 1**. And when I turned there in my Bible, I was floored by what I found myself reading. Peter writes to churches, including churches in Asia (and possibly the Church in Philadelphia), and what he says in **VV.13–25** is essentially a summary of Jesus' letter to the Church in Philadelphia. I encourage you to read it for yourself and ask the Lord to show you the many connections to **Revelation 3:7–13.**

REVELATION 3:14-22

THE CHURCH IN LAODICEA

In the previous letter, we studied the church every believer should want to be part of—the Church in *Philadelphia*. They kept God's Word and did not deny His name. They held fast, and Jesus promised to keep them from *the* Tribulation. Along with Smyrna, they're the only church to receive no criticism from the Lord and the promise of eternal rewards. In this letter to the Church in Laodicea, we'll examine the church *no believer* should want to be part of.

What does the city's name tell us about the Church in Laodicea? It's a Greek compound word made up of the words "laos" and "dike." The word "laos" means "a people" and the root word behind "dikē"[102] refers to giving some sort of presentation, such as a teaching. The gist of the compound word is "the people's teaching" or "the teaching of the people."

Democracy as we know it is a relatively new political system, with the twentieth century seeing waves of democratization sweep

---

[102] Deiknyō.

the globe followed by waves of resistance seeking to reverse those changes.

Similarly, board-run or congregationally run churches are a recent development within the Church. Only in the last couple of centuries have we seen churches ruled by the people who attend them. It is now normal to see congregations hire the pastor they want and fire the pastor they don't.

I'm very aware that what I'm getting at will offend some, but the obvious parallels must be pointed out. We have congregations that have the power to fire their pastor should he fail to meet their desires and expectations. There's no way around the fact that in that church model, the pastor is an employee of the people, and they are the ones ruling the church.

It's the rule of the laity, the Laodicean church. And here's what you need to know: there is no biblical precedent for this church model. None whatsoever. In the Old Testament, nothing good ever comes from God's people wanting to rule themselves. It's always disastrous. What you find God doing in Scripture is using specific people who are more concerned with being obedient to Him than pleasing the people. God uses those kinds of people, often against the *protests* of the people.

While I would love to get into a study on ecclesiastical polity (church governance structures), I will limit myself to this simple statement: I believe that we should derive our models of church governance from the Scriptures—specifically, governance used by the Early Church during the apostles' lifetimes. How did they structure church leadership in Jerusalem, Antioch, and Ephesus, for example?

The short answer is that we find churches led by elders, with "elder" being used as a synonym for "pastor." The New Testament model has churches being led by a plurality of pastors. There is simply no other leadership model for churches presented in Scripture. As I said, I'd love to talk more about that, but we need to stay on track.

Unfortunately, we're seeing more and more churches advertising pastoral positions with job descriptions resembling Fortune 500 companies rather than the New Testament requirements for elders. Why? Because many churches are no longer looking to the Scriptures for guidance, they're looking to the culture and the business world.

I pray I never end up at a church where the pastor is more afraid of his people than God. Because that pastor will not tell me the truth. He'll do what he needs to do to keep his job and feed his family. And that is not a recipe for a healthy church. It's like seeing a doctor who only gets paid if he gives his patients a favorable report, and therefore doesn't end up helping anybody.

Sadly, that was the situation in Laodicea.

HISTORY AND CULTURE OF LAODICEA

Laodicea was founded in the third century BC by King Antiochus II Theos of the Seleucid dynasty, who named the city after his wife, Laodice.

It was situated on an important trade route from the east and served as a crossroads to other major cities in the region. This privileged location caused the city to prosper rapidly and become the wealthiest city in Asia Minor. It was a center of commerce, banking, and even fashion. So prosperous and progressive was Laodicea that Rome granted it the status of a free city, allowing it to govern itself (under Roman observation).

The city hosted a large textiles industry renowned for its unique production of glossy black wool. The locals mastered the art of raising entire herds of black sheep. This place was so trendy that even their *sheep* wore black.

They were also famed for their medical center, which boasted the world's leading specialists in ophthalmology—the branch of medicine dealing with *eye* disorders. They produced an *ointment* that was famed for helping all kinds of eye conditions; it was exported across the Empire and was even used and written about by Aristotle.

In AD 60 the city was devastated by an earthquake that ravaged the region. While other cities relied on financial relief from Caesar Nero in Rome, Laodicea turned down the offer because the people had the resources and wealth to rebuild the city themselves. Unsurprisingly, the city became extremely *prideful* because they felt that they were completely *self-sufficient*.

The city was located on a high platform between three rivers but none of that water reached Laodicea. So, they employed mind-blowing technology to pump in the water they needed from several miles away.

Most of their supply came from the Baspinar spring in the city of Denizli, but there was a problem: Baspinar was a *hot* spring. By the time the water arrived in Laodicea, it was *lukewarm* and murky from the multi-mile journey through dirty aqueducts.

"Lukewarm" also describes the city's political climate and military policy. Their reliance on an external water supply meant their city was, for all intents and purposes, indefensible. So, the city and its people survived by learning to be *flexible*—politically and culturally. They were always willing to change to *fit in* with the dominant regional power. They wouldn't put up a fight or take a stand; they'd simply fall in line with the changing times. They were *pragmatists* who focused on being relevant, relatable, and accepting of whatever the current cultural expectations were. The approach worked well and allowed the Laodiceans to live comfortable lives through multiple significant political changes in the region.

Today, the ruins of Laodicea reveal a city packed with theaters, gymnasiums, a 30,000-seat stadium, steam baths (where people would hang out and socialize), temples, a bouleuterion (Senate House), and many shops. It was a wealthy, trendy city that loved *luxury* and *entertainment*.

The city had a large church but unfortunately, it had become infected with the spirit of the place. Archippus, the Bishop of Colossae, oversaw the Laodicean church and had to be specifically rebuked (verbally slapped upside the head) by the Apostle Paul, who told him:

> ***Take heed to the ministry which you have received in the Lord, that you may fulfill it.***
>
> —Colossians 4:17

Paul asked the Church in Colossae to forward that epistle to the Church in Laodicea,[103] and after studying this letter, I encourage you to read **Colossians 1**. You'll find that in it, Paul addresses all the criticisms Jesus will raise here in **Revelation 3**, decades later. And it'll be obvious that despite Paul's rebuke of Archippus, things did *not* get better in Laodicea.

A Prophetic Look at Laodicea

Prophetically, Laodicea will be the last of the seven churches to emerge before Jesus comes for His Church. The Laodicean Church

---

[103] Cf. Colossians 4:16.

began between 1850 and 1900 and continues today. She is best described as "the Lukewarm Church."

When I say these seven letters lay out 2,000 years of Church history, keep in mind that this prophetic pattern couldn't be identified until most of it had already unfolded. Enough of the pattern had to appear for it to be *identifiable* as a pattern. Earlier churches couldn't recognize it, in part because they didn't have access to information and archaeology that has become available over the last couple of centuries.

What I find especially compelling is that some theologians recognized this prophetic pattern in the 1800s, *before* it had been fully revealed. And using the pattern, they were able to *predict*, with stunning accuracy, what would happen next in Church history.

In 1865 a theologian named Joseph Seiss published three volumes of lectures on the apocalypse. In Volume 1, he writes about the Laodicean church as something that he was beginning to see but that was primarily *yet to come*. After studying Revelation, this was what Seiss believed the Laodicean church era would look like:

> *It is Laodicean—conformed in everything to the popular judgment and will—the extreme opposite of Nicolaitane. Instead of a Church of domineering clericals, it is the Church of the domineering mob, in which nothing may be safely preached except what the people are pleased to hear—in which the teachings of the pulpit are fashioned to the tastes of the pew, and the feelings of the individual override the enactments of legitimate authority.*
>
> *It is lukewarm—nothing decided, partly hot and partly cold— divided between Christ and the world—not willing to give up pretension and claim to the heavenly, and yet clinging close to the earthy—having too much conscience to cast off the name of*

Christ, and too much love for the world to take a firm and honest stand entirely on His side.[104]

Seiss described a future where pastors wouldn't ask, *"What does my congregation **need** to hear?"* but *"What does my congregation **want** to hear?"* Unfortunately, he envisioned a time when pastors would select their sermon content based upon the desires of the congregation, with cultural approval serving as the primary goal.

In the prophetic layer of the letter to Laodicea, Seiss foresaw the seeker-sensitive movement more than *a century* before it arrived. The Apostle Paul did even better, calling it around 1,800 years beforehand and describing it like this in **2 Timothy 4:3–4** (NLT):

> **...a time is coming when people will no longer listen to sound and wholesome teaching. They will follow their own desires and will look for teachers who will tell them whatever their itching ears want to hear. They will reject the truth and chase after myths.**

Laodicea and the Modern Church

Modern church growth theory says that if you want to grow a church, you shouldn't teach too much of the Bible because people don't want to hear that. Rather, teach on something positive like love or self-esteem or chasing your dreams, and then throw in a few verses that vaguely tie into the subject. That's what people *really* want.

The key is to figure out what people are interested in and from there, well, it's not rocket science—just give them what they want!

---

[104] Joseph A. Seiss, *The Apocalypse: Lectures on the Book of Revelation* (New York: Cosimo Classics, 2007), 84–85.

Do a series on spicing up your sex life or *"Getting the Life You Deserve"* and watch your church grow! The secret is to let the desires of the people drive your preaching.

And you don't need to take my word for it. If you live in North America, then you probably live within an hour's drive of one or more churches that fit the description I just shared (and they're probably *packed*).

The way many evaluate the health of a church sounds something like this: *"If the church is growing and the people are having a good time, then God must be blessing whatever that church is doing!"*

But imagine if I told you, *"You know, we've got six kids, and we were thinking the other day about how we could improve our meals. And then it hit me—who better to come up with the menu than the people who are going to be eating the food? So, we've started letting our kids decide what they want to eat. We're on day five of pizza and ice cream, and they're having a blast! And I can tell you this: you won't find happier kids at anybody else's dinner table. It's clear that God is blessing our approach to feeding our children."*

Would you be impressed with me, as a father? Maybe a little, but only in a similar manner to how impressed you are with someone who can eat 30 hot dogs in one sitting. It's kind of amazing but also disturbing and clearly a bad idea, especially as regular behavior.

So, what would you think of a *pastor* who said, *"I'm not going to teach you the deeper things of God's Word. We're gonna stay away from the difficult truths of the Scriptures. I'm committed to sticking with whatever **you** want to talk about and whatever makes **you** feel good."*

It's a father's job to be a father, and it's a shepherd's job to be a shepherd. But the Laodicean church doesn't want a shepherd. They want a positive-thinking life coach.

Modern Philosophical Movements

How did the modern Church end up here? Well, around 1920, during the Philadelphia church age (the missionary-sending, evangelical, get-back-to-the-Bible church), some within the Church began to embrace what's known as "higher criticism."

Higher criticism is a school of thought that has been around for centuries but only began to enter mainstream Christianity in the late nineteenth to early twentieth centuries. It holds a very "low" view of Scripture (which I'll explain in a moment) and is generally not confessional (i.e., it rejects most orthodox confessions of Christianity, such as the "5 Fundamentals of the Faith").

Birthed in Germany, higher criticism was the result of liberal scholars and theologians such as Rudolf Karl Bultmann embracing the work of Enlightenment and Rationalist thinkers such as John Locke (1632–1704), David Hume (1711–1776), Immanuel Kant (1724–1804), Gotthold Lessing (1729–1781), Gottlieb Fichte (1762–1814), G. W. F. Hegel (1770–1831), and the French rationalists.

Higher criticism promoted ideas such as a non-Mosaic (i.e., not Moses) authorship of the Torah, multiple "Isaiahs" penning the book that bears his name, a nonliteral interpretation of the Bible's miracles (instead viewing them figuratively), and many other unorthodox beliefs about the Scriptures.

Higher criticism quickly spread across Europe to England, and then across the Atlantic to America and Canada. And as Modernism came to cultural prominence in the 1930s, seminaries, Bible colleges, and churches were caught up in this seemingly "enlightened" academic movement.

Modernist thinkers believed there were better ways of doing practically everything, but these new ways could only be discovered by challenging and shedding the traditional paradigms, conventions, and expectations that had been established in culture.

This shift is embodied in the differences between modern art and the works of the Renaissance. Modern art was all about fleeing the literalism of the past, and instead embracing the abstract and unconventional. Modernist philosophy explained that because art and beauty are subjective and relative concepts, art can be whatever its creator considers it to be. The modern, enlightened man or woman was to question everything and spur societal progress by helping to break down conventional ways of thinking about the arts, architecture, philosophy, and yes—theology and religion.

Modernism took hold in the '40s, rose to popularity in the '50s, and drove the countercultural movement of the '60s.

But while the broader culture was still in the throes of Modernism, the philosophical world was in turmoil. There had been a general expectation that the "enlightened" thinking of the twentieth century would lead to the dawning of a new age of peace and prosperity—that it would be a century marked by quantum leaps in almost every aspect of humanity.

If you know your history, then you know what followed was the *bloodiest century in history*. World War I was soon followed by World War II, and America (the world's new cultural epicenter) soon entered the Korean and Vietnam wars. Atheistic Communism killed dozens of millions in Stalin's Russia and Mao's China while battling democracy in seemingly endless proxy wars. And on and on I could go. Modernism completely failed to deliver on its promise.

As a result, contemporary philosophy became jilted, jaded, and truly hopeless. And these changes led Modernism to morph into *Postmodernism*—a movement skeptical of *any* type of truth claim. It finds the concept of truth to be outdated, instead embracing the view that truth is *relative*. Unsurprisingly, it completely rejects rigid theology, which is built on *the* truth of Jesus Christ.

Postmodernism began to manifest in the arts and philosophy, where it encouraged the world to reject any kind of restrictions, embracing everything and everyone because life shouldn't be taken too seriously.

While appearing to throw out the rule book, Postmodernism was, in reality, writing a new one that included commands to never judge anyone, be inclusive, applaud all lifestyle decisions, not be so arrogant as to claim that there is an exclusive truth, and more. And as this new rule book began to work its way into the culture, not only were exclusive truth claims rejected but they were also branded as "narrow-minded" and soon, "bigoted."

And as Modernism and Postmodernism crept into the Church, the result was, and is, *Laodicea*—a church that seeks the approval of the *culture* above the approval of *Jesus*. It is a church that believes theology needs to *evolve* with society (because nothing in the Bible is absolute anyway), and a church that believes Jesus' greatest concern is our present happiness.

> **Note:** It's a conversation for another day, but as I write this in 2023, postmodernism is unquestionably in its final throes. There is currently no consensus on the terminology to be used for the neo-modernism and rigid progressive idealism that has recently risen to prominence.

INTO THE TEXT

Let's dive into the text at **Revelation 3:14**:

> [14] *And to the angel of the church of the Laodiceans write,* ...

The letters to the other six churches are all addressed relative to their *city*. Each letter begins with, *"to the angel of the Church in _____"* or *"of_____,"* referencing the *city*. Laodicea is the only letter that instead references the *people*.

That's because, while Jesus is supposed to be the leader of the Church, He is not the leader of *this* Church. In fact, we'll discover that Jesus is not even *in* this Church!

... These things says the Amen, the Faithful and True Witness, the Beginning of the creation of God:

Based on the title Jesus uses for Himself here, it appears there are three things Laodicea needs to remember: Jesus is Truth Incarnate, the Martyr, and the Creator.

Jesus Is *"the Amen"*—Truth Incarnate

"Amen" means, *"firm, trustworthy, surely, so be it, verily."* When you're reading John's Gospel and Jesus prefaces a statement with the phrase, *"Verily, verily"* or *"Most assuredly,"* what He actually said was, *"Amen, amen."* He was saying that what He's about to tell them is the truth.

This is the only place in Scripture where "Amen" is used as a *title*. Jesus is claiming to be the embodiment of absolute truth, meaning that the assessment of this Church He is about to share is *absolutely truthful*.

Prophetically, Laodicea has forgotten even the *concept* of absolute truth. When on the earth as a man, Jesus dismissed all notions of pluralism and relativism by claiming to be the exclusive path to God:

I am the way, the truth, and the life. No one comes to the Father except through Me.

—John 14:6

Referring to Himself as *"the truth,"* Jesus also said:

> *... you shall know the truth, and the truth shall make you free.*
> —John 8:32

Jesus Is "the Faithful and True Witness"—The Martyr

The word *"Witness"* is the word "martus" in the original Greek, from which we derive "martyr." Laodicea needs to remember that Jesus became a martyr for them when He gave up His blood and life on the Cross to save them and bring them into the family of God.

Both in AD 96 and prophetically in the present day, this church departed from the belief that we need Jesus to save us from our sins and embraced ideas like pluralism, which rejects the truth of **John 14:6** and teaches many paths to God.

In the Laodicean Church of our time, I believe this refers to the church that doesn't want to talk about the Cross, the blood of Jesus, and how He died for us because, as hymnist Isaac Watts wrote, Jesus' sacrifice demands, *"my soul, my life, my all."*[105] Laodiceans have no interest in a Gospel that includes a *personal cost*.

However, Jesus was always clear about the cost of following Him, openly teaching ideas like this:

> *... whoever desires to save his life will lose it, but whoever loses his life for My sake and the gospel's will save it.*
> —Mark 8:35

We can only receive salvation because Jesus gave His life for us. And as we receive His gift of eternal life, we relinquish ownership

---

[105] Cf. *"When I Survey the Wondrous Cross"*

of our lives. Jesus comes into our lives as *King*. We get off the throne and ask Him to take it because the Bible tells us that we were **"bought at a price."**[106]

And as Jesus directs our lives through His Spirit, He leads us to *live* as He did, which sometimes leads people to *treat us* as He was treated. Unsurprisingly, not everyone wants to hear that kind of talk, which is why we don't see verses like **2 Timothy 3:12** on coffee mugs or bumper stickers:

> **. . . all who desire to live godly in Christ Jesus will suffer persecution.**

Apparently, the Laodiceans need to be reminded of all this. Perhaps because subjects like martyrdom, suffering, and sacrifice are hard to fit in when all you are preaching is earthly victory, prosperity, abundance, and positivity.

You can't talk about the Cross without talking about sin. And you can't talk about sin without talking about a standard of truth and righteousness (which we fail to meet). And that can seem judgmental to some. The conviction of the Gospel can make people feel bad and realize that they desperately need saving. So, wouldn't it be better if we just talked about *"5 Reasons God Loves You Just the Way You Are"?*

I can sense some of you yelling at me that the horse is dead and that I should stop beating it. I am belaboring this point because I do not want you to miss that *right now*, we are living in a time when many churches view things like the Cross, the death of Jesus, and the blood of Jesus as *barriers* that need to be edited out of our message because they may prevent people coming to church or stop

---

[106] 1 Corinthians 6:20.

them feeling comfortable in church. While still claiming to believe in such doctrines, far too many churches never speak of them from the pulpit and then justify their editorializing as an evangelistic strategy.

Our brother Paul described this as **"having a form of godliness but denying its power."** And counseled us, **"from such people turn away!"**[107]

I think Jesus is *grieved* as He sees churches sweeping His atoning work on the Cross under the proverbial rug in the name of evangelism. Without the Cross, there could *be* no evangelism because there would be no salvation! Quoting Paul again:

> **... God forbid that I should boast except in the cross of our Lord Jesus Christ, by whom the world has been crucified to me, and I to the world.**
> —Galatians 6:14

Most pastors know that talking about *sacrifice* is a terrific way to shrink your church. It's not uncommon for those who call their congregants to serve at church once or twice a month to be met with responses like, *"That's just way too much commitment for me right now."* And yet when that same congregant hears their child's coach say, *"Games are on weekends. There will be two practices per week, and whatever else I feel is needed."* They'll nod their head and respond, *"That seems reasonable. People gotta be committed."*

In our first-world churches, a regular church attender is generally defined as someone who attends at least once every six weeks.

When Christians learn about trusting the Lord with their finances, they're often *shocked* and sometimes accuse the Church of

---

[107] 2 Timothy 3:5.

being out to steal their money. And yet those same Christians can often be found signing up for a credit card with a 22% interest rate (or worse). That credit card will then be used to buy things they can't afford, with no real plan of how they're going to pay it off.

In many cities, Christians "church shop." They look for a church that makes them feel good, has a musical style they like, a children's ministry with the "wow factor," recreational programs they want, and checks everything else on their wish list. In so doing, they exclude questions like:

Does this church teach the Bible?
Which church do You want me to join, Jesus?
What needs could I help meet at this church?

To these Laodiceans who want to be served rather to serve others, Jesus says, *"the Son of Man did not come to be served, but to serve, and to give His life as a ransom for many."*[108] But Laodicea didn't want to hear it.

Jesus Is the Beginning of the "Creation of God" – The Creator

The literal translation has Jesus declaring Himself to be the *"origin of the creation of God."* Around AD 96, Laodicea had likely bought into a heretical gnostic teaching that Jesus was a *created* being—a teaching of many cults to this day. Paul had to set the Colossians straight on this issue too, and so he stated the truth as plainly as possible:

> **... by Him [Jesus] all things were created that are in heaven and that are on earth, visible and invisible, whether**

---
[108] Matthew 20:28.

> **thrones or dominions or principalities or powers. All things were created through Him and for Him. And He is before all things, and in Him all things consist.**
> —Colossians 1:16–17

Inspired by the Holy Spirit, John felt this issue was so important that his Gospel opens with these three verses (referring to Jesus as "the Word"):

> **In the beginning was the Word, and the Word was with God, and the Word was God. He was in the beginning with God. All things were made through Him, and without Him nothing was made that was made.**

Prophetically, the Laodicean church doesn't seem to struggle with the heresy that Jesus is a created being, but they do seem to struggle with orthodox biblical teaching related to creation—the belief that Jesus created the universe from nothing, including the first fully-formed man and woman.

For the first time in Church history, the past several decades have seen many believers, churches, and even denominations embrace teachings that seek to credit Jesus with the bare minimum of creation. Bombarded by cultural pressures, many have embraced *theistic evolution*—the belief that God created the biological building blocks of humanity and then handed them over to natural processes, which ran their course, bringing us to where we are today.

There are many excellent books by Christian scientists and biologists that do a far better job explaining the problems with theistic and neo-Darwinian evolution than I ever could, so I'm not going to even try to speak to that issue at length here and now.

Although I believe the Bible to be scientifically accurate, the Lord did not set out to write a science textbook in Genesis 1 and 2. He had a higher purpose in mind. And whatever your view on creation is (old earth, young earth, literal, allegorical, etc.), any honest interpretation of **Genesis 1–2** will conclude a few key truths the Lord wanted the reader to understand:

- God created *everything* that exists in the universe.
- God created because He *wanted* to, and so He created with purpose, design, and order.
- God created men and women as *finished products* (i.e., not needing to evolve).

The creation account God placed in His Word cannot be reconciled with evolution—theistic or otherwise. The only way to even try to harmonize the two is by demanding that Scripture bows to the theory of evolution.

And if you're willing to make *that* compromise solely because of cultural pressures, then why wouldn't you compromise again the next time something challenging comes up in the Torah? And if you can't trust the Torah's key statements, then how can you trust the rest of the Old Testament, which is built upon the Torah? Suddenly you're left questioning whether you can trust *anything* the Bible declares as absolute truth, including the Resurrection and the Gospel message.

Jesus believes His Church cannot be confused about who He is, as revealed in **Genesis 1–2**. It's such a big deal to Him that He takes the time to specifically remind the church of the Laodiceans that *He* is the Creator.

Jesus Has No Commendation for the Church of Laodicea

Let's get into Laodicea's report card.

> ¹⁵ *I know your works, . . .*

The lifestyle of the Laodiceans exposed their true spiritual condition. As the Epistle of James[109] explains, we are not saved by our works. However, our works *reveal* whether the Holy Spirit is present in our lives because the Spirit naturally produces fruit in the form of good works.

No fruit = No Holy Spirit = No salvation

> *. . . that you are neither cold nor hot. I could wish you were cold or hot.* ¹⁶ *So then, because you are lukewarm, and neither cold nor hot, I will vomit you out of My mouth.*

Jesus has *no* commendation for this Church. He has nothing good to say about them. To state the obvious, whatever problems are in this Church, they are *serious*.

Scholars generally agree that in this context, the temperatures refer to different spiritual conditions. *"Cold"* refers to those who are not saved, while *"hot"* refers to those who are (and are producing the fruit of good works as evidence of their conversion). But Jesus calls the Laodiceans *"lukewarm"*—a spiritual condition so repulsive, it elicits the equivalent of an involuntary gag reflex. I feel a little more detail may be helpful.

The idea behind the word *"vomit"* (or whatever verb your Bible uses) is really *to spew*. As a father of six children, my wife and I are quite frankly experts on the nuances of vomiting. For example, I can tell you that the difference between vomiting and spewing is

---

[109] Cf. James 2:14–26.

distance. When one vomits, one is at risk of throwing up on oneself. When one spews, one is at risk of throwing up on other people. I promise I'm only sharing this level of detail to be faithful to the text.[110]

If being *"cold"* equates to being unsaved, and being *"hot"* refers to being saved, what spiritual condition does *"lukewarm"* refer to? And why is it so disgusting to Jesus?

The rest of the letter to the Laodiceans makes it clear Jesus considers these *"lukewarm"* church attenders to be *unsaved*—and not in the sense that they're backslidden believers. Rather, they've *never* been saved, but they think they are. Their spiritual condition disgusts Jesus for two main reasons:

1. **He has been revealed to them, and they're just not that interested.**

    They attend church services (semi-regularly). They own Bibles. Their church may not preach the full Gospel, but they're still close enough to it that if they wanted more truth, they could easily reach out and grab it.

    Instead, they are like the religious leaders of Jesus' day. They were blessed with the ultimate revelation—God in the flesh, standing right in front of them. And they said, *"Nah. We're good."*

    In **Matthew 7:24–27**, Jesus put it like this:

    > *... whoever hears these sayings of Mine, and does them, I will liken him to a wise man who built his*

---

[110] Or because fathering six children has caused me to retain a juvenile sense of humor.

> *house on the rock: and the rain descended, the floods came, and the winds blew and beat on that house; and it did not fall, for it was founded on the rock.*
>
> *But everyone who hears these sayings of Mine, and does not do them, will be like a foolish man who built his house on the sand: and the rain descended, the floods came, and the winds blew and beat on that house; and it fell. And great was its fall.*

When Jesus judges these unsaved men and women, they will have no excuse. They will not be able to say, *"We didn't know!"* They received much revelation but did not desire the true Gospel. Instead, they eagerly embraced a false gospel.

2. **Their hypocrisy is bringing disrepute to the name of God.**

Those who are spiritually *"cold"* do not claim to love Jesus, follow Him, or belong to Him. In that sense, they're not hypocrites. Those who are spiritually *"hot"* claim to love Jesus, actively follow Him, and belong to Him. They are not hypocrites either.

These Laodiceans, on the other hand, claim to be Christians but do not care at all about how Jesus has asked His followers to live. They are hypocrites, and they are taking His name **"in vain"** (as we discussed in our previous study).

Being spiritually *"lukewarm"* is the most dangerous place one can be because they have deluded themselves into believing that they are walking with Jesus when, in reality, they are walking *"the way that leads to destruction."*[111]

People will not take medicine if they believe they are not sick. Addicts will not overcome their addiction if they do not believe they have a problem. And sinners will not be saved if they believe themselves to be already righteous. Such was the disastrous spiritual condition of the religious leaders who rejected Jesus.

To truly grasp the seriousness of the *"lukewarm"* man or woman's condition, we must understand they are the ones Jesus was speaking of when He prophesied regarding the Day of Judgment:

> *Many will say to Me in that day, "Lord, Lord, have we not prophesied in Your name, cast out demons in Your name, and done many wonders in Your name?" And then I will declare to them, "I never knew you; depart from Me ... "*
> —Matthew 7:22–23

The Corinthian church took a very "modern" approach to a *"lukewarm"* man in their congregation who was unrepentantly living in sin—they showed him "grace" by letting his sin slide while patting each other on the back for being such a gracious congregation. When Paul heard about this, he sent these instructions:

> **In the name of our Lord Jesus Christ, when you are gathered together, along with my spirit, with the power of our Lord Jesus Christ, deliver such a one to Satan for the destruction of the flesh, that his spirit may be saved in the day of the Lord Jesus.**
> —1 Corinthians 5:4–5

---

[111] Matthew 7:13.

In other words, *"Kick him out of the church because you are allowing him to believe that he is saved when there is no evidence of salvation in his life. And before a man can be saved, he must realize that he is lost."*

That's how serious the *"lukewarm"* condition is. It's life and death. And allowing someone who is destined for hell to believe they are destined for Heaven is not love. It is not grace. It is selfishness. Paul confronted the Corinthians just as Jesus confronts the Laodiceans— out of *love*.

We don't have room to study it here, but I encourage you to read **Matthew 22:1–14**, where Jesus teaches the Parable of the Wedding Feast. In it, Jesus speaks of the *"lukewarm"* believer, the Tribulation, the Marriage Supper of the Lamb, and more. There is much waiting to be discovered by those who dive deep into those verses.

Just as the hot water pumped from Denizli became lukewarm as it traveled several miles through the aqueducts, this Church had taken on the spiritual temperature of the world around it. It had been so influenced *by* the culture that it became practically indistinguishable *from* the culture. The Laodicean Church compromised repeatedly in the name of survival and cultural relevance. They took their cues from society rather than the Word of God. In this Church, the greatest sin was not having the approval of the world. And in their desperate efforts to gain and maintain that approval, they had lost the only thing of true worth they had to offer the world—*Jesus*.

In **V.17** Jesus, the One who is truth incarnate, lays bare the reality of the *"lukewarm"*:

> [17] *Because you say, "I am rich, have become wealthy, and have need of nothing"—and do not know that you are wretched, miserable, poor, blind, and naked—*...

This is a *shock* to the Laodiceans because they thought they were doing great. The truth was they had built a Gospel and church to themselves, not the Lord Jesus.

In the original Greek, the word *"wretched"* appears only one other place in the New Testament—**Romans 7:24**, where Paul exclaims:

O wretched man that I am! Who will deliver me from this body of death?

Jesus is writing this letter to elicit that same reaction from the Laodiceans, that He might offer them the same antidote he offered Paul—salvation through His blood.

This might shock you, but I believe God *does* want you to be healthy, wealthy, and happy. What's the alternative—a God who wants you to be sick, poor, and miserable? The issue is that our Heavenly Father has an even greater, better goal for each of us—making us more like His Son, Jesus.

I believe our Father blesses us as much as He can until it impedes us becoming more like Jesus. I believe God would make us all billionaires if the truth wasn't that pretty much all of us would quickly stop depending on Him and walking by faith if He did. Wealth tends to create a delusional sense of self-sufficiency in our hearts, producing the exact *opposite* of the character God said would be blessed, in the Sermon on the Mount.[112]

Making us more like Jesus is the greatest good God can work in the life of a believer; it's the good that will benefit us most in eternity. But Laodicea was/is all about the here and now, and so

---

[112] Cf. Matthew 5:2–11.

they don't want to hear those pesky teachings of Jesus where He promises we'll have troubles in this life.

The text reveals that this Church was into *wealth*. Like the Pharisees of Jesus' day, they associated wealth with God's approval. It gave them a false sense of spiritual security and righteousness that blinded them to their true condition.

The Laodicean Church and the Church Today

We can easily deduce that on a *prophetic* level, the Laodicean Church today must primarily exist in first-world countries where a relatively high level of wealth is enjoyed (although sadly her errant doctrines are now also rapidly spreading in the second and third worlds). You and I live in the wealthiest period in Church history that the world has ever known. If you live in a first-world country, then you enjoy daily luxuries most of the world can't even fathom. If your household brought in $32,400 (USD) or more in 2019, you were in the top 1% of the world's earners.[113] Suffice it to say, the Laodicean church isn't in Iran or China; it's in places like the USA and the UK.

What a contrast this is to the Suffering Church in Smyrna. They viewed themselves as impoverished, but Jesus tells them that from His perspective, they are rich. The Laodiceans viewed themselves as rich, but Jesus tells them that from His perspective, they are impoverished. Laodicea lost sight of the fact that the Church exists first and foremost for *Jesus*. Instead, they embraced the belief that Jesus and the Church existed for *them*.

The belief that God cares more about your comfort than your

---

[113] GlobalRichList.com as of 2019.

character fits under the umbrella of the term, "The Prosperity Gospel." Perhaps you've seen its proponents on TV—they're usually preaching a message in which God is a glorified genie who exists to fulfill your earthly dreams, passions, and desires. *"Name it and claim it . . . Blab it and grab it . . . Believe and receive."* You'd think pastors who preach such things wouldn't be mentioned in the Scriptures, but they are. In fact, we just read about them:

> **. . . *you say, "I am rich, have become wealthy, and have need of nothing" . . .***

Those who espouse the Prosperity Gospel tell their followers to *literally* "confess" such statements "by faith" as a means of manifesting wealth. But Jesus says that they:

> **. . . *do not know that you are wretched, miserable, poor, blind, and naked . . .***

For clarity's sake, let me say that I believe that we *are* called by God's Word to speak in faith, but here's the caveat: we are called to speak in faith by *agreeing with God's Word*. We are not to simply speak our fleshly desires into the ether and expect God to go to work manifesting them.

The Solution to Lukewarm Faith

Jesus is so gracious. His Words have the power to open our eyes, even when we are blind. If you're reading this and thinking, *"This is describing me! I think I might be Laodicean! What do I do?"* Jesus gives us the solution:

> [18] ***I counsel you to buy from Me gold refined in the fire, that you may be rich; and white garments, that you may be clothed, that***

the shame of your nakedness may not be revealed; and anoint your eyes with eye salve, that you may see.

1 Peter 1:7 refers to faith as ***"being* much more precious than gold that perishes, though it is tested by fire."**

If the Holy Spirit is revealing to you that you've become lukewarm in your faith, Jesus has some heavy-duty advice for you. But be warned, this is gutsy stuff and is not for the faint of heart.

Jesus tells us to pray for *trials*. Yes, really. Because when we're lukewarm, trials shake us out of our reliance on our health and wealth and force us to depend on Jesus. And as we're driven back into intimate relationship with Him, the world begins to lose its grip on us, and we find that what we've really been craving is fellowship with the Lord.

The crisis of being lukewarm is more serious than the difficulty found in any trial. It is far better to be on fire for Jesus in a season of difficulty than lukewarm in a time of comfort. If your faith is lukewarm, I believe that Jesus would say to you, *"I counsel you to buy from Me gold refined in the fire, that you may be rich . . . "*

James 1:2–4 counsels us to . . .

. . . count it all joy when you fall into various trials, knowing that the testing of your faith produces patience. But let patience have *its* perfect work, that you may be perfect and complete, lacking nothing.

As we've gone through these seven letters, have we found that persecution and difficulty affect the Church positively or negatively? Have wealth and comfort been good or bad for the Church? Unquestionably, we have found that persecution and trials make the Church more like Jesus and bring the Church closer to Jesus.

I pray that we would be men and women who have the guts to pray, *"Father, do whatever You need to do to make me more like Your Son, Jesus, and stop me from becoming lukewarm."*

The Believer's Righteousness in Jesus

While they may have trendy clothing and an outward appearance that impresses the culture, what they need most are *"white garments"* that only Jesus can provide (in contrast to the *black* wool garments for which Laodicea was famous). In the letter to Sardis, we learned that *"white garments"* are a reference to being forgiven and justified through Jesus and put in right relationship with God.

Isaiah 61:10 declares:

> **I will greatly rejoice in the Lord,**
> **My soul shall be joyful in my God;**
> **For He has clothed me with the garments of salvation,**
> **He has covered me with the robe of righteousness . . .**

In contrast, **Isaiah 64:6** declares that our *own* works (apart from Christ) are like *"filthy rags."*

The believer's righteousness comes from *Jesus*. It is literally *His* righteousness. It's a gift from God. And that righteousness naturally produces good works in our lives, not *so that* we can be saved but because we *are* saved.

When we reach **Revelation 19:8**, we'll read:

> **. . . to her** [the Church] **it was granted to be arrayed in fine linen, clean and bright, for the fine linen is the righteous acts of the saints.**

The church of the Laodiceans is not characterized by people who have been truly converted and made a **"new creation."**[114] For the most part, the people in this Church haven't backslidden into a lukewarm faith; they've *never* been saved.

I'd love to tell you that the point of these verses is not to scare us, but I think that is the point. Because He loves us, the Lord wants us to evaluate whether we're truly saved—committed to serving and following Jesus, whatever the cost. There is simply no issue in all of life of greater importance.

> [19] *As many as I love, I rebuke and chasten. Therefore be zealous and repent.*

Jesus' motivation in saying all of this is His *love* for us. And if He knows that we are destined for hell because we've bought into a false gospel, He wouldn't be a loving God if He didn't do everything in His power to reveal that to us. And so, He does.

Let this sink in: Jesus' letter to the Laodiceans is a prophecy that is being fulfilled *right now*. And I'm begging you not to be part of the fulfillment of this prophecy. Don't let it be you. Don't be the one who, on that day, finds themselves in church but naked and blind and spewed out of the mouth of Jesus. This is a picture of the last Church, but it doesn't have to be a picture of you.

Jesus Is Not in Laodicea

> [20] *Behold, I stand at the door and knock. If anyone hears My voice and opens the door, I will come in to him and dine with him, and he with Me.*

---

[114] 2 Corinthians 5:17.

In the other six letters, Jesus is *in the midst* of each church. But not in Laodicea. Here we find Him *outside* the Church, knocking on the door. Don't miss this—Jesus is *not in* the church of the Laodiceans. He's not among them.

There is so much commentary I am tempted to offer on this point, but I'm only going to say this: The Laodiceans are doing church in such a way that the Holy Spirit is *not present* . . . and they haven't even noticed. Apparently, they've developed a way of doing church that does not require the Holy Spirit. And as I examine the evangelical landscape, I believe the same is true of many churches today.

Take another look at **V.20** and notice the language:

Behold, I stand at the door and knock. If anyone hears My voice and opens the door, I will come in to him and dine with him, and he with Me.

Jesus isn't appealing to the Church in Laodicea; He's extending an invitation to *individuals* within the Church. This verse is both sobering and hopeful. It's sobering because this Church will not get better. There will not be a revival or reformation in this Church. As an organization, Jesus has written them off. But the good news is that Jesus hasn't given up on the individuals who make up the Church in Laodicea.

As always, God is a perfect gentleman. He will never force His way into someone's life (including yours and mine). Instead, He knocks. Whether we open the door is up to us. Most in this Church will not. They'll reply through it, *"Thanks, but no thanks. We're not interested in the Jesus who is Truth Incarnate, the Martyr, and the Creator."* But some will open the door and invite Jesus into their lives. And when they do, He will come in and make Himself at home.

If you're realizing that you are part of the Church of the Laodiceans (i.e., in terms of the church you attend and/or your attitude toward Jesus) and if you sense the Lord calling you out of it, be zealous, repent, and invite Him into your life:

> [21] **To him who overcomes I will grant to sit with Me on My throne, as I also overcame and sat down with My Father on His throne.**

I like Young's Literal Translation of **V.21 (YLT)**:

> *He who <u>is</u> overcoming—I will give to him to sit with me in my throne, as I also did overcome and did sit down with my Father in His throne.*

In this context, the overcomer is the believer who doesn't give in to the self-serving Gospel of comfort being preached by Laodicea, who cares more about the truth than finding a church that teaches what their flesh wants to hear, and who has truly given their life to Jesus. They understand they are not their own, and they are *all in* on following Jesus, regardless of the cost.

The Church of the Laodiceans is preaching a false gospel of prosperity that appeals to fleshly desires for comfort, status, wealth, and power. It's not a coincidence that Jesus promises the overcomer all of that . . . but in eternity, where it matters and lasts forever.

Read **V.21** again slowly. What Jesus promises the overcomer is *incredible*:

> *He who is overcoming—I will give to him to sit with me in my throne, as I also did overcome and did sit down with my Father in His throne* (YLT).

Jesus promises that this type of overcomer will *reign with Him* in the ages to come. It's a promise so astounding, it sounds almost blasphemous. But it's not. It's the heart of Jesus. The more accurate present tense in Young's Literal Translation (YLT) also tells us some will be actively overcoming *when* Jesus comes for His Church. And we'll tie all that together in the next chapter of this book.

A quick note for the Bible nerds: Jesus says, **"I will grant to sit with Me on My throne."** He describes a future reward for the overcomer that involves *His* throne. But did you know that the Bible tells us Jesus is not sitting on *His* throne presently?

Jesus has a very specific throne that will be His in the future. The angel Gabriel declared to Mary that Jesus would one day be given *"the throne of His father David."*[115] We talked about that in the letter to the Church in Philadelphia. Jesus is not sitting upon the throne of David at this moment, and He never has. But He *will*.

Where is Jesus right now? He tells us He is *"with My Father on His throne."* As we study Revelation together, Jesus is seated at the right hand of the Father, on His *Father's* throne.

What Does Being an Overcomer Mean?

After reading all seven letters, we've heard Jesus give seven different promises to the overcomer. And if you're like me, you want to be that overcomer! So, let me encourage you with something John[116] wrote about what it means to be an overcomer:

> **…whatever is born of God** [*i.e., whoever is born again*] **overcomes the world. And this is the victory that has**

---

[115] Luke 1:32.

[116] John the Apostle, who recorded the Book of Revelation.

> overcome the world—our faith. Who is he who overcomes the world, but he who believes that Jesus is the Son of God?
> —1 John 5:4–5

If you've placed your faith in Jesus as Lord and Savior and been born again, then you *are* and *will be*, an overcomer, wherever life takes you. As with all the Christian life, being an overcomer isn't about anything we can do or anything we can stir up in ourselves. It's Jesus who, in us and through us, by His Spirit, empowers us to live as overcomers. We offer ourselves to Jesus, completely, and *He* makes us overcomers.

> [22] *He who has an ear, let him hear what the Spirit says to the churches.*

APPLICATION TO ALL CHURCHES

The Church exists for Jesus and is destined to be His Bride. Therefore, the Church's highest goal should be to be beautiful in *His* eyes, even if that means being detestable in the eyes of the culture.

Jesus wants a Church that treasures and teaches the truth and worships Him as **"the way, the truth, and the life."** May His desires be fulfilled in our churches.

APPLICATION TO ALL BELIEVERS

Does Jesus have to remind *you* that He is the Creator? It has been well said that if you can believe **Genesis 1:1**, you'll have no problem with the rest of the Bible. That opening verse declares:

In the beginning God created the heavens and the earth.

If you'd like to further your understanding of the intellectual evidence for Christianity, I recommend following the ministries of apologists like Frank Turek, J. Warner Wallace, and Sean McDowell.

Perhaps you've begun to doubt God's Creator credentials because you don't want to sound like a simpleton in front of your friends, coworkers, and family. Like you, I like it when people consider me to be a reasonably intelligent person. When I get into Gospel-related conversations, I do my best to come across as thoughtful. But if you're a Christian, sooner or later you're going to discover there's not always a perfect answer that lets you preserve your dignity and worldly reputation. You're going to run into people who will think you're a fool or a bigot for believing what the Bible teaches, regardless of how gracious and articulate your explanations are.

When that happens, we are faced with the choice to either offend *people* or offend *God*. Let me encourage you to decide, here and now, that you'll choose to offend people rather than your Creator. Follow Jesus, no matter the cost.

Are you *lukewarm?* Are you in need of some trials to shake you out of your spiritual malaise? Do you want comfort, or do you want to be made more like Jesus? May our Lord find us sincerely praying, *"Make me more like You, Jesus."*

Jesus lived under the specter of His looming crucifixion, and yet His Word tells us that He was ***"anointed with the oil of gladness, more than all His fellows."***[117] We need God to work *in us* even more than we need Him to work on our circumstances.

If Jesus is your greatest passion, does anybody else know that? Because if He is, He'll show up in every area of your life—your

---

[117] Psalm 45:7; Hebrews 1:9.

relationships, family, finances, work, service—all of it. Does that describe your life? Or would people be *surprised* if you told them that Jesus was the center of your life?

Go all-in on following Jesus. Put Him first in everything. Don't block Jesus out of certain areas of your life and in so doing, allow yourself to be lulled into a lukewarm spiritual condition. Take responsibility for your spiritual growth. Get yourself to a healthy church and get involved in the life of that body. Don't be a once-every-six-weeks church attender. Don't be somebody who blows the dust off your Bible on Sundays. Be *zealous*.

I would be remiss if I did not ask anyone reading this to stop and make absolutely sure you are saved—that you are *born again*. I'm not asking if you're perfect, I'm asking if there is undeniable evidence that a change has taken place in your life because of Jesus.

The Church of the Laodiceans is full of people who think they're saved but are living lives that prove nothing's really changed. They're still living for themselves and not for the Lord. I pray that none of us would so delude ourselves. I pray that we have all opened the door and let Jesus into our whole lives. And if you haven't, do it now!

> *If anyone hears My voice and opens the door, I will come in to him and dine with him, and he with Me.*
> —Revelation 3:20

CLOSING THOUGHTS ON THE SEVEN CHURCHES – THE END IS APPROACHING

The first of the seven letters was addressed to Ephesus, and Jesus didn't say anything about coming back for His Church. All He said was that they should come back to their first love—the Lord Jesus.

The second letter went to Smyrna. In it, Jesus warned that they would go through intense suffering and that they needed to be faithful unto death. But there was no mention of Him coming back.

Then came Pergamos, the "unacceptable marriage" church. And Jesus didn't talk to them about His coming either.

Then suddenly, something changed.

We came to the Church in Thyatira—the church focused on the woman who had brought all kinds of paganism into the Church. Jesus warns the people in that Church who have bought into that paganism that they will go into *"great tribulation."* More specifically, *the* Tribulation. To those in that Church who have *not* bought into that paganism, Jesus says, **"Hold fast what you have till I come."**[118] If Jesus is telling some in this Church to hold fast *until* He comes, then this Church must *exist* until He comes. And if some in this Church will go *into* the Tribulation, then this Church will have to also *exist* until the Tribulation.

Out of the Church in Thyatira came the next church in history—Sardis, the Reformation or Denominational Church. They receive both good and bad news, and Jesus also talks to them about His coming. He says, **"you will not know what hour I will come upon you."** Although this Church reformed many things, they never reformed their eschatology—their end-times theology. Using His own language from the Olivet Discourse and Paul's in his letter to the Thessalonians, Jesus warns the Sardians that most people in their Church are not ready for His coming because they're not saved. This means the Church in Sardis must exist when Jesus comes for His Church.

Then we came to Philadelphia. And we heard Jesus tell them that

---

[118] Revelation 2:25.

He is *"coming quickly!"* In the original Greek, the word *"quickly"*[119] means *"suddenly"* or *"soon."* When Jesus comes for His Church, He will come suddenly, but He also tells us here that He will come *soon*, relative to Philadelphia's position in Church history. We might not feel like His timing is soon, but in terms of world history, Jesus is coming *very* soon. And if Jesus encouraged Philadelphia by telling them He is coming soon, then their church also must be on the earth when He comes.

In the final letter, written to Laodicea, Jesus said, **"Behold, I stand at the door and knock."**[120] The Weymouth New Testament puts it like this: **"I am now standing at the door and am knocking."** That last church won't hear Jesus say, *"I'm coming quickly!"* They'll hear Him say that He's here, at the door, and this is the last call.

The final four churches come into existence *sequentially* (one after the other). But all four churches exist *simultaneously* (at the same time) until Jesus comes for His Church. The first three churches do not mention His coming. The last four churches *all* mention His coming. Therefore, those last four churches must be in existence at the time of the Rapture.

Revelation 4 will begin with the words, *"After these things"* Something has *ended*, and something new is about to *begin*. Are you ready?

---

[119] Tachu.

[120] Revelation 3:20.

THE RAPTURE

REFLECTING ON THE LETTERS TO THE SEVEN CHURCHES

Take a few moments to reflect on the prophetic nature of the letters to the seven churches and how they perfectly lay out ~2,000 years of Church history. When we see the historical parallels and specific details in each letter and realize that the prophetic pattern wouldn't work if the letters were in any other order, I believe we're left with only two options: Either these letters are indeed prophetic, or their arrangement is a coincidence of preposterous proportions.

The more I study Bible prophecy, the more I am convinced that God's Word does not deal in coincidences. That's why I want to challenge you to reach a *conclusion* regarding the data. If we don't believe in the prophetic application of the letters, then we must provide a reasonable alternative explanation. It's not acceptable to simply say, *"Bah! I don't buy it!"* That's not a valid argument or a productive way to study the Bible.

If you're not quite there yet, perhaps I can provide some comfort in an alternative approach. We should all be open to changing our opinions regarding Scripture. If we're not, that means there's no room to grow. I hope I have some different opinions 10, 20, and

30 years from now because I desire to *grow* in my understanding of God's Word. So, let me suggest this approach—believe in the prophetic application of the seven letters unless you find a better explanation for the evidence.

I believe that in *any* area of theological study, we are obligated to hold to the best explanation in light of common sense and the whole counsel of Scripture (as best we know at the time). By the end of our time together, I believe you will agree that no approach to the Book of Revelation better interprets the information in a way that harmonizes *everything* the Bible says about the end-times. And that's really the key test. It's easy to pluck a verse here and there and use it out of context. But any view on the end-times must work *everywhere* in the Bible, which I believe this view does.

If the prophetic application of the seven letters is designed to help us understand the *state* of the Church in the end-times (i.e., the four churches that exist during the end-times), then what happens at the *end* of the Church Age? If Revelation is (for the most part) a chronological account of the end-times, what happens next? *The Rapture.*

The late Chuck Missler said of the Rapture:

> *"This, of course, is the most preposterous doctrine in Christianity.... The only thing it has going for it is that it is very clearly described in the Scriptures."* [121]

So, what *is* the Rapture? It's the term used for a specific future worldwide event in which Jesus calls His Church to meet Him **"in**

---

[121] Chuck Missler, "The Seven Myths of Eschatology," Post Falls, ID: Koinonia House, August 1, 2012, https://www.khouse.org/articles/2012/1072/.

the clouds."[122] The moment Jesus issues that call, every believer alive on the earth will instantaneously disappear from the earth and find themselves in the presence of Jesus.

If this is the first time you're hearing this, you now know why most churches don't talk about it very much. If you've got some first-time guests checking out your church, they might think they've accidentally hopped on the train to Crazy Town and look to make a quick exit.

But before you seek to join them, remember that this is *God* we're talking about—the same God who created the world from nothing. And if He is powerful enough to *create* the universe the way He wanted to, then He is powerful enough to *end* the universe the way He wants to. So, let's see what He has revealed in His Word before forming our opinion.

INTO THE TEXT (REVELATION 4:1–2)

Revelation 4 opens with two *massive* verses. The Church Age has ended. The first and second divisions of the Book of Revelation have been completed, and now something changes. The Apostle John writes:

> [1] **After these things I looked, and behold, a door** *standing* **open in heaven. And the first voice which I heard** *was* **like a trumpet speaking with me, saying,** *"Come up here, and I will show you things which must take place after this."*
>
> [2] **Immediately I was in the Spirit; and behold, a throne set in heaven, and** *One* **sat on the throne.**

---

[122] 1 Thessalonians 4:17.

V.1 is *significant* because it harkens back to **Revelation 1:19**, where Jesus told John to write about three distinct subjects. The third of those subjects was *"the things which will take place after this."*

Here in **Revelation 4:1**, Jesus tells John to join Him in Heaven so He can show him *"things which must take place after this."* In the original Greek, **Revelation 1:19** and **Revelation 4:1** include the same phrase, *"meta tauta."* In fact, it's the very next place in the book that phrase shows up after **Revelation 1:19**. Jesus made it intentionally easy to connect these two verses. All you have to do is look for the next place the phrase "meta tauta" shows up. The Holy Spirit does this because He does not want us to miss that this is a *dividing line* in the narrative. This is where the Church Age ends, and something else begins. The scene shifts *dramatically*.

Symbolically, John the Apostle is us—the believers, the Church. And as the Church Age comes to a close, the believer sees **"a door standing open in heaven"** and hears a voice **"like a trumpet"** speaking to him. What voice would that be? Well, back in **Revelation 1:10-11**, John wrote:

> **. . . I heard behind me a loud voice, as of a trumpet, saying,** *"I am the Alpha and the Omega, the First and the Last,"* **. . .**

And we learned that voice belonged to *Jesus*. So, John (a.k.a. the believer, the Church) hears Jesus speak to him again. Jesus calls to him and says, *"Come up here."* Jesus doesn't say, *"You stay there, John. I'm coming down to you."* Jesus is not the one changing location; the *believer* is called *"up."*

Jesus then tells the believer that once he has come *"up here,"* He will show him *"things which must take place after this."* Not things that *might* take place but things which *"must"* take place, meaning they will happen with 100% certainty *"after this."*

After what? The end of the Church Age and the Rapture. I want to make sure we understand that Jesus is telling John there are things He has ordained to take place only *after* the believer has been removed from the earth and brought *"up here."*

In **Acts 2**, Pentecost *begins* the Church Age. In **Revelation 4:1**, the Rapture *ends* the Church Age.

² **Immediately I was in the Spirit;** . . .

As opposed to what? Being in an earthly body on earth. Faster than the blink of an eye, **"Immediately,"** John is in a different type of body and dimension. Jesus calls the believer up, and the believer is instantly **"in the Spirit."** There's been a change of body and a change of location.

Every believer who leaves the earth—in the Rapture or by physical death—will arrive in the presence of Jesus in a new, resurrected body. The theological term for this is being *"translated,"* and I like that because our earthly bodies are not fit for the environment of Heaven. They're infected with sin and sickness and can't withstand the glory we will encounter in the Lord's presence. We'll need new bodies, and the good news is that your resurrected body will be *perfect*.

When Jesus rose from the dead, He rose in a *resurrected body*. Was it a *physical* body? Absolutely! The disciples and hundreds of other people saw Him and touched Him. Thomas felt the wounds in Jesus' hands and side. Jesus even ate food to prove that He wasn't a ghost.[123] But His body was also *more* than physical (as we

---

[123] Luke 24:39–43.

define it). We are three-dimensional beings that generally interact with a three-dimensional world. While we don't know how many dimensions Jesus' resurrected body exists in, we do know it's more than three because, after His resurrection, He passes in and out of our three-dimensional world,[124] seemingly no longer constrained by the laws of physics (as we understand them). And in eternity, we're going to receive bodies like His!

John gives us further insight in his first epistle:

> **Behold what manner of love the Father has bestowed on us, that we should be called children of God! Therefore the world does not know us, because it did not know Him. Beloved, now we are children of God; and it has not yet been revealed what we shall be, but we know that when He is revealed, we shall be like Him, for we shall see Him as He is.**
>
> —1 John 3:1–2

In other words, we have no paradigm for what we will become in eternity. Whatever you're thinking, it's more. It's better. It's greater. We will be made **"like Him."** Read that last part of **1 John 3:2** again. What it says is so glorious, it's *scandalous*. How amazing will our resurrected bodies be? They'll be just like Jesus' body, according to His Word. Trust me when I tell you we have no grasp on just how much God plans to bless us in eternity. His kindness is truly outrageous.

I can't wait to be **"in the Spirit"** because I am so tired of being in my flesh. I am so tired of living in a body that resists the will of God.

---

[124] Cf. John 20:26.

I am so tired of having to crucify my flesh every day. Like Paul, I am so tired of doing the things that I don't want to do and not doing the things that I want to do.[125] He wrote about the Rapture and our coming translation in **1 Corinthians 15:51–57**, saying:

Behold, I tell you a mystery: ...

The idea is that Paul wants to *reveal* something that has been a mystery *up to this point*.

We shall not all sleep [i.e., we won't all die], **but we shall all be changed—in a moment, in the twinkling of an eye, at the last trumpet. For the trumpet will sound, and the dead will be raised incorruptible** [i.e., imperishable; they'll never die again], **and we shall be changed.**

Paul tells us there will be some believers who won't die a physical death. That implies there will be a final generation of the Church on the earth when the Rapture occurs. He also says the Rapture will occur **"in a moment, in the twinkling of an eye,"** just as John experienced it happening **"Immediately"** in **Revelation 4:1**.

Paul says that in the Rapture, **"we shall all be changed,"** just as John was changed to be **"in the Spirit"** and wrote that we will be made **"like Him"** [i.e., Jesus]. And when does Paul say this will happen? **"At the last trumpet."** How did John describe the voice of Jesus that called him to *"Come up here"*? He said it sounded **"like a trumpet."**

The phrase *"the twinkling of an eye"* can be likened to the time it takes light to travel through the human eye. We don't have

---

[125] Cf. Romans 7:15–20.

space for the long scientific explanation, but I can tell you that the amount of time we're talking about is the shortest unit of time that can exist. It's commonly referred to as "Planck time," and measures 10^{-43} seconds.

When you examine the descriptions written by John and Paul, it becomes clear the Rapture will not involve us slowly floating off the earth. It will be *instantaneous*. We will be here one second and gone the next. Paul continues, and referring to our coming translation writes:

> **For this corruptible must put on incorruption, and this mortal *must* put on immortality. So when this corruptible has put on incorruption, and this mortal has put on immortality, then shall be brought to pass the saying that is written: *"Death is swallowed up in victory."***
>
> ***"O Death, where is your sting?***
> ***O Hades, where is your victory?"***
>
> **The sting of death *is* sin, and the strength of sin *is* the law. But thanks *be* to God, who gives us the victory through our Lord Jesus Christ.**

What a moment that's going to be! Let's get back to John in **Revelation 4:2**. He is now in a resurrected body and a spiritual dimension, and he describes what he sees as he looks around:

> **. . . and behold, a throne set in heaven, and *One* sat on the throne.**

The Holy Spirit wants to be crystal clear that John is *in Heaven* at this point, beholding the glory of the Lord. John saw a door open in Heaven; he heard the voice of Jesus call him up; he was translated into a resurrected body and is now in Heaven before the throne of God. John has been *raptured*.

JESUS ON THE RAPTURE

Did you know that Jesus Himself promised He would rapture His Church? **John 14:1–3** records Him sharing these words with His disciples:

> *Let not your heart be troubled;* ...

What Jesus is going to share is intended to be a *comfort* to believers who are *"troubled."*

> *... you believe in God, believe also in Me. In My Father's house are many mansions; if it were not so, I would have told you.*

The first comfort is knowing there is enough room in Heaven for all who belong to Jesus.

> *I go to prepare a place for you. And if I go and prepare a place for you, I will come again and receive you to Myself; that where I am, there you may be also.*

Jesus tells His disciples that part of the reason He's going to leave them is to *"prepare a place"* for them. Where did Jesus *"go"* at the end of His earthly ministry? He ascended to *Heaven*. The place Jesus is preparing for believers, which He calls *"My Father's house,"* is *Heaven*.

Jesus then promises He's going to *"come again"* for the purpose of *receiving* believers *to* Himself. This receiving of us will not involve Jesus coming *down* to us but rather us going *up* to Him. And to make sure we understand that we are the ones who will be changing location, Jesus adds the explanation *"that where I am, there you may be also."*

Jesus says this to ensure we understand He is *not* referring to the Second Coming when He will descend to the earth and rule from the Throne of David in Jerusalem for the thousand years of the Millennial Kingdom. He wants us to understand that He is talking about the Rapture, a *separate event* from the Second Coming. Jesus will come again to receive believers to Himself and take them to where He is—*Heaven*.

We're going to learn that at the Rapture, Jesus comes *for* His Church (we *leave* the earth to be with Him), while at the Second Coming, Jesus comes *with* His Church (we *return* to the earth with Him).

It is genuinely puzzling to me how someone could read **John 14:1–3** and say, *"Nope, that's not talking about the Rapture. It must be talking about the Second Coming."* That conclusion can only be reached through some combination of willful ignorance and egregious exegesis. Just *read it!* It's plain and simple and one of the most explicit passages of Scripture on the doctrine of the Rapture.

PATTERN IS PROPHECY: THE TRADITIONAL JEWISH WEDDING

There's another layer to the words of Jesus we just read from **John 14**. In the Greek model of prophecy, which is the model we're most familiar with, prophecy is based on *prediction* and *fulfillment*. But in the Hebrew model of prophecy, there are three components: prediction, fulfillment, and *pattern*.

THE RAPTURE

When Jesus' disciples heard His words, the vocabulary would have brought to mind a traditional Jewish *wedding*, which would begin with the *mohar*,[126] which is the bride's agreed-upon *price*, known in some cultures as the *dowry*. Until this price was paid, the wedding could not move forward. Once the groom had paid the *mohar*, the bride would be considered *set apart* (which is what the word "sanctified" means), betrothed, off the market. Everybody would know that she had been *purchased*, and even though she was not yet *with* her husband, she *belonged* to him.

Next, the groom would return to his father's house, where He would prepare the bridal chamber—a room addition to the family home. Simultaneously, the bride would occupy herself with preparing for her groom's imminent return, even though she wouldn't know exactly *when* her groom would show up. It was a bit of a game in which she had to keep herself *ready*, and he would do his best to surprise her.[127]

Even though the modern bride would *murder* her future husband for surprising her like this, both the bride and groom enjoyed the game back then.

One day, the bride would hear a *shout* from her approaching groom and his party. He would appear (along with up to half the town) and *claim his bride*. They would ride together back to the house of the groom's father, where the bride would undergo ritual *cleansing* before the *chupah* (the wedding ceremony).

The happy couple would then disappear into the bridal chamber, everybody would scatter and give them privacy, and then return later

---

[126] Later incorporated into the *ketubah* (the wedding contract).

[127] This scenario is the basis for Jesus' "Parable of the Wise and Foolish Virgins" in Matthew 25:1–13.

that same day to celebrate their *marriage supper*, which would last for *seven days*.

It all paints a stunning prophetic picture of Jesus, the Church, and the Rapture:

- Our bridegroom, Jesus,[128] has purchased His bride, the Church, with His blood and life on the Cross.[129]

- Because our price had been paid, we are now *sanctified*—set apart and reserved to be the eternal Bride of Christ in the future.

- Jesus has returned to His Father's house, Heaven, to prepare a place for us.[130]

- While He does that, the Church is to occupy herself by *preparing* for His return. That means studying His Word and learning how we can be the most beautiful bride possible for our King. Even though we don't know precisely *when* our groom will return, we know that it could happen *at any time*.[131]

- Jesus is going to come and collect His Bride, the Church, and take us back to His Father's house (Heaven).[132]

- Before our "wedding ceremony" can take place, we will need to undergo *ritual cleansing* in the form of translation,

---

[128] Cf. John 3:28–29.

[129] Cf. Acts 20:28; 1 Corinthians 6:19–20, 11:25; Ephesians 5:25–27.

[130] Cf. John 14:2.

[131] Cf. Matthew 24:36, 25:1–13.

[132] Cf. John 14:3; 1 Thessalonians 4:13–18.

where we will receive new, resurrected, sinless, perfect bodies. Our ritual cleansing may also include the judgment of our works (to determine rewards, not salvation).[133]

- We will then come together with Jesus for *"the marriage supper of the Lamb,"* a celebration made up of every tribe, tongue, and nation.[134]

- How long does a traditional Jewish marriage supper last? Seven *days*. How long will the Church be in Heaven with Jesus while the Tribulation takes place on Earth? We'll soon discover the answer is seven *years*. Then Jesus will return to the earth, with His bride, to establish His Millennial Kingdom.

In the Bible, *pattern* is *prophecy*.

THE RIGHTEOUS ARE SPARED FROM GOD'S WRATH

Many Christians and churches believe the Church will *not* be spared from the Tribulation. Some believe we'll be raptured halfway through the seven years ("mid-Trib"). Others believe in a rapture *after* the Tribulation ("post-Trib"), while others believe there won't be *any* type of Rapture.

Because pattern is prophecy in Scripture, I want to point out that nowhere in the Bible, Old Testament or New, do we see God's punishment of the wicked fatally "spill over" onto the righteous.

---

[133] Cf. 1 Corinthians 3:12–15.

[134] Cf. Matthew 22:1–14; Revelation 19:7–9.

There is no text where God pours out His wrath in judgment on unrighteous people and allows the righteous to die as collateral damage. It never happens.

- Noah and his family are safe in the Ark when the earth is flooded.[135]
- Lot and his family are taken out of Sodom before God destroys it with fire.[136]
- Rahab and all those in her household are safe as Jericho falls around them.[137]

And I could share several other examples. Anyone who believes there is no Rapture and that the Church will be left on the earth to suffer through the Tribulation must believe in something God has *never done* and something that, I will argue, goes against His fundamental character—allowing the *righteous* to experience His *wrath*.

The Lord simply does not do that. Remember Paul's assurance in **1 Thessalonians 5:9**:

…God did not appoint us to wrath, but to obtain salvation through our Lord Jesus Christ…

Let me try to be absolutely clear about the claim I am making: The Church has been experiencing the wrath of *man* and *Satan* since the days of **Acts 2**. Believers can experience God's *discipline* as a loving correction. But believers never have and never will experience the *wrath* of *God*.

---

[135] Cf. Genesis 7.
[136] Cf. Genesis 19:22.
[137] Cf. Joshua 6:17.

The Tribulation will not be God *disciplining* believers for the purpose of *correction;* it will be God pouring out His *wrath* on the earth that has rejected Him before He returns to rule and reign.

I encourage you to search the Scriptures for yourself on this. I believe you will find great comfort in the realization that because we are God's children, we will *never* be objects of His wrath.

THE SECOND COMING OF CHRIST

After spending the Tribulation in Heaven with the Lord, the Church will return to the earth with Jesus at the Second Coming, which will mark the *end* of the seven-year Tribulation. Remember that the Rapture is Jesus coming *for* His Church;[138] the Second Coming is Jesus coming *with* His Church.

Paul used the phrase **"the coming of our Lord Jesus Christ with all His saints"** to describe the Second Coming in **1 Thessalonians 3:13**, and we'll see that event unfold in **Revelation 19**.

But to state the obvious, before Jesus can return to the earth *with* His saints, He must come *for* His saints. We must first be *with* Jesus in Heaven before we can *return* to the earth with Him. Therefore, He must first come and *get us*. Jesus can't return to the earth **"with all His saints"** right now because **"all His saints"** are not *with* Him! That's part of the purpose of the Rapture.

Look at **Revelation 4:1–2** again where John writes:

> After these things I looked, and behold, a door *standing open in heaven.* And the first voice which I heard *was* like a trumpet speaking with me, saying, *"Come up here,*

---

[138] Cf. John 14:1–3.

and I will show you things which must take place after this." **Immediately I was in the Spirit; and behold, a throne set in heaven, and *One* sat on the throne.**

Most of the Book of Revelation will unfold *chronologically*. And I want you to notice that in the flow of the narrative, John and the Church are now up in Heaven before the throne of God, *before* God's wrath begins coming upon the earth in **Revelation 6:16**—that is, before the Tribulation begins.

In **Revelation 5:9–10**, John will see a group of people singing to Jesus before the throne of God in Heaven:

> *. . . they sang a new song, saying:*
> *"You are worthy to take the scroll,*
> *And to open its seals;*
> *For You were slain,*
> *And have redeemed us to God by Your blood*
> *Out of every tribe and tongue and people and nation,*
> *And have made us kings and priests to our God;*
> *And we shall reign on the earth."*

"They" sing to Jesus that He has *"redeemed us to God by Your blood."* Is Israel singing this? No, because **"they"** are *"Out of every tribe and tongue and people and nation"*—**"They"** are the Church.

Revelation 1:7 is the only other place in the Bible where we encounter the phrase *"kings and priests,"* and John uses it to describe what Jesus has made every believer into.

Look at the last line of **Revelation 5:10**:

- *"And we . . . "*—those who are there in Heaven before the throne.

- "*...shall reign...*"—future tense, meaning it's something that's going to happen *after* the Church has been taken up to Heaven.
- "*...on the earth.*"—Don't miss this: **"they"** are in Heaven, singing about how they will return to earth to reign with Jesus in the future.

In **Revelation 4:1**, the Church is taken *up* to Heaven when Jesus comes *for* His saints. In **Revelation 6**, God's *wrath* comes *down*. In **Revelation 19**, Jesus returns *with* His saints to reign on the earth for 1,000 years. That's the big picture of what happens to the Church in the end-times.

WHAT THE TIME OF THE RAPTURE WILL LOOK LIKE

The arrival of the end-times was announced by something miraculous—the State of Israel rising from the dead after ~1,900 years. And what's even more impressive is that thousands of years ago,[139] the Bible predicted it would happen. But that's not all. Jesus Himself further prophesied that this event would mark the final generation—the generation of the Church that will be alive on the earth when the Rapture takes place.[140]

In a monologue called "The Olivet Discourse," Jesus describes the *signs* that will mark the last days. You can (and should) read it in **Matthew 24–25** and **Luke 17**. Jesus lists some specific things that will happen, and if you go through His list item by item, I don't

---

[139] Cf. Isaiah 11:11–12; Ezekiel 37:21–22.
[140] Cf. Matthew 24:32–33.

think you'll conclude that Jesus is speaking about things that have already taken place.

Matthew 24 opens with Jesus prophesying to His disciples that the Temple in Jerusalem will be destroyed; that happened in AD 70. Then in **V.3**, we read:

> **Now as He sat on the Mount of Olives, the disciples came to Him privately, saying,** *"Tell us, when will these things be? And what will be the sign of Your coming, and of the end of the age?"*

The disciples ask Jesus three questions:

- When will these things happen?
- What will be the sign of Your coming?
- What will be the sign of the end of the age?

In the two chapters that follow (**Matthew 24–25**), Jesus answers their questions, and not surprisingly, it's worth studying what He tells them.

BIRTH PANGS

The term **"last days"** applies to the entire Church Age, which began around AD 32 on Pentecost and continues *today*. While describing all the signs of the last days, Jesus says this in the Olivet Discourse:

> *. . . all these things are merely the beginning of birth pangs.*
> —Matthew 24:8 NASB

Notice that He describes the signs of the last days as being like labor pains, which get more *intense* and *frequent* before things *really* start to happen. Paul describes the attitudes and behaviors that will mark the last days. They began in his time but have gotten more *intense* and *frequent* in ours:

> ... in the last days perilous times will come: For men will be lovers of themselves, lovers of money, boasters, proud, blasphemers, disobedient to parents, unthankful, unholy, unloving, unforgiving, slanderers, without self-control, brutal, despisers of good, traitors, headstrong, haughty, lovers of pleasure rather than lovers of God, having a form of godliness but denying its power [*e.g., the church of the Laodiceans*]. And from such people turn away!
> —2 Timothy 3:1–5

Let's examine each of these signs:

- The original Greek for **"perilous times"** refers to *harsh, fierce,* or *savage* times of trouble. When we look across the earth, do we see societies getting *more* violent or *less* harsh, fierce, and savage? Are crime statistics generally going *up* or *down?* How about attitudes? How many of us grew up without a security alarm system in our homes? How many of us have one now? Why? Because violence is increasing on the earth. How many tragedies and how much violence is recorded and posted to the Internet by people who should be helping? Why? Because these are **"perilous times"**—increasingly harsh, fierce, and savage.

- The self-help movement seems to have flowed right into the age of social media, producing new generations of **"boasters"** who are **"proud."** We now exalt what we used to call narcissism as children are raised to be **"lovers of themselves"** in the name of self-esteem. The older folk have to read books and seek counseling to figure out how they can catch up and also learn to love themselves more deeply.

If you and I look at a group photo, what criteria determine whether it's a good photo? How *I* look, obviously! I am always on my mind, but Paul says that the last days will be characterized by a *dramatic* increase in the obsession with self. And what better encapsulates such a movement than the selfie? *"Check it out; it's a photo of me! Just me. That's all it takes to make it an amazing photo."*

- The word **"unforgiving"** is the Greek word *"aspondos,"* and it means to be *"irreconcilable"* or *"without truce."* The age will be marked by people who cannot be reasoned with and refuse to make peace.

One of the modern geopolitical realities that continue to astound me is the number of high-ranking political figures who seem to genuinely believe that, at the end of the day, everybody is reasonable. They go into negotiations with rogue states and groups, assuming they're dealing with *reasonable* people.

Yet we know that North Korea is led by a dictator who was raised to believe he was the chosen one. He actually believes that. He is *not* reasonable. The real power brokers in Iran and groups like ISIS are devoted to the Shia form of Islam, which teaches that things like the destruction of Israel and the establishment of a unified Islamic state may hasten the return of the twelfth Imam, the Mahdi who is their messiah figure. These leaders would gladly give their lives and the lives of their people in return for the destruction of the State of Israel. They are not *reasonable*.

In North America and Europe, we see more and more "progressive" liberal groups who are no longer willing to be *reasonable*. They believe there can be no tolerance for other views. The only acceptable view is theirs, and you must celebrate it or suffer the consequences.

All these things are manifestations of the last days attitude that is *irreconcilable* and *without truce*.

- **"Without self-control"**—Addiction in our generation is at a level *unparalleled* in the scope of history. From painkillers to mood-altering medications to Internet porn, our belief in our right to instant happiness and pleasure drives us to indulge our base desires more readily and easily than ever before.

- **"Despisers of good"**—You can't hand out Bibles in a school, but you can hand out condoms and flyers educating preteens about access to abortion and "gender-affirming" surgeries. We started by *allowing* increased evil into our society, but we've long since moved on to *celebrating* it. Things have already gotten so crazy that it can seem like the world has gone mad—until you realize that this is precisely what the Lord told us we'd see in the last days.

Again, the attitudes and behaviors Paul describes have been evident since AD 32 but will (and have) become more *intense* and *frequent* as the Rapture approaches.

Everything Paul says points to what Jesus said; that is, the last days will be a time when things are, in reality, very *unusual,* but almost everyone will think it's business *as usual.* The world will be (and is) like a frog in boiling water, failing to discern the radical changes occurring until circumstances become *catastrophic.*

THE DAYS OF NOAH AND LOT

In the Olivet Discourse, Jesus makes it clear that while He doesn't want us to get into date setting, He does expect us to recognize the *generation* of His return and look for it with expectation and longing. And to help us do that, He shares this in **Matthew 24:37–39**:

> *. . . as the days of Noah were, so also will the coming of the Son of Man be.*

Jesus doesn't say, *"as the days of Isaiah were"* or *"as the days of Ezekiel were".* He says, *"as the days of Noah were."*

> *For as in the days before the flood, they were eating and drinking, marrying and giving in marriage, until the day that Noah entered the ark, and did not know until the flood came and took them all away, so also will the coming of the Son of Man be.*

Though the world was on the verge of *catastrophic judgment,* life outside Noah's family continued as usual up to the moment the rains of the Great Flood began to fall. Jesus is pointing out a specific parallel that will exist between the days of Noah and the end-times. In both instances, there will be obvious warning signs that almost everybody will miss as they go about life as usual, right up to the moment God's wrath begins to fall upon the earth.

The story of the Flood of Noah can be found in **Genesis 6**, and I want to highlight something the text tells us about the state of humanity just before the waters began to rise. In **Genesis 6:11**, we read:

The earth . . .

Not just one region (i.e., the ancient near east) but the *whole earth*.

. . . also was corrupt before God, and the earth was filled with *violence.*

In the eyes of God, *violence* was one of the defining characteristics of the earth in the days of Noah. And while the earth has known violence ever since Cain killed Abel, there was something *dark* in peoples' hearts that inclined them toward violence in a greater way in the days of Noah, and so it shall be in the days leading up to the Rapture.

But don't forget the good news that even in the days of Noah, God had a plan for those who belonged to Him. He put them in an Ark that they entered through a *door*. Once they were inside, God Himself closed that *door* and kept them *safe* as His wrath was poured out on the earth through the Flood. Does that sound familiar?

Luke's Gospel records an additional sign mentioned by Jesus in the Olivet Discourse. In **Luke 17:28–30**, Jesus says:

> *Likewise as it was also in the days of Lot: They ate, they drank, they bought, they sold, they planted, they built; but on the day that Lot went out of Sodom it rained fire and brimstone from heaven and destroyed them all. Even so will it be* [i.e., it will be just the same] *in the day when the Son of Man is revealed.*

Jesus points out that life was going on as usual in Sodom—right up to the moment God began pouring out His wrath on the city, raining down fire and brimstone. The people of Sodom were not even remotely anticipating what was about to happen. They were drinking, buying and selling, planting and building for the future when catastrophe came upon them in the blink of an eye. They thought it was just another ordinary day.

And Jesus says it will be like that on the day He comes for His Church.

THE RAPTURE WILL BE A GLOBAL EVENT

In case we're not grasping that the Rapture will be a *worldwide* event, Luke's Gospel also includes this detail shared by Jesus in the Olivet Discourse:

> *I tell you, in that night there will be two men* [meaning "people"] **in one bed: the one will be taken and the other will be left. Two women will be grinding** [wheat] *together: the one will be taken and the other left. Two men will be in the field* [harvesting]*: the one will be taken and the other left.*
>
> —Luke 17:34–36

Jesus describes an instantaneous event taking place at different times of the day. Jesus taught that when this event happened, it would be early morning in one location (when women ground wheat), the main part of the day in another (when men would work in a field), and *"night"* in another. That means He *cannot* be speaking about an event that took place or will take place in only one region (i.e., Israel).

1 THESSALONIANS 4:13–18

We looked at this passage in an earlier chapter, but it's worth revisiting, as it is likely the most well-known text on the Rapture in all of Scripture.

Paul likely spent no more than a total of six months in the city of Thessalonica, and during that time, he established a church there. Paul was faced with the question, *"What does a group of new believers most need to be taught?"* And when he thought through the essentials of the faith, Paul concluded that the end-times and the Rapture needed to be among them. Think about that for a moment. Paul had very limited time with this group of new believers, and he taught them *eschatology*.

Paul had to flee the city, and five or six months later, Silas and Timothy visited the young church. They found believers who loved the Lord and were living for Him faithfully but had also *misinterpreted* Paul's teachings about the end-times. Some had even quit their jobs in anticipation of Jesus' imminent return! Others were concerned about the persecution they were beginning to experience, as it left them wondering if they had possibly *missed* the Rapture. Furthermore, some wondered if their loved ones who had died had missed out on Heaven because they hadn't lived to see the Rapture.

To address their concerns and clear up misunderstandings, Paul wrote 1 Thessalonians. Let's read from **1 Thessalonians 4:13–17:**

- **...I do not want you to be ignorant** [uninformed]**, brethren, concerning those who have fallen asleep** [died]**, lest you sorrow as others who have no hope.**

  Paul does not want them to grieve over death like nonbelievers do because, as believers, they have hope! For all who love the Lord will be together with Him in eternity.

- **For if we believe that Jesus died and rose again, even so God will bring with Him those who sleep in Jesus.**

    If we believe Jesus died and rose again, then we can believe that at the Rapture, He will bring with Him every believer who died before, including our loved ones.

- **For this we say to you by the word of the Lord, ...**

    Paul wants us to know that what he is teaching comes straight from the Lord as revealed to him. Indeed, this is God's Word.

    ... that we who are alive *and* remain until the coming of the Lord will by no means precede those who are asleep.

When we're raptured to be with the Lord, every other believer from all of history will be there too.

And then Paul explains *how* this is all going to happen:

For the Lord Himself will descend from heaven with a shout, with the voice of an archangel, and with the trumpet of God. And the dead in Christ will rise first. Then we who are alive *and* remain shall be caught up together with them in the clouds to meet the Lord in the air. And thus we shall always be with the Lord.

The Lord Jesus will descend, but not down to the earth. He will let out a shout with His voice that sounds like a trumpet, and we will hear some version of the words, *"Come up here."*

"Immediately," we will be **"caught up"** and find ourselves in new, resurrected, eternal bodies, in the presence of the Lord in Heaven.

The text seems to imply that believers who have died will be with the Lord a split second before those on the earth at the moment of the Rapture. And all of this will take place **"in the twinkling of an eye."**

How is that possible? We'll find out soon enough. One possibility is that Heaven exists in multiple dimensions that our current reality does not. Time almost certainly functions differently there, likely in ways we cannot even fathom. If time is linear[141] on earth, time in Heaven almost certainly works differently. For example, it is theoretically possible that all who love the Lord arrive in Heaven at the same time, despite leaving earth's timeline at different points.

I'm not saying that's how it works. I'm sharing that to make the point that there are explanations and possibilities we don't even know to consider, and in Himself, the Lord has *infinite* options available to accomplish His will.

Jesus will receive us *to* Himself. We're not going to meet Him on the *earth*; we're going to *leave* the earth and meet Him **"in the air," "in the clouds,"** in heavenly places, in another *dimension*. And from that moment on, we will be with the Lord *forever*.

The story of every believer's life really will end with, "and they lived happily ever after."

HARPAZO

One of the most repeated myths regarding the Rapture says, *"The word 'rapture' isn't even in the Bible."* Before we go any further, I need to clear this up.

Until the 300s, the Bible existed in parts and in multiple languages—Greek, Aramaic, and some Hebrew. A wise decision was made to translate the complete text into one document and a

---

[141] That it, it functions on a line, with time moving from left-to-right.

single language. Latin was chosen because it was a "dead" language, meaning it was no longer used by any society as their main dialect and had therefore finished evolving. This meant that Latin would be the same in a thousand years, making it an excellent choice for source and reference documents.

In **1 Thessalonians 4:17**, which we just read, we see the phrase **"caught up."** When Paul wrote in Greek, the word he used was *"harpazo."* When the Bible was translated into the Latin Vulgate, *"harpazo"* was translated to *"raptus,"* from which we get the English word "rapture." Both "harpazo" and "raptus" refer to being *"caught up"* or *"snatched up."*

So, to be clear, the word "rapture" is absolutely in the Bible. It's simply been translated as "caught up" in our English Bibles. This myth is based entirely on ignorance of Bible translation history.

Some who don't believe in the Rapture will say that when Paul talks about us being **"caught up,"** he is referring to an earthly experience where we are *emotionally overwhelmed* by the Lord's presence. The problem with that line of thinking is that the future rapture of the Church is not the only rapture that takes place in the Bible. It may surprise you to learn that the Scriptures record multiple people being raptured in various ways:

- *Enoch* was taken by God and **"did not see death."**[142]
- *Elijah* was taken to Heaven in a whirlwind.[143]
- *Jesus* ascended to Heaven.[144]

Revelation 12:5 even uses the same *"harpazo"* to describe the

---

[142] Cf. Genesis 5:24; Hebrews 11:5.

[143] Cf. 2 Kings 2:1, 11.

[144] Cf. Mark 16:19; Acts 1:9–11; Revelation 12:5.

Ascension of Jesus that Paul used to describe the Rapture of the Church in **1 Thessalonians 4**. There's an issue here in the realm of Biblical interpretation. When a word appears in the Scriptures, it must be interpreted consistently unless there's a compelling reason not to.

In Jesus' *"harpazo,"* did He literally ascend to Heaven and leave the earth? Of course, He did! Therefore, when Paul writes that the Church will ascend to Heaven and leave the earth in a "harpazo," it means *the same thing*. There is no compelling reason to interpret the text differently.

And there are more examples:

- *Philip* was raptured, caught up, from one location to another.[145]
- The Apostles *Paul* and *John* were temporarily raptured to Heaven.[146]
- And the seventh rapture recorded in the Bible is the coming rapture of *the Church*.

Those examples prove that when the Bible talks about being *"caught up"* or *"snatched up,"* it's not being figurative. The Bible is speaking literally, and we know that because raptures have already happened to multiple men in Scripture.

BACK TO 1 THESSALONIANS 4

This is how Paul wraps up his explanation of the Rapture to the Thessalonians in **V.18**:

Therefore comfort one another with these words.

---

[145] Cf. Acts 8:39.

[146] Cf. 2 Corinthians 12:2–4; Revelation 4:1.

Jesus shared the Rapture with His disciples for the same reason Paul shared it with the Thessalonian believers—to *comfort* them. And that's the reason Jesus has shared it with us in His Word. He wants us to be *comforted* by the knowledge that the Church will not experience His wrath on the earth during the Tribulation (or ever!).

If I said, *"I'm Post-Trib. I believe there will be a seven-year Tribulation in which God's wrath is poured out on the earth, killing most of us. But when it's all over, Jesus will return for the few of us left."* Would you find that comforting?

If I said, *"I'm Mid-Trib. I believe there will be a seven-year Tribulation of death, doom, and destruction. Most of us will die horrific deaths under God's wrath, but halfway through those seven years, Jesus will come for those who have managed to survive."* Would that be comforting?

What if I said, *"Just as Noah, Lot, Rahab, and other righteous men and women were spared from the wrath of God, Revelation 4:1 tells us the Church will be taken up to Heaven before God's wrath comes upon the earth. We will be with Jesus during the seven-year Tribulation and never experience His wrath."* Would that be comforting? *Absolutely.*

CLOSING THOUGHTS

In **Matthew 24:44**, Jesus said:

> **... *you also be ready, for the Son of Man is coming at an hour you do not expect.***

We can't know the *day*. We can't know the *hour*. But we can know the *generation* when the Rapture will take place if we'll take God's Word seriously. Most people (including most Christians) won't see it coming.

It's not a cliché to ask, *"If the Rapture happened five minutes from now, would you be ready?"* The reality is that it really *could* happen five minutes from now. And if it does, you don't want to realize that you weren't truly saved. You don't want to be the one left in the field.

Make sure you're right with the Lord. Be sure of your salvation *today*. May we be comforted by these words of John the Apostle:

Behold what manner of love the Father has bestowed on us, that we should be called children of God! Therefore the world does not know us, because it did not know Him. Beloved, now we are children of God; and it has not yet been revealed what we shall be, but we know that when He is revealed, we shall be like Him, for we shall see Him as He is.

—1 John 3:1–2

REVELATION 4

THE CHURCH IN HEAVEN

As we discussed in the previous chapter, the Church is taken to Heaven *before* the wrath of God is poured out on the world that has rejected Him. To understand this, all you have to do is remember the book's outline in **Revelation 1:19** and understand that (for the most part) the rest of the book unfolds *literally* and *chronologically*. It's that simple. No master's degree required.

In **Revelation 4–5**, we see the Church *in Heaven*. In **Revelation 6**, God begins to pour out His wrath on the earth. And here's the amazing thing—in both Greek and English, the numbers four and five come before the number six. Always have, always will. Jesus devotes two entire chapters to driving home the point that the Church is in Heaven *before* His wrath is poured out on the earth.

Over the following two chapters, we will be treated to a glorious preview of Heaven—the hope of believers living in a broken world since Adam and Eve were removed from the Garden of Eden. I urge you to soak in these feel-good chapters because we know what's coming down in **Revelation 6**—the wrath of God. And it goes on for a while. So, enjoy these two chapters and comfort yourself with the reality they relate to the *believer* during the

Tribulation. We will watch **Revelation 6–19** unfold *from Heaven*. Thank You, Jesus!

THE THRONE ROOM OF HEAVEN

Let's revisit the first couple of verses of **Revelation 4**:

> **¹After these things I looked, and behold, a door *standing* open in heaven. And the first voice which I heard was like a trumpet speaking with me, saying, *"Come up here, and I will show you things which must take place after this."***
>
> **² Immediately I was in the Spirit; and behold, a throne set in heaven, and *One* sat on the throne.**

As **Revelation 4** opens, the Church is raptured to Heaven. Specifically, the throne room of Heaven, which is the center not only of the universe but of *everything*.

I'm very skeptical of people who claim to have visited Heaven and been sent back by God to write a book and make a low-quality movie about it. And one reason I'm skeptical is because their "testimony" is usually focused on themselves. It's all about the cool stuff they got to do, their extraordinary newfound abilities, the fuzzy feelings—it's all about me, me, me.

But when you read **Revelation 4–5** and the visions of John, Isaiah,[147] Ezekiel,[148] Micaiah,[149] and Daniel,[150] their glimpses of

---

[147] Cf. Isaiah 6:1.
[148] Cf. Ezekiel 1:26–28.
[149] Cf. 1 Kings 22:19.
[150] Cf. Daniel 7:9–10.

Heaven were consumed by one thing—the glory of God. Heaven is all about *Him*, and that is what makes it so wonderful.

With his limited human vocabulary, John attempts to describe for us what He sees in Heaven's throne room:

> **³ And He who sat there was like a jasper and a sardius stone in appearance; and *there was* a rainbow around the throne, in appearance like an emerald.**

Remember that when John uses the word **"like,"** he is telling us that He's *not* speaking literally; he's doing his best to describe something *indescribable*. He's not saying the one on the throne *was* a jasper and a sardius stone; He's saying that something about His appearance *resembled* a jasper and a sardius stone.

Jasper was a precious stone that could be one of several colors. Most scholars consider it to be a clear diamond, while others believe it to be a blue opal.

The sardius stone (also called the "sardine stone") was mentioned in the letter to the Church in Sardis. Some speculate it's a ruby, as we know it was blood red.

Readers with a Jewish background would have recognized these as the first and last stones found in the high priest's breastplate.[151] Similarly, we've seen Jesus identify Himself as the First and the Last, the Alpha and the Omega, the beginning and the end.

Exodus 28:21 tells us each of the stones in the high priest's breastplate was engraved with the name of one of the 12 tribes of Israel, which were founded by the 12 sons of Jacob. The first and last sons of Jacob were Reuben and Benjamin. Reuben means, *"behold a son,"* while Benjamin means, *"son of my right hand."*

---

[151] Cf. Exodus 28:17–20.

That's the scene here in **Revelation 4**, in the throne room of Heaven—Jesus, the Son of God, seated at the right hand of His Father.

As John looks at the throne and the one seated upon it, he sees things in dimensions we can't perceive in our current bodies. And all John can say is that the throne was radiant, beautiful, and colorful, like a diamond and a blood-red stone.

In Greek, the word translated as *"rainbow"* is "iris." And the word *"around"* doesn't mean *"over,"* as we think of a rainbow. It means *"roundabout, from all sides, all around."* The idea is a spectrum of color radiating in every direction from the throne of God: light, light, and more light.

John alludes to this in his first epistle:

This is the message which we have heard from Him and declare to you, that God is light and in Him is no darkness at all.

—1 John 1:5

When John refers to the rainbow's appearance as being **"like an emerald,"** he's likely referring to the way light reflects off and refracts through an emerald because he describes the colors as **"a rainbow."** Here's the point: God's appearance is *light*.[152]

Everything will be illuminated in the presence of God, including our understanding. We will understand the reason behind every yes and no we received from the Lord. We will grasp the complete plan of God and how our joys and sufferings were woven into it. All our whys will fade away in His presence as our understanding is

---

[152] Cf. 1 Timothy 6:16.

illuminated, and we are left with the inevitable conclusion that God is and has always been, great, glorious, gracious, and good.

When we trust the Lord in the absence of answers, it's only a *temporary* trust. We won't need to fill in the blanks with faith forever. We're saying, *"I'm OK waiting to get the answer because I know my moment of illumination is coming. And when I have it, I know I will be satisfied."*

THE 24 ELDERS

> ⁴ **Around the throne *were* twenty-four thrones, and on the thrones I saw twenty-four elders sitting, clothed in white robes; and they had crowns of gold on their heads.**

Who are these 24 elders? It's time for some detective work. The Greek word used for *"elders"* is *"presbyteros,"* from which we get our English word "Presbyterian." This has caused some to suggest there will only be 24 Presbyterians in Heaven. Obviously, that's preposterous. Scholars agree there may be as many as 30.

I'm joking! I love my Presbyterian brothers and sisters.

Remember, everything in the Book of Revelation that *seems* hard to understand is explained somewhere else in the book or the Scriptures. Let's look ahead a little bit to **Revelation 5:8–9**. I'll explain the context in the next chapter, but for now, I just want you to notice the *lyrics* of the song the elders are singing:

> **Now when He had taken the scroll, the four living creatures and the twenty-four elders fell down before the Lamb, each having a harp, and golden bowls full of incense, which are the prayers of the saints. And they sang a new song, saying:**

"You are worthy to take the scroll,
And to open its seals;
For You were slain,
And have redeemed us to God by Your blood"

Clearly, the 24 elders are believers, not angels. Jesus didn't die to redeem angels; He died to redeem *people*. The following line of the song gives us another important clue:

Out of every tribe and tongue and people and nation,

That means these elders cannot represent only Israel or Old Testament saints.[153] At a minimum, their identity must include the Church. Additionally, their **"white robes"** and **the "crowns of gold on their heads"** were both mentioned as being given to believers in the letters to the seven churches.[154]

But what's the significance of the number 24? *Before* the death and resurrection of Jesus, God worked on the earth through *Israel*. *After* the death and resurrection of Jesus, God works on the earth through *the Church*.

God established Israel through 12 tribes. God established the Church through 12 apostles.

12+12 = 24

While *ethnic* Israel has her own destiny,[155] which will emerge later, *spiritual* Israel is now comprised of Old Testament saints and

---

[153] Believers who died before the death and resurrection of Jesus.

[154] Cf. Revelation 2:10; 3:4–5, 11, 18.

[155] Cf. Romans 11.

the Church.[156] We have been **"grafted in,"**[157] as Paul wrote. That's why in **Revelation 21**, we see the creation of the **"New Jerusalem"** as a home for this "new Israel." And in that New Jerusalem, guess what we find.

> **... she had a great and high wall with twelve gates, and twelve angels at the gates, and names written on them, which are *the names* of the twelve tribes of the children of Israel ...**
>
> —Revelation 21:12

> **... the wall of the city had twelve foundations, and on them were the names of the twelve apostles of the Lamb.**
>
> —Revelation 21:14

Twelve tribes and twelve apostles, together in the New Jerusalem, as the new spiritual Israel.

And if we go back to the Old Testament, in **1 Chronicles 24**, we read of King David (who is a *type* of Jesus) dividing the Levitical priesthood into 24 teams. Each team was to serve in the Temple (that Solomon would later build) on a rotating basis.[158] And when the king wanted to communicate with the priesthood, he would summon the 24 elders who represented the *entire* priesthood.

The Church doesn't have a separate priesthood because *every* believer is a priest. As our brother Peter wrote:

> **... you *are* a chosen generation, a royal priesthood, a holy nation, His own special people, that you may proclaim the**

---

[156] Cf. Romans 2:28–29.

[157] Romans 11:17.

[158] Each team would serve a total of two weeks per year, in addition to the feasts.

praises of Him who called you out of darkness into His marvelous light . . .

—1 Peter 2:9

Finally, in **1 Chronicles 25:2–4**, we find David appointing 24 singers and musicians to lead the praise and worship of God at the Temple. For me, the picture is *clear*. The 24 elders represent the royal priesthood of believers, consisting of Old Testament saints and the Church. And as we look at the text of **Revelation 4–5**, we see this priesthood doing precisely what they were created to do—ministering to the Lord.

Did you notice what the elders (i.e., believers) are *doing* before Jesus? They each have **"a harp"** and are worshipping Him with whatever the Heavenly version of music is. They're also pouring out **"bowls,"** which John describes as **"full of incense."** The image we're supposed to form in our minds is of a type of smoke filling the throne room of God, enveloping the proceedings. Except, in some mystical way that we can't fully grasp, that incense is **"the prayers of the saints."**

How do you think God perceives *your* prayers? They're not annoyances. They're not tiresome to the Lord. They are like incense rising around Him because every prayer testifies that He is the only one who can help, save, deliver, rescue, redeem, and restore. Our prayers are worship to Him because they reveal our trust in Him, and they surround Him in His throne room, lingering like incense.

If we can grasp this reality, it will transform the way we pray. We'll *believe* God's Word when it tells us we should **"come boldly to the throne of grace, that we may obtain mercy and find grace to help in time of need."**[159]

---

[159] Hebrews 4:16.

Your prayers bless the Lord, and that should encourage you. For a rewarding personal study, I recommend reading all of **Ephesians 2** and comparing it to this scene with the 24 elders in **Revelation 4**. See how many similarities you can find!

A STORM BREWING

> ⁵ **And from the throne proceeded lightnings, thunderings, and voices.**

We see this theme of light radiating from the throne continuing, along with sounds like thunder and the incense of the prayers of the saints. This is an *intense* scene.

Why does the text use the plural form—"**voices**"? It could be because Jesus is on that throne *with* His Father, though we can't be sure.[160] As we've mentioned before, Jesus will take His *own* throne, the throne of David, during the Millennium.[161]

Since man's first few decades outside Eden, humanity has observed the wrongs of this world, such as the innocent being slaughtered and abused, and cried out, *"God, aren't You going to do something?!"* The answer is *"Yes."* And we will see it play out across the Tribulation in **Revelation 6–18**.

The day of God's wrath is coming, and once the Church has been raptured, we see a *storm* brewing on the throne of God. In **Psalm 73:3, 17**, the psalmist writes:

> **. . . I *was* envious of the boastful,**
> **When I saw the prosperity of the wicked. . . .**

---

[160] Cf. Mark 16:19; Hebrews 1:3, 10:12, 12:2.

[161] Cf. Isaiah 9:7; Luke 1:32.

Until I went into the sanctuary of God;
***Then* I understood their end.**

Back to Revelation 4:5:

Seven lamps of fire *were* burning before the throne, which are the seven Spirits of God.

You'll recall from **Revelation 1** that **"the seven spirits of God"** refer to the Holy Spirit,[162] who is also before the throne of God.

SEA OF GLASS

⁶ Before the throne *there was* a sea of glass, like crystal.

Again, we see the word **"like."** This is *not* a crystal or glass sea; it's just the best way John can describe it. We should take from this that there seems to be a beautiful, open, and serene *expanse* before the Lord's throne.[163]

What a contrast this must create: a rainbow of light *exploding* outward from the throne, smoke, the incense of the prayers of the saints, sounds like thunder and voices—juxtaposed with an ocean of *peace*.

The prophet Jeremiah summed up this contrast beautifully when he wrote:

A glorious high throne from the beginning is the place of our sanctuary.

—Jeremiah 17:12

---

[162] Cf. Isaiah 11:1–2.
[163] Cf. Exodus 24:9–10.

The place of God's overwhelming and awesome glory is also our place of sanctuary—our refuge.

In the Temple, "the Sea" was a water basin constantly stirred up by the priests who used it to wash before ministering. In Heaven, the Sea is glass, like crystal. Why? Because *Jesus* is our high priest. He is entirely without sin, so He does not need to be purified before ministering on our behalf.

THE FOUR LIVING CREATURES

Continuing in **V.6**:

> **And in the midst of the throne, and around the throne,** *were* **four living creatures full of eyes in front and in back.** ⁷ **The first living creature** *was* **like a lion, the second living creature like a calf, the third living creature had a face like a man, and the fourth living creature was like a flying eagle.** ⁸ *The* **four living creatures, each having six wings, were full of eyes around and within.**

To make sense of this seemingly bizarre description, we must remember that this scene unfolds in *Heaven*. We've left the three-dimensional universe with which we're familiar and are now in a place with only God knows how many dimensions.

There's a hint of that where we are told that the four living creatures **"were full of eyes around and within."** What does it mean to have eyes **"within"**? My earthly human brain has no idea.

If your Bible says "beasts" instead of **"creatures,"** just know that these are not evil beings. And when we see them, we will find them spectacular, beautiful, and amazing.

Before we reach Heaven, each of us will undergo a dramatic change when we are translated and receive a new, resurrected, eternal body. Before puberty hits, we see people kissing and think, *"Ugh. Gross! Cooties!"* And then suddenly, puberty hits, and there's an awakening, a revelation, as what was once disturbing becomes beautiful, intriguing, and amazing. I'm confident our translation into resurrected bodies will result in an even greater awakening than that brought on by puberty! That's why, as John looks at these creatures in his temporarily translated body, he's in awe.

These four creatures are likely those described in greater detail in **Ezekiel 1:5–25** and referred to in **Isaiah 6:2** as **"seraphim."** From those accounts, we understand they are not four different creatures with four different faces but rather four identical creatures, each possessing *all four faces* (a lion, a calf, a man, and an eagle). As John looked at them, each apparently faced him from a different angle, revealing a different face.

There's not a consensus on the *meaning* of the four faces, and it's not central to the narrative of Revelation. Therefore, I suggest we be content to know these creatures as high-level supernatural beings created by Jesus, who worship and serve Him. Take a look at what they were doing:

> **And they do not rest day or night, saying:**
> *"Holy, holy, holy,*
> *Lord God Almighty,*
> *Who was and is and is to come!"*

Some suggest they say *"Holy, holy, holy"* because they're worshipping the *triune* God—Father, Son, and Spirit.

R. C. Sproul's insight on this point is profound:

> *Only once in sacred Scripture is an attribute of God elevated to the third degree. Only once is a characteristic of God mentioned three times in succession. The Bible says that God is holy, holy, holy. Not that He is merely holy, or even holy, holy. He is holy, holy, holy. The Bible never says that God is love, love, love; or mercy, mercy, mercy; or wrath, wrath, wrath; or justice, justice, justice. It does say that he is holy, holy, holy, that the whole earth is full of His glory.*[164]

They also specifically praise God for His *eternality*—the fact that He has always existed. Most of us are familiar with God's omnipresence in the sense that He is *everywhere* simultaneously. We are less familiar with His omnipresence in the sense that He is in every *moment* simultaneously. He is omnipresent throughout *time*. He is the Alpha and Omega, the beginning and the end; He **"Who was and is and is to come!"**

> [9] **Whenever the living creatures give glory and honor and thanks to Him who sits on the throne, who lives forever and ever,** [10] **the twenty-four elders fall down before Him who sits on the throne and worship Him who lives forever and ever, and cast their crowns before the throne, saying:**
>
> > [11] *"You are worthy, O Lord,*
> > *To receive glory and honor and power;*
> > *For You created all things,*
> > *And by Your will they exist and were created."*

---

[164] R. C. Sproul, *The Holiness of God*, 2nd ed. (Carol Stream, Illinois: Tyndale House Publishers, 1998), 25.

We will spend considerable time in Heaven wearing out the word *"Wow."* I reckon I'll spend at least the first thousand years grabbing the person closest to me and yelling, *"Are you seeing this right now?!"* That's what's happening here as the Church and the angels and the creatures praise God together. It's not a chore. It's not a burden. It's a higher state of joy and glory than we can imagine! It's the result of God allowing us to see Him as He truly is. The best word we have for this is "awesome." Heaven is going to be, quite simply, *awesome*.

CROWNS AS REWARDS

In Scripture, three judgments occur in the end-times: the Judgment Seat of Christ, the Sheep and Goats Judgment, and the Great White Throne Judgment.

The Judgment Seat of Christ is for believers only, and it is to determine eternal rewards. Paul described it to believers this way in **2 Corinthians 5:10**:

> **. . . we must all appear before the judgment seat of Christ, that each one may receive the things *done* in the body, according to what he has done, whether good or bad.**

"Good or bad" just means "acceptable or unacceptable." Paul described this judgment in greater detail in **1 Corinthians 3:11–15**:

> **. . . no other foundation can anyone lay than that which is laid, which is Jesus Christ. Now if anyone builds on this foundation *with* gold, silver, precious stones, wood, hay, straw, each one's work will become clear; for the Day will**

declare it, because it will be revealed by fire; and the fire will test each one's work, of what sort it is. If anyone's work which he has built on *it* endures, he will receive a reward. If anyone's work is burned, he will suffer loss; but he himself will be saved, yet so as through fire.

Everything we've done in our lives will be passed through the fire. Everything we've done out of selfish motivations will be burned up. Everything we've done in sincerity for the Lord will come out the other side, and *those* are the things for which we will be rewarded.

It will be a moment of great joy for every Christian who has endeavored to live their life for Jesus and a moment of profound regret for every Christian who has wasted their life living primarily for themselves.

When will the Judgment Seat of Christ take place? Jesus said:

> *... the Son of Man will come in the glory of His Father with His angels, and then He will reward each according to his works.*
>
> —Matthew 16:27

I believe Jesus is saying that eternal rewards will be given to the Church shortly following the Rapture. And that fits with the fact that we see the 24 elders wearing *crowns* in Heaven. And I suggest the text also tells us they only *recently* received those crowns. Why do I say that? Let me explain.

Two Greek words refer to a crown. One is a *diadem*, something a king would wear. The other is a *stephanos*, something given to the victor in a competition. **V.10** refers to the latter. It refers to a *reward*, something that has been *won*. There are likely more variations of

Heavenly crowns than the Bible records, but here are the ones the Bible reveals:

- The crown of *life* for those who have endured temptation, trials, and suffering for Jesus.[165]
- The crown of *righteousness* for those who lived and longed for the coming of Jesus.[166]
- The crown of *glory* for those who discipled the Church.[167]
- The crown of *rejoicing* for those who share the Gospel.[168]

The crowns are not the actual rewards. The true rewards will include things like greater responsibility when we rule the earth with Jesus in the Millennial Kingdom, and other privileges we're currently not aware of. These crowns represent the *glory* associated with the rewards. And what do we see believers *doing* with their crowns—even those who earned them by being martyred?

. . . the twenty-four elders fall down before Him who sits on the throne and worship Him who lives forever and ever, and cast their crowns before the throne, saying:

> [11] *"You are worthy, O Lord,*
> *To receive glory and honor and power . . ."*

Apparently, when we see the Lord, our instinctive reaction will be to cast anything we have of value at His feet. The greatest reward you can receive in Heaven is having something to honor God with

---

[165] Cf. James 1:12; Revelation 2:10.
[166] Cf. 2 Timothy 4:8.
[167] Cf. 1 Peter 5:4.
[168] Cf. 1 Thessalonians 2:19.

because it's all about *Him*. This is also why I believe the elders only *recently* received their crowns—specifically, at the Judgment Seat of Christ shortly following the Rapture.

The day is coming when *we* will bow before the throne of God. And when crowns are being cast at His feet, will you have anything to offer? That moment is going to be incredible. And the rewards that Jesus will distribute will be more wonderful than we can fathom. Some believers adopt an attitude of, *"I'm not worried about rewards. As long as I get into Heaven, that's good enough for me. I don't care about crowns."* You will when they're revealed. I promise you will.

Decades before John received this revelation, the Apostle Paul was shown a vision of Heaven.[169] It's fascinating because Paul says that the Lord *forbade* him from sharing what he saw. And a few decades later, the Lord revealed why: Jesus wanted *John* to write about Heaven.

But if you read through the writings of Paul, you'll notice that his tone changes dramatically after his Heavenly experience, and he becomes even more obsessed with living for eternity. In **Philippians 1:21**, he writes:

. . . to live *is* Christ, and to die *is* gain.

Then in **Philippians 3:13–15**, he writes:

Brethren, I do not count myself to have apprehended; but one thing *I do*, forgetting those things which are behind and reaching forward to those things which are ahead, I press toward the goal for the prize of the upward call of God in

---

[169] Cf. 2 Corinthians 12:1–4.

Christ Jesus. Therefore let us, as many as are mature, have this mind; and if in anything you think otherwise, God will reveal even this to you.

Learning about Heaven and eternity is not a *distraction* to the Christian; it's *fuel* for the Christian! The exhortation is clear: Don't waste your life; spend it on Jesus.

The Sheep and Goats Judgment will determine who among those left on the earth at the end of the Great Tribulation enter the Millennial Kingdom. We'll study that when we reach **Revelation 19**.

The Great White Throne Judgment will be exclusively for nonbelievers and will take place at the end of the Millennium. We'll study that when we reach **Revelation 20**.

JESUS, THE CREATOR

Recall that, in His letter to the Laodiceans, Jesus reminds them that He is *"the beginning of the creation of God"* a.k.a. the Creator because they are buying into the idea that He *isn't* the Creator of all things. With that in mind, notice what else the 24 elders/royal priests are singing to Jesus in Heaven:

> *For You created all things,*
> *And by Your will they exist and were created.*

Heaven is not confused about who created and sustains all things.

And while we're on that subject, I want to quickly draw your attention to something every person needs to know. On the chance there's someone reading this who has never heard this before or needs to hear this again, I want you to recognize that **V.11** tells you that you exist because God *created* you. He made you because He *wanted* you to exist. You were created *by* God and *for* God. You were created to know Him and be known by Him. You were created to love Him and be loved by Him. You are not an accident or the result of chance. To paraphrase Augustine:[170]

> *"You have made us for yourself, O Lord, and our heart is restless until it rests in you."*[171]

You have a maker. And you will find the meaning of life in loving Him and being loved by Him.

JESUS SEATED AT THE RIGHT HAND OF THE FATHER

Let's talk more about the glass sea, which is like crystal.

V.10 refers to **"Him who sits on the throne, who lives forever and ever."** That's a clear reference to the *resurrected* Jesus, and it's significant that He's *sitting* on the throne because, in the Holy of Holies in the Temple, there was no throne. There was nowhere for the high priest to sit because a priest's work was never done. People were constantly sinning, so there was always a sacrifice that needed to be made—until Jesus. **Hebrews 4:14** tells us:

> **. . . we have a great High Priest who has passed through the heavens, Jesus the Son of God . . .**

Jesus was and is our high priest. And in the throne room of Heaven, He's *sitting down*. Why? Because as He said just before

---

[170] Of Hippo.

[171] Allan D. Fitzgerald, ed., *Augustine Through the Ages: An Encyclopedia* (Grand Rapids, Michigan: William B. Eerdmans Publishing Company, 1999), 228.

He died for us on the Cross, *"It is finished!"* Hebrews 10:12 says:

> **...this Man, after He had offered one sacrifice for sins forever, sat down at the right hand of God...**

When your life hits a storm, remember what Jesus is doing in Heaven right now. He's not pacing back and forth frantically; He's not yelling *"What are we gonna do?!"* at His Father; He's not anxious or stressed; He is sitting beside His Father on Heaven's throne with a perfectly calm sea of glass before them because the work is *finished*.

Jesus has it all figured out. He has orchestrated an ending where you and I emerge more blessed than we can fathom. Paul says it like this:

> **...being confident of this very thing, that He who has begun a good work in you will complete *it* until the day of Jesus Christ...**
>
> —Philippians 1:6

If you are a parent, you know that kids can read fear on your face. They can hear it in your voice and intuitively read it in your body language. I'm scared of heights but don't want my kids to be. So, when we cross the Lynn Canyon Suspension Bridge in North Vancouver, I go in the back so that I only have to hide my fear for the few moments they turn around as we cross (I smile, give a thumbs-up, and lie straight to their faces, saying something like, *"Isn't this fun?"*) because little kids look at their parents to figure out whether or not everything is OK.

And when we're in the middle of a difficult season in life, we're supposed to look at Jesus, who is the direct reflection of His Father, our Heavenly Father. They are both *sitting* on the throne. They're at peace, which tells us we should be too. Because, unlike me, they're not faking it!

Do you remember when the disciples were caught in a deadly storm on the Sea of Galilee?[172] The story *begins* with Jesus telling them how their journey will *end*. Jesus says, *"We're going to the other side."* And when the storm hits, what is Jesus doing? He's sleeping! He's at rest, not losing his mind in fear. The disciples should have followed His example and lay next to Him for a quick nap. Instead, they cry out:

Teacher, do You not care that we are perishing?

Listen to Jesus' response:

Then He arose and rebuked the wind, and said to the sea, "Peace, be still!" And the wind ceased and there was a great calm.

One way or another, in this life or the next, Jesus will calm every storm in our lives. In Heaven and in our lives now, before the throne of God, the wind ceases, and chaos gives way to peace. And after calming the storm, Jesus said to His disciples:

Why are you so fearful? How is it that you have no faith?

If your life is in a storm, look to Jesus. He is at rest, and so are all who come before His throne.

CLOSING THOUGHTS

Revelation 4 reminds us that Jesus is at the center of everything. It all revolves around Him. And that leads us to ask ourselves critical

---

[172] Cf. Mark 4:35–41.

questions: *"Is Jesus at the center of **my** life? Does **my** life revolve around Him?"*

If not, ask the Lord to show what changes you need to make to truly place Him at the center of your life.

REVELATION 5

THE TITLE DEED

In **Revelation 4**, we were raptured with John to Heaven and got a sneak preview of the awesome throne room of God. There is no break between **Revelation 4** and **5**; the former flows immediately into the latter.

In **Revelation 5**, we'll peek behind the curtain of the entire cosmos and get a glimpse of *ultimate* reality. Everything that has happened, is happening, and will happen, is related to what we'll study in this chapter. And, incredibly, I'm still *underselling* the importance of **Revelation 5**.

Among this chapter's revelations, we'll learn why there's pain and suffering in the world and why a loving God seems to allow it. Students of Scripture will find much to dig into by comparing **Revelation 4–5** with **Daniel 7:9–13**, as the events and the setting appear identical. To a lesser degree, there are also similarities to God's judgment of Israel in **Ezekiel 1–2**. We don't have room to get into those passages in this chapter, but I encourage you to do so in your own studies.

THE SCROLL

> ¹ And I saw in the right *hand* of Him who sat on the throne a scroll . . .

If your Bible doesn't use the word **"scroll,"** write it in there because it's significant.

> . . . **written inside and on the back, sealed with seven seals.**

Our scene opens with God the Father on His throne in Heaven. And in His hands is a *scroll*. Let's unpack this a bit because there's some background information we must understand, not only for this study but as followers of Jesus.

HISTORY OF THE TYPICAL TITLE DEED SCROLL

When Revelation was recorded, books and codices weren't widely used. *Scrolls* were the preferred method. They were made from paper derived from a variation of papyrus and could easily be dozens of feet long. Scrolls would be smooth on the inside (which was used for writing) and rough on the outside.

But we notice *this* scroll has writing on the **"inside and on the back."** The only type of scrolls with writing on the rough outside were contracts, wills, and title deeds. The details would be written on the inside, while the contract title (e.g., "Bob & Brenda Smith's Marriage Contract") would be written on the outside as a reference. Scrolls of such legal importance would often be sealed with seven seals.[173] Jews reading Revelation in John's day would have

---

[173] Caesars Augustus and Vespasian did this with the wills they left for their successors.

immediately understood all this from his description of the scroll. The question is, what is this scroll a deed or contract *for*? We'll get to that answer in a minute, but first, there's some more background and biblical typology you need to be aware of.

When Israel took possession of the Promised Land, God had them distribute the land among the 12 tribes. Within each tribe, the land was further distributed among families. Even back then, people would sometimes find themselves in debt and need to sell their property. However, God's laws forbade any Jew from permanently selling their portion of the Promised Land. Every fiftieth year was a year of Jubilee when all debts were canceled, and all property returned to its original owner. It was a blessing from God that kept wealth equitably distributed among His people and prevented a small group from ending up with most of the land. Consequently, anyone buying property was, essentially, renting it until the next Year of Jubilee.

Additionally, God's law preserved the right of every property owner to *buy back* their property at any time if the redemption requirements were met.[174]

When a property was sold, the title deed—including the requirements for redemption (i.e., the price and terms of buying back the property)—would be recorded and sealed in a scroll like the one John saw in Heaven.

THE TITLE DEED TO THE EARTH

I'm going to give you the punchline up front: As we unpack **Revelation 5**, I believe it will become clear that this scroll is

---

[174] Cf. Leviticus 25:23–25.

the title deed to the *earth*. And how it ended up in the hands of God the Father, unopened, in Heaven, is the story of *everything*. It is the story of the cosmos. It is the story behind every world event and all of human history. It is the story of Jesus. And it is our story.

Before Adam and Eve and the Garden of Eden, there was God—the Trinity—in Heaven. And out of a desire to share Himself and His goodness, God created a son and daughter, Adam and Eve. He placed them upon a beautifully and perfectly designed earth, in a universe that proclaimed His glory.

God gave man a special place in His creation—close enough to His glory that man could find Him but far enough not to be overwhelmed by it. As a result of this arrangement, man could have genuine free will and the choice to follow or reject His maker. In other words, God gave man sovereignty.

And He did that because for love to be real, it must be based upon a *choice*. It must be a *free-will decision*. If love is simply the result of programming, then it is meaningless. It's not real love. And God desired a relationship with His children based on real love.

And God went even further—giving Adam, His new creation, the *title deed* to the earth.[175]

This special creation of God was astonishing to the angels in Heaven. It was wondrous to them but offensive to one—the most beautiful angel in Heaven, the archangel Lucifer. He watched as God created the universe and blessed Adam and Eve, and jealousy stirred within his heart. He felt that any new creation or blessings should flow in his direction and result in him receiving greater glory. Lucifer began to share his thoughts with other angels, telling them

---

[175] Cf. Genesis 1:28.

they deserved more glory too. He stirred up a revolt against God, citing a need for equality in Heaven. He didn't desire to be *greater* than God; he said, *"I will make myself like the Most High."*[176] The pitch was, *"We should **all** be gods!"*

Lucifer's coup attempt didn't go so well. God didn't even budge from His throne. He had the archangel Michael cast Lucifer and his co-conspirators—a third of the angels[177]—out of Heaven, and they fell to the earth.[178] Today, Lucifer is most widely known as Satan, and the angels aligned with him are known as fallen angels.

Once he was on the earth, how did Satan respond? He appeared before Eve in the Garden of Eden with the same pitch he made to the angels in Heaven, essentially saying: *"You deserve to be a god too! Take and eat the fruit, and you will be like God."* And utilizing her God-given free will, Eve took and ate the fruit. When Adam found out, he didn't cry out to God in repentance or for help; he joined Eve in her sin.

The Bible says, **"All we like sheep have gone astray; we have turned, every one, to his own way."**[179] The point is this: what Adam and Eve did, we too have done in our own way, over and over again. We would have done the same thing if placed in their situation.

When we (the human race) sinned in the Garden, something catastrophic happened. Sin entered the world as, at that moment, we rejected God in favor of ourselves. There are only two kingdoms—God's and Satan's. And when we rejected God's rule and reign in

---

[176] Isaiah 14:14.

[177] Cf. Revelation 12:4.

[178] Cf. Revelation 12:7–9.

[179] Isaiah 53:6.

favor of ruling ourselves, we chose to be ruled by Satan. At that moment, we handed *Satan* the title deed to the earth.[180]

God restrained Satan's power on the earth to a certain degree but make no mistake; Satan held the title deed.

In **Ephesians 2:2**, Satan is called **"the prince of the power of the air."**

In **John 12:31**, Jesus calls him *"the ruler of this world."*

In **1 John 5:19**, we are told, **"the whole world lies *under the sway of* the wicked one."**

And in **2 Corinthians 4:4**, Paul calls him **"the god of this age."**

During the Temptation of Christ, Satan takes Jesus to a place where all the nations of the earth are visible and says, *"All these things I will give You if You will fall down and worship me."*[181] Jesus doesn't reply, *"Don't be ridiculous! You don't own the earth; I do!"* Jesus does not dispute Satan's claim to have dominion over the nations of the earth.

This is not some fringe theological theory. Jesus, John, and Paul all testify to Satan's rule over the earth—even after the death and resurrection of Jesus.

When we rebelled against God and fell into sin, handing Satan the title deed to the earth, whose fault was it? Was it Satan's fault? No, we had free will. Was it God's fault? No, we had free will. We

---

[180] Cf. Romans 5:14.
[181] Matthew 4:9.

chose to disobey Him. We chose to reject His lordship over our lives. *We chose.*

And when all that happened, Eden, which was God's gift of a perfect earth; our humanity; and the universe were all torn apart. Disease, anger, bitterness, pain, selfishness, and everything wrong with the world today came flooding into reality as the earth became Satan's domain. It wasn't long before Adam and Eve endured the pain of their two sons occupying both sides of the first murder in human history. In other words, it didn't take long for things to start unraveling. As lives and families and society crumbled around us, did we repent? Did we turn back to the Lord? No. Instead, we came up with accusations against God that we repeat to this day:

"How can God be good when there's so much pain and suffering in the world?"

"How can God be loving when my life is filled with so much darkness?"

"If God cares, why is there senseless violence across the earth?"

Humanity rejected its Creator. And to this day, we ignore His Word and reject His lordship while blaming Him for everything *we've* done. We blame Him for the state of the world ruined by the work of *our* hands. It's *our* fault! May God forgive us for our blasphemy.

Instead, we should ask:

*"How can **humanity** be good when there's so much pain and suffering in the world?"*

*"How can **humanity** be loving when my life is filled with so much darkness?"*

*"If **humanity** cares, why is there senseless violence across the earth?"*

*"How can **humanity** be good when he rapes and murders, abuses, enslaves, and destroys?"*

How can humanity be good? We *can't!* Because we *aren't!* The psalmist wrote truthfully:

> **. . . They have done abominable works,**
> **There is none who does good.**
> **The Lord looks down from heaven upon the children of men,**
> **To see if there are any who understand, who seek God.**
> **They have all turned aside,**
> **They have together become corrupt;**
> ***There is** **none who does good,**
> **No, not one.**
>
> —Psalm 14:1–3

Humanity *fell*. We severed our relationship with the Lord. We chose our own way, and we can imagine Satan smugly saying to the Lord, *"What a surprise, they didn't choose You! It's over. What will You do with Your creation now, all-loving God?"*

Satan knows that God is perfect and without sin. He's *holy*. And because of that, God is morally obligated to judge sin. Just as you and I are morally bound to judge the murderers in our society, God is qualified and obligated by His very nature to judge *all* sin. It's *all* as unacceptable to Him as the murder of an innocent is to us. And just as we have an inherent need and hunger for justice, so does He.

Satan must have thought, *"Checkmate. God must judge their sin. And the only appropriate punishment for rejecting the God of the*

Universe is eternal death." No angel in Heaven could have imagined what God would do next.

Isaiah 53:6 *begins* with the words we read earlier:

All we like sheep have gone astray;
We have turned, every one, to his own way; . . .

But in the most incredible plot twist that will ever exist, **Isaiah 53:6** *ends* with these words:

And the Lord has laid on Him the iniquity of us all.

Jesus, the perfect, sinless, innocent, holy Son of God, came to the earth as a man to die in the place of all mankind. Instead of God's righteous wrath and judgment falling upon us, as we deserve, the Father stored it all up and poured it out upon *Jesus*, who willingly accepted it.

Jesus died for us. He settled the debt we could never repay. He redeemed us. He purchased us. And when He did that, He also bought back the earth that we had sold to Satan. He paid the redemption price and took back the *title deed* as was His right as the original owner.

During the three days He was in the grave, Jesus descended into Hades ("Sheol" in Hebrew), where a host of Old Testament saints were waiting in the place the Hebrews called **"Abraham's bosom."**[182] As sinners unable to enter the holy presence of God, they had been waiting for atonement to be made for their sins.[183] Jesus showed up with *"the keys to death and Hades"*[184] and said,

---

[182] Luke 16:22.

[183] Cf. Luke 16:19–31; Ephesians 4:8–10.

[184] Revelation 1:18.

"Tetelestai![185] *It is finished! Your sin debt has been paid in full, and Heaven is waiting."*

Jesus returned to the earth in His resurrected body for forty days before His Ascension.[186] And we can only imagine the glorious pandemonium that ensued in Heaven when Jesus returned with the title deed to the earth, which He handed to His Father as He sat down at His right hand on the throne because the work was *finished*.

Since the Resurrection, God has held the title deed to the earth. But He has not yet *opened it* and reclaimed the earth. Why? Because certain things will happen when He does. For example, He will have to judge the sin that is taking place in His house, and that will mean devastating consequences for those who reject the Lord. **Second Peter 3:9** tells us:

> **The Lord is not slack concerning *His* promise, as some count slackness, but is longsuffering toward us, not willing that any should perish but that all should come to repentance.**

God is being gracious by giving people more time to repent and be adopted into His family. When the Lord reclaims the earth, the window of opportunity will close quickly before closing *completely*. Jesus has authority over the nations, but He has not yet *exercised* that authority.

Jesus has paid for everyone's sins, but that payment is only valid for your life if you accept it. That's what we're doing when we receive Jesus as our Savior. We're saying, *"Jesus died in my place and made*

---

[185] Cf. John 19:30.
[186] Cf. Acts 1:3.

the full payment for my sins. He traded His life for mine, so my life now belongs to Him."

Those who reject Jesus' sacrifice and payment on their behalf are choosing to reject God Himself. And God will ultimately give them what they want—an eternity apart from Him. It is a deadly serious thing to look at Jesus, who was tortured and crucified on our behalf, and say, *"No, thanks."*

And when Jesus begins to judge those who have rejected Him, He doesn't want even a drop of His wrath falling on those who are His. So, He will *remove* those who are His, in the Rapture.

The Father, in His mercy, has been waiting. Jesus has been waiting. The Holy Spirit has been waiting. All of Heaven has been waiting. The martyrs from across the centuries have been waiting. The universe has been waiting.[187] And we have been waiting for the moment when the Father hands the title deed, the scroll, to Jesus and says, *"It's time."*

And here in **Revelation 5**, *it's time.*

² Then I saw a strong angel proclaiming with a loud voice, *"Who is worthy to open the scroll and to loose its seals?"*

Not, *"Who is willing?"* but *"Who is worthy?"* There have always been men and groups *willing* to rule the earth. Hitler, Genghis Khan, Alexander the Great, Napoleon, Google, the United Nations, and the WEF were or are *willing*. But none are *worthy*.

To redeem a title deed, a person had to meet four criteria:

1. They had to be the original owner of the property or their close relative who, if permitted by the original owner,

---

[187] Cf. Romans 8:22.

could function as a *kinsman-redeemer*. [188, 189] Jesus is the Son of God *and* the Son of Man. He's fully God and fully Man. He is the original owner *and* a kinsman of Adam.

2. They had to be able to meet the redemption requirements of the title deed. As the only man to ever live a perfect, sinless life, Jesus was the only one who could offer Himself as an acceptable sacrifice in our place.

3. They had to be willing to meet the requirements. Nobody forced Jesus to lay down His life for us; He chose to offer it willingly.[190]

4. They had to assume all the obligations of the beneficiary. Jesus is ready, willing, able, and worthy to rule the earth in righteousness.

V.3 tells us that a *search* was conducted to see if any person who has ever lived was both worthy and able to redeem the earth's title deed.

³ . . . no one in heaven or on the earth or under the earth was able to open the scroll, or to look at it.

---

[188] Cf. Leviticus 25:25.

[189] To learn more about kinsman redeemers, I recommend that you investigate two sections of Scripture and look for parallels to the ministry of Jesus: (1) In Jeremiah 32, the Lord tells Jeremiah to act out prophecy by serving as the kinsman redeemer for a piece of property owned by his cousin. (2) The Book of Ruth is a prophetic picture of God's plan for Israel and the Church in the end-times, and I'll give you the keys to unlock it: Boaz represents Jesus; Naomi represents Israel; and Ruth represents the Church. This little book is absolutely packed with insights into Revelation and eschatology.

[190] Cf. John 10:18.

Some Bibles more accurately translate the phrase as **"no man in heaven"** rather than **"no one in heaven."** I point that out because at this moment in time, as this scene is unfolding in Heaven, there are men **"in heaven," "on the earth,"** and **"under the earth."** And we know they're all *alive* because, in **V.13**, they're all going to *speak*.

- **"In heaven"** refers to every believer who has ever lived, including those taken in the Rapture.
- **"On the earth"** refers to nonbelievers who have not been taken in the Rapture. Some of them will become believers in the Tribulation.
- **"Under the earth"** refers to nonbelievers who have died and are in Hades, awaiting the Great White Throne Judgment.[191]

I share those details because we must understand that every person who has ever lived is still alive right now, somewhere.

V.3 described a *dire* situation, with no one being found worthy to redeem the earth's title deed. And John responds appropriately:

⁴ So I wept much, because no one was found worthy to open and read the scroll, or to look at it.

When it says that John **"wept much,"** it means that he was *convulsing* with tears. He was wailing in emotional agony. If I think of this cinematically, I envision a montage that changes every second and reveals one scene after another from our fallen world—wars, ethnic cleansing, slavery, child soldiers, famine, murder, abuse, and on and on and on. John is so deeply grieved because if there is no

---

[191] Cf. Revelation 20:11–15.

one worthy to open the scroll, it means the world will stay as it is—broken and getting worse and worse until it destroys itself. John is overwhelmed by the reality that there is no hope for our world. We cannot fix it.

That's the truth of how hopeless our lives would be without Jesus. We were all born into a hopeless situation from which we could not save ourselves. Our sin had doomed us. We were a lost cause. To grasp even a small part of this truth, apart from Jesus, is to investigate the deepest despair a person can know.

> ⁵ **But one of the elders said to me,** *"Do not weep. Behold, the Lion of the tribe of Judah, the Root of David, has prevailed to open the scroll and to loose its seven seals."*

Who is *"the Lion of Judah"?*[192] Who is *"the Root of David"?*[193] We know His name. It's *Jesus*. The one who is both the son of man *and* the son of God. When there was no other way, there was no hope, when I was irredeemable and in debt so deep that I could never get out; when all was lost, *"Behold, the Lion of the tribe of Judah."* Take that in for a moment. Meditate on it. Thank God for it.

Two more brief notes:

1. Paradoxically, Jesus is the *Root* of David. In other words, David came from Jesus. And yet, Jesus also came from the family line of David.

2. Twenty-four titles were used for Jesus in **Revelation 1–3**. These titles apply to Him in His present role, as He is revealed to the Church. Starting here in **Revelation 5**,

---

[192] Cf. Genesis 49:8–10.

[193] Cf. Isaiah 11:1, 10.

we'll see primarily *Jewish* titles used for Jesus. That's because *ethnic Israel* is about to take center stage in our story as the climax of human history approaches.

It will significantly expand your understanding of not only Revelation but the whole Bible if you recognize that the Scriptures describe different promises, destinies, and roles for ethnic Israel and the Church in the end-times. After the Church has been raptured, one of the key items on the agenda becomes the unfilled earthly promises God has made to ethnic Israel. And we're going to see them fulfilled in later chapters.

⁶ And I looked, and behold, in the midst of the throne and of the four living creatures, and in the midst of the elders, stood a Lamb as though it had been slain, having seven horns and seven eyes, which are the seven Spirits of God sent out into all the earth.

This is how Jesus appears to John, so let's see if we can break this down and understand it better.

In the previous chapter, we talked at length about **"the throne," "the four living creatures,"** and **"the elders."** Regarding the **"seven horns,"** we find that throughout the Bible, horns symbolize power[194] and honor.[195] We also know that the number seven is often connected to wholeness and holiness in the Bible. When you put all that together, the point seems to be that the Jesus John saw had total and perfect *power* and *honor*.

---

[194] Cf. Deuteronomy 33:17; 1 Kings 22:11; Zechariah 1:18; Psalm 75:4.

[195] Cf. 1 Samuel 2:1–10; Psalm 89:17, 24; Psalm 112:9–10, 148:14.

As far as the **"seven eyes"** go, the same verse tells us that they **"are the seven Spirits of God sent out into all the earth."** You will no doubt recall that the **"seven Spirits of God"** is a reference to the Holy Spirit. John tells us that as He looks at Jesus, the Holy Spirit is clearly upon Him.

JESUS' PERMANENT SCARS

The description of Jesus as the Lamb is not unusual. What *is* remarkable is that His appearance is described as **"a Lamb as though it had been slain."** I would wager that in almost all the paintings you've seen of the resurrected Jesus, He has scars on His hands. But we forget those weren't the only scars the Cross left Him with. Notice that this prophetic description is found back in **Isaiah 52:14**:

> **Just as many were astonished at you,**
> **So His visage** [Jesus' external appearance] **was marred more**
> **than any man,**
> **And His form more than the sons of men...**

His crucifixion experience—the beatings, the pulling out of His beard, the scourging—so disfigured Jesus that people couldn't bear to look at Him. It was that disturbing to behold. He didn't just suffer physically; the emotional, psychological, and spiritual torment was even worse. The fear and stress of knowing what was coming caused Jesus to sweat blood from His face in the Garden of Gethsemane.[196] And in His darkest, most trying hour, He endured the anguish of being separated from His Heavenly Father for the

---

[196] Cf. Luke 22:44.

first time in eternity. On the Cross, Jesus was *"forsaken"*[197] by His Heavenly Father and the people He had created to know, love, and enjoy Him.

We have no idea—no concept—of what Jesus went through for us. *Nobody* has been scarred as Jesus was scarred for us. When represented in art, Jesus usually still has a beautiful face and an untouched body, but that's not what happened. All those scars are still with Him, in a way that was still discernable to John.

Do you remember when, after the Resurrection, Mary goes to the Garden and encounters Jesus but doesn't recognize Him? She thinks He's the gardener[198] until she hears Him speak her name. He then appears to the disciples while they are fishing. And when they find Him cooking on the beach, John's Gospel records:

> **Jesus said to them, *"Come and eat breakfast."* Yet none of the disciples dared ask Him, *"Who are You?"*—knowing that it was the Lord.**
>
> **—John 21:12**

They knew in their spirits that this man was Jesus, but He didn't look like Jesus. The experience of the Cross left Jesus changed forever, scarred forever. It's been said that the only man-made things in Heaven will be the scars on Jesus. That's why when John sees Jesus in Heaven, He appears as **"a Lamb as though it had been slain."**

Remember that Heaven is a place with many more dimensions than our current reality, so you should not walk away from this text with the impression that Jesus will eternally appear grotesque,

---

[197] Matthew 27:46; Mark 15:34.
[198] Cf. John 20:15.

like a lamb that has been killed. Revelation also describes His appearance as a lion, a man dressed in white, and several other things. Apparently, the dimensionality of Heaven allows for all of that, possibly simultaneously.

What we should take from this is that Jesus' work on the Cross left scars that will remain with Him forever. And that work was so important, so central to everything, that we will be reminded of it every time we look at Him. The Cross *defines* Jesus in a profound, eternal way.

In **V.5**, one of the elders describes Jesus to John as ***"the Lion of the tribe of Judah,"*** which contrasts with His description in the next verse, where He appears as **"a Lamb."** Jesus is the Lion *and* the Lamb, which is key to understanding Him and His Kingdom.

The four Gospels present Jesus' First Coming, His Incarnation when He came to the earth as the Lamb of God—the sacrifice made in our place—offering the hope of salvation to all humanity. Revelation presents Jesus' Second Coming, when He will return to the earth as the Lion of Judah—the conquering king who will rule the nations and judge sin. It's the same Jesus, coming at two different times in two different roles. And we would be wise to welcome Him as the *Lamb* because He is coming again as the *Lion*.

Think of it this way. If you were to come to my house any night around seven o'clock and knock on my door, I'd let you in if I'd invited you or liked you. I'd bring you into our kitchen or living room where you'd see my whole family, including my children. We'd make some coffee, sit down and chat for a bit, and then you'd be on your way.

Now imagine what would happen if you tried to break into my house at three o'clock in the morning and I caught you climbing in the window of one of my kids' bedrooms. Do you think you'd get the same welcome as if you'd stopped by at seven o'clock in the evening and knocked on the front door? *Nope.* You're going to be dealing with a very different Jeff, in a very different state of mind! The version of me you get depends on when and how you approach me. Similarly, Jesus can be approached as the Lamb of God because we're in the age of grace. But it won't last forever. The Lion of Judah is coming.

> **⁷ Then He came and took the scroll out of the right hand of Him who sat on the throne.**

When Jesus is given this title deed by His Father, it's so that He—the only one who is willing, worthy, and able—can *open* it. And when He does, things are going to begin changing dramatically. **Hebrews 2:8** says:

> **. . . in that He** [the Father] **put all in subjection under him** [Jesus]**, He** [the Father] **left nothing** *that is* **not put under him** [Jesus]**. But now we do not yet see all things put under him.**

That verse sums up the present situation: Jesus has conquered death on the Cross; the ending is written in stone, and there's nothing Satan can do about it; the title deed to the earth is in the hands of God the Father; Jesus has authority over all things, but He has not yet fully *exercised* that authority by opening the scroll and laying claim to the earth.

I don't need to tell you that the world is crazy right now. Evil things are called "good," and good things are called "evil."[199] When I

---

[199] Cf. Isaiah 5:20.

preached on this, I listed several examples, but I've learned that our world is sliding downhill so fast that by the time you read this, there will be even more egregious examples of what I'm talking about!

As we discussed earlier, current affairs can drive you crazy if you don't remember that God's Word tells us that the world is under Satan's influence and power. Then it all suddenly makes sense. But it's not going to be that way forever. There's a change comin', and it begins in **Revelation 5:7**.

"WORTHY IS THE LAMB"

In **V.8**, we see Heaven's response as Jesus is handed the title deed by His Father:

> **⁸ Now when He had taken the scroll, the four living creatures and the twenty-four elders fell down before the Lamb, each having a harp, and golden bowls full of incense, which are the prayers of the saints.**

All our prayers make it to the throne room of God. Some of them are answered, but some are *stored* because there are things we long and ache for that can only occur *after* Jesus reclaims the earth.

> ⁹ *And they sang a new song, saying:*
>   *"You are worthy to take the scroll,*
>   *And to open its seals;*
>   *For You were slain,*
>   *And have redeemed us to God by Your blood*
>
>   *Out of every tribe and tongue and people and nation,*
> ¹⁰ *And have made us kings and priests to our God;*
>   *And we shall reign on the earth."*

In the previous chapter, we learned that these 24 elders are the royal priesthood of believers, consisting of Old Testament saints and the Church. And at this moment, they're in *Heaven*. But they're singing about their future destiny—reigning with Jesus **"on the earth."**

I'd be remiss if I didn't point out that the first thing the elders sing about in Heaven is the *blood of Jesus*. In much of the modern Church, our savior's blood is viewed as something that makes first-time guests uncomfortable and, therefore, shouldn't be sung about. Even speaking about it seems to give many pastors pause, as it demands we address the reality of sin—another topic that may cause first-time guests to squirm.

And yet it's the *focus* of our *celebration* in Heaven! We'll be singing about Jesus, the Lamb who was slain and who has redeemed us by His blood. Decades ago, the late J. Vernon McGee candidly observed:

> *Down here, many denominational churches are taking the blood from their hymnbooks.... And I guess maybe that's the reason the Lord's not gonna embarrass them by taking them to Heaven, because they'd have to sing about the blood.*[200]

May we never be embarrassed or ashamed of the blood our Savior shed. We'll be singing about it in Heaven, so let's sing and speak of it with joy and gratitude on the earth now.

---

[200] J. Vernon McGee, "Revelation 5:7–10" (Blue Letter Bible Audio), https://www.blueletterbible.org/audio_video/popPlayer.cfm?id=9316&rel=mcgee_j_vernon/english/rev.

THE DIVINE COUNCIL

While we're here, I need to show you one more thing that we don't have room to fully explore in this book. I encourage you to explore the role of *the Divine Council* on your own; I'm convinced that you will find further study beneficial.

Notice the *tenses* in **V.10**—the royal priesthood of believers is in place, and we discussed them ministering to the Lord in Heaven in the previous chapter. But it also says we've been made *"kings"* at this point. That speaks of *ruling*. And that's interesting because the *tense* used for reigning with Jesus on the earth is *future* in **V.10**. Here's my point—our being *"kings"* and reigning with Jesus is not something that only happens on the earth during the Millennial Kingdom. It's a status we're given and will hold *in Heaven*.

That's because we are destined to join Jesus on what's known as "The Divine Council." It's a council God has assembled in the heavenly realms that consists of Himself and supernatural beings He has created. And the Lord has chosen to involve these beings in His affairs. That's the oversimplified explanation, and you can find a couple of the most explicit references to this in **Job 1:6–12** and **Daniel 4:17**.

Our destiny is to join Jesus on the Divine Council. This is what Paul is referring to when he writes in **1 Corinthians 6:2**:

> **Do you not know that the saints will judge the world?...**

And then, in the next verse (**1 Corinthians 6:3**), he adds:

> **Do you not know that we shall judge angels?...**

We are destined to join Jesus on the Divine Council, where we will participate in the judgment of the natural and supernatural worlds. In fact, the Divine Council is almost certainly the context in which **Revelation 5** is taking place.

If you'd like to learn more about this view, its most ardent contemporary supporter was the late Dr. Michael S. Heiser, who wrote about it extensively in his book, *The Unseen Realm*.[201] And while I don't agree with all his conclusions, I think they are compelling and worth exploring.

> **[11] Then I looked, and I heard the voice of many angels around the throne, the living creatures, and the elders; and the number of them was ten thousand times ten thousand, and thousands of thousands, ...**

The idea is that there is a *countless* number of angels.

> **... [12] saying with a loud voice:**
> *"Worthy is the Lamb who was slain*
> *To receive power and riches and wisdom,*
> *And strength and honor and glory and blessing!"*

When this happens, something *else* happens that is very interesting. We've just read what's happening in *Heaven;* now, check out **V.13**:

> **[13] And every creature which is in heaven and on the earth and under the earth and such as are in the sea, and all that are in them, I heard saying:**
> *"Blessing and honor and glory and power*
> *Be to Him who sits on the throne,*
> *And to the Lamb, forever and ever!"*

---

[201] Michael S. Heiser, *The Unseen Realm* (Bellingham, WA: Lexham Press, 2015), 354–357.

The Greek word translated here as "creature"[202] is used in Scripture to refer to all peoples and animals. As best we can understand, it seems that at the moment Jesus takes the title deed to the earth, there is an *eruption* across all dimensions, as every person in Hades, Heaven, and on the earth is *compelled* to join with every creature on the earth in blessing the Lord.

If I'm correct in my understanding, one can imagine the *shock* of unbelievers on the earth as they hear themselves involuntarily speak these words of blessing to the Lord!

¹⁴ Then the four living creatures said, *"Amen!"* And the twenty-four elders fell down and worshiped Him who lives forever and ever.

As we close **Revelation 5**, Heaven is exploding with worship for Jesus, the Lion and the Lamb, who is about to open the seven seals on the scroll and reclaim the earth.

CLOSING THOUGHTS

I can tell you one thing about the Tribulation with absolute certainty: you don't want to be on the earth when it happens! Right now, you can encounter Jesus as the Lamb, embrace Him, become part of His family, receive Him as your savior, and begin a life with Him that will last into eternity. Believe me when I say you don't want to wait until the Tribulation to give your life to Jesus. Do it *now*.

I think what God's Word has shown us in this chapter should help us understand the seriousness of **James 4:4**, which we referenced when studying the letter to the Laodiceans:

---

[202] Ktisma.

> **Adulterers and adulteresses! Do you not know that friendship with the world is enmity with God? Whoever therefore wants to be a friend of the world makes himself an enemy of God.**

We need to understand that the Bible tells us that the world's system is *Satan's* system. If we love the world, we're saying, *"I'm actually OK with earth's current management."* And that means what we really love is the kingdom of Satan.

If, however, you love the Kingdom of God, you will *ache* for the world. You will mourn over her brokenness. You will see tragedy, inequality, and injustice, and your spirit will cry, *"Come quickly, Lord Jesus!"*

We're citizens of Heaven. We're pilgrims and sojourners on the earth. We are in the world but not of the world because we love and belong to the Kingdom of God.

The Cross left Jesus permanently changed. He's the Lamb that was slain... *forever*. And the Cross leaves *us* permanently changed too. We are called to live our lives, every day, as though we have died to ourselves—because we have. Paul said it like this:

> **I have been crucified with Christ; it is no longer I who live, but Christ lives in me; and the *life* which I now live in the flesh I live by faith in the Son of God, who loved me and gave Himself for me.**
>
> —Galatians 2:20

The version of me who lives for me is *dead*. I live for Jesus now. How are you doing with that?

> **...we know that the whole creation groans and labors with birth pangs together until now. Not only *that*, but we**

also who have the firstfruits of the Spirit, even we ourselves groan within ourselves, eagerly waiting for the adoption, the redemption of our body.

—Romans 8:22–23

The day of the Lion and the Lamb is almost here. And it won't be long before the earth is back in the hands of the only one worthy to rule it—Jesus Christ.

Before you close this book for now or move on to the next chapter, would you take a moment to pray and bless the Lord—to celebrate and thank Him for His precious blood and what it has accomplished in your life?

REVELATION 6

THE FIRST SIX SEALS

In **Revelation 5**, we looked at the story of *everything*. We learned there is a title deed to the earth, and although God possesses it, Satan is currently managing the earth. But the day is coming when Jesus will reclaim it by opening that title deed—the scroll with seven seals. And when He does, the wrath of God will begin to be poured out upon the earth.

But we are not fearful because we know that those who belong to Jesus won't be on the earth at that time. The royal priesthood of believers will be in Heaven, casting their crowns at His feet in worship—even *before* He receives the scroll from His Heavenly Father.

ISAIAH 61 AND THE DAY OF VENGEANCE

One day during His earthly ministry, Jesus went into the synagogue in His hometown of Nazareth and read from **Isaiah 61**.[203] That passage is a prophecy about Messiah, and it reads:

---

[203] Cf. Luke 4:16–30.

The Spirit of the Lord is upon Me,
Because He has anointed Me
To preach the gospel to the poor;
He has sent Me to heal the brokenhearted,
To proclaim liberty to the captives
And recovery of sight to the blind,
To set at liberty those who are oppressed;
To proclaim the acceptable year of the Lord

Luke's Gospel tells us:

Then He closed the book, and gave *it* **back to the attendant and sat down. And the eyes of all who were in the synagogue were fixed on Him. And He began to say to them,** *"Today this Scripture is fulfilled in your hearing."*

—Luke 4:18–21

I imagine the room fell silent after Jesus finished reading because everyone present would have known that this was a prophecy about Messiah and understood that in saying, *"Today this Scripture is fulfilled in your hearing,"* Jesus was claiming that *He* was its fulfillment. He was claiming to be Messiah!

Not only are the verses Jesus quoted of note, but so is the fact that he stopped quoting *before* the end of the prophecy—something else everyone would have noticed. Look at what comes next in **Isaiah 61**:

. . . And the day of vengeance of our God . . .

Jesus' First Coming saw Him herald *"the acceptable year of the Lord"*—the dawning of the age of grace. Jesus didn't read that next line of **Isaiah 61** because it was not intended to be fulfilled during the Incarnation. **"The day of vengeance"** is *yet to come.* And as surely as Jesus fulfilled the first part of **Isaiah 61**, He will fulfill the rest of **Isaiah 61**. That latter program will begin when Jesus receives the scroll, as described in **Revelation 5:7**.

THE PURPOSE OF THE TRIBULATION

The Tribulation will serve three purposes:

1. **A last call to unbelievers**

   If the overwhelming evidence of the signs and wonders of the Tribulation doesn't cause a person to turn to Jesus, then nothing will. It will be the final invitation to join God's family, and He will make it *loud*.

   Now, I must mention something because some will hear this and think, "*Well then, I'll just wait until the Tribulation to get saved and do what I want until then.*" Let me be blunt. If you can't bring yourself to follow Jesus now when there's no real persecution, what in the world makes you think you'll have the courage to begin following Him at a time when it will cost you your earthly life? Don't fool yourself.

2. **To wake up ethnic Israel**

   During the Tribulation, Israel will finally recognize Jesus as her savior, her long-awaited Messiah. But to bring her to that point, God will have to break her by leading her to the point of desperation through persecution (as He did more than once in the Old Testament). In that moment of desperation, Israel will cry to the Lord for deliverance, and He will deliver her.

3. **To complete the Kingdom**
    When the first two purposes are accomplished, everyone who is part of the family of God will be united to enjoy eternity in the glory of God's presence.

UNDERSTANDING GOD'S WRATH

When you preach on God's wrath, you quickly become aware of how uncomfortable many people are with the concept. Many struggle to reconcile the idea of a wrathful God also being a loving God. This prompts questions like, *"How can wrath be poured out by a loving God?"* Let's see if we can shed some light on this.

I believe the answer can be found within each of us. My wife and I watched a TV show called *"Behind the Mask."* It's a documentary series about people who are mascots, and it's much more interesting than it sounds. One of the featured characters on the show was a guy in his twenties with reasonably advanced autism. He suffered from panic attacks and crippling anxiety because of the brutal teasing and abuse he suffered at school as a child.

As I was watching, I got choked up and angry. Because all I could think was, *"Why was nobody there to punch those bullies in the face? Why was nobody there to stand up for that guy when he was a kid?"* He didn't need somebody to share an encouraging word after the abuse. He needed somebody to step in and stop it. He needed someone to say, *"This is not right!"* and use force to stop it. And because nobody did that for him, he grew up believing he was not worth defending or fighting for.

There are many situations I've heard of that make me wish I could have been there to "lay hands" on someone because some people will only stop doing evil when someone stronger than them forces them to.

We have no idea how many people are literally in bondage around the world, how many people are in emotional bondage, and how many people feel worthless because there is nobody to fight for them. Many of those people pray *every day* for someone who cares about what is right to show up—someone who can and will pour out *wrath* on those who are abusing them. Are they wrong for wanting that? We know they're not. Because deep down, we all recognize the desperate need for *righteous wrath* on the earth.

The desire for justice that we feel is there because we were created Imago Dei (i.e., in the image of God).[204] We've worked hard to mess it up, but there are still things built into the fabric of our being that reflect who God is. And one of those things is an innate desire for justice.

Having children dramatically changes your understanding of justice. If anyone were to seriously harm or kill one of my children, their only hope would be getting to jail before I get to them. Because as a parent, you don't tolerate people messing with your children. We get that from God. That's how He feels about His children, you and me.

Even while He was on the earth as the Lamb, Jesus felt this way about His brothers and sisters. In **Matthew 18:6–7**, He said:

> *... whoever causes one of these little ones who believe in Me to sin, it would be better for him if a millstone were hung around his neck, and he were drowned in the depth of the sea. Woe to the world because of offenses! For offenses must come, but woe to that man by whom the offense comes!*

Jesus feels *strongly* about His family.

We all recognize the need for a strong hand to bring justice to the earth. Every prayer from every person who has been abused,

---

[204] Cf. Genesis 1:26.

tormented, or enslaved has been heard by God. He has listened to their cries across millennia and *always* planned to respond. And when He finally does, it's what we call "wrath."

As unpleasant as this may be, let's explore a scenario in which the person who means the most to you is the victim of a brutal crime in which they are kidnapped, abused, and then murdered. Fortunately, the perpetrator is arrested, charged, and found guilty based on overwhelming evidence. Now, imagine being in the courtroom for their sentencing and hearing the judge say:

"This man is clearly guilty. But I believe in love. And because I'm a man of peace, I can't sentence this man to receive wrath. So, I'm going to let him go. We all have our faults and punishing this man would just perpetuate the destructive cycle of negativity."

Would you consider that judge to be acting in love? Would you call his actions "loving"? Of course not. Because there's a connection between love and justice. And when wrath is poured out to bring about justice, it's a right expression of *love* toward those who have been wronged.

Deep down, we all understand that righteous wrath is necessary to bring about justice. We all believe there are wrongs that need to be righted, even by force. We all recognize that there is a necessary time and place for wrath. And Jesus agrees.

Most people are OK with the idea of Hitler receiving God's wrath, but they have a hard time with the idea of someone they consider a good person potentially receiving God's wrath simply because they did not choose to follow Jesus.

Here's the problem with that line of thinking: When we talk about rejecting the invitation of the God who created you, loved you, and died for you, we are talking about the most severe crime any human being could ever commit. A *lifetime* of charitable deeds cannot make up for the blasphemy of rejecting Jesus.

And when we imply that "good" people shouldn't receive God's wrath for "only" rejecting Jesus, what we're really saying is, *"Rejecting Jesus isn't that big of a deal."* But it is. He's *God!* Heaven forbid we devalue the infinite worth of Jesus by adopting such views.

THE COMING "DAY OF THE LORD"

You also need to be aware that the phrase **"the Day of the Lord"** is used about 35 times in the Bible to describe the coming time when God will judge the earth and those who have rejected Him. It includes the Great Tribulation, breaks for the thousand years of the Millennial Kingdom, resumes for the final satanic rebellion, and concludes with the Great White Throne Judgment.

I believe it makes the most sense to view the first four seal judgments as preliminary (for lack of a better term) and unfolding over the first three and a half years of the seven-year Tribulation.[205]

It seems that the fifth seal is opened around the halfway point of the Tribulation, followed shortly by the sixth seal at the beginning of the second half of the Tribulation.

That sixth seal appears to mark the beginning of the *Great* Tribulation and the Day of the Lord. I say that because **Joel 2:31** prophesies:

> **The sun shall be turned into darkness,
> And the moon into blood,** ...

That will happen with the sixth seal judgment in **Revelation 6:12** ...

---

[205] See Appendix B to learn how we know the Tribulation will last for seven years.

... Before the coming of the great and awesome day of the Lord.

And then, in **V.17**, we still hear those on the earth cry out *"the great day of His wrath has come."*

As we enter the text in **Revelation 6**, the Church is in Heaven. Those left on the earth have, thus far, rejected Jesus. It's important to realize that Jesus decrees every judgment that unfolds in **Revelation 6–19**. Even Satan and his demons will be used as instruments of judgment by God for His own higher purposes. None of these horrors occur outside God's sovereign control and will. They are His righteous judgments upon the earth that has rejected Him.

First up are the famed Four Horsemen of the Apocalypse.

THE FIRST HORSEMAN/SEAL: ANTICHRIST

> **¹ Now I saw when the Lamb opened one of the seals; and I heard one of the four living creatures saying with a voice like thunder, *"Come and see."* ² And I looked, and behold, a white horse. He who sat on it had a bow; and a crown was given to him, and he went out conquering and to conquer.**

I'll do the big reveal upfront, and then we'll investigate the details: the first horseman is *antichrist*.

Over 30 different titles are used in Scripture for antichrist (e.g., **"man of sin"** and **"son of perdition"** in **2 Thessalonians 2:3**), but the term "antichrist" is only used in John's epistles[206] to describe a *spirit*. Contrary to what you may have heard, "antichrist" doesn't

---

[206] Cf. 1 John 2:18, 22, 4:3; 2 John 1:7.

mean *"against Christ"*; it means *"instead of Christ"* or *"in place of Christ."* It describes the spirit that desires the praise and glory that belongs to Jesus, and we've seen it in men across history, such as the ten Caesars who persecuted the Early Church and claimed divinity, Hitler, Mao, and far too many others.

The man we think of when we refer to "antichrist" will be the ultimate embodiment of this spirit, but it is not his title. However, the term "antichrist" is heavily ingrained in Church culture, so I'll refer to him by that title to avoid confusion.

The two most common questions about antichrist are:

- When will he appear?
- Who is he?

Regarding the first question, he's making his entrance right here in **Revelation 6:2**. Regarding the second question, we need to put something to rest. The Bible specifically tells us that antichrist will not be revealed until *after* the Church has been raptured. Paul cautioned the Thessalonian believers:

> **Let no one deceive you by any means; for *that Day will not come* unless the falling away comes first, and the man of sin is revealed, the son of perdition . . .**
>
> —2 Thessalonians 2:3

Then he goes on to say:

> **For the mystery of lawlessness is already at work; only He who now restrains *will do so* until He is taken out of the way. And then the lawless one will be revealed, whom the Lord will consume with the breath of His mouth and destroy with the brightness of His coming.**
>
> —2 Thessalonians 2:7–8

The forces behind antichrist are already at work in the world, but they're being *restrained* by something that will be **"taken out of the way."** And *only then* can antichrist (**"the lawless one"**) **"be revealed."**

The question is, who or what is **"He who now restrains"**? Who or what is the force keeping antichrist from being revealed and holding back his rise to prominence on the world stage?

In **Job 1:6–12**, we are given a peek behind the curtain into the true reality of the supernatural realm. We learn that Satan's work on the earth occurs only within parameters established by God. *God* is the ultimate restrainer of Satan's earthly activities.

In Matthew's Gospel, we see Jesus "deputizing" his disciples, and by extension the Church, with a significant degree of this same authority:

> *... I will give you the keys of the kingdom of heaven, and whatever you bind on earth will be bound in heaven, and whatever you loose on earth will be loosed in heaven.*
>
> —Matthew 16:19

This is possible through the Holy Spirit, who takes up residence in every believer in the Church. Wherever believers are, the Holy Spirit is there. The same power that raised Jesus from the dead is there.

Therefore, when the Church is raptured, the presence of the Holy Spirit on the earth will *dramatically decrease*. Although the Holy Spirit will continue His work of calling nonbelievers to Jesus, there will be a tremendous change in the earth's *spiritual climate*. And though God will continue to be the ultimate restrainer, He will restrain Satan less after the Rapture. As a result, Satan will finally have the operational latitude he needs to fuel antichrist's rise.

Let me say it one more time: Antichrist *will* only and *can* only be revealed *after* the Church has been raptured. I realize this may devastate some of you because it means there's no point in playing that classic Christian game, *"Guess the Antichrist."* And it means the political party you don't like is probably not being led by the antichrist. If you belong to Jesus, you'll be out of here before antichrist takes the stage.

Despite what I just said, I think it is likely that Satan has had an antichrist candidate ready to go throughout the Church Age because he has no idea when the Rapture will occur. He's just waiting for the restrainer to be removed so that he can move forward with his diabolical plans.

The Bible tells us that antichrist will be an intellectual genius, charismatic speaker, shrewd politician, financial mastermind, forceful military leader, powerful organizer, and unifying religious guru. He's going to be, for a while, universally adored. He'll be so well-liked that those who say, *"Something's wrong with that guy,"* will be perceived as crazy.

Let's look at these first couple of verses again:

> **¹ Now I saw when the Lamb opened one of the seals; and I heard one of the four living creatures saying with a voice like thunder,** *"Come and see."* **² And I looked, and behold, a white horse. He who sat on it had a bow; and a crown was given to him, and he went out conquering and to conquer.**

In the Bible, white horses are symbolic of victory and conquering. People who look at these verses in isolation often assume this is Jesus because He's on **"a white horse."** However, as we examine the company this horseman keeps, it'll become clear this is not Jesus. Remember, Jesus is the Lamb opening the scroll. He's not the one released when the scroll is opened. We will find, however, that this rider *resembles* Christ to many people.

The crown this horseman wears is a "stephanos"—a victor's crown. When John was writing, a victor's crown would have been made from olive branches, a well-known symbol of peace. But like natural olive branches, the peace this rider will offer will not last.

We're told that this crown is **"given to him."** When you study what the Bible tells us about antichrist, I think it's clear he will be given this crown by those who dwell upon the earth because they will *want* him to rule over them.

THE SIGNIFICANCE OF THE BOW

We also notice that he has a **"bow."** There are two main theories regarding its meaning, and I'll share both.

First, some scholars point out that the word used for **"bow"** is the same Greek word[207] used in the Septuagint for **"rainbow"** in **Genesis 9:13**, where God tells Noah that the rainbow will be a symbol of peace between man and God—a covenant promise from God to never again destroy the earth with a flood.

Daniel prophesied this about antichrist:

> *"Through his cunning* [likely meaning "policy"]
> *He shall cause deceit* [literally, "craft"] *to prosper under his rule;*
> *And he shall exalt himself in his heart.*
> *He shall destroy many in their prosperity* [better translated as "by peace he shall destroy many"].

---

[207] Toxon.

> *He shall even rise against the Prince of princes* [that's Jesus];
> *But he shall be broken without human means* [i.e., supernaturally; not by human intervention]."
>
> —Daniel 8:25

As scholars look at these and other verses I'll share in a moment, many conclude that the emerging picture has antichrist rising to prominence on the world stage shortly after the Rapture by presenting an unprecedented *peace plan*. The world will view him as a transcendent man of *peace*, and many who have studied eschatology suspect he will solve the tensions between Israel and the Palestinians, the holy grail of diplomacy.

How could that ever happen? Likely because the Jews will initially receive him as their long-awaited *Messiah*. Jesus was speaking of antichrist when He said this to the Jews, His own people:

> *I have come in My Father's name, and you do not receive Me; if another comes in his own name, him you will receive.*
>
> —John 5:43

Antichrist will show up and perform one of the grand signs the Jews are expecting from the Messiah—he will pave the way for rebuilding the Temple.

But what about the Dome of the Rock, which sits on the Temple Mount? It's hard to imagine Muslims being OK with destroying it in favor of a Jewish Temple. While this theory is contested, several archaeologists posit that the original Temple site may have been *next to* the space occupied by the Dome of the Rock. If true, this would allow the Temple to be rebuilt without interfering with the mosque.

I'm not saying this is a certainty. I'm sharing this to remind us that there are possibilities we may not have considered that will allow difficult biblical prophecies to be fulfilled literally.

It's also interesting to note the mission and work of the Temple Institute.[208] They are a group of Israelis committed to seeing the Jewish Temple rebuilt on the Temple Mount. They are building and gathering everything required for this task—the furniture, the priestly robes, priests with the right bloodline—everything. And they have most of it ready to go.

The Bible teaches that the Temple will be rebuilt, and sacrifices will occur again. Daniel prophesied:

> *Then he* [antichrist] ***shall confirm a covenant with many for one week*** [7 years]***;***
> ***But in the middle of the week*** [3.5 years into it]
> ***He shall bring an end to sacrifice and offering.***
> ***And on the wing of abominations shall be one who makes desolate,***
> ***Even until the consummation, which is determined,***
> ***Is poured out on the desolate.***
> —Daniel 9:27

After three and a half years, antichrist will storm the rebuilt Temple, declare himself to be God, and demand to be worshipped. When that happens, the scales will begin to fall from the eyes of Israel as they realize this man is *not* Messiah. And that will start a traumatic process, a breaking of Israel, that will culminate in her finally recognizing Jesus as her Messiah.

Those who hold this view also point out that the **"bow"** antichrist

---

[208] templeinstitute.org.

bears has no arrows and should therefore be taken as a reference to a *peace covenant* (similar to the rainbow shown to Noah).

The second theory is equally compelling and points to the striking similarities between antichrist and Nimrod, who shows up in **Genesis 10** as the world's first antichrist leader:

> ... he [Nimrod] **began to be a mighty one on the earth. He was a mighty hunter before the Lord** ...
>
> —Genesis 10:8–9

The word **"before"** is more accurately translated as "against," which would render the phrase "was a mighty hunter **against** the Lord." And, as a hunter, Nimrod would be associated with the *bow*.

Nimrod was the founder of Babylon and the Babylonian mystery religion (i.e., paganism). He also united the world's men to build the Tower of Babel. **Genesis 11** tells us their goal was to **"make a name"** for themselves,[209] which sure sounds a lot like the motivation behind *Satan's* insurrection in Heaven. Remember how he put it? *"I will be like the most high."*[210]

If you dig into the similarities, you'll soon see why many consider antichrist to be "Nimrod II." And we'll deal with antichrist in greater detail when we reach **Revelation 13**.

The word **"bow"** could refer to a weapon or rainbow, and I think both theories could be on to something because antichrist is going to *"by peace ... destroy many."*[211] He's going to use peace as a weapon to subjugate the world.

---

[209] Genesis 11:4.

[210] Isaiah 14:14.

[211] Daniel 8:25 KJV.

What we do know is that this first horseman is antichrist, and his ascension to global political prominence is the first significant development on the earth following the Rapture.

I remember when Barack Obama won his first term as president. I'd never seen anything like it: the speech he made at a packed Mile High Stadium in Denver to accept the Democratic nomination, on a stage lined with Roman-styled columns; the joy in newspapers, on TV screens, and on the streets of countries around the world after he won the election; the widespread optimism that a new day of peace was dawning. You may recall that less than a year after taking office, he was presented with the Nobel Prize—not because of anything he had done, but because of what people assumed and hoped he *would* do.

As I watched all this unfold, I remember thinking, *"I know he's not antichrist. But, man, the world sure is hungry and ready for antichrist."* The world was, and is even more so today, longing for a man of peace to rise up with solutions to our ever-increasing list of problems. If nothing else, Obama's rise proved that the world *wants* to believe that someone like that can exist.

Now, imagine if Obama *had* been able to broker peace in the Middle East. Imagine the blind devotion that would've been stirred up in the world's population. Imagine how eagerly most would've handed him unlimited power. The antichrist will be all that and do all that, and more.

A SIDENOTE ON TIMING

Let's clear up a common misconception regarding the end-times timeline: The Tribulation will not necessarily begin *immediately* after the Rapture. The signing of a peace treaty created by antichrist is what marks the beginning of the seven-year Tribulation, not the Rapture.

How long will the gap be between the Rapture and the start of the Tribulation? We don't know. It could be weeks or a few years. But it must be long enough for a relatively unknown antichrist to rise to a position powerful enough to broker peace in the Middle East.

THE SECOND HORSEMAN/SEAL: WAR

> ³ **When He opened the second seal, I heard the second living creature saying,** *"Come and see."* ⁴ **Another horse, fiery red, went out. And it was granted to the one who sat on it to take peace from the earth, and that *people* should kill one another; and there was given to him a great sword.**

Antichrist will come to power through *peace*, but he will soon be followed by the second horseman, who brings *war*. And not just local war but a *spirit* of war that causes conflicts to break out across the globe. Every ethnic and national tension that could flare up *will*. Murders rates will soar in the cities and small towns, and those who search for peace will not find it.

Despite this, people will continue to follow and only grow in their affection for antichrist. We are then told what all that war leads to.

THE THIRD HORSEMAN/SEAL: FAMINE

> ⁵ **When He opened the third seal, I heard the third living creature say,** *"Come and see."* **So I looked, and behold, a**

black horse, and he who sat on it had a pair of scales in his hand. ⁶ **And I heard a voice in the midst of the four living creatures saying,** *"A quart of wheat for a denarius, and three quarts of barley for a denarius; and do not harm the oil and the wine."*

The third horseman is *famine*. Let's break down the details of his description. Black is associated with famine at least three times in the Bible,[212] and the practice of eating bread by weight was a Jewish expression to describe a time of dire food scarcity.[213]

A **"denarius"** was the standard day's wage for a commoner in the Roman Empire at this time in history. A quart of wheat was enough food to feed one man for one day. It was the daily ration given to every Roman soldier. *"A quart of wheat for a denarius"* describes an economy where the price of food is so high that the average man or woman must work all day just to buy enough wheat to feed themselves. Barley was typically used to feed animals because it was not as filling as wheat. But people will eat it at this time because it will be the only way they can feed their families.

The text describes disastrous famine and catastrophic inflation.

Then we see the phrase *"and do not harm the oil and the wine."* Oil and wine were luxury items in John's day, like expensive perfumes, vintage bottles of wine, and gold-covered steaks (it's a thing) are in ours. In the middle of this horrific food shortage and hyperinflation, there will still be an elite class who will be concerned about their supply of luxury items. As is always the case, when tragedy and war strike the planet, the elites get richer, and

---

[212] Cf. Lamentations 4:4–8, 5:10; Jeremiah 14:1–2.

[213] Cf. Leviticus 26:25–33; Ezekiel 4:10–11, 16.

the poor become destitute. But as the Tribulation unfolds, we'll see even the wealthy and powerful unable to escape the wrath of God.

The tragedy of most famines is that they occur because of politics, not scarcity. The scarcity tends to be brought about by the abuse of political power. And that seems to be the case here, with the third horseman/seal.

Antichrist will still be rising and ruling as these other horsemen/seals wreak havoc on the earth. And it won't be long before antichrist controls the world's economy and food supply. We see that in **Revelation 13:16–17**, where we find these infamous verses:

> **He causes all, both small and great, rich and poor, free and slave, to receive a mark on their right hand or on their foreheads, and that no one may buy or sell except one who has the mark or the name of the beast, or the number of his name.**

Antichrist is going to burst onto the scene with a miraculous peace plan. But he'll be shortly followed by war. That war will lead to worldwide famine. And that leads us to the fourth seal, the final horseman.

THE FOURTH HORSEMAN/SEAL: WIDESPREAD DEATH ON EARTH

> [7] **When He opened the fourth seal, I heard the voice of the fourth living creature saying,** *"Come and see."* [8] **So I looked, and behold, a pale horse. And the name of him who sat on it was Death, and Hades followed with him. And power was given to them over a fourth of the earth, to kill with**

sword, with hunger, with death, and by the beasts of the earth.

The fourth horseman/seal, simply and terrifyingly, is *death*. And he will claim a quarter of the earth's population. A quarter! We're talking about the potential of 1.5–2 billion people being killed in a very short time.

The Greek word used for **"pale"** is the word *"chloros,"* from where we get our words "chlorine" and "chlorophyll." It refers to a sickly bleached or green paleness, like that brought on by death. In the Book of Leviticus, it's the color of leprosy.[214] The appearance of this **"pale horse"** is sickly and zombie-like.

The grim reality is that when a quarter of the earth's population dies in a short time, it will be impossible to process all the corpses properly. That will inevitably result in all kinds of diseases and plagues running rampant, leading to even more death.

"Death" refers to the death of the earthly, physical body. **"Hades"** refers to the death of the eternal spirit. The idea is that this horseman is killing people's physical bodies on the earth, and Hades (the destination of nonbelievers awaiting the Great White Throne Judgment) is immediately claiming their spirits. Apparently, those killed by this fourth horseman/seal have rejected Jesus.

And that raises the intriguing and (I think) likely possibility that once someone on the earth turns to Jesus during the Tribulation, they are saved from the wrath of God (i.e., they are unaffected by the judgments of His wrath), though not from the wrath of Satan or man.

---

[214] Cf. Leviticus 13:49.

This would be consistent with God's practice of never allowing His people to be harmed by His wrath—even collaterally. It would also harmonize with the plagues of Egypt being a *type* of the Tribulation. Remember, the Book of Exodus tells us that from the fourth plague on, only the Egyptians were affected by the plagues.

When it talks about the **"beasts of the earth,"** some scholars point out that the original Greek word[215] applies to creatures of any size—even *microscopic*. They posit this phrase could be referring to a *pandemic*. They also see a parallel to **Ezekiel 14:21**:

> **... thus says the Lord God:** *"How much more it shall be when I send My four severe judgments on Jerusalem—the sword and famine and wild beasts and pestilence—to cut off man and beast from it?"*

Again, it would seem to make sense that diseases would run wild with exposed corpses everywhere. But, on the other hand, this is God we're talking about. While we know the broad details, we're speculating on the specifics. It's equally possible that antichrist confiscates all personally owned weapons (in the name of peace, of course), and then *bears* come down from the mountains and start mauling people! My point is that we need to remember that the Tribulation will be an unparalleled time of God's judgment and supernatural activity on the earth. We don't need to explain everything naturalistically. If God wants wild animals to kill a billion people, it'll happen.

And with that, we wrap up the Four Horsemen. But things are just getting started . . .

---

[215] Therion.

THE FIFTH SEAL: THE CRY OF THE MARTYRS

⁹ When He opened the fifth seal, I saw under the altar the souls of those who had been slain for the word of God and for the testimony which they held.

"The word of God" is also a title for Jesus.[216] These **"souls"** are the fifth seal, and they are those who have become believers *during* the Tribulation, up to this point, and been martyred for turning to Jesus.

If you've been keeping score, things are going really badly on the earth at this time. And when bad things happen, people want someone to blame. In the days of the Black Plague, one out of every four people died. The only group of people who were spared was the *Jews*. Today, we know it was because they were following Old Testament hygiene laws. But suspicious people at the time became convinced the Jews were the *reason* for the Plague and so, they viciously persecuted them.

The same thing will probably happen in the Tribulation. Imagine how the world will react when they realize it is *Jesus* pouring out these catastrophes on the earth, and they learn some people are *worshipping* this same Jesus. Then they notice that those who worship Jesus seem to be *exempt* from these catastrophes. The wrath of *man* will fall upon Christians (post-Rapture converts) because those on the earth will *hate* them. How much? They'll *kill* them for following Jesus.

We must remember that John is again describing something he sees *in Heaven*. And as we've discussed, Heaven is a place with greater dimensionality than earth. It's a fuller reality that is beyond

---

[216] John 1:1.

our current comprehension. John can only do his best to describe it for us, using his earthly vocabulary and life experiences, which are both inadequate for the task.

John's description here is centered on an *altar* in Heaven. With our earthly paradigms, most of us read it and imagine many cramped people, reaching their hands out from underneath a regular-sized altar, like prisoners in a small cage. But that's not what's going on here. Whatever this altar is, it's huge and comfortable, and these **"souls"** are happy to be there—even as they long for God to bring justice to the earth.

> [10] **And they cried with a loud voice, saying,** *"How long, O Lord, holy and true, until You judge and avenge our blood on those who dwell on the earth?"*

They're crying out for God to execute justice on the earth. They're asking God to make things right and pay back ***"those who dwell on the earth,"*** who killed them and their families. They're asking for God to display His wrath.

When Jesus was dying on the Cross, He cried out, *"Father, forgive them, for they do not know what they do."*[217] When Stephen was being stoned to death, he cried out, *"Lord, do not charge them with this sin."*[218] But here in **V.10**, the martyrs are crying out, *"How long, O Lord, holy and true, until You judge and avenge our blood on those who dwell on the earth?"* Why? Because the time of Jesus the Lamb is over, and it's now the time of Jesus the Lion. The window of grace has almost closed, and the window of wrath has been flung wide open.

---

[217] Luke 23:34.

[218] Acts 7:60.

¹¹ Then a white robe was given to each of them; and it was said to them that they should rest a little while longer, until both *the number of* their fellow servants and their brethren, who would be killed as they *were*, was completed.

Just as there is an appointed *time* for the Rapture, there is an appointed *number* of Gentiles who will be saved in the Tribulation.[219] When that number has been reached, Jesus will return to the earth at the Second Coming and avenge the Tribulation saints (among other important activities). Jesus comforts these **"souls"** with this knowledge and encourages them to be patient because this time gap is only being permitted that more people might be saved.

THE SIXTH SEAL: COSMIC DISTURBANCES

¹² I looked when He opened the sixth seal, and behold, there was a great earthquake; and the sun became black as sackcloth of hair, and the moon became like blood. ¹³ And the stars of heaven fell to the earth, as a fig tree drops its late figs when it is shaken by a mighty wind. ¹⁴ Then the sky receded as a scroll when it is rolled up, and every mountain and island was moved out of its place.

The sixth seal consists of supernatural events in the natural universe. But what does it all mean? Many commentators read this and see a nuclear winter, the aftereffects of nuclear war. Others suggest these will be *literal events*, without any earthly cause, and we always want to be open to that possibility. Remember, God is *God*. He can do whatever He wants.

---

[219] Cf. Romans 11:25.

There's no reason to not take the **"great earthquake"** literally. And if this is indeed a global event, it would mean tectonic plates slipping all over the place, causing volcanos to erupt across the earth, spewing ash into the sky that we know is more than capable of blotting out the sun and causing the moon to appear blood red.

With regards to the **"stars of heaven"** falling to the earth, it could very well refer to meteors pummeling the earth, but I suspect this may be referring to the expulsion of all those who presently interact with the Divine Council and are not allies of the Lord.[220] This may be the time when those the Bible refers to as the corrupt gods of the nations are removed from the Divine Council and have their access revoked.

If you're thinking, *"What is Jeff talking about? What about corrupt gods ruling the nations?"* I recommend digging into a study of **Psalm 82** and **Daniel 10**.

When John says, **"the sky receded as a scroll when it is rolled up,"** it may be referring to the dissolution, in some way, of the veil that currently conceals the supernatural dimension from earthly view.

Isaiah 34:4 describes this same event:

All the host of heaven shall be dissolved,
And the heavens shall be rolled up like a scroll . . .

There is one thing we know with certainty regarding this sixth seal: it's not something that can be explained by solely natural or manmade developments because even those on the earth who hate God give Him credit for these signs. They don't say, *"We need to rethink our nuclear policies."* Look at how they respond:

---

[220] Cf. The use of "star" or "stars" in Isaiah 14:12–13; Revelation 9:1, 12:4.

¹⁵ **And the kings of the earth, the great men, the rich men, the commanders, the mighty men, every slave and every free man, hid themselves in the caves and in the rocks of the mountains, . . .**

And their doomsday bunkers . . .

¹⁶ **. . . and said to the mountains and rocks,** *"Fall on us and hide us from the face of Him who sits on the throne and from the wrath of the Lamb!* ¹⁷ *For the great day of His wrath has come, and who is able to stand?"*

While the events of the first four seals (the four horsemen) could be attributed to natural and/or human causes, something changes dramatically when this sixth seal is opened. And **V.16** clarifies that those on the earth are no longer confused about who or what is causing these catastrophes.

Most of the world's leaders, and a large percentage of people, will *not* cry out to Jesus for deliverance in the Tribulation. Faced with His awesome power, they will stubbornly refuse to repent. They will have no case to make before Jesus when they are judged in **Revelation 19** because they knew Jesus was God, yet they refused to worship Him as God.

So deceived[221] are those who dwell on the earth at this point that they still don't grasp the eternal nature of their spirits. Facing the supernatural wrath of God on earth, they cling to philosophical naturalism, thinking physical death will afford them escape from the judgment of God.

Did you notice that **V.15** referred to **"every slave"**? Apparently,

---

[221] Cf. 2 Thessalonians 2:11–12.

slavery will again become mainstream in the Tribulation. If you know anything about Islam and sharia, then you know that slavery is permitted and encouraged in the Quran. In fact, many territories in the Middle East and Africa currently controlled by Islamic extremist groups have reinstituted public slave markets. Even more (allegedly) developed nations like Qatar and Dubai have massive problems with slaves being sold on social media. **V.15** could be referring to adopting these types of Islamic practices, or it could be that in this time of extreme famine, people are selling themselves into slavery to survive.

LOOKING AHEAD

Revelation 6 concludes with the people of the earth crying out, *"the great day of His wrath has come, and who is able to stand?"* **Revelation 7** is going to answer that question and reveal the *identity* of the mysterious 144,000.

If you've been paying attention, you may have noticed that only six of the seven seals have been opened. The seventh seal will be opened when we reach **Revelation 8**. It's as though the Lord felt that after reaching the sixth seal, we need to take a break. And so, He'll give us a chapter with more detail about something else, and then go to the seventh seal in **Revelation 8**.

When we reach that seventh seal, we'll find that it consists of seven *sub*-judgments, known as the *trumpet* judgments. And after the sixth *trumpet* judgment, there will be *another* pause for several chapters before we go to the seventh trumpet judgment. When we do, we'll find that *it too* consists of seven *sub*-judgments, known as the *bowls of wrath*.

The idea is that, like birth pangs, God's judgments during the seven years of the Tribulation increase in *intensity* and *frequency* as the Second Coming approaches.[222]

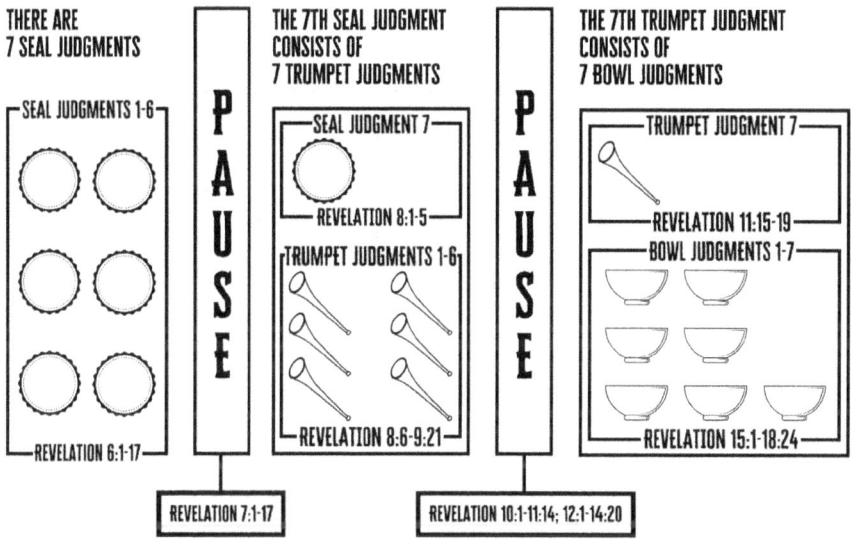

CLOSING THOUGHTS

What should we take from **Revelation 6**? I'll say it again: If you're not saved, if you haven't given your life to Jesus and decided to follow Him as your Lord and Savior, do it *right now*. **Hebrews 10** makes it clear:

> ... if we sin willfully after we have received the knowledge of the truth, there no longer remains a sacrifice for sins,

---

[222] Appendix B explains how we know the Tribulation will last for seven years.

> **but a certain fearful expectation of judgment, and fiery indignation which will devour the adversaries.**
>
> —Hebrews 10:26–27

> **It is a fearful thing to fall into the hands of the living God.**
>
> —Hebrews 10:31

For those of us who are saved, I'd argue that for good portions of our study into the Tribulation, there won't be any practical life lessons for us because we'll be in Heaven with the Lord when it happens. What these chapters should do is compel us to pray for and seek opportunities to share the hope of Jesus with those in our lives who do not yet know Him, and thank God for the gracious and glorious truth of **1 Thessalonians 5:9**:

> **...God did not appoint us to wrath, but to obtain salvation through our Lord Jesus Christ...**

As the world increasingly falls apart around us, we should find ourselves increasingly moved to thank the Lord that our destiny is in Heaven, with Him, around His throne.

REVELATION 7

THE 144,000 AND THE GREAT REVIVAL

In **Revelation 6**, we read about the beginning of the Tribulation, when God's wrath begins to fall upon the earth that has rejected Him. As difficult as that subject may be, without an understanding of God's righteous judgment and wrath, we cannot properly appreciate our salvation or understand what happened to Jesus on the Cross and what He has saved us from. The reality that we deserve wrath but have received mercy is what makes the Gospel good news!

For most of us, the subject of God's wrath is problematic not because it is illogical but because of the names and faces that come to mind—a spouse, a sibling, a dear friend. And we are filled with dread at the thought of them running out of time to be saved. If that's you, I think you'll be encouraged by this chapter because we'll learn that there may well be more people saved in the Tribulation than in all the years that preceded it.

A RENEWED FOCUS ON ISRAEL

But before we get into that, I want to remind you of something I mentioned briefly in an earlier chapter. **Revelation 2–3** focus entirely on the Church and the Church Age. When the Church is removed from the earth in the Rapture, God's focus will return to *ethnic* Israel.

Throughout the Bible, we are told that God will bring ethnic Israel back into her homeland in the end-times. For example, God spoke through the prophet Zechariah:

> ***Behold, I will make Jerusalem a cup of drunkenness to all the surrounding peoples, when they lay siege against Judah . . .***
>
> —Zechariah 12:2

That's a reference to the nation of Israel.

> ***. . . and Jerusalem. And it shall happen in that day that I will make Jerusalem a very heavy stone for all peoples; all who would heave it away will surely be cut in pieces, though all nations of the earth are gathered against it . . .***
>
> —Zechariah 12:2–3

> ***. . . but Jerusalem shall be inhabited again in her own place— Jerusalem.***
>
> —Zechariah 12:6b

God is driving home the point that in the end-times, He's going to restore Israel as the homeland of the Jewish people, and it's going to be a real problem for the rest of the world.

Sadly, instead of *celebrating* the extraordinary fulfillment of biblical prophecy, many Christians today are *frustrated* that Israel has become a nation again. These misguided believers side with the Palestinians because they fail to recognize that God is the One behind Israel's national resurgence.

God promises that at the end of the Tribulation, Jesus will reveal Himself to His people, Israel, with remarkable results:

> *... I will pour on the house of David and on the inhabitants of Jerusalem the Spirit of grace and supplication; then they will look on Me whom they pierced. Yes, they will mourn for Him as one mourns for his only son, and grieve for Him as one grieves for a firstborn.*
>
> —Zechariah 12:10

There is a coming moment when Jesus will reveal Himself to ethnic Israel, the **"blindness"** Paul wrote of in **Romans 11:25** will be lifted, Israel will recognize Jesus as her Messiah, **"And so all Israel will be saved."**[223] As we shall see, that moment will arrive at the Second Coming.

Writing about Israel's fate in the Great Tribulation, the prophet **Joel** penned these words given to him by the Lord:

> *And it shall come to pass afterward*
> *That I will pour out My Spirit on all flesh;*
> *Your sons and your daughters shall prophesy,*
> *Your old men shall dream dreams,*
> *Your young men shall see visions.*
> *And also on My menservants and on My maidservants*
> *I will pour out My Spirit in those days.*
> *And I will show wonders in the heavens and in the earth:*
> *Blood and fire and pillars of smoke.*
> *The sun shall be turned into darkness,*
> *And the moon into blood, ...*
>
> —Joel 2:28–31

---

[223] Romans 11:26

We saw this happen in **Revelation 6:12** at the sixth seal judgment.

> *...Before the coming of the great and awesome day of the Lord.*
> *And it shall come to pass*
> *That whoever calls on the name of the Lord*
> *Shall be saved.*
> *For in Mount Zion and in Jerusalem there shall be deliverance,*
> *As the Lord has said,*
> *Among the remnant whom the Lord calls.*
>
> —Joel 2:31–32

And in **Zechariah 13:6**, we read this incredible interaction that will take place when Jesus reveals Himself as Messiah to ethnic Israel:

> **And** *one* will say to him, *"What are these wounds between your arms?"* Then he will answer, *"Those with which I was wounded in the house of my friends."*

Even though they arranged His murder, Jesus still calls Israel His *"friends"*—present tense.

WHO CAN STAND?

Revelation 6 ended with the people of the earth crying out, *"the great day of His wrath has come, and who is able to stand?"* **Revelation 7** will answer that question by telling us about two groups: The *sealed* servants (**VV.1–8**) and the *saved* servants (**VV.9–17**).

THE SEALED SERVANTS

¹ After these things I saw four angels standing at the four corners of the earth, holding the four winds of the earth, that the wind should not blow on the earth, on the sea, or on any tree.

In the previous chapter, we saw the devastating effects of the first six seals being opened, including the four horsemen of the apocalypse—antichrist, war, famine, and death. The four horsemen were not events but rather ongoing judgments that will continue to affect the earth throughout the Tribulation. And it makes the most sense to view the **"four winds"** as those same four horsemen.[224]

Before the seventh seal is opened, God presses the Pause button on everything to give those on the earth a moment to reflect and an opportunity to repent. And amid the Tribulation, we will see God gloriously pour out His mercy in an astonishing way.

² Then I saw another angel ascending from the east, having the seal of the living God. And he cried with a loud voice to the four angels to whom it was granted to harm the earth and the sea, ³ saying, *"Do not harm the earth, the sea, or the trees till we have sealed the servants of our God on their foreheads."*

This type of *sealing* refers to the shipping trade of John's day. If you wanted to move cargo from one place to another, you would pour some hot wax on your items and then press your signet ring

---

[224] See the parallels to the four horsemen in Zechariah 6:1–8; the Hebrew "rûaḥ" in Zechariah 6:5 can refer to "spirit" or "wind"; wind is used in reference to God's judgment in Jeremiah 49:36; 51:1, 16.

into the wax, leaving them marked with your personal, unique seal. When that cargo reached the end of its journey, the only person who could claim it would be someone who had a matching signet ring (i.e., you or someone you gave a copy of the ring to). These *"servants"* in **V.3** will be marked/sealed as God's property.

Some attempt to apply an environmental agenda to **V.3**, claiming it proves God's overriding concern for nature, even in the Tribulation. Those who hold this view should note the presence of the word *"till,"* which tells us this is just a *pause* before the earth, the sea, and the trees *are* harmed by the wrath of God.

Who are these *"servants of our God"?*

⁴ And I heard the number of those who were sealed. One hundred *and* forty-four thousand of all the tribes of the children of Israel *were* sealed:

While not as popular as *"Guess the Antichrist,"* many still enjoy a good round of *"Guess the 144,000."* Several groups have claimed to be the 144,000, especially over the past century and a half or so. I'm going to mention some of them here, and if you're offended, please do some of your own research before emailing me because everything I'm about to tell you is factual religious history.

Most of you have probably heard the 144,000 referenced by Jehovah's Witnesses (JWs). Their movement was founded with the teaching that JWs would be the 144,000. That was all well and good until the 1930s when the number of JWs began to *exceed* 144,000. Fortunately, it was nothing a few theological tweaks couldn't solve. The identity of the 144,000 was revised to be a group chosen by God to go to Heaven where they will rule over all the other believers, who will be spending eternity on a remade, paradise-like earth.

REVELATION 7

Brigham Young, the second president of the Church of Jesus Christ of Latter-day Saints, claimed the Mormons were the 144,000. However, they too grew beyond that number and had to revise their theology.

At a minimum, both groups are guilty of failing to plan ahead.

Ellen G. White, the founder of Seventh Day Adventism, said: *"Let us strive with all the power that God has given us to be among the hundred and forty-four thousand."*[225]

And while most Seventh Day Adventists no longer believe or teach that, their founder unquestionably did. Suffice it to say, all these groups were way off because, as you've probably discerned by now, the only way to be part of the 144,000 is to read *this book*.

I'm kidding! So, who are the 144,000, *really?*

⁴ And I heard the number of those who were sealed. One hundred *and* forty-four thousand of all the tribes of the children of Israel *were* sealed:

We can save ourselves much confusion by noting what the text plainly tells us. These 144,000 are **"of all the tribes of the children of Israel."** In other words, they're *Jewish*.

While we're here, I want to offer what I think is an important challenge to my friends who are Jehovah's Witnesses: What is the basis for claiming that the *number* of the 144,000 is literal, but their *ethnicity* is figurative? What is the hermeneutical justification for switching from a literal to figurative interpretation—in the *same*

---

[225] Ellen G. White, "God's Purpose for Us," *The Review and Herald*, March 9, 1905 (quoting from a sermon preached in Oakland, California on Sunday, April 12, 1903).

sentence of the *same verse?* Respectfully, I don't think there is any reasonable justification for it, or for ignoring what the text plainly says.

I suggest God knew people would try to distort or dismiss the identity and ethnicity of the 144,000 as merely figurative. So, He was as redundant, plain, and specific as He could be. To avoid any confusion, the Lord used a bunch of real estate in the Book of Revelation to list out exactly where these 144,000 come from and who they are:

> ⁵ **of the tribe of Judah twelve thousand *were* sealed;**
> **of the tribe of Reuben twelve thousand *were* sealed;**
> **of the tribe of Gad twelve thousand *were* sealed;**
> ⁶ **of the tribe of Asher twelve thousand *were* sealed;**
> **of the tribe of Naphtali twelve thousand *were* sealed;**
> **of the tribe of Manasseh twelve thousand *were* sealed;**
> ⁷ **of the tribe of Simeon twelve thousand *were* sealed;**
> **of the tribe of Levi twelve thousand *were* sealed;**
> **of the tribe of Issachar twelve thousand *were* sealed;**
> ⁸ **of the tribe of Zebulun twelve thousand *were* sealed;**
> **of the tribe of Joseph twelve thousand *were* sealed;**
> **of the tribe of Benjamin twelve thousand *were* sealed.**

I get the feeling that when somebody says, "*I don't think it's talking about Jews.*" God must be thinking, "*Just stop. What else do you want Me to do? It's right there! Just read it! I numbered them! I named the tribes! I said they were from the* **tribes** *of* **Israel**!"

Obviously, God doesn't do that. He's all-knowing and, therefore, never surprised by our stupidity. These are 144,000 Jewish men—12,000 from each of the twelve tribes of Israel.

When we reach **Revelation 14:3-4**, we're going to read this about the 144,000:

> **They sang as it were a new song before the throne, before the four living creatures, and the elders; and no one could learn that song except the hundred *and* forty-four thousand who were redeemed from the earth. These are the ones who were not defiled with women, for they are virgins.**

Here's what we know from Scripture: The 144,000 are male Jewish virgins who evangelize the world and are supernaturally marked/sealed by God, enabling them to survive the Tribulation.

We know they will not be saved at the time of the Rapture because they will still be on the earth *after* the Rapture. But *in* the Tribulation, they will receive the revelation that Jesus is Messiah and will follow Him.

When you think about it, why would you *want* to be in the 144,000? Why would you want to be on earth for the Tribulation when you could be in Heaven with the Lord? The latter sounds like a much better plan to me.

Tragically, many scholars and pastors across the centuries have refused to acknowledge the Jewish ethnicity of the 144,000 because they believe in supersessionist theology.[226] They believe God is "through with the Jew," so when ethnic Israel comes up in eschatology, they are *pre-committed* to finding an alternative explanation. Because regardless of how plain the text is, if the literal Jewish ethnicity of the 144,000 is acknowledged, then supersessionism must be abandoned.

---

[226] See Appendix C for an explanation of the theology of supersessionism.

SEALING IN THE OLD TESTAMENT

When God seals these 144,000 Jewish missionaries, nobody, including antichrist, will be able to touch them. They're going to be supernaturally protected by the Lord during this time. And this is not without biblical precedent.

Ezekiel 9:3–5 records a time when the nation of Israel was in rebellion against God, and He needed to step in and correct their behavior. These verses give us a *preview* of how the 144,000 will be sealed in the Tribulation:

> **Now the glory of the God of Israel had gone up from the cherub, where it had been, to the threshold of the temple. And He called to the man clothed with linen, who *had* the writer's inkhorn at his side; and the Lord said to him, . . .**

There's a whole story behind this, but for now, I just want us to focus on what the Lord says next:

> *Go through the midst of the city, through the midst of Jerusalem, and put a mark on the foreheads of the men who sigh and cry over all the abominations that are done within it.*

God *marks/seals* those who are His—those who are grieving over Israel's sin.

> **To the others He said in my hearing,** *"Go after him through the city and kill; do not let your eye spare, nor have any pity."*

Several times in the Old Testament, God *sealed* His people before He poured justice and wrath on those who were hostile to Him. That's what we're seeing take place here in **Revelation 7**. God is *sealing* the 144,000 *before* the wrath continues in **Revelation 8**.

As I shared in the previous chapter, I suspect something changed dramatically at the sixth seal judgment, and the spiritual dimension became perceivable to those on the earth (in some way). Therefore, I suspect those on the earth will be able to somehow *perceive* the "seal" God places on the 144,000.

IS PURE TRIBAL DNA POSSIBLE?

One of the questions that people have wrestled with is: *"How can the DNA of the twelve tribes still be pure after 2,000 years of inter-tribal marriage?"* Without getting into the technical details, a research paper published in 1997 revealed that, as incredible as it may seem, Jewish males with Levitical heritage carry distinct, unique genetic markers.[227] And this method of testing has been employed for over 17 years to identify men qualified to serve in the priesthood of the new, Third Temple.

For 2,000 years, God was able to keep the DNA of the tribes of Israel *intact*. And I point that out to remind us that when God makes a plan, He dots the i's and crosses the t's. He's got all the angles covered.

THE "MISSING" TRIBES

If you examine the twelve tribes listed in **VV.5–8** and compare that to other lists of the twelve tribes in Scripture, you'll notice the tribes of Dan and Ephraim are missing, and the tribes of Levi and Joseph have been added in their place.

---

[227] Karl Skorecki et al. "Y Chromosomes of Jewish Priests" *Nature* 385, no. 32 (1997). https://doi.org/10.1038/385032a0.

This is likely because Dan and Ephraim became heavily involved in idolatry[228] and, in so doing, forfeited their role in the ministry of the 144,000. However, both tribes will be redeemed and present when Jesus reigns over Israel and the earth in the Millennial Kingdom.[229]

The 144,000 will be sent out and become the most effective evangelists the world has ever known. And through them, in earth's darkest hour, Israel will finally fulfill her original calling to be a light to the nations.[230]

If you'd like to investigate these things further, I encourage you to pour over **Isaiah 49**. It is an astonishing prophecy that includes much of what we discuss in this chapter.

THE SAVED SERVANTS

> [9] **After these things I looked, and behold, a great multitude which no one could number, of all nations, tribes, peoples, and tongues, standing before the throne and before the Lamb, clothed with white robes, with palm branches in their hands, . . .**

In **V.14**, we will discover that this **"great multitude"** is not the Church or Old Testament saints but the *fruit* of the evangelism of the 144,000. Their ministry will be so effective that John says, **"no one could number"** those who will turn to Jesus and be saved through it.

---

[228] Cf. Genesis 49:17 for Dan; Isaiah 7:17 and Hosea 4:17 for Ephraim; both violated the covenant of Deuteronomy 29 and received the penalty of V.21.

[229] Cf. Ezekiel 48:1–2, 5–6, 32.

[230] Cf. Genesis 12:1–3; Psalm 67: 2, 7

REVELATION 7

The fact that those saved will be from **"all nations, tribes, peoples, and tongues"** tells us that the 144,000 will minister *worldwide*.

Don't miss this little nugget: How does John know that these people are from **"all nations, tribes, peoples, and tongues"**? I suggest it's because he can see it in their physical appearance and hear it in how they speak and sing.

Clearly, in Heaven, ethnic differences don't completely disappear. We won't all become clones. Our ethnic differences seem to be eternal. That means God wants those differences to exist because, in some way, they bring glory to Him. He is blessed by the diversity and different expressions of worship in His family.

Heaven doesn't resolve ethnic tensions by removing our ethnic differences. It resolves ethnic tensions by redeeming our ethnic differences before the Throne of God. That's possible because we are *all* equal before His throne. We are all sinners who could not save ourselves. We are all redeemed saints by the grace of God. We are all adopted children of the Father. We are brothers and sisters—not just in theory, but in a more genuine sense than we are related to our earthly siblings.

Give us more of that perspective here and now, Lord!

PALM BRANCHES

We also notice that these saints worship Jesus **"with palm branches in their hands."** To explain the significance of that, we need take a quick look at three most prominent annual Jewish feasts:

- The **Feast of Passover** was established in the Old Testament to help Israel remember how God had freed them from slavery in Egypt. Specifically, they were to remember how the Lord broke Egypt's will through the tenth plague—the death of every firstborn son of the Egyptians. If any Israeli family followed God's instructions and painted the blood of a lamb on their doorposts, death "passed over" their household.

Jesus became the greater Passover Lamb when He was crucified on a Passover for all sins—past, present, and future—saving us from eternal death.

- The second feast, the **Feast of Pentecost**, was established by the Lord to help Israel remember the giving of the Law, specifically, the Ten Commandments.

The greater Pentecost is documented in **Acts 2** when the Holy Spirit first came upon believers, on the day of the Feast of Pentecost.

God has already fulfilled the greater prophetic purposes of Passover and Pentecost. In the Hebrew calendar, those two spring feasts are followed by a long summer and a final major feast in the fall. I agree with Bible scholars who hold that the summer parallels the Church Age—the ~2,000 years of Church history. I believe that because the last feast is the Feast of Trumpets and Tabernacles.

- The **Feast of Trumpets and Tabernacles**.[231] The Feast of Trumpets is a one-day event. If you research it, you'll discover that it's not really an observance of any past

---

[231] Cf. Leviticus 23:23–25.

event. All God tells Israel is that it's a holy day, a day of rest, and a day to blow trumpets.

And that's intriguing when you consider that the Feast of Trumpets has not yet been fulfilled in a greater way. I suspect it speaks prophetically of the Rapture. Do you remember what Paul wrote about the Rapture in **1 Thessalonians 4:16?**

> **... the Lord Himself will descend from heaven with a shout, with the voice of an archangel, and with the trumpet of God.**

Then we have the Feast of Tabernacles, sometimes called the Feast of Booths.[232] God had the Israelites make booths out of branches and wood and live in them for a week while worshipping Him. This helped them remember the Lord had brought Israel out of Egypt, which is always a picture of the world in Scripture. And while they were in the wilderness, on their way to the Promised Land, Israel lived in temporary shelters (i.e., booths).

This feast has also not been fulfilled in a greater way. I believe it will be when we arrive in Heaven and spend a temporary season there during the Tribulation before returning to the earth with Jesus to reign with Him for the Millennium.

---

[232] Cf. Leviticus 23:33–44.

Here's the connection to palm branches: the only other places in the Bible where they are used in worship is when God lists them as one of the items to be used in building booths to celebrate the Feast of Tabernacles,[233] and when the crowd waves them before Jesus on Palm Sunday as He publicly reveals Himself as the Messiah.[234]

John sees these Tribulation saints in Heaven, worshipping Jesus and waving palm branches:

> ... [10] **and crying out with a loud voice, saying, *"Salvation belongs to our God who sits on the throne, and to the Lamb!"***

Did you notice they're not whining? There is no whining in Heaven (and all the parents said, *"Amen!"*). They're not asking, *"Lord, how could You let us go through that? How could You let me be beheaded?"* Rather, they're thanking and praising the Lord because they realize that the Tribulation is what brought them to Him; it's what got them into the Kingdom. And that is why we find them celebrating that Jesus is righteous in all His judgments.

Are you whining about something God is allowing you to go through so that you might be brought closer to Him? Or to Him for the first time?

> [11] **All the angels stood around the throne and the elders and the four living creatures, and fell on their faces before the throne and worshiped God,** [12] **saying:**
>
> *"Amen! Blessing and glory and wisdom,*
> *Thanksgiving and honor and power and might,*

---

[233] Cf. Leviticus 23:40; Nehemiah 8:15.
[234] Cf. John 12:12–13.

Be to our God forever and ever.
Amen."

This is a snapshot of Heaven caught up in the worship of the Lord, in awe of what He has done and how He has done it.

¹³ Then one of the elders answered, saying to me, *"Who are these arrayed in white robes, and where did they come from?"* **¹⁴ And I said to him, *"Sir, you know."***

John recognized the Church in **Revelation 4–5** but doesn't recognize this multitude. And that's because they're not the Church.

We notice that the *angels* are thrilled by the presence of this multitude. Jesus told us that when one person joins the family of God, all of Heaven breaks out in praise.[235] So, just imagine the celebration that breaks out when this multitude begins to arrive in Heaven because *this* is who they are:

So he said to me, *"These are the ones who come out of the great tribulation, and washed their robes and made them white in the blood of the Lamb."*

We saw this group when the fifth seal was opened in **Revelation 6:9–11**. At that point, the group included those martyred for turning to Jesus in the first half of the Tribulation.

When John sees this vision, we're in the second half of the Tribulation, and the 144,000 have been preaching the Gospel across the earth. And as a result, the number of those saved has swelled to **"a great multitude which no one could number, of all nations, tribes, peoples, and tongues."**

---

[235] Cf. Luke 15: 7, 10.

John recorded the seven letters Jesus wrote to the seven churches. He was aware that only one small church of the seven will still exist and be faithfully following Jesus when the Rapture occurs. John had seen the chaos and destruction of the Tribulation.

John had heard Jesus say, *"narrow is the gate and difficult is the way which leads to life, and there are few who find it."*[236] So, imagine John's joy when the elder explained, *"These are those who turned to Jesus in the Tribulation."*

I would wager that almost all of us have people in our lives who don't know the Lord and for whom we care deeply. Keep the faith. Have hope. Keep asking the Lord to open their eyes to the Gospel and keep telling them about Jesus because the greatest revival the world has ever seen is going to take place *after* the Rapture. All those seeds you sow into their lives will be given every possible chance to grow in the Tribulation when God will do absolutely everything to bring people into His family. They might not respond today, but the Lord may well use your faithfulness to prime their hearts to respond during the Tribulation.

THREE DISTINCT GROUPS

To recap, the Church, the 144,000, and Tribulation saints are distinct and separate groups. The Church is promised to be kept *from* the Tribulation. We saw that in **Revelation 3:10**, where Jesus said:

> *Because you have kept My command to persevere, I also will keep you from the hour of trial which shall come upon the whole world, to test those who dwell on the earth.*

---

[236] Matthew 7:14.

We learned in **V.4** that the 144,000 will be preserved *through* the Tribulation.

And here in **V.14**, we are told there is a multitude that *"come out of the great tribulation."* They lose their lives on the earth during the Tribulation and are not part of the Church.

> *¹⁵ Therefore they are before the throne of God, and serve Him day and night in His temple. And He who sits on the throne will dwell among them. ¹⁶ They shall neither hunger anymore nor thirst anymore; the sun shall not strike them, nor any heat; . . .*

Apparently, these believers were experiencing hunger, thirst, and oppressive heat wherever they came from. We discussed those conditions in the previous chapter and how they relate to the infamous Four Horsemen of the Apocalypse.

> *. . . ¹⁷ for the Lamb who is in the midst of the throne will shepherd them and lead them to living fountains of waters. And God will wipe away every tear from their eyes.*

During the Tribulation, there will be many tears shed. But for these saints, that all ends now. They're safely home, and nothing bad will ever happen to them again.

For the sake of further clarity, let's highlight the differences between the Church and the Tribulation saints:

- The Church is *kept from* the Tribulation, while these saints *come out* of the Tribulation.
- John *recognizes* the Church in **Revelation 4–5** but has no idea who the multitude is.

- The Church receives *crowns* as rewards, but these saints do not.
- The Church has *harps* in their hands while the Tribulation saints have *palm branches*.
  - The Church *sits on* God's Throne with Jesus[237] while these saints *stand before* the Throne.[238]
  - The Church will *reign* with Jesus;[239] these saints will *serve* Him night and day in His temple.[240] It's beautiful but not *as* wonderful as reigning with the Lord.

As an aside, the temple in **V.15** will be on the earth in the Millennium. We know this because **Revelation 21:22** tells us there will be no Temple building when the new heavens and earth are created, **"for the Lord God Almighty and the Lamb are its temple."**

The Church and the Tribulation saints will have unique experiences and roles in eternity. Right now, our lives are empowered by the Holy Spirit. We have the opportunity to serve Jesus. In the Tribulation, there won't really be an opportunity to serve Jesus, only to *die* for Jesus.

Everyone in Heaven will have a wonderful and glorious experience. But I need to be precise—it will be significantly better to be in Heaven as part of the Church than as a Tribulation saint. Those who serve Jesus now, *before* the Rapture and Tribulation, will

---

[237] Cf. Revelation 3:21.

[238] Cf. Revelation 7:9.

[239] Cf. Luke 12:37; 1 Corinthians 6:2–3; 1 Peter 2:9; Revelation 1:6, 5:10.

[240] Cf. Revelation 7:15.

hold a higher position (there's no other way to say it). If you think that sounds weird, just remember what Jesus told Thomas when He appeared to him after the Resurrection:

> *... because you have seen Me, you have believed. Blessed are those who have not seen and yet have believed.*
> —John 20:29

PALM SUNDAY

The signs that Jesus told us to watch for, which He said would mark the last days leading up to the Rapture, have become dramatically more clear, frequent, and pronounced in our lifetimes. So, if the Bible is true (which it is), then this is all going to come to fruition very soon. Jesus really is going to come back for His Church. And after that happens, many people will say, *"It was true! It wasn't just a fairy tale. It really was true!"* And at that moment, many will realize they need to give their lives to Jesus, which will cost them their earthly lives.

We talked earlier about Palm Sunday and the crowd that cried out, **"Hosanna! Hosanna! Blessed is the King who comes in the name of the Lord!"** as Jesus rode into Jerusalem on a donkey. They were referencing Psalms that spoke prophetically of Messiah. Having heard that Jesus had raised Lazarus from the dead the day before, the masses who had been intrigued by His miracle-working ministry had become convinced that He was the Messiah.

However, they were not anticipating a Messiah who would be a suffering servant, but one who would be in the line of David, *politically*—a conquering king who would bring peace to Israel by vanquishing her enemies. After all, Israel was under the boot of the Romans. She needed a *militant* savior—not a spiritual one.

After riding into Jerusalem as Messiah, Jesus looked over the city and *wept*. He cried out:

> *... If you had known, even you, especially in this your day, the things that make for your peace! But now they are hidden from your eyes.*
>
> —Luke 19:42

Jesus had known that His people would reject Him; and He had previously lamented over Jerusalem:

> *See! Your house is left to you desolate ...* [241]

Why? Don't miss this:

> *... because you did not know the time of your visitation.* [242]

Jesus held Israel responsible for failing to recognize that they lived in the time when the savior of their souls had come among them. From God's perspective, they had the Scriptures and the prophets—more than enough to recognize the season of history they were living in. And we all know the story: Less than 40 years later, Israel was wiped out and did not exist as a nation for almost 1,900 years.

I say all that to say this: *don't miss the signs*. Don't miss what the Bible is telling us about when Jesus will come again. He laid it out in Scripture for His First Coming; He has laid it out in Scripture for His Second Coming; and He expects us to *recognize* the season of history we are living in.

---

[241] Matthew 23:38.

[242] Luke 19:44.

CLOSING THOUGHTS

We read about the 144,000 who will be **"sealed"** by God so that Satan will not be able to touch them. They will be God's property, and even in the worst days the world has ever seen, He will protect them. He will not lose even one of them. That fills my heart with hope because in **Ephesians 1:13–14**, Paul writes using similar vocabulary and the same concept (sealing one's property):

In Him you also *trusted*, after you heard the word of truth, the gospel of your salvation; in whom also, having believed, you were sealed with the Holy Spirit of promise, who is the guarantee of our inheritance until the redemption of the purchased possession, to the praise of His glory.

When you give your life to Jesus, you really do become His property. And as we just read, He then *seals* you—not with wax but with the Holy Spirit. No matter how much Satan may want to steal you, he can't because the Holy Spirit inside you marks you as Jesus' property. And Jesus will be there on the other side of your journey, waiting to receive you, because you belong to Him.

Whatever difficulties you're facing in life at this time, I pray you would know the deep and transcendent peace that is rooted in the glorious truth that you have been *sealed* with the Holy Spirit. You belong to Jesus. And **Ephesians 4:30** tells us we've been **"sealed for the day of redemption."**

REVELATION 8

THE FIRST FOUR TRUMPETS

In **Revelation 6,** we saw Jesus, the Lamb of God, open the first six seals of the title deed to the earth, unleashing wrath upon the earth that had rejected Him. In **Revelation 7**, God pressed the Pause button to do something amazing. He sealed/marked 144,000 Jewish men to be evangelists, sparking the greatest revival the world will ever see.

Here in **Revelation 8**, God is about to press the Play button again, and what will unfold will be *astonishing*. As we enter what can seem like a very dark section of Revelation, we should remember that God's wrath is not a trivial matter. I pray that as you study, you will be moved by what we've been saved *from* and what we've been saved *to*.

PRELUDE TO THE SEVENTH SEAL: SILENCE IN HEAVEN

¹ **When He [Jesus] opened the seventh seal, there was silence in heaven for about half an hour.**

As the seventh seal is opened, Heaven falls so silent you could hear a pin drop. Why? Because everyone in Heaven understands the *gravity* of the coming judgment.

I hope we all understand that while it is right for God to judge sin, it is never something to celebrate when a person hardens their heart and chooses to live as God's enemy. That's why Heaven is silent here. God's wrath is just and righteous but also a serious and somber matter. God is not rushing to judgment. He's waited until the *last possible moment* to render His verdict. And so, Heaven holds its collective breath in anticipation of what is about to be revealed.

In **Zephaniah 1:7**, the prophet captures this moment perfectly:

Be silent in the presence of the Lord God; for the day of the Lord *is* at hand . . .

Half an hour may not seem like a long time, but it's a long time to wait in absolute silence with a massive group of people. Such a reaction was appropriate given the weight of what was about to unfold.

² And I saw the seven angels who stand before God, and to them were given seven trumpets.

Here we discover that the seventh *seal* judgment consists of seven *trumpet* judgments and seven sub-judgments. Later, we'll learn that the seventh *trumpet* judgment is made up of seven *bowl* judgments and seven more sub-judgments. The *trumpet* judgments will be worse than the *seal* judgments, and the *bowl* judgments will be worse than the *trumpet* judgments.

This period of silence followed by seven trumpets recalls the fall of Jericho in **Joshua 6**, where the Israelites circled in silence for seven days before seven priests blew seven trumpets, resulting in the destruction of the city. And there are some further parallels there you can explore in your own studies.

The Bible reveals that the Lord's angels are organized by rank, like an army. It's clear these seven angels are higher ranking because they are called **"the seven angels who stand before God."** And later, these same seven angels will be tasked with pouring out the seven bowl judgments.

> **³ Then another angel, having a golden censer, came and stood at the altar. He was given much incense, that he should offer *it* with the prayers of all the saints upon the golden altar which was before the throne. ⁴ And the smoke of the incense, with the prayers of the saints, ascended before God from the angel's hand.**

In both the Tabernacle and the Temple, every morning and evening, a priest would use a censer to scoop hot coals from the brazen altar, where sacrifices were offered, and carry them into the Holy Place. In the Holy Place, there was a golden altar upon which a bowl containing incense rested. As the priest placed the coals into this bowl, it would ignite the incense, releasing its smoke and fragrance,[243] which served as a physical representation of the prayers of God's people rising to Him. God wanted His people to understand that He viewed their prayers as sacred and beautiful, and received them as one would a sweet-smelling fragrance. And, of course, that's still true today.

All of this is referenced in **Luke 1:8–10** regarding Zacharias, the father of John the Baptist. He was a Levite; therefore, he was on the rotation of those who served as priests in the Temple.

---

[243] Cf. Exodus 30:7, 8; 2 Chronicles 29:11; 1 Kings 7:50.

> ... while he was serving as priest before God in the order of his division, according to the custom of the priesthood, his lot fell to burn incense when he went into the temple of the Lord. And the whole multitude of the people was praying outside at the hour of incense.

Can you picture this in your mind? The people would pray outside the Holy Place while a priest went in and offered incense, which represented the prayers of those outside rising to the Throne of God in Heaven.

Switching back to Heaven, we know that the *earthly* Tabernacle and Temples were copies of the *heavenly* Temple. **Hebrews 8:5** talks about those:

> ... who serve the copy and shadow of the heavenly things, as Moses was divinely instructed when he was about to make the tabernacle. For He said, *"See that you make all things according to the pattern shown you on the mountain."*

This is why we find a golden altar and bowls of incense in Heaven too.

In **Revelation 5:8**, John saw:

> ... golden bowls full of incense, which are the prayers of the saints ...

And in **Revelation 6:9**, John wrote:

> ... I saw under the altar the souls of those who had been slain for the word of God and for the testimony which they held.

We learned earlier those were Tribulation martyrs—people who came to faith in Jesus during the Tribulation and were then martyred for making that choice.

In the days of the Tabernacle and the Temples, there was a connection between *sacrifice* and *prayers* offered to God. Remember that the priest would take hot coals from the brazen altar, where sacrifices were made, and use them to ignite the incense, representing the prayers of God's people.

Here in **Revelation 8**, in Heaven, we see a connection between the *sacrifice* of the Tribulation martyrs, who have laid down their lives for Jesus, and the *prayers* being offered to God. You might recall that in **Revelation 6:10,** those same Tribulation martyrs offered up this prayer:

> *How long, O Lord, holy and true, until You judge and avenge our blood on those who dwell on the earth?*

The picture here is the prayers of those Tribulation martyrs (the **"great multitude"** who have been saved thus far in the Tribulation) mixing with the prayers of the saints (the Church and Old Testament saints) and rising to God, enveloping His throne.

These are prayers for God to judge wickedness, avenge believers who were martyred, destroy sin and Satan, and take complete control of the earth. Before the Church was established, Jesus told His disciples to pray, *"Your kingdom come. Your will be done,"*[244] and we've been praying that ever since, for almost 2,000 years. Have you noticed that the Kingdom hasn't come to earth yet? Well, what happens next is God *responding* to all those prayers.

---

[244] Matthew 6:10; Luke 11:2.

⁵ Then the angel took the censer, filled it with fire from the altar, and threw *it* to the earth. And there were noises, thunderings, lightnings, and an earthquake.

Fire is often associated with *judgment* in the Scriptures. In **Ezekiel 10:2**, the prophet sees a vision of a man scattering hot coals over Jerusalem as a picture of God judging wickedness. That's what's happening here in **V.5**. The prayers of God's people align with His will, and so He moves to act and continue His escalating judgment of the earth.

As those in Heaven watch the angel cast down fire upon the earth, those on the earth will see fire fall from the heavens over the first three trumpet judgments.[245]

⁶ So the seven angels who had the seven trumpets prepared themselves to sound.

The seven trumpets can be divided into two categories:

- The first four affect thirds of the environment (you'll see what I mean as we get into the text).
- The last three affect every person on earth.

Whatever your stance on global warming, this chapter should settle one thing: one way or another, the earth is destined to experience catastrophic global warming. It's coming! But when it hits, nobody will be able to stop it by driving electric cars or eating less meat.

I believe in the biblical principle of stewardship regarding the environment. But Christian, please hear me on this: according to

---

[245] Cf. Revelation 8:7–8, 10.

the Bible and the words of Jesus, we are not going to succeed in environmentally saving a planet that God has promised to devastate in the Tribulation and destroy at the end of the Millennium.[246]

God's plan for saving the planet does not include more robust recycling legislation. He plans to simply remake the earth and undo all the damage we have done. And to that, I say, *"Amen!"* So, take care of the earth the Lord has put you on. But keep in mind that He has also promised it will cease to exist one day. *Steward* the earth; don't *worship* the earth.

FIRST TRUMPET: VEGETATION IS STRUCK

⁷ The first angel sounded: And hail and fire followed, mingled with blood, and they were thrown to the earth. And a third of the trees were burned up, and all green grass was burned up.

The seventh *seal* has been opened, unleashing a wave of seven *trumpet* judgments.

The original Greek word translated as **"grass"**[247] refers to vegetation that provides food for people and animals (e.g., crops, hay). After the hyperinflation and famine brought on by the four horsemen during the first four seal judgments, things get even worse as this judgment causes massive hail and (most likely) lightning storms (**"fire"**) that destroy a third of the fields still producing food on the earth.

---

[246] Cf. 2 Peter 3:11–13.

[247] Chortos.

This parallels the seventh plague of Egypt.[248] We will see some obvious parallels to those plagues across the first five trumpet judgments. It's a project you can dig into in your own studies if you'd like, but I'll let you know the punchline: the plagues of Egypt and the Exodus of the Jewish people were also a type—a prophetic foreshadowing—of the Tribulation. And I believe that one of the reasons God does this is to make it clear that the Tribulation judgments in Revelation are *literal*, just as the plagues of Egypt were.

Some believe the first four trumpet judgments result from a nuclear holocaust, either entirely or partially. Since everyone on the earth will understand these disasters to be judgments from God,[249] I believe they will simply be decreed by God and happen just as the plagues of Egypt literally happened. No other explanation is required. The hail is hail, the fire that comes down from Heaven is lightning (based on **Exodus 9:23**), and the blood is just that—a horrific rain of blood from the heavens, supernatural in its origins.

In **Luke 21:25–26**, Jesus shares what will be unfolding on the earth during the second half of the Tribulation, which is the time we're reading about here in **Revelation 8**:

> *... there will be signs in the sun, in the moon, and in the stars; and on the earth distress of nations, with perplexity, the sea and the waves roaring; men's hearts failing them from fear and the expectation of those things which are coming on the earth, for the powers of the heavens will be shaken.*

---

[248] Cf. Exodus 9:13–35.

[249] Cf. Revelation 6:16–17.

"Shaken"[250] means *"to be set off-balance."* In my opinion, this continues to line up with the idea that something changes dramatically when the sixth seal is opened. The "veil" concealing the supernatural world from those on the earth begins to dissolve, which is why those on the earth can recognize these events as judgments of God (and not in the general sense but from Jesus, specifically[251]). When men look up at the sky during this time, it will be *terrifying*. They will see fire, smoke, hail, glimpses of Heaven sending down judgment, supernatural beings—and who knows what else.

SECOND TRUMPET: THE SEAS ARE STRUCK

> **⁸ Then the second angel sounded: And *something* like a great mountain burning with fire was thrown into the sea, and a third of the sea became blood. ⁹ And a third of the living creatures in the sea died, and a third of the ships were destroyed.**

The second trumpet destroys all life in a third of the world's *oceans*.

Notice again that John uses the word **"like."** That means this is just the best John can do to explain what he's seeing with what he knows at this time. And in this instance, he tells us it was like watching a mountain on fire fall from the sky and crash into the ocean.

I think John is almost certainly describing a giant *meteor* that crashes into one of the three main oceans, destroying all sea life,

---

[250] "Saleuo" in the original Greek.
[251] Cf. Revelation 6:16–17.

boats, and ships in that ocean and assumedly launching devastating tsunamis.

Because of the obvious parallels to the first plague of Egypt, I believe this ocean will literally turn to blood just as the Nile River literally turned to blood in Exodus.[252] *Everything* in one of the earth's three major oceans will be destroyed.

Interestingly, around one-third of the world's seawater is in the Atlantic Ocean. That's the size of the calamity we're talking about—every ship and sea creature in the Atlantic Ocean destroyed, and the water turned to blood.

THIRD TRUMPET: THE WATERS ARE STRUCK

> [10] **Then the third angel sounded: And a great star fell from heaven, burning like a torch, and it fell on a third of the rivers and on the springs of water.** [11] **The name of the star is Wormwood. A third of the waters became wormwood, and many men died from the water, because it was made bitter.**

This third trumpet judgment sees a third of the world's *fresh water* destroyed. For centuries, people have debated the meaning of this **"great star"** being named **"Wormwood."** It seems like every time NASA tells us there's a meteor that has a tiny chance of hitting the earth, I see tabloids and online articles exclaiming, *"It's Wormwood, the ancient doomsday biblical prophecy!"*

But I don't think it's a meteor because John describes the second and third trumpets *differently*, meaning they can't both be meteors. And the effect of the second trumpet seems to imply a meteor much

---

[252] Cf. Exodus 7:14–25.

more strongly than the effects of this third trumpet, which are seemingly unrelated to a meteor.

So, what could this third trumpet judgment be? As always, it could just literally be a star that God throws to the earth. But the fact that this single **"star"** falls upon a third of the world's fresh water without being so large an object that the earth is destroyed, and the fact that it *poisons* the water it falls upon causes many (including me) to suspect this may not be a *literal* **"star."**

I think there's a good chance this is a nuclear weapon (or weapons) that explodes in the atmosphere, causing radiation to fall upon a third of the world's freshwater supply (e.g., lakes and rivers).

It could be that antichrist is at war with a nation that won't submit to him, like China, they're firing missiles at each other, and God causes them to explode mid-flight. Or it could be that as those on the earth see these judgments coming from Heaven, they attempt to launch a nuclear missile at God! And if you think such behavior sounds crazy, take a quick look ahead at **Revelation 19:19** or **20:7–9**.

In 1985, America deployed the LGM-118 missile, which could be launched into space, where it would release up to 12 nuclear warheads that could be precision-guided to different targets.[253]

Nuclear fission, created by nuclear weapons or reactors, produces isotopes such as Strontium-90 and radioactive iodine. As these are released into the atmosphere, they contaminate soil, food, and water with potentially deadly consequences.

---

[253] While LGM-118 missiles were officially decommissioned in 2005, I believe it's reasonable to assume that the United States' weaponized nuclear technology has advanced and not regressed.

Though we are speculating, it's not hard to see some striking similarities between the known effects of nuclear fallout and this **"great star"** that contaminates one-third of the world's fresh water, causing men to die from drinking it.

WORMWOOD

But what about this star's mysterious name, **"Wormwood"**? The original Greek word[254] refers to bitterness (literally or figuratively) and/or calamity (figuratively), and the potent liqueur known as "absinthe" derives its name from the Greek. Wormwood is one of the most bitter herbs in existence, and its bitterness is a warning as it causes convulsions, paralysis, and even death if taken in large doses.

In the Old Testament, the word "wormwood" was used in relation to the bitter consequences of immorality,[255] specifically, forcing the hand of God in judgment. **Revelation 8:11** is the only use of the word in the New Testament.

Incredibly, there is a city on earth named "Wormwood," but nobody lives there. It's a ghost town. And it's not referred to by the name "Wormwood" because it's known by its Russian name, *Chernobyl*. Predictably, some on the Internet have gone wild with this and decided that this proves we're in the Tribulation because the Chernobyl meltdown happened in 1986. Here's what those Internet "scholars" need to remember: According to the Bible, when Wormwood hits the earth, a third of the world's fresh water

---

[254] "Apsinthion."

[255] Cf. Deuteronomy 29:17–18; Proverbs 5:4; Jeremiah 9:15, 23:15; Lamentations 3:15, 19; Amos 5:7.

will become contaminated. That did not happen when the nuclear reactor at Chernobyl melted down. The Lord put these specifics in Scripture so we would not be confused.

However, I do think there may be a clue in this, as I find it hard to believe the Chernobyl-Wormwood-nuclear link is purely coincidental.

FOURTH TRUMPET: THE HEAVENS ARE STRUCK

> **[12] Then the fourth angel sounded: And a third of the sun was struck, a third of the moon, and a third of the stars, so that a third of them were darkened. A third of the day did not shine, and likewise the night.**

I don't think John is saying that the length of a day changed in terms of time because he says, **"and likewise the night."** The most reasonable interpretation would seem to be that the *brightness* of the sun, moon, and stars is diminished by a third, from the perspective of those on the earth.

Because of the intentional parallels to the ninth plague of Egypt,[256] I believe this is simply God turning down the brightness dial on the celestial bodies visible from earth.

Others suspect it may be the result of nuclear weapons detonating at the third trumpet—part of what's known as a "nuclear winter." Hiroshima's "Little Boy" bomb was *tiny* by today's nuclear standards. But scientists tell us that if 50 of them were detonated anywhere on earth around the same time, the average temperature would drop by 9.5 degrees Celsius.

---

[256] Cf. Exodus 10:21–29.

Despite all this, most people on the earth *still* won't repent. And things are about to get even worse. The first four trumpets are sometimes called "The Judgment of the Thirds" because we see destruction to:

- A third of the world's food-producing vegetation
- A third of the world's oceans
- A third of the world's fresh water
- A third of the brightness of the sun, moon, and stars

In contrast, the bowl judgments will be *whole* judgments. They're going to affect *all* the earth, not just a third. Just as the seal judgments were warnings of what was to come in the trumpet judgments, these trumpet judgments (terrifyingly) are only warnings of what is to come in the bowl judgments.

¹³ And I looked, and I heard an angel flying through the midst of heaven, . . .

Some other translations render it **"mid-heaven."** It's a reference to what we would call "the sky" (as seen from earth).

. . . saying with a loud voice, "Woe, woe, woe to the inhabitants of the earth, because of the remaining blasts of the trumpet of the three angels who are about to sound!"

This angel is not saying *"Woe, woe, woe"* because of what has happened or is happening, but because of what is about to occur over the remaining three trumpet judgments (hence the threefold use of **"woe"**).

I've shared my belief that the sixth seal judgment began to dissolve the veil concealing the supernatural world from the natural world. In **Revelation 9**, the judgments will become *entirely* supernatural.

We're seeing that foreshadowed here, as this angel flies across the skies, visible and audible to everyone on earth.

WOE TO EARTH'S INHABITANTS

In **V.13**, please note the phrase *"the inhabitants of the earth."* This refers to the people on the earth who have rejected Jesus and are determined to reject Him, no matter what.[257] As I've mentioned before, Revelation also refers to this group as **"those who dwell on the earth," "earth dwellers,"** and several other terms. This group does not include Tribulation saints; rather, these are those who have determined that the earth is their home.[258] They are very different from believers, who quickly realized that—like us—the earth is *not* their home. You'll recall that the Bible calls believers **"sojourners and pilgrims."**[259]

The angel in **V.13** reminds us once more that the Lord takes no pleasure in judging the wicked. Because He is holy, He must judge sin. The earth and its people cannot reject Him forever. At some point, the issue must be dealt with.

The angel is making this proclamation for one reason—to call the people of earth to repent. He is warning them that this is not just a season; this is not something that will simply pass, allowing them to go back to life as normal; no, they must choose between Jesus and Satan—between the kingdom of God and the kingdom of this world.

---

[257] Cf. Revelation 13:8.

[258] See Revelation 3:10; 6:10; 8:13; 11:10; 12:12; 13:8, 12, 14; 14:6; 17:2, 8. "Inhabitants" is "katoikeo" in Greek. It means *"to settle down in a dwelling, to dwell fixedly in a place."*

[259] 1 Peter 2:11; Philippians 3:18–21.

God's heart will surely be breaking as this unfolds, and ours along with His. Not because the judgment is wrong or unjust but because it is tragic to behold hardhearted people who would rather serve Satan than Jesus, even in the face of overwhelming evidence.

CLOSING THOUGHTS

If we truly believe these things are imminent, how should we live? When Peter was writing about the end-times scenario we've studied in this chapter, he said:

> **Therefore, since all these things will be dissolved, what manner** *of persons* ought you to be in holy conduct and godliness, looking for and hastening the coming of the day of God, because of which the heavens will be dissolved, being on fire, and the elements will melt with fervent heat? Nevertheless we, according to His promise, look for new heavens and a new earth in which righteousness dwells.
>
> —2 Peter 3:11–13

A couple of things hit me in those verses. First, we're not going to save the earth by going green. Even within Christianity, there's a lot of talk about how we're going to redeem the earth and make things better because we're *"trending up,"* but that's not happening. And to reach that conclusion, all you have to do is look at the world around you and pay a modicum of attention. The Bible doesn't teach that things will gradually improve; it says the exact opposite! Things get worse, and we're raptured. Things get *way* worse, and then Jesus comes back, redeems the earth, and reigns for a thousand years before bringing an end to this universe and creating new heavens and a new earth.

In light of all that, Peter tells us to live our lives in holiness. We represent the Lord on the earth. We bear His name. And right now, God wants to use each of us to bring as many people to Him as possible in this special and unique season of world history. Even when people aren't responding as much as we'd like, we are called to be a city on a hill—a holy people, living for Jesus, amidst a world falling ever deeper into darkness.

The truth is that this is not Heaven. That's why Heaven, where we'll be with Jesus, is our hope! If you call yourself a Christian but all your hope is here on the earth and everything you're living for and motivated by is here on the earth, you're in for a life of great disappointment because our hope as believers is that we're going to leave all this and be united with the Lord.

Considering what Peter says, I think it's wise to examine our lives and, if need be, reprioritize things based on what's truly important and eternal. We've all heard people say, *"If you only had six months to live, what would you do?"* Most of us would probably write some sort of "bucket list" in the hopes of making the most of our remaining time. Well, if you knew the Rapture was going to happen in six months, what would you do? What changes would you make to how you live? What would become important, and what would immediately become unimportant? I don't think it's for me to tell you, but I think it's worth taking some time to pray, seek the Lord, and ask Him.

Second, I'm reminded of the Parable of the Talents (or "Minas") found in **Luke 19:11–27**. At the time, "talents" represented a sum of money, and in the parable, they represent resources like money but also abilities, gifts, and so on. In the parable, the nobleman (who represents the Lord) must leave for a time. Before he leaves, he tells his servants (who represent us), **"Do business till I come."** This is

God's word to those of us wondering what we should do while Jesus is away. I think the message of Scripture is clear: We are to do the very best we can with what the Lord has given us. Put it to work. Don't just sit around and wait for Him to return. Don't spend all day gazing up at the sky. Don't hide in a bunker. We've got work to do!

The King James Version has the nobleman saying, *"Occupy till I come."* As believers await the Lord Jesus, there's no call to retreat or hide, only the call to go forward in the things God has called you to regardless of what's happening around you.

Many believers are talking about bunkers and trying to find ways to remove themselves from the cities and suburbs. Listen, Church: we're called to be the light of Jesus in our world, no matter what, even if our lives become endangered. And as we do our best to live this out, we should remember the many times God has promised to show up in the believer's life in a world falling apart. So many of the great stories in the Bible document God showing up when everything is unraveling, which is why David writes in **Psalm 23:5**:

> **You prepare a table before me in the presence of my enemies; You anoint my head with oil; my cup runs over.**

David paints a picture of the Lord blessing him, preparing a table for him, anointing his head with oil, and providing for him materially, spiritually, and emotionally while he's surrounded by people who want to kill him. He says, **"my cup runs over."** When is David's life overflowing with blessings? When the whole world seems to be against him. The Lord loves to give believers this type of testimony.

Now is not the time to run, hide, or try to blend in. It's time to live by radical faith because the Lord said, *"Do business till I come."*

Everything we read about in this chapter is really going to happen one day soon. That's why we need to be shining, taking steps of faith, living fearlessly, doing business until He comes, and living holy lives.

If you are living a sold-out life for Jesus, then you will be ready for whatever comes next—*whatever* it is, *whenever* it is.

REVELATION 9

TRUMPETS FIVE AND SIX

Revelation 8 ended with this ominous verse:

> And I looked, and I heard an angel flying through the midst of heaven, saying with a loud voice, *"Woe, woe, woe to the inhabitants of the earth, because of the remaining blasts of the trumpet of the three angels who are about to sound!"*
>
> —Revelation 8:13

The idea being, *"As awful as the things that have already taken place are, there is worse yet to come."* They say the best scary stories are the true ones. And that makes the story we're about to dive into absolutely terrifying.

FIFTH TRUMPET: LOCUSTS FROM THE BOTTOMLESS PIT

> ¹ Then the fifth angel sounded: And I saw a star fallen from heaven to the earth. To him was given the key to the bottomless pit.

The word **"him"** tells us this **"star"** is not a *what* but a *who*. And pretty much all commentators agree that this star is an *angel*. While some suggest he is a *fallen* angel due to the word **"fallen"** in this verse, I believe that the context will make it clear this is an angel of God who has descended to the earth to fulfill His instructions.

In **Revelation 20:1–3**, we will encounter an angel who casts Satan into this same **"bottomless pit"** and imprisons him there for a thousand years. Those verses will also tell us that the angel has **"the key to the bottomless pit."**

The most logical explanation is that the angel here in **9:1** is the same angel mentioned in **20:1–3** because it seems unreasonable to suggest that Jesus gives a *fallen* angel a key to the Bottomless Pit and then later has a *good* angel imprison Satan in that same Bottomless Pit. Obviously, the fallen angel would simply re-release Satan.

So, don't get hung up on the word **"fallen"** in this instance. It's better interpreted as "descended."

THE ABYSS

But what is this **"bottomless pit"** or **"abyss,"** as some translations render it? In the original Greek, it's the word "abyssos." And while we don't have space for a complete study on the Abyss, I can share a few notes that will help you understand what's going on:[260]

- The Bible teaches a three-tiered cosmological model. There are the heavenly places, including heaven, the earth, and the underworld known as "Hades" (Greek) or "Sheol" (Hebrew).

---

[260] For a more detailed Bible study on the Abyss, you can listen to my message on Luke 16:19–31, "A Peek Behind the Curtain," (June 5, 2016), gospelcity.ca/media/messages/a-peek-behind-the-curtain.

- There are three distinct areas, or compartments, in Hades: Paradise (also known as Abraham's bosom[261]), death (or the grave), and between them, the Abyss (or **"the bottomless pit"**).

- If a person dies rejecting God, their spirit goes to the *death* side of Hades. It's a place of torment and suffering, where they await the Great White Throne Judgment of **Revelation 20:11–15**.

- If a person died with faith in God *before* Jesus died on the Cross, they would go to the Paradise side of Hades to await salvation. It was a place of rest and comfort, but it was not a place of full joy because Jesus was not there. Why did they have to wait for salvation? Why couldn't they go straight to Heaven? Because Jesus had not yet paid for their sins with His life and blood on the Cross.

  When Jesus died, He descended with **"the keys of Hades and of Death"**[262] and led all those awaiting their atonement up to Heaven in victory. From that moment on, the Paradise side of Hades has been empty and always will be.

  The death side of Hades continues to grow, as all who reject God arrive there following the end of their earthly lives, to await their final judgment.

---

[261] Cf. Luke 16:22.

[262] Revelation 1:18.

- Between the Paradise and death sides of Hades is a great gulf that no one can cross,[263] known as **"the abyss"** or **"the bottomless pit."**
- The Abyss is a place of torment where God imprisons demonic entities who have done things so wicked that they cannot be allowed to remain free—even in our age of evil.

  We know their number includes fallen angels who participated in the abomination of **Genesis 6** that produced the Nephilim.[264, 265]

Do you remember the story of the demon-possessed man in Gadara and his encounter with Jesus?[266] Jesus confronts two men possessed by thousands of demons, a **"Legion."** If you're unfamiliar with the text I'm referring to, it's a great bedtime story for the kids (I'm joking).

I'd like to draw your attention to a few details from that incident. In **Luke 8:28**, we read:

> **When he** [the demon-possessed man] **saw Jesus, he cried out, fell down before Him, and with a loud voice said,** *"What have I to do with You, Jesus, Son of the Most High God? I beg You, do not torment me!"*

---

[263] Cf. Luke 16:26.

[264] Cf. 2 Peter 2:4; Jude 6 .

[265] For a detailed Bible study on fallen angels and the Nephilim, you can listen to my message on Genesis 6, "The Days of Noah," (April 15, 2018), gospelcity.ca/media/messages/the-days-of-noah.

[266] Cf. Matthew 8:28–34; Mark 5:1–20; Luke 8:26–39.

The demons inside this man speak with one voice, and they recognize who Jesus is. But, as we just said, they're *demons*. What could Jesus possibly do that would *"torment"* them? Well, a few verses later in **V.31**, we find the answer:

> **... they begged Him that He would not command them to go out into the abyss.**

Again, the Greek translated there as **"abyss"** is "abyssos"—the same word translated in **Revelation 9:1** as **"bottomless pit."** It's the *same place*.

The demons Jesus encountered during His earthly ministry knew who He was. And when Matthew records the same story, he adds a little more detail regarding the protests of those demons:

> *... Have You come here to torment us before the time?*
> —Matthew 8:29

These demons knew they had a future destiny of destruction and that Jesus had authority over them, so they ask Jesus to let them go into something or someone else. Jesus tells them that they can go into the pigs. And they do. They know their future is the Abyss, and they beg Jesus not to send them there yet because apparently, it is so awful that even demons are terrified of being sent there.

In **Revelation 20:1–3**, we learn that Satan Himself will be imprisoned in the Abyss:

> **... I saw an angel coming down from heaven, having the key to the bottomless pit and a great chain in his hand. He laid hold of the dragon, ...**

Just in case we're confused about who **"the dragon"** is, Jesus spells it out for us:

> **...that serpent of old, who is *the* Devil and Satan, and bound him for a thousand years; and he cast him into the bottomless pit, and shut him up, and set a seal on him, so that he should deceive the nations no more till the thousand years were finished...**

According to the Scriptures, **"the bottomless pit"/"the abyss"** is a place of torment where God imprisons demonic entities for egregious offenses.

The demonic entities currently in the Abyss are worse than anything we've ever seen. And they have been imprisoned and tormented for a long, long time. They're not going to be happy when they get out, and when they do, it will be hell on earth.

> **² And he** [the angel] **opened the bottomless pit, and smoke arose out of the pit like the smoke of a great furnace. So the sun and the air were darkened because of the smoke of the pit.**

If you and I were standing in seventeenth-century London right now, we would find ourselves enveloped in the smoke of various fires that burned day and night. This was because the intelligentsia of the day had identified *fresh air* as the cause of the Black Death, the plague that killed around a third of Europe's population. Today we know the real problem was fleas spreading the bacteria to rats. But at the time, such a suggestion would have been viewed as ridiculous.

In our world today, the intelligentsia scoffs at the idea of demons. They say, *"We now understand that demons are merely projected manifestations of fear, anxiety, and other psychological issues."* They were way off in the seventeenth century, and they're way off today. The Bible says demons are at work, causing people to experience depression, emotional distress, and relational trauma.[267] Inspired by the Holy Spirit, Paul said we do not wrestle against flesh and blood but very real demonic forces.[268]

While we can't yet know, some scholars believe the Abyss to be in the center of the earth, in a spiritual dimension, because it is described in this chapter as a **"pit"** beneath the earth's surface. Wherever it is, **V.2** tells us that it's opened at this moment in the Tribulation. And the description we read makes it sound as though a hole literally tears open in the earth. Yes, it will be just as terrifying as it sounds and more.

³ Then out of the smoke locusts came upon the earth.

As we read this chapter, I think it becomes clear that John is not saying they were *literal* locusts. He is saying their *number* was so great that as they poured out of the Abyss, they *looked* like a swarm of locusts. They were so numerous that their presence blocked out the sun as they spread across the earth. And the darkness they bring is undoubtedly more than physical—they are an unspeakable evil unleashed on the earth.

I'll share the punchline up front: these locusts are clearly *demonic entities* of some sort. And our first clue is relatively obvious: they come out of **"the bottomless pit."**

---

[267] Please understand that I am not claiming these maladies to be exclusively caused by demonic activity.

[268] Cf. Ephesians 6:12.

> **And to them was given power, as the scorpions of the earth have power. ⁴ They were commanded not to harm the grass of the earth, or any green thing, or any tree, but only those men who do not have the seal of God on their foreheads.**

There is an obvious parallel here to the eighth plague in **Exodus 10**. Just as that plague fell exclusively upon those who were opposed to God, this judgment shall fall solely upon those who are opposed to God. The 144,000 of **Revelation 7** and those on the earth who have turned to Jesus will *not* be affected by this judgment, which will only make those who *are* affected hate and persecute them with even greater ferocity.

Even during the Tribulation, the words of **2 Timothy 2:19** ring true:

> **. . . the solid foundation of God stands, having this seal:** *"The Lord knows those who are His . . . "*

Revelation 9 describes the things that come out of the Abyss as being like **"locusts,"** and it says they torment men like stinging scorpions:

> ⁵ **And they** [the locusts] **were not given** *authority* **to kill them, but to torment them** *for* **five months. Their torment** *was* **like the torment of a scorpion when it strikes a man.**

But we also see that they must have permission to do this. **V.3** says they were **"given power"**; **V.4** says, **"They were commanded"**; **V.5** says, **"they were not given authority to kill them."**

Satan and his allies would *love* to kill everybody on earth because it would prevent anybody else from being saved. Instead, the Lord permits them to torment those on the earth that they might be brought to repentance. As always, God is calling the shots, and these demons are subject to His authority.

For those on the earth who are opposed to God, this **"torment"** will continue for five months.[269] **V.6** describes the effect of these horrific **"locusts"**:

⁶ In those days men will seek death and will not find it; they will desire to die, and death will flee from them.

That is *dark*.

Because these **"locusts"** are demonic entities, we can assume the torment they inflict is not only physical but also spiritual. We're likely talking about millions of people being *possessed* by demons. It will be so unbearable that people will want to commit suicide but will be unable to.

This is what we see when the Bible describes cases of demonic possession. The person is not in control of themselves, so they can't kill themselves, even though they want to. They are just *tormented*. They cut, harm, and hurt themselves but don't kill themselves. And even if they can get a knife, gun, or some pills, they won't work. This torment will be inescapable.

Just as literal locusts destroy all traces of life, turning once green fields into deserts, this demonic swarm will also destroy all traces of life in those who refuse to turn to the Lord—turning once sovereign men and women into slaves of darkness.

God is giving those who reject His offer of salvation a preview of the alternative. These demons will be their brethren for all eternity, where suffering and unfulfilled desire for death will continue forever.

---

[269] Five months happens to be the average lifespan of a locust.

> ... men will seek death and will not find it; they will desire to die, and death will flee from them.

Tragically, we'll learn that few (if any) will repent. And this will go on, all over the world, for five months.

V.7 gives us more detail regarding these *things* that come out of the Abyss:

> ⁷ The shape of the locusts was like . . .

Meaning John's doing his best to describe what he sees with his limited vocabulary.

> ... horses prepared for battle. On their heads were crowns of something like gold, ...

The crowns mentioned there are "stephanos" in the Greek—victor's crowns—because, for these five months, they will be permitted to *conquer*.

> ... and their faces *were* like the faces of men. ⁸ They had hair like women's hair, and their teeth were like lions' *teeth.* ⁹ And they had breastplates like breastplates of iron, and the sound of their wings *was* like the sound of chariots with many horses running into battle. ¹⁰ They had tails like scorpions, and there were stings in their tails. Their power *was* to hurt men five months.

If you visualize this scene, it's terrifying. I believe these are most likely *fallen angels*.

We're not explicitly told that people on earth can *see* these demonic entities. Because John is in Heaven, watching from the supernatural dimension, he can perceive the natural and supernatural worlds. But by now, you know my personal belief, which is that those on the earth can also see beings in the supernatural dimension at this time.

The Bible tells us that angels can take physical human form, which was true of the fallen angels in **Genesis 6**. But here in **Revelation 9**, with the supernatural veil removed, these fallen angels can be seen in their true form by those on the earth.

> [11] **And they had as king over them the angel of the bottomless pit, whose name in Hebrew *is* Abaddon, but in Greek he has the name Apollyon.**

Both **"Apollyon"** and **"Abaddon"** mean *"destroyer."* And this destroyer rules over whatever is released from **"the bottomless pit"** as their king. Jesus revealed Satan's agenda in **John 10:10**:

> *The thief does not come except to steal, and to kill, and to destroy...*

In the Old Testament Hebrew mind, Abaddon was the personification of the insatiable appetite of the tormenting side of the underworld (Sheol). When this **"angel of the bottomless pit"** leads this army, it will be as though the evil of the underworld has been unleashed on the surface of the earth.

I'm struck by **Proverbs 30:27**, which seems oddly out of place in Scripture—so much so that it causes one to think, *"That's a strange observation to include in the Bible."* The verse reads:

> **The locusts have no king, yet they all advance in ranks...**

That verse speaks of literal locusts, but the locusts of **Revelation 9:11** *do* have a king. The Holy Spirit tucked that verse away in

Proverbs so we would understand that these locusts in **Revelation 9** are *not* literal locusts. They are demonic entities under the leadership of Satan.

> ¹² **One woe is past. Behold, still two more woes are coming after these things.**

One woe down, two more to go. One of the things we're discovering is that Revelation is (for the most part) laid out *chronologically*. The phrase **"after these things"** clarifies that whatever is about to happen next follows what has just happened. Logical enough, right?

SIXTH TRUMPET: ANGELS FROM THE EUPHRATES

> ¹³ **Then the sixth angel sounded: And I heard a voice from the four horns of the golden altar which is before God,** ¹⁴ **saying to the sixth angel who had the trumpet,** *"Release the four angels who are bound at the great river Euphrates."*

These are four *fallen* angels (angels allied to Satan) who did something wicked in the past that caused God to imprison them **"at the great river Euphrates,"** where they remain to this day.

The location of their imprisonment is an interesting one. It was part of the boundary of both the Garden of Eden[270] and the Promised Land.[271] The region was the cradle of civilization, and as we shall see in later chapters, will also be the casket of civilization.

The river Euphrates flows through present-day Syria and Iraq—

---

[270] Cf. Genesis 2:14.

[271] Cf. Genesis 15:18.

the region of *Babylon*, an area that has been a demonic stronghold since Adam and Eve committed the first sins there.[272] It was the site of the first murder[273] and the world's first mass rebellion against God at the Tower of Babel under the leadership of Nimrod,[274] the first "antichrist" and father of paganism.

The Bible teaches that there are powerful demonic entities, sometimes referred to as "gods" or "gods of the nations" in the Old Testament, who are territorial. They are "based" in geographic locales, and the spiritual activities of people in that region seem to affect their power.[275]

Without getting into what could easily be its own book, I'll simply say that I agree with the view that these regional demonic entities are supernatural beings who sit on the Divine Council but have rebelled against God. They were given authority over certain regions but became corrupted. And instead of ruling righteously, they have used their power for their own evil purposes.

It seems plausible that these fallen angels operated in this geographic region and participated in something egregious, leading God to bind and imprison them there, preventing them from any further actions . . . until this appointed future time.

At the sixth trumpet judgment, these wicked angels are unleashed upon the earth once again.

¹⁵ So the four angels, who had been prepared for the hour and day and month and year, were released to kill a third of mankind.

---

[272] Cf. Genesis 2:14–15, 3:6–7.

[273] Cf. Genesis 4:8.

[274] Cf. Genesis 10–11.

[275] For example, Daniel 10:9–13.

Death, given a leave of absence for the fifth trumpet, returns to the earth with a vengeance. At this point, the world has lost hundreds of millions of people in the Rapture. The fourth seal judgment killed a quarter of the earth's population.[276] A **"great multitude"** has been martyred. The other judgments have killed countless people. And now, a third of those left on the earth are wiped out by these four fallen angels. Conservatively, we're talking about the deaths of over three billion people thus far in the Tribulation.

Notice the phrase **"the hour and day and month and year."** It's one of those little clues that Jesus put in the Book of Revelation to let us know that this is not all allegorical. It's not all spiritual or mystical. It doesn't all apply to all of Church history. This is about a specific *hour*, *day*, *month*, and *year*. Jesus couldn't be clearer.

¹⁶ Now the number of the army of the horsemen *was* two hundred million; I heard the number of them.

John doesn't count this army; he's told they number 200 million (**"I heard the number of them"**).

There are a couple of possibilities regarding the *identity* of this army. Some say this could be a *human* army. This idea gained significant traction when people were stunned by China's claim in a 1965 edition of *TIME Magazine*[277] that it could field an army of 200 million people with just a month's notice.

It may be that at this time, an army from a country or countries that do not want to submit to antichrist's leadership revolt against

---

[276] Cf. Revelation 6:8.

[277] "Red China: Firecracker No. 2," *TIME Magazine,* May 21, 1965, https://content.time.com/time/subscriber/article/0,33009,901693,00.html.

him. They refuse to follow Jesus, but they also refuse to follow antichrist. And the war their march sparks kills countless millions of people.

When I read John's description of this army over the next few verses and note the supernatural shift at the fifth trumpet, it leads me to believe this is a *demonic* army being led by the four fallen angels released from the Euphrates. The supernatural and natural worlds continue to collide and merge as these supernatural entities cause physical death and destruction.

It may be that human beings are working in partnership with this demonic army, but I think John is most likely describing an army of supernatural beings.

If you find the idea of a demonic army preposterous, you should know there is a *precedent* for spiritual armies in the Bible. In **2 Kings 6:13–17**, we read about the prophet Elisha who prayed for his assistant to see into the spiritual dimension when they seemed doomed. Sure enough, the man's spiritual eyes were opened, and he saw an *army* of God's angels, including horses and chariots. And if *angels* can organize into an army, then *fallen* angels can surely do the same thing.

^{17} And thus I saw the horses in the vision: those who sat on them had breastplates of fiery red, hyacinth blue, and sulfur yellow; ...

We don't understand the significance of those colors today, but I'm sure it will be apparent when the time comes.

... and the heads of the horses *were* like the heads of lions; and out of their mouths came fire, smoke, and brimstone. ^{18} By these three *plagues* a third of mankind was killed - by the fire and the smoke and the brimstone which came out

of their mouths. ¹⁹ For their power is in their mouth and in their tails; for their tails *are* like serpents, having heads; and with them they do harm.

By this point in the Great Tribulation, the dream of a secular humanistic one-world utopian society lies in ruins. The earth has been devastated by one judgment after another. Most of the population has been killed or murdered. The streets are littered with corpses. Men and women have been reduced to living and thinking like animals. The idea that people have power has been exposed as a farce, and antichrist has been exposed as an impotent fraud.

So, how do people respond?

²⁰ But the rest of mankind, who were not killed by these plagues, did not repent of the works of their hands, that they should not worship demons, and idols of gold, silver, brass, stone, and wood, which can neither see nor hear nor walk.

The idea in **VV.20–21** is that those on the earth refuse to repent of the evil they have been doing since the days leading up to the Rapture. Despite all the evidence and warnings God has given them, they continue their wicked ways, even after the sixth trumpet.

Our brother John explains why people do this, writing:

> ...this is the condemnation, that the light has come into the world, and men loved darkness rather than light, because their deeds were evil. For everyone practicing evil hates the light and does not come to the light, lest his deeds should be exposed.
>
> —John 3:19–20

Why don't these people repent? For the same reason people don't repent today. They love their sin. They love the darkness more than they desire the light.

It may very well be that those on the earth who refuse to repent after the fifth trumpet lose the ability to *ever* repent. This would again parallel the Exodus plagues, where Pharaoh repeatedly hardened his *own* heart[278] before God finally hardened it.[279] It is a disturbing biblical truth that one can blaspheme the Holy Spirit and lose the opportunity to ever be saved[280] long before one's earthly death. There is a point where a person hardens their heart in the face of such overwhelming evidence that it becomes clear they will *never* turn to the Lord. Such was the case with Pharaoh, some of the religious leaders in Jesus' day,[281] and most of Israel.[282]

Some might think, *"Come on, Jeff. We don't worship those kinds of idols in the twenty-first century."* Really? We don't need gold or silver made into anything; we'll worship it just for being gold and silver! We'll devote our lives to working for it. Look at any parking lot and tell me that nobody is worshipping idols made of metal. How many people do you know who idolize the home they're killing themselves to earn enough gold and silver to buy? Trust me, we worship idols made of wood and stone.

The overarching point is that these people are wholeheartedly committed to earthly, material things. They are not interested in or

---

[278] Cf. Exodus 8:15, 32.

[279] Cf. Exodus 9:12.

[280] Cf. Matthew 12:31.

[281] Cf. Matthew 13:10–15.

[282] Cf. Luke 19:41–42.

concerned with spiritual or eternal things. Everything they desire and crave is *on the earth*.

Like Pharaoh, when faced with the overwhelming power of God over Egypt, we see those who hate God dig their heels in even deeper in stubborn rebellion against the Lord.

²¹ And they did not repent of their murders or their sorceries or their sexual immorality or their thefts.

Interestingly, John says they wouldn't repent of **"their murders."** It has never been legal in any functional society to kill your neighbor because you cannot build a functioning society if that behavior is permitted. So, what form of murder could we be talking about here that is seemingly widespread and socially acceptable under antichrist? I suggest the answer is *abortion*. In most first-world countries, the government uses taxpayer money to subsidize the murder of the unborn. We live in an age when killing babies in utero (and even after birth) is not considered a sin but a women's right, and something that ought to be celebrated.

"Sorceries" is the Greek word "pharmakeia," from which we derive the word "pharmacy." I understand that there are legitimate psychiatric medical conditions. Some people have imbalanced brain chemistry, and medication is needed to help with that. But we also all know that *many* people are on mood-altering drugs because they are filled with the existential angst and emptiness caused by being out of relationship with God. When a nonbeliever looks at the world and concludes that their life is meaningless and hopeless, they are seeing things clearly. Life *is* pointless without Jesus! And the solution is not to try and medicate away the conviction of the Holy Spirit; the answer is to receive the Holy Spirit and discover the abundant life that is only found in Jesus Christ.

A 2014 study concluded that 19.1% of American adults had taken some type of antidepressant in the preceding month.[283] That's one out of every five adults. **V.21** is not about legitimate medical issues related to brain chemistry; it's about people who would rather self-medicate than repent and turn to Jesus.

And then, it mentions "**their sexual immorality**," which is the word "porneia" in the original Greek, from which we derive the word "pornography." I'm sure I don't need to tell you that thanks to the Internet, pornography is part of mainstream culture on an unprecedented scale. Its usage is not only accepted in our society; it's assumed. Thirty years ago, those who wanted to view pornography would have to sneak into a store to buy it, risking public embarrassment. They'd have to order it through the mail and wait for an unmarked package to arrive. Most boys would only come across it if somebody discarded a magazine in the woods. Today, it's already in our homes, in our pockets on our phones, freely available, and always waiting for us.

I tried but couldn't figure out a non-sketchy way to say, *"I did some research into this . . . "* So, please know that this was *statistical* research. While exact figures can be hard to find, I did learn that:

- One in five Internet searches on a mobile device is for porn.[284]

---

[283] Lea Winerman, "By the Numbers: Antidepressant Use on the Rise," *American Psychological Association*, 48, no. 10 (November 2017) https://www.apa.org/monitor/2017/11/numbers.

[284] Maryam Kamvar and Shumeet Baluja, "A Large Scale Study of Wireless Search Behavior: Google Mobile Search," *Proceedings of the SIGCHI Conference on Human Factors in Computing Systems*, April 22, 2006, 701–709, https://dl.acm.org/doi/10.1145/1124772.1124877.

- 90% of teens and 96% of young adults are either encouraging, accepting, or neutral when they talk about porn with their friends.[285]
- 56% of teens and young adults age 13–24 believe not recycling is wrong, while only 32% believe viewing pornographic images is wrong.[286]

The percentage of men and women viewing Internet porn regularly is staggering. And tragically, there is no discernable statistical difference between the habits of Christians and non-Christians; in a 2015 study, 64% of Christian men and 18% of Christian women said they use porn regularly.[287] The Church is still lagging way behind reality in confronting this issue. Most churches are silent on one of the sins with which their congregation is most likely struggling.

It won't take you very long to realize that porn will destroy your thought life, your emotional life, your marriage, your sex life, and your relationship with Jesus. I don't need to sell you on sexual purity. If you're dabbling with porn, then you are already experiencing the consequences, and you need to repent. Jesus is calling you to repent *right now*.

When I talk about repenting from porn, the goal is not to have you cry your eyes out and dramatically pledge to never do it again. If that happens, that's OK, but it's not the goal because genuine

---

[285] Josh McDowell, Barna Group, *The Porn Phenomenon: The Impact of Pornography in the Digital Age* (Ventura, CA: Barna Group, 2016), 14.

[286] McDowell and Barna Group, *The Porn Phenomenon*, 14.

[287] McDowell and Barna Group, *The Porn Phenomenon*, 33.

repentance is about much more than just a temporary emotional response.

Like any addiction or sin, we cannot repent unless we are willing to make serious changes in our lives. But if you *are* ready to do that, then there's hope. Do whatever it takes. Install accountability software on all your computers, tablets, and phones. Make your spouse your accountability partner (yes, really). Stop watching shows that fill your head with pornographic images (no, you're not "mature enough to handle it"). Go through a recovery program. Freedom really is possible.

Of course, porn is just one manifestation of the sexual immorality sweeping our culture. Meaningful, godly relationships have been traded for apps that provide one-night stands and strictly physical sexual relationships. The people you hook up with and how you hook up with them is driven by a single value—what you crave at the moment. Whatever you want is justified because you want it. Such is the sexual ethos of our culture. Those on the earth during the Tribulation will have no interest in giving up their sexual immorality. They would rather go to war with God than allow Jesus to be Lord over their sexuality.

As the love of many grows cold,[288] our society has less and less of a conscience regarding **"thefts."** Politicians and corporate leaders become increasingly brazen in their corruption. More people tend to cheat on their taxes and fake sick days. More people over-bill for their time, cut corners, and help themselves to things they want but can't afford. After all, it's OK to steal from wealthy corporations, right?

And if you think thievery and corruption are bad today, what

---

[288] Cf. Matthew 24:12.

will it look like in the Great Tribulation, when it's every person for themselves? I would argue that as we look at the world around us *today*, we already see a society that refuses to repent of these behaviors.

CLOSING THOUGHTS

If you're not saved, you don't know how many chances you will get. This may be your last one before your heart becomes so hardened that there's no way back. The Bible says four times:

> ***Today, if you will hear His voice, Do not harden your hearts.***

If the Tribulation teaches us anything, it's that God will do whatever it takes to help us realize just how desperately we need Him. When it comes to our salvation, all options are on the table. He loves us enough to let the bottom fall out of our lives if that's what it takes to get us to Him.

If you're not saved right now, Jesus is calling out to you. Repent. Turn to Him. Place your faith in Him. Trade His life for yours. Be forgiven. And He will go to work making you whole.

For those who are saved, the list of things we will not repent of reveals various ways we can give Satan a foothold in our lives. Because we are Christians, Satan may not be able to be *possess* us, but we can be *oppressed*. And there are many other secret sins, addictions, idols, and substitutes for God that we can find ourselves trapped by simply because we gave Satan a crack in our spiritual armor to exploit.

If you've given Satan a foothold in your life, repent now. And again, I don't mean cry about it and make a bunch of promises to God that you don't intend to keep. I mean choose to stop believing the lies you've been telling yourself, like, *"This isn't hurting anyone"* and *"I'm doing fine. It's not affecting me."*

Repent. Confess to the Lord what you've gotten yourself into and do whatever is necessary; make whatever changes are required to walk in freedom and turn away from those sins. Repentance is in the change, not just the emotions.

No matter how long or far you've gone into a secret sin, if you repent, the Holy Spirit will bring you peace and comfort. He'll go to work healing you and making you whole again. Why? Because your Heavenly Father loves you—always, and no matter what.

REVELATION 10-11:2

As Jesus unrolled the scroll that is the title deed to the earth, a judgment was poured out with the opening of each seal. After six seal judgments, there was a *pause* in **Revelation 7** before the seventh and final seal was opened. When it was opened, we learned that it consisted of seven sub-judgments, called "trumpet judgments." After six trumpet judgments, there will be *another* pause before the final trumpet judgment is blown.

This pause is not due to God's wrath temporarily ceasing. Rather, it is a *literary* pause to allow John the opportunity to fill us in on some of the other events that have been taking place during the Tribulation. We've focused on the judgments thus far, but there have been other things happening that we need to catch up on.

When we reach the final trumpet judgment, we will learn that it too consists of seven sub-judgments called "bowl judgments." And after six bowl judgments, there will be *another* pause (albeit for just a single verse) before the final, final, final judgment—the seventh bowl judgment.[289]

---

[289] For an overview of the seal, trumpet, and bowl judgements, see "The Judgments of Revelation" chart on pages 224–225.

THE MIGHTY ANGEL WITH THE LITTLE BOOK

¹ I saw still another mighty angel coming down from heaven, clothed with a cloud. And a rainbow *was* on his head, his face *was* like the sun, and his feet like pillars of fire.

As always, we remember that whenever we see the word **"like,"** it means John is doing his best to describe what he sees even though it's beyond description.

In **Revelation 4**, we learned that the original Greek word translated here as **"rainbow"** means "halo." The idea is that light is *radiating* from the **"face"** and head of this angel. He is glorious and beautiful. **"His feet like pillars of fire"** because he brings a message of *judgment* to the earth.

Some say this angel is Jesus, while others say it is an angel. Those who claim it is Jesus do so because:

- They see parallels to the Old Testament appearances of Jesus as **"the angel of the Lord."**[290]

- There are similarities between the description of this **"angel"** and Jesus in **Daniel 7:13** and **Revelation 1**.

- There is a clear Old Testament counterpart to this chapter found at the end of Ezekiel Chapter 2 and the beginning of Chapter 3.[291] God gives Ezekiel a scroll to eat, and some posit that the **"little book"** John is given

---

[290] Cf. Genesis 16:7–12, 21:17–18, 22:11–18; Exodus 3:2; Judges 2:1–4, 5:23, 6:11–24, 13:3–22; 2 Samuel 24:16; Zechariah 1:12, 3:1, 12:8.

[291] Ezekiel 2:7–3:4, 14.

to eat in this chapter must therefore also be given to him by God, not an angel.

I'm in the camp of those who believe this is an angel and not the Lord Jesus. I hold that view because:

- When Jesus came to the earth, He identified Himself as the Son of God. He never appears as the Angel of the Lord after the Incarnation because He is forever the Son of God and the Son of Man.

- Angels can be glorious and beautiful. Just read the description of Lucifer in **Ezekiel 28:11–13**.

- In **VV.5–6**, this **"angel"** will swear by the Creator God in such a way that it's clear the God he's swearing by is in Heaven while this **"angel"** is on the earth. In the New Testament, Jesus is the only member of the Trinity credited as the Creator.

- The use of the Greek word *"allos"* instead of *"heteros."* If I say to you, *"Can you give me another pencil?"* it can be confusing because it's not apparent whether I'm asking you to give me another pencil like the one I already have or another pencil that is *different* from the one I already have. In Greek, there are two variations of the word "another": *"allos"* means "another of the same kind," while *"heteros"* means "another of a different kind."

The word in **Revelation 10:1** is *"allos,"* meaning "another of the same kind." That is, it means the same kind of angels we saw in the previous chapter blowing the trumpets. To put it another way, there are no angels like Jesus. Therefore, this angel cannot be another (*allos*) Jesus.

Whatever you conclude, it doesn't make any meaningful difference. It doesn't change the context; it doesn't affect the narrative; it's not a big deal either way.

² He [the mighty angel] **had a little book open in his hand. And he set his right foot on the sea and *his* left *foot* on the land, . . .**

This angel is not standing on a beach with one foot in the water and one foot on the sand. This is a giant, massive (think hundreds of feet tall) angel with one foot in the sea and one foot on land to demonstrate his power and authority as God's messenger to the earth.

We'll learn that it's a **"little book"** because it's going to be given to *John*. This vision wouldn't work if the book were sized for this giant angel, as John would be crushed when it was given to him!

Most Bible scholars believe this **"little book"** to be the Word of God—the Scriptures. And we'll see why as we continue.

. . . ³ and cried with a loud voice, as *when* a lion roars. When he cried out, seven thunders uttered their voices.

This angel speaks loudly and authoritatively. His proclamation demands attention.

After he speaks, thunder roars, and there are voices in the thunder that say specific things John can understand. We know that because of what John writes next:

⁴ Now when the seven thunders uttered their voices, I was about to write; but I heard a voice from heaven saying to

me, *"Seal up the things which the seven thunders uttered, and do not write them."*

I wish Jesus would have told John to just not mention this because it's like somebody saying, *"Oh, man, I've got something unbelievable to tell you! Actually, you know what? I don't want to gossip. Forget I mentioned it."* And you're left thinking, *"What was it?! Just tell me!"* But for whatever reason, God said this is not for us to know. If He wanted us to know, He would have revealed it. That means that we would be wasting time if we tried to figure out what He said.

This is the only sealed thing in this unsealed book. And I'm OK with that because if you've been following Jesus for more than a couple of years, you've realized that there are some things we're just not going to know or understand until we get to Heaven. We've all got unanswered questions. But we're OK with that because we've seen enough of God and developed a close enough relationship with Him to trust His character through those unanswered questions. As Paul said, **"I know whom I have believed . . ."**[292]

> [5] **The angel whom I saw standing on the sea and on the land raised up his hand to heaven** [6] **and swore by Him who lives forever and ever, who created heaven and the things that are in it, the earth and the things that are in it, and the sea and the things that are in it, . . .**

As I mentioned earlier, if this **"angel"** is swearing by the Creator God who is up in Heaven—who is Jesus, then this **"angel"** cannot also *be* Jesus.

The point of the language used here is that this angel delivers

---

[292] 2 Timothy 1:12.

a message to John from the One who has total authority over all things. And by swearing, this angel indicates that what he is about to share is truthful and important.

> **... that there should be delay no longer, ⁷ but in the days of the sounding of the seventh angel, when he is about to sound, the mystery of God would be finished, as He declared to His servants the prophets.**

The Greek word rendered **"delay"** in **V.6** means "time."[293] The idea is that there will be no more delays, no more waiting, and no more time for the earth and its inhabitants. The final act is in motion, and it's not going to last very long. The bowl judgments will be poured out *rapidly*—likely over days and weeks rather than months and years.

In **Revelation 6:10–11**, the first group of Tribulation martyrs cried out to God,

> *How long, O Lord, holy and true, until You judge and avenge our blood on those who dwell on the earth?*

And we were told,

> **... it was said to them that they should rest a little while longer, until both** *the number of* **their fellow servants and their brethren, who would be killed as they** *were,* **was completed.**

Now, in **Revelation 10:6**, this angel declares there will **"be delay no longer."**

---

[293] Chronos.

I suspect the implication is that there are no more Tribulation martyrs to come. Heaven is not waiting for anybody else. As I mentioned previously, it's likely those who do not repent following the fifth trumpet judgment forsake the possibility of *ever* being saved.

"The mystery of God" is language used by Jesus[294] and Paul[295] to refer to the Gospel, but it includes the totality of God's plans for humanity. We're talking about things like the Law, the Incarnation, the Cross, the Resurrection, the Rapture, the Tribulation, Israel's hardening and redemption, predestination versus free will—all of it. As we watch from Heaven, *everything* will be revealed and made clear. We'll see God's plan, formed before the world was created, fully realized.

Perhaps you've enjoyed a great movie or TV show, where all the loose ends and seemingly unrelated storylines suddenly come together in a final act that blows your mind. It will be like that by a factor of . . . whatever the largest number known to humanity is! The **"mystery"** will be **"finished."**

The phrase **"as He declared to His servants the prophets"** refers to the last remaining unfulfilled prophecies in the Old Testament that are about to be fulfilled in this final stage of the Tribulation. It's as though this angel holding the **"little book,"** which contains all those prophecies, is telling John, *"Everything in here is about to be fulfilled. We're almost there."*

---

[294] Cf. Mark 4:11.

[295] Cf. Romans 11:25, 16:25; 1 Corinthians 2:7, 15:51; Ephesians 1:9, 3:9, 6:19; Colossians 1:27, 2:2, 4:3; 1 Timothy 3:9, 16.

JOHN EATS THE LITTLE BOOK

⁸ Then the voice which I heard from heaven spoke to me again and said, "Go, take the little book which is open in the hand of the angel who stands on the sea and on the earth."
⁹ So I went to the angel and said to him, "Give me the little book."
And he said to me, "Take and eat it; and it will make your stomach bitter, but it will be as sweet as honey in your mouth."

Don't get distracted by the surface-level weirdness here. It's a simple idiom that we still use today. Have you ever heard someone say something like, *"I loved that book! I just devoured it."* There's a similar idea in play here. It's a picture of absorbing the Word of God and letting it affect the deepest parts of oneself. And if you've been around the Bible for a while, then you know that likening God's Word to food for our souls is an idiom used several times in the Scriptures.[296]

This is a picture of what it looks like when God's Word is not only being added to the data bank in your mind but also affecting your heart, your emotions, the way you look at people and the world around you, the way you see yourself, and the way you see God.

It's a picture of what it means to meditate on the Word of God. To not only say, *"What does this text mean?"* but also, *"Lord, what do You want this text to do in me? Is there an action You want me to take? Is there a belief You want me to change? Is there an attitude that needs to be adjusted? Is there a perspective that needs to be altered?"*

---

[296] Cf. Psalm 19:10, 119:103; Jeremiah 15:16; Matthew 4:4; 1 Corinthians 3:1–2; Hebrews 5:12-14; 1 Timothy 4:6; 1 Peter 2:2.

¹⁰ Then I took the little book out of the angel's hand and ate it, and it was as sweet as honey in my mouth. But when I had eaten it, my stomach became bitter.

You'll recall that almost everything in the Book of Revelation is explained in the Old Testament. Revelation contains over 800 allusions to the Old Testament, and one of the reasons many people think it's hard to understand is because they're not familiar with the Old Testament—especially compared to those to whom John was writing at the time.

By this point in our study of Revelation, you're probably having a similar experience to John in this sense: We're going through an amazing book of the Bible; we're understanding it (perhaps for the first time); we're learning new things; we're having the future destiny of the earth and the Church revealed to us; and we're gaining insight into what's going on in the world around us. It's fascinating, faith-building, and reassuring. Yet, if we're really taking this in with our minds and spirits, Revelation is also *deeply disturbing* because we are reading about real people who will choose to reject God and experience His wrath. *Real people* who will refuse to worship Jesus, instead siding with Satan. And these are real judgments that will fall upon the earth we currently inhabit.

David wrote in **Psalm 119:103**:

How sweet are Your words to my taste,
***Sweeter* than honey to my mouth!**

The prophet Jeremiah said:

Your words were found, and I ate them,
And Your word was to me the joy and rejoicing of my heart . . .
—Jeremiah 15:16

But it's also bitter when you realize that most of the world doesn't know any of this is coming because most don't care. This part of Revelation is sweet in the mouth and bitter in the stomach.

Because the text has taken us there, I want to share a practical exhortation. Precious Christian, flee from preachers and teachers who are only ever sweet. The Church today is full of these guys (and girls), and they're usually among the most popular "preachers" in evangelicalism. According to the Bible, if their words only ever leave you with a sweet taste, it's probably because they're leaving the other half out.

Jesus said:

Enter by the narrow gate; for wide is the gate and broad is the way that leads to destruction, and there are many who go in by it. Because narrow is the gate and difficult is the way which leads to life, and there are few who find it.

—Matthew 7:13–14

The *sweet* news is that there is a way that leads to life, and you can find it. The *bitter* news is that it's not easy, which is why most don't choose it and end up on the way that leads to destruction.

There are many preachers and teachers out there who aren't spreading lies; they're saying what the Bible says. The problem is not in what they're saying, it's in what they're *not* saying. They just never seem to get around to sharing the whole truth of God's Word. They never seem to share the sweetness *and* the bitterness.

In the last letter he wrote, Paul issued this warning to a young Pastor Timothy:

. . . the time will come when they [those who call themselves Christians] **will not endure sound doctrine, but according**

to their own desires, *because* they have itching ears, they will heap up for themselves teachers; and they will turn *their* ears away from the truth, and be turned aside to fables.

—2 Timothy 4:3–4

In the last days, the days we're living in, people will not want the whole truth; they will want **"fables"** like these:

"All you must do to be saved is raise your hand and say a prayer. Then you can just keep living life however you want."

"If you love and serve Jesus, everything in your life will work out. You'll get that promotion. You'll always have an abundance of money. You'll be immune from sickness."

"Jesus came to the earth to die so that you would have Holy Spirit power to make your dreams come true!"

I expect believers who are not in the Word to be deceived. Do not be one of them. Don't give your time or attention to preachers and teachers who are only ever sweet, sweet, sweet. In their efforts to make God's Word sweeter, they lead many to destruction because they lead people to believe they're saved when they are not.

The end-times prophecies of Scripture are, like the rest of the Bible, sweet. They are a blessing. But if we're really taking them in, they will also leave us disturbed by the reality of how lost the world around us is. They will leave us nauseated over how sick and lost our culture is. And that's the way it should be. That's the Word of God doing what it does and producing in us a holy discontent.

[11] And he said to me, *"You must prophesy again about many peoples, nations, tongues, and kings."*

John is told that the end is near, and it's going to be sweet, but first, a few more things must take place on earth. These things will be difficult to comprehend and, for the most part, people will continue to reject the Lord. Their fate is going to leave John with a bitter aftertaste. Ultimately, the end will be *sweet* because God finally deals with the problem of evil on the earth, and good triumphs in the end. But it will be *bitter* because many choose evil and their own destruction over Jesus and salvation.

THE NEW TEMPLE IN JERUSALEM

Continuing into **Revelation 11**:

> ¹ **Then I was given a reed like a measuring rod.**

This bamboo-like staff was a simple measuring instrument used in John's day. It was hollow and light, yet rigid, and was probably around ten feet long. Whenever somebody uses a measuring rod in the Bible, it's a symbol of, or precursor to, judgment.[297] Because we are not given the measurements John took, we can reasonably deduce that his actions were to convey something else—most likely God marking Israel, symbolized by the Temple, for protection and deliverance as He judged the earth.

Nothing in this chapter gives us reason to believe the text is speaking allegorically or mystically. And that's important because the text is going to speak of a future development that seems impossible today.

---

[297] Cf. 2 Kings 21:13; Isaiah 34:11; Jeremiah 31:38–39; Lamentations 2:8; Ezekiel 40:2ff; Amos 7:8; Zechariah 2:1–2; Revelation 2:27, 12:5, 19:15.

And the angel stood, . . .

A couple of key historical manuscripts do not contain the phrase **"And the angel stood."** It's more likely the voice of *God* that now begins speaking to John.[298]

> **. . . saying, *"Rise and measure the temple of God, the altar, and those who worship there. ² But leave out the court which is outside the temple, and do not measure it, for it has been given to the Gentiles. And they will tread the holy city underfoot for forty-two months."***

Here's a massive plot twist: The Jewish Temple will be rebuilt in Jerusalem, on the Temple Mount, during the first half of the Tribulation.

Remember that Israel will be God's primary agenda during this final phase of the Great Tribulation because there remain unfulfilled promises God has made to Israel, extending as far back as the Book of Genesis. And God *always* keeps His Word. And so, we now see the focus zooming in on one particular city—the holy city,[299] Jerusalem.

According to Jesus Himself, the Temple must be rebuilt before the Tribulation's midway point. After prophesying the destruction of the Temple[300] (which took place in AD 70), Jesus continued prophesying about end-times events and said in **Matthew 24:15**:

> **. . . *when you see the "abomination of desolation," spoken of by Daniel the prophet, standing in the holy place*** (whoever reads, let him understand) **. . .**

---

[298] This is supported by the use of the phrase *"my two witnesses"* in Revelation 11:3.
[299] Cf. Nehemiah 11:1, 18; Isaiah 52:1; Daniel 9:24; Matthew 4:5, 27:52–53.
[300] Cf. Matthew 24:2.

Here's the part I want you to notice: Jesus prophesies a future time when an *"abomination of desolation"* will stand **"in the holy place."** The Holy Place is a room inside the Temple. Here's what I'm getting at: Jesus' prophecy can only be fulfilled if the Temple is *rebuilt*.

The *"abomination of desolation"* Jesus refers to is a term taken from **Daniel 11–12**. It's a reference to antichrist. And the detail you need to know is that around the halfway point of the Tribulation (three and a half years in), antichrist will enter the **"holy place"** of the rebuilt Temple, set up a throne for himself, and demand to be worshipped as God. Our brother Paul prophesies this about antichrist:

> **. . . who opposes and exalts himself above all that is called God or that is worshiped, so that he sits as God in the temple of God, showing himself that he is God.**
>
> —2 Thessalonians 2:4

Up to that point, Israel will have viewed antichrist as a blessing (possibly even as Messiah) because he will have brokered peace in the Middle East, placating Israel's enemies and facilitating the impossible—the building of a new Temple. But at the halfway point of the Tribulation, he will desecrate the Temple and set his sights on annihilating ethnic Israel. This turning point will initiate the worst season of persecution the Jewish people have ever experienced—yes, even worse than the Holocaust. According to **Zechariah 13:8**, two out of every three Jews will lose their lives during this horrific wave of satanic persecution.[301]

---

[301] Cf. Zechariah 13:8.

For most of the past 1,800 years, biblical scholars generally believed that prophecies like **Matthew 24:15** and **2 Thessalonians 2:4** had to be allegorical or mystical because Israel had been a wasteland since the second century. The idea of Israel returning to life as a political nation and rebuilding the Temple seemed increasingly laughable as the centuries passed. And yet, as we now know, the first of those two seemingly impossible events occurred on May 14, 1948.

Daniel 11:31 and **12:11** give us the additional detail that *sacrifices* will resume at this newly rebuilt Temple, but antichrist will put a stop to that when he takes it over.

Perhaps you're wondering why religious Jews are so passionate about rebuilding the Temple in Jerusalem. As believers in Jesus, you and I know He paid for our sins with His blood on the Cross. But if you're religiously Jewish, you don't believe Jesus is the Messiah. You believe the Messiah is yet to come. And, according to your Scriptures, that means you should still be offering *sacrifices* to be made right with God.[302] Therefore, you are heartbroken over the fact that nobody has been able to make a sacrifice for almost 2,000 years because there has been no Temple in Jerusalem since it was destroyed in AD 70. Devout Jews believe that they're not genuinely practicing their religion if they don't have a Temple in Jerusalem where they can offer sacrifices. *That's* why they are passionate about rebuilding the Temple.

What's the hold-up with rebuilding the Temple? The cultural nuclear bombs known as "The Dome of the Rock" and the Al-Aqsa Mosque. We'll talk more about those in a minute.

In the Olivet Discourse, Jesus prophesied the destruction of Israel

---

[302] Cf. Leviticus 17:11.

and the scattering of her people. Speaking of Jews in Jerusalem, he predicted this in **Luke 21:24**:

...they will fall by the edge of the sword, and be led away captive into all nations....

That's precisely what happened between the fall of Jerusalem in AD 70 and the rebirth of the State of Israel in 1948. Then He said,

... And Jerusalem will be trampled by Gentiles until the times of the Gentiles are fulfilled.

Politically, Israel has been restored. *Spiritually*, she is still as blind as ever. And that is symbolized in our time by the fact that Israel controls Jerusalem but not the Temple Mount—the center of religious Judaism. That's what Jesus was prophesying. He was saying that from the time the Temple was destroyed (in AD 70), the Temple Mount would be under the control of Gentiles *"until the times of the Gentiles are fulfilled."* That time will arrive when we reach the end of the Tribulation in **Revelation 19**. And only then will Israel and Jerusalem truly fulfill their destiny.

Look at the first sentence in **Revelation 11:2** again:

² But leave out the court which is outside the temple, and do not measure it, for it has been given to the Gentiles.

The Second Temple (the Temple of Jesus' day) included the Temple structure and multiple courtyards for Jewish men and women. But most of the Temple Mount area was designated as the Court of the Gentiles. As the name suggests, it was for Gentiles who had converted to Judaism. They were not allowed as close to the Temple as Jews. Remember, the whole Temple was centered on the Holy of Holies, so the closer you got to it, the more sacred the ground became.

In the original Greek, there are two different words for **"temple."** One refers to the entire Temple compound *(heiron;* i.e., the entire Temple Mount), while the other refers to just the main portion of the Temple *(naos;* i.e., everything except the Court of the Gentiles). The word used in **VV.1-2** is the latter. And that could be an important detail because when you add John's word choice to the fact that the angel tells John to ignore *"the court which is outside the temple,"* it raises the possibility that the Bible is telling us that it's not the whole Temple compound that will be rebuilt. It may be just the smaller, main part that excludes the Court of the Gentiles.

Even though there is a rebuilt Temple in Jerusalem for John to measure in this vision, the Temple Mount will still be **"given to the Gentiles"** because **"the times of the Gentiles"** will only be **"fulfilled"** at the end of the Tribulation.

All this lines up with the theory that antichrist will pave the way for the reconstruction of the Temple *adjacent* to the Dome of the Rock and the Al-Aqsa Mosque, on a Temple Mount that will continue to be governed by Gentiles.

THE TEMPLE MOUNT AND A PEACE PLAN

Perhaps you're wondering how Israel came to have control over all of Jerusalem except the Temple Mount. It's clear Israel would love to have it. The famous Wailing Wall is only frequented as a place of prayer because it is the only surviving portion of the Second Temple (a foundational wall) where Jews are permitted to pray (they are forbidden from praying on the Temple Mount). The story of how we got here is, in a word, *inexplicable*.

In 1967, the Six-Day War erupted. Egypt, Syria, and Jordan prepared to attack Israel in what was repeatedly described by Egyptian President Gamal Abdel Nasser and other Arab leaders as a war of annihilation to eradicate the Jewish state of Israel and her people.

Israel's intelligence services learned an attack was coming, and so Israel launched a *pre-emptive* attack that crippled the Arab militaries to such an extent that the conflict was over in just six days.

As she beat back her attackers from her borders, Israel took *territory*, including all of biblical Jerusalem. This meant the Temple Mount was under Jewish control for the first time in almost 1,900 years.

But then Israel did the strangest thing. Not wanting to inflame tensions in the Middle East, General Moshe Dayan ordered his soldiers to lower the Israeli flag they had just raised after taking the Temple Mount. Out of a desire to establish peace with the nations that had just tried to eradicate them, Israel immediately returned control of the sacred Temple Mount to the Arab Muslims, who control it to this day through the Jordanian Authority.

Think about that for a minute. Israel didn't build anything on the Temple Mount or make any changes, even though the people who worship there had just tried to commit *genocide* against them. As I mentioned, Jews cannot even *pray* on the Temple Mount today. Israel's actions seem baffling and misguided unless you understand biblical prophecy. It simply was not yet the time God has ordained. **"The times of the Gentiles"** had not been **"fulfilled."**

But this has left Israel with an obvious problem. They *want* to build a new Temple on the Temple Mount but can't do it without risking World War III.

Interestingly, most devout Jews believe that one of the things

Messiah will do for Israel is rebuild the Temple. I know peace between Israel and the Palestinian Authority seems impossible. But imagine what a game-changer it would be if someone showed up with a plan that gave Israel a new Temple! You can see why they would welcome such a proposal and the man who brings it. They may well receive him as the Messiah—and think how *that* would affect any political negotiations.

When that man appears, he will be *antichrist*, and he will not be a man of peace for very long. We know that war will follow close behind him, but he will go much, much further than that.

3.5 YEARS

Look again at the second sentence in **Revelation 11:2**:

> *...And they* [the Gentiles] ***will tread the holy city underfoot for forty-two months.***

V.2 tells us that sometime after the Temple is rebuilt, sentiment in Jerusalem will turn against the Jewish people. As I mentioned earlier, this shift will occur at the halfway point of the Tribulation, when antichrist takes over the Temple, demands to be worshipped as God, and begins viciously persecuting the Jewish people.

We're told this treading underfoot of Jerusalem will last for a specific length of time: *"forty-two months."* That's exactly three and a half years—the length of the second half of the Tribulation. **Daniel 9:27** tells us this, and I want you to focus on the word *"week"*:

> *Then he* [antichrist] ***shall confirm a covenant with many for one week;***
> ***But in the middle of the week***
> ***He shall bring an end to sacrifice and offering.***

And on the wing of abominations shall be one who makes desolate,
Even until the consummation, which is determined,
Is poured out on the desolate.

Don't worry about understanding everything in that verse. The part I want to bring to your attention is that the word *"week"* is the Hebrew word *"sabua."* It refers to a period of seven—typically days or years. In numerology, it's known as a *"heptad."*

While we use the word "decade" for ten years, the Hebrews used the word *"sabua"* to refer to a heptad of seven years. That's how the word is used in **Daniel 9:27**. The term *"week"* refers to a heptad of seven years.[303]

When it says that antichrist *"shall confirm a covenant with many for one week,"* it means that he will lead Israel to sign a peace plan with her enemies that has a seven-year term. That event will mark the *beginning* of the Tribulation.

When it talks about him bringing *"an end to sacrifice and offering"... "in the middle of the week,"* it means he will take over the Temple at the *halfway point* of those seven years.

Hang with me because I'm going somewhere with this.

Now, let's take a quick look at **Revelation 12:6**. I'll explain this fully when we study it, but for now, I just want you to notice the *length of time* mentioned:

Then the woman [Israel] fled into the wilderness, where she has a place prepared by God, that they should feed her there one thousand two hundred and sixty days.

---

[303] Cf. Genesis 29:18, 20, 27–28, 30 for the hermeneutical principle of "first mention."

This is again talking about the second half of the Tribulation, and I need to walk you through the math here:

The Bible is generally based upon the Hebrew solar calendar, while we use the Gregorian calendar. On the Hebrew solar calendar, a month is always 30 days, making a year always 360 days. If we do the math, **"one thousand two hundred and sixty days"** divided by 30 days comes out to 42 months or 3.5 years.

The Holy Spirit references this specific length of time in multiple places in Scripture. And He references it in days,[304] months,[305] and years[306] (1,260 days; 42 months; 3.5 years).

The Holy Spirit has been so specific because He wants us to understand that this verse is speaking *literally*. Just as He did with the 144,000, the Holy Spirit has broken the information down repeatedly, as if to say, *"What else can I do to make it clear that I'm speaking* **literally***?"*

And if the Holy Spirit went to such great lengths to help us understand that this *time* is literal, then doesn't it make sense to begin with the assumption that the *events* ascribed to it are equally literal?

Speaking of time, I'll share one more reference. **Daniel 7:25** tells us this about antichrist:

> **He shall speak** *pompous* **words against the Most High,**
> **Shall persecute the saints of the Most High,**
> **And shall intend to change times and law.**

When antichrist rises to power on the world stage, he will make significant changes to the legal system. We know that because one of the defining things he'll do is implement what is commonly

---

[304] Cf. Revelation 12:6.
[305] Cf. Revelation 11:2.
[306] Cf. Daniel 9:27.

known as "the mark of the beast"—a mark without which people cannot buy or sell.[307] But according to this verse, antichrist will also want to *"change times."* As I write this, it's 2023. That means we're 2023 years from the birth of Jesus (yes, I know it may not be exact). However, if you're a Muslim, your "year zero" is the year we know as AD 622 because that was the year Muhammad emigrated from Mecca to Medina. Apparently, in his quest to rid the world of every reference to Jesus, antichrist will seek to revise the dating system that revolves around the birth of Christ.

Then *the saints* shall be given into his hand
For a time and times and half a time.

The phrase **"time and times and half a time"** seems confusing to us today. That's because we're used to the concepts of singular and plural. We're not used to the concept known as a "dual," which appears in some languages (e.g., Aramaic). In those languages, a single is one, and a plural is more than one, but there's also a concept between those two, which is called a "dual." The closest equivalent we have in English is the word "both." If I said, *"I had all my friends over for a party last night—both of them."* that would be an example of a dual.

In this verse, **"time"** is singular, and **"times"** is a dual. And if you look up the Aramaic word used here for **"time"**[308] in a Bible dictionary, it will tell you that it's referring to a *year*. Here's how it works:

"time" = singular, one year
"times" = dual, two years
"half a time" = 6 months

---

[307] Cf. Revelation 13:16–17.
[308] Iddan.

The phrase **"time and times and half a time"** is simply another way of referring to three and a half years—specifically, the second half of the Tribulation.[309]

It's interesting to me that Daniel says that during the first half of the Tribulation, antichrist will **"persecute the saints of the Most High"** but in the second half of the Tribulation, **"*the saints* shall be given into his hand."**

Daniel tells us that something changes in the second half of the Tribulation. It could be that the persecution of Christians in the first half of the Tribulation is not state-sanctioned. In other words, antichrist may have discriminatory policies against believers in the first half of the Tribulation, but the state is not rounding them up and killing them yet (other countries and mobs might). That seems to change in the second half of the Tribulation, when he seeks to wipe out the saints and, for the most part, is permitted to succeed.

CLOSING THOUGHTS

This chapter doesn't have a neat and tidy conclusion. So, keep reading!

---

[309] If this number stuff is a bit confusing, I recommend that you listen or watch portions of our sermon series, "World History from Daniel to Jesus," 2017, http://gospelcity.ca/sermon/world-history-from-daniel-to-jesus/.

REVELATION 11:3-19

THE TWO WITNESSES

As mentioned previously, John the Apostle is taking a literary pause between the sixth and seventh trumpet judgments to fill us in on other events unfolding during the Tribulation.

And next up in **Revelation 11** is a mysterious duo who have been the subject of much speculation across the centuries. They show up seemingly out of thin air as part of God's plan, much to the chagrin of Team Satan. But what are they doing and, most intriguingly, who are they?

Let's pick things up in **Revelation 11:3** with God speaking to John:

> *³ And I will give power to my two witnesses, and they will prophesy one thousand two hundred and sixty days, clothed in sackcloth.*

A more accurate translation of *"my two witnesses"* would be *"the two witnesses of Mine."* The implication being they've functioned in this capacity in the past, and if we've read the Scriptures, we will be familiar with them and their ministries.

These two witnesses show up on the earth and begin to *"prophesy,"* declaring the truth. They will preach the Gospel; explain what God is doing and what He will do next; and expose Satan, antichrist, and their evil schemes.

While their ministry will have a global reach, its primary purpose will probably not be evangelistic. An extremely unglamorous aspect of being an Old Testament prophet was serving as part of God's judgment and condemnation of a person or people. God would sometimes send His prophets to preach to hostile and unrepentant people who may even kill them, so that it could not be said that God did not give them an opportunity to repent and turn to the truth. Such appears to be the primary role of these two witnesses.

We've also learned that the seven years of the Tribulation will be divided into two halves of three and a half years, with a significant shift taking place at the halfway point. Here, once again, the Bible is explicit that this length of time is *literal*. The Holy Spirit couldn't be any more specific than to say, **"*one thousand two hundred and sixty days*"**—the exact length of three and a half years by the Hebrew solar calendar.

They will prophesy for the duration of the *Great* Tribulation—the latter half of the seven years of the Tribulation. And as we go through this chapter, I think it'll become clear how we can deduce that. Their ministry will be primarily to the Jews of Jerusalem,[310] as God's focus shifts to ethnic Israel during the Great Tribulation.

We're told they're **"*clothed in sackcloth.*"** It's exactly what it sounds like. Picture a burlap sack with a hole for the head and arms—that's the general idea. In the days of the Old Testament,

---

[310] Cf. Revelation 11:8.

prophets[311] and men who were repenting[312] or in mourning[313] wore sackcloth. These two witnesses will do the same as they grieve the desecration of the Temple, antichrist's power over Jerusalem, and the continued wickedness of the world in the face of God's terrible judgments. They are indeed prophets and will call people to repent. But we'll discover that, as was often the case with the prophets of the Old Testament, their message does not go down well with their audience.

Why *two* witnesses? Because under Jewish law, two witnesses are required to establish a matter as truth.[314] That's why there were two truthful witnesses sent to spy on the Promised Land (Joshua and Caleb) and two angels at the tomb of Jesus following His resurrection. It's also one of the reasons Jesus sent out His disciples in pairs.[315]

You may remember from earlier chapters that the word "witness" is the word "martys" in the original Greek, from where we get our word "martyr." That's a clue as to what will happen to these two witnesses.

⁴ These are the two olive trees and the two lampstands standing before the God of the earth.

This is a reference to a vision seen by Zechariah the prophet.[316] And if you dig into the parallels, you'll discover it's a picture of these

---

[311] Cf. Job 16:15; Isaiah 20:2; Daniel 9:3.

[312] Cf. 2 Kings 6:30, 19:1; 1 Chronicles 21:16; Matthew 11:21; Luke 10:13.

[313] Cf. Genesis 37:34; 2 Samuel 3:31.

[314] Cf. Deuteronomy 17:6 ,19:15; Matthew 18:16; John 8:17; 2 Corinthians 13:1; 1 Timothy 5:19; Hebrews 10:28.

[315] For example, Mark 6:7; Luke 10:1.

[316] Cf. Zechariah 4:11–14.

two witnesses being continuously filled and empowered by the Holy Spirit to deliver the Word of the Lord.

It seems worth asking the logical question, *"If the majority of the people on earth hate Jesus and are killing His followers at this time, then how are these two men able to survive preaching publicly in Jerusalem for three and a half years?"* The next verse provides the answer:

> **⁵ And if anyone wants to harm them, fire proceeds from their mouth and devours their enemies. And if anyone wants to harm them, he must be killed in this manner.**

That explains it! Devouring your enemies with fire from your mouth is an effective means of dealing with hecklers. The Lord will give the two witnesses this power for two reasons:

1. **To authenticate their ministry** and make it clear they are messengers from God, not just two crazy men ranting in the streets. Remember, miracles alone are not evidence that someone is a messenger from God. Their message must align with the ultimate message, the Scriptures, and direct glory to Jesus.

2. **To protect their ministry.** It is the will of God that these men prophesy for three and a half years, even though antichrist and others will desire to stop them. The fire is a practical solution to ensure the fulfillment of their ministry.

When Jesus was on earth, James and John once suggested calling down fire from Heaven to deal with a hostile audience.[317] Jesus

---

[317] Cf. Luke 9:54–56.

rebuked them and made it clear He had come to *save* people. But the Great Tribulation is a different deal. Time has run out because people have been given more than enough opportunities to turn to the Lord.

⁶ **These** [the two witnesses] **have power to shut heaven, so that no rain falls in the days of their prophecy; and they have power over waters to turn them to blood, and to strike the earth with all plagues, as often as they desire.**

Slow down and imagine this: Two men appear in Jerusalem and start preaching in a crowded area. I'm sure it'll be somewhere prominent. I suspect it will be on the Temple Mount, which would be interesting, as antichrist would also be on the Temple Mount, sitting in the rebuilt Temple. I can't help but smile at the thought of antichrist having to share the Temple Mount with these two witnesses, who he can't kill or get rid of—witnesses who spend all day glorifying Jesus, preaching the Gospel, calling people to repentance, and declaring the wickedness and evil of antichrist and his regime. I don't think he would appreciate that, to put it mildly!

Imagine the first day they appear and begin to prophesy. Security guards will be dispatched to remove them, but *fire* will come out of their mouths and vaporize them. Multiple tactical military teams will likely be sent in. They will try to shoot them, producing the same result. The attackers will be vaporized, and the two witnesses will return to preaching *("As I was saying . . . ")*.

Then, they will throw out this little detail: *"Until further notice, there will be no rain."* Somebody asks, *"What else are you going to do?"* And they reply, *"We'll see what happens. We've been given the power to strike the earth with any plague we feel is needed, as often as we feel it is needed."*

Suffice it to say, they will go viral on social media within *minutes* of beginning their ministry.

THE IDENTITY OF THE TWO WITNESSES

You're probably wondering, *"Who are these guys?"* If we're honest, we won't know for sure until the time comes. And until it does, all we can do is speculate. So, let's go ahead and speculate! Because if nothing else, it's good clean fun and causes us to dig into our Bibles.

I believe all the clues point to the two witnesses being *Elijah* and *Moses*. Let me explain why. Back in Deuteronomy, God told Moses to speak this prophecy over Israel:

> ***The Lord your God will raise up for you a Prophet like me from your midst, from your brethren. Him you shall hear . . .***
>
> —Deuteronomy 18:15

And then, a couple of verses later, God addresses Moses:

> ***I will raise up for them a Prophet like you from among their brethren, and will put My words in His mouth, and He shall speak to them all that I command Him. And it shall be that whoever will not hear My words, which He speaks in My name, I will require it of him.***
>
> —Deuteronomy 18:18–19

Because of those prophecies, an expectation grew among the Jewish people that it wasn't a prophet *like* Moses that would appear in the future but *Moses himself*. Right or wrong, that became their expectation.

And in the last chapter of Malachi, the final book in the Old Testament, God says:

> *Behold, I will send you Elijah the prophet before the coming of the great and dreadful day of the Lord.*
> —Malachi 4:5

This caused the Jews to also expect the reappearance of *Elijah* at some point in the future.[318] *"The great and dreadful day of the Lord"* mentioned in **Malachi 4:5** refers to the worst part of the end-times season of God's judgment, the Great Tribulation. God promised to send Elijah *"before"* that time.

You ask, *"Couldn't that be referring to John the Baptist, Jeff?"* While Jesus was on the earth, He said this regarding John the Baptist:

> *...if you are willing to receive it, he is Elijah who is to come.*
> —Matthew 11:14

While our first inclination may be to dismiss the phrasing as an odd translation, it is precise and correct. Look closely at what Jesus says: John the Baptist *"is Elijah,"* present tense, *"who is to come,"* future tense. Jesus said that while John the Baptist was ministering in the *spirit* of Elijah, Elijah *himself* was still *"to come."*

Some of your Bibles may translate that verse *"was to come,"* but it should have a footnote for that phrase that says something like, *"literally it means 'is to come.'"* The idea is that Elijah himself would still come in the future.

In **Matthew 17:11–13** Jesus gives us further insight as He converses with His disciples:

> **Jesus answered and said to them, *"Indeed, Elijah is coming first and will restore all things. But I say to you that Elijah***

---

[318] See also Malachi 3:1–7.

has come already, and they did not know him but did to him whatever they wished. Likewise the Son of Man is also about to suffer at their hands." **Then the disciples understood that He spoke to them of John the Baptist.**

Jesus affirmed that John the Baptist came in the *spirit* of Elijah.[319] That is, the same powerful anointing that was upon Elijah also rested upon John, but he was *not* Elijah. In the spirit of Elijah, John the Baptist preached a message of repentance to prepare people for Jesus' *First* Coming. Elijah himself will return to the earth to preach a message of repentance to prepare people for Jesus' *Second* Coming.

Finally, the Jews were also expecting the future appearance of the *Messiah* due to the 300-plus Old Testament prophecies that predicted His coming. Beginning centuries before the Incarnation, there was a Jewish expectation of three future "comings": Moses, Elijah, and the Messiah.[320]

THE DEATHS OF ELIJAH AND MOSES

The *deaths* of Elijah and Moses are also worth investigating. Elijah didn't die; he was *raptured*. In **2 Kings 2:11**, we read:

> **Then it happened, as they continued on and talked, that suddenly a chariot of fire *appeared* with horses of fire, and separated the two of them; and Elijah went up by a whirlwind into heaven.**

---

[319] Cf. Luke 1:15–17.

[320] Cf. John 1:19–21.

After leading the endlessly stubborn and faithless Israelites through the wilderness, Moses' patience finally ran out when they complained about being thirsty (if you've parented small children, then you understand). In anger, Moses struck a rock with his staff, causing water to miraculously flow from it. But that was not what the Lord told Moses to do; his actions made the people think God was mad at them. God was displeased because Moses had misrepresented Him to the people, so He told Moses that he would not enter the Promised Land with the people.

Harsh, right? Rejoice that you are living in the age of grace! So, God took Moses up a mountain, where he could look across into the Promised Land. And **Deuteronomy 34:5–7** tells us:

So Moses the servant of the Lord died there in the land of Moab, according to the word of the Lord. And He buried him in a valley in the land of Moab, opposite Beth Peor; . . .

Did you catch *who* buried the body of Moses? God Himself.

. . . but no one knows his grave to this day.

The Lord buried Moses somewhere *secret*. Hmmm . . .

Moses *was* one hundred and twenty years old when he died.

Note this strange little detail recorded in God's Word:

His eyes were not dim nor his natural vigor diminished.

One gets the sense that Moses may have some unfinished business. Additionally, there is this verse in the Book of Jude **(V.9a)** that is flat-out *odd:*

> **... Michael the archangel, in contending with the devil, when he disputed about the body of Moses ...**

Michael the archangel got into a dispute with Satan because Satan wanted the *body* of Moses. Why in the world would Satan want the body of Moses? What's so special about it? Perhaps, in some way we can't fully understand, Moses will need it again in the future. And maybe Satan knew this and thought he could somehow thwart the plans of God by destroying it. We're speculating, but I have heard no other plausible explanation of **Jude 9**.

When you look at the details, I believe the deaths of both Moses and Elijah qualify as exceptional. And by that, I mean they are both *exceptions* to how people typically die.

During the ministry of Jesus, an event takes place known as "The Transfiguration." Jesus goes up a mountain to pray with Peter, James, and John, and in **Luke 9:30–31** we are told:

> **... two men talked with Him, who were Moses and Elijah, who appeared in glory and spoke of His decease which He was about to accomplish at Jerusalem.**

Moses typically represents the Law, while Elijah typically represents the Prophets. So, at the Transfiguration, you have Jesus, the Law, and the Prophets gathered together. You'll understand the significance if you've been around the Bible for a while.

ELIJAH AND FIRE FROM HEAVEN

When you look at the *miracles* performed in **Revelation 11:5–6**, you'll find they correspond with the ministries of Elijah and Moses. For instance, using fire to devour enemies. The only person known for doing that in the Bible is Elijah.

In **2 Kings 1**, King Ahaziah falls through the lattice at his palace and is injured. He wants to know whether he will live or die, so he seeks advice from the local god, Ba'al (more specifically, Ba'al-zebub). He sends a delegation to "ask" Ba'al, *"Am I going to live?"* and while they're traveling, they encounter Elijah, the prophet of the Living God. In **2 Kings 1:3**, Elijah asks them, *"Is it because there is no God in Israel that you are going to inquire of Ba'al-zebub, the god of Ekron?"* Moreover, Elijah instructs the messenger to tell the king he's going to die.

They take Elijah's message back to the king, and he angrily says that Elijah always has bad things to say about him. The king declares that he hates Elijah and vows to put an end to this immediately, so he sends 50 men to capture Elijah. They find him sitting on a rock and tell him that the king wants to see him right away. They order him to come down, but Elijah replies, *"If I am a man of God, let fire come down from Heaven and consume you"* (**2 Kings 1:10**). And boom! That's exactly what happens. It's a beautiful story.

Word gets back to the king, who gets even angrier and says that he's *done* with Elijah, so he sends another group of men to capture him (he's a slow learner). They do the same thing, and Elijah responds the same way. More toasty soldiers.

The king is *incensed* at this point, so he sends *another* group of 50 men. But these guys were more intelligent than the king. When they reach Elijah, they bow down and say something along the lines of, *"We recognize that you're a man of God, have mercy on us. We work for the king. He's an idiot, a jerk, and we all know it. You're awesome, and we're unworthy."* They nicely ask, *"Would you please come with us to see the king?"* Elijah says, *"Yeah, sure. No problem."* And off they go.

Read **2 Kings 1** and **1 Kings 18:20–40**. They are great stories, and you'll learn that Elijah is *the* fire-from-Heaven guy in the Bible.

OTHER POWERS OF THE TWO WITNESSES

Elijah also *stopped the rain*,[321] which is interesting because **Revelation 11:6** says:

> **These** [the two witnesses] **have power to shut heaven, so that no rain falls in the days of their prophecy…**

And **James 5:17** says:

> **Elijah was a man with a nature like ours, and he prayed earnestly that it would not rain; and it did not rain on the land for…**

Guess how long?

> **…three years and six months.**

That's a total of 3.5 years. 42 months. 1,260 days. Coincidence? I think not.

Revelation 11:6 told us, "**they have power over waters to turn them to blood.**" Who did that in the Old Testament? Moses, for the first plague in Egypt.[322]

And then finally, **Revelation 11:6** also tells us these two witnesses have the power "**to strike the earth with all plagues, as often as they desire.**" Who did God use to bring the plagues upon Egypt? *Moses.*[323]

---

[321] Cf. 1 Kings 17–18.

[322] Cf. Exodus 7:19–20.

[323] Cf. Exodus 7–12.

THE TWO WITNESSES KILLED

⁷ **When they finish their testimony, the beast that ascends out of the bottomless pit will make war against them, overcome them, and kill them.**

Despite their earthly deaths, their testimony is not cut short. It is not interrupted. It ends when it is *finished*, from God's perspective. When you're faithfully serving Jesus, you are immortal until you have fulfilled God's purposes for your earthly life. God has a plan for you, and if you live your life in agreement with that plan, you can trust that you won't go until it's your time to go. And when it is your time to go, you'll go.

This is the first time **"the beast"** is mentioned in Revelation. We'll learn much more about him in the coming chapters, and as those details emerge, you'll understand how we determine his identity.

In this chapter, we're told he comes **"out of the bottomless pit"** (the Abyss), which is the prison for wicked spiritual beings that is opened in the Tribulation. **"The beast"** is a reference to the powerful demonic spirit that is subject to Satan and will possess the man known as "antichrist."

And in the final days of the Great Tribulation, **"the beast"** is permitted by God to kill the two witnesses:

⁸ **And their dead bodies *will lie* in the street of the great city which spiritually is called Sodom and Egypt, where also our Lord was crucified.**

As an intentional insult, antichrist will order the bodies of the two witnesses left to lie in the street in view of the watching world.

To ensure we're not confused, **V.8** tells us that this takes place in the city **"where also our Lord was crucified"**—meaning Jerusalem.

So, why does it say that this city is **"spiritually . . . called Sodom and Egypt"**? Those are two locations referenced in Scripture as the epitome of the sinful, fallen world under Satan's sway.[324] Both were described as places believers needed to escape because they were hopelessly corrupt. **V.8** tells us that in the Great Tribulation, Jerusalem will become *like* Sodom and Egypt—sinful, worldly, full of hatred toward the Lord, and apparently a home base for antichrist. It shouldn't surprise us that Satan would want to blaspheme God's holy city on earth to a shocking degree.

This description of Jerusalem only makes sense after *"the abomination of desolation"* has occurred midway through the Tribulation, placing the two witnesses in the Great Tribulation when Jerusalem is being trodden underfoot by the Gentiles for **"42 months."**[325]

> ⁹Then *those* from the peoples, tribes, tongues, and nations...

In other words, the whole world.

> **. . . will see their dead bodies three-and-a-half days, and not allow their dead bodies to be put into graves.**

Imagine how this would sound to the reader just a hundred years ago. *"People from all over the world will look at these dead bodies as they lie in the street? That's impossible! They wouldn't even be able to **get** to Jerusalem in three and a half days. Obviously, this can't be a literal event."*

As I mentioned earlier, there's no question these events will be

---

[324] Cf. 1 John 5:19.

[325] Cf. Revelation 11:2.

live-streamed to the whole world. It happens every day. My kids watch live streams of animals from around the world. Once again, what was once impossible is now ordinary.

> ¹⁰ **And those who dwell on the earth . . .**

Remember that in Revelation, phrases like **"those who dwell on the earth"** are always a reference to those who continue to stubbornly reject Jesus during the Tribulation.

> **. . . will rejoice over them, make merry, and send gifts to one another, because these two prophets tormented those who dwell on the earth.**

This is the only time the Bible records those who reject Jesus in the Tribulation rejoicing. And they do it when God's prophets are killed. Why? Because they had **"tormented"** them with their message of truth, their calls to repentance, and the plagues God empowered them to inflict. They knew it was true but didn't want to hear it. And so, they react to their deaths by shouting, *"Woohoo! The men who were making us feel convicted over our sins are dead! Our problems are solved!"*

THE TWO WITNESSES RESURRECTED

Get ready for a tasty plot twist:

> ¹¹ **Now after the three-and-a-half days the breath of life from God entered them, and they stood on their feet, and great fear fell on those who saw them.**

While wicked men and women are dancing around their corpses and taking selfies, the two witnesses spoil the party by *standing to their feet*—unquestionably causing many to experience what we'll term "significant fluid loss." Can you imagine the fear that will grip people?

> [12] **And they** [the two witnesses] **heard a loud voice from heaven saying to them,** *"Come up here."* **And they ascended to heaven in a cloud, and their enemies saw them.**

This differs greatly from the Rapture. The Rapture, you'll recall, is an *instantaneous* event. Paul wrote it would happen **"in the twinkling of an eye."**[326] Nobody on the earth will see believers leave the earth in the Rapture. We'll simply disappear, from their perspective. The two witnesses return to life and leave the earth by *ascending* into the sky, in full view of everyone watching. Suffice it to say, their enemies will be terrified.

While I have no scriptural evidence to back up this point, I believe the two witnesses will probably be holding their fingers to their foreheads, making the L-for-loser sign, as they ascend to Heaven in front of those who celebrated their deaths. I think that because God seems to be intentionally messing with His enemies throughout this incident. He gives those who hate Him three and a half days to celebrate—just enough time to send gifts to each other and *really* get the party started—and *then* He brings the two witnesses back to life. I'm kidding.

Obviously, God is doing more than simply messing with people. He's showing that Satan cannot kill these men. God is in control. He's still doing whatever He wants, and there's nothing Satan, antichrist, or anybody else can do about it.

---

[326] 1 Corinthians 15:52.

And it gets *worse* for those in Jerusalem who have just had their "Dead Witnesses" rave ruined:

¹³ In the same hour there was a great earthquake, and a tenth of the city fell. In the earthquake seven thousand people were killed, and the rest were afraid and gave glory to the God of heaven.

A note in newer translations correctly renders this phrase **"seven thousand men of names."** The idea is that 7,000 notable people are killed in this earthquake—meaning it likely also claims the lives of multiplied thousands of regular people in Jerusalem.

Because antichrist will have taken over the Temple and Jerusalem at this time, it will be one of the trendiest cities on earth. And when the two witnesses are killed, the party will be *massive*. Dignitaries and celebrities will flood into the city, but the celebration will be cut short when the two witnesses revive and return to Heaven, unleashing an earthquake that crosses 7,000 names off the "Who's Who" list.

The statement, **"the rest were afraid and gave glory to the God of heaven,"** clearly refers to the rest of the inhabitants of the city of Jerusalem who do not perish in the earthquake.

While it's technically possible for this statement to include sincerely repentant Gentiles, it seems unlikely. The Jews of Jerusalem will have fled into the wilderness at the halfway point of the seven years or stayed and been murdered by antichrist (this will be explained in **Revelation 12**). There is nothing in the text (now or in upcoming chapters) to indicate repentance by the Gentiles in Jerusalem at this point in the narrative.

A more likely explanation is that these are Gentiles who are forced by fear to acknowledge the omnipotence and authority of God but refuse to submit to Him. Multiple places in Scripture refer to nonbelievers acknowledging God's power and reality without submitting to His lordship,[327] and that seems to be the case here in **V.13**.

As we head into a break in the wrath narrative, we leave with this ominous cliffhanger:

> [14] **The second woe is past. Behold, the third woe is coming quickly.**

"**The second woe**" was the sixth trumpet judgment, which is now complete. Only "**the third woe**" remains—the seventh trumpet judgment, which will (likely) unfold over the final days and weeks of the Great Tribulation.

THE SEVENTH TRUMPET BEGINS

> [15] **Then the seventh angel sounded:** . . .

The final trumpet is blown. And as we know, this final trumpet judgment will consist of seven bowl judgments. However, we won't get to those bowl judgments until **Revelation 16**. There are still other significant things taking place that John needs to catch us up on.

Those who believe in a "Mid-Trib" view[328] suggest this is the trumpet of the Rapture, mentioned by Paul in **1 Thessalonians 4:16**. There are a bunch of problems with that interpretation, not the least of which is that this trumpet is one of seven sounded by an *angel*, while the trumpet God refers to is *the* trumpet of *God*. That

---

[327] Cf. 1 Samuel 6:5; Proverbs 1: 24–32; Jonah 1:10, 16; Acts 12:23; Philippians 2:10–11; 1 Peter 2:12; Revelation 14:7.

[328] That is, the Church will be raptured at the halfway point of the Tribulation.

difference alone makes it clear that these are separate and distinct events.[329] Like the six that preceded it, this trumpet is to herald the coming king, Jesus Christ.[330]

And while the seventh trumpet is blown here in **Revelation 11**, we will not see its effects until **Revelation 15**.

> **...And there were loud voices in heaven, saying, *"The kingdoms of this world have become the kingdoms* of our Lord and of His Christ, and He shall reign forever and ever!"**

I can't wait to hear Heaven say those words.

Around 2,000 years ago, Jesus was in the wilderness. He was being tested by Satan after fasting for 40 days in preparation for the start of His ministry. In **Matthew 4:8–10**, we read:

> **...the devil took Him up on an exceedingly high mountain, and showed Him all the kingdoms of the world and their glory. And he said to Him, *"All these things I will give You if You will fall down and worship me."***
>
> **Then Jesus said to him, *"Away with you, Satan! For it is written, 'You shall worship the Lord your God, and Him only you shall serve.'"***

Psalm 84:11 declares:

> **...No good *thing* will He withhold**
> **From those who walk uprightly.**

---

[329] If you would like more information about this issue, you can read my blog post at gospelcity.ca/blog/trumpet-confusion-1-corinthians-15-vs-1-thessalonians-4-vs-revelation.

[330] Cf. 2 Samuel 15:10; 1 Kings 1:39; 2 Kings 9:13, 11:12, 14.

If there is anything you or I desire that is **"good,"** in the true sense of the word, the Lord will give it to us. It may happen during our earthly lives, or it may happen after our earthly lives. But He'll give it to us. The question is, will we trust Him while we wait?

It can be challenging to exercise faith in the form of patience when we have an enemy who loves to show up and offer us a *shortcut* to get what we want. That's what Satan was trying to do with Jesus. He was trying to tempt Him with a shortcut that would bypass the trial of the Cross. And that's what Satan does to us; he offers us a shortcut to get what we want *now*.

But there's always a catch. There's always a price. If Jesus had bowed down to Satan, He would have been given **"the kingdoms of the world,"** but Satan would've become heir to the cosmos because Jesus would've been acknowledging Satan to be His superior. There will always be a price for you and me when we take Satan's offer of a shortcut, and the price is, generally, catastrophic.

May we find encouragement from the One who is always our example—our brother, savior, and king, Jesus, who has patiently remained faithful to His Heavenly Father and will soon hear Heaven erupt with **"loud voices"** crying:

The kingdoms of this world have become the kingdoms of our Lord and of His Christ, and He shall reign forever and ever!

Those who are Mid-Trib will say, *"See? The seventh trumpet sounds and 'The kingdoms of this world have become the kingdoms of our Lord.'"* The problem is that the verb translated *"have become"* is in the proleptic aorist tense in the original Greek. And that matters because, in New Testament Greek, verbs can have different tenses. And in this instance, the tense used means, *"The kingdoms of this world **are becoming** the kingdoms of our Lord."*

It is what is known as a *proleptic* statement, and it denotes a future event so certain that it is referred to as if it has already occurred. It's a perfect term for Bible prophecy.

Isaiah 53:5 speaks prophetically of Jesus when it says, **"He was wounded for our transgressions, He was bruised for our iniquities."** Had this event happened when Isaiah penned these words? No. And yet he recorded it in the *past tense* because it was as certain as if it had already happened.

In **Romans 8:17 and 30**, we learn that we've been **"glorified."** Have you looked in the mirror lately? I don't know about you, but when I look in the mirror, what I see doesn't make me say, *"Yep, I've definitely been glorified!"* So, why does Paul say that? Because one day we will be. It's a fact.

When God declares the future, something that is yet to happen becomes as certain as something that already has. If you want to be a Christian who lives by faith, you've got to develop a *proleptic* view of God's promises in Scripture. Instead of asking God for things He has already promised He'll do, start thanking Him that His Word will come to pass.

When the Israelites faced the Reed Sea[331] while being chased by the Egyptian army, they thought they were dead. They wanted to kill Moses. A short time later, Miriam led them in worship[332] because the Lord had opened a path for them through the water and closed it on their pursuing enemies. Praise is good, but how much

---

[331] "Red Sea" in our Bibles is the Hebrew term, *"cuwph yam,"* meaning "sea of reeds" or "sea of papyrus reeds." For several compelling reasons, I agree with scholars who hold that Israel did not cross the Red Sea but a different body of water called "The Reed Sea," which may have flowed into the Red Sea.

[332] Exodus 15:20.

better would it have been if the Israelites had praised God in faith *before* the miracle?

"The kingdoms of this world have become the kingdoms of our Lord." That's the language of Heaven. If you want Heaven in your heart or your home, speak *proleptically* as you praise God *prolifically*.

Many Christians are shocked to learn that God has never reigned on the earth. Some of you just read that and are wondering if I've finally revealed myself to be a heretic (I'm not).

God created the earth and placed *who* in charge of it? *Adam.*

Man sinned and in so doing gave *who* authority over the earth? *Satan.*

Jesus won back the earth's title deed through His death and resurrection, but up to this point, He has not "cashed it in" and laid claim to the earth by fully opening the scroll. The Lord intervenes in our world in various ways and to different degrees, but up to this point, Jesus has not ruled and reigned over the earth. That glorious day is yet to come, and it's almost here as the final trumpet sounds:

> [16] **And the twenty-four elders who sat before God on their thrones fell on their faces and worshiped God,** [17] **saying:**
> *"We give You thanks, O Lord God Almighty,*
> *The One who is and who was and who is to come,*
> *Because You have taken Your great power and reigned."*

I love this (I say that a lot when it comes to the Word, but it's true every time I say it!). We see the 24 elders representing the royal priesthood of believers overwhelmed with joy, bowing down, and worshipping Jesus. They thank Him because one of their greatest desires, prayers, and longings is being fulfilled: Jesus is beginning His reign over the earth.

This desire is found in every person who truly loves the Lord.

We recognize that all power, glory, and authority belong to Him, so we desire our *experiential* reality to line up with *spiritual* reality.

The royal priesthood continues speaking praise to Jesus:

¹⁸The nations were angry, . . .

Not repentant, just *"angry."*

. . . and Your wrath has come,

Literally, *"is come."* It's another proleptic aorist verb, meaning it's as good as done. **V.18** continues:

And the time of the dead, that they should be judged,
And that You should reward Your servants the prophets and
the saints,
And those who fear Your name, small and great,
And should destroy those who destroy the earth.

When it talks about *"those who destroy the earth,"* it's not making an ecological statement. That phrase is better translated as *"those who corrupt the earth."* It's referring to people who follow the destroyer, Satan.

¹⁹ Then the temple of God was opened in heaven, . . .

We've been looking at the new Temple on earth, and now we're shifting our focus to the true Temple in Heaven.

. . . and the ark of His covenant was seen in His temple.

You might think, *"What? The Ark of the Covenant is in Heaven?"* It's always been in Heaven. Remember, the Tabernacle and the Temple are replicas of what has always existed in Heaven. The Lord instructed the earthly Ark of the Covenant be made according to the pattern He gave, which was based on the Ark that exists in Heaven.

God opens the Temple in Heaven and invites His people into His presence, showing that as Jesus prepares to return to the earth, His people are invited into all that He is doing. We will not be simply spectators. As our brother Paul told us, we are **"joint heirs with Christ, if indeed we suffer with *Him*, that we may also be glorified together."**[333]

And if you're wondering whether the earthly Ark of the Covenant will ever be found again, the answer is, *"Probably not."* In fact, **Jeremiah 3:16** tells us that in the last of the last days and the Millennium, the Ark won't even be mentioned. (Sorry, Indy.)

> **And there were lightnings, noises, thunderings, an earthquake, and great hail.**

God's presence and power are stirring in Heaven as the final act of the Great Tribulation begins to unfold, and Jesus prepares to return to the earth in victory with His saints.

We'll pick up this narrative thread in **Revelation 15**, but starting in **Revelation 12**, John will pause again to bring us up to speed on more events that have been unfolding during the Tribulation.

CLOSING THOUGHTS

If God is bringing conviction and correction into your life right now, I want to ask you a serious question: Do you desire freedom from your *sin*, or do you desire freedom from the *consequences* of your sin?

---

[333] Romans 8:17.

Those on the earth during the Tribulation were being tormented by their sin—spiritually, emotionally, physically—in every sense. But they didn't want to repent because they loved their sin. That's why they celebrated when the two witnesses were killed. If you're in sin, repent. Hate your sin. Because if you don't, I can promise you that any relief it may bring will be temporary. There is no peace apart from the Prince of Peace. You don't need freedom from the consequences of your sin; you need freedom from your sin. And there is no freedom apart from Jesus.

In **Ezekiel 2–3,** we read about God assigning Ezekiel to preach the Word of the Lord, regardless of whether the people listened. The Lord has given you and me the same assignment. We're called to proclaim the good news of the Gospel, even though it will (increasingly) be received as bad news by those we share it with.

Perhaps you are living this out in your workplace, school, or family. Maybe you feel like the two witnesses because you're sure everyone is glad to see you go, and it's like you're tormenting them whenever you try to share Jesus with them.

Psalm 118:6 says:

The Lord *is* on my side;
I will not fear.
What can man do to me?

If you were paying attention in this chapter, you know that man *can* kill you. But you also know that God can raise you. And He will. One way or another, you'll be raised to God's presence in Heaven, where you'll hear Him say, *"Well done, good and faithful servant."* Keep sharing the Gospel.

And remember that success in the Christian life has nothing to do with the results you get. Success in the Christian life is simply obeying Jesus. That's it.

Finally, let me encourage you to exercise a *proleptic* faith. If you're a believer, the question, *"How are you doing?"* should really be viewed as two distinct questions:

- How are your circumstances?
- How are you doing?

Because if you're a believer, you should be able to give honest answers like these:

My circumstances are terrible right now. Standing for Jesus in my workplace, school, or family is creating all kinds of problems. But it is well with my soul. I'm full of joy and peace. Because I know that, in a real sense, the kingdoms of this world are becoming the kingdoms of our Lord.

I know that **Ephesians 1:4–7** *declares:*

. . . God, who is rich in mercy, because of His great love with which He loved us, even when we were dead in trespasses, made us alive together with Christ (by grace you have been saved), and raised *us* up together, and made *us* sit together in the heavenly *places* in Christ Jesus, that in the ages to come He might show the exceeding riches of His grace in *His* kindness toward us in Christ Jesus.

So, while my circumstances are difficult, I am doing well, thanks. I'm doing well.

When God is involved, something that is yet to happen becomes as certain as something that already has happened. Jesus has told us how the story ends. He's shown us our future destiny, and it is glorious. *That* is our hope.

The kingdoms of this world ARE BECOMING the kingdoms of our Lord.

Hasten the day, Lord!

REVELATION 12:1-6

THE ENIGMA OF ISRAEL

On our timeline, the seventh trumpet has been blown, marking the final judgment of the Tribulation. But we will not see its *effects* until we pick up that narrative thread in **Revelation 16**.

When we reach **Revelation 12:7**, we'll discuss a *war* that unfolds in the heavenly places. But for now, we're going to look at **VV.1–6** because John is going to give us some necessary background and history on the key figures in that war.

In the Great Tribulation,[334] God's focus returns to Israel because He has unfinished business with them. Specifically, there are unfilled promises that He intends to fulfill.

Unfortunately, many professing believers hold to a theology that teaches God is done with the Jewish people, abandoning them in favor of the Church. The only problem with that idea is the Bible. For example, in **Jeremiah 31:37**, we read:

> Thus says the Lord:
> *If heaven above can be measured,*
> *And the foundations of the earth searched out beneath,*

---

[334] The second half of the seven years of the Tribulation.

I will also cast off all the seed of Israel
For all that they have done, says the Lord.

In other words, God says it's *impossible* that He would cast out Israel from His heart and plans.

VV.1–6 will explain at least part of the enigma that is ethnic Israel, the Jewish people. Why has this group been hated and persecuted despite being a relatively tiny population and country (when it even had a country)? Jews make up ~0.2% of the world's population, while Muslims make up ~24.1%. Why is Israel such a lightning rod? If they are God's chosen people, why do they seem to be both the victims and the cause of so much turmoil? A closer look at **VV.1–6** will give us the answer.

THE WOMAN, THE CHILD, AND THE DRAGON

> [1] **Now a great sign appeared in heaven: . . .**

Our scene changes, and we find ourselves looking at something else: **"a great sign"** that appears before John in Heaven. As we've worked through Revelation, we've always started with the assumption that the text is speaking literally, unless there is a compelling reason to interpret it another way. And such is the case here, where we are explicitly told this is **"a great sign."** That is, the vision John is about to see contains *symbolism*.

> **. . . a woman clothed with the sun, with the moon under her feet, and on her head a garland of twelve stars.** [2] **Then being with child, she cried out in labor and in pain to give birth.**

There's been much speculation across the centuries regarding the identity of this **"woman."** Some say she is the Church, but that's problematic because the Bible always implies that the Church is a virgin bride for Christ,[335] not somebody who has been married before, had a child with someone else, or is pregnant out of wedlock. And there's no mention of the Church ever being pregnant.

Some say this **"woman"** is Mary, but we're going to find that while she is involved, there's something even greater going on here that makes it impossible for this woman to be Mary.

I'll give you the punchline, and then we'll unpack it: the **"woman"** is *ethnic Israel*.

By now we know that pretty much everything in Revelation is explained elsewhere in the book or in the Old Testament. The symbolism we see here—the stars, the sun, and the moon together—only shows up in one other place in the Bible.

In Genesis, we encounter a man named Jacob. God changes Jacob's name to "Israel" at a certain point in his life. Jacob/Israel has twelve sons, one of whom is Joseph. Joseph has a dream in which he appears powerful and successful, and he tells his brothers about it with exactly zero tact (as siblings are apt to do):

> **Then he dreamed still another dream and told it to his brothers, and said,** *"Look, I have dreamed another dream. And this time, the sun, the moon, and the eleven stars bowed down to me."*
>
> —Genesis 37:9

The dream offends Jacob, and his response explains why:

> **... his father rebuked him and said to him,** *"What is this dream that you have dreamed? Shall your mother and I and*

---

[335] Cf. 2 Corinthians 11:2; Revelation 19:7–9.

your brothers indeed come to bow down to the earth before you?"

—Genesis 37:10

The implication is that in Joseph's dream, Jacob is the sun; Rachel (Joseph's mother), Leah, or Jacob's wives (collectively) are the moon;[336] and the 11 stars are his brothers. Joseph is the twelfth star. We bump into that same symbolism here in **Revelation 12:1**, where John sees:

> **... a woman clothed with the sun, with the moon under her feet, and on her head a garland of twelve stars.**

The twelve sons of Jacob/Israel would grow to become the famous twelve Tribes of Israel. The nation of Israel came from these twelve sons. So, the big thing we need to understand to make sense of this **"great sign"** is that this **"woman"** is *ethnic Israel*, and she is about to give birth to a *child*.

> **³ And another sign appeared in heaven: ...**

We're reminded again that God is revealing things to John using symbolism, and we are changing scenes again, as John sees **"another sign"** related to the first sign.

> **... behold, a great, fiery red dragon having seven heads and ten horns, and seven diadems on his heads.**

---

[336] Rachel had died by this time, so Jacob's reference to Joseph's "mother" may be intended to communicate something along the lines of, "Will your mother rise from the dead and bow to you?" It may also be a reference to Leah, who may have stepped into the motherly role in Joseph's life. Finally, it may be a collective reference to all of Jacob's wives. Whatever the case may be, it makes no difference in the context of our study.

Even if you're not a Christian, you get no points for figuring out who the **"fiery red dragon"** is. It's *Satan*. **V.9** will make that clear.

The "diadema"[337] on his heads are the crowns worn by conquering *kings* and *political rulers*.

We don't have time to unpack all the symbolism here, but we will in upcoming chapters. I'll satisfy your curiosity by letting you know that the "seven heads" refer to seven world empires that opposed Yahweh—six from history and one that is yet to come. On the other end of history, the **"ten horns"** are yet to come. They refer to the leaders of ten nations or regions that will make up a type of revived Roman Empire, which will be ruled by antichrist during the Tribulation.[338]

In **Revelation 12–13**, we'll also see the emergence of an *unholy trinity*, consisting of Satan (the dragon), antichrist (the beast), and the false prophet (antichrist's soon-to-be-revealed minister of propaganda), who will together form a reprobate imitation of the Father, Son, and Holy Spirit.

LUCIFER'S FALL

We have been introduced to Israel, the woman about to give birth to a child, and Satan, the dragon who has persecuted Israel throughout history and will rule the earth through antichrist during the Tribulation. Let's see what else we learn about the origins of Satan, the dragon.

> **⁴ His tail drew a third of the stars of heaven and threw them to the earth.**

---

[337] In the original Greek.

[338] Cf. Daniel 7:23–25; Revelation 13:1; 17:12.

As in several other places in Scripture, these **"stars of heaven"** are *angels*.[339] And we notice that because those **"stars"** were following the dragon, they were cast from Heaven to the earth along with him. When Lucifer rebelled against God in Heaven, incredibly, a third of the angels sided with him. But if you know the story, it didn't go well. They were thrown out of God's Kingdom and cast down **"to the earth."** The archangel Lucifer became known as "Satan," and the angels allied to him became known as "fallen angels."

And if you're doing the math, this means that in the realm of angels; Satan is outnumbered two-to-one.

WHY SATAN TRIES TO DESTROY ISRAEL

Now we learn what the dragon, Satan, is determined to do:

And the dragon stood before the woman who was ready to give birth, to devour her Child as soon as it was born.

We're meant to understand that Satan has been bitter since he was cast out of Heaven. He has hated God. And he was listening when God spoke the Protoevangelium, the first recorded prophecy, in **Genesis 3:15**, saying to Satan:

> *. . . I will put enmity*
> *Between you and the woman,*
> *And between your seed and her Seed;*
> *He shall bruise your head,*
> *And you shall bruise His heel.*

---

[339] For example, Job 38:7; Jude 1:13; Revelation 1:20; 9:1.

From this, Satan grasped the idea that God was planning to save humanity from sin through a male child. And as Satan listened in on God's promises to Abraham, Isaac, and Jacob, it became clear which people this male child would come from and where they would dwell on the earth. That's why we see Satan, in this symbolic scene, waiting to *devour* the child that would come from the woman, Israel. Obviously, the child we are referring to is *Jesus* the Messiah.

This is why there has been anti-Semitism for as long as the Jewish people have existed. *This* is why empire after empire set their sights on Israel, a tiny and seemingly inconsequential people. It's because they are *not* insignificant. They were right in the middle of God's plan to save humanity and are still a massive part of God's plan.

There is hatred in the collective heart of humanity toward the Jew, and it has been put there by Satan himself. He hates God, he hates God's son, and he hates those whom God loves.

When we understand this, so much of what is happening in the Middle East begins to make sense, as does much of Old Testament narrative:

- Cain slew his righteous brother, Abel. John explains in his first epistle:

  ...Cain *who* was of the wicked one and murdered his brother. And why did he murder him? Because his works were evil and his brother's righteous.

  —1 John 3:12

- **Genesis 6**[340] tells us that Satan sent fallen angels to procreate with human women to corrupt the gene pool in an attempt to render humans irredeemable.

---

[340] Genesis 6:1-4.

- After Joseph had been forgotten, Satan attempted genocide by stirring the hearts of Pharaohs in Egypt to kill Hebrew babies and enslave their families.
- In the centuries of the judges of Israel, Satan attempted to spiritually annihilate God's people through surrounding pagan cultures, including repeated attempts to lure the Jews into cults that practiced child sacrifice.[341]
- Satan used King Saul to try to assassinate David, knowing Messiah was destined to be born of his lineage.[342]
- When Israel was a divided kingdom, the Messianic line was twice reduced to a single child.[343]
- Satan again attempted genocide through Haman, but God thwarted those plans through a young Queen Esther.
- Satan worked through Herod the Great, who issued a command to kill all baby boys under the age of two in and around Bethlehem following news of the birth of Jesus.[344]
- During Jesus' ministry, Satan tried to stir up the people of His hometown, Nazareth, to kill Him,[345] and later tried to drown Jesus in a storm on the Sea of Galilee.[346]

---

[341] Cf. Leviticus 18:21; 2 Kings 16:3; 2 Chronicles 28:3; Psalm 106:37–38; Ezekiel 16:20.

[342] Cf. 1 Samuel 18:10–11.

[343] Cf. 2 Chronicles 21:17; 22:10–12.

[344] Cf. Matthew 2:13–16.

[345] Cf. Luke 4:28–30.

[346] Cf. Matthew 8:23–27; Mark 4:35–41; Luke 8:22–25.

- The events leading up to the crucifixion of Jesus were fueled by Satan in an attempt to destroy Him.

However, as we know, Satan was an unwitting participant in the redemptive plan of God. In Satan's defense (not a phrase I use often), can you blame him for not seeing it coming? Can you blame him for not even considering the possibility that Jesus would die for our sins? You can't because it's so wonderful that it didn't even enter the mind of Satan, the angels, or anybody else. It's too good. It's too gracious. It's too merciful. It's too kind. It's too outrageous.

Since Adam and Eve were placed in the Garden of Eden, Satan has been trying to wipe out the people of God. Why? Because Satan believed that by eliminating the Jews, he could thwart God's plans, embarrass Him, and ruin His plans to redeem humanity. Unfortunately for Satan, before the world was made, God had already incorporated all his demonic efforts into His master plan.

Having failed to prevent Jesus from coming as Messiah at His *First* Coming, Satan now seeks to undermine Jesus' *Second* Coming. How? If Satan can destroy the Jewish people, God won't be able to fulfill His promises to Israel, and, in some twisted way, Satan will score a "win" by making God out to be a liar.

- *Satan* is the reason for the violent persecution and anti-Semitism that has marked the past 2,000 years.

- *Satan* is the reason Hitler was obsessed with wiping out the Jews.

- *Satan* is the reason why, on the day Israel became a nation again in 1948, the armies of Egypt, Jordan, Syria, and Iraq joined together in an attempt to eliminate her.

- *Satan* is actively at work, trying to thwart God's promise to redeem Israel (spoiler alert: Wile E. Coyote has a better chance of catching the Road Runner).

⁵ **She** [the woman/Israel] **bore a male Child who was . . .**

If your Bible says **"was,"** put a line through it and write, **"is."** That's the more accurate rendering, and I'll explain why it matters:

When Jesus Christ incarnate was ministering on the earth, the Jews (and the world) collectively said, *"We will not have this man to reign over us."*[347] What would have happened if they had said, *"We will have this man to reign over us"*? It's a fascinating question that I'll leave you to discuss with your Church family. All we know for sure is that humanity rejected the rule and reign of Jesus at that time, which is why **V.5** should read:

She bore a male Child who was IS to rule all nations with a rod of iron.

This is a reference to **Psalm 2:9**, which speaks prophetically of the coming Messiah. More specifically, it speaks of His Second Coming, which takes place in **Revelation 19**. The reference to a **"rod of iron"** doesn't mean Jesus' Millennial reign will be marked by brutality but rather that His government will be strong, unshakable, and just. He will destroy all corrupt earthly systems—political, economic, and social. He will have the power to enforce justice on the earth. And, incredibly, Jesus told us in **Revelation 2:26–27** that He will share that authority with us!

---

[347] Luke 19:14.

And her Child [Jesus] was caught up to God and His throne.

Ultimately, Satan could not stop Jesus' earthly ministry from succeeding, and Jesus returned to Heaven victorious. The scenes John has been shown have been a broad overview of the history we've just discussed.

ISRAEL FLEES

Between **V.5** and **V.6** lies the Church Age. And the scene now returns to the Tribulation:

> ⁶ **Then the woman fled into the wilderness, where she has a place prepared by God, that they should feed her there one thousand two hundred and sixty days.**

Remember how long **"one thousand two hundred and sixty days"** is? It's three and a half years—exactly half of the seven-year Tribulation. Anytime we see this number expressed as days, months, or years, it's a reference to the back half of the Tribulation, the *Great* Tribulation.

And we learn here that at the halfway point of the Tribulation, Israel will need to flee for safety. Why? What changes at the halfway point of the Tribulation? As we've learned, *everything* changes for Israel halfway through the Tribulation. Antichrist commits the **"abomination of desolation,"** kicking the Jews off the Temple Mount, entering the rebuilt Temple and setting up a throne for himself, demanding to be worshipped as God, and launching a genocide against the Jewish people.

But our omniscient God has a plan in place to protect Israel by providing a place of shelter in **"the wilderness."**

Jesus talked about this in the Olivet Discourse in **Matthew 24:15–22**:

> *... when you see the "abomination of desolation," spoken of by Daniel the prophet, standing in the holy place"* (whoever reads, let him understand), *then let those who are in Judea flee to the mountains. Let him who is on the housetop not go down to take anything out of his house. And let him who is in the field not go back to get his clothes.*

Jesus gives Israel a *stern warning:* When they see antichrist committing the abomination of desolation, things are about to take a dark turn in a way that will make the Holocaust look tame by comparison. When this happens, they are to flee immediately—no time to grab their things, pack, or call their friends.

> *But woe to those who are pregnant and to those who are nursing babies in those days!*

Because nobody will be able to slow down for them.

> *And pray that your flight may not be in winter ...*

This may surprise you, but mountainous parts of Israel and Jordan to the south can become completely impassable due to winter snowstorms. That's why Jesus tells them to pray this doesn't happen in winter because their escape route will be cut off.

> *... or on the Sabbath.*

This is not a warning for the Church (who will be raptured before the Tribulation begins). Jesus says this is for *"those who are in Judea"* and an area affected by the observance of *"the Sabbath."* Jesus is clearly speaking to *Jews*.

As a day of the week, the Sabbath (Saturday) doesn't change anything for Gentiles other than being part of our weekend. But in Israel, everything shuts down. Society grinds to a halt. That's why Jesus says it will be especially challenging for them if this happens on the Sabbath.

Then Jesus gives a warning to Israel:

For then there will be great tribulation, such as has not been since the beginning of the world until this time, no, nor ever shall be.

Would you agree that as far as sources go, Jesus is pretty good? Of course! Considering that, I don't want us to miss that Jesus Himself tells Israel that what they will experience in the Great Tribulation will be worse than anything they ever have experienced or ever will experience after. It will be worse than the fall of Jerusalem in AD 70—and worse even than the Holocaust.

It's critical to understand the implications of this verse because it destroys eschatological systems that teach things like, *"The Book of Revelation is about things that have already happened. It's about the fall of Israel between AD 70 and 120."* No, it's not. Because Jesus said:

For then there will be great tribulation, such as has not been since the beginning of the world until this time, no, nor ever shall be.

The time Jesus is speaking about will be as bad as it will ever get for Israel. As bad as the events of AD 70–120 were, the Holocaust was significantly worse. That means Jesus could not have been referring to first- and second-century events.

And to underscore His point, Jesus adds:

And unless those days were shortened, no flesh would be saved; but for the elect's sake those days will be shortened.

Unless God limited the length of this *"great tribulation,"* everyone on earth would die. But God *will* limit the length of those days to exactly three and a half years.

WHERE DOES ISRAEL GO?

In **Isaiah 16:1–5,** the question of *where* Israel will flee is addressed prophetically:

**Send the lamb to the ruler of the land,
From Sela to the wilderness, . . .**

Wherever Israel goes will involve journeying through **"the wilderness."**[348]

**. . . To the mount of the daughter of Zion . . .
. . . Hide the outcasts,
Do not betray him who escapes.
    Let My outcasts dwell with you, O Moab;
    Be a shelter to them from the face of the spoiler . . .**

Some translations have Israel hiding from "the destroyer" instead of **"the spoiler."**

For the extortioner is at an end, . . .

---

[348] See also Zechariah 14:5.

Things are wrapping up.

> **. . . Devastation ceases,**
> **The oppressors are consumed out of the land.**

God declares there is a place called **"Sela"** in the land of **"Moab."** Moab is in present-day Jordan. The Jews in Jerusalem and Israel will flee south to Jordan during the Great Tribulation, as there will be enemies in every other direction.

"Sela" means "the rock" in Hebrew, and if you look it up in a *Strong's Concordance*, you will find that it refers to "the rock-city of Idumaea." In Greek, that same city is called "Petra." When you put it all together, you learn that **"Sela"** is Petra, the rock city of Idumaea.

That's kind of mind-blowing because there *is* a city in Moab/Jordan that is called "Petra" (or "Sela" in Hebrew). It's about 140 miles southeast of Jerusalem and 2,700 feet above sea level in the mountains. It was carved into rock around 2,500 years ago and is most famous for being featured in the 1989 movie, *Indiana Jones and the Last Crusade*.

You might recognize its treasury from this photo:

Al Khazneh/The Treasury; Petra, Jordan;
by Dimitris Vetsikas from Pixabay

Petra is a fantastic place. Through ingenious engineering, the Edomites who built it created a system that captures rainwater in massive cisterns, providing hydration in a desert environment. This enabled the development of an entire civilization that once lived and thrived there. Staggeringly, the rock city of Petra could still hold a population of up to two million people. But for now, it's a tourist attraction and designated as one of the "New 7 Wonders of the World."[349]

As always, I encourage you to do your own research, but I am personally convinced that Petra is where Israel will flee during the Great Tribulation.[350]

But if you're still not convinced, I've got one more exhibit of evidence to share. Daniel the prophet wrote that antichrist would . . .

> . . . enter the Glorious Land, . . .

That references Israel and infers that antichrist will conquer political Israel.

> . . . and many *countries* shall be overthrown; but these shall escape from his hand: Edom, Moab, and the prominent people of Ammon.
>
> —Daniel 11:41

What modern-day country includes Edom, Moab, and Ammon? Jordan, whose capital is Amman. Where did we learn that Petra is located? Moab. Daniel prophesies that, for some reason, antichrist

---

[349] https://world.new7wonders.com.

[350] See also Psalm 60:9–12 for a possible prophetic application in David's cry.

will not conquer the nation of Jordan during his Tribulation reign. I suggest we know the reason why.

Israel and Jordan currently enjoy peace thanks to a treaty they signed in 1994. That treaty also (literally) paved the way for a major highway connecting the two countries today.

Let's read **V.6** one more time:

> ⁶**Then the woman fled into the wilderness, where she has a place prepared by God, that they should feed her there one thousand two hundred and sixty days.**

It was prepared by God 2,500 years ago, and God has preserved it ever since.

ISRAEL'S PRESERVATION IN ISAIAH

The preservation of Israel's remnant through the Tribulation is described in the Old Testament Book of Isaiah, where he prophesies from the perspective of the Lord:

> **Come, my people, enter your chambers,**
> **And shut your doors behind you;**
> **Hide yourself, as it were, for a little moment,**
> **Until the indignation is past.**
> **For behold, the Lord comes out of His place**
> **To punish the inhabitants of the earth for their iniquity . . .**
> —Isaiah 26:20–21

God's people are told to **"hide"** in their **"chambers"** **"for a little moment."** This is a *temporary* relocation **"until the indignation is past."**

What is **"the indignation"**? We're told that it is God pouring out His wrath on **"the inhabitants of the earth for their iniquity."** And that's exactly what God will do during the Great Tribulation.

CLOSING THOUGHTS

In the Great Tribulation, Jesus Messiah, the stumbling stone and rock of offense[351] to the Jewish people, will become the rock of their salvation as He shelters them in the rock city of Petra.

And just as Jesus has prepared a place for the Jewish people in the Great Tribulation, He has prepared a place in eternity for all those who love Him.

> *... I go to prepare a place for you. And if I go and prepare a place for you, I will come again and receive you to Myself; that where I am, there you may be also.*
>
> —John 14:2–3

As Christians, we should find it encouraging to read of God's faithfulness to Israel across millennia. Because when we see God's absolute commitment to keep His promises, we are reminded of just how secure we are in His promises to us.

In **Jeremiah 31:37**, we read:

> **Thus says the Lord:**
> *"If heaven above can be measured,*
> *And the foundations of the earth searched out beneath,*
> *I will also cast off all the seed of Israel*
> *For all that they have done, says the Lord."*

---

[351] Cf. Romans 9:33; 1 Peter 2:8.

God says that it's *impossible* for Him to disown Israel. They're His people.

In **2 Timothy 2:13**, Paul writes this about us—those who belong to Jesus:

> **If we are faithless,**
> **He remains faithful;**
> **He cannot deny Himself.**

When we place our faith in Jesus, He puts His seal on our lives by placing His Spirit—the Holy Spirit—in us. And He has promised to never take His Spirit from us, telling His disciples, *"I am with you always."*[352]

When we mess up, foolishly choose sin, rebel, don't honor Jesus the way we should, and fail, He doesn't leave us. It's impossible for Him to disown us because He is in each of us and disowning us would be disowning Himself.

God will not keep His promises to Israel because they deserve it. And God will not keep His promises to us because we deserve it. God will keep His promises to Israel and the Church for one reason: His name's sake. No one will ever be able to accuse Him of failing to keep His promises or lacking love, mercy, grace, and compassion. He is just *good*—only, ever, and always. I am so thankful for the truth our brother Paul shared in **Romans 8:38–39**:

> **... I am persuaded that neither death nor life, nor angels nor principalities nor powers, nor things present nor things to come, nor height nor depth, nor any other created thing, shall be able to separate us from the love of God which is in Christ Jesus our Lord.**

---

[352] Matthew 28:20.

REVELATION 12:7-17

HOW TO OVERCOME

Revelation has pressed the Pause button on the narrative describing the judgments of God being poured out upon the earth. This pause gives us some time to catch up on other events that have transpired during the Tribulation so that we have a fuller understanding of what's taken place before the Play button is pressed again.

In the first six verses of **Revelation 12**, we met three of the key figures in this chapter—Israel, Satan, and Jesus—who will all be involved in a *war* that breaks out in Heaven in **V.7**. But before we get into that, I need to take a minute to correct a common misconception we often have about Satan.

If you read the Bible, you've hopefully realized that Satan is not walking around covered in red body paint and a trench coat, carrying a pitchfork. But you may still believe that he is currently in charge of hell. The Bible doesn't say that. In fact, the Bible doesn't teach that Satan has *ever* been to hell. He will be cast into the lake of fire at the end of the Millennium,[353] but even then, he will not oversee it; he will be suffering more than anyone or anything else.

---

[353] Cf. Revelation 20:7–10.

So, where *does* Satan dwell? According to Satan himself[354] and Peter[355]—*on the earth*. Additionally, as we've discussed before, as the current ruler of the earth, Satan has access to the Divine Council in Heaven,[356] where, according to **V.10**, he accuses us before God, day and night.

INTO THE TEXT

⁷ **And war broke out in heaven: . . .**

While Satan currently has access to the Divine Council, he is not able to trespass anywhere he wants. Heaven is *secure*. The term **"heaven"** used here is better understood to refer to the heavenly places, the supernatural dimension where the Kingdom of God and the kingdom of darkness have been battling since Lucifer's fall. It's what Paul refers to in **Ephesians 6:12**:

> **. . . we do not wrestle against flesh and blood, but against principalities, against powers, against the rulers of the darkness of this age, against spiritual *hosts* of wickedness in the heavenly *places*.**

We have no idea or clue as to what sparks this war or how long it lasts. When we talk about angels fighting fallen angels and demons, we have no idea how that works. None whatsoever. It's so far beyond our understanding and paradigms that we cannot even speculate.

---

[354] Cf. Job 1:7.

[355] Cf. 1 Peter 5:8.

[356] Cf. Job 1:6–12; Luke 22:31.

> **... Michael and his angels fought with the dragon** (Satan); **and the dragon and his angels fought, ⁸ but they did not prevail, nor was a place found for them in heaven any longer. ⁹ So the great dragon was cast out, that serpent of old, called the Devil and Satan, who deceives the whole world; he was cast to the earth, and his angels were cast out with him.**

Your first response to reading this passage may be, *"We know that story. It's the one we talked about earlier in VV.3–4."* Those verses covered Satan's fall from God's Kingdom, and I don't believe the Bible is being needlessly redundant here in **VV.7–9**. All signs point to this being a *separate* incident.

Exactly when this war takes place is a matter of speculation. I suspect it is around the halfway point of the Tribulation:

- Satan and the gods of the nations lose their access to the Divine Council and are cast down to the earth.

- Satan leads antichrist to commit **"the abomination of desolation"** and persecute the Jewish people.

- The earthly presence of Satan and all other fallen supernatural entities is likely why we see a dramatic shift toward supernatural/demonic judgments during the Great Tribulation, as Satan rages against God and humanity, knowing he has but a short time before his destruction.

The big idea is this: At some point in the Tribulation, the armies of Yahweh are attacked by Satan and all those who oppose the Lord, and the result is the expulsion of all God's enemies from the heavenly places. In **V.12**, the royal priesthood of believers in Heaven will make this clear when they cry out:

> ... *Woe to the inhabitants of the earth and the sea! For the devil has come down to you, having great wrath, because he knows that he has a short time.*

Because the text raises the issue, I want to ensure we don't miss an essential truth about this so-called "battle" between God and Satan; *there is no battle*. Even many believers view Jesus and Satan as counterparts, yin and yang or rivals, but the reality is that Jesus has no rival. He is unmatched in every way, and we see that here as the text reveals that Satan's counterpart is the archangel Michael, not Jesus.

Lucifer was an archangel, like Michael. Jesus is God. Angels are created beings; Jesus is uncreated. And when God wanted Satan dealt with, He didn't even get off His throne. He gave the assignment to Michael, and Michael prevailed. God and Satan are *not* counterparts. There is no scale of comparison that can contain both Satan and God because God is so completely "other." He is peerless. Never forget that.

I pray that understanding changes the way you read verses like **1 John 4:4**, which tells us:

> ... **He who is in you is greater than he who is in the world.**

Lucifer said, *"I will be like the Most High,"*[357] but Michael's name means, *"Who is like God?"* The answer? *No one.*

---

[357] Isaiah 14:14.

SATAN'S TACTICS

V.9 also tells us that Satan **"deceives the whole world."** Since his fall, one of Satan's primary tactics has been *deception*. We've all been deceived by him at various points in our lives, and we all know people who are being deceived by him right now. It's just what he does. **2 Corinthians 4:4** describes nonbelievers as those:

> **…whose minds the god of this age has blinded, who do not believe, lest the light of the gospel of the glory of Christ, who is the image of God, should shine on them.**

When somebody doesn't believe the Gospel, the Bible teaches that Satan has blinded their spiritual sight and understanding. I should clarify here that no one is deceived against their will. Those who are deceived are deceived willingly. Remember **John 3:19**:

> **… light has come into the world, and men loved darkness rather than light, because their deeds were evil.**

Remember Paul's warning to Timothy:

> **… the time will come when they will not endure sound doctrine, but according to their own desires, *because* they have itching ears, they will heap up for themselves teachers; and they will turn *their* ears away from the truth, and be turned aside to fables.**
>
> —2 Timothy 4:3–4

Those who desire the light of truth shall receive it. Those who don't have that desire shall continue to be deceived by Satan. So, how do *we* avoid being deceived? In **John 17:17**, Jesus prayed this over His disciples:

Sanctify them by Your truth. Your word is truth.

One of the most important life lessons the Holy Spirit has taught me (through repeated failure) is that my emotions are not a reliable means of determining what is true. My emotions lie all the time. Just because I *feel* something does not mean it is true, nor does it make it true. That's just one of the reasons why I am so thankful for God's Word. While my emotions often resemble a rollercoaster, God's Word is constant and unchanging. That's why it is a firm foundation for anyone's life. It *always* tells us the truth, no matter how we're feeling. Every day, I work at believing the Scriptures over my emotions. And when, by the grace of God, I'm able to do that, I protect myself from being deceived by my emotions, which Satan loves to manipulate.

I had a pastor who once insightfully observed that most Christians can't tell the difference between their emotions and the Holy Spirit. They think that if they have an emotional experience or reaction, it must be the Holy Spirit. Such thinking is, quite simply, false. And the only way to learn the difference between your emotions and thoughts and the voice of the Holy Spirit is to learn what the voice of the Holy Spirit sounds like. We do that by constantly taking in the Word of God, which teaches us who God is and what His character is like. When the voice we hear aligns with God's character as revealed in His Word, we know it's the Holy Spirit speaking. And guess what: His voice doesn't sound like ours!

> *"For My thoughts are not your thoughts,*
> *Nor are your ways My ways," says the Lord.*
>
> —Isaiah 55:8

If you want to avoid being deceived by Satan, take God's Word into your heart so that you can learn His voice and then *respond* to

His voice. This is the renewing of our minds that Paul said we need every day[358] because we don't naturally think like Jesus.

Choose to believe His Word over your feelings. Choose to obey His Word over your emotions. If you build your life upon the truth of God's Word, Satan will have a tough time deceiving you.

Conversely, those who are *not* taking in the Word regularly, *not* building their lives on the Word, *not* believing the Word over their emotions, and *not* obeying the Word over their feelings are easily deceived by Satan and allow him to fill their mind with beliefs that are not true.

MORE OF SATAN'S TACTICS

[10] **Then I heard a loud voice saying in heaven, . . .**

This is the collective voice of the royal priesthood of believers.

. . . Now salvation, and strength, and the kingdom of our God, and the power of His Christ have come, for the accuser of our brethren, who accused them before our God day and night, has been cast down.

When it says, *"have come,"* it's another proleptic statement like the ones we learned about in **Revelation 11**. To refresh your memory, a proleptic statement refers to a future event so certain that it is spoken of in the past tense (e.g., **Isaiah 53**).

The believers in Heaven *rejoice* because Satan, his allies, and the gods of the nations have been cast from the heavens, down to the earth. This means that it won't be long before they are cast from the

---

[358] Cf. Romans 12:2; 2 Corinthians 4:16; Ephesians 4:23.

earth into the Abyss for the duration of the Millennium, after which they will be cast into the lake of fire for eternity.

The believers in Heaven refer to Satan as *"the accuser of our brethren, who accused them before our God day and night."* Satan loves to *deceive,* and then he loves to *accuse.* That's his second main tactic. He accuses us in three arenas:

1. **Satan accuses us before God:**

    "I can't believe You love those people. Are You seeing what I'm seeing? Do You see how fleeting their devotion to You is? Do You see how hard they work at everything except loving You? Look at them! They're committing that sin again!"

    Praise God for what the Bible tells us about Jesus:

    He is also able to save to the uttermost those who come to God through Him, since He always lives to make intercession for them.

    —Hebrews 7:25

    . . . if anyone sins, we have an Advocate with the Father, Jesus Christ the righteous.

    —1 John 2:1

    Jesus is in Heaven right now, defending you and me against Satan's accusations. He's answering something like this: *"Those accusations might be true, Satan. But what's also true is that I've paid for all their sins with My blood, and their debt is paid in full."*

    If our salvation hinges upon *our* righteousness, then we're done for. But thanks to Jesus, our salvation rests upon *His* righteousness. And that is why our salvation is secure.

2. **Satan accuses us directly:**

We all experience that voice of accusation, don't we? Sometimes, we hear that voice saying, *"God doesn't love you. You messed up again? You are worthless. God can't do anything with your life. God's blessings are not for you."* If we listen to that voice and agree with and entertain those accusations, we'll still be saved, but we won't experience the fullness of life God has for us. If we refuse to walk in agreement with what God says about us, we will handicap His power in our lives[359] just as the citizens of Jesus' hometown of Nazareth missed out on miracles **"because of their unbelief."**[360]

The solution is to declare the whole truth: *"I am broken. I still make mistakes and sin, but the blood of Jesus covers me. My hope is not in myself but in the power of Christ in me. The same power that raised Jesus from the dead is at work in my life, making me more like Him. And despite all my failures, even those to come, He will never leave nor forsake me."*

Do you see what happens when we do that? Instead of feeling shame and condemnation, we allow Satan's accusations to remind us of the greatness of the grace of

---

[359] Cf. Amos 3:3.
[360] Matthew 13:58.

God. We return to the Cross, to the table of Communion, with fresh gratitude and say, *"Thank You, Jesus."*

Some of us are handicapping ourselves because we don't know the truth of God's Word. And if we don't *know* it, how will we *declare* it? How will we stand upon it when the accuser shows up in our lives? We need to get God's Word into our souls. We must learn who God is and who we are in Him. Until we do, we will be highly susceptible to deception.

3. **Satan leads us to accuse others:**

When we accuse one another, we are joining Satan in his ministry. *Yikes.* I could write a whole chapter on this, but for now, I'll settle for reminding us to speak truth and grace. We are called to speak the whole truth, but we are to be led by the Holy Spirit in all things. That means allowing *Him* to determine the time and manner in which we deliver that truth and grace.

HOW TO OVERCOME SATAN

Satan and all other rebellious spiritual entities are cast out of the heavenly places, down to the earth, for the final act of the Great Tribulation. Satan is in an evil fervor, knowing he has only a short time left to persecute the Jewish people and those on the earth who have turned to Jesus. But look at what **V.11** tells us about those Satan will turn into martyrs in that time:

[11] And they overcame him [Satan] by the blood of the Lamb and by the word of their testimony, and they did not love their lives to the death.

What a tremendously powerful verse. God's kids will *overcome* Satan. Even as Satan is killing them, they are overcoming him. Let me explain.

During this time, as He has throughout the Church Age (including today), Jesus will provide three weapons for believers that empower us to overcome Satan and his tactics:

1. **"The blood of the Lamb"**

    If you've ever found it strange how much we talk about the blood of Jesus, I need to explain why the Bible and the Church can't stop mentioning it: The blood of Jesus reminds Satan and us that Jesus has paid for our sins. And we need to remember this because Satan is *constantly* accusing us. And so, to help us, Jesus gave us Communion.

    Remembering the blood of Jesus protects us from being deceived by Satan's accusations. When I get an automated phone call telling me that my account at TD Bank has been suspended, I am not concerned. Do you know why? Because I don't have an account at TD Bank! So, I know the call is obviously a scam. When Satan says, *"God doesn't love you. You're such a filthy sinner. You're worthless."* I am not concerned. Do you know why? Because all my sin—past, present, and future—is covered by the blood of Jesus. So, I know the accusations are obviously part of a fraudulent scam.

    And when that glorious truth becomes rooted in our thinking, Satan's attempts to condemn us only cause us to marvel even more at the greatness of our salvation because they remind us that we have been forgiven much and therefore have much to be thankful for.

The blood of Jesus marks us as forgiven and stands as immovable evidence that we belong to God.

2. *"The word of their testimony"*

Your testimony is what *God* has done for *you*. Not what *you* have done for *God*, but what *God* has done for *you*. In **Psalm 40:2**, David testifies about what God did for him:

> **He also brought me up out of a horrible pit,**
> **Out of the miry clay,**
> **And set my feet upon a rock,**
> ***And* established my steps.**

Many of us are familiar with the troubling words of Jesus in **Matthew 7:22–23**, where He says:

> *Many will say to Me in that day, "Lord, Lord, have we not prophesied in Your name, cast out demons in Your name, and done many wonders in Your name?" And then I will declare to them, "I never knew you; depart from Me, you who practice lawlessness!"*

We read that and get scared because we think, *"It sounds like they were doing good things. What's the problem? Why does Jesus call their good works 'lawlessness'?"* The problem is that their testimony is all about what *they* did for God, not what *God* did for them. As we've read through Revelation, have we come across any Heavenly songs about what we've done for God? *Nope.* They're all about what God has done for us.

All cults reverse that by emphasizing what we do for God and using that fear and guilt to control people and spread their message. The truth is that focusing on yourself is a great way to become depressed because you'll *never* be good enough. You'll *never* measure up to God. If you want to be profoundly unhappy and unsatisfied, live a life focused on yourself and your accomplishments.

This is your testimony: God loved you. The Father sent His Son, Jesus, to save you by purchasing you from death with His life and blood. The Holy Spirit called you and lavished the grace of God upon you. I like the way Paul says it in **Ephesians 1:6–7**:

> **. . . to the praise of the glory of His grace, by which He made us accepted in the Beloved.**
>
> **In Him we have redemption through His blood, the forgiveness of sins, according to the riches of His grace . . .**

Some will argue, *"Grace is the **starting** point, but now you've got to do all these other things . . . "* and they begin to add to the list of what's required to be saved. But grace is not the starting point; it *is* the point. I love my kids because they are mine, not because they are good. And that's a good thing because they're like me—not always good. Grace gets you *into* the family of God, and grace *keeps* you in the family of God. Our testimony is and will always be what *God* has done for us.

3. *"They did not love their lives to the death"*

Christians love Jesus above all else, including their earthly lives. As unlikely as it sounds, martyrdom is a *weapon* against Satan. Because when you reach the place where you value Jesus more than your earthly life, the fear of death no longer has power over you. As His Word says, **"death is swallowed up in victory."**[361] Satan is rendered impotent when his trump card, death, no longer has any power over us.

SATAN ON BORROWED TIME

¹² Therefore rejoice, O heavens, and you who dwell in them! Woe to the inhabitants of the earth and the sea! For the devil has come down to you, having great wrath, because he knows that he has a short time."

Heaven rejoices as Satan and every other rebellious spiritual entity are expelled from the heavenly places. The earth receives Satan, who is full of *"great wrath"* because he knows his time is short. He is furious, raging like a snake with its head cut off, destined for death but still thrashing around, trying to do as much damage as possible before it's all over.

How short a time does Satan have left at this point? I'll go out on a limb and suggest he has exactly 1,260 days, 42 months, or 3.5 years.

---

[361] 1 Corinthians 15:54.

THE WOMAN/ISRAEL IS PERSECUTED

¹³ Now when the dragon saw that he had been cast to the earth, he persecuted the woman who gave birth to the male Child.

Remember, **"the woman"** is ethnic Israel. And now we understand another reason why Satan begins to persecute the Jews so ferociously during the Great Tribulation: he knows his time is almost up, and raging with anger, he frantically seeks to destroy anything he can find that is precious to the Lord which, of course, includes Israel.

¹⁴ But the woman was given two wings of a great eagle, that she might fly into the wilderness to her place, where she is nourished for a time and times and half a time, from the presence of the serpent.

You'll recall that the phrase **"time and times and half a time"** is also used in **Daniel 7:25** and is another way of describing three and a half years. We learned in **Revelation 12:6** that, in all likelihood, Israel will be provided for (**"nourished"**) in the **"wilderness"** in Petra for the three and a half years of the Great Tribulation.

Some speculate the **"two wings of a great eagle"** is a reference to some sort of airlift operation that will be conducted to evacuate the Israeli people to Petra. Some believe the **"great eagle"** reference points to American involvement.

What we know with certainty is that the language is connected to **Exodus 19**, where we read:

Moses went up the mountain to God, and the Lord called to him from the mountain: *"This is what you must say to* *the house of Jacob and explain to the Israelites: 'You have seen what I did to the Egyptians and how I carried you on eagles' wings and brought you to myself. Now if you will carefully listen to me and keep my covenant, you will be my own possession out of all the peoples, although the whole earth is mine, and you will be my kingdom of priests and my holy nation.' These are the words that you are to say to the Israelites."*

—Exodus 19:3–6

When God says, *"I carried you on eagles' wings,"* He is referring to the way He delivered Israel out of Egypt. Did He do that by *literally* carrying Israel on eagles' wings? No. The Lord was speaking poetically, and that's almost certainly what He's doing here in **V.14**. That's why I don't subscribe to the airlift theory.

During our studies, we've seen many similarities between the Exodus and the Tribulation, and we'll continue to see even more—especially as it relates to Israel. The point we need to understand is that just as God moved supernaturally to get His people beyond *Pharaoh's* reach, He will move supernaturally to get them beyond *antichrist's* reach. And just as God supernaturally provided for the practical needs of Israel in the wilderness during the Exodus, He will supernaturally provide for the practical needs of Israel in the wilderness during the Great Tribulation.

¹⁵ So the serpent spewed water out of his mouth like a flood after the woman, that he might cause her to be carried away by the flood.

There are multiple places in Scripture where floods and drowning are used as imagery for God's people being persecuted by enemies from which God delivers them,[362] and that's the most logical way to interpret the **"flood"** referred to here. We're being told that as Israel flees to Petra, antichrist will give chase, seeking to kill them all.

> **[16] But the earth helped the woman, and the earth opened its mouth and swallowed up the flood which the dragon had spewed out of his mouth.**

Just as He did in the Exodus by drowning the Egyptian army in the Reed Sea, God will once again supernaturally use elements of the natural world to protect and deliver Israel. The Reed Sea *literally* swallowed the Egyptian army. Based on the text, something similar will happen to the soldiers and weapons antichrist employs to pursue Israel in Petra. Perhaps the earth will swallow them up, as it did Korah and those who participated in his insurrection against Moses.[363]

Some pastors and authors talk about how great Petra is as a defensive position because of its canyons, elevation, and other geographic features. But I think that's missing the point. Israel won't be protected in Petra because of its natural characteristics; Israel will be protected in Petra because *God* will *supernaturally* protect her.

> **[17] And the dragon was enraged with the woman, . . .**

Infuriated by God supernaturally protecting Israel, Satan shifts his focus.

> **. . . and he went to make war with the rest of her offspring, who keep the commandments of God and have the testimony of Jesus Christ.**

---

[362] Cf. 2 Samuel 22:5; Psalms 18:4, 16; 46:3; 66:12; 69:1–2, 14–15; 124:4–5; 144:7–8, 11; Isaiah 43:2; 59:19; Jeremiah 46:8; Daniel 9:26.

[363] Cf. Numbers 16:31–33.

Like the Egyptians who pursued Israel in the Exodus, Satan will have no choice but to give up his pursuit of Israel in Petra because God will supernaturally protect her. The fulfillment of **Romans 11:26** is inevitable: **"all Israel will be saved, as it is written."**

"**Enraged**," Satan will try to persecute and murder every Jesus follower he can find. This may include ethnically Jewish believers, Gentile believers, and the 144,000 (whom he will be unable to kill).

CLOSING THOUGHTS

Don't miss the vital lessons for the Christian life raised in this portion of the text. If you're going to be an overcomer, you must know what God's Word says about you and live your life in agreement with it.

Can two walk together, unless they are agreed?

—Amos 3:3

You can't walk with God while agreeing with what Satan says about you. God, His Word, and the precious blood of Jesus all declare the same truths: You are forgiven, you are redeemed, you belong to Jesus, you are in the family of God; and nothing can separate you from His love.

If you're not in God's Word on a daily or near-daily basis, you are not at risk of losing your salvation, but you are at risk of being deceived by Satan and having your mind filled with beliefs that are not true. The Bible will keep you grounded in the truth, free from condemnation, and enable you to see reality clearly.

If you don't have a daily time with God's Word, then schedule one. Set aside a daily time with your Bible, a notebook, and a cup of coffee. Listen to Bible studies in the car or on your way to and from work. Whatever it needs to look like in your life, *figure it out*. God's Word will change your life radically, for the better.

Finally, I want to encourage you to adopt the practice of testifying to the goodness of God *out loud*. Instead of grumbling and complaining, declare to others and yourself what God has done for you. It'll change your mindset, shift your focus, and build your faith.

REVELATION 13:1-10

THE ANTICHRIST'S REGIME (PART 1)

The Pause button is still pressed on our narrative as John backtracks to fill us in on some additional developments that will unfold in the Tribulation.

In **Revelation 12**, we saw Israeli Jews flee to what is likely the ancient rock city of Petra in Jordan, where God will supernaturally protect them from Satan and antichrist during the Great Tribulation.

We also learned that (likely) around the halfway point of the Tribulation, Satan and all supernatural entities who oppose Yahweh will lose all access to the heavenly places forever as Michael and his angels repel their attack and cast them down to the earth.

Aware that his time is rapidly running out, Satan will be determined to thwart God's plans in any way he can. As a result, the second half of the Tribulation—the *Great* Tribulation—will be *far worse* than the first half.

In **Revelation 13**, we will cover antichrist, the Mark of the Beast, and the False Prophet. It's going to be fascinating and a bit dark; hopefully, it will debunk some wild theories that have run rampant in the Church for far too long.

THE BEAST FROM THE SEA

As we dive into the text, we must begin by addressing a *translation issue* in **V.1**. The oldest and most reliable texts begin with "Then he," *not* "Then I." And if you look at the last verse of **Revelation 12**, it's clear who the "he" is; it's the dragon, Satan. That means **V.1** *should* begin with, "Then the dragon":

> ¹ **Then I** [the dragon] **stood on the sand of the sea. And I saw a beast rising up out of the sea, having seven heads and ten horns, and on his horns ten crowns, and on his heads a blasphemous name.**

Remember what we've already learned: the dragon is *Satan*,[364] and this **"beast"** is *antichrist*.

For the sake of clarity, we should note that the term "beast" is used in Scripture to refer to the *person* of the antichrist, the *spiritual power* that will possess him, and the *kingdom* he will rule over during the Great Tribulation.

In the first-century Jewish worldview, the sea was a place of darkness and chaos—characteristics that will be embodied by antichrist. Additionally, the sea is sometimes used in Scripture as an idiom for the Gentile nations of the world.[365] For this reason, many scholars believe antichrist will rise to power in a Gentile nation (i.e., not Israel). In the Book of Isaiah, the prophet refers to antichrist as *"the Assyrian."*[366]

Because he rebuilds the Temple, leading the Jews to likely welcome him as *Messiah*, many believe antichrist will be at least

---

[364] Cf. Revelation 12:9.

[365] Cf. Isaiah 17:12; 57:20–21; Revelation 17:15.

[366] Cf. Isaiah 10:5, 12, 24; 14:25.

half *Jewish*. In **John 5:43**, Jesus contrasted Himself with antichrist, saying:

> *I have come in My Father's name, and you do not receive Me; if another comes in his own name, him you will receive.*

Do you remember the two Greek words for "another"—"allos" and "heteros"? The word used here by Jesus is "allos," meaning "another of the same kind," referring to another of the same *ethnicity*.

When you put all the scriptural hints and evidence together, it seems to point to antichrist being ethnically half Jewish and half Gentile and rising to power in a Gentile nation during the first half of the Tribulation.

All that to say that the first part of **V.1** seems to be showing us (symbolically) **"the dragon"** (Satan) using his power to bring **"a beast"** (antichrist) out of **"the sea"** (the Gentile nations).

It's easy to get overwhelmed whenever we see a phrase like **"seven heads and ten horns, and on his horns ten crowns,"** but remember, almost everything in Revelation is explained somewhere else in the book or in the Old Testament.

The *"seven heads"* that each have *"a blasphemous name"* represent seven world empires that opposed Yahweh—six from history and one that is yet to come. A detailed explanation of that will be found in **Revelation 17**.

The **"ten horns"** represent the leaders of ten nations or regions that will make up a *revived Roman Empire*, which will be ruled by antichrist during the Great Tribulation. I'll explain further later in this chapter. Each horn has a crown because they each represent a king, president, or ruler.

Remember, we saw this same description applied to the dragon, Satan, in **Revelation 12:3**. Thus, it is clear that the kingdom of *antichrist* is one and the same as the kingdom of *Satan*.

DANIEL 7 UNLOCKS V.2

> ² **Now the beast which I saw was like a leopard, his feet were like *the feet of* a bear, and his mouth like the mouth of a lion.**

What a strange picture this is. The key to understanding **Revelation 13** is understanding its Old Testament counterpart, **Daniel 7**. In it, the Lord gives Daniel a prophetic dream that includes the Empire of Babylon (where he was captive at the time) and the subsequent three empires that would conquer Israel up to and including the time of Jesus.

So, let's look at **Daniel 7**, starting with **VV.1-8**. While we don't have room to study this in-depth, I hope to illuminate a few things that will help us understand **Revelation 13** more clearly.

> **In the first year of Belshazzar king of Babylon, Daniel had a dream and visions of his head *while* on his bed. Then he wrote down the dream, telling the main facts. Daniel spoke, saying, "I saw in my vision by night, and behold, the four winds of heaven were stirring up the Great Sea."**

In **Revelation 13:1**, John saw the beast/antichrist coming out of what? **"The sea"**—the Gentile nations of the world.

Then, Daniel sees four beasts, each representing an *empire*. Their characteristics appear again in the description of the beast in **Revelation 13** but in *reverse order*. Some scholars suggest the reason is that Daniel was looking *ahead* in time while John was looking *back* in time. Whatever the reason, the point is that the empire of the beast of **Revelation 13** contains *all* the characteristics of the empires that conquered Israel.

And four great beasts came up from the sea, each different from the other. The first was like a lion, ...

This speaks of the ferocious and boastful Babylonians.

And suddenly another beast, a second, like a bear.

This speaks of the overpowering and dominant military of the Medo-Persians.

After this I looked, and there was another, like a leopard ...

This speaks of the lightning-fast Greek Empire that rapidly conquered all rivals under the leadership of Alexander the Great[367] (who was Macedonian).

Then Daniel sees a strikingly *different* kind of beast—the terrifying Roman Empire:

After this I saw in the night visions, and behold, a fourth beast, dreadful and terrible, exceedingly strong. It had huge iron teeth; it was devouring, breaking in pieces, and trampling the residue with its feet. It was different from all the beasts that were before it, and it had ten horns.

This last beast is an empire of ten kingdoms/nations, as antichrist's *future* empire will be.[368] The same spirit behind the Roman Empire will be behind a revived "Roman Empire" in the Great Tribulation.

As Daniel contemplates what he has seen in his dream thus far, the Lord "zooms in" on the fourth beast, the Roman Empire,

---

[367] This is further detailed in Daniel 8.
[368] Cf. Revelation 17:12.

and shows Daniel some details that will unfold when this empire is *revived* in the Great Tribulation:

> *I was considering the horns, and there was another horn, a little one, coming up among them, before whom three of the first horns were plucked out by the roots. And there, in this horn, were eyes like the eyes of a man, and a mouth speaking pompous words* [or "great boasts"].

The little horn Daniel sees is antichrist. He will rise up amidst this ten-kingdom union and, in one quick blow, take out three political leaders (i.e., assume leadership of their kingdoms).

As we travel through Revelation, it will be confirmed that antichrist will be a gifted and charismatic orator who is constantly boasting and speaking blasphemies. Skip down to **Daniel 7:11**:

> *I watched then because of the sound of the pompous words which the horn was speaking;* . . .

Let's jump to **Daniel 7:15**:

> *I, Daniel, was grieved in my spirit within my body, and the visions of my head troubled me. I came near to one of those who stood by, and asked him the truth of all this. So he told me and made known to me the interpretation of these things: 'Those great beasts, which are four, are four kings* [or "kingdoms]" **which arise out of the earth.**

Referring to the Babylonian, Medo-Persian, Greek, and Roman empires.

Skip ahead to **Daniel 7:19:**

> *Then I wished to know the truth about the fourth beast* (the Roman Empire), *which was different from all the others,*

exceedingly dreadful, with its teeth of iron and its nails of bronze, which devoured, broke in pieces, and trampled the residue with its feet; . . .

This *"fourth beast"* was so much worse, so much more brutal than the first three; Daniel *had* to know more about it. In **V.23**, he is given this explanation:

**. . . The fourth beast shall be
A fourth kingdom on earth,
Which shall be different from all *other* kingdoms,
And shall devour the whole earth,
Trample it and break it in pieces.**

When the Roman Empire existed, it spanned what was then considered **"the whole earth."** When antichrist rules his *revived* Roman Empire, it seems it will span a similar territory. But regardless of borders, empires, and official titles, Scripture makes it clear that antichrist will control almost the entire world.

Jumping back to **V.20**, Daniel shares that he also wanted to know more about . . .

. . . the ten horns that were on its head, and the other horn [the little horn] *which came up, before which three fell, namely, that horn which had eyes and a mouth which spoke pompous words, whose appearance was greater than his fellows.*

In **V.24**, Daniel gets an explanation of the ten horns:

**The ten horns *are* ten kings
Who shall arise from this kingdom.
And another shall rise after them;**

He shall be different from the first *ones,*
And shall subdue three kings.

And in **Revelation 17:12**, we receive confirmation that this interpretation is also *prophetic*, as an angel explains to John:

> *The ten horns which you saw are ten kings* [or "kingdoms"] *who have received no kingdom as yet, but they receive authority for one hour* [one time period] *as kings with the beast.*

I know we're jumping all over the place but hang with me. Let's go back to **Daniel 7:21**:

> *I was watching; and the same horn* [the little horn which is antichrist] *was making war against the saints, and prevailing against them*[369], *until . . .*

Antichrist's power to persecute and kill the saints in the Great Tribulation *ends* when . . .

> *. . . the Ancient of Days* [Jesus] *came, and a judgment was made in favor of the saints of the Most High, and the time came for the saints to possess the kingdom.*

This refers to the Second Coming when Jesus returns to the earth to deal with Satan and his crew and establish the Millennial Kingdom (we'll read about that in **Revelation 19**).

Skip down to **Daniel 7:25**:

> *He* [antichrist] *shall speak pompous words against the Most High, Shall persecute the saints of the Most High, And shall intend to change times and law.*

---

[369] Cf. Revelation 13:7.

We talked about that back in **Revelation 10**. Daniel continues in **V.26**:

Then **the saints shall be given into his hand**
For a time and times and half a time.

As we know, *"time and times and half a time"* is another way of describing the three and a half years of the Great Tribulation.

Many people will come to faith in Jesus during the Tribulation. And in the *Great* Tribulation, antichrist will seek to *kill* those believers until Jesus appears at the Second Coming.

THE ROMAN EMPIRE

Perhaps you're a bit confused by all this talk of the ***"fourth beast"**/* Roman Empire being revived in the Great Tribulation under the leadership of antichrist. Let's see if we can shed some more light on this.

The revived Roman Empire will be directed by the same *spirit* that worked behind the scenes during its first incarnation. It will govern in a similar fashion, using overwhelming force and fear, and once again, its leader will declare himself to be God and demand to be worshipped.

History sometimes smooths the rough edges of reality, and when many think of the Roman Empire, they think of the *Pax Romana* (the "Roman Peace") that brought peace to the known world by uniting her under a single authority. What we forget is just how *bloody* that authority was. If you were walking into a town in the Empire, it was common to pass several rotting, crucified corpses just outside the city, positioned to send the message, *"Global peace is here. Embrace it, or this is what will happen to you."* It's incredible how many people become "committed" to world peace when the only alternative is a torturous death. The Roman Empire *butchered* the world into submission.

We don't have room to dive into it, but **Daniel 2** prophesies that while the Roman Empire would fall away, it would *return* in the last days—the same last days that will include the Second Coming.

One of the interesting things about the Roman Empire is that it wasn't really ever *conquered*; it mostly crumbled over time under the weight of its decadence and hedonism. It split, and one half quickly faded away while the other half took over a thousand years to dissolve. Unbelievably, there was still a Caesar on the throne in Rome in the 1100s (though he only held the authority of a mayor). Since that time, various men have *tried* to revive the Roman Empire. Napoleon tried and failed. Hitler tried and failed. But in the last days, there will be one who *will* bring back the Empire.

Earlier, I explained how Satan will construct a fraudulent trinity, consisting of himself, antichrist, and the false prophet. Antichrist's revived Roman Empire will be a fraudulent version of the Millennial Kingdom. Under antichrist in the Great Tribulation, the world will see what things are like when Satan reigns on the earth with little restraint. Under Jesus in the Millennial Kingdom, the world will see what things are like when Jesus reigns on the earth.

For those who are conspiratorially inclined, I recommend doing some Internet research into the Treaty of Rome. It's a document written in the 1950s that outlines the foundational principles and goals of what is today the European Union. You'll discover that the vision was to unite Europe around a common language, economy, and much more. Sort of like a *revived Roman Empire*.

THE SOURCE OF ANTICHRIST'S POWER

Let's jump back into **Revelation 13:2**:

> **The dragon** [Satan] **gave him** [antichrist] **his power, his throne, and great authority.**

Satan will give power, prestige, and authority to antichrist, and in return, antichrist will direct the world to worship Satan.

How is Satan able to do this? Remember, while Jesus holds the earth's "title deed," He has not yet fully opened it and ushered in the Kingdom Age (a.k.a. the Millennial Kingdom). Currently, Satan is still technically **"the god of this age,"**[370] as Paul put it. Additionally, we know that God will remove the restraining power of the Church from the earth during this time.[371] And finally, the Lord will *permit* Satan to do this as part of His plan.[372]

ANTICHRIST'S "RESURRECTION"

John the Apostle is the only biblical author to use the term "antichrist," and he only uses it in his first two epistles. He uses it to refer to a *spirit* rather than a person. The word "antichrist" is generally viewed as meaning *"against God,"* and while that's accurate, it's more accurate to view it as meaning *"in place of God."* It's the satanic spirit that desires to be in the *place* of God, and it's the spirit personified by Lucifer's attempted rebellion in Heaven. Therefore, as this satanic spirit possesses antichrist, we will see him embody the Luciferian spirit.

---

[370] 2 Corinthians 4:4.

[371] Cf. 2 Thessalonians 2:7.

[372] Cf. Revelation 13:7.

³ And I saw one of his [antichrist's] **heads as if it had been mortally wounded, ...**

Around the halfway point of the Tribulation (I'll explain how we know that in a minute), antichrist will be *killed* in what will most likely be an assassination attempt. The original Greek allows the text to say he will be killed or will appear to be killed; based on typology and the rest of the text in Revelation, it's my personal belief that he really is assassinated.

Zechariah 11:16–17 gives more detail about the *wounds* antichrist will suffer:

> *... I will raise up a shepherd in the land who will not care for those who are cut off, nor seek the young, nor heal those that are broken, nor feed those that still stand. But he will eat the flesh of the fat and tear their hooves in pieces.*

Who is the *"great Shepherd"*[373] in Scripture? *Jesus.*

Zechariah prophesied a *false "shepherd"* would emerge in Israel *("in the land")*. At first, he'll be welcomed by the Jewish people as one who cares for them (I suggest he'll be received as Messiah), but he'll soon reveal his true nature as he rips them apart and *devours* them.

> *Woe to the worthless shepherd,*
> *Who leaves the flock!*
> *A sword shall be against his arm*
> *And against his right eye;*
> *His arm shall completely wither,*
> *And his right eye shall be totally blinded.*

---

[373] Hebrews 13:20.

How's that for being specific? This (likely) assassination attempt will leave antichrist blind in one eye and paralyzed in one arm. He will come back to life but will be left with these *scars*.

Think with me for a moment: We worship someone who came back to life but still bears *scars*.[374] **Revelation 13** refers to antichrist's fatal wound three times. It becomes one of his defining characteristics, and his *scars* become known to the whole world.

Back to **Revelation 13:3** for the plot twist:

. . . and his deadly wound was healed.

Antichrist is (likely) killed in an assassination attempt. However, he will *rise from the dead*. Some suggest this will be a *faked* resurrection, but I see no reason to read that into the text. It seems likely that this is the moment the satanic spirit from the bottomless pit[375] enters and possesses antichrist.

We need to slow down for a second and let this sink in. This is not some magic trick or illusion. This is a legitimately supernatural and miraculous recovery that will be medically documented. Can you imagine? A real, undisputed miracle from the leader of the New World Order. No wonder many will begin to say, *"He has the **right to demand worship because, apparently, he is God!"***

And that's just the response we see in **V.3**:

And all the world marveled and followed the beast.

In addition to a fraudulent trinity and a fraudulent kingdom, Satan will be permitted to concoct a fraudulent *resurrection* and fraudulent *scars* for his fraudulent *savior*.

---

[374] For example, John 20:25–27; Revelation 5:6.

[375] Cf. Revelation 11:7, 17:8.

We've made this point before, but **V.3** provides another example. Just a century ago, the idea that antichrist's resurrection would be seen by **"all the world"** was considered *impossible*. And for that reason, almost all Bible scholars believed these verses should be interpreted as symbolic. Today, we all understand how easily the world will be able to see, hear, and marvel together at an internationally newsworthy event.

We don't follow God because of signs and wonders because God is *not* the only one who can perform signs and wonders. While there's no comparison between God's power and Satan's power, Satan *does* have the ability to work miracles on the earth, and he's been doing it for millennia.

Do you recall Jannes and Jambres,[376] the two magicians of Pharaoh's court? When Moses threw down his staff, which turned into a snake, they were able to do the *same thing*[377] through the occultic power of Satan.

If you're only following Jesus because of signs and wonders, you'll find yourself constantly searching for *more* of them. And sooner or later, you'll end up following someone who's not doing them by the power of God.

So, how *do* we evaluate the legitimacy of a ministry? We ask, *"Is it faithful to the Scriptures?"* And we examine who gets the glory. Is it *Jesus* or someone/something else?

V.4 tells us who gets the glory when *antichrist* rises from the dead:

⁴ So they worshiped the dragon who gave authority to the beast; and they worshiped the beast, saying, *"Who is like the beast? Who is able to make war with him?"*

---

[376] Cf. 2 Timothy 3:8.

[377] Cf. Exodus 7:10–11.

The world's reaction to antichrist's resurrection is to praise him as a god and declare, *"Who is able to make war with him?"* In other words, *"Who can stop him? He's invincible!"*

Jesus was raised from *earthly* and *eternal* death; Satan will be permitted to raise antichrist from *earthly* death.

Jesus, the Son, directed glory to His Heavenly Father; antichrist, Satan's "son," will direct glory to his "father"—Satan/**"the dragon."**

In **1 Corinthians 10:20**, Paul observes:

> **... the things which the Gentiles sacrifice they sacrifice to demons and not to God ...**

The Gentiles thought they were sacrificing to their gods, but they sacrificed to the demons *behind* those gods. Similarly, those who worship antichrist will be honoring the power behind him—*Satan*.

And just as Jesus has been given all authority by His Father (which he will exercise at the Second Coming), antichrist will be given authority *on earth* by *his* "father," Satan. Antichrist will enter the rebuilt Temple in Jerusalem, claim to be the only god worthy of worship, and the world will *agree*.

> **⁵ And he was given a mouth speaking great things and blasphemies, ...**

Just as we read in **Daniel 7**:

> **... and he was given authority to continue for forty-two months.**

Or 1,260 days, 3.5 years, or **"time, times, and half a time."**

This is how we know this assassination attempt happens around the halfway point of the Tribulation. Antichrist is killed, raised by

Satan, imbued with power and authority by Satan, and allowed by God to continue **"for forty-two months"**—the length of the Great Tribulation.

By the power of Satan, antichrist will become a master of *deception*. He will have Satan's gift for charismatic speech and will serve as his mouthpiece. How good are Satan's oratory skills? Well, he talked a third of the angels into joining his rebellion against God. He persuaded Eve to do the one thing she was forbidden to do. And he has successfully deceived all of us, at one time or another. People will eat up antichrist's words and view him as an **"angel of light."**[378]

Now, notice *who* antichrist blasphemes:

> **⁶Then he opened his mouth in blasphemy against God, to blaspheme His name, His tabernacle, and those who dwell in heaven.**

This is almost certainly a reference to **"the abomination of desolation,"** which happens around the halfway point of the Tribulation.

The phrase **"those who dwell in heaven"** refers to us, the raptured Church. Antichrist will declare something to this effect: *"Good riddance! Those Christians were always the real problem. Now we can come together and build the world we've always dreamed of, free of outdated and imagined moral constraints and constructs."* That's not hard to imagine at all, is it?

It's political tradition for the current administration to blame problems on the previous administration. That's precisely what antichrist will do after we're removed, and it will unite the world in killing those who turn to the Lord during the Great Tribulation.

---

[378] 2 Corinthians 11:14.

⁷ It was granted to him to make war with the saints and to overcome them.

This is the moment we read about in **Revelation 12:17**. Unable to touch the Jews in Petra, Satan, via antichrist, directs his wrath toward anyone he can find who pledges allegiance to Jesus. You'll recall that **Daniel 7:21–22** also described this:

> *...the same horn was making war against the saints, and prevailing against them, until the Ancient of Days came, and a judgment was made in favor of the saints of the Most High, and the time came for the saints to possess the kingdom.*

During the Great Tribulation, antichrist's earthly schemes against believers will *succeed*. **V.7** declares he will **"overcome them,"** and that's one more reason we know this cannot be referring to the Church. I say that because of what Jesus said in **Matthew 16:18**:

> *...I will build My church, and the gates of Hades shall not prevail against it.*

Jesus promised that even though empires, tyrants, and armies would try to wipe out the Church, none of them would succeed. The Church would keep going and would *not* be overcome. In the Great Tribulation, we see no such protection granted to Gentile believers because they are *not* part of the Church. They will be part of a distinct group in Heaven, which we discussed in **Revelation 7**.

The bottom line is that these Gentile saints who are being **"overcome"** by antichrist are those who are saved *after* the Rapture. The Tribulation will result in the greatest revival the world has ever seen. But almost all those who turn to the Lord in that time will do so at the expense of their earthly lives.

The rest of **V.7** tells us:

And authority was given him [antichrist] **over every tribe, tongue, and nation.**

We know that antichrist will lead a revived Roman Empire, and this verse tells us that he will be given the power to do *even more*—ruling over an empire larger than any leader before could even imagine. While he may *officially* rule over a revived Roman Empire, the leaders of the world will bow and submit to his rule, believing him to be the savior of earth.

⁸ All who dwell on the earth will worship him, whose names have not been written in the Book of Life of the Lamb slain from the foundation of the world.

There will be no agnostics, atheists, or neutrals on the earth in the Great Tribulation. *Everyone* will either worship antichrist and Satan or Jesus.

We know those **"who dwell on the earth"** is a term used in Revelation for people who have determined to make the earth their home instead of Heaven. In other words, those who have rejected Jesus are following antichrist and will never change their allegiance. **V.8** clarifies that everyone who worships antichrist during the Great Tribulation is *damned*.

The only people who will *refuse* to worship him will be those who have turned to Jesus and the ethnic Jews who will flee to Petra and turn to Jesus when He appears at the Second Coming.

When John refers to Jesus as **"the Lamb slain from the foundation of the world,"** he means that it was *always* God's plan for Jesus to die for our sins. It was the plan before the world was created because God has always known how things would play out.

And here's the wonderful part: God has always known how each person's *life* would play out. He has always known who would choose Him. And **Revelation 17:8** declares that the names written in the Book of Life have also been there **"from the foundation of the world."**

Those who love Jesus and belong to Him will *not* be deceived by antichrist. They will *not* worship him. In eternity, they will overcome him by the blood of the Lamb and the word of their testimony.

What will be true of them is true of the Church today. Believers do not overcome to *earn* their place in the Book of Life; believers overcome because their names *are written* in the Book of Life.

Believers do not stand in their own strength. Believers do not overcome Satan by their own power. Believers stand because *Jesus* enables us to stand. Believers overcome Satan because *Jesus* empowers us to overcome Satan.

⁹ If anyone has an ear, let him hear.

Every time we've seen this phrase in Revelation, it's been followed by the words, "what the Spirit says to the churches." Why don't we see that here? Because it's not for us! The Church will be in Heaven during the Great Tribulation.

This is an appeal to the man or woman reading the Book of Revelation *after* the Rapture. It's an exhortation to understand what will happen during the Great Tribulation and choose the Lord's side.

I cannot imagine the gravity these words will hold for the person who reads them seeking answers after the Rapture and watches things unfold *exactly* as they are written.

¹⁰ He who leads into captivity shall go into captivity; he who kills with the sword must be killed with the sword. Here is the patience and the faith of the saints.

This doesn't translate well into English, but here's the gist of what the Lord is saying:

Those who turn to Me after the Rapture will not be called to armed resistance against antichrist and his agenda. Their hope will be the knowledge that I am ultimately in control. They are called to trust their souls and lives to Me and stay faithful even to death.

There will be no miraculous earthly deliverance for these Gentile Tribulation saints. On *earth*, Satan will overcome them. But in *eternity*, they will overcome Satan.

CLOSING THOUGHTS

As we've been studying through Revelation, I hope you've realized that we are *so close* to the Rapture. I hope you've begun to see the plans of God unfolding around us as the signs of the times increase in frequency and intensity.

And I also hope you've noticed something else important—we are not called to try to stop these signs from appearing. We are not called to armed resistance against the plans of God. When teaching His disciples about these things, Jesus told them:

See that you are not troubled; for all these things must come to pass . . .

—Matthew 24:6b

Our hope is not in getting our preferred political candidates elected. Our hope is in Jesus and the knowledge that He has a good plan that will result in us being with Him and enjoying His presence forever. *That's* our hope.

And until that day, we are called to do what Christians have always been called to do: faithfully follow Jesus, obey His commands, preach the Gospel, love the saints, and (most importantly) abide in Him.

Jesus has not called us to forcefully topple governments and redeem the global political system. He has called us to establish His Kingdom in our personal worlds—our hearts, marriages, families, homes, and churches.

And you know what? That's a big enough task for us. That's a challenging enough call to keep us busy for the rest of our lives.

The Kingdom of God will be established across the earth *when?* When Jesus returns to the earth.

REVELATION 13:11-18

THE ANTICHRIST'S REGIME (PART 2)
The Second Beast (the False Prophet)

[11] Then I saw another beast coming up out of the earth, and he had two horns like a lamb and spoke like a dragon.

"Another" is the Greek word "allos," meaning "another of the same kind." Like the first beast (antichrist), this beast will also be a *person*.

This second beast comes **"up out of the earth"**—the idea being the fiery depths of the earth. A terrifying place, but not as foreboding as the dark and chaotic sea (in the mind of a first-century Jew) because this second beast is not quite as fearsome as antichrist.

This idea is reinforced in the description of him appearing **"like a lamb,"** in contrast to the first beast, who was likened to a leopard, a bear, and a lion. In Scripture, horns speak of authority and honor. And while the first beast had ten horns, this beast has two. Despite his meeker and gentler appearance, he is fueled by the same Luciferian power as antichrist—a fact betrayed in his *speech*. We are told that he **"spoke like a dragon."** No matter what this second beast looks like on the outside, his true satanic nature is revealed when he opens his mouth.

A person who presents themselves as a lamb *externally* while having the character of the dragon *internally* brings to mind this warning from Jesus, which was later repeated by Paul to the elders of the Church in Ephesus:

> ***Beware of false prophets, who come to you in sheep's clothing, but inwardly they are ravenous wolves.***
>
> —Matthew 7:15

This is where the phrase "a wolf in sheep's clothing" comes from, and it's exactly what the second beast will be. Because false prophets generally arise from *within* the Church, many suspect the second beast will too. But that would require a church to still be on the earth *after* the Rapture. Hmmm. We'll revisit that controversial possibility in a future chapter.

¹² And he exercises all the authority of the first beast in his presence, and causes the earth and those who dwell in it to worship the first beast, whose deadly wound was healed.

Satan will give the second beast the same authority and power as antichrist. The second beast will use it to direct people to worship antichrist—a deception that will be turbocharged when antichrist miraculously rises from the dead. And when people worship antichrist, they'll really be worshipping the power behind him—*Satan*.

Perhaps you're wondering who this second beast is. For the answer, let's look ahead at **Revelation 19:20**:

> **. . . the beast was captured, and with him the false prophet who worked signs in his presence, by which he deceived**

those who received the mark of the beast and those who worshiped his image . . .

The second beast is not *a* false prophet; he is *the* false prophet who will lead the global antichrist cult. Though we're meeting him for the first time here in **Revelation 13**, the false prophet will have been a notable figure on the earth for years, likely even before the Rapture. Antichrist will come on the scene as a *political* figure and take control of a revived Roman Empire. In contrast, the false prophet will be a *religious/spiritual* figure who will lead the people of earth to worship antichrist.

We've mentioned that Satan will construct a counterfeit Trinity during the Tribulation. The false prophet will be the third part of it, impersonating the Holy Spirit. Directing people to worship the "son," antichrist, will be the "ministry" of the false prophet, just as the real Holy Spirit never talks about Himself but always directs people to worship Jesus.[379]

[13] He performs great signs, so that he even makes fire come down from heaven on the earth in the sight of men.

The false prophet will be able to call down fire from the sky. Not in some figurative sense but *real* fire, called down at will.

The obvious comparison is the two witnesses of **Revelation 11**—*genuine* prophets that God will send to Jerusalem in the Great Tribulation. We learned they will likely be Elijah and Moses, and we read of their power to use *fire* to destroy anyone who tries to stop them from preaching.[380] Through the false prophet, Satan

---

[379] Cf. John 15:26, 16:13–15.

[380] Cf. Revelation 11:5.

will apparently equal this miracle (at least partially) in the hopes of assuring those on the earth that antichrist has the same power as Yahweh, just as Jannes and Jambres did for Pharaoh in duplicating Moses' miracle of turning his staff into a snake.[381] And people will follow these signs, just as Jesus predicted when He said:

> *... false christs and false prophets will rise and show great signs and wonders to deceive, if possible, even the elect.*
> —Matthew 24:24

By the way, that verse is making the point that the only thing that will prevent *everyone* from being deceived in the Great Tribulation is the fact that *some* will be *"elect"*; they will belong to Jesus. That's how strong the antichrist and false prophet's deceptions will be.

And I'll say it again while we're on the subject: Christians need to recognize that miracles alone do not validate a ministry. If they did, then the false prophet would be a legitimate man of God. Obviously, he's not. One reason the Bible does not instruct us to follow miracles and signs is because it's possible for them to be performed by demonic power. Miracles can validate words that align with the Scriptures, but miracles cannot validate words that do not align with the Scriptures.

Next, the false prophet comes up with a big idea:

¹⁴ And he deceives those who dwell on the earth ...

While the Holy Spirit opens eyes and ears to the truth, bringing *enlightenment*, the false prophet *deceives*. And remember, **"those who dwell on the earth"** refers to those on the earth who have rejected

---

[381] Cf. Exodus 7:8–12.

Jesus and will never repent. They are willingly *self-deceived* before they are ever deceived by the false prophet.

> **... by those signs which he was granted to do in the sight of the beast, telling those who dwell on the earth to make an image to the beast who was wounded by the sword and lived.**

We know that by the halfway point of the Tribulation, the construction of a new Jewish Temple in Jerusalem will be completed. We also know that antichrist will enter that Temple around that same time, set up a throne for himself, and demand to be worshipped as God as prophesied by Daniel,[382] Jesus,[383] and the Apostle Paul.[384] Shortly after those events, the false prophet will arrange for this **"image"** of antichrist to be placed in the Holy of Holies of the Temple.

> [15] **He** [the false prophet] **was granted** *power* **to give breath to the image of the beast, ...**

Without getting too technical, the original Greek[385] clarifies we're not talking about the image simply being able to move; we're talking about the appearance of being *truly alive*—being *sentient*. As bizarre as it sounds, somehow this **"image of the beast"** will be brought to life by the false prophet, whom Satan will empower.

Because it's called **"the image of the beast,"** we know it will be some sort of visual representation of antichrist. We don't know if this will be a statue, a hologram, a robot, a genetic clone, or artificial intelligence.

---

[382] Cf. Daniel 9:26–27.

[383] Cf. Matthew 24:15–22.

[384] Cf. 2 Thessalonians 2:1–12.

[385] Pneuma.

We don't know if this **"image"** will be demonically possessed or somehow conscious. Whatever it is, we know it will *come alive*.

And note what this **"image"** is brought to life to *do:*

> **...that the image of the beast should both speak and cause as many as would not worship the image of the beast to be killed.**

The **"image"** will command people to worship antichrist, identify those who refuse, and arrange their execution.

My personal speculation is that **"the image of the beast"** will be related to artificial intelligence, as I believe the ability to create human consciousness is the domain of God alone. I suspect it will be some digital form of antichrist—possibly to imitate the omnipresence of God. It could be a means for antichrist to be everywhere, with everyone, at all times. This may work something like saying, "Hey Google" or "Hey Siri" but *giving* instructions rather than taking them.

It will almost certainly constantly sift through all the data provided by the world's surveillance apparatus (such as satellites, cell phones, CCTV, home security cameras, webcams, smart home assistants, or browser activity) and use it to identify anyone who refuses to worship antichrist.

Most of those who reject Jesus in the Tribulation will be completely convinced that antichrist is the best thing to ever happen to humanity. They will watch in amazement as he brokers peace in the Middle East and then rises from the dead. And as he declares an end to all religions by calling the world to worship him, most will say, *"Finally! An end to the divisiveness of religion. This is going to be like John Lennon's song, 'Imagine,' brought to life!"* Nonbelievers will perceive the execution of those who refuse to worship the image of the beast as a necessary price to pay for world peace.

Antichrist's regime will be a revived form of the Roman imperial cult, which was initiated by Augustus. As discussed in the letter to Smyrna in **Revelation 2**, an annual pinch offering was required from every citizen, along with the words, *"Kaiser Kurios" ("Caesar is Lord")*. Those who refused to offer the required worship and confession were executed.

Most Gentiles who refuse to take the mark will be executed during the Great Tribulation. They are the Tribulation saints we encountered in Heaven in earlier chapters of Revelation. A small percentage of Gentile Tribulation saints will survive and be alive on the earth when Jesus returns at the Second Coming.[386]

We know that a remnant of the Jewish people will be preserved through the Great Tribulation and turn to Jesus at the Second Coming. However, **Zechariah 13:8–9** tells us that two out of every three Jews on the earth will die in the Great Tribulation.

Not only will the false prophet lead the global antichrist cult, but he will unite *all* non-Christian religions under antichrist. Something like this must occur because we don't see any mention in biblical eschatology of anyone except Christians resisting antichrist on religious grounds. Islam has around 1.8 billion adherents. Hinduism has about 800 million. Orthodox Islam teaches that those who reject Muhammed's teachings should be executed.[387] This is the theology behind the actions of Islamic terror groups such as Al-Qaeda and ISIS. There is increasing radicalism and violence among India's Hindus, who also believe in the exclusive nature of their faith. Islam and Hinduism are the second and third most popular religions in the world today.

---

[386] Cf. Isaiah 65:20–23; Matthew 25:31–40.

[387] Cf. Qur'an 2:191, 193; 8:12, 17, 65; 9:5, 14, 123; 47:4; 69:30–37.

Back in **V.3**, we read, **"all the world marveled and followed the beast."** I want us to take note of the phrase **"all the world"** because that includes Islam, Hinduism, and all other non-Christian religions. Somehow, they will all accept and submit to antichrist as their central religious figure.

How could that be? If you dig into other cults and religions, you'll find that almost all of them have an eschatology and/or prophesies that antichrist could fulfill. For example, to Shia Muslims, antichrist may be received as *Imam al-Mahdi* (the Twelfth Imam/the Mahdi). We've talked about how the Jews will likely receive him as *Messiah*. The Mormons will probably welcome him as the fulfillment of what's known as *"The White Horse Prophecy."*

Islam is particularly interesting as it relates to **V.15**, as it is the only major religion to stipulate *beheading* as the standard method of execution, and **Revelation 20:4** tells us that is how believers will be martyred in the Tribulation.

THE IMAGE OF ANTICHRIST AND DANIEL 3

This talk of antichrist directing the world to worship an image of himself recalls **Daniel 3**, where King Nebuchadnezzar of Babylon constructs a massive statue of himself and demands the populace bow down to it or face the death penalty.

The *dimensions* of Nebuchadnezzar's statue are fascinating. It was 60 cubits high, with a base measuring six cubits by six. It points to 666, the mark of the beast (which we'll discuss in a moment).[388]

---

[388] As a fun fact, did you know that the base of the Washington Monument in Washington, DC, measures 666 inches x 666 inches? And its height is 6,666 inches. "Let the reader understand . . ."

Those heroes of the Bible—Shadrach, Meshach, and Abed-Nego—who refused to bow down to the statue, were cast into a fiery furnace. But instead of being destroyed in the fire, they were supernaturally protected and encountered their Savior, Jesus, amid the flames. The only thing burned by the fire were the ropes used to bind them, and they walked out of the fire as free men. This is what will happen to the Jews through the Tribulation. Amid their fiery trial, they will encounter Jesus, who will protect and reveal Himself to them that they might be set free.

Daniel 3 also raises an interesting question: *Where's Daniel?* Being one of the most important government officials in Babylon, we can only deduce that Daniel must have been out of the country as there is no record of him attempting to intervene or being arrested for refusing to bow to the statue (which would have undoubtedly been his response).

If (in this event) Shadrach, Meshach, and Abed-Nego serve as a prophetic picture of the Jewish people in the Great Tribulation, whom does Daniel represent? *The Church.* Just as Daniel is absent from **Daniel 3**, so is the Church absent from **Revelation 6–19** and the Tribulation. Praise God!

WHAT IS THE IMAGE?

For centuries, people have driven themselves crazy trying to figure out what this **"image"** and the mark of the beast will be. In **Daniel 12:4**, Daniel is given these instructions:

> *...shut up the words, and seal the book until the time of the end; many shall run to and fro, and knowledge shall increase.*

Daniel was told that the prophecies he had been given regarding the end-times would be *"shut up"*[389] (i.e., sealed) *"until the time of the end."* In other words, nobody would be able to clearly understand them until the *very* end-times—the days in which they would soon be fulfilled. Why? Because Christians in AD 300 or 1200 didn't need to understand the details of antichrist's schemes and regime. But do you know who *will* need to understand them? The generation that is alive when it happens—those left on the earth following the Rapture.

And when that time arrives, the Bible declares that *"knowledge shall increase."* God's Word promises that those who read the prophecies recorded in Daniel will finally be able to *understand* them in the last of the last days. This is a recurring theme in biblical eschatology. Things that were *impossible* to understand even 50 years ago now make sense. Technology has evolved. The world has changed. Pieces have been moved into place. And God is giving His Church *understanding* in these last of the last days, just as He promised Daniel He would.

While we don't know exactly what this **"image"** of antichrist will be, we know it will be clear in the Tribulation. When the time comes, those who *need* to understand *will* understand.

THE MARK OF THE BEAST

And now we come to the infamous "mark of the beast":

> ¹⁶ **He** [the false prophet] **causes all, both small and great, rich and poor, free and slave, to receive a mark on their**

---

[389] Daniel 12:4.

right hand or on their foreheads, ¹⁷ and that no one may buy or sell except one who has the mark or the name of the beast, or the number of his name.

First and foremost, we must understand that this mark will signify *allegiance* to the antichrist. It will serve two purposes:

1. Clearly distinguish those who worship antichrist from those who do not.
2. Create intense financial pressure to worship antichrist.

These verses reveal that antichrist's regime will control most of the world's financial system in the Great Tribulation. Nobody will be able to buy, sell, or conduct any type of financial transaction in his empire unless they bear his mark.

Incredibly, this was foreshadowed all the way back in **Leviticus 19:28**, where God instructed His people:

Do not cut your bodies for the dead or put tattoo marks on yourselves . . .

If you have a tattoo, don't worry! Back then, marks on the body, such as tattoos and cuts, were primarily used to show devotion to a *pagan cult*—hence God's command. That same ancient pagan concept will again come into play with the mark of the beast.

Because of **Leviticus 19:28**, Satan knows there's no chance a devout Jew will take the mark. It's one more method Satan will employ in his attempts to track them down so that he can kill them.

V.16 mentions **"free and slave."** As we've pointed out before, slavery will apparently become mainstream again. Guess what major world religion allows, and even encourages, slavery? *Islam*.

And my guess is that along with beheading those who refuse to worship antichrist, they'll be at the center of a revived slave trade in his empire.

The mark of the beast is yet another facet of eschatology that was widely considered figurative until less than 50 years ago because the idea of a mark allowing you to buy and sell things seemed *crazy*. Today, none of us are scoffing at that notion. We have tiny RFID chips that are easily implanted and could be read by scanners on every street corner to track our movements. Small QR codes can be tattooed on the skin and read by cameras. In fact, as I write this, hundreds of people are already using both technologies for their COVID vaccine passports. If you have a smartphone, you're being tracked. Where you go, how long you stay there, the audio of your conversations and surroundings—it's *all* being tracked, and we all know it. It's not a conspiracy theory; it's how tech companies figure out what ads to show you.

For as long as there have been societies, people have adjusted their appearance to emulate people they admire. When I was a kid, I had a passion for tennis. And in the tennis world at that time, Andre Agassi was *it*. He'd wear Spandex shorts underneath his regular shorts, so I did the same (regrettably).

People will show their allegiance to antichrist by taking his mark on their *forehead* or *hand*. What parts of antichrist's body are left scarred by the attempt on his life? His *eye* and his *arm*. It could be that there's a connection there, and the marks' locations are a type of tribute to antichrist's resurrection scars.

But here's the trajectory I find most compelling: Just as Satan will construct a false trinity during the Tribulation, I believe there's something similar going on with the mark of the beast.

- **Revelation 7:3** told us the 144,000 will be sealed with a mark placed on their foreheads by God.

- In **Ephesians 1:13**, Paul tells us that the Holy Spirit in us is God's seal upon us, marking us as His property.

- In multiple Old Testament texts, we find the Lord telling Israel to physically place His Law upon their *foreheads* and *hands*.[390] Jewish men still do this today using *phylacteries*, which are small leather cases that hold little scrolls upon which are written verses from the Torah; these are bound to their foreheads and hands. Jews believe this represents agreement with God ideologically (the forehead) and a desire to live out that ideology practically (the hand).

The idea of the mark of the beast seems to be Satan imitating or mocking the concept of God's mark upon His people by marking a people for himself who are committed to *his* ideology. Instead of bearing the name of *Yahweh*,[391] those on the earth will take the name of *Satan*. Whereas the 144,000 were marked to protect them from God's wrath against the *wicked*, antichrist's followers will be marked to protect them from Satan's wrath against the *righteous*.

Let me assuage some of your fears regarding the mark of the beast. *Nobody* who desires to follow Jesus will take the mark unintentionally, unwittingly, or against their will. God will go to

---

[390] Cf. Exodus 13:9, 16; Deuteronomy 6:8; 11:18.

[391] Cf. Exodus 19:6; Numbers 6:27.

extraordinary lengths to ensure everybody understands the gravity of taking the mark. In **Revelation 14:9–10**, we are told:

> **... a third angel followed them, saying with a loud voice,** *"If anyone worships the beast and his image, and receives his mark on his forehead or on his hand, he himself shall also drink of the wine of the wrath of God, which is poured out full strength into the cup of His indignation. He shall be tormented with fire and brimstone in the presence of the holy angels and in the presence of the Lamb."*

Have you ever seen an angel flying around in the sky, declaring those things? Has anybody? Nope. Because it hasn't happened yet. But it will happen before the antichrist regime implements the mark. When that time comes, there will be no confusion about what is happening. Nobody will take the mark in ignorance—*nobody*.

THE NUMBER OF THE BEAST

> [18] **Here is wisdom. Let him who has understanding calculate the number of the beast, for it is the number of a man: His number** *is* **666.**

What's the deal with 666? There are a couple of possibilities that I think are plausible:

- It could be related to what's known as "gematria." Without getting bogged down in the details, it's an alphanumeric code where a numerical value is assigned to a name, word, or phrase based on its letters. Every letter has a value, and the value of a word is calculated by the sum of the value of its letters. Some suggest that antichrist's name will add up to 666 using gematria.

- Alternatively, and more plausibly, 666 is meant to be the numerical representation of ultimate *fallen-ness*. In the Bible, 6 is the number of man—sinful, fallen, broken man. It's the number of the flesh. Repeating something three times may simply be for emphasis, as we sing the phrase, *"Holy, holy, holy."* It could be that 666 simply emphasizes the Great Tribulation and the antichrist empire as the pinnacle of fallen-ness on the earth.

People have been trying to guess the antichrist using gematria for decades. They've also driven themselves crazy using various other forms of numerology. *"Wait a minute, 'Barack' has six letters!"* Or *"'Ronald Wilson Reagan' has six letters in each of his names . . . 666!"* And on and on and on. Remember, Paul told us antichrist won't be revealed until *after* the Church has been raptured[392]—meaning that it is impossible to guess his identity if you're part of the Church. So please, don't try! Don't forward that message or share that post!

The number of the beast will be helpful to those who are searching the Scriptures in the Tribulation. And to *them*, the meaning will be clear.

WHAT SCRIPTURE SAYS ABOUT THE MARK AND NUMBER OF THE BEAST

There is so much misinformation regarding the mark and number of the beast. And let me just say this: People who are worried about the

---

[392] Cf. 2 Thessalonians 2:6–8.

mark of the beast but aren't interested in giving their lives to Jesus are no different from those who will take the mark in the Tribulation. Because both are like Pharaoh in the Book of Exodus; they are concerned with the *signs*, but not with the one who *sends them*.

I also don't understand why anyone would take the Bible seriously enough to worry about the mark of the beast but *not* take the Bible seriously enough to worry about its central message that they are a sinner who needs to be saved by faith in Jesus! That doesn't make any sense to me.

The misinformation around this subject is even more astonishing when you consider that pretty much everything the Bible tells us about it can be found in only five verses: three verses in **Revelation 13** and two verses in **Revelation 14**. That's all! Think of all the misinformation that could be avoided if people would just read *five verses*.

Please note these *facts* regarding the mark of the beast, revealed in those five verses, lest we unwittingly contribute to the cesspool of misinformation:

- It has nothing to do with class warfare waged by the Illuminati or global elite. We know this because it will be required of **"all, both small and great, rich and poor."**

- It bears the seal, symbol, or name of the beast—antichrist. And Scripture clarifies everybody will *know* that. They will *understand* that they are pledging allegiance to antichrist, just as those in the Roman Empire understood they were pledging allegiance to the emperor when they gave the pinch offering.

- Taking the mark is irreversible. **Revelation 14:9–10** tells us that if you take the mark, it's over. There's no going back. Some suggest this points to genetic modification, which is possible, but I suspect it's a spiritual issue. If you've lived through the first half of the Tribulation, seen the signs and wonders, seen and heard the angels' warnings, and *still* choose to follow the beast, then you've reached a spiritual point of no return. If everything you've seen up to that point is still not enough for you, nothing ever will be. You're rejecting Jesus with your eyes wide open.

- The mark is physical. It is an externally visible mark *on* or *in* your forehead or hand. So, abstract statements like *"Islam is the mark of the beast"* make little sense.

- The mark is not *a* number; it's *his* number, and people *know* it's his number.

- Since the 1980s, some people have been freaking out over any identifying mark related to numbers—credit cards, Social Security numbers, you name it. But they all miss the fact that the Bible specifically tells us that it's **"the mark or the name of the beast, or the number of his name."** The mark is not a number that identifies people individually; it's a number associated with *antichrist*. Those who take the mark will bear *his* number.

- The evidence points to computerized data recognition of some sort. Because you cannot buy, sell, or conduct business without the mark, it seems clear that it will be connected to one's personal data and finances. If you've ever visited a store that doesn't take cash, that's the type of scenario we're talking about. Imagine all stores only taking the mark as a method of payment.

- Finally, it could be something we can't imagine because it doesn't exist yet. Technology is progressing so rapidly; people will use tech just ten years from now that we can't even imagine today.

Please understand that we must look at *everything* the Word says about the mark of the beast. A program or initiative fulfilling one or two of the characteristics of the mark does not make it the mark. It must satisfy *all* the criteria.

CLOSING THOUGHTS

If you're worried about the mark of the beast, you don't need to become an expert in understanding it so that you can identify it when it happens; you need to be *saved!* You need to give your life to Jesus!

If you're on the earth when it happens, identifying it as the mark of the beast won't save you. Only faith in Jesus will save you—just as only faith in Jesus will save you today. And if you'll put your faith in Jesus, you won't need to fear antichrist or the mark of the beast. You won't need to fear a revived Roman empire. You won't need to fear death or hell. You need the perfect love that casts out fear,[393] and His name is *Jesus*.

As I write this, it's 2023, and we're still dealing with the fallout of COVID vaccines and restrictions. During the last few years, I have heard some pondering out loud, *"Could mRNA vaccines be the mark of the beast?"* I hope that looking into the specifics of God's Word has provided us with clarity and made it clear that the mark will not be anything like a vaccine.

---

[393] Cf. 1 John 4:18.

But I also think we'd be ignorant to not recognize that some of the things unfolding around us are clearly preparatory for things to come in antichrist's regime. We've seen infrastructure and logistics developed to facilitate the global roll-out of vaccines. When the mark of the beast is implemented, these things will need to be in place and ready to go. Thanks to COVID, they will be.

We've seen the implementation of health passports around the globe. Once we digitize data, the logical next steps are digitizing our health records, driver's licenses, and more into one sort of "Multipass" (if you've seen the sci-fi classic *The Fifth Element*, you'll get that reference).

Our society is becoming increasingly *cashless*. All financial transactions are going digital. That's significant because all financial transactions can then be tracked and interfered with; CBDCs (central bank digital currencies) rolled out over the next few years and that will create the infrastructure for antichrist's financial system.

If you don't know what the Trusted News Initiative[394] is, it's worth looking up. It was rolled out by the BBC in 2020 and is an agreement between the world's major news organizations and social media companies to censor what they consider "misinformation" and promote stories they feel are in the interest of the public good. The world's media is openly conspiring to censor information they deem harmful and promote information they think is "helpful." That is happening *right now*.

Mass surveillance and tracing of the public continue to increase in the name of safety against terrorism, battling climate change, and controlling pandemics. But perhaps the most compelling

---

[394] Trusted News Initiative (website), British Broadcasting Corporation, https://www.bbc.co.uk/beyondfakenews/trusted-news-initiative.

development we've witnessed over the past several years has been the rise of the sociological phenomenon known as "othering." Let me explain.

World War II fascinates me because of the endless stories and subplots. It's a seemingly infinite field of study. But the part of WWII that I find most interesting is this: *"How did ordinary German citizens go from living next door to Jewish people and viewing them as neighbors to casually watching them and their families be executed and their bodies dumped into mass graves?"* How does that happen?

The answer is "othering." It happens when we view a group of people as "other"—not part of *our* group or team. Othering can be based on ethnicity, nationality, political views, athletic ability, or practically anything.

And what psychology has figured out is that most people need to "other" a group of people before they can justify mistreating them. We need to be able to tell ourselves that "those people" are not like us. They're not part of us. That thinking quickly develops into viewing them as *less* than human. And once we view someone as subhuman, we feel *released* from our moral obligations to treat them with human dignity.

That's what happened in Germany with the Jewish people. They were turned into *caricatures*. They were turned into *creatures* rather than people. All the frustrations of the German people were focused on the Jews, who were "othered" all the way to concentration camps and gas chambers.

Let me tell you what othering sounded like in 2020:

"We shouldn't let the unvaccinated have access to the healthcare system."

"We should put the unvaccinated in camps."

"It's understandable if nurses abuse and offer a lower standard of care to the unvaccinated."

"We need restrictions to punish people for not being vaccinated."

"I couldn't care less if an unvaccinated person dies from COVID."

Please understand that my point is not to advocate for or against vaccines. My point is the *othering* we saw come to the surface of our society so rapidly around this issue. And I hear people talk this way about all kinds of issues.

It's not difficult to imagine a day when the world will say, *"We need to get rid of these subhumans who follow Jesus and refuse to worship antichrist. He's leading us into a glorious new age of humanity, and we can't be held back by fools any longer."*

If you're guilty of othering any group in a manner that devalues them in an unbiblical way, I urge you to repent. We cannot follow Jesus and engage in "othering" because we will never love people we have "othered."

And no matter what's happening around us, praise God; our reality never changes. Every day, our hope, peace, joy, and fulfillment can be found in the same place—abiding in Jesus. May the Lord help us to never forget that.

REVELATION 14

Before the chronological narrative resumes in **Revelation 15**, John the Apostle has been filling us in on some additional developments that will unfold in the Tribulation so that we have a fuller understanding of the big picture.

In **Revelation 14**, it's as if John is saying, *"There are just a few more things I want you to know before we get back to the main story."* This chapter is parenthetical in that it contains multiple scenes from multiple points in time rather than one primary incident or subplot. They are additional details not laid out in any specific order, given to us to enhance our understanding of the meta-narrative.

THE LAMB AND THE 144,000

Our first scene unfolds at some point *after* the Tribulation when Jesus is reigning on the earth from the Throne of David in Jerusalem.[395]

> [1] **Then I looked, and behold, a Lamb standing on Mount Zion, . . .** [396]

---

[395] Cf. Isaiah 24:23; Luke 1:32.

[396] Cf. Psalm 2:6–9.

As we know by now, in the Bible, the Lamb is always *Jesus*.

. . . and with Him one hundred *and* forty-four thousand, having His Father's name written on their foreheads.

These are the 144,000 Jewish men chosen by God to be powerful, effective, and immortal evangelists who preach the Gospel worldwide during the Tribulation. In **Revelation 7**, we saw them *sealed* by God. And here in **Revelation 14**, we see them standing with Jesus at the end of the Tribulation. Not 143,999 of them but exactly 144,000. They all made it. Jesus didn't lose even one.

And that brings me great comfort because, in **Ephesians 1:13–14**, Paul writes this about us:

In Him you also *trusted*, after you heard the word of truth, the gospel of your salvation; in whom also, having believed, you were sealed with the Holy Spirit of promise, who is the guarantee of our inheritance until the redemption of the purchased possession, to the praise of His glory.

I get excited when I see the word **"guarantee"** associated with my salvation! Jesus *sealed* the 144,000, and they all made it. Jesus has *sealed* those of us who have placed our faith in Him, and so, we will make it too. Not because we're faithful. Not because we won't mess up. But because the Lord has *sealed* us. We *will* arrive in His presence one day. Nothing can change that. The One who saved us is the same One who will sustain us.

These 144,000 went through the worst tribulation the world will ever see. But it did not have the power to change the ending of their story. And here we see them, at the finish line, with Jesus. No matter how much tribulation life throws at you, if you've given your life to Jesus, your story will end with Him meeting you at the finish line. He *guarantees it:*

> *My sheep hear My voice, and I know them, and they follow Me. And I give them eternal life, and they shall never perish; neither shall anyone snatch them out of My hand. My Father, who has given them to Me, is greater than all; and no one is able to snatch them out of My Father's hand.*
>
> —John 10:27–29[397]

Our brother Paul reached this conclusion:

> **...I am persuaded that neither death nor life, nor angels nor principalities nor powers, nor things present nor things to come, nor height nor depth, nor any other created thing, shall be able to separate us from the love of God which is in Christ Jesus our Lord.**
>
> —Romans 8:38–39

And in **Philippians 1:6,** he writes that he is:

> **...confident of this very thing, that He who has begun a good work in you will complete** *it* **until the day of Jesus Christ...**

The Bible declares that God is the One who *began* the work in you, God is the One who is *doing* the work in you, and God will be the one to *finish* the work in you. So, when God says you're going to make it, you're going to make it. God declares that with total confidence because *He* is the One who will make it happen. Praise God for our salvation.

---

[397] See also John 6:39.

This truth would have been a great comfort to John's readers around AD 96. They faced persecution and death under Caesars who hated Jesus—being burned at the stake and fed to lions. But as they read about these 144,000 who didn't compromise and were sustained by the power of Jesus through the greatest time of tribulation the world will ever see, they would have been filled with hope.

Because this is the last time we'll see them, I'll mention that the 144,000 will enter the Millennial Kingdom as human men. They will likely continue their evangelistic mission throughout the thousand years of Jesus' earthly reign. Because while only redeemed human beings will *enter* the Millennium, there will be some born who will grow up and choose *not* to submit to the lordship of Jesus. We'll talk more about that in future chapters but suffice it to say there will still be a need for Gospel proclamation in the Millennial Kingdom.[398]

² And I heard a voice from heaven, like the voice of many waters, and like the voice of loud thunder. And I heard the sound of harpists playing their harps.

John hears a song coming from Heaven, overflowing down to the earth.

"Harps" refers to stringed instruments in general, meaning there could be people shredding on guitar in Heaven (sorry if you were banking on Heaven being a return to organ-only worship). Whatever the case, let's just be grateful that there are apparently no bagpipes in Heaven.

---

[398] Cf. Isaiah 60:3; Zechariah 8:23.

³ They sang as it were a new song before the throne, before the four living creatures, and the elders; . . .

We talked about them back in **Revelation 4**.

. . . and no one could learn that song except the hundred *and* forty-four thousand who were redeemed from the earth.

There's a specific song being sung in Heaven that only the 144,000 can join in at this moment. It seems likely that Heaven is giving them a song that is *unique* to their experience.

During the Tribulation, most of the world will want to kill them. We know they won't be able to because God will make them temporarily invincible but remember, they will still be tasked with publicly preaching the Gospel *in the Tribulation*. It's not going to be an easy assignment. Most will hurl abuse and try to kill them everywhere they go. People will abuse and kill those who *do* respond to their preaching. And I think it's safe to assume that Satan will do everything he can to try to get these guys to fall into sin.

And yet, after all that, when they're standing with Jesus, they're not whining. They're not saying, *"Lord, what was up with all that persecution?"* or *"God, that was so hard!"* Nope. They're singing. They're making music to the Lord.

And the song they sing will be born of the sum of their experiences with Jesus. It's *their* song, not yours or mine. You and I will have our own song to sing, so to speak, and it too will be born of the sum of our experiences with the Lord. It will be *our* testimony of God's faithfulness and goodness. And believe me, we will sing it at the top of our lungs.

How are the 144,000 able to complete such a trying task so joyfully? In the same way Paul and Silas found the strength to sing while imprisoned in chains.[399] Please don't miss this because I'm about to share with you one of the great truths about how the Holy Spirit works in our lives: God always provides the grace that is needed for the calling.

When God calls you to a task, He makes available the grace, mercy, strength, peace, and joy you need. Whatever is needed, He will provide it. When you face great difficulty, great grace is made available to you. When you meet a little difficulty, a little grace is available to you. In both instances, the grace God gives is enough—enough to fill your spirit with a song, even in the darkness of a prison cell.

This can be hard to accept because it means we can't complain to others and say, *"I have a right to complain! I have a right to grumble and moan! You don't know what I'm going through! If you did, you'd be complaining too!"* The reality is that you may be going through something I can't possibly understand, but I know that the Lord understands it. He sees it all. And He has made available the grace you need to walk through your trial with joy.

"But Jeff, if what you're saying is true, I don't get to look for sympathy from everybody." Exactly!

"Then I can't be mad when people don't respond to my attention-seeking social media posts!" Right!

"Are you saying my suffering isn't more significant than everybody else's?" Yes, that's precisely what I'm saying.

Ouch. That hurts me too. Because you better believe I want your sympathy when I'm suffering (man colds are no joke). But if I believe the Bible, I must believe God has provided all I need, and that His

---

[399] Cf. Acts 16:25.

mercies are new every morning. And that means He has given me the grace I need for *today*—the grace that finds a song to sing, the song that only I can sing, no matter how difficult my circumstances.

If you need to be encouraged in this, take **Lamentations 3** to heart. Slow down for a moment, and let these verses minister to your soul:

> ***Through* the Lord's mercies we are not consumed,**
> **Because His compassions fail not.**
> ***They are* new every morning;**
> **Great *is* Your faithfulness.**
> **"*The Lord is my portion,*" says my soul,**
> **"*Therefore I hope in Him!*"**
>
> **The Lord *is* good to those who wait for Him,**
> **To the soul *who* seeks Him.**
> ***It is* good that *one* should hope and wait quietly**
> **For the salvation of the Lord.**
>
> —Lamentations 3:22–26

I pray that those verses describe our response to seasons of tribulation. Instead of complaining and giving voice to our doubts and fears, may we **"hope and wait quietly for the salvation of the Lord."** Because in that stillness, we will find the grace and the song that God is giving *us*.

Have you ever had a brother or sister in Christ share a challenge or problem, and you had no idea what to say or suggest or how to help? Can I tell you what is *always* helpful? Listening well, letting them know you love them, and praying with them. Praying in faith and thanking God that He will provide everything needed. Because we *all* need those encouraging reminders, and prayer is powerful. It is good to build each other up in the truth.

⁴ These are the ones who were not defiled with women, for they are virgins. These are the ones who follow the Lamb wherever He goes.

One of the defining characteristics of the 144,000 will be their radical purity. In a world gleefully submitted to the lusts of the flesh, they will remain devoted to God and sexually righteous.

I shared in the previous chapter how the Lord instructed His people to bind His commands between their eyes (on their forehead) and onto their hands. And I shared how they viewed this as representing agreement with God, ideologically (the forehead/mind) and practically (the hand). It visualized every believer's desire to agree with God in their *thinking* and *behavior*.

In **V.1**, we read that the 144,000 have **"His Father's name written on their foreheads."** I believe that points to one of the secrets of the 144,000 and how they will remain sexually pure in a deviant world: their *minds* will be focused on the Lord, and they will meditate upon His Word.

Because of sexual sin, many of us struggle with the mental side of the Christian walk. Yes, our sins are forgiven. Yes, there's grace for us. But our sins can leave us with mental scars and images that stick around for a long time. God will forgive you if you make a terrible decision and watch something you shouldn't. But those images, thoughts, and ideas seem to live on in our minds, working against our desire to live in purity. We can't meditate on the things of God and simultaneously fill our minds with the things of this world.

Let's ensure we're being honest about how we're wired so we don't sabotage ourselves. Let's take **Psalm 101:3** to heart: **"I will set nothing wicked before my eyes."** Whatever you need to change, whatever you need to get rid of to make that happen—*do it*.

Isaiah 26:3 gives us this tremendous promise:

You will keep *him* in perfect peace,
***Whose* mind *is* stayed *on* You,**
Because he trusts in You.

When the Holy Spirit convicts us of sin, our thoughts become restless. But the mind that trusts in the Lord finds peace. In most cases, the solution for our mental anguish is the simple truth of **Isaiah 26:3**. If you're dealing with stress, worry, or anxiety, I recommend you take some time to honestly evaluate whether you're trusting the Lord. In my life, I have found that the degree of worry and fear I have about the future is always directly related to how I'm doing with trusting God.

And yes, I understand that mental health and brain chemistry are real things. I'm saying that we should always *start* by evaluating whether we're trusting God and His Word before we also seek counseling or medication.

How will the 144,000 stay pure? How will they not freak out from worry and stress in the Tribulation? By keeping their *minds* free of worldly things and focused on the Lord.

While we're on the 144,000 and their example, I should remind us of another simple truth about the Christian life that we often forget: If we want to see God *move* through our lives, we need to *sanctify* our lives. We must decide to set our lives apart for the Lord's purposes and glory. Why? Because sin will stop the flow of God's power in our lives. I speak from experience, as I'm sure you can too.

Perhaps as you read that, you think, *"Come on, Jeff. The 144,000 are a special deal. They've got special power to live righteously."* Do they? Remember what Jesus said to His disciples before His Ascension:

> ...*you shall receive power when the Holy Spirit has come upon you; and you shall be witnesses to Me in Jerusalem, and in all Judea and Samaria, and to the end of the earth.*
>
> —Acts 1:8

Last time I checked, that same Holy Spirit is available to you and me. The same Holy Spirit that operated in the disciples and will operate in the 144,000 is available to us. But we must choose to live for the Lord *before* the test comes. If we put off living wholeheartedly for the Lord, thinking we'll just flick some "faith switch" when the moment of trial or temptation comes, we're delusional. We need to choose Jesus *now*.

General George S. Patton Jr. paraphrased Shakespeare when he famously wrote, *"Fatigue makes cowards of us all."*[400] When we're going through tribulation, it seems so *easy* to justify sin:

> "I deserve it. How else am I supposed to cope with this? Nobody can judge me because they don't know what I'm going through."

When the 144,000 are tired or feeling the pressure of the Tribulation, they won't run to an antichrist or idol. Their strength, power, authority, and energy will come from being intimately connected to Jesus, *"the vine"*[401] that will make them fruitful.

John's readers needed this encouragement. They needed this word. They needed to be reminded that when tribulation hits our

---

[400] George S. Patton, Jr., *War As I Knew It* (New York: Bantam Books, 1980), 288, Ebook edition.

[401] John 15:1–8.

lives, we don't need to fear death or pain or suffering. We can have peace and joy amid it all if we set our minds on Jesus.

These were redeemed from *among* men, *being* firstfruits to God and to the Lamb.

In the Tribulation, the 144,000 will be the **"firstfruits."** Of what? The harvest of ethnic Israel returning to the Lord, as prophesied. Ultimately, God's Word tells us that **"all Israel will be saved"**[402] through the Great Tribulation.

When you read the story of Israel's history in the Scriptures, you learn she failed to fulfill her God-given destiny because she kept getting entangled with the world's idols and sexual immorality, and usually both simultaneously. The 144,000 will fulfill Israel's destiny to preach the Gospel to all nations while remaining faithful to the Lord and set apart for Him. They will be the **"firstfruits"** in that sense, also:

⁵ And in their mouth was found no deceit, for they are without fault before the throne of God.

These incredible men will live lives that back up everything they're preaching. There won't be a hint of hypocrisy in them. They'll be the real deal in every sense of the phrase.

THREE ANGELS SPEAK FROM THE SKY

Our next scene takes place around the halfway point of the Tribulation, as the whole earth sees and hears the declarations of three angels. Their messages will be the *final call* to those on the

---

[402] Romans 11:26.

earth before the mark of the beast is rolled out, and everyone still alive is forced to choose between antichrist and the Lord.

> ⁶**Then I saw another angel flying in the midst of heaven,** . . .

John sees this angel flying around the sky.

> . . . **having the everlasting gospel to preach to those who dwell on the earth—to every nation, tribe, tongue, and people—** . . .

Before we go any further, there's a translation issue we need to deal with. The New King James Version of the Bible, which I'm using, employs the phrase, **"those who dwell on the earth."** We know that phrase refers to those on the earth who have rejected Jesus and will never repent. But in the original Greek, that's not the phrase used. It should be rendered **"those who LIVE on the earth."** That's important because this angel will preach to *everyone* on earth, including those who can and will choose to repent and follow Jesus.

Many of us have probably heard something like, *"The Bible teaches that when the Gospel has been preached to everyone on the earth,* **then** *Jesus will come back. So, we need to reach every person, and when we finally do, Jesus will return."* That idea comes from Jesus in **Matthew 24:14**:

> . . . *this gospel of the kingdom will be preached in all the world as a witness to all the nations, and then the end will come.*

Jesus was talking about *this moment* in **Revelation 14:6**, around the halfway point of the Tribulation, when an angel will fly across the skies, preaching the **"gospel of the kingdom . . . " " . . . to every nation, tribe, tongue, and people."** When this happens, everyone on earth will hear the Gospel, and Jesus' criteria for **"the end"** will be met.

And this will be the angel's message:

> ...⁷ **saying with a loud voice,** *"Fear God and give glory to Him, for the hour of His judgment has come; and worship Him who made heaven and earth, the sea and springs of water."*

As we've mentioned many times, things will be *crystal clear* by this point in the Tribulation. The world will understand that this is the Kingdom of God versus the Kingdom of Satan. No apologetics will be needed because when watching an angel preach from the sky, questions like, *"How do I even know that the supernatural world is real? What evidence do you have?"* no longer need to be addressed. Suffice it to say atheism will not survive the Tribulation.

When we share the Gospel today, we can tell people that God has a plan for their life, things for them to do and that He is the best way to experience life on earth. The Gospel this angel shares is significantly more concise. He is telling them that this is their last chance. Their Creator is about to judge the earth, and they will want to be on His side when He does. So, they should give their lives to Him *right now*.

This angel lists four things that people need to do to be saved at this time. It's an all-encompassing list, and regardless of the time, anyone who does these things can be assured they've sided with Jesus:

1. Fear God—even more than the Tribulation and antichrist's regime. It's the beginning of wisdom.[403] Remember how Jesus counseled His disciples:

   > ... *do not fear those who kill the body but cannot kill the soul. But rather fear Him who is able to destroy both soul and body in hell.*
   >
   > —Matthew 10:28

---

[403] Cf. Psalm 111:10; Proverbs 1:7, 9:10.

2. Give God glory, not *any* antichrist.

3. Worship God; direct your affections toward Him, not earthly things.

4. Acknowledge God as the Creator; He created you for a relationship with Him.

As discussed in the previous chapter, God will go to incredible lengths to save people in the Tribulation. **"The Lord is . . . not willing that any should perish but that all should come to repentance."**[404] And we see God's heart displayed in His sending of this angel to preach the Gospel to everyone on earth.

> **⁸ And another angel followed, saying, *"Babylon is fallen, is fallen, that great city, because she has made all nations drink of the wine of the wrath of her fornication."***

The term "Babylon," used here for the first time in Revelation, can be a bit confusing because it is used in Scripture to refer to something literal, something abstract and mystical, and sometimes both simultaneously.

Literally, Babylon is a city located in present-day Iraq. It is one of the most notable cities of antiquity, serving as the capital of empires and the world's cultural center for centuries.

In the abstract and mystical sense, Babylon refers to the *world system*—all the systems established by the world's current ruler, Satan. This includes economic, governmental, religious, sexual, entertainment, and values systems—basically all of secularism. They are all Babylon.

---

[404] 2 Peter 3:9.

This angel's declaration comes partially from **Isaiah 21:9**, which prophesied the idols of literal Babylon being destroyed. This angel's declaration is a proleptic statement destined to be fulfilled in **Revelation 17–18** and, ultimately, at the Second Coming.

It will be a *shocking* statement to those on the earth—not only because an angel will make it, but also because they will believe that the antichrist's empire is an unstoppable force. At this moment in the Tribulation, he will wield more power than any man on earth has ever had (since Adam). But this angel will declare that the destruction of his empire is inevitable and already almost here.

We'll study Babylon in greater detail when we reach **Revelation 17–18**.

⁹ **Then a third angel followed them, saying with a loud voice, . . .**

How loud? Loud enough for every single person on earth to hear!

. . . If anyone worships the beast and his image, and receives his mark on his forehead or on his hand, ¹⁰ *he himself shall also drink of the wine of the wrath of God, which is poured out full strength into the cup of His indignation. He shall be tormented with fire and brimstone in the presence of the holy angels and in the presence of the Lamb.*

The idea is that those who reject Jesus will experience the full wrath of God—not anything watered down or restrained. I know many believers never read the Book of Revelation because of the rumors that it's hard to understand. But I also know that many don't want to touch it, or the subject of eschatology, because they've read or heard a few snippets that left them thinking, *"Wow, God can be incredibly harsh."*

To that person, I would simply say, *"Read your Bible!"* Revelation tells us the Lord will send an angel to warn everyone *not* to take the beast's mark, but most will still choose to do it. Those arrogant enough to say, *"I'll believe it when I see it,"* will be without excuse.

God: *"Don't take the mark, or you'll be damned."*
People: *"I'm going to take the mark anyway."*
God: *"Then you're damned."*
People: *"I always knew You weren't a loving God!"*

I honestly don't know what else the Lord could do to be more straightforward and clear.

¹¹ *And the smoke of their torment ascends forever and ever; and they have no rest day or night, who worship the beast and his image, and whoever receives the mark of his name.*

The first phrase is similar to **Isaiah 34:9–10**, which details God's destruction of Edom. The idea in both cases is that the systems of the wicked are destroyed and will never be rebuilt again.

This is one of the places where the Bible clarifies that those who reject God will spend eternity in a very real place, where they will ***"have no rest"*** *forever*. They will not simply cease to exist. They will not get a second chance to work out their karma or graduate from purgatory.

It's a tragic reality that Satan will drag many with him to eternal destruction by convincing them of what they desire to believe—that such a future cannot exist. But the Bible tells us otherwise. Jesus said, in **Matthew 13**:

The Son of Man will send out His angels, and they will gather out of His kingdom all things that offend, and those who practice lawlessness, and will cast them into the furnace of fire. There will be wailing and gnashing of teeth.

—Matthew 13:41–42

The angels will come forth, separate the wicked from among the just, and cast them into the furnace of fire. There will be wailing and gnashing of teeth.

—Matthew 13:49b–50

Jesus wanted everyone to understand the *reality* of eternity. In fact, Jesus talked more about Sheol, Gehenna, and Hades than He did about Heaven (during earthly His ministry). Those who belong to Jesus will experience eternal *life*. Those who reject Jesus will experience eternal *death*.[405]

And I would not be loving you well if I did not plainly share that truth with you.

Like you, when I hear that, I'm disturbed. We should be. Though we tend to feel apologetic for the reality of eternity, we shouldn't because the very concept of salvation *presupposes* our damnation. It presupposes there is something we need saving *from*. We shouldn't apologize for the reality of sin and death because the glory of the Gospel is how God *responded* to the reality of our damnation. He did the unthinkable to save us—laying down *His* life for us.

If we don't actually *need* saving, then the Cross was just an ultimately pointless attempt at some sort of morality-based performance art. But we *do* need salvation. And the reality of eternal death is what necessitated the reality of Jesus' death and resurrection. We should not be embarrassed or ashamed of the existence of sin

---

[405] Cf. Matthew 25:46.

and death because the glory of the Gospel is what the Lord did to *save us* from death.

Do you know why there isn't an angel flying across the sky, preaching the Gospel today? Because for now, preaching the Gospel is our job. Jesus gave the task to the Church that we might have an opportunity to participate in His work and store up treasures in Heaven.

"But people won't listen to me!" Most people won't listen to this angel either, so don't feel bad if they don't listen to you. Most people didn't listen to the apostles, the prophets, or even Jesus. When the Church was born on Pentecost, there were 120 people in the Upper Room.[406] Three years of ministry by *God in the flesh* produced 120 people. Don't be discouraged. Preach the Gospel anyway because, for now, it's our job.

Before anybody takes the mark of the beast, these angels will fly across the sky, preaching the Gospel and warning everyone to ally themselves with Jesus and refuse the mark. Again, *nobody* is going to take the mark unwittingly or unwillingly. Sadly, the overwhelming majority will take it anyway because, as John wrote, **"men loved darkness rather than light, because their deeds were evil."**[407]

COMFORT FOR TRIBULATION SAINTS

The next scene is one of comfort for those on the earth who turn to Jesus in the Tribulation and are martyred for His name's sake.

> **¹² Here is the patience of the saints; here *are* those who keep the commandments of God and the faith of Jesus.**

---

[406] Cf. Acts 2:15.

[407] John 3:19.

When you and I become believers, we join in the *mission* Jesus has given His Church: proclaiming the Gospel and making disciples. In contrast, those who become believers in the Great Tribulation are given a different task: *persevere*. All Jesus asks them to do is keep the faith, even to death. And the comfort of these verses is God's promise that He will sustain the faith of those who belong to Him, no matter what happens, until they arrive in His presence.

As the next verse will reveal, death is actually the best thing that can happen to a believer in the Great Tribulation:

¹³ Then I heard a voice from heaven saying to me, "Write: 'Blessed are the dead who die in the Lord from now on.'"
"Yes," says the Spirit, "that they may rest from their labors, and their works follow them."

For those who turn to the Lord in the Great Tribulation, death will be a blessing because their tribulation will be over. While we can take encouragement from this verse, it's another one that's not really for us. It's written to reassure those who will turn to Jesus in the Great Tribulation. Things will be so chaotic and intense; they'll need reassurance.

This part of Jesus' promise is true for every believer who dies before the Rapture and during the Tribulation: *"that they may rest from their labors, and their works follow them."* Everyone who loves Jesus has an eternity waiting for them in which there is no more labor. We'll have things to do, but they won't be laborious; they'll only be a joy. It's going to be so good!

And don't you love what this verse says about the *"works"* of those who belong to the Lord? It's telling us that the only thing that leaves the earth with us are the works we did for the Lord. Praise God for that! I'll be more than happy to leave everything else behind.

This is why Paul wrote, *"to live is Christ, and to die is gain."*[408] If the Lord allows me to wake up tomorrow morning, I'll have another opportunity to serve Jesus on the earth and store up treasures in Heaven. If I die before tomorrow comes, my work is over. I'll rest for eternity, and I'll have treasures in Heaven waiting for me. Because of the Cross, life or death is a win-win situation for the believer.

THE FULLNESS OF THE GENTILES

There are a lot of different views regarding **VV.14–20**. I'll share my conclusions, but, as always, you do your own research and draw your own conclusions.

> **¹⁴ Then I looked, and behold, a white cloud, and on the cloud sat *One* like the Son of Man, having on His head a golden crown, and in His hand a sharp sickle.**

If you read **Daniel 7:13–14**, you'll find this is unquestionably Jesus, preparing to return to the earth as its conquering king as indicated by the crown he is wearing. It's a *stephanos,* a victor's crown, rather than a royal crown.

> **¹⁵ And another angel came out of the temple [in Heaven], crying with a loud voice to Him who sat on the cloud, *"Thrust in Your sickle and reap, for the time has come for You to reap, for the harvest of the earth is ripe."***

When you examine the original language, it's clear this other angel is not *commanding* Jesus; He's *announcing* what Jesus is about to do. He's serving as a herald.

---

[408] Philippians 1:21.

ⁱ⁶ **So He who sat on the cloud thrust in His sickle on the earth, and the earth was reaped.**

Some scholars believe this *reaping* refers to the seven bowl judgments, which will begin in **Revelation 15**. But there's some confusion because reaping is used in Scripture as an idiom for both wrath and salvation.

I look at **V.13** and see God *comforting* Tribulation saints by saying, *"Blessed are the dead who die in the Lord from now on."* For that reason, I believe this refers to a final harvest of Gentiles—the last non-Jews who will be saved in the Great Tribulation. We know such a number exists. Paul described it as **"the fullness of the Gentiles."**[409]

And interestingly, Paul wrote that number must be reached *before* Israel's spiritual blindness can be lifted—an event that will happen when Jesus appears to Israel at the Second Coming.

THE GRAPES OF WRATH

Following that harvest of salvation is a harvest of wrath:

¹⁷ **Then another angel came out of the temple which is in heaven, he also having a sharp sickle.**
¹⁸ **And another angel came out from the altar, who had power over fire, . . .**

This seems to be the angel who oversees the incense altar in Heaven, where we saw the prayers of the saints collected in **Revelation 8:3–5**. And he is announcing that God had decreed it

---

[409] Romans 11:25.

time for this prayer to be answered: *"Your Kingdom come. Your will be done on earth as it is in Heaven."*[410]

> **. . . and he cried with a loud cry to him who had the sharp sickle, saying, *"Thrust in your sharp sickle and gather the clusters of the vine of the earth, for her grapes are fully ripe."*
> [19] So the angel thrust his sickle into the earth and gathered the vine of the earth, and threw *it* into the great winepress of the wrath of God. [20] And the winepress was trampled outside the city, and blood came out of the winepress, up to the horses' bridles, for one thousand six hundred furlongs.**

Clearly, we're talking about a harvest of *wrath*. And keeping our focus on the big picture, this appears to be looking ahead to the famous "Battle of Armageddon" at the Second Coming.

From the rest of Scripture, we know that **"the city"** in **V.20** is Jerusalem. This event will unfold **"outside the city"** about 60 miles north of Jerusalem, on the Plain of Esdraelon near Mount Megiddo. As unbelievable as it sounds, antichrist, the false prophet, human military forces, and evil spiritual forces will be gathered in Megiddo and will turn their weapons against Jesus when He returns to the earth. It won't go well for them.

Imagine harvesting grapes with a sickle. Nobody would ever do that because if you don't harvest grapes by hand, you'll *crush* and *burst* them. If you use a sickle, it's going to be a mess. And Armageddon is going to be a *bloody mess*.

If you're paying close attention, you might realize that the term

---

[410] Cf. Matthew 6:10; Luke 11:2.

"Battle" in the phrase "Battle of Armageddon" is a misnomer. There is no battle, only annihilation. The Old Testament prophet Joel prophesied about this time, writing:

> *Put in the sickle, for the harvest is ripe.*
> *Come, go down;*
> *For the winepress is full,*
> *The vats overflow—*
> *For their wickedness is great.*
>
> **Multitudes, multitudes in the valley of decision!**
> **For the day of the Lord *is* near in the valley of decision.**
> —Joel 3:13–14

The imagery employed here tells us the enemies of God will be gathered in Megiddo, like grapes being tossed into a winepress, where Jesus will *crush* them.

Look again at the disturbing observations of **V.20**:

> **... the winepress was trampled outside the city, and blood came out of the winepress, up to the horses' bridles, for one thousand six hundred furlongs.**

Does this mean there will *literally* be blood four feet deep over an area of hundreds of square miles? Probably not. It more likely means the blood of people dying will *spray up* to the height of the horse's bridles. Yes, it's going to be a bloody mess. And I'm sorry, but there's not really any way for me to get around that. It's what the text says.

The blood spilled by this second "harvest" will cover a distance of **"one thousand six hundred furlongs."** A furlong is about 600 feet, making this distance around 176 miles.

What city is located **"one thousand six hundred furlongs"** from the Valley of Megiddo? *Petra*. Another name for Petra is "Bozrah," and it was used by Isaiah when he prophesied:

> **Who *is* this who comes from Edom,**
> **With dyed garments from Bozrah,**
> **This *One who is* glorious in His apparel,**
> **Traveling in the greatness of His strength?—**
> *"I who speak in righteousness, mighty to save."*
> **Why *is* Your apparel red,**
> **And Your garments like one who treads in the winepress?**
> —Isaiah 63:1–2

The answer to Isaiah's question, of course, is *Jesus*. He is the One who will be treading this winepress and completely overwhelming the enemies of God at Armageddon.

It seems possible that Jesus' enemies will either flee from Megiddo and head south toward Petra to escape or head south toward Jerusalem and then Petra in the hopes of landing a final blow against the Lord by harming His city and people. In either event, the result will be their dead bodies strewn from Armageddon to Petra.

And if Jesus does indeed end up at Petra, it would be fascinating as it would also be the ordained moment for Him to reveal Himself to Israel and finally be welcomed as her messiah.

CLOSING THOUGHTS

The purpose of animal sacrifices under the Old Covenant was to teach Israel and us that sin always creates an *effect*. There are always *consequences*, and the Bible tells us what they are: **"the wages of sin is**

death."[411] Those sacrifices pointed to the reality that only innocent blood could cover our sins. And ultimately, it all pointed to Jesus and the precious blood He would shed in our place.

This chapter reminds us there is no neutral ground. I will either receive the wages of death for my sins or accept Jesus' glorious offer to receive those wages on my behalf. At this very moment, each of us has chosen to be *judged* by Jesus or *saved* by Jesus. There are no other options.

Physical death is the separation of the spirit from the body. *Spiritual* death is the separation of the spirit from the presence of God.[412] And *nobody* is prepared for the gravity of what that actually means. If you have not taken your place in the family of God, please, choose Him now!

If you are facing tribulation of any sort, remember the promise of **Isaiah 26:3**:

> **You will keep *him* in perfect peace,**
> ***Whose* mind *is* stayed *on You*,**
> **Because he trusts in You.**

Choose faith and thank Jesus that He's *got you*. Then meditate on that thought and allow the peace of God to cover your mind.

> ***Through* the Lord's mercies we are not consumed,**
> **Because His compassions fail not.**
> ***They are* new every morning;**
> **Great *is* Your faithfulness.**
> **"*The Lord is my portion*," says my soul,**

---

[411] Romans 6:23.

[412] Cf. Jude 1:12; Revelation 2:11, 20:6, 14, 21:8.

"Therefore I hope in Him!"
The Lord *is* good to those who wait for Him,
To the soul *who* seeks Him.
It is good that *one* should hope and wait quietly
For the salvation of the Lord.

—Lamentations 3:22–26

REVELATION 15-16

THE SEVEN BOWL JUDGMENTS

Revelation 6–9 walked us through the first two sets of judgments unleashed upon the earth in the Tribulation. They started with seven *seal* judgments, and when we reached the seventh seal judgment, we learned it consisted of seven *trumpet* judgments.

But when we reached the seventh trumpet judgment, John pressed the Pause button to fill us in on some additional details from the Tribulation so that we would have a fuller understanding of events before the Play button was pressed again. In **Revelation 15–16**, that Play button is pressed, and our chronological narrative resumes.

You might recall that the seventh trumpet was sounded back in **Revelation 11**, but we have not yet seen its *effects* because we've been in Pause mode.

We'll discover that just as the seventh *seal* judgment was made up of seven *trumpet* judgments, the seventh *trumpet* judgment will consist of seven *bowl* judgments.

We're going to look at **Revelation 15** and **16** together because they offer two perspectives on the same events. **Revelation 15** describes what takes place in Heaven, while **Revelation 16** describes what simultaneously unfolds on the earth.

SETTING UP THE BOWL JUDGMENTS

> **¹ Then I saw another sign in heaven, great and marvelous: seven angels having the seven last plagues, for in them the wrath of God is complete.**

These seven bowl judgments will **"complete"** the pouring out of God's wrath upon the earth.

The word **"last"** confirms there is indeed a *chronology* to the judgments of Revelation. These are the **"last"** judgments, coming *after* the seal and trumpet judgments.

We can be so hypocritical in how we think about God. Many will say, *"How can you believe in a loving God when Hitler was allowed to do what he did?"* But those same people will then ask, *"How could a loving God order the extermination of the Canaanites?"*

Here's the hypocrisy—we want God to deal *justly* with great evil, yet we accuse Him of being *unjust* when He does! History tells us that every people group God commanded killed (e.g., the Canaanites) was wicked in ways that I will only describe as *unspeakable*. Suffice it to say, they were an entire society of Hitlers who were raising generation after generation of little Hitlers, conditioned from birth to be evil and perverse beyond belief. And yet, God gave them *hundreds* of years to repent. But they would not.

God will only pour out His wrath on the earth after giving humanity *thousands* of years to repent. And the lack of repentance by those who reject Jesus to the very end proves they would *never* have repented under any circumstances. Like the Canaanites, the earth will have reached the point where it cannot merely be reformed. The slate will have to be wiped clean.

The logical question isn't, *"How could God judge humanity so harshly?"* The logical question is, *"Why has He given humanity so much time to repent?"* **2 Peter 3:9** tells us the Rapture and Tribulation haven't happened yet for one reason:

> ... [God is] **longsuffering toward us, not willing that any should perish but that all should come to repentance.**

God is just, and patient, and desires everyone be saved. The only reason anyone will experience the wrath of God will be because, ultimately, they *choose* to. They choose *wrath* over *Jesus*. Jesus is the One who gave His body and blood to offer everyone a place in His family. That's why it's nothing short of blasphemy to suggest that God is not loving. Any attempt to argue that point falls apart at the foot of the Cross, where Jesus died in our place to save us from the punishment we deserve.

> **² And I saw *something* like a sea of glass mingled with fire, and those who have the victory over the beast, over his image and over his mark *and* over the number of his name, standing on the sea of glass, having harps of God.**

The people John sees are those who were martyred in the Great Tribulation for refusing to worship antichrist or take his mark. You'll recall that in **Revelation 12:11**, we read:

> **...they overcame him by the blood of the Lamb and by the word of their testimony, and they did not love their lives to the death.**

We've talked about how earthly Tabernacles and Temples mirrored the true Temple in Heaven. This **"sea of glass"** in Heaven was mirrored on earth by the brass "sea"—a laver or basin used by the priests for ceremonial washing. In **Ephesians 5:26**, Paul tells us that we are sanctified and cleansed not by washing with water but by washing with the Word. The picture we're meant to understand is that, symbolically, these precious Great Tribulation martyrs are standing on the Word of God, not in a disrespectful sense, but in the sense that the promises of God are their *firm foundation*.

Remember that antichrist will openly commit *genocide* against Jews and believers in the Great Tribulation. He'll think he's succeeding, but in reality, he'll just be running a shuttle service to Heaven, which is a much better place to be during the Great Tribulation!

The **"fire"** points to God's *judgment*, and we'll see how that's connected in a moment.

> ³ **They sing the song of Moses, the servant of God, and the song of the Lamb, saying:**
>
> *"Great and marvelous are Your works,*
> *Lord God Almighty!*
> *Just and true are Your ways,*
> *O King of the saints!* [literally "nations"]
> ⁴ *Who shall not fear You, O Lord, and glorify Your name?*
> *For You alone are holy . . . "*

These Tribulation martyrs are singing **"the song of Moses,"** the first song recorded in Scripture back in **Exodus 15:1–18**, and **"the song of the Lamb,"** first heard in **Revelation 5:8–14**.

A few hours before **"the song of Moses"** was sung for the first time, the Israelites were in a hopeless situation, pinned against the Reed Sea with the Egyptian army bearing down on them and nowhere to run. The triumph of evil over good seemed inevitable. Yet, just a few hours later, they found themselves standing safely on the other side, watching the water close around the Egyptians, burying them in the depths. That is precisely what will happen to those martyred in the Great Tribulation. In the blink of an eye, they will be transported from their *darkest* hour to their *greatest* hour through death. They will be delivered by the Lord and watch as He deals with their enemies.

How perfect it is then that as they sing the Bible's *first* song, they also make it the Bible's *final* song.[413] When following Jesus gets you killed, it might seem *strange* to then sing words like:

Great and marvelous are Your works, . . .
Just and true are Your ways, . . .

But the reality of Heaven completely changes the equation for those who belong to the Lord. Don't ever lose sight of Heaven. These martyrs left the earth in a wave of persecution, suffering, and death. They were *losers* on earth but *champions* in eternity. The reality of Heaven changes *everything*.

The final part of their song says this in **V.4**:

. . . For all nations shall come and worship before You,
For Your judgments have been manifested.

The word *"shall"* tells us that this is speaking in the *future* tense. It pertains to what will occur *after* the Tribulation and the Second

---

[413] Portions of the Bible's first song are also repeated in Psalm 118 in celebration of the end of the Babylonian Exile and in Isaiah 12 by those in the Millennial Kingdom.

Coming, in the Millennial Kingdom. **Zechariah 14:16** talks about this time and gives us some additional details:

> **. . . everyone who is left of all the nations which came against Jerusalem shall go up from year to year to worship the King, the Lord of hosts, and to keep the Feast of Tabernacles.**

In the Millennial Kingdom, which will begin with the Second Coming, the Mosaic Feast of Tabernacles will be *reinstated*. Each of the Hebrew feasts points to a future fulfillment. The most obvious example is Jesus laying down His life as the ultimate Passover lamb, fulfilling Passover. In **Acts 2**, we see the fulfillment of Pentecost, as the Spirit is given because Christ has fulfilled the Law. The fulfillment of the Feast of Tabernacles will take place in the Millennium. Instead of celebrating the exodus of the Israelites from *Egypt* to the *Promised Land*, we will celebrate the Lord bringing us out of the *world* and into *His Kingdom*.

But incredibly, Zechariah tells us in the next verse that not everyone will accept the invitation:

> **. . . it shall be *that* whichever of the families of the earth do not come up to Jerusalem to worship the King, the Lord of hosts, on them there will be no rain.**
>
> —Zechariah 14:17

In the Millennium, this will serve as a *physical* manifestation of what is already a *spiritual* truth. We've all been invited to fellowship with the Lord today. But it's our choice. And if we decline the invitation, we will find our souls dry. That's what happens when we choose to say, *"I can't make it to the place where God's people are gathering. I've just got a lot going on right now."* If you dig into the

Scriptures, you'll find that the Lord loves it when His people get together. He blesses those times. He moves in those gatherings. He revives us through them. So don't decline His invitation.

Back to **Revelation 15**:

> [5] **After these things I looked, and behold, the temple of the tabernacle of the testimony in heaven was opened.**
>
> [6] **And out of the temple came the seven angels having the seven plagues, clothed in pure bright linen, and having their chests girded with golden bands.**

White robes speak of righteousness, and these angels are dressed like priests. Now we see the *judgment* that the *fire* back in **V.2** was alluding to. These angels are preparing to pour out the final portion of God's righteous judgments upon the earth:

> [7] **Then one of the four living creatures gave to the seven angels seven golden bowls full of the wrath of God who lives forever and ever.** [8] **The temple was filled with smoke from the glory of God and from His power, and no one was able to enter the temple till the seven plagues of the seven angels were completed.**

FIRST BOWL: SORES

Let's continue into **Revelation 16**, which describes the *contents* of each bowl of wrath.

> [1] **Then I heard a loud voice from the temple saying to the seven angels,** *"Go and pour out the bowls of the wrath of God on the earth."*

These seven bowl judgments will be *rapid* and immediately followed by the Second Coming. So, we know they will take place very close to the *end* of the Great Tribulation—likely over the final few weeks.

² So the first went and poured out his bowl upon the earth, and a foul and loathsome sore came upon the men who had the mark of the beast and those who worshiped his image.

Those who embraced the leadership of antichrist and Satan by taking the mark will experience an unexpected side effect—a torturous *sore* on their body. If I were speculating (and I am), I would guess the sore occurs on the part of their body where they received the mark.

These people rejected God and took the mark because they believed it would solve all their problems. We do the same thing every time we reject God's ways in favor of our own. We *know* what God's Word says, but we believe *something else* will bring us greater relief. And what happens? Scripture tells us that sin is pleasurable *for a season*.[414] It tastes sweet at first. But inevitably, it always eventually brings pain and destruction. *Always*.

Perhaps you've been through a season where you wrestled with viewing God as a *killjoy*—a Big Brother-type overlord who sees everything and uses that power to find out if anyone is having fun so that He can put a stop to it ASAP. That view of God changes when you take an honest look at how your sin affects your life because it's never pretty.

Too often, we fail to grasp the reality that sin has *natural* consequences. And 99.9% of the time, Jesus forgiving our sins does not exempt us from experiencing them. When facing those natural consequences, we have no right to blame God for anything. We're merely reaping what we have sown.

---

[414] Cf. Hebrews 11:25.

You're only hurting yourself if you're still trying to get away with sin. It's a fool's errand. You are sowing seeds that you do not want to reap. And God loves you enough to tell you in His Word, *"You don't want to do that."* The wise man or woman eventually realizes that sin is *stupid*. It's almost as stupid as being angry with God when faced with the natural consequences of our sins.

Last, on this first bowl judgment, I want to make sure we notice it is *specific* to those who have taken the mark of the beast and worship antichrist. This judgment will not affect those who have chosen Jesus and are still alive on the earth. And you can make the case that they will, somehow, be protected from *all* the bowl judgments.

SECOND BOWL: THE SEA OF BLOOD

> ³ **Then the second angel poured out his bowl on the sea, and it became blood as of a dead *man;* and every living creature in the sea died.**

The text clearly says that the sea turned to blood, *literally*—the kind that flows out of **"a dead man."** And as a result, **"every living creature in the sea died."** Did you catch that? *All life* in the oceans and seas will *die*.

Those on the earth rejected the blood and water that flowed from Jesus' side on the Cross, the blood and water that speaks of *salvation*, and now they must deal with blood and water that speaks of *condemnation*.

Some people confuse these bowl judgments and think John repeats his description of judgments from earlier chapters. The short answer is that these are *distinct* judgments. To ensure we don't get confused, God divided the judgments into three sets of seven, with each set given a different "format" (seal, trumpet, and bowl).

THIRD BOWL: OTHER WATERS TURNED TO BLOOD

> ⁴ Then the third angel poured out his bowl on the rivers and springs of water, and they became blood.

The implication seems to be that the second bowl judgment turns all *saltwater* into blood, while this third bowl judgment turns all *fresh water* into blood. Morbidly, this means blood will be all that's available to drink for those who have rejected the Lord.

While some might cry, *"That's horrible! That's not fair!"* note the explanation provided by this third angel:

> ⁵ And I heard the angel of the waters saying:
> *"You are righteous, O Lord,*
> *The One who is and who was and who is to be,*
> *Because You have judged these things.*
> ⁶ *For they have shed the blood of saints and prophets,*
> *And You have given them blood to drink.*
> *For it is their just due."*
> ⁷ And I heard another from the altar saying, *"Even so, Lord God Almighty, true and righteous are Your judgments."*

The angel affirms that this is a righteous judgment because these people have rejected the Lord's blood sacrifice and delighted in spilling the blood of His saints. So, the Lord is just in giving them blood to drink. Yes, it's pretty dark stuff. But maybe we can shed some light on it.

If you're a parent, you probably know how it pushes a button in you if anyone messes with one of your kids. You might be a peace-loving Christian man or woman, but if someone messed with one of your kids in a serious way, they'd see a different side of you real fast!

God is so gracious because, unlike me, His first response is *never* wrath upon those who have harmed His kids. Unbelievably, His first response is to invite those people to be adopted into His family too, that they might experience His love, have a change of heart, and be brought to the place where they cry out, *"Father, please forgive me!"*

That's what Jesus did for the Apostle Paul, a man who had devoted himself to persecuting Christians. But what do you think happens when God extends that amazing grace, going above and beyond, offering the life of His only begotten Son to call those people to repentance, and they respond by saying, *"Yea, I know You're God, and I know they're Your kids. But I don't care, and I'm not going to stop. I just love killing Your kids."*

You know what happens? **Revelation 16** happens. And the response of all of us in Heaven, along with the angels, will be, *"This is righteous and just."*

FOURTH BOWL: HEAT WAVE

> **⁸ Then the fourth angel poured out his bowl on the sun, and power was given to him to scorch men with fire. ⁹ And men were scorched with great heat, and they blasphemed the name of God who has power over these plagues; and they did not repent and give Him glory.**

This bowl is poured out on the *sun*. It changes something about the sun, stirring up unusual activity on its surface. Perhaps it will be solar flares of an intensity and multitude that will cause burning on the bodies of those on the earth.

Isaiah wrote about this time:

> The earth mourns *and* fades away,
> The world languishes *and* fades away;
> The haughty people of the earth languish.
> The earth is also defiled under its inhabitants,
> Because they have transgressed the laws,
> Changed the ordinance,
> Broken the everlasting covenant.
> Therefore the curse has devoured the earth,
> And those who dwell in it are desolate.
> Therefore the inhabitants of the earth are burned,
> And few men *are* left.
>
> —Isaiah 24:4–6

FIFTH BOWL: A PREVIEW OF THE OUTER DARKNESS

> [10] Then the fifth angel poured out his bowl on the throne of the beast, and his kingdom became full of darkness; . . .

The ninth plague of the Exodus was also a plague of darkness—darkness the Lord described as ***"darkness which may even be felt."***[415] That description tells us it was also a *spiritual* darkness—a small preview of the eternal **"outer darkness"**[416] awaiting those who reject the Lord. We can safely assume the darkness of the fifth bowl judgment will be similar in nature.

The text seems to imply this darkness will be *limited* to the kingdom of antichrist. Perhaps places like Petra and possibly other

---

[415] Exodus 10:21.
[416] Cf. Matthew 8:11–12, 22:12–14, 25:29–30.

parts of the world not ruled by antichrist will be exempt from this judgment. If so, it would parallel God's distinguishing between the Israelites and the Egyptians during most of the Exodus plagues.

> **. . . and they gnawed their tongues because of the pain.**

The idea is that they're chewing their tongues to try and release just a *drop* of moisture in their mouths. There will be *scorching heat* and nothing to drink but *blood* in a darkness that can be *felt*.

The Puritans used to say, *"The same sun that melts the ice hardens the clay."* **V.11** shows us that in the Tribulation, God's invitation of salvation and the urgency He conveys through plagues and other judgments will harden, rather than melt, the hearts of those on the earth:

> **11 They blasphemed the God of heaven because of their pains and their sores, . . .**

From the first bowl judgment.

> **. . . and did not repent of their deeds.**

The Church has been removed from the earth; the **"fullness of the Gentiles"** has been added to the family of God, and the door of salvation for the Gentiles has closed. Almost all remaining Jews are hiding in Petra after fleeing Jerusalem, and antichrist is on his throne in the desecrated Temple. It will be a time of darkness on every level, the likes of which the world has never seen, nor will ever see again.

Back in **Revelation 13:4**, those who rejected Jesus were in awe of antichrist:

> **. . . they worshiped the dragon who gave authority to the beast; and they worshiped the beast, saying, *"Who is like the beast? Who is able to make war with him?"***

At this point in the Great Tribulation, the Lord is answering their question with sobering clarity.

SIXTH BOWL: EUPHRATES DRIED UP

¹² Then the sixth angel poured out his bowl on the great river Euphrates, and its water was dried up, so that the way of the kings from the east might be prepared.

The Euphrates River is referred to 25 times in the Bible. It constitutes the northernmost boundary of the land God promised to Abraham and his descendants[417] and is *antithetical* to the Jordan River. The Jordan leads to the Promised Land, while the Euphrates leads to Babylon.

This plague serves a specific purpose: the Euphrates will be dried up so that **"kings from the east"** can move across it to the western side. The implication is that these **"kings"** will lead *armies*.

When John recorded this, **"the east"** was anywhere east of *Israel*. In modern western thinking, we take it to mean somewhere like China or Japan but remember, the magi (or "wise men") who came to visit Jesus as a toddler also came from **"the east,"**[418] which was *Babylon* (modern-day Iraq). I think these **"kings from the east"** will most likely be from China and/or India, but there's room (technically) for many countries to fit under the umbrella of that term.

Where are these **"kings from the east"** going with their armies? I suggest if we look ahead to **V.16** for a moment, we'll find our answer:

---

[417] Cf. Genesis 15:18.
[418] Matthew 2:1.

And they gathered them together to the place called in Hebrew, Armageddon.

All indicators are that these armies are heading to the Valley of Jezreel in northern Israel, better known as "Armageddon." Why? We'll discuss that in just a few verses' time.

People used to scoff at the idea of the Euphrates drying up, but that all changed when Turkey completed the Ataturk Dam in 1994—a project primarily undertaken for political reasons. Turkey lies upstream of Syria and Iraq, and this dam allows them to *cut off* the flow of the Euphrates for up to a year, should they feel the need to do so—which they did as recently as May 16, 2014.

In the political world, Turkey wants to see Syrian dictator Bashar Assad ousted. Turkey has tried to accomplish this in recent years by arming Syrian rebels. However, once Russia came to Assad's aid, such an outcome became impossible. One of Turkey's other tactics was strategically cutting off Syria's water supply from the Euphrates. Tragically, all this did was devastate Syrian and Iraqi civilians, who rely on the Euphrates for many essentials of life.

Even more recently, Turkey has built several new dams to generate hydroelectricity and has also sought to prosper its agricultural industry by using more water than it previously has. As a result, the level of the Euphrates is now dangerously low in countries that lie further downriver.

Some Bible teachers speculate these kinds of geopolitical issues could cause most of the Euphrates to be *already* dried up by the time this judgment takes place, ensuring hard ground for things like tanks to drive across (as opposed to a swamp). As always, we must remember that we don't *need* a naturalistic explanation for these judgments. God can just make them happen. But I felt these details were interesting enough to share.

And speaking of preparing the world for Armageddon, check out **V.13**:

> [13] **And I saw three unclean spirits like frogs *coming* out of the mouth of the dragon, out of the mouth of the beast, and out of the mouth of the false prophet.**

They're not *literally* frogs, but to John, their appearance is somehow **"like frogs."** One of these things comes out of each member of the unholy trinity (Satan, antichrist, and the false prophet), and the next verse tells us what they *are* and what they *do:*

> [14] **For they are spirits of demons, performing signs, *which* go out to the kings of the earth and of the whole world, to gather them to the battle of that great day of God Almighty.**

These **"frogs"** are demonic spirits that will come out of the unholy trinity and be sent to perform amazing signs for the kings of the earth. We don't know what that means, and we should be honest about that. We don't know if these demons will appear directly to kings of the earth or if they will possess human messengers sent by antichrist. We just don't know.

While these armies will assemble at Armageddon, multiple Old Testament prophecies[419] seem to clarify that their target will be *Jerusalem,* which is 60 miles to the south. Satan will realize he's at the end of the endgame and seek to do whatever harm he can in the

---

[419] For example, Zechariah 12:9–11.

very little time he has left. And, apparently, one of his goals will be to wipe Jerusalem off the face of the earth.

It could be that things are so devastated by this point that antichrist doesn't have the military resources to take out Jerusalem on his own. It's also possible that the plan will be to move on to *Petra* and try once again to wipe out the Jews being sheltered there by the Lord.

Why they all end up at Armageddon doesn't really matter. The point is that, ultimately, it will be the *Lord* who causes them to be gathered there like grapes tossed into a winepress.

In **V.15,** Jesus says:

¹⁵ Behold, I am coming as a thief. Blessed is he who watches, and keeps his garments, lest he walk naked and they see his shame.

This is both an *encouragement* and a *warning* to those on the earth who will read this during the Great Tribulation. Jesus came **"as a thief"** to rapture His Church,[420] and many did not see it coming. Jesus will come again at His Second Coming **"as a thief,"** and many will not see it coming. So, Jesus counsels the man or woman who will read this in the Great Tribulation to stay committed to Him and continue walking in righteousness, no matter the cost.

When we give our lives to Jesus, He graciously wraps us in robes of His righteousness. Knowing that, Christians need not fear being ashamed when they stand before the Lord.

¹⁶ And they gathered them together to the place called in Hebrew, Armageddon.

---

[420] Cf. Matthew 24:42–44; Luke 12:38–40.

The armies of the world rally together to partner with the armies of antichrist, meeting at Armageddon. If you do an image search for "Jezreel Valley," you'll find photo after photo of a massive valley about 60 miles north of Jerusalem—20 miles long and 15 miles wide. This beautiful valley is where the Great Tribulation will reach its conclusion.

It's a place with a remarkable history of war, having been the site of more battles than any other location on earth. The ground is rich with the spilled blood of soldiers. It is where Samson fought the Philistines; Gideon overcame the Midianites with just 300 men; King Josiah was killed by Pharaoh Necho and King Saul by the Philistines; Deborah and Barak defeated Sisera and Jabin's 900 chariots; and the Turks, Muslims, Syrians, Egyptians, and Europeans all waged war.

In 1799 Napoleon faced the Ottomans here, emerging victorious and calling this valley *"the most natural battleground of the whole earth."*

SEVENTH BOWL: THE EARTH UTTERLY SHAKEN

The sixth bowl was preparation for Armageddon—moving the pieces into position. Now the seventh and final bowl judgment is unleashed.

> **17 Then the seventh angel poured out his bowl into the air, and a loud voice came out of the temple of heaven, from the throne, saying,** *"It is done!"*

This angel pouring **"out his bowl into the air"** references Paul's description of Satan as **"the prince of the power of the air"**[421] referring to his reign as ruler of the earth. While Satan has been confined to earth by this point in the Tribulation, this is a *cleansing*, of sorts, of his former domain.

---

[421] Ephesians 2:2.

God's voice will declare, *"It is done!"* marking the end of His judgment of the earth.

You'll recall from **Revelation 14** that when the armies of antichrist and the kings of the earth are gathered in Armageddon, Jesus will return at the Second Coming, and they will all turn their weapons on *Him*. But there will be no battle. Jesus will simply *annihilate* them, like grapes being crushed in a winepress.

> [18] **And there were noises and thunderings and lightnings; and there was a great earthquake, ...**

This scene harkens back to the earthquakes that hit Jerusalem during Jesus' First Coming as He died on the Cross[422] and again when He rose from the dead.[423]

> **... such a mighty and great earthquake as had not occurred since men were on the earth.**

Look at what this earthquake does:

> [19] **Now the great city [Jerusalem] was divided into three parts, and the cities of the nations fell.**
> **And great Babylon was remembered before God, to give her the cup of the wine of the fierceness of His wrath.**

We'll explain this in greater detail when we study Babylon in **Revelation 17–18**.

> [20] **Then every island fled away, and the mountains were not found.**

---

[422] Matthew 27:54.

[423] Matthew 28:2.

What seems to be going on with this **"great earthquake"** is not a *judgment* but rather a *preparation* of the earth's geography for the return of Jesus.[424] It will *terraform* the planet and return it to its pre-Flood condition, which seems to be free of isolated islands, inaccessible mountain ranges, deserts, tundra, and the like. We don't know why Jerusalem will be split into three parts, but it seems to have something to do with preparing the city for Jesus' imminent return.

> **[21] And great hail from heaven fell upon men,** *each hailstone* **about the weight of a talent.**

A **"talent"** weighs 86–135 lbs. I'm pretty sure the exact number is irrelevant because if you're struck by a hailstone that "only" weighs 86 pounds, you're still very much dead.

> **Men blasphemed God because of the plague of the hail, since that plague was exceedingly great.**

The hard hearts of those on the earth will yet again be on full display. They blasphemed God in **VV.9** and **11**, so God sends catastrophic hail on them. How do they respond? By blaspheming God for sending the hail!

It's interesting to note that under the Law, the punishment for blasphemy was . . . *stoning.*[425]

CLOSING THOUGHTS

I've mentioned this before, but it's worth mentioning again. If you ever feel God's wrath and eternal hell are unjust, cruel, or extreme,

---

[424] Cf. Isaiah 35:1; 40:4; Zechariah 14:4–10.
[425] Cf. Leviticus 24:10–16.

you need to understand this: Any sound justice system assigns a punishment that fits the crime. The more severe the crime, the more severe the punishment. For example, a *person's* life should be more valuable than an *animal's* life.

With that in mind, let me ask you: What is the value of *God?*

God's worth is, quite simply, *infinite*. It is *incalculable*. Therefore, the wrath of God and eternity in hell is the appropriate punishment for spitting in His face and rejecting Him. It's just. It's right. It's in proportion with the offense.

We've got to understand—and I know this is a hard truth—that any desire to *lessen* the severity of God's wrath or the seriousness of hell is also an appeal to lower God's *value*.

If the punishment must fit the crime for justice to be done, then the only way to reduce the punishment is to reduce the *severity* of the crime. And the only way to do that is to reduce the *value* and *worth* of God.

I know that's hard. But the worth of God must not, cannot, be reduced so that we can claim that hell and His wrath are unjust. God is *infinitely* worthy. He has loved us *infinitely* and rejecting Him is *infinitely* wicked.

The severity of God's wrath is *proportionate* to God's worth.

Finally, as we read through wrath upon wrath upon wrath, remember that this is only a tiny glimpse into the punishment our sin deserves. It's also only a tiny glimpse of what was poured out upon Jesus on the Cross *in our place*. And when we get to Heaven and understand all that Jesus went through for us, we too will say, **"Righteous are Your judgments, Lord."**

I will never get over the fact that Jesus took the wrath appointed for me upon Himself.

> **...God demonstrates His own love toward us, in that while we were still sinners, Christ died for us.**
>
> —Romans 5:8

> **He who did not spare His own Son, but delivered Him up for us all, how shall He not with Him also freely give us all things?**
>
> —Romans 8:32

Not only in eternity but right now: *"Righteous are Your judgments, Lord."*

When my prayers go unanswered and I don't know why: *"Righteous are Your judgments, Lord."*

When I experience tribulation and difficulty in my life: *"Righteous are Your judgments, Lord."*

When I'm faithful to God and it seems like it only results in more things going wrong: *"Righteous are Your judgments, Lord."*

When I experience the natural consequences of my sins, even though I'm forgiven: *"Righteous are Your judgments, Lord."*

REVELATION 17

THE WOMAN OF HIGHLY QUESTIONABLE CHARACTER

Revelation 16 saw the final bowl judgment poured out, completing God's judgment of the earth, and bringing us to the end of the Great Tribulation. Next on the schedule is the return of Jesus to the earth in the event known as "The Second Coming." That will unfold in **Revelation 19**.

Revelation 17–18 are *parenthetical*, meaning they press the Pause button on the main timeline to fill us in on some additional information before we continue. And that additional information concerns the destruction of *Babylon*.

You might recall that in **Revelation 14:8**, as the second half of the Tribulation began, an angel flew across the skies declaring for all the world to hear:

> *Babylon is fallen, is fallen, that great city, because she has made all nations drink of the wine of the wrath of her fornication.*

We talked about how that was a *proleptic* statement, meaning Babylon's destruction was so *inevitable* that it could be said to have *already happened*. We will learn that Babylon's judgment and destruction began at the halfway point of the seven years of the Tribulation and unfolded over the remaining three and a half years.

In our study of **Revelation 14**, I summarized the biblical concept of Babylon, but it's brief enough for me to repeat here:

The term "Babylon" can be a bit confusing because it is used in Scripture to refer to something *literal*, something *abstract* and *mystical*, and sometimes *both* simultaneously. Literally, Babylon is a city located in the present-day country of Iraq. It is one of the most notable cities of antiquity, serving as the capital of empires and the world's cultural center for centuries. In the abstract and mystical sense, Babylon refers to the *world system*—all the systems established by the world's current ruler, Satan; that includes economic, governmental, religious, sexual, entertainment, values—all of secularism. They are all *Babylon* from a biblical perspective.

So, when we study Scripture and see Babylon referenced, we need to examine the *context* to discern whether it's referring to the literal city, the mystical concept, or both. **Revelation 17–18** describe the destruction of mystical *and* literal Babylon during the Great Tribulation.

Revelation 17 focuses on *religious* Babylon, while **Revelation 18** focuses on *economic* Babylon. **Revelation 17** is structured so that a *mystery*, a hidden truth, is presented and then explained. I think the most helpful way to make sense of the text is to read through the mystery, go through the explanation in detail, and then reread the mystery, incorporating our newfound understanding.

THE MYSTERY (VV.1–6)

[1] Then one of the seven angels who had the seven bowls came and talked with me, saying to me, *"Come, I will show*

you the judgment of the great harlot who sits on many waters, ² *with whom the kings of the earth committed fornication, and the inhabitants of the earth were made drunk with the wine of her fornication."*

³ So he carried me away in the Spirit into the wilderness. And I saw a woman sitting on a scarlet beast *which was* full of names of blasphemy, having seven heads and ten horns. ⁴ The woman was arrayed in purple and scarlet, and adorned with gold and precious stones and pearls, having in her hand a golden cup full of abominations and the filthiness of her fornication. ⁵ And on her forehead a name *was* written:

MYSTERY, BABYLON THE GREAT,
THE MOTHER OF HARLOTS
AND OF THE ABOMINATIONS
OF THE EARTH.

⁶ I saw the woman, drunk with the blood of the saints and with the blood of the martyrs of Jesus. And when I saw her, I marveled with great amazement.

If you're reading this for the first time, you should have no problem agreeing that these verses are indeed a *mystery*.

WHO IS THE HARLOT?

The first clue we must solve is the identity of *"the great harlot."*

Sidenote: The first time I taught this chapter in church was on a Mother's Day Sunday (really!).

Who is this woman? After lots of study into the different views, I believe she represents *religious* Babylon in the mystical sense. She represents all religious and spiritual systems that are *false* in that they do not point to Jesus as the way, the truth, and the life.

This woman's appearance in this chapter is to reveal her role in the first half of the Tribulation and her *final judgment* at the halfway point of it. The text indicates that we're going to see two main ideas emerge:

- Some type of *unification religious movement* will emerge in the first half of the Tribulation. We know it won't be a one-world religion because there will be Jews worshipping at the rebuilt Temple in Jerusalem. Rather, it will be a new openness toward and cooperation around a type of *universalism*—the belief that all religious roads essentially lead to the same destination. This new openness will extend even to Judaism and Islam.

- Some type of *world council of religious cooperation* will emerge, led by the false prophet. And all of this, as we shall see, will be in preparation for the antichrist cult that will emerge at the halfway point of the Tribulation.

But why is this woman presented as a **"harlot,"** a prostitute? It's because, in the Old Testament, God uses sexual immorality as a metaphor for *spiritual* unfaithfulness. Every man and woman was created to worship God, and when we don't, it's the spiritual equivalent of a wife cheating on her husband. God views a person engaging with false religions, paganism, or idolatry as a husband would view his wife going out and working as a *prostitute*. It's that awful, wicked, heartbreaking, and abhorrent to God.

To use that same type of biblical imagery, the false religious system represented by this woman will be the *embodiment* of spiritual whoredom.

THE EXPLANATION (VV.7–18)

⁷ But the angel said to me, *"Why did you marvel? I will tell you the mystery of the woman and of the beast that carries her, which has the seven heads and the ten horns."*

We just talked about who the woman is, and you should recall that *"the beast"* is *antichrist*. The *"seven heads"* and *"ten horns"* will be explained in a few verses.

⁸ *The beast that you saw was, and is not, and will ascend out of the bottomless pit and go to perdition* [destruction].

There are a few different views on this verse. I'll share my thoughts, but, as always, do your own research and come to your own conclusions:

- The angel refers to *"The beast,"* antichrist, and tells John that he *"was"*—in other words, he existed in the past; *"is not"*—he does not exist today; but in the future, he will return from *"the bottomless pit."*

  Remember, the term "the beast" refers to antichrist the *person* and who he becomes when Satan empowers him. The man who becomes the antichrist will be possessed by a spirit that comes from *"the bottomless pit."*

- When did the beast exist in the past? I suspect it was in the form of a man named Nimrod in the Book of Genesis. He was the first version of *the* antichrist, so to speak. I suspect Nimrod may have even been possessed by the same spirit that will possess *the* antichrist.

We find a redemptive example of this concept in **Luke 1:17**. An angel comes to a man named Zacharias and tells him that his son will minister in the **"spirit"** of Elijah. That son would be John the Baptist, and the angel meant that the same *anointing* that was on Elijah would be upon John—and it was.

That's the idea with Nimrod and the antichrist, but (unfortunately) in a *demonic* sense.

- The beast was *"not"* on the earth around AD 96 when John recorded the Book of Revelation, and he is not on the earth today. However, the *person* who will *become* the beast is likely alive right now.

- At the halfway point of the Tribulation, the spirit that (likely) possessed Nimrod will emerge from the Bottomless Pit and enter a rising global political leader who has just been assassinated, bringing him back to life as *the beast*—*the* antichrist.

MORE ON NIMROD

I want to share a bit more about Nimrod because it'll help you understand why I hold the suspicions I just mentioned.

The Bible tells us that Nimrod was a great-grandson of Noah. His name means, *"we will rebel."* In **Genesis 10:9–10**, we are told this about him:

> **He was a mighty hunter before the Lord; therefore it is said, *"Like Nimrod the mighty hunter before the Lord."* And the beginning of his kingdom was Babel, Erech, Accad, and Calneh, in the land of Shinar.**

The phrase **"before the Lord"** is a mistranslation. The original manuscripts and traditional Jewish understanding are that it should read, "Like Nimrod the mighty hunter *in defiance* of the Lord."

Genesis 6:4 tells us there were Nephilim (i.e., *giants*) on the earth before and after the Flood (that is a story for another day). That same verse calls them **"mighty men."** Because **Genesis 10:9** calls Nimrod **"a mighty hunter,"** some believe Nimrod to be the first Nephilim giant to appear in Scripture after the Flood.

Genesis 10:10–11 tells us that Nimrod began his empire with four cities, including *Babel*. We don't know if he founded them or conquered them. After those first four cities, he founded another four, including *Nineveh*. The Bible presents Nimrod as the ruler of the first *empire* in world history. And I'll show you in a moment that he was likely also the first *global dictator*.

Genesis 11:1–9 tells us that under Nimrod's rule, a great tower was built in Babel. In defiance of the Lord's command to humanity to spread out across the earth and multiply, Nimrod led people to disobey God. Under Nimrod's leadership, they stayed together and built a great tower, which marked Babel as the world capital of those who did not fear the Lord.

In the centuries that followed, the location of the Tower of Babel would grow into a mighty city-state named "Bab-El-on" or *Babylon*. And that's pretty much everything the Bible tells us about Nimrod.

There are many historical writings that *aren't* in the Bible but talk about things related *to* the Bible. They are not divine truth like the Word of God is, but they can sometimes help us understand how historians, scholars, and Hebrews of the ancient world viewed the Scriptures.

For example, Josephus writes:

> ... God also commanded them to send colonies abroad, for the thorough peopling of the earth, that they might not raise seditions among themselves, but might cultivate a great part of the earth, and enjoy its fruits after a plentiful manner. But they were so ill instructed that they did not obey God; for which reason they fell into calamities... ... when they flourished with a numerous youth, God admonished them again to send out colonies; but they, imagining the prosperity they enjoyed was not derived from the favour of God, but supposing that their own power was the proper cause of the plentiful condition they were in, did not obey him. Nay, they added to this their disobedience to the Divine will, the suspicion that they were therefore ordered to send out separate colonies, that, being divided asunder, they might the more easily be oppressed.
>
> ... Now it was Nimrod who excited them to such an affront and contempt of God. He was the grandson of Ham, the son of Noah: a bold man, and of great strength of hand. He persuaded them not to ascribe it to God, as if it was through his means that they were happy, but to believe that it was their own courage which procured that happiness. He also gradually changed the government into tyranny; seeing no other way of turning men from the fear of God, but to bring them into a constant dependence on his own power.
>
> ... Now the multitude were very ready to follow the determination of Nimrod, and to esteem it a piece of cowardice to submit to God; and they built a tower... [426]

---

[426] Flavius Josephus, *The Works of Josephus*, trans. William Whiston (Peabody, Massachusetts: Hendrickson Publishers, 1985), 30.

Nimrod was a *tyrant* who ruled by making men fear him more than they feared God. In *Targum Jonathan*, we read the following from **Genesis 10:9**:

> *From the day that the world was created there hath not been as Nimrod, mighty in hunting, and a rebel before the Lord.*[427]

And *Targum Jerusalem* states the following for **Genesis 10:9**:

> *He* [Nimrod] *was mighty in hunting and in sin before the Lord; for he was a hunter of the sons of men in their languages.*

Not *literally*, but *spiritually*. In regard to **Genesis 10:9**, Targum Jerusalem says here's how Nimrod "hunted" men:

> *... he* [Nimrod] *said to them, "Leave the judgments of Shem* [the commands of Yahweh], *and adhere to the judgments of Nimrod." On this account it is said, "As Nimrod the mighty, mighty in hunting and in sin before the Lord."*[428]

He was a wicked person. For all these reasons and more, Nimrod is considered by many to be the first appearance of the *spirit* that will possess *the* antichrist in the Tribulation and make him, in a sense, Nimrod II.

---

[427] Jonathan Uzziel, *Targum Pseudo-Jonathan: The First Five Books of the Bible*, ed. Tov Rose, trans. J. W. Etheridge (London: Longman, Green, Longman, and Roberts, 1862–1865), 23. Kindle Edition.

[428] Tov Rose, ed., *Targum Jerusalem*, trans. J. W. Etheridge (London: Longman, Green, Longman, and Roberts, 1862), https://www.sefaria.org/Targum_Jerusalem%2C.

BACK TO THE TEXT

Let's continue in **V.8**:

> *And those who dwell on the earth will marvel, whose names are not written in the Book of Life from the foundation of the world, when they see the beast that was, and is not, and yet is.*

As we've discussed, everyone on the earth who will *never* belong to Jesus will marvel when antichrist rises from the dead as the beast. They'll say, *"This man must be a god!"*

All the bits and pieces of information we're accumulating will come together in a clear picture over the coming verses...

> ⁹ ***Here is the mind which has wisdom:***

That's a way of saying, *"Think about what I'm about to share with you. Meditate on it."*

> ***The seven heads are seven mountains on which the woman sits.***

The key to understanding this strange statement is found in **Daniel 2**, where we find Daniel living in *Babylon*. Not a coincidence. He is a Hebrew exile serving as a counselor to King Nebuchadnezzar. The king has a dream, and only Daniel can interpret his dream. In that dream, the king saw a massive statue of a man, and Daniel describes it:

> *This image's head was of fine gold, its chest and arms of silver, its belly and thighs of bronze, its legs of iron, its feet partly of iron and partly of clay. You watched while a stone was cut out without hands, which struck the image on its feet of iron and clay, and broke them in pieces. Then the iron, the clay, the bronze, the silver, and the gold were crushed together, and*

became like chaff from the summer threshing floors; the wind carried them away so that no trace of them was found. And the stone that struck the image became a great mountain and filled the whole earth.

—Daniel 2:32–35

Daniel then explains the dream to the king by revealing that each material used in the statue represents an *empire*. First was the Babylonian Empire, which included Nebuchadnezzar. The Medo-Persian, Greek, and Roman empires followed it. And the *last empire* will be the revived Roman Empire, ultimately ruled by *antichrist*.

Daniel wraps up his interpretation of the king's dream by explaining that the *"stone"* that destroyed the statue was *Jesus*, coming to establish His Kingdom on the earth. Daniel tells Nebuchadnezzar:

. . . in the days of these kings . . .

In the season of history of that final earthly kingdom:

. . . the God of heaven will set up a kingdom which shall never be destroyed; and the kingdom shall not be left to other people; it shall break in pieces and consume all these kingdoms, and it shall stand forever. Inasmuch as you saw that the stone was cut out of the mountain without hands, and that it broke in pieces the iron, the bronze, the clay, the silver, and the gold— the great God has made known to the king what will come to pass after this. The dream is certain, and its interpretation is sure.

—Daniel 2:44–45

We see mountains used as a metaphor for *kingdoms* in the Old Testament,[429] and here in **Daniel 2**, God uses a mountain as a metaphor for *His* kingdom.

In the king's dream, Jesus is *"the stone"* that was *"cut out of the mountain without hands."* Jesus *willingly* came to the earth as a man from the *Kingdom* of God.[430] He was not extracted from Heaven or *"cut out"* of God's Kingdom by force. He will return to the earth, destroying antichrist's kingdoms and *all* earthly kingdoms. The Kingdom of Jesus will *"stand forever"* and fill *"the whole earth."*

All of that needs to be understood so that we can reach this conclusion: the **"seven mountains on which the woman sits"** are seven *kingdoms*.

¹⁰ *There are also seven kings.*

The angel continues to speak of these seven kingdoms, the seven *"mountains,"* telling us that:

Five have fallen, one is, and the other has not yet come.

Here's the punchline: These seven kingdoms are the seven great empires that dominated the Israelites. The Bible is *Israel-centric*, and so these seven empires are the ones that affected and will affect *Israel*. That's why there's no allusion in Scripture to empires like the Maya and Inca or the Chinese dynasties.

- *"Five have fallen"* refers to the empires of Egypt, Assyria, Babylon, Medo-Persia, and Greece.
- *"one is"* refers to the Roman Empire in power when John recorded the Book of Revelation.

---

[429] Cf. Psalm 30:7; Isaiah 2:2; Jeremiah 51:25.
[430] Cf. John 10:17–18; Philippians 2:5–8.

- *"the other has not yet come"* refers to the revived Roman Empire that will ultimately be ruled by antichrist.

¹¹ ***The beast that was, and is not, is himself also the eighth, and is of the seven, and is going to perdition*** ["destruction"].

This is a little tough, but hang with me, and I'll walk you through it:

- We know *"The beast"* is antichrist.

- We explained the phrase, *"that was, and is not"* back in **V.8**.

- The meaning of *"is himself also the eighth, and is of the seven"* is a little convoluted, but the idea is that antichrist will be *part* of the seventh empire, the revived Roman empire, as a politician during the first three and a half years of the Tribulation.

  He will be assassinated, possessed, and resurrected at the halfway point of the seven years. At that time, he will take complete control of the empire, and it will evolve into an *"eighth"* empire, so to speak. That's why antichrist is *"of the seven"* (he'll be *part* of the seventh empire) but *"also the eighth"* (he'll take complete control of that empire, morphing it into an eighth empire).

- John is reminded that antichrist *"is going to perdition."* His ultimate destiny of destruction is *fixed* and God Himself will destroy that eighth empire.

V.11 continues, and we read:

And when he [antichrist] ***comes, he must continue a short time.***

His empire will be short-lived. How short? It will last 3.5 years; 42 months; 1,260 days; time, times, and half a time.

> ¹² *"The ten horns which you saw are ten kings who have received no kingdom as yet, but they receive authority for one hour as kings with the beast.*

Daniel 7:24 tells us that during the first half of the Tribulation, the revived Roman Empire will be divided into ten regions (i.e., nations, territories), each with a ruler or "king." As antichrist rises on the political scene, he will overthrow three of those ten kings and assume control of their regions. In the second half of the Tribulation, when he is the uncontested leader of the empire, antichrist will appoint *"ten kings"* to serve under him.

These ten kings also appear in **Daniel 2**[431] as the ten *toes* of the statue in Nebuchadnezzar's dream, and in **Daniel 7**,[432] as ten horns.

The phrase *"one hour"* does not refer to a literal hour but rather a *passage* of time. We still use this in phrases like "their finest hour." In this instance, the "hour" refers to the three and a half years of the Great Tribulation.

> ¹³ *These* [the ten kings] *are of one mind, and they will give their power and authority to the beast.*

These kings will be regional supervisors with one job—following antichrist blindly.

> ¹⁴ *These* [the ten kings] *will make war with the Lamb* [Jesus], *and the Lamb will overcome them, for . . .*

---

[431] Daniel 2:41–42.

[432] Daniel 7:7–8, 20, 24.

How is it possible that Jesus will overcome ten kings? Because . . .

. . . He is Lord of lords and King of kings; . . .

I love that. I love the juxtaposition of the ten earthly kings and the introduction of Jesus as the *"King of kings."* We sometimes forget that's who He is. In a proper, old-school monarchy, the king spoke, and it was *done*. He had absolute, unquestioned authority. The gap between a commoner and a great king was incalculable and insurmountable. Think of how a commoner would have looked at a king. Think of how a Babylonian farm worker would have looked at Nebuchadnezzar, unassailable in the heights of his glory and power. Now understand this: that is how *God* is compared to every earthly and supernatural power. That's how *they* view *Him*. He is the *King* of kings. He is the *Lord* of lords. He speaks, and they obey. There is no other option. He commands, and it is accomplished. He has *absolute, unquestioned* authority.

These will make war with the Lamb, and the Lamb will overcome them, for He is Lord of lords and King of kings; and those who are with Him are called, chosen, and faithful.

If you have given your life to Jesus, it was because He *called* you. It was because He *chose* you. And He has placed His spirit in you to give you the power to live your life faithfully for Him.

The word *"faithful"* is an intentional contrast to those who reject Jesus. God views them as engaged with *"the great harlot,"* but He regards those who belong to Him as *"faithful."*

It blesses me so much to hear God refer to me as *"faithful"* because that's not how I tend to view myself. But this precious word reminds me that just as Jesus makes us *righteous*, His Spirit empowers us to remain *faithful*. And for 2,000 years, His Spirit has empowered believers to face persecution and even death and stay *faithful* to the end. If you belong to Him, He will make you able to stand, no matter what you face. He calls us *"faithful."*

If you want to practice some biblical, righteous personal affirmation, start praying this regularly: *"Lord, thank You that I am called, chosen, and that by Your power, I will be faithful."*

> **¹⁵ Then he said to me, *"The waters which you saw, where the harlot sits, are peoples, multitudes, nations, and tongues."***

Finally, a *simple* explanation! As the world's religions unite, the whole planet will be drawn into spiritual fornication in the first half of the Tribulation. Only those who belong to Jesus will not participate.

> **¹⁶ *And the ten horns which you saw on the beast, these will hate the harlot, make her desolate and naked, eat her flesh and burn her with fire.* ¹⁷ *For God has put it into their hearts to fulfill His purpose, to be of one mind, and to give their kingdom to the beast, until the words of God are fulfilled.***

Remember, the *"ten horns"* are ten kings who will serve under antichrist in his empire.

At the halfway point of the Tribulation, antichrist will rise from the dead, and you'll recall that he will enter the Holy of Holies in the rebuilt Temple in Jerusalem and declare *himself* to be God. He will abolish all other religions and demand the worship of all peoples. The false prophet will facilitate this and direct the empire to worship antichrist, which they will. The emergence of a revived Roman Empire and a spirit of universalism will *pave the way* for antichrist the beast.

That's what's being pictured here. Antichrist and the world's religions will peacefully coexist for the first three and a half years of the Tribulation. But then, at the halfway point of the seven years, antichrist will be possessed and *devour* all other religions, replacing them with himself with the help of his ten kings and the false prophet.

¹⁸ *And the woman whom you saw is that great city which reigns over the kings of the earth.*

We'll reread **V.5** in a moment, but you might recall that *"the great harlot"* has the title **"MYSTERY, BABYLON THE GREAT, THE MOTHER OF HARLOTS"** written on her forehead. **Revelation 17–18** and the title on her forehead clarify that the *"great city"* this woman represents is *Babylon*; I'll touch on why that matters in a moment. To summarize, **V.18** tells us the woman is part of *mystical* Babylon. As we said earlier, she is *religious* Babylon.

WHY THE WOMAN IS NOT THE ROMAN CATHOLIC CHURCH

Some believe that the woman in **Revelation 17** is the Roman Catholic Church, and Babylon is *Rome*. They hold this view for a few main reasons:

- *... The seven heads are seven mountains on which the woman sits* (Revelation 17:9).

    The original Greek word translated as *"mountains"*[433] can also be translated as "hills." And *Rome* has been famously known throughout history as "The City of Seven Hills."

---

[433] Oros.

- *...the woman whom you saw is that great city which reigns over the kings of the earth"* (Revelation 17:18). When John was recording Revelation, *"that great city which reigns over the kings of the earth"* would have obviously been Rome.

Scripture and history teach that Babylon was the birthplace of paganism. And it's Babylon where we see some of the most enduring pagan archetypes of the ancient world emerge. Notably, the concept of the feminine divine and mother-son worship.

The feminine divine is, essentially, the concept that certain feminine traits are *divine*. At its root, it comes from men, inspired by Satan, who became sexually obsessed with women. And therefore, traditional forms of the feminine divine tended to be highly sexualized in their mythology, the physical appearance of their deities, and their worship rituals. The concept comes from a desire to worship sex and is, of course, ultimately driven by Satan's desire to pervert God's good design.

Instead of having Yahweh as God, men leading their families in righteousness, and sex being sacred in marriage, Satan created a form of paganism where false gods are worshipped, womanhood is reduced to carnal sexuality, and all of society becomes driven by *lust*.

In Babylon, we also see a mother-son model of paganism emerge, where the feminine divine has a *son*, and both are worshipped because of their intimate connection.

This model appears in multiple ancient mythologies, and the Bible records *Israel* getting caught up in this type of paganism. For example, Jeremiah[434] rebukes them for worshipping *"the queen of heaven,"* who their forefathers had also worshipped.

I believe the pagan concepts of the feminine divine and mother-son worship are alive and well today in Roman Catholicism. The Mary of the Vatican is not the mother of Jesus but *"the queen of heaven."* This is why Rome teaches that Mary is *divine*, even though the Bible does not present the mother of Jesus that way.

And so, because of the Babylon/feminine divine/mother-son paganism that traces back to Babylon, there is a view that the woman of **Revelation 17** is the Roman Catholic Church.

Let me share why I *don't* hold this view:

V.5 tells us she has **"MYSTERY, BABYLON THE GREAT"** written on her forehead.

- *Babylon* and the Euphrates River, which runs through it, are the focus of **Revelation 17–18**.

- Pretty much everything in this chapter is *figurative*. For example, the waters upon which the woman sits. What is our justification for switching to a literal interpretation of the *"seven mountains"*?

---

[434] Jeremiah 44:15–19, 20–27.

- While the Greek word translated *"mountains"* in **V.9**[435] *is* translated as "hills" three times in Scripture, it is translated as "mountain" 41 times and "mount" 21 times.

- If he were referencing seven *hills*, it would have been obvious to John and his readers that the angel was referring to Rome. The angel would not have needed to include the preface, ***"Here is the mind which has wisdom,"*** appealing to the reader to exercise special discernment.

- While the links to Babylonian pagan mythology are valid, many of the *specifics* used to draw parallels with Roman Catholic doctrine are *not* verifiable. Most of them trace back to a book titled *The Two Babylons*, written by Alexander Hislop in 1853.[436]

For example, Hislop was the first to claim that *Easter* derived its name from the ancient pagan goddess *Ishtar*. Unfortunately, it turns out he based that claim on nothing more than noticing that the words *sounded* similar.

We can check claims made by authors, speakers, and pastors regarding essential theology by examining the Scriptures. However, historical and anecdotal claims (e.g., sermon illustrations) were challenging to verify before the proliferation of the Internet. Christians tended to believe the things they were told by authors, speakers, and pastors they considered godly men. And those godly men were often repeating the historical and

---

[435] Oros.

[436] Alexander Hislop, *The Two Babylons*, 7th ed. (Crossreach Publications, 2017).

anecdotal claims of other men, whom they also thought godly.

Unfortunately, when we trace things back to the source, we sometimes discover that the original author, speaker, or pastor was *incorrect* or *negligent* in their research. Such is the case with many of the claims made by Alexander Hislop in *The Two Babylons*. And his claims have been repeated for over a century and a half by many authors, speakers, and pastors. I'm sure they're almost all godly men, but unfortunately, they have not fact-checked their sources by tracing the information back to its origins.

- Last, Babylon is *more* than just a literal city, just as *Zion* is more than just a literal city. However, Babylon *is also* a literal city, just as Zion *is also* a literal city. Whenever there is a literal geographic location associated with Babylon in Scripture, it's always *Babylon* just as whenever there is a literal geographic location associated with Zion in Scripture, it's always *Jerusalem*.

Babylon is *not* literal, geographic Rome. And the woman is *not* the Roman Catholic Church. That being said, the Roman Catholic Church is almost unquestionably *part* of religious Babylon.

BACK TO THE SCARLET WOMAN AND THE SCARLET BEAST

Let's return to the *mystery* laid out in the first six verses of this chapter and see if we can wrap our minds around it now:

> **¹ Then one of the seven angels who had the seven bowls came and talked with me, saying to me,** *"Come, I will show*

you the judgment of the great harlot who sits on many waters, ² with whom the kings of the earth committed fornication, and the inhabitants of the earth were made drunk with the wine of her fornication."

This angel tells John that he's going to show him how the Lord will judge Babylon in the Tribulation.

Once the Church leaves the earth in the Rapture, the earth will rapidly descend into an orgy of ungodliness, as the people unite in their hatred of God and their love of sin in every sphere of life.

The *judgment* of religious Babylon is that when it reaches the state that every false religion envisions—world harmony, unity, peace, and understanding, it will culminate in the empire of antichrist, which will usher in *hell on earth*. That is how God will expose, judge, and destroy religious Babylon.

³ So he carried me away in the Spirit into the wilderness. And I saw a woman sitting on a scarlet beast *which was* full of names of blasphemy, having seven heads and ten horns. ⁴ The woman was arrayed in purple and scarlet, and adorned with gold and precious stones and pearls, having in her hand a golden cup full of abominations and the filthiness of her fornication. ⁵ And on her forehead a name *was* written:

> **MYSTERY, BABYLON THE GREAT,**
> **THE MOTHER OF HARLOTS**
> **AND OF THE ABOMINATIONS**
> **OF THE EARTH.**

⁶ I saw the woman, drunk with the blood of the saints and with the blood of the martyrs of Jesus. And when I saw her, I marveled with great amazement.

We should be able to understand this scene now. The woman is *religious* Babylon whose universalist spirit will intoxicate the world with false promises of peace, unity, and financial prosperity during the first three and a half years of the Tribulation.

She is riding the beast, antichrist, as they partner together for those first three and a half years to prepare the world for a single religion that will worship antichrist alone during the Great Tribulation.

One aspect of that partnership will be the fierce persecution of Christians. The world will hate righteousness to such a degree that they want to *kill it* everywhere they find it.

Antichrist will seize control of the final world empire, the revived Roman Empire, and appoint ten kings under His rule. And He will lead the world into sin, darkness, and evil to a degree we cannot even imagine.

CLOSING THOUGHTS

Universalism is not only logically incoherent; it's *demonic*. It will be used to unite the world in rejecting God and, ultimately, worshipping Satan. Our world romanticizes the idea of universalism in things like bumper stickers that read "COEXIST." But the reality is that there are only two kingdoms—the Kingdom of God and the kingdom of darkness. Satan loves universalism because he doesn't care what flavor of spirituality you choose; he just cares that it isn't *Jesus*. Universalism is indeed about unity, but only in the sense that Satan wants to deceive *everyone* into rejecting Jesus.

REVELATION 18

THE FALL OF ECONOMIC BABYLON

In the previous chapter, we learned that **Revelation 17** and **18** are *parenthetical*. The Pause button has been pressed on our main narrative so that an angel can reveal to John the Lord's judgment of Babylon in the Tribulation.

Babylon was the birthplace of *paganism* and the first world empire. It was ruled by the world's first tyrant, a man who was likely the *first* antichrist—*Nimrod*.

Revelation 17 detailed God's judgment of *religious* Babylon, and here in **Revelation 18**, we will see God's judgment of *economic* Babylon.

The world's economic system is not *impartial*. It is not *amoral*. God's judgment of it will reveal that He considers it to be a great *evil*. I believe the world's financial system is one of the most explicit pieces of evidence that man is *not* inherently good and cannot save himself. We mastered global travel and trade, but instead of using it to elevate the welfare of everyone, we used it to exploit the poor on the other side of the globe. We created a class of modern-day slaves, putting even children to work. Why? Because we realized we could have *more* and pay *less* for it. *We* made that system. *We* turned medicine into big business, creating a world where thousands of people die every day from curable diseases solely because the poor can't afford to buy those medications. *We* created an agricultural economy where warehouses full of food *rot* to keep their market value inflated while people *starve* within a day's journey by boat or plane.

Under Satan's influence, *we*—the fallen people of earth—created this system. Not God. *Us*. And that system is so *extensive*, *wicked*, and *intricate* that none of us will ever be able to truly reform it. We won't. The best we can do is replace it with a different evil system, like communism. Therefore, we hope and pray and long for the day when *Jesus* rules as king because He is the *only* good king. *Communism* is not the answer. *Socialism* is not the answer. *Capitalism* is not the answer. *Jesus* is the answer. We need the *only* good king to come and reign over the earth.

Revelation 18 details God's judgment of *economic* Babylon, the world's financial system. And as best we can tell, God will accomplish this by destroying the *literal* city of Babylon.

Now, that statement can be challenging for some to accept because if you hop on Google Earth and look at Babylon today, you'll find that it comprises ancient ruins visited by less than 100,000 Iraqis per year, farmland because of its proximity to the Euphrates River, and a few small towns. There is not much going on there, nor is anything significant currently planned.

While several pastors and authors claim that antichrist will rule his empire from Babylon, nothing in the biblical text indicates that. Instead, we see antichrist occupying the *rebuilt Temple* in Jerusalem and desecrating the Holy of Holies by using it as his throne room.

And yet, I believe the text of **Revelation 18** points to a *literal*

Babylon being destroyed, and her destruction resulting in the collapse of the world's economic system. How could that be possible?

I'm speculating, but I think of the relationship between Washington, DC and New York City. Washington, DC is the *legislative* capital of the United States of America, but New York City is, essentially, the *financial* capital. It's entirely feasible that antichrist could designate Babylon the *financial* capital of his empire. Imagine all transactions being processed through a software system headquartered in Babylon, a system that prevents anyone from buying or selling without the beast's mark. Imagine a new type of *exchange* being established there, where all stocks and commodities trading, global shipping transactions, and individual and corporate banking pass through antichrist's financial servers.

But why would antichrist build that in *Babylon?* Because, as we've discussed previously, while Jerusalem is *God's* sacred location on the earth, Babylon is *Satan's*. The significance of both cities is far greater than we realize and transcends our geopolitical paradigms.

Revelation 18 describes a *literal* Babylon being destroyed and her destruction resulting in the collapse of the world's economic system—perhaps, because the software systems controlling global trade will be *wiped out*. All currency will be digital at that time, and it will simply *cease to exist* when God judges economic Babylon. I suspect that's the kind of idea being presented in this chapter.

In terms of the timeline, it appears the judgment of economic Babylon unfolds around the same time as the seventh and final bowl judgment. **Revelation 16:17–19** described that judgment:

> **...the seventh angel poured out his bowl into the air, and a loud voice came out of the temple of heaven, from the throne, saying, *"It is done!"* And there were noises**

and thunderings and lightnings; and there was a great earthquake, such a mighty and great earthquake as had not occurred since men were on the earth. Now the great city was divided into three parts, and the cities of the nations fell. And great Babylon was remembered before God, to give her the cup of the wine of the fierceness of His wrath.

INTO THE TEXT

And with that, let's get into the details of the text. Because while there are lots of *theories* about the end-times, many of them fall apart when you get into the *details* of Scripture. This chapter is undoubtedly not black-and-white, but, as always, the details give us greater clarity about what's going on.

> [1] **After these things . . .**

After being shown a vision of the destruction of religious Babylon, John is shown *another* vision.

> **. . . I saw another angel coming down from heaven, having great authority, and the earth was illuminated with his glory.**

Recall that the bowl judgments will likely unfold in rapid succession, creating a *cumulative* effect, rather than each judgment ending before the next begins. That means that when this angel appears, antichrist's empire will still be in *darkness* because of the fifth bowl judgment,[437] making the appearance of this glorious angel even more striking.

---

[437] Cf. Revelation 16:10.

² And he [the angel] cried mightily with a loud voice, saying, "Babylon the great is fallen, is fallen, and has become a dwelling place of demons, a prison for every foul spirit, and a cage for every unclean and hated bird!"

This is another pronouncement of judgment upon Babylon, another *proleptic* statement. And everyone who dwells on the earth will hear these words. The judgment pronounced back in **Revelation 14:8** will soon be *complete*.

The word *"bird"* is used as an idiom for demons and foul spirits in this context. It's intended to convey the filthy nature of scavenging birds, whose presence is associated with death and destruction.[438]

Interestingly, the angel calls destroyed Babylon *"a prison for every foul spirit, and a cage for every unclean and hated bird."* It seems that, at the end of the Tribulation, God will gather all the demonic entities permitted to roam the earth in the Tribulation[439] and *imprison* them in the vicinity of Babylon in preparation for their imminent destruction.

Antichrist and the false prophet will *not* be imprisoned in Babylon, as God has a *different plan* for them that we'll learn about soon.

³ For all the nations have drunk of the wine of the wrath of her fornication, the kings of the earth have committed fornication with her [economic Babylon], *and the merchants of the earth have become rich through the abundance of her luxury.*

---

[438] Cf. Jeremiah 50:39. The Christian Standard Bible offers "desert demons" as an alternative translation for "desert creatures."

[439] For example, Revelation 9:1–11, 13–16; 12:4–9.

I mentioned in the previous chapter that God created every man and woman to worship *Him*. Because we derive our meaning from what we worship, He would not be a good God if He instructed us to worship anything other than Him. He is the best thing for us and the only source of true life in existence. God likens it to *harlotry* when any man or woman chooses to worship something or someone else. He considers idolatry to be *spiritual adultery*.

In **Revelation 17**, God addressed the idolatry of *false religion*. In **Revelation 18**, He addresses the idolatry of *material wealth*, referring to those who worship *money*, the god called "Mammon"[440] in the Scriptures.

The phrase *"all the nations"* is employed because the *whole world* has been and will be seduced by economic Babylon and the *lure* of material wealth.

The biblical event that best parallels this chapter is ancient Babylon on the night she was taken by Cyrus the Great. The story is found in **Daniel 5**. It documents *Belshazzar*, an indulgent and arrogant king, throwing a lavish party despite being aware of Cyrus' hostile presence outside the city walls. Belshazzar wasn't at all concerned because Babylon's walls were famously *impregnable*. A river ran through the city. They had so many supplies that it was said the city could survive a 20-year siege. Everyone in Babylon assumed they were *untouchable*.

But God crashed the party, wrote His judgment on a wall with His finger, and then inspired Cyrus to cut off the river's flow, allowing his army to walk *under* the walls of Babylon. Belshazzar and his pagan nobles were killed that very night, and Babylon fell. That's the picture here. Babylon will once again think herself

---

[440] Cf. Matthew 6:24; Luke 16:13.

impregnable and indestructible, and God will bring it to nothing in just one day.

Here's the counsel God gives those who have turned to Him in the Tribulation and are still alive on the earth at this time:

> ⁴ **And I heard another voice from heaven saying,** *"Come out of her* [Babylon], *my people, lest you share in her sins, and lest you receive of her plagues."*

God warns everyone to get as far away from Babylon as they possibly can because He's about to destroy her. It's similar to the instructions given to Lot and his family to flee the city of Sodom.[441] God's call to His people to come out of Babylon is *timeless* and still applies to believers today. We live *in* Babylon, yet we are called to not be *of* Babylon. The New Testament speaks of this principle repeatedly.[442] For example, when Jesus is praying for His disciples on the night of His arrest, He prays this to His Heavenly Father:

> *They are not of the world, just as I am not of the world. Sanctify them by Your truth. Your word is truth.*
>
> —John 17:16–17

If you're going to follow Jesus, you must view yourself as *"not of the world."*[443] Although we *live* in this world (for now), we don't live and work and build and store up stuff as though this is our *forever home* and the only life we're going to have.

But how do we practically *live* in this world without getting

---

[441] Cf. Genesis 19:12–13.

[442] Cf. Romans 12:2; 2 Corinthians 6:14–17; James 1:27, 4:4; 1 John 2:15.

[443] John 15:9; 17:14, 16.

caught up in this world? How do we *use* the world's money but not be used *by* the world's money? Jesus' request of His Heavenly Father, on our behalf, gives us the answer: **"Sanctify them by Your truth. Your word is truth."**

In the Tribulation, *God's Word* will give direction to believers, just as it does today. It lays out a path—a way of living that allows us to *live* in Babylon without becoming *part of* Babylon. How do you avoid getting caught up in *religious* Babylon? Believe and practice what the Word commands regarding *spiritual* matters. How do you avoid getting caught up in *economic* Babylon? Believe and practice what the Word commands regarding *financial* matters.

God says that if we embrace Babylon as our *home*, we will join in her sins and receive the natural consequences. Sin *always* leads to destruction and death. So, if you embrace a culture that loves sin, destruction and death will show up sooner or later in your life, including in your relationships and finances.

This is the same warning God repeatedly gave the Israelites, and they never seemed to listen. He warned them not to intermarry with the surrounding pagan cultures and not to mingle with them because He knew they would be seduced by their wickedness and join them in it. Don't think you can take fire in your lap and not be burned.[444] Don't fall in love with Babylon because you won't change Babylon; Babylon will change *you*. Babylon will stand until *Jesus* tears it down. Until that glorious day, we are called *out* of Babylon.

> **⁵ For her sins have reached to heaven, and God has remembered her iniquities.**

---

[444] Cf. Proverbs 6:27.

When you give your life to Jesus, you receive forgiveness for every sin you've committed and will commit. Jesus paid that debt on your behalf on the Cross. Those sins are not hanging over your life, and they will not follow you into eternity. But the sins of those who reject Jesus hang over them, never disappearing into the passage of time but waiting for the inevitable day of judgment.

The Lord says that the sins of Babylon have piled up, like a tower reaching to Heaven, *demanding* a response from Him. God *remembers* every evil committed by Babylon and those who have fornicated with her. He remembers every genocide, every abuse, every disease that could have been cured, every slave trader, every bit of human oppression and exploitation, and He will judge it *all*.

> **⁶ Render to her just as she rendered to you, and repay her double according to her works; in the cup which she has mixed, mix double for her.**

In other words, because Babylon's *wickedness* was extraordinary, it is just that her *punishment* be equally extraordinary.

> **⁷ In the measure that she glorified herself and lived luxuriously, in the same measure give her torment and sorrow; for she says in her heart, "I sit as queen, and am no widow, and will not see sorrow." ⁸ Therefore her plagues will come in one day—death and mourning and famine. And she will be utterly burned with fire, for strong is the Lord God who judges her.**

V.7 describes the *appeal* of economic Babylon, the *reason* people worship and fornicate with her. It's the enticement of living *"luxuriously"* and having a life where wealth *insulates* and *protects* them from the trials of life experienced by "ordinary" people. It's the lure of *glory* and *prestige*, feeding the insatiable appetite of one's ego. And yet the Lord declares that Babylon *"will be utterly burned with fire,"* and those who worship her are destined for a similar fate in eternity.

V.8 tells us that, incredibly, economic Babylon will burn to the ground in a *single day*.

> ⁹ *The kings of the earth who committed fornication and lived luxuriously with her will weep and lament for her, when they see the smoke of her burning,* ¹⁰ *standing at a distance for fear of her torment, saying, "Alas, alas, that great city Babylon, that mighty city! For in one hour your judgment has come."*

Notice that *"The kings of the earth"* and the *"merchants"* do not mourn in repentance or lamentation over their idolatry; they grieve over the destruction of *Mammon*, the god they devoted their lives to serving.

VV.9–10 and **15–16** are the strongest indicators that we're talking about a *literal* city, as *"The kings of the earth"* and the *"merchants"* are described watching from a distance as Babylon burns, fearing coming any closer, lest they share in her fate. This clearly describes the destruction of a *literal* Babylon and not just a *mystical* Babylon.

We also see the word "city" used repeatedly in this chapter,[445] and there are several Old Testament prophecies[446] that foretell the *permanent* destruction of a *literal* Babylon. For example, Isaiah prophesied:

> **... Babylon, the glory of kingdoms,**
> **The beauty of the Chaldeans' pride,**
> **Will be as when God overthrew Sodom and Gomorrah.**

---

[445] VV.10, 16, 18, 19, 21.

[446] For example, Isaiah 13:19–22; 14:22–23; Jeremiah 50:13, 39; 51:26, 37.

> **It will never be inhabited,**
> **Nor will it be settled from generation to generation;**
> **Nor will the Arabian pitch tents there,**
> **Nor will the shepherds make their sheepfolds there.**
> —Isaiah 13:19–20

How did God destroy Sodom and Gomorrah? By raining *literal fire* and *brimstone* from the sky.[447] That's what will *literally* happen when Babylon is *"utterly burned with fire."* We also know Isaiah's prophecy hasn't been fulfilled yet because people live in Babylon right now. But when God is through judging her, *nobody* will *ever* set foot there again.

> [11] *And the merchants of the earth will weep and mourn over her, for no one buys their merchandise anymore:* . . .

Those who sell merchandise will mourn over the loss of their wealthy customers because the world financial system will be *eviscerated*. It will *cease to exist*.

Apparently, the world's *elites* were the ones to whom these merchants were selling. We know that because we are told in the following two verses what *kinds* of items these merchants were selling.

> . . . [12] *merchandise of gold and silver, precious stones and pearls, fine linen and purple, silk and scarlet, every kind of citron wood, every kind of object of ivory, every kind of object of most precious wood, bronze, iron, and marble;* [13] *and cinnamon and incense, fragrant oil and frankincense, wine and oil, fine flour and wheat, cattle and sheep, horses and chariots, and bodies and souls of men.*

---

[447] Cf. Genesis 19:24.

This list includes things like gold and silver; diamonds; the most refined fabrics; the most expensive and exotic building supplies such as ivory, specialty woods and metals, and marble; the costliest spices and fragrances; the best wines; the purest cooking and baking ingredients; livestock; exotic cars and private jets. Then you reach this strange phrase: *"bodies and souls of men."* Greek scholars generally agree that *"bodies"* should be translated as *"slaves."*[448] The phrase *"souls of men"* refers to the *essence* of a person—their life, mind, heart. Scholars with whom I agree deduce that these terms are being used to point to sex trafficking.

In **V.14**, God speaks this judgment over economic Babylon and those who worship her:

¹⁴ The fruit that your soul longed for has gone from you, and all the things which are rich and splendid have gone from you, and you shall find them no more at all.

Those who worship wealth will be left with empty *hands* and empty *souls*. Those who rejected Jesus longed for the fruit of material wealth. Those who love Jesus long for the fruit of the Spirit, which is love that produces joy, peace, patience, kindness, goodness, faithfulness, gentleness, and self-control.[449]

¹⁵ The merchants of these things, who became rich by her, will stand at a distance for fear of her torment, weeping and wailing, ¹⁶ and saying, "Alas, alas, that great city that was clothed in fine linen, purple, and scarlet, and adorned with gold and precious stones and pearls! ¹⁷ For in one hour such

---

[448] "Soma" in Greek.

[449] Cf. Galatians 5:22–24.

great riches came to nothing." Every shipmaster, all who travel by ship, sailors, and as many as trade on the sea, stood at a distance [18] and cried out when they saw the smoke of her burning, saying, "What is like this great city?"

[19] *They threw dust on their heads and cried out, weeping and wailing, and saying, "Alas, alas, that great city, in which all who had ships on the sea became rich by her wealth! For in one hour she is made desolate."*

And here's how the saints, the Church, you, and I are told to respond:

[20] **Rejoice over her, O heaven, and you holy apostles and prophets, for God has avenged you on her!**

If you love the Lord and righteousness, then you will *rejoice* when the world economic system comes tumbling down. We will *rejoice* when the righteousness of Heaven invades earth and triumphs over evil. We will *rejoice* when Jesus is exalted, and the way is made straight for His return to reign as king over the earth.

[21] **Then a mighty angel took up a stone like a great millstone and threw *it* into the sea, saying, *"Thus with violence the great city Babylon shall be thrown down, and shall not be found anymore."***

This angel creates a *visual metaphor* of what Babylon's destruction will be like. A millstone was between four and five feet across and one foot thick. And as this angel throws a millstone into the ocean, there is doubtless a massive, sudden impact; then the stone disappears beneath the waters, never to be seen again. So shall Babylon's final destruction be.

²² The sound of harpists, musicians, flutists, and trumpeters shall not be heard in you anymore. No craftsman of any craft shall be found in you anymore, and the sound of a millstone shall not be heard in you anymore.

If a rebuilt Babylon becomes the world's financial capital, it will undoubtedly attract the elite. And from this verse, we learn that, until she is judged, Babylon will be filled with the sounds of parties and entertainment in the Great Tribulation.

²³ The light of a lamp shall not shine in you anymore, and the voice of bridegroom and bride shall not be heard in you anymore. For your merchants were the great men of the earth, . . .

Now isn't this an interesting bit of Bible prophecy? Babylon will be destroyed in an age when *"the great men of the earth"* are not Caesars, emperors, or kings but *"merchants."* Titans of industry, trade, and commerce who acquire their wealth and power by fornicating with Babylon. I know it's hard to imagine such a time, but it's what the Bible says (I'm being facetious).

For your merchants were the great men of the earth, for by your [Babylon's] **sorcery all the nations were deceived.**

Everyone who doesn't belong to Jesus will fornicate with economic Babylon because the appeal of material wealth will seduce them.

²⁴ And in her was found the blood of prophets and saints, and of all who were slain on the earth.

If you haven't noticed, Babylon—in *all* her forms—*hates* God and those who worship Him. I find **V.24** interesting because God declares that Babylon is guilty of the *"blood of the prophets and* *saints"* and *"all who were slain on the earth."* The values of Babylon—selfishness, greed, and jealousy—lead to murder.

CONSPIRACIES AND COMPARISONS

There's an old saying: *"Public policy makes the world go round."* I'm sorry, I messed that up. I meant to say, *"Democracy makes the world go round."* Wait, that's not right either. *"Honest business makes the world go round."* Now I remember: *"**Money** makes the world go round."*

I think everybody now understands that the world does not function as it appears on the surface. Democratically elected politicians do not determine the direction of the world. And if you're a Christian, you should know this because Scripture tells us that Satan is pulling the strings behind the scenes, and he uses *people* to do it.

> **. . . the whole world lies *under the sway of* the wicked one.**
> —1 John 5:19

If you are concerned about influential people trying to take over the world and seize control by fornicating with economic Babylon, you need to remember what the Bible says:

> **. . . we do not wrestle against flesh and blood, but against principalities, against powers, against the rulers of the darkness of this age, against spiritual *hosts* of wickedness in the heavenly *places*.**
> —Ephesians 6:12

Stopping evil people will not bring down economic Babylon because the driving forces behind it are *spiritual*. We must understand this. We need to learn how to fight in the *spiritual* arena, using weapons such as prayer, worship, and the declaration of God's

Word. I mentioned this earlier, but I want to repeat it: *according to the Bible*, Babylon—in *all her forms*—will exist and only *grow* in power between now and the end of the Tribulation. She will not be stopped until *Jesus* steps in and destroys her. I can't think of anything more foolish than spending one's time, money, and energy working against the fulfillment of biblical prophecy. If God has ordained it, it's *going to happen.*

"What are you saying, Jeff? Are you saying we're just supposed to do ***nothing?!*** *Are we not supposed to* ***resist evil?"*** I'm not saying we're to do nothing. Far from it. I'm saying that Jesus has revealed in His Word what we're called to do, how we're called to live, and how we're called to fight. You likely recall from a previous chapter that Jesus told His followers, including you and me, **"Do business till I come."**[450] In other words, *"Be about My business until I return."* That means don't check out. Don't hide in a bunker. Don't build a compound and disappear. Live for Jesus, according to His Word, and represent His Kingdom wherever you find yourself.

We are Heaven's ambassadors,[451] and we are called to shine the light of God's Kingdom. We are called to bring mercy, grace, truth, and justice to our spheres of influence such as our relationships, marriages, families, churches, social circles, workplaces, and schools. Jesus said:

> *You are the light of the world. A city that is set on a hill cannot be hidden. Nor do they light a lamp and put it under a basket, but on a lampstand, and it gives light...*
>
> —Matthew 5:14–15

---

[450] Luke 19:13.

[451] Cf. 2 Corinthians 5:20.

Does it give light to all who are in the world? *No.* "*. . . it gives light to all who are in the house.*"

When you're immature in the faith, you get frustrated when you hear that, and you think, *"I want to do something bigger! I want to bring a revolution that changes everything and kicks Babylon out of my country!"* When you become mature in the faith, you look at your relationships, your marriage, your family, your church, your social circle, your workplace, or your school, and you think, *"Reflecting the light of Jesus in these places is more than enough of a challenge to keep me busy for the rest of my life."*

Every now and then, God calls us to walk through a door that leads to a place of incredible influence. But that's not the norm for believers. About 99.99% of the time, our calling is to represent Heaven in our highly localized spheres of influence.

Spiritually, it has been *night* on the earth since Adam and Eve fell into sin. It's night right now. It's dark on the earth. And it will only turn to day when Jesus returns to usher in the new day of His Millennial Kingdom. Don't try to find a light switch that will illuminate the whole world. Try to let your light shine in the spheres of influence God has given you. *That's* the call.

"BABYLONIANS" COMPARED TO LAODICEANS

In **V.7**, we read of the *arrogance* of those who have placed their trust in the world and material wealth:

> **. . . *she says in her heart,* "*I sit* as queen, and am no widow, and will not see sorrow."**

That sounds a lot like the tone struck by the Last Days Church—the age we're living in—back in **Revelation 3:17–22**. Do you remember what Jesus said to the Church at Laodicea, which loved the world system?

> *... you say, "I am rich, have become wealthy, and have need of nothing"—and do not know that you are wretched, miserable, poor, blind, and naked—I counsel you to buy from Me gold refined in the fire, that you may be rich; and white garments, that you may be clothed, that the shame of your nakedness may not be revealed; and anoint your eyes with eye salve, that you may see. As many as I love, I rebuke and chasten. Therefore be zealous and repent. Behold, I stand at the door and knock. If anyone hears My voice and opens the door, I will come in to him and dine with him, and he with Me. To him who overcomes I will grant to sit with Me on My throne, as I also overcame and sat down with My Father on His throne.*
>
> *He who has an ear, let him hear...*

Let me remind you of some fundamental truths about material wealth:

- It cannot satisfy your soul.
- It cannot bring you peace with God.
- It's all going to burn, and you cannot take it with you.

Jesus said:

> *... what will it profit a man if he gains the whole world, and loses his own soul?*
>
> —Mark 8:36

And Jesus told this parable:

> *... The ground of a certain rich man yielded plentifully. And he thought within himself, saying, "What shall I do, since*

> *I have no room to store my crops?" So he said, "I will do this: I will pull down my barns and build greater, and there I will store all my crops and my goods. And I will say to my soul, 'Soul, you have many goods laid up for many years; take your ease; eat, drink, and be merry.'" But God said to him, "Fool! This night your soul will be required of you; then whose will those things be which you have provided?"*
>
> *So is he who lays up treasure for himself, and is not rich toward God.*
>
> —Luke 12:16–21

In other words, God calls the man or woman who devotes their life to the pursuit of material wealth while ignoring Him a fool because they refuse to recognize the realities of life, death, and eternity. And to the believer, Jesus says:

> *Do not lay up for yourselves treasures on earth, where moth and rust destroy and where thieves break in and steal; but lay up for yourselves treasures in heaven, where neither moth nor rust destroys and where thieves do not break in and steal.*
>
> —Matthew 6:19–20

Jesus doesn't say, *"Don't worry about acquiring treasure."* Jesus tells us to instead store up treasures for ourselves in *eternity*, where we will be able to enjoy it *forever*. How do you do that? By offering God everything in your life and asking Him, *"What do You want me to do with this?"* And as we daily hear Him answer in His Word and by His Spirit, and we obey Him, we store up for ourselves treasure in Heaven.

If you're worshipping material wealth, you are worshipping

Mammon, and the destiny of your god is documented in **Revelation 18**.

WHAT JAMES SAYS ABOUT THE COMING DESTRUCTION OF BABYLON

You may not expect the Epistle of James to have any connections to the judgment and destruction of Babylon, but it was *undoubtedly* inspired by the Lord to address things we've been studying in this chapter. Just look at the first four verses of **James 5**:

> **Come now, *you* rich, weep and howl for your miseries that are coming upon *you!* Your riches are corrupted, and your garments are moth-eaten. Your gold and silver are corroded, and their corrosion will be a witness against you and will eat your flesh like fire. You have heaped up treasure in the last days.**

Do you remember back in our study of **Revelation 6**, when the Four Horsemen of the Apocalypse—the first four seal judgments—rode out? Following antichrist and war were global famine and poverty. And there was this strange verse that said, *"do not harm the oil and the wine."* We talked about how the rich just get richer even during global poverty. That's what James is referring to here. Those who fornicate with Babylon's economic system are willing to get wealthy through the pain and suffering of everybody else.

> **Indeed the wages of the laborers who mowed your fields, which you kept back by fraud, cry out; and the cries of the reapers have reached the ears of the Lord of Sabaoth ["Hosts"].**

Isn't it interesting that God specifically notes the elite's practice of gaining wealth by mistreating and underpaying their employees? China has hundreds of thousands of unjustly imprisoned men and women working in factories. India, Pakistan, and Malaysia have longstanding practices of mistreating workers. But you don't even have to go that far. Just learn what's going on in your local Amazon distribution warehouse. The abuse of workers happens worldwide because greed is a *global* phenomenon. And God sees it *all*.

You have lived on the earth in pleasure and luxury; you have fattened your hearts as in a day of slaughter.

The elites spend their lives pursuing luxury and ease. The truth is, they're like pigs that think they're enjoying a life of endless buffets when the reality is that they're being prepared for slaughter.

You have condemned, you have murdered the just; he [the just man] **does not resist you.**

The just man does not take vengeance into his own hands; he leaves it to the Lord. The wicked wealthy man thinks he's getting away with taking advantage of the just man, but **Revelation 18** tells us the Lord sees, the Lord remembers, and the Lord will *judge*.

In light of that, James addresses you and me **(5:7–8)**:

Therefore be patient, brethren, until the coming of the Lord. See *how* the farmer waits for the precious fruit of the earth, waiting patiently for it until it receives the early and latter rain. You also be patient. Establish your hearts, for the coming of the Lord is at hand.

I'm so thankful that the Lord has given us His Word and made these things *plain*. The secret knowledge that the world's elite believes they have is *nothing* compared to what our Heavenly Father has revealed to us. He has pulled back the curtain, disclosing how the world really works and where the world is headed. I'm so thankful that the Lord has revealed to me the *emptiness* of Babylon, and I'm so grateful that the Lord has invited me to store up treasure in Heaven instead.

Christian, don't fall in love with money. God tells us we will *rejoice* when this world's economic system is destroyed. Don't fall in love with something that will never satisfy and is destined for destruction. *Use* money for the glory of God. Be *generous*. Do *good* in Babylon. If handling your money and your business with integrity costs you, remember that it's only costing you here on earth. You're gaining treasure in Heaven, where moth and rust do not destroy.

Believers view *everything they have* as belonging to the Lord and want Him to use it all for His glory. Let's live like *that*. Let's be light in the darkness of Babylon. Trust in the Lord. Hope in the Lord. Be fulfilled in the Lord. He is coming soon, so store up treasure in Heaven. Do business until He returns. And rejoice that the day will come when Babylon is destroyed, and we will watch it happen in the presence of the Lord.

CLOSING THOUGHTS

Do you have a hard time trusting God to take care of your practical needs when it comes to money? If so, you need to memorize these verses. Many of us know them, but we don't *know* them. They're in our *heads*, but not in our *hearts*. Jesus said:

> *...I say to you, do not worry about your life, what you will eat; nor about the body, what you will put on. Life is more than food, and the body is more than clothing. Consider the*

ravens, for they neither sow nor reap, which have neither storehouse nor barn; and God feeds them. Of how much more value are you than the birds? And which of you by worrying can add one cubit to his stature? If you then are not able to do the least, why are you anxious for the rest? Consider the lilies, how they grow: they neither toil nor spin; and yet I say to you, even Solomon in all his glory was not arrayed like one of these. If then God so clothes the grass, which today is in the field and tomorrow is thrown into the oven, how much more will He clothe you, O you of little faith?

And do not seek what you should eat or what you should drink, nor have an anxious mind. For all these things the nations of the world seek after, and your Father knows that you need these things. But seek the kingdom of God, and all these things shall be added to you.

Do not fear, little flock, for it is your Father's good pleasure to give you the kingdom. Sell what you have and give alms; provide yourselves money bags which do not grow old, a treasure in the heavens that does not fail, where no thief approaches nor moth destroys. For where your treasure is, there your heart will be also.

—Luke 12:22–34

REVELATION 19:1-10

THE SECOND COMING (PART 1)

Revelation 19 finds us at the *end* of the Tribulation. Religious and economic Babylon has fallen. The seal, trumpet, and bowl judgments have concluded. The armies of antichrist and the armies of the north, south, and east are converging at Armageddon. The surviving ethnic Jewish population of Israel is hiding in Petra. And the hour that creation itself groans and longs for has arrived—the return of the King, also known as "The Second Coming."

To help us keep the big picture in mind over the following few chapters, I want to point out five things that will take place at the Second Coming. Jesus will:

- Defeat all forces of evil, freeing the earth of Satan's influence.
- Reveal Himself to ethnic Israel, and their relationship will be restored.
- Purge the earth of those who have rejected Him.
- Host the marriage supper of the Lamb, where He will be joined to His bride, the Church.

- Inaugurate the Millennial Kingdom and begin His reign over the earth from Jerusalem.

HEAVEN REJOICES OVER THE DEATH OF BABYLON

¹ **After these things . . .**

That is, after the destruction of *literal* and *mystical* Babylon:

I heard a loud voice of a great multitude in heaven, saying, "Alleluia! Salvation and glory and honor and power belong to the Lord our God! ² **For true and righteous are His judgments, because He has judged the great harlot who corrupted the earth with her fornication; and He has avenged on her the blood of His servants shed by her."**

Here we see Heaven rejoicing again at the *demise* of Babylon, which was recorded in **Revelation 17–18**.

This **"great multitude"** of voices likely belongs to the *angels* because the *Church* responds in **V.4** and is called to rejoice in **V.5**.

³ **Again they said,** *"Alleluia! Her smoke rises up forever and ever!"*

That phrase simply means that Babylon's judgment is *final* and *irreversible*.[452]

⁴ **And the twenty-four elders and the four living creatures fell down and worshiped God who sat on the throne, saying,** *"Amen! Alleluia!"*

---

[452] Cf. The judgment of Edom in Isaiah 34:10.

You may recall from our study of **Revelation 4–5** that "**the twenty-four elders**" represent the royal priesthood of believers, consisting of Old Testament saints and the Church.

"Amen" means, *"so be it."* "Hallelujah" or *"Alleluia"* is a compound word. "Halal" is the Hebrew word for *"praise,"* and "Jah" is one of the Hebrew words for *"God."* So, when you put them together as "Halal Jah" or "Hallelujah," it simply means *"praise God"* or *"Praise the Lord."*

The first time the phrase appears in Scripture is in **Psalm 104:35**. Notice what it says:

May sinners be consumed from the earth,
And the wicked be no more.
Bless the Lord, O my soul!
Praise the Lord!

Even more interesting is that the phrase appears only four times in the New Testament, and they're all *right here* in **Revelation 19**, where the people of God celebrate the destruction of Babylon and God's righteous judgment of the wicked.

If we are going to be people of faith, we must master the habit of declaring these two phrases in every life situation: *"so be it"* and *"praise God."* *"Amen"* and *"Alleluia."*

Those are the words, the sentiments, and the prayers that flow from the hearts of *mature* believers. Mature believers recognize that when we have complete understanding in Heaven, it will be clear how God's judgments were perfect in every situation. When shown the whole picture, we will *all* say, *"True and righteous are Your judgments, O Lord."* Therefore, mature believers (here and now) declare:

> *I have faith in the **judgment** of my God because I have faith in the **character** of my God. So, where I don't understand yet, I choose to*

simply say, "Amen. Alleluia." Because I know that sooner or later, I'll say that anyway. So, I'm going say it now, in faith.

Mature believers recognize the *pattern* of God's perfect goodness and faithfulness in their lives. When they doubt God and are proven wrong by His faithfulness, mature believers actually *take note.* The immature believer *never* recognizes the pattern. It doesn't matter how many times they doubt God and are proven wrong by His faithfulness, immature believers never learn that *God is faithful.*

If you're honest, which description fits you? Are you *confident* in the character of your Heavenly Father? You can be because He loves you more than you could imagine. He is faithful and He *deserves* your trust.

Mature believers know God's character and are therefore able to say, *"Amen"* ("so be it") and *"Alleluia"* ("praise God"), in faith, in every circumstance of life.

This chapter can be awkward for some people because we see that believers in Heaven are *glad* all of this is happening. And this causes some to ask:

"How can a loving God and the Kingdom of a loving God be happy about wrath being poured out on people like this?"

I don't want to shock you with horror stories in this commentary, but I do think you should get yourself a copy of *Foxe's Book of Martyrs* and spend an evening reading about what those who have hated Jesus across the centuries have done to believers, simply because they loved Jesus. I hope you have some idea of the atrocities that ISIS and their counterparts have committed against Christians within the past decade and what's going on in places like Nigeria, China, and North Korea today. The Book of Revelation speaks of the coming time when God will declare that enough is enough. And with His family all accounted for, the justice He had been delaying in His mercy will be delayed no longer.

And all of Heaven—including you and me—won't say, *"That's so unfair!"* or *"Wait longer anyway!"* We'll say, *"It's about time. Amen. Alleluia."*

> ⁵ **Then a voice came from the throne, saying, "Praise our God, all you His servants and those who fear Him, both small and great!"**

> ⁶ **And I heard, as it were, the voice of a great multitude, as the sound of many waters and as the sound of mighty thunderings, saying, "Alleluia! For the Lord God Omnipotent reigns!"**

Handel's famous *Hallelujah Chorus* was inspired by this text—the moment Heaven *roars* with praise over Jesus' victory over Babylon and His imminent return to the earth.

THE MARRIAGE SUPPER OF THE LAMB IS ANNOUNCED

> ⁷ *Let us be glad and rejoice and give Him glory, for the marriage of the Lamb has come, and His wife has made herself ready.*

In other words, the Church is ready to step into her destiny as the Bride of Christ.

> ⁸ **And to her** [the Church] **it was granted . . .**

That means it was *given*, not *earned*.

> **. . . to be arrayed in fine linen, clean and bright, for the fine linen is the righteous acts of the saints.**

What do you wear to the greatest party the universe has ever seen? Scripture tells us that the only thing to be seen in will be *righteousness*.

When a man tries to *earn* His way to salvation with good works, God rightly views his woefully inadequate attempts as **"filthy rags."**[453] But when a man places his faith in Jesus, He is robed in the righteousness of *Jesus*. **Isaiah 61:10** declares:

> **I will greatly rejoice in the Lord,**
> **My soul shall be joyful in my God;**
> **For He has clothed me with the garments of salvation,**
> **He has covered me with the robe of righteousness . . .**

And when we have been made into new creations[454] by the indwelling of the Holy Spirit, we can now actually do works that God views as *good* because those works flow from the righteousness of *Jesus* that dwells in us.

We learn in **V.8** that at the marriage supper of the Lamb, we will be adorned, in a somehow visible way, with the good works that the Lord produced in our earthly lives through His Spirit in us.

All who love Jesus are presently robed in His righteousness. We are *innocent* before the Father because Jesus has imputed His righteousness to us. That righteousness enables us to stand in right relationship with God today, and it ensures that we are judged worthy of being in His family. Praise God!

But I want to suggest that God's plan for us in eternity goes beyond even *imputed* righteousness and includes *intrinsic* righteousness. Let me explain.

---

[453] Cf. Isaiah 64:6.

[454] Cf. 2 Corinthians 5:17.

Were Adam and Eve created righteous? *Absolutely.* God called them **"good."**[455] Were they righteous with the *imputed* righteousness of Jesus? *No.* They were righteous because they were created without sin. Their righteousness was *intrinsic*. When we are translated into our resurrected bodies, we will be remade and imbued with *intrinsic* righteousness. But unlike Adam and Eve, we will not have to contend with an external tempter (as Satan will be cast into the lake of fire), and we will have a complete understanding of the *consequences* of sin. We will have tasted both sin and righteousness, death and life, so we will be able to fully grasp the glory of the grace lavished upon us. We will have the knowledge, nature, and holiness to faithfully serve the Lord in righteousness for eternity.

As I've shared before, God's scandalously good plans for us are summed up in **1 John 3:2**, where our brother John writes:

Beloved, now we are children of God; and it has not yet been revealed what we shall be, but we know that when He is revealed, we shall be like Him, for we shall see Him as He is.

However good you think God's plans for you are, I promise they're *even better*.

⁹ **Then he ...**

The angel who was still with John from **Revelation 18**:

... **said to me,** *"Write: 'Blessed are those who are called* ["invited"] *to the marriage supper of the Lamb!'" And he said to me, "These are the true sayings of God."*

---

[455] Genesis 1:31.

Here we have the famous *"**marriage supper of the Lamb**."* The phrase, *"**These are the true sayings of God**,"* means *"You can bet your life on this. It's going to happen."*

The Bible describes the relationship between Jesus and His Church as the relationship between a *groom* and his chaste, pure *bride*. One of the things that makes marriage sacred is the fact that Jesus intended it to reflect His relationship with His Church.[456] The love of God, *agape* love, is sacrificial and rooted in a free-will decision to love the other person. It's a relationship based on a *commitment*, not behavior, performance, or emotions. That's how God loves us as His Church, and it's how He desires husbands and wives love each other.

The Church is not a *guest* at the marriage supper of the Lamb: the Church is the bride. So, who are the ones *invited* to this wedding?

- **All those who died in faith in the Old Testament era:** Saints such as Abraham, David, and the prophets.[457] Their *spirits* have been with the Lord in Heaven since the death and resurrection of Jesus. However, they have not yet received resurrected *bodies*. As best we can tell from Scripture,[458] Old Testament saints will receive their new bodies at the Second Coming, so that they might participate in the wedding and the Millennial Kingdom.

- **Tribulation saints:** Those who placed their faith in Jesus *after* the Rapture.

---

[456] Cf. Ephesians 5:24–27.

[457] Cf. Matthew 8:11; Luke 13:28.

[458] For example, Daniel 12:1–2.

- **Redeemed Israel:**[459] The 144,000 and all ethnic Jews who turn to Jesus after the Rapture, including all Israel still alive on the earth when He appears to them at the Second Coming.

PARALLELS BETWEEN A TRADITIONAL JEWISH WEDDING AND THE CHURCH'S DESTINY

There are some striking parallels between a traditional Jewish wedding and the destiny of the Church as the Bride of Christ. It's difficult to verify every bit of information, but I've done my best to (hopefully) convey the big picture accurately:

- First, the father would identify where they believed the perfect bride resided. It could be their small village, it could be a few villages up the road, or it could be even further away.

- The bride would be chosen by an intermediary (his father, a servant, or a relative) on the groom's behalf.

- Assuming the woman was agreeable to the proposal, the intermediary and her father would negotiate a marriage contract *(the Ketubah)*, including a *purchase price*—what some cultures call the dowry.

- That price was established based on three factors:

    First, the father's wealth. If the groom's father were a rich man, he would pay a high price to not appear cheap.

---

[459] Cf. Isaiah 25.

Second, the bride's worth. If she were beautiful or otherwise gifted, her price would be higher.

Third, the groom's work. It was sometimes up to the groom to pay the price.

- If the woman was willing and the price was satisfactory, the couple would become *engaged*—betrothed. Even though they were not yet married, they would be joined in a legal, binding agreement at that point. The bride would be considered "set apart." That's literally what the word "sanctified" means. She had a future husband, and even though she was not yet *with* him, she belonged *to* him.

- The bridegroom would then begin construction at his father's house, adding a room to the structure. The bride, both families, and all their friends could observe the progress, and it would tell them how close they were to the wedding day.

- Eventually, the time would arrive when the groom would put the final touches on the room addition. Everybody would notice this, especially the bride, who would gather her friends and prepare herself for the wedding. The bride wouldn't know what *day* of the week it would happen, but she could discern what *week* it would happen.

- She had to keep herself *ready*, and it was a bit of a game because the bridegroom would make it his goal to *surprise* her. The groom, however, would only leave to get his bride when his father said, *"Now is the time."*

- When that time arrived, the groom would wait for nightfall, suit up, and begin his processional toward his bride's house, accompanied by his friends and family blowing trumpets, shouting, and cheering.

- When the bride heard the trumpets, she would rise, receive a blessing from her father, and go out to greet her groom, accompanied by her bridesmaids.[460]

  Culturally, if you were in the village and saw this, you would stop what you were doing and join the procession, cheering it along. As the procession traveled through the village, it would get larger and larger.

- The groom would finally arrive at his bride's house, collect her, and bring her back to his father's house for the wedding ceremony.[461]

  That ceremony wouldn't be where promises were made but where the agreement—the contract or covenant—that had been agreed to earlier would be reread, and a blessing pronounced over the couple.

- The wedding feast would immediately begin, lasting for seven days. During those seven days, the newlyweds would do no work, instead devoting themselves to enjoying the festivities and spending time together in their room.

---

[460] Cf. Matthew 25:1–13.

[461] Cf. Matthew 25:1–13.

- They would be dressed and treated like *royalty*, and if the father were wealthy enough, he would even provide *clothing* for all the guests.

- The wedding feast would last for seven days, but the *marriage supper* was a specific event at the *end* of the seven days. This also allowed time for other guests from farther away to receive word that the wedding festivities had commenced and make the journey to join the celebration.

If you've been around the Bible for more than a year, the prophetic parallels should be apparent:

- God chose us to be the Bride of Christ. We were chosen **"before the foundations of the world."**[462]

- We have been *purchased* at the *highest price*—the precious blood of Jesus.[463] That's the value God has placed upon us.

- Jesus has made His Church beautiful by the way He has loved her. He loved us all the way from death to life, wickedness to righteousness, and sinfulness to spotless beauty.[464]

- We are now *sanctified*—set apart as the soon-to-be bride of Christ.

---

[462] Ephesians 1:4.

[463] Cf. 1 Corinthians 6:19–20.

[464] Cf. Ephesians 5:25–27; Revelation 19:8.

- We have the contract, the Word of God, that assures us He is coming for us.[465]

- Jesus has returned to His Father's house, Heaven, to prepare a place for us.

- **First Peter 1:6–8** describes our longing and expectation over the arrival of our groom, Jesus Christ:

> **In this you greatly rejoice, though now for a little while, if need be, you have been grieved by various trials, that the genuineness of your faith, *being* much more precious than gold that perishes, though it is tested by fire, may be found to praise, honor, and glory at the revelation of Jesus Christ, whom having not seen you love. Though now you do not see *Him*, yet believing, you rejoice with joy inexpressible and full of glory . . .**

- While Jesus prepares a place for us, it's our job to prepare for His imminent return. So, we watch for the signs He gave us in His Word. We recognize that "construction" is almost finished. Everything is in place. And we understand that He could come for us *at any moment.*

- When He comes for us, He will take us back to His Father's house to be with Him.[466]

- How long did the wedding feast last? Seven *days*. How long will the Church be tucked away in Heaven with Jesus while the Tribulation unfolds on the earth? Seven *years*.

---

[465] Cf. Ephesians 1:13–14.

[466] Cf. 1 Thessalonians 4:16–17.

That is why the Marriage Supper of the Lamb occurs at the *end* of the seven-year Tribulation and not at the *beginning* of the seven-year Tribulation. Jesus told His disciples:

In My Father's house are many mansions; if it were not so, I would have told you. I go to prepare a place for you. And if I go and prepare a place for you, I will come again and receive you to Myself; that where I am, there you may be also.

—John 14:2–3

While some believe the marriage supper of the Lamb takes place in Heaven, I think it takes place on the earth following the Second Coming and the Sheep and Goats Judgment. I hold this view because there will still be some believers on the earth when Jesus returns. Additionally, Israel will be reconciled to God. Are those two groups going to be *excluded* from the marriage supper of the Lamb, even as guests? That doesn't seem like a reasonable assumption.

[10] And I fell at his feet to worship him [John fell at the feet of the angel]. **But he said to me, "See that you do not do that! I am your fellow servant, and of your brethren who have the testimony of Jesus. Worship God! For the testimony of Jesus is the spirit of prophecy."**

This is the standard operating procedure for angels in the Bible. Whenever anyone tries to worship them, they always instruct them to stop and worship God instead. They know they are simply messengers, and only the Lord is deserving of worship. To point out the obvious, the Bible makes it clear that *we do not worship angels.*[467]

---

[467] Cf. Colossians 2:18.

However, people regularly responded to *Jesus* in like manner—falling at His feet or kneeling before Him.[468] And not once did He respond by saying anything like, *"Don't worship me! I'm not God."* So, when Mormons or JWs tell you that Jesus was just an angel, the only problem with that is *the Bible*. The angels don't accept worship because they are *not* God. Jesus accepts worship because He *is* God.

When the angel says, **"the testimony of Jesus is the spirit of prophecy,"** he's saying that everything Jesus says, everything He testifies to, is destined to happen. It's a *given*. If Jesus prophesied it, then it will happen.

CLOSING THOUGHTS

If life is difficult right now, if you're in a season of tribulation, or if there seems to be no answers or explanation from God, let me encourage you to make *"Amen. Alleluia."* your prayer. Trust the Lord. Recognize the pattern of His faithfulness in your life. Remember that Jesus proved His love for you with His blood, so you need not doubt His compassion and care for you.

If you do that, I believe you'll find your burden lightened. You'll experience peace coming over your mind, not because you suddenly understand everything but because you remember that you don't *need* to understand everything because you understand *enough*.

God is good. Your Heavenly Father knows what you need. And *He loves you.* My goodness, He loves you.

So, amen. Alleluia. So be it. Praise God.

---

[468] For example, Joshua 5:13–15; Luke 5:8; John 20:28.

REVELATION 19:11-21

THE SECOND COMING (PART 2)

Let's continue in **Revelation 19:11**:

> ¹¹ **Now I saw heaven opened,** . . .

Heaven opened in **Revelation 4:1** for *the Rapture*, the event where Jesus comes *for* His Church. Let's look at it one more time:

> **After these things I looked, and behold, a door *standing open* in heaven. And the first voice which I heard *was* like a trumpet speaking with me, saying, *"Come up here, and I will show you things which must take place after this."***

The believer moves from earth to Heaven in the event described in that verse. Remember that Jesus told His disciples, *"I will come again and receive you to Myself."*[469] Here in **Revelation 19:11**, we see Heaven open again for *the Second Coming*—the event where Jesus comes *with* His Church. And we'll see that the believer now moves from Heaven to earth. Paul referred to this as **"the coming**

---

[469] John 14:3.

of our Lord Jesus Christ with all His saints,"[470] and **Zechariah** prophesied:

> ... **the lord my God will come,** *and* **all the saints with You.**
> —Zechariah 14:5

When you examine the *details* of the Rapture and the Second Coming, it soon becomes apparent that they cannot possibly be the same event, as some suggest. They're so different; they are undeniably *mutually exclusive*. At the Rapture, Jesus comes *for* His Church. At the Second Coming, Jesus comes *with* His Church. In **Revelation 4:1**, Heaven opens for *the Rapture*. In **Revelation 19:11**, Heaven opens for *the Second Coming*. And the seven-year Tribulation takes place *between* those two events.

Continuing in **V.11**:

> ... **and behold, a white horse. And He who sat on him** *was* **called Faithful and True, and in righteousness He judges and makes war.**

"**Faithful and True**" is how Jesus referred to Himself back in **Revelation 3:14** in His letter to the Last Days Church, the Church in Laodicea. Just as Jesus was "**Faithful**" to do His Father's will at His *First* Coming, He will be faithful to do His Father's will at His *Second* Coming. And just as He was "**True**" to every promise He made in His Word regarding His First Coming, He will be faithful to every promise He has made in His Word regarding His *Second* Coming.

Note the phrase, *"in righteousness He judges and makes war."*

---

[470] 1 Thessalonians 3:13.

In light of everything we see happen in the Book of Revelation, we must never forget that everything God does is *righteous*—it's right. Some people choose to get tattoos that read, *"Only God can judge me."* By this point in our study, I hope we understand such notions are valid but should *terrify* those who do not belong to Jesus because He *will* judge every man and woman! But here's the glorious truth: if you belong to Jesus, God has *already* judged you. The Father judged *Jesus* for your sins in your place. The punishment for your sins—past, present, and future—was rendered unto Jesus just outside the city of Jerusalem almost 2,000 years ago.

¹² His eyes *were* like a flame of fire, and on His head *were* many crowns.

Fire often speaks of *judgment* in the Scriptures, and this description of Jesus' eyes is intended to convey that He is coming to judge the earth.

The reference to **"many crowns"** points to Jesus' absolute authority over everything and everyone on the earth.

He had a name written that no one knew except Himself.

In the Bible, one's name tends to reveal one's *nature*. And what is suggested here is that there is a side to Jesus that nobody knows but God. When we see Him face-to-face, we will be awed by what we behold because even the most devoted among us don't know Jesus today the way we will know Him then. Paul tells us in **1 Corinthians 13:12**:

> **. . . now we see in a mirror, dimly, but then face to face. Now I know in part, but then I shall know just as I also am known.**

One day we will know Jesus the way He knows us. And we will spend eternity appreciating the infinite nuances and facets of His glory.

¹³ He *was* clothed with a robe dipped in blood, and His name is called The Word of God.

The Second Coming of Jesus is *literal*. Aspects of it that we'll read about in a moment, like a sword coming out of His mouth, the rod of iron, and the winepress at Armageddon, are *symbolic*. The robe of Jesus that is dipped in blood is *symbolic*. We know this because, at this moment, Jesus has not yet personally and directly engaged His enemies on the earth.

It may symbolize the fact that Jesus is the judge of the earth, and the one who *ordered* the devastating seal, trumpet, and bowl judgments.

Or it may point to what is *about to* unfold on the earth as Jesus returns as a conquering warrior. If you saw a soldier holding a knife with blood sprayed on his clothes, you would immediately recognize that this is a *warrior*, not an ambassador coming to offer peace terms. That may be the idea here—imagery that foreshadows Jesus coming as the Lion of Judah, not a sacrificial lamb.

Notice **V.13**. **"The Word of God"** is one of Jesus' *names*. It's who He *is*. His Word is intimately and inseparably part of His identity. John, who just told us that Jesus' name is **"The Word of God,"** began his Gospel with these words:

In the beginning was the Word, and the Word was with God, and the Word was God.

—John 1:1

He then writes in **V.14** of that same chapter:

> **...the Word became flesh and dwelt among us, and we beheld His glory, the glory as of the only begotten of the Father, full of grace and truth.**

Jesus is His Word, and His Word is Him. It's a mystical truth that Jesus and His Word are inseparably connected. And when we interact with God's Word, we interact with God. That's why we approach the Bible so reverently and take it so seriously.

> **[14] And the armies in heaven, clothed in fine linen, white and clean, followed Him on white horses.**

Who is **"clothed in fine linen, white and clean"** in Heaven? The saints.[471] You and me. We saw that in **Revelation 19:7–8**.

Revelation 7:9 told us that white robes will also be given to Tribulation saints—those who turn to Jesus after the Rapture, in the Tribulation. This army will also certainly include the Old Testament saints, who will have just received their resurrected bodies,[472] and the angels, who are prophesied to be with Christ at His return.[473] So, to summarize, the **"armies in heaven"** will include the Church, Tribulation saints, Old Testament saints, and the angels. Jesus' return is going to be *spectacular*.

Keep in mind that Jesus doesn't need any backup. Armageddon isn't going to be a *war;* it will be an *appointment*—and a very short appointment at that. We won't be there to fight; Jesus will take care of everything. We'll have one job at Armageddon—to

---

[471] Cf. Zechariah 14:5.

[472] Cf. Daniel 12:1–2.

[473] For example, Matthew 25:31.

serve as the greatest hype posse the world has ever seen. We'll be waving towels, high-fiving each other, singing, and shaking each other by the shoulders as we yell in each other's faces, *"Did you see that?!"*

¹⁵ Now out of His mouth [the mouth of Jesus] **goes a sharp sword, that with it He should strike the nations.**

As I mentioned a moment ago, I don't think we should view this literally because the Bible uses a sharp sword as an idiom for the Word of God in places like **Hebrews 4:12**, and **V.13** just highlighted the fact that one of Jesus' names is **"The Word of God."**

All Jesus has to do is speak His will, and reality bends to fulfill it. The words of Jesus *created* humanity, and the words of Jesus will ultimately *destroy* those on the earth who reject Him. Jesus speaks judgment, and His enemies are judged. Jesus speaks destruction, and His enemies are destroyed. That's the idea here.

And He Himself will rule them [the nations] **with a rod of iron.**

The phrase **"rod of iron"** is also figurative and is based on an ancient expression. It means that Jesus will be in *absolute control* of the earth when He rules from the throne of David in Jerusalem. His enemies will not rise and overthrow Him. He will have the power to enforce righteousness on the earth. When somebody does something evil, it will be immediately identified and righteously judged.

I want to point out that according to **V.15**, the time when Jesus rules the nations comes *after* His return to the earth. This chapter makes that obvious. So, to anyone who would say, *"We're in the Millennium right now."* I would respectfully ask, *"Did I miss* something? Because I don't remember the Second Coming having taken place yet."

The first part of **V.15** reveals that the **"them"** in question are **"the nations."** Why is that important? Well, if there is *no* Millennium, as Amillennialists believe, then when *does* Jesus rule the nations **"with a rod of iron"**?

I am baffled by those who believe we are presently in the Millennial reign of Christ because I don't know about you, but when Jesus reigns over the earth, I have *much* higher expectations. Call me crazy, but I think that Jesus literally ruling over the nations will produce a better world than the one we're currently living in! When the Jesus I read about in the Scriptures reigns over the earth, it will inevitably be the most glorious season of history the world will ever see. Whether someone takes **V.15** literally or figuratively, I just don't know how in the world they could conclude that Jesus is *actively* ruling over the nations. If He is, it's been going horribly for the past 2,000 years. Ergo, He is not.

And that's why I can't wait for the day when this verse is *truly* fulfilled.

V.15 continues:

He Himself [Jesus] treads the winepress of the fierceness and wrath of Almighty God.

We talked about this **"winepress"** imagery at length in our study of **Revelation 14**.

¹⁶ **And He has on *His* robe and on His thigh a name written: KING OF KINGS AND LORD OF LORDS**

I used to get fired up because, at first reading, this seems to be implying that Jesus has a *tattoo*. Some scholars still hold that view, but I don't because having a tattoo violates the Old Testament Law which Jesus kept perfectly as a man,[474] and it seems likely never has and never will violate.

The more likely explanation is that **"KING OF KINGS AND LORD OF LORDS"** is written on the hem of His garment—the bottom edge where one's family pedigree was traditionally indicated in Hebrew culture, and His robe is simply pulled up to his thighs because He's riding a horse.

Nevertheless, what a scene this is going to be! There is a moment coming when we will be in our resurrected bodies, join the angels and saints, and return to the earth with Jesus when He comes in glory as the **"KING OF KINGS AND LORD OF LORDS."**

THE BEAST AND HIS ARMIES DEFEATED

> [17] **Then I saw an angel standing in the sun; . . .**

The original word is "mid-Heaven," which refers to our sky or atmosphere. You can't miss this angel because he is as prominent in the sky as the sun.

> **. . . and he cried with a loud voice, saying to all the birds that fly in the midst of heaven,** *"Come and gather together for the supper of the great God,* [18] *that you may eat the flesh of kings, the flesh of captains, the flesh of mighty men, the flesh of horses and of those who sit on them, and the flesh of all people, free and slave, both small and great."*

---

[474] Cf. Matthew 5:17.

Talk about a bad omen for the armies of antichrist and all those on the earth who hate the Lord! This angel tells all meat-eating birds to prepare to feast because the enemies of God are all about to *die*.

There's an intentional contrast in the phrasing here—those who don't want to be part of the marriage supper of the Lamb will instead be part of *"the supper of the great God."*

The phrase *"the flesh of all people, free and slave, both small and great"* refers to the fate of those on the earth who reject Jesus throughout the Tribulation. They will not be permitted to enter the Millennial Kingdom. Instead, they will be *judged*, their earthly bodies will be *executed*, and as we shall see later in this study, their spirits will be immediately condemned to the lake of fire for eternity.

Lest you think this sounds harsh, please remember that we are talking about people who will *refuse* to turn to Jesus despite all the signs, wonders, and judgments displayed over the seven years (**seven years!**) of the Tribulation. We are talking about people who will take the beast's mark and pledge their allegiance to antichrist, despite seeing and hearing an angel warning them it will result in their eternal damnation.[475] They are people who will *cheer* as those who love Jesus are murdered. But most of all, we are talking about people who will simply be given *what they want*. They won't want to serve Jesus. They won't want a relationship with Him. They won't want to be part of His family. They won't want to be under His leadership and authority. And so, Jesus will give them what they want—eternity apart from Him.

Those who aren't killed at Armageddon will be judged and executed at the Sheep and Goat Judgment, which will also take

---

[475] Cf. Revelation 14:9–11.

place around the time of the Second Coming and is described by Jesus in **Matthew 25:31–46**:

When the Son of Man comes in His glory, and all the holy angels with Him, then He will sit on the throne of His glory.

In Jerusalem.

All the nations will be gathered before Him, and He will separate them one from another, as a shepherd divides his sheep from the goats. And He will set the sheep on His right hand, but the goats on the left.

At the Second Coming, after Armageddon, everyone alive on the earth will be gathered before Jesus, and He will separate those who belong to Him from those who do not.

Then the King [Jesus] *will say to those on His right hand* [the sheep], *"Come, you blessed of My Father, inherit the kingdom prepared for you from the foundation of the world: . . . "*

This is another one of those little clues about our future destiny that we miss because what it's saying is so incredible that it doesn't even enter our minds to consider. It seems scandalous. It seems blasphemous. But Jesus Himself referred to His Kingdom as being prepared for *us "from the foundation of the world."*

When the Bible teaches that we have become adopted sons and daughters of the Father, it also teaches that our adoption has made us brothers and sisters of the Father's Son, Jesus. He is our Savior, He is our Lord, and He is also our *brother*. And one of the things I cannot wrap my head around is the reality that Jesus is excited to share *everything He has* with *us*. We didn't earn *any of it*. He earned it all and was rewarded with it by His Father.

And yet, even though Jesus earned it through the worst suffering anyone will ever endure, all He wants to do with His Kingdom is share it with those who love Him, saying, *"Come, you blessed of My Father, inherit the kingdom prepared for you from the foundation of the world."* As David mused when He pondered the ways of the Lord,

> *Such* knowledge *is* too wonderful for me; **It is high, I cannot attain** it.
>
> —Psalm 139:6

Jesus continues in **Matthew 25:42–46** and says:

> *. . . for I was hungry and you gave Me food; I was thirsty and you gave Me drink; I was a stranger and you took Me in; I was naked and you clothed Me; I was sick and you visited Me; I was in prison and you came to Me.*
>
> *Then the righteous will answer Him, saying, "Lord, when did we see You hungry and feed You, or thirsty and give You drink? When did we see You a stranger and take You in, or naked and clothe You? Or when did we see You sick, or in prison, and come to You?" And the King will answer and say to them, "Assuredly, I say to you, inasmuch as you did it to one of the least of these My brethren, you did it to Me."*
>
> *Then He will also say to those on the left hand, "Depart from Me, you cursed, into the everlasting fire prepared for the devil and his angels: for I was hungry and you gave Me no food; I was thirsty and you gave Me no drink; I was a stranger and you did not take Me in, naked and you did not clothe Me, sick and in prison and you did not visit Me."*

Then they also will answer Him, saying, "Lord, when did we see You hungry or thirsty or a stranger or naked or sick or in prison, and did not minister to You?" Then He will answer them, saying, "Assuredly, I say to you, inasmuch as you did not do it to one of the least of these, you did not do it to Me." And these will go away into everlasting punishment, but the righteous into eternal life.

Matthew 25:41 seems to make it clear that those who reject Jesus and are still alive on the earth at the Second Coming will be judged, executed, and their spirits immediately condemned to the lake of fire *("the everlasting fire prepared for the devil and his angels")*.

Jesus also described this time of judgment in **Matthew 13**. Beginning in **V.24**, He shares what is known as "The Parable of the Tares":

Another parable He put forth to them, saying: *"The kingdom of heaven is like a man who sowed good seed in his field; but while men slept, his enemy came and sowed tares among the wheat and went his way. But when the grain had sprouted and produced a crop, then the tares also appeared. So the servants of the owner came and said to him, 'Sir, did you not sow good seed in your field? How then does it have tares?' He said to them, 'An enemy has done this.' The servants said to him, 'Do you want us then to go and gather them up?' But he said, 'No, lest while you gather up the tares you also uproot the wheat with them. Let both grow together until the harvest, and at the time of harvest I will say to the reapers, "First gather together the tares and bind* *them in bundles to burn them, but gather the wheat into my barn."' "*

—Matthew 13:24–30

Starting in **V.37**, Jesus *explains* the parable:

He answered and said to them: "He who sows the good seed is the Son of Man [Jesus]. The field is the world, the good seeds are the sons of the kingdom, but the tares are the sons of the wicked one. The enemy who sowed them is the devil, the harvest is the end of the age, and the reapers are the angels. Therefore as the tares are gathered and burned in the fire, so it will be at the end of this age. The Son of Man will send out His angels, and they will gather out of His kingdom all things that offend, and those who practice lawlessness, and will cast them into the furnace of fire. There will be wailing and gnashing of teeth. Then the righteous will shine forth as the sun in the kingdom of their Father. He who has ears to hear, let him hear!"

—Matthew 13:37–43

The Second Coming will be *glorious* and *joyful* for those who love the Lord, but *doom* and *terror* for those who hate Him.[476] Note that the phrase **"gnashing of teeth"** means that even at their time of judgment, they will *still* display the hostility toward God revealed in their stubbornness throughout the Tribulation—like Pharaoh in the face of God's miracles in Egypt. They will not repent or beg for a second chance; they will continue to resent God for bringing their kingdom of wickedness to ruin.

---

[476] Cf. Zephaniah 1:14–18.

¹⁹ And I saw the beast, the kings of the earth, and their armies, gathered together to make war against Him who sat on the horse and against His army.

These armies will be **"gathered together"** on the plain of Jezreel, in the valley in northern Israel more famously known as *Armageddon*. Antichrist's plan will be a final and decisive destruction of ethnic and political Israel, starting with Jerusalem.

Revelation 16:12 and **16** tell us that armies from **"the east"** will be gathered at Armageddon. According to **Daniel 11**, **"the South,"** which includes the Pan-African nations and the Arab states, will band together and head north into this conflict, as will **"the king of the North"** (likely Russia). And as they converge around Armageddon, they will look up and see *Jesus* returning to the earth. Knowing their end is near, their response will be to turn all their weapons upon Him in the greatest fool's errand the world will ever witness.

Notice the *epic back-and-forth* battle between Jesus and Satan (I'm being facetious):

²⁰ Then the beast was captured, and with him the false prophet who worked signs in his presence, by which he deceived those who received the mark of the beast and those who worshiped his image. These two were cast alive into the lake of fire burning with brimstone.

It happens like the snap of one's fingers. In an instant, antichrist—**"the beast"**—and the false prophet are captured and cast into the lake of fire. If you're thinking, *"What about Satan?"* He gets dealt with first thing in the next chapter.

The **"lake of fire"** is the *final* destination of Satan, antichrist, the false prophet, all supernatural entities opposed to God, and all men and women who reject Jesus as Lord and Savior.

²¹ And the rest [the armies opposing Jesus] **were killed with the sword which proceeded from the mouth of Him who sat on the horse** [Jesus]**. And all the birds were filled with their flesh.**

The voice that calmed the storm, cast out demons, healed the sick, raised the dead, and created the universe will speak a word, and antichrist and the false prophet will be cast into the lake of fire. He will speak a word, and physical life will flee from their armies. Jesus' victory will be *effortless* and *instantaneous*.

In the passage that unquestionably inspired the face-melting-Nazis scene in the movie *Raiders of the Lost Ark*, the prophet Zechariah describes Jesus' wrath against His enemies at Armageddon:

> **. . . this shall be the plague with which the Lord will strike all the people who fought against Jerusalem:**
>
> **Their flesh shall dissolve while they stand on their feet,**
> **Their eyes shall dissolve in their sockets,**
> **And their tongues shall dissolve in their mouths.**
>
> **It shall come to pass in that day**
> ***That* a great panic from the Lord will be among them.**
> **Everyone will seize the hand of his neighbor,**
> **And raise his hand against his neighbor's hand; . . .**
>
> —Zechariah 14:12–13

Their bodies will rapidly decay where they stand, or their fellow soldiers who will be seized by absolute panic will kill them.

MORE SCRIPTURES ON THE SECOND COMING

I want to share some more verses with you that speak of these future events. In **2 Thessalonians 1:7–10,** Paul writes:

> ...**the Lord Jesus is revealed from heaven with His mighty angels, in flaming fire taking vengeance on those who do not know God, and on those who do not obey the gospel of our Lord Jesus Christ. These shall be punished with everlasting destruction from the presence of the Lord and from the glory of His power, when He comes, in that Day, to be glorified in His saints and to be admired among all those who believe...**

Jude tells us that Enoch, the first man to be raptured,[477] was a *prophet*:

> **Now Enoch, the seventh from Adam, prophesied about these men** [apostates] **also, saying,** *"Behold, the Lord comes with ten thousands of His saints, to execute judgment on all, to convict all who are ungodly among them of all their ungodly deeds which they have committed in an ungodly way, and of all the harsh things which ungodly sinners have spoken against Him."*
>
> —Jude 14–15

Jesus also talked about these events in **Matthew 24:27–31**:

> ... *as the lightning comes from the east and flashes to the west, so also will the coming of the Son of Man be.*

---

[477] Cf. Genesis 5:24.

The idea is that when Jesus returns it will be *sudden*, and *everyone* will see Him because His glory will light up the entire sky. And then Jesus says:

> *For wherever the carcass is, there the eagles will be gathered together.*

For years, I would teach on that verse with no idea what Jesus was referring to. Every commentary I could find either ignored it or offered an explanation that was clearly a stretch. After more than 15 years, the Holy Spirit graciously connected the (annoyingly obvious) dots for me. It's an allusion to **Revelation 19:17–18**, where the angel calls the meat-eating birds to feast on the dead bodies of God's enemies. It's referencing the time when eagles will gather around dead bodies at the Second Coming.

So, be encouraged. I still have *lots* of questions about the Bible! The Lord is gracious to answer them over time, so write down your questions, share them with other believers who love the Scriptures, and you'll be amazed how the Lord will grow your understanding over the years.

Jesus continues in **Matthew 24**:

> *Immediately after the tribulation of those days the sun will be darkened, and the moon will not give its light; the stars will fall from heaven, and the powers of the heavens will be shaken. Then the sign of the Son of Man will appear in heaven, and then all the tribes of the earth will mourn, and they will see the Son of Man coming on the clouds of heaven with power and great glory. And He will send His angels with a great sound of a trumpet, and they will gather together His elect from the four winds, from one end of heaven to the other.*

The elect on the earth—those who turned to Jesus in the Tribulation—will be gathered and invited to the marriage supper of the Lamb. Those who rejected the Lord will *"mourn"*—not in *repentance*, but because Jesus has returned to claim the earth.

ISRAEL'S DESTINY

One group of people *will* mourn in repentance at the Second Coming—*ethnic Israel*. This refers to all ethnic Jews who are still alive on the earth at the Second Coming and have not yet recognized Jesus as Messiah. Because they collectively rejected Jesus at His First Coming, Israel has had her eyes blinded to the truth ever since. Because they *would not* believe in Jesus, God made it so they *could not* believe in Jesus.

And the Lord did this to be *merciful* because every person who rejects God will be judged based on the degree of revelation they received. The greater the revelation, the greater the sin of rejecting Jesus.[478] Knowing they would continue to reject Jesus throughout the centuries, God chose to limit Israel's revelation, sparing them even greater judgment. When He was on the earth, Jesus wept over Israel's hard hearts, crying out:

> *O Jerusalem, Jerusalem, the one who kills the prophets and stones those who are sent to her! How often I wanted to gather your children together, as a hen gathers her brood under her wings, but you were not willing! See! Your house is left to you desolate; and assuredly, I say to you, you shall not see Me until*

---

[478] Cf. Luke 10:12, 14; 12:47–48; Revelation 20:11–15.

the time comes when you say, "Blessed is He who comes in the name of the Lord!"

—Luke 13:34–35

Paul writes about this reality in **Romans 11:25**:

... blindness in part has happened to Israel until the fullness of the Gentiles has come in.

At the Second Coming, that moment arrives, and the **"blindness"** that is currently upon Israel is *lifted*. In the very next verse,[479] Paul tells us that the destiny of Israel is that **"all Israel will be saved."**

Zechariah 12:10 tells us that when they see Jesus at the Second Coming, Israel will be made able to recognize Him as the Messiah they've been waiting for. Prophesying through Zechariah, the Lord promises this:

... I will pour on the house of David and on the inhabitants of Jerusalem the Spirit of grace and supplication; then they will look on Me whom they pierced. Yes, they will mourn for Him as one mourns for his only son, and grieve for Him as one grieves for a firstborn.

Jesus will return to the earth, deliver Israel from her enemies, and pour grace upon her, lifting her **"blindness."** They will recognize Jesus as Messiah and *"grieve"* in collective repentance over their 2,000 years of rejecting Him and involvement in His death. And Jesus will forgive them, just as He has forgiven us. Their relationship will be restored, and they will enter the Millennial Kingdom as part of the family of God.

---

[479] Romans 11:26.

God has not abandoned His promises to Israel, as some claim. Paul explains all this in detail in **Romans 9–11**, three chapters that speak to Israel's *past, present,* and *future*. I'm so glad we serve a God who keeps *all* His promises.

If you'd like to dig into the Lord's plans and heart for Israel a little bit more, you can check out **Isaiah 25**[480] and **Isaiah 54:5–17**. Both passages prophesy regarding the Lord's plans for Israel at the Second Coming and in the Millennium.

CLOSING THOUGHTS

I don't know how **Revelation 19** feels to you, but it feels almost too *abrupt* to me. We've had tribulation and judgments and wrath being detailed for a *really* long time, and then suddenly it's all over? Just like that?

Yes, just like that. It's as instantaneous as our salvation. One moment we're *dead*; the next, we're *alive* in Christ. It's as instantaneous as eternity with Jesus. One moment we're in this **"body of death,"**[481] and the next, we're clothed in white robes in Heaven with Jesus.

The Book of Revelation desperately wants us to understand how *quickly* things can change. Jesus, writing through the Apostle John, wants us to grasp the truth that when it looks like everything is collapsing and Satan is winning, a greater reality and plan are unfolding right on schedule.

And because *Jesus'* victory is certain, we know that *our* victory is certain. Because He is our victory. We keep the faith because we

---

[480] The mountain in view is Mount Zion (Cf. Isaiah 24:23).
[481] Romans 7:24.

know that for all of us, one way or another, *everything* is going to change in an instant, **"in the twinkling of an eye."**[482]

When that moment comes for *you*, how will you feel about how you lived your life? How will you feel about the things you prioritized? Will the things you spent your life devoted to, the things you spent your life serving, *matter?* I want to leave you with this exhortation from our brother Paul in **Galatians 6:9**:

> **. . . let us not grow weary while doing good, for in due season we shall reap if we do not lose heart.**

Live for Jesus with your whole life, and do not lose heart. *Do not lose heart.*

---

[482] 1 Corinthians 15:52.

REVELATION 20:1-6

THE MILLENNIAL KINGDOM

We are studying the thousand years of the future golden age of the earth known as "The Millennial Kingdom." It will be a time when Christians need no longer pray, *"Thy Kingdom come, Thy will be done"* because Jesus and His Kingdom will *reign on the earth*.

It won't be Heaven, but it will be an excellent *warm-up* for Heaven. It won't be where righteousness dwells; it will be where righteousness is *enforced*. There's a big difference. It will be a *temporary* redemption of creation under the reign of Jesus before the universe as we know it is destroyed and replaced by new heavens and a new earth.

And it is going to be *wonderful*.

EXPLORING MILLENNIAL VIEWS

In the Introduction, I shared the main eschatological views and explained that they are based on how one interprets key end-times events such as the Rapture, the Millennium, and the Tribulation period. Christians generally *agree* that **Revelation 19** describes the Second Coming of Christ, but they *disagree* broadly over what **Revelation 20** describes.

I hold to a *Premillennial* and *pre-Tribulation* ("pre-Trib") eschatological interpretation. I believe that we should always start by taking the Bible *literally* and only move to a figurative interpretation if there's a compelling reason to do so, and I listed some good and bad reasons to interpret a biblical text figuratively in the Introduction.

Here's why I mention all that: pretty much all Christians believe that Jesus' Second Coming will be *literal* (i.e., it will actually happen). That's what **Revelation 19** describes. So, if a person believes *that*, why wouldn't they also believe in a literal *Millennial Kingdom*, as described in **Revelation 20**? If a person interprets the primary subject of **Revelation 19** *literally*, what's their justification for interpreting the primary subject of **Revelation 20** *figuratively?* Especially when the phrase **"thousand years"** is used *six times* in **Revelation 20**.

Origen was possibly the most important "father" of the figurative approach to eschatology. While living and working in Alexandria (AD 220–230), he was part of a school of Christianity that enjoyed the relative favor of Roman officials. But it turned out the Roman leaders didn't like it when Christians taught that the kingdoms of this world were destined to fall away and be replaced by the kingdom of Jesus. So, to protect the political favor he was enjoying, Origen began to allegorize those types of texts and instead teach that Jesus was going to rule in the hearts of men—a doctrine that posed no threat to emperors with god complexes.

In the fourth century, Augustine ran with Origen's approach and evolved it into Amillennialism, which teaches that the Millennium will not be literal.

Regardless of this historical background, I think a person is obligated to provide a compelling *reason* for not taking such a specific number literally. And when you dig into the offered explanations for that hermeneutical flip-flop, I think you'll reach the same conclusion I have—namely, that the explanations are *unsatisfying* and *unreasonable*. As we study **Revelation 20**, you'll find that the text provides no compelling reason to allegorize the Millennial Kingdom.

One final comment on this matter. I would be remiss if I didn't mention an interesting detail regarding the Millennium. Jesus created the universe in six days. What did He do on the seventh day? He *rested*. In **2 Peter 3:8**, as the Apostle Peter is writing to believers and encouraging them to be patient regarding the coming of Jesus, he shares this:

> **... beloved, do not forget this one thing, that with the Lord one day *is* as a thousand years, and a thousand years as one day.**

Interestingly, we live in the generation when Israel has re-emerged as a political nation, placing us in the generation that will see the return of Jesus, according to biblical prophecy. And it's interesting that when you lay out the genealogies and timeline of the Bible, it puts the age of humanity at around 6,000 years (and I know that's opening a whole other can of worms that we don't have room for in this book).

Some have suggested that the pattern of six days of creation followed by a day of rest is *mirrored* in the story of humanity. There will be six "days" of a thousand years of work followed by a single "day" of a thousand years of rest. And those thousand years of rest will, of course, be *the Millennium*. At the very least, it's interesting that these things seem to harmonize.

SATAN BOUND 1,000 YEARS

In the previous chapter, we saw *antichrist* and *the false prophet* cast into the lake of fire,[483] and I stated that Satan would be dealt with first thing in **Revelation 20**.

> ¹ **Then I saw an angel coming down from heaven, having the key to the bottomless pit...**

This is not the lake of fire; it's the *Abyss*[484] that we looked at in detail in our study of **Revelation 9**. It's the darkest, most tormenting place in Hades that serves as a *prison* for some of the most heinous supernatural entities. When someone or something is cast into the lake of fire, they're there forever. When someone or something is imprisoned in the Abyss, they can be released later, which we'll learn is going to be the case with Satan.

> **... and a great chain in his hand.**

John sees a mighty angel come down from Heaven with the key to the Abyss and **"a great chain"** in one hand.

> ² **He laid hold of the dragon, that serpent of old, who is *the Devil and Satan*, ...**

---

[483] Cf. Revelation 19:20.

[484] "Abyssos" in Greek.

We know that we're talking about Satan wherever we see a reference to a *dragon* in the Book of Revelation. John also tells us that Satan is **"that serpent of old."** That's a reference to **Genesis 3**, where Eve is tempted to eat the forbidden fruit by a *serpent*. If we were ever confused, **Revelation 20:2** makes it clear that it was *Satan* in the Garden of Eden who tempted Eve to sin, who in turn enticed Adam, which resulted in the fall of humanity into sin and death.

> **... and bound him for a thousand years; ³ and he cast him into the bottomless pit, ...**

Satan is *imprisoned* in the Abyss for the thousand years of the Millennial Kingdom.

In **Revelation 12**, we read about a war in the heavenly realms that will likely unfold around the halfway point of the Tribulation, where Satan and his legions will attempt to seize control of Heaven. Obviously, it doesn't work. I pointed out that God didn't even enter that fight because Satan is not God's rival. God has no rival. Satan began his existence as an archangel *created* by God. And so, God has the archangel Michael and the other faithful angels cast Satan and his allies out of the heavenly realms and down to the earth. Michael has no problem doing that because God *delegates* all the power and authority to Michael that he needs.

I revisit all that because I notice here that when it's time to imprison Satan in the Abyss, God again does not budge from His throne. Instead, He delegates power and authority to this nameless angel (who may well be Michael), who *by himself* is able to arrest Satan and cast him into the Abyss.

We need to understand that God's authority and power are

unmatched. Whatever power Satan and the gods of the nations currently possess is only theirs because God permits it—for reasons that would be an entire study unto itself.

Isaiah tells us what our reaction will be when we *see* Satan. We'll squint and cock our heads to the side and say:

> **...*Is this the man who made the earth tremble, Who shook kingdoms*...**
>
> —Isaiah 14:16

This event is just one example that clarifies the Millennium is *literal*. **James 4:7** tells us to **"Resist the devil and he will flee from you."** We wouldn't need to **"Resist the devil"** if he was currently bound in the Abyss, would we? Therefore, we are *not* presently in the Millennium.[485] As many have observed, *"If we're in the Millennium right now, then Satan's chain is too long."* Thankfully, the truth is that the Millennium will be markedly different from the world we're living in today because while Satan is not bound *now*, he will be *then*.

Continuing in **V.3**:

> **... and [the angel] shut him up, and set a seal on him, so that he should deceive the nations no more...**

The phrase **"deceive the nations no more"** clarifies that Satan *is presently* deceiving the nations. When we look at the state of our world and ask, *"What is going on?"* this verse gives us the answer:

---

[485] See also Matthew 13:39; Acts 5:3; 10:38; 1 Corinthians 7:5; 2 Corinthians 2:10–11; 4:4; 11:14; 12:7; Ephesians 2:2; 4:27; 6:10–20; 1 Thessalonians 2:18; 2 Thessalonians 2:9; 1 Timothy 5:15; 2 Timothy 2:26; James 4:7; 1 Peter 5:8.

Satan is deceiving the nations. By and large, the rulers of our world are *puppets* of his kingdom of darkness.

And this makes me so grateful that God's Word tells us we can have **"the mind of Christ."** Through the Holy Spirit, we can think with truth and clarity despite living in a very *murky* world. Paul writes in **1 Corinthians 2:14–16:**

> **... the natural man does not receive the things of the Spirit of God, for they are foolishness to him; nor can he know** *them,* **because they are spiritually discerned. But he who is spiritual judges all things, yet he himself is** *rightly* **judged by no one. For** *"who has known the mind of the Lord that he may instruct Him?"* **But we have the mind of Christ.**

Satan is *bound up* so that he cannot deceive anyone during the Millennium. Then we read:

> **... till the thousand years were finished. But after these things he must be released for a little while.**

At the end of the Millennium, Satan will be released one final time. And we'll discuss that when we reach **V.7**.

The time is coming when the one the Bible calls the **"ruler of this world"**[486] and the **"god of this age"**[487] will no longer be. And in his place, *Jesus* will rule the nations.

---

[486] John 12:31.

[487] 2 Corinthians 4:4.

WHO GOES INTO THE MILLENNIUM?

It's easy to lose track of who will go *into* the Millennium. So, let's summarize for the sake of clarity. Here's who will enter the Millennial Kingdom:

- **The Church**, who will receive their resurrected bodies at the Rapture.

- **Old Testament saints**, who will receive their resurrected bodies at the Second Coming.

- **Tribulation saints**, those who turned to Christ during the Tribulation and are still alive on the earth at the Second Coming will enter the Millennium in their earthly bodies. Those who died in the Tribulation will receive their resurrected bodies at the Second Coming.

- **Surviving ethnic Israel**, who will enter the Millennium in their earthly bodies.

Let's talk a bit more about each group.

If you have placed your faith in Jesus as your Savior and have welcomed Him into your life as Lord ("master"), you are part of the Church. And the Church is going to reign *with* Jesus on the earth, in the Millennial Kingdom. We will have assignments that will include judging and enforcing righteousness on the earth. Jesus will establish the civil laws of the world, and they will be *perfect*. They will bring freedom and safety and *life* to the earth.

Why will enforcement be needed? Even though Satan, the tempter, will be bound during the Millennium, there will still be people on the earth in their earthly bodies, like ethnic Israel, who will still have to deal with their sinful nature because they will still be in *unredeemed* bodies.

And if you're thinking, *"I don't want to be a supernatural security guard and party-pooper for a thousand years. That sounds like a major downer."* Remember that ruling with Jesus will be a *reward*. It's going to be something we'll love. And I think that's because we will actively participate in making things *right*. In the Millennium, we will help prevent all the evil we wish we could stop today. And *that* sounds amazing to me.

The second group that goes into the Millennium is **Old Testament saints**, who will serve in the same capacity as the Church.

The third group will be the **Tribulation saints**—those who turn to Jesus *after* the Rapture. Most of this group will have died or been martyred in the Tribulation. They include the souls under the altar we read about back in **Revelation 6:9**, as well as those who lost their lives for refusing to take the mark of the beast and worship antichrist.

Some Tribulation saints will survive until the Second Coming. Maybe they're preppers, finally being spectacularly proven right, or perhaps they live in a remote region beyond antichrist's reach.

Those who died before the Second Coming will enter the Millennium in *resurrected* bodies. Those who are still alive on the earth when Jesus returns will enter the Millennium in their *earthly* bodies.

The fourth group will be **surviving ethnic Israel**—all ethnic Jews who are alive on the earth at the end of the Tribulation will receive Jesus as Messiah when He opens their eyes to recognize Him at the Second Coming. Scripture tells us that only a *third* of the earth's ethnic Jews will survive the Tribulation. But in **Zechariah 13:9**, the Lord goes on to say this:

> *I will bring the one-third through the fire,*
> *Will refine them as silver is refined,*
> *And test them as gold is tested.*

They will call on My name,
And I will answer them.
I will say, "This is My people";
And each one will say, "The Lord is my God."

And these will enter the Millennium in their *earthly* bodies.

⁴ And I saw thrones, and they sat on them, and judgment was committed to them.

I think the best way to discern *who* ("**them**") is being spoken of in **V.4** is to look at who the Bible says will be entrusted to judge the earth with Jesus in the Millennium. And that group seems to be the *royal priesthood of believers*, composed of Old Testament saints and the Church.[488]

Now, John sees those who were *martyred* for their faith in the Tribulation (i.e., Tribulation Saints):

Then *I saw* the souls of those who had been beheaded for their witness to Jesus and for the word of God, who had not worshiped the beast or his image, and had not received *his* mark on their foreheads or on their hands. And they lived and reigned with Christ for a thousand years.

Notice that John sees them as "**souls**," and then he says, "**they lived and reigned with Christ for a thousand years.**" The idea is that they received their *resurrected* bodies at this time—at the Second Coming.

Tribulation Saints reign with Jesus in the Millennium, like the Church and the Old Testament saints, but *judgment* is not committed

---

[488] Cf. Daniel 7:27; Matthew 19:28; 1 Corinthians 6:2–3; Revelation 2:26.

to them. They're in a slightly different category. It's wonderful to be in the Kingdom of God in any capacity, but it's better to be part of the royal priesthood of believers—those who serve God in faith *before* the Tribulation.

As an aside that I've mentioned previously, notice the specific *method* of execution referenced in **V.4** that will be used on those who choose Jesus in the Tribulation. It's *beheading*. That's interesting because today, the only countries that officially execute that way are *Muslim*. And they do that because of verses contained in the Quran. For example, the 47th surah *("The Surah of Muhammad")* says in V.4: *"When you encounter the infidels,* [those who do not believe in Islam] *strike off their heads until you have made a great slaughter among them, and of the rest make fast the fetters."*

Remember, all worldly religions, including Islam, will unify under antichrist because they will likely receive him as their end-times savior figure. And based on the method of death, it appears that Islam will provide the *executioners* for antichrist's regime.

⁵ But the rest of the dead did not live again until the thousand years were finished.

"The rest of the dead" refers to all who rejected Jesus and died before the Second Coming. At the end of their earthly lives, their spirits descend into *Hades,* a place of torment where spirits await their final judgment before being cast into the lake of fire for eternity.

And **V.5** tells us that final judgment will occur at the end of the Millennium. It's called "The Great White Throne Judgment," and it'll come up in **V.11**.

While a person's spirit is in Hades, they are considered **"dead,"** even though they are conscious and present. From a biblical perspective, to be in Hades is to be counted among the dead. When

V.5 tells us these **"dead"** will **"live again,"** it's referring to the fact that they will leave Hades and appear in the land of the living before Jesus for their final judgment. Getting to leave Hades, even for a brief time, is considered "living." And that is *sobering*—almost as sobering as the reality that their return to "life" will only be a pit stop on their journey to eternal death in the lake of fire.

This *is* the first resurrection.

The **"first resurrection"** is better understood as a large *class* of people rather than an individual *event*. It includes everyone who belongs to Jesus and is destined to receive a resurrected body, fit for the ages to come. Our brother Paul rightly described Jesus as the **"first fruits"** of the first resurrection[489] because He was the first to rise from the dead to eternal life.

To be clear, **"the first resurrection"** refers to the translation (receiving a resurrected body fit for eternal life) of all those who belong to Christ.

[6] Blessed and holy *is* he who has part in the first resurrection. Over such the second death has no power, . . .

Those born once will die twice, but those born twice only die once. I mentioned this in our study of the letter to the Church at Smyrna, but I'll share it again: Almost everyone will experience the first death, which is the end of our earthly lives. But the Bible teaches that our *spirit* continues to live forever, one way or another. Our eternity will be spent in one of two conditions: eternal *life* or eternal *death*. Those who belong to Jesus will experience never-ending *life*.

---

[489] 1 Corinthians 15:20, 23.

Those who do not belong to Jesus will experience never-ending *death*, **"the second death."**

When you place your faith in Jesus as Savior and welcome Him into your life as Lord, He described what takes place as being ***"born again."***[490] The Holy Spirit joins itself to your dead spirit, bringing it to life and making you **"a new creation."**[491]

A person who is only born *once* (physically) will die at the end of this earthly life and then experience death for *eternity*. The person born *twice* (physically *and* spiritually) will die at the end of this earthly life but then *live* again for eternity. This is what **V.6** is referring to when we read:

Blessed and holy *is* he who has part in the first resurrection. Over such the second death has no power . . .

Everyone who is born again (i.e., born twice), will be part of the first resurrection unto eternal *life*. Everyone born *once* will be part of a second resurrection, unto eternal *death*.

Christian, if everything else in your life is going wrong, you're still *blessed* because you will spend eternity with Jesus, and **"the second death has no power"** over you. We'll talk more about **"the second death"** when we reach **V.14**.

V.6 continues speaking of those who are part of **"the first resurrection"** and says:

. . . but they shall be priests of God and of Christ, and shall reign with Him a thousand years.

---

[490] Cf. John 3:3, 7.

[491] 2 Corinthians 5:17.

Everybody who belongs to Jesus will reign *with* Him and minister *to* Him in the Millennium.

THE MILLENNIUM

The Millennium is going to be *incredible*. It's going to be *wonderful*. We are going to see everything wrong with the world made right. Imagine a world where creation is restored to its original quality and beauty. Every trace of damage to the environment is *undone*. The air and water quality are pristine *everywhere*. You'll be able to drink from rivers that today would make you sick. The deserts will turn into lush forests.[492] **Isaiah 11:6–9** prophesies:

> *The wolf also shall dwell with the lamb,*
> *The leopard shall lie down with the young goat,*
> *The calf and the young lion and the fatling together;*
> *And a little child shall lead them.*
>
> *The cow and the bear shall graze;*
> *Their young ones shall lie down together;*
> *And the lion shall eat straw like the ox.*
> *The nursing child shall play by the cobra's hole,*
> *And the weaned child shall put his hand in the viper's den.*
> *They shall not hurt nor destroy in all My holy mountain,*
> *For the earth shall be full of the knowledge of the Lord*
> *As the waters cover the sea.*

The creatures and animals will all become vegetarian and not harm anyone. Insects won't annoy, bite, or terrify us. That's right;

---

[492] Cf. Isaiah 35:1–2, 7.

there is a day coming when we won't hate spiders! You'll be able to lie down anywhere outside, take a nap, and not worry about *anything*. Wolves and bears and deer will roam among us, and children will *play* with them.

And speaking of children, every parent will be a "free-range" parent because the world will be so *safe*. Children will be able to roam and play and explore. Children will be treasured and watched over by everyone. Orphanages will close because there will be no orphans.

There will be no armies, for there will be no war. **Isaiah 2:2–4** describes this:

> **Now it shall come to pass in the latter days**
> ***That*** **the mountain of the Lord's house**
> **Shall be established on the top of the mountains,**
> **And shall be exalted above the hills;**
> **And all nations shall flow to it.**
> **Many people shall come and say,**
> ***"Come, and let us go up to the mountain of the Lord,***
> ***To the house of the God of Jacob;***
> ***He will teach us His ways,***
> ***And we shall walk in His paths."***
> **For out of Zion shall go forth the law,**
> **And the word of the** LORD **from Jerusalem.**
> **He shall judge between the nations,**
> **And rebuke many people;**
> **They shall beat their swords into plowshares** [farming tools],
> **And their spears into pruning hooks** [kitchen knives];
> **Nation shall not lift up sword against nation,**
> **Neither shall they learn war anymore.**

Hospitals will close because there will be no sickness.[493] **Isaiah 35:5–6 declares:**

> **Then the eyes of the blind shall be opened,**
> **And the ears of the deaf shall be unstopped.**
> **Then the lame shall leap like a deer,**
> **And the tongue of the dumb** [the mute] **sing.**
> **For waters shall burst forth in the wilderness,**
> **And streams in the desert.**

Did you know that different *languages* only exist because of God's curse on humanity at the Tower of Babel? In the Millennium, that too will be reversed! In **Zephaniah 3:9,** the Lord promises:

> *For then I will restore to the peoples a pure language,*
> *That they all may call on the name of the Lord,*
> *To serve Him with one accord.*

The impact of our sin on the universe will be *undone*. Everything will be restored to God's original design. And when we see it, we will declare as He did when He made it, *"This is good."*

Imagine a world where Satan, the gods of the nations, and all demonic entities are *absent*. They don't tempt or deceive *anybody*. The reins of power will sit firmly in the hands of the righteous, who will serve under the leadership of Jesus. On the rare occasion when someone commits an injustice, it will be known and dealt with *immediately* and *perfectly*. Nobody will be able to abuse or oppress.

Neither will anyone accumulate wealth at the expense of another. There will be no lower class, middle class, upper class, or elite because

---

[493] Cf. Isaiah 33:24.

everyone will be able to enjoy abundance.[494] *Everyone* will have all they need to enjoy life in peace, full of joy and adventure.

Work will not be *labor;* it will be rewarding, fulfilling, and enjoyable. And people will enjoy *each other* as never before. Freed from all our insecurities, scars (of all kinds), anxieties, selfishness, lust, and every other negative issue, humanity will experience relationships as God intended—full of *love, life,* and *joy.*

It will be the greatest season of history the world will ever know because *Jesus* will reign as king.

WE CRAVE LIFE IN THE MILLENNIUM

A compelling argument for the God of the Bible is the *longing* in our souls for a world that looks like the Bible's description of the Millennium. We look at the world and have this existential sense that things are not as they should be. We don't look at the world and think, *"All things are as they ought to be. The pain, chaos, violence, hatred, abuse, and exploitation are simply evolution and natural selection doing their thing. We shouldn't expect anything more."*

We look at the world and *lament* and *grieve* over its condition. When death interrupts a child's life, we don't say, *"Well, it's just a statistical reality that a certain number of children will die from cancer. Objectively, we have nothing to be upset about."* When confronted with death, we are all struck by how *wrong* it seems. We can sense in the deepest parts of us that things should not be like this.

Where does that come from? How do we just *know* that something has gone terribly wrong with the world? We know because we are all made in the image of God. And He has placed

---

[494] Cf. Isaiah 30:23–24; Joel 2:21–27.

in our souls a *hunger* for the kind of reality that can only exist under the reign of Jesus.

And we either *recognize* that and turn to Jesus, or we refuse to accept the testimony of our souls because we want to be our *own* god more than we want the life that Jesus offers. And if we do that, we spend our lives embracing the delusional belief that even though humanity is the *cause* of everything wrong with the world, humanity is somehow the *solution* to everything wrong with the world. The folly of such thinking is painfully apparent.

If you want to get serious about spirituality and philosophy, you must seek to answer two critical questions:

- What has gone wrong with the world?
- What is the solution?

The Bible teaches that *our sin* is what has gone wrong with the world, but praise God, there is a solution. And His name is *Jesus*.

THE MILLENNIUM IN ISAIAH 65

Look at what **Isaiah 65:18–26** prophesies about the Millennium. This is God speaking to ethnic Israel, who will enter the Millennium in earthly bodies:

> *... be glad and rejoice forever in what I create;*
> *For behold, I create Jerusalem as a rejoicing,*
> *And her people a joy.*
> *I will rejoice in Jerusalem,*
> *And joy in My people;*
> *The voice of weeping shall no longer be heard in her,*
> *Nor the voice of crying.*

Perhaps the most contentious real estate on the planet, Jerusalem will become the safest, most peaceful place on earth.

No more shall an infant from there live but a few days,

There will be no more miscarriages, and no more sudden infant deaths.

Nor an old man who has not fulfilled his days;
For the child shall die one hundred years old,
But the sinner being one hundred years old shall be accursed.

At the age of 100, someone will still be considered a *"child."* And if someone dies a natural death at the age of 100, it will only be because they grievously rebelled against God, and He ended their life.

They shall build houses and inhabit them;
They shall plant vineyards and eat their fruit.

I like to think this means everything I try to build and grow will actually work!

They shall not build and another inhabit;
They shall not plant and another eat;

Nobody will work for another person. All employer-employee relationships will cease. There will be more than enough for everybody.

For as the days of a tree, so shall be the days of My people,
And My elect shall long enjoy the work of their hands.
They shall not labor in vain,

The norm will be *centuries* to enjoy whatever you build.

Nor bring forth children for trouble;

Pregnancy and labor won't hurt anymore, and there will be no medical emergencies caused by giving birth.

For they shall be the descendants of the blessed of the Lord,
And their offspring with them.
"It shall come to pass
That before they call, I will answer;
And while they are still speaking, I will hear.
The wolf and the lamb shall feed together,
The lion shall eat straw like the ox,
And dust shall be the serpent's food.
They shall not hurt nor destroy in all My holy mountain,"
Says the Lord.

To wildly understate things, it's going to be *incredible*.

CLOSING THOUGHTS

Is there *chaos* and *brokenness* in your soul? If so, make sure you're bringing it to Jesus. Make sure you're serving Him as Lord by doing with your chaos and brokenness that which He asks you to do. And what does He ask?

- He asks us to cast our cares upon Him because He cares for us.[495]

- He calls us to confess our sins to Him and be forgiven.[496]

---

[495] Cf. 1 Peter 5:7.

[496] Cf. 1 John 1:9.

- He calls us to confess our sins to one another and be healed.[497]

- He encourages us to seek wise counsel from mature brothers and sisters.[498]

- He gives us our church family to pray with us and for us.[499]

- He calls us to ask the elders to lay hands on us and pray for healing.[500]

- He calls us to fast and pray.[501]

If that's you, then obey Jesus. Follow Jesus. Do what He tells you to do. Let His Kingdom reign in your life and over your chaos and brokenness, and you *will* experience His life, joy, peace, and hope.

---

[497] Cf. James 5:16.
[498] Cf. Proverbs 19:20.
[499] Cf. Romans 12:12.
[500] Cf. James 5:14
[501] Cf. Acts 13:2–3; 14:23.

REVELATION 20:7-15

THE FINAL JUDGMENT

In the first six verses of **Revelation 20,** we looked at some of the beautiful details of the Millennial Kingdom revealed in Scripture. Our focus now moves to significant events that occur at the *end* of those glorious thousand years.

Some of this section will be difficult to read. It'll be heavy, and it should be. My goal is simply to share the truth, and the truth does not change based on whether we find it pleasant or hard to swallow. What happens to us after we die is not affected by what we think *should* happen to us. In these verses, we'll hear from Jesus—the One who will judge everyone in eternity. Considering that reality, we would be wise to listen to what He wants us to know.

SATANIC REBELLION CRUSHED

> ⁷ **Now when the thousand years have expired, Satan will be released from his prison** [in the Abyss] ⁸ **and will go out to deceive the nations which are in the four corners of the earth,** . . .

If you belong to Jesus, Satan will *not* deceive you at the end of the Millennium. We will be in resurrected bodies, free from sin. That means we'll have a spirit *and* a body that loves Jesus. We will also have knowledge and experience with the devastating consequences of sin, so nobody would be able to convince us that sin is somehow better.

If you're wondering whom exactly Satan *will* deceive, remember there will be many born *during* the Millennium. They will be the children of Tribulation saints[502] and ethnic Jews who were still alive on the earth at the Second Coming and entered the Millennium in fallen, earthly bodies. Like their parents, they will be born with fallen, earthly bodies.

Those born in the Millennium will generally live for at least centuries, and they'll have kids. If you have a thousand years of good health where you're aging slowly, and pregnancy and childbirth aren't even uncomfortable, you're going to make a bunch of babies!

All they will know is life on a redeemed earth under the excellent and righteous reign of Jesus. Yet even under those ideal conditions, some will live *begrudgingly* under His rule. Satan will be bound and unable to tempt them from without, but some will succumb to evil desires that come from within (i.e., their fallen flesh) to be their *own* god.

Remember that Lucifer's pride and covetousness emerged even though all he had ever known was the glory, beauty, and goodness of Heaven. And so, sadly, there will be those who will live in the most incredible age the world will ever see, submitted to Christ's governmental reign only because there will be no other choice. For this reason, at the end of the Millennium, Jesus will *give them* a choice.

---

[502] Those who turned to Jesus after the Rapture.

If you belong to Jesus, then you have already made your choice. You've already *chosen to be chosen*. You've already *selected to be elected*. So, you have nothing to worry about.

I believe there are three main reasons why the Lord will allow this at the end of the Millennium:

1. God doesn't want anyone in His eternal kingdom who doesn't *want* to be there. Love cannot exist apart from free will. God desires a relationship of love with His children. Therefore, our love must be based on the *mutual choice* of God to love us and us to love Him.

2. The release of Satan and the subsequent human rebellion will destroy the argument of those who claim, *"If it weren't for my bad upbringing and the environment I was raised in, I wouldn't have any issues. I'd be perfectly good."* Those who claim their sins are merely the result of being set up to fail won't have a leg to stand on after being raised in the abundant goodness of the Millennial Kingdom. It will be apparent that *our sin* is what went wrong with humanity and the earth.

3. And all this will prove that there truly is *nothing* that satisfies and fulfills except knowing Jesus and being known by Him. Those who say, *"I'd have peace and joy and fulfillment if I had a billion dollars!"* or *"... if I just had _____!"* or *"... if I just didn't have _____!"* will be proven wrong.

In the Millennium, people will grow up in *paradise* with Satan bound and with everything provided for them; they will have no hardship and no sickness. They'll play badminton with bears and leapfrog with lions, yet some will *still* be miserable! The futility and emptiness of life without Jesus will be revealed when all the earth's problems are healed, and every need is met, but some are *still* not happy.

Why? Because joy is not found in everything being perfect. It's not found in a perfect body, perfect stuff, a perfect climate, or even in a perfect world. We were made to *know God*. We have been engineered so that nothing else can fill the space in our soul that was made to be filled by Him.

We will be satisfied in the Millennium the same way we are satisfied now—*in Christ.*

Yes, it will be easier for us to be satisfied in Christ in the Millennium because we'll be in resurrected, righteous bodies. Still, we do not have to *wait* for the Millennium to experience God's satisfaction, peace, and joy. Those things are available through Jesus *right now*. He will fulfill us then, and He can fulfill us now. The Holy Spirit is working on the heart of every person who loves Jesus, and one of the lessons He's trying to teach us is that our contentment and joy do not have to be connected to our circumstances. In **Psalm 144:15,** David wrote:

Happy *are* the people whose God *is* the Lord!

God's plan is not that we would be miserable in this life and say, *"At least I'll be happy in the Millennium."* God's plan is that we would find our joy in Him here and now! He wants the Millennium to be *gravy* for you and me. Our hope is not the Millennium; our hope is Jesus. And He is *available* to us. We can say, *"It is well with my soul"* today for the same reason we'll be able to say it in the Millennium—God is with us. It's not a perfect world that satisfies; it's Jesus.

Incredibly, there will be those in the Millennium who will honor Jesus only to the legally required degree. They will not worship Him as Lord. They will give in to the part of themselves that desires to be their own god, just as Lucifer did. And as the men of Jerusalem cried out during Jesus' First Coming, so too some will cry out at the end of the Millennium: *"We will not have this man to reign over us."*[503]

The text then tells us that Satan . . .

> **. . . will go out to deceive the nations which are in the four corners of the earth, Gog and Magog, to gather them together to battle, whose number *is* as the sand of the sea.**

Before any of you Bible nerds get excited at the mention of **"Gog and Magog,"** let me just say that I don't think this is a reference to the war described in **Ezekiel 38–39**. **Ezekiel 39** describes the *aftereffects* of that war, and they just don't align with the text here in **Revelation 20** because the earth as we know it *won't exist* after the Millennium comes to an end (we'll talk more about that later).

This verse seems to be simply telling us that the number of people who will side with Satan will be *significant* (**"as the sand of the sea"**) and include people from practically every nation on the earth (**"the nations which are in the four corners of the earth"**).[504]

> ⁹ **They went up on the breadth of the earth and surrounded the camp of the saints and the beloved city.**

---

[503] Luke 19:14.

[504] For more on the differences between Gog and Magog in Ezekiel 38–39 and Revelation 20, see Appendix D.

The **"beloved city"** is, of course, Jerusalem. Satan will plan to attack Jerusalem because it will be where Jesus is reigning over the earth from the throne of David. You might be thinking, *"Haven't we seen this movie before at Armageddon?"* and you'd be right. But maybe there will be more of an epic battle this time around. Let's keep reading and see . . .

And fire came down from God out of heaven and devoured them.

Never mind! And just like that, it'll be *over*.

[10] **The devil, who deceived them, was cast into the lake of fire and brimstone where the beast and the false prophet *are*.**

With Satan's purposes in God's plans fulfilled, he will be cast into the lake of fire forever to join antichrist and the false prophet, who will have already been there for a thousand years.

And they will be tormented day and night forever and ever.

They won't be *destroyed*; they'll be *tormented forever*.

THE GREAT WHITE THRONE JUDGMENT

God doesn't leave anything unfinished. Having given us a thousand years to observe and experience the paradise of the earth under His governance, it will be time for the next order of business. And with that, the earth and the entire universe will *cease to exist*.

Second Peter 3:10 tells us about this moment:

. . . the day of the Lord will come as a thief in the night, in which the heavens will pass away with a great noise, and

the elements will melt with fervent heat; both the earth and the works that are in it will be burned up.

The creative process that birthed the universe will be *reversed*. The universe will be *uncreated* in the same manner it was created—by the Word of God. The One who holds the universe together will simply *let go*.

As our universe comes to an end, the living and the dead are transported into the heavenly realms, where John sees a *cosmic courtroom* and Jesus seated on a white throne, which speaks of His sinless perfection that qualifies Him to righteously judge humanity.

Seeing this and immediately understanding what is about to happen, those who have rejected Jesus will frantically look for anywhere to flee, any hole to crawl into, but will find none.

[11] Then I saw a great white throne and Him who sat on it, from whose face the earth and the heaven fled away. And there was found no place for them.

This is the Great White Throne Judgment, and it is no exaggeration to call it the most tragic and sobering passage in all of Scripture. For in it, those who hate and reject Jesus are brought face-to-face with Him for their *first* and *final* audience with the God of the universe.

[12] And I saw the dead, small and great, standing before God, . . .

Note the reference here to **"the dead."** These are not believers; they are those who died rejecting God and have been in *Hades* awaiting this, their final judgment.

As I mentioned earlier, the glorious news for you and me is that we've *already* been judged because Jesus was judged in our place, for our sins, on the Cross. And I am so thankful for that!

THE SECOND RESURRECTION

In **V.6**, we talked about the **"first resurrection."** We learned it refers to a large *class* of people that includes everyone who belongs to Jesus and is therefore destined to receive a resurrected body, fit for the ages to come. That first resurrection is *completed* at the Second Coming.

To refresh our memories, **V.6** says:

Blessed and holy *is* he who has part in the first resurrection. Over such the second death has no power, but they shall be priests of God and of Christ, and shall reign with Him a thousand years.

We need to discuss why it's called the **"first resurrection."** The phrase implies a *second* resurrection. And indeed, that is what we see unfolding here at the end of the Millennium. In **John 5:24–29**, Jesus explained it this way:

Most assuredly, I say to you, he who hears My word and believes in Him who sent Me has everlasting life, and shall not come into judgment, but has passed from death into life. Most assuredly, I say to you, the hour is coming, and now is, when the dead will hear the voice of the Son of God; and those who hear will live. For as the Father has life in Himself, so He has granted the Son to have life in Himself, and has given Him authority to execute judgment also, because He is the

Son of Man. Do not marvel at this; for the hour is coming in which all who are in the graves will hear His voice and come forth—those who have done good, to the resurrection of life, and those who have done evil, to the resurrection of condemnation.

The **"first resurrection"** in **V.6** is a resurrection to eternal *life*. The second resurrection occurs at the Great White Throne Judgment and is a resurrection to eternal *death*.

The term **"resurrection"** refers to receiving a new body that is fit for the ages to come—a body that will last for eternity. When Jesus was resurrected, He received a new, eternal body.

Paul spoke of the first resurrection and wrote:

...now Christ is risen from the dead, *and* has become the firstfruits of those who have fallen asleep. For since by man came death, by Man also came the resurrection of the dead. For as in Adam all die, even so in Christ all shall be made alive. But each one in his own order: Christ the firstfruits, afterward those who are Christ's at His coming.

—1 Corinthians 15:20–23

When the Bible speaks of resurrection, it is not referring to simply being *conscious*. Nobody in the Bible is referred to as being resurrected in a *disembodied* state. In Scripture, resurrection always includes a *physical body*.

Remember that in **Revelation 6:9–10**, John saw and heard the *disembodied souls* of Tribulation martyrs under the altar in Heaven, crying out to Jesus. But it was only at the first resurrection in **Revelation 20:4** that John says they **"lived."** What did John mean? He meant that they received their new *physical bodies*.

Here's the heavy bottom line:

- The first resurrection sees new eternal bodies given to all who *belong* to Jesus to free us from the sinful desires of our flesh and equip us for the weight of *glory* that awaits us in eternity.

- The second resurrection sees new eternal bodies given to all who *reject* Jesus because their current bodies could not endure the *torment* that awaits them in eternity.

To say it another way:

- Those who *belong* to Jesus will be equipped to enjoy an eternity of *pleasure* in God's presence.

- Those who *reject* Jesus will be equipped to endure an eternity of *torment* that is existence completely separated from God.

Jesus taught this plainly when He told His disciples:

. . . do not fear those who kill the body but cannot kill the soul. But rather fear Him who is able to destroy both soul and body in hell.[505]

—Matthew 10:28

- The first resurrection gives believers new bodies for eternity *with* God.

- The second resurrection gives unbelievers new bodies for eternity *apart* from God.

---

[505] "Gehenna."

That's the truth. And I would not love you if I misled you regarding what the future holds for those who love Jesus and those who reject Him. The issue is submitting your life to God or spitting in His face and choosing to be your own god. These Scriptures are in the Bible because God does not want us to be confused about the gravity of our decision. In the Bible, God's desire for us to be with Him for eternity is repeatedly made clear.

> **The Lord is . . . not willing that any should perish but that all should come to repentance.**
>
> —2 Peter 3:9

But it's *our decision*. God will not force us to love Him. If He did, it would not be love. And so, He will not force us to spend eternity with Him. We must choose for ourselves.

A LOGICAL PROBLEM WITH ANNIHILATIONISM

Those who advocate for *annihilationism*[506] face this logical problem with the second resurrection: It doesn't make sense that God would give unbelievers a new physical body, only to immediately *execute* them, *separating* them from that new physical body.

BACK TO THE TEXT

Continuing in **V.12**, we read:

> **. . . and books were opened. And another book was opened, which is *the Book* of Life. And the dead were**

---

[506] The belief that there is no eternal torment for unbelievers, only an absolute end to their existence.

judged according to their works, by the things which were written in the books. ¹³ The sea gave up the dead who were in it, and Death and Hades delivered up the dead who were in them. And they were judged, each one according to his works.

"Books" are opened, and some seem to contain a record of everything each person has done, neglected to do, spoken, and thought about during their lifetime.[507] Solomon prophesied:

> ... God will bring every work into judgment,
> Including every secret thing,
> Whether good or evil.
> —Ecclesiastes 12:14

Also, among the books will be the Scriptures. In **John 12:48**, Jesus said:

> *He who rejects Me, and does not receive My words, has that which judges him—the word that I have spoken will judge him in the last day.*

Another book that sits open is the ***"Book* of Life."** This book contains the names of everyone who is a citizen of Heaven.[508] If you belong to Jesus, then your name is in there. But the names of all who reject Jesus are not. And because they declined Jesus' offer of salvation—His offer to be judged in their place—they will stand before Him and have their life judged according to *His* standards.

One of the most foolish spiritual beliefs embraced by many

---

[507] Cf. 1 Samuel 2:3; Matthew 12:36–37; 16:27; Jude 1:15.

[508] Cf. Philippians 3:20.

sounds like this: *"I'm just going to do my best to live my life as a good person. Then, whatever's on the other side, I'll be ready."* It's foolish because it assumes that whatever is on the other side of death shares our definition of "good." What would make us think that God is constantly updating His definition of "good" to keep up with ours?

We generally define "good" by figuring out a standard we believe we *can* live up to and *want* to live up to. If we change our minds and want to do something we previously considered to be less than "good," we simply *revise* our definition to align with our new desires.

And we do this because we seem to believe that all we must do to pass whatever test follows death is be able to point out a handful of people who were worse than us. *"I'm not as bad as Hitler. I'm not as bad as that jerk that I worked with. And I can name at least five other people that I'm definitely better than."* We don't consider the possibility that perhaps one of the things that makes God *God* is that He's not like us. The Bible teaches that God is perfect, without sin or flaw, and He intends to judge us according to *His* standards, not ours. God shared this about Himself through the prophet Isaiah:

> ... *"My thoughts are not your thoughts,*
> *Nor are your ways My ways,"* **says the Lord.**
> *"For as the heavens are higher than the earth,*
> *So are My ways higher than your ways,*
> *And My thoughts than your thoughts."*
>
> —Isaiah 55:8–9

Nobody can live up to God's standards. That's why we need Jesus. And it's why the Great White Throne Judgment won't be a *trial;* it'll be a *sentencing.*

ACCOUNTABILITY FOR REVELATION RECEIVED

Scripture also implies the amount of *revelation* each person received in their earthly life will be included under the umbrella of their **"works."** The greater the revelation, the greater the evil of rejecting God, and the worse the eternal torment will be. In **Luke 10**, Jesus sends out 70 of His disciples in pairs to preach the Gospel, and He shares these instructions:

> *... whatever city you enter, and they do not receive you, go out into its streets and say, 'The very dust of your city which clings to us we wipe off against you. Nevertheless know this, that the kingdom of God has come near you.' But I say to you that it will be more tolerable in that Day for Sodom than for that city.*
>
> —Luke 10:10–12

The idea is that because these cities received greater revelation than Sodom and then *rejected* that revelation, their eternal punishment would be *worse* than Sodom's. Jesus continued and addressed cities that had apparently already rejected Him:

> *Woe to you, Chorazin! Woe to you, Bethsaida! For if the mighty works which were done in you had been done in Tyre and Sidon, they would have repented long ago, sitting in sackcloth and ashes. But it will be more tolerable for Tyre and Sidon at the judgment than for you.*
>
> —Luke 10:13–14

Because Jesus did wondrous works in Chorazin and Bethsaida, giving them far greater *revelation* than Tyre and Sidon received, their citizens would be judged by a higher standard. Two chapters later, in **Luke 12,** Jesus shares this observation as part of His explanation of a parable:

> *...that servant who knew his master's will, and did not prepare himself or do according to his will, shall be beaten with many stripes. But he who did not know, yet committed things deserving of stripes, shall be beaten with few. For everyone to whom much is given, from him much will be required; and to whom much has been committed, of him they will ask the more.*
>
> —Luke 12:47–48

You can also make the case that at a certain point in His ministry, Jesus switched to teaching publicly only in parables[509] so that those who wanted to reject Him could not understand what He was saying and, therefore, would not be *accountable* for rejecting even more significant revelation. It was an act of *mercy* by Jesus.

Every nonbeliever will be judged, and their degree of eternal torment will be determined by their works, including the amount of revelation they received.

REFUTING PARTIAL ANNIHILATIONISM REGARDING TIME

I mentioned annihilationism earlier, and I want to address another version of it because some believe that the varying degrees of punishment in the lake of fire will be accomplished through the method of *time*. In other words, the more wicked a person is, the *longer* they will have to spend in the lake of fire before they cease to exist.

---

[509] Cf. Matthew 13:1–15.

The problem with this is the parable Jesus tells in **Luke 16:19–31** of the rich man and Lazarus. In that parable, Jesus teaches that Hades is a place of *torment* for those who have rejected God (**V.24**). Hades is where unbelievers await the Great White Throne Judgment. Jesus also teaches that time in Hades runs *parallel* to time on the earth (**VV.27–31**). That means that right now, there are people in Hades, in torment, who have been there for *thousands of years*. When Hades is emptied for the Great White Throne Judgment, there will be people who were in there for mere *days*, having died just days before the end of the Millennium.

My point is this: Even though Hades is a place of *torment*, God is not concerned that people are spending different lengths of *time* there before the Great White Throne Judgment. That doesn't make sense if God intends to use time to differentiate between levels of punishment in the lake of fire. Why would God use time as a measure of justice in the lake of fire but not in Hades?

Because God is not concerned with the length of time unbelievers are tormented in Hades, it only makes sense to hold to the plain reading of Scripture that the unbeliever's ultimate torment in the lake of fire is indeed *eternal*.

BACK TO THE BOOKS

If anyone judged by Jesus objects and says, *"I'm not perfect, but I certainly don't deserve to go to the lake of fire!"* The Lord will simply say, *"Open the books."* and everything will be laid bare—every good deed done with an ulterior motive, every moment of envy, every evil wished upon another, every lustful thought, every moment of sinful stubbornness, every unnecessary conflict due to pride—*every single sin*. And if that happens, I believe God won't get anywhere close to the end of that person's chapter before they cry out, *"Stop! It's all true. I'm guilty."* When the books are opened, *nobody* will be able to argue their innocence.

The Great White Throne Judgment is *sentencing* to determine the *severity* of punishment. The matter of guilt was determined long ago, as Jesus Himself said in **John 3:18**:

> *He who believes in Him is not condemned; but he who does not believe is condemned already, because he has not believed in the name of the only begotten Son of God.*

In **Revelation 20**, we are told:

> [14] **Then Death and Hades were cast into the lake of fire.**

This is the *death* of death. Satan, his kingdom, and death itself will be **"cast into the lake of fire."** God will create *new* heavens and a *new* earth (we'll see that in **Revelation 21**). As part of that process, sin must be dealt with *definitively*. And the Great White Throne Judgment is a necessary part of the final judgment of sin and death.

This is the second death.

Recall our previous discussion: Those born *once* will die *twice*. Those who are born *twice* will die *once*.

> [15] **And anyone not found written in the Book of Life was cast into the lake of fire.**

That is the sobering truth of the eternity that awaits all who reject the love, grace, and blood of Jesus.

CLOSING THOUGHTS

Let's read a little bit more of what Peter wrote:

> . . . the day of the Lord will come as a thief in the night, in which the heavens will pass away with a great noise, and the elements will melt with fervent heat; both the earth and the works that are in it will be burned up. Therefore, since all these things will be dissolved, what manner *of persons* ought you to be in holy conduct and godliness, looking for and hastening the coming of the day of God, because of which the heavens will be dissolved, being on fire, and the elements will melt with fervent heat? Nevertheless we, according to His promise, look for new heavens and a new earth in which righteousness dwells.
>
> —2 Peter 3:10–13

Every one of us needs to regularly ask ourselves this question posed by Peter:

> **Therefore, since all these things will be dissolved, what manner *of persons* ought you to be in holy conduct and godliness?**

Jesus has told us how this universe will end. He has said that this is not our home. Therefore, how should we live? I've said it before, and I'll repeat it: don't waste your life. Don't spend your life on things destined to **"be dissolved."** Spend your life on *Jesus*. Live for Him radically, not recreationally. And do not get caught up in the cares of this world.[510]

---

[510] Cf. Mark 4:19

In the Book of Deuteronomy, Moses constantly reminds Israel of their history—what God had done for them and the things they would most need to remember in the future. Over and over, Moses says, *"Remember"* or *"Do not forget."* He uses the word "remember" 15 times in Deuteronomy. And one of his appeals is to watch out for spiritual *complacency*. When the struggles are over, when the battles are done, when life starts getting good, *that's* when we're especially vulnerable. In **Deuteronomy 8:11–18,** Moses says this to Israel:

> *Beware that you do not forget the Lord your God by not keeping His commandments, His judgments, and His statutes which I command you today, lest—when you have eaten and are full, and have built beautiful houses and dwell in them; and when your herds and your flocks multiply, and your silver and your gold are multiplied, and all that you have is multiplied; when your heart is lifted up, and you forget the Lord your God who brought you out of the land of Egypt, from the house of bondage; who led you through that great and terrible wilderness, in which were fiery serpents and scorpions and thirsty land where there was no water; who brought water for you out of the flinty rock; who fed you in the wilderness with manna, which your fathers did not know, that He might humble you and that He might test you, to do you good in the end—then you say in your heart, "My power and the might of my hand have gained me this wealth."*
>
> *And you shall remember the Lord your God, for it is He who gives you power to get wealth . . .*

If you've been around the Church for a while, you've seen this type of thing play out. People finally get something they've longed for, and they just *tune out*. They shift into cruise control in their walk with Jesus. They become complacent and lose their spiritual hunger and zeal.

I've seen it happen when people get into a romantic relationship they've longed for. I've seen it happen when people start having kids. I've seen it happen when a career or business finally starts taking off. I've seen it happen when people retire.

We get *distracted* and *complacent*, and God slips down the priority list. If we allow ourselves to fall into that type of spiritual malaise, we can waste *years* living for meaningless things. We can waste entire *seasons* of our lives.

Nate Saint was the pilot that flew Jim Elliot and three others into the remote Ecuadorian jungle in 1956, where they hoped to reach an isolated tribe with the Gospel. All five team members were murdered by that tribe when they first encountered them. (If you don't know what happened after that, you should read the story because it's *incredible*.)

Here are two quotes from Nate Saint that I think are worth reflecting on:

> *People who do not know the Lord ask why in the world we waste our lives as missionaries. They forget that they too are expending their lives. They forget that when their lives are spent and the bubble has burst they will have nothing of eternal significance to show for the years they have wasted.*[511]

---

[511] Russell T. Hitt, *Jungle Pilot* (Grand Rapids, Michigan: Discovery House Publishers, 1997), 142.

> *When life's flight is over, and we unload our cargo at the other end, the fellow who got rid of unnecessary weight will have the most valuable cargo to present to the Lord.*[512]

Don't waste your life. If you become great at anything, let it be *loving Jesus*.

The One who will fill you with joy and peace in the Millennium offers His joy and peace to you *today*. Jesus will be our source *then*, and He is our source *now*. Even a perfect world won't satisfy many in the Millennium because *nothing* satisfies apart from knowing Jesus. If you are holding on to the hope that something changing in your life will make everything better, you are in for disappointment. It may make your life easier. It may make your life more enjoyable. But it won't satisfy your soul. Only Jesus can do that.

If you've been chasing fulfillment anywhere other than in Jesus, let me encourage you to take some time to repent and confess to the Lord:

> *"I'm so sorry for placing my hope in something other than You. Forgive me, God. What I really need is You—more and more of You. Please give me You."*

Is your name written in the Book of Life? I don't want to create unnecessary doubt, but you need to be *sure*.

In eternity, everyone will be given what they truly desire. The sick man who declines the help of a doctor is *choosing* sickness. So too, the man who rejects the invitation to step into the light *chooses* the darkness. The man who says, *"I don't want God"* is *choosing* an eternity without Him. Jesus, on the other hand, said, *"I am choosing*

---

[512] Hitt, *Jungle Pilot*, 157.

you, even though it will cost Me My life." Jesus died for you, so that if you want to know Him, you can. If you want to be part of His family, you can. If you want to know His love, peace, and joy, you can. But it's *your choice*. Everybody will get what they want in eternity. The only catch is that you must make your choice *before* you get there. This life is the only chance you get. And you have all the information you need to make the wise choice.

Finally, may this chapter remind us how much the lost need Jesus. They are perishing and destined for destruction unless they repent and turn to Him. Pray for those the Lord has put in your life who don't yet know Him. Ask the Holy Spirit to illuminate opportunities for you to share the Gospel with them. And if you've grown cold or callous to the fate of those whose names are not written in the Book of Life, ask the Lord to give you *His* heart for them once again. Ask Him to stir your spirit with *His* love for them.

REVELATION 21:1-5

THE HOPE OF HEAVEN

The reality of Heaven and eternity with Jesus has provided hope and motivation to the believer since the advent of the Church on the Day of Pentecost:

> Heaven is where we see Jesus face-to-face.
> Heaven is where those who love Him store their treasure.
> Heaven is where our inheritance awaits.
> Heaven is where we receive new bodies, free from sin and frailty.
> Heaven is where our citizenship resides.
> And Heaven is the home we were made for.

If you love Jesus, then your heart *yearns* for Heaven. The Apostle Paul exhorted the Colossians:

> **If then you were raised with Christ, seek those things which are above, where Christ is, sitting at the right hand of God. Set your mind on things above, not on things on the earth.**
>
> —Colossians 3:1–2

The Apostle Peter summed up the longing in the heart of every believer when he wrote:

> **... we, according to His promise, look for new heavens and a new earth in which righteousness dwells.**
>
> —2 Peter 3:13

Revelation 21 and **22** are *travel brochures* for Heaven. These final chapters should spark our imaginations with thoughts of the Lord and eternity in His presence and Kingdom. So, let's meditate on and dream about Heaven together.

The Scriptures provide only a few snippets of information about Heaven. There is much mystery, and I think there are two main reasons for that:

1. We currently lack the capacity and ability to *fathom* all that Heaven will be.

   Can you imagine describing a new color to someone if that color had no relationship to any they'd seen before—or if it wasn't a lighter or darker version of anything that currently exists? It would be impossible!

2. If you're a parent, you know (or will soon learn) the special joy of *surprising* your children with something wonderful.

   Be it a Christmas or birthday gift or something entirely out of the blue, there's not much better than surprising your children with something they love. Their reaction blesses your heart deeply. And at that moment when they're overwhelmed with joy, the *cost* of that gift does not compare to the joy you feel because their joy is *priceless* to you. We get that from being made in the image of God. Because it's how He feels about *us*. Do you know what is greater than the suffering Jesus endured on the Cross? The joy He experiences when sinners repent and are adopted into His family. God *delights* in blessing you.

I remember one Christmas when we were living in South Florida, and we got our whole family annual passes to Disney World. When our kids opened those cards on Christmas morning, there was much dancing and jumping and screaming; it was the best!

I remember a couple of years after we planted our church in Vancouver, Canada, and our family hadn't had a vacation for several years. We didn't have the money for it, so we told our kids to pray (because God can't seem to turn down the prayers of children—pro tip). Two families from thousands of miles away sent us checks to pay for a vacation. Charlene and I planned the whole trip and kept it a secret. I rented an RV, parked it in front of our house, and then took the kids into it and sat them down at the kitchen table. And then I got to tell them,

"You know how you've been praying for our family to go on vacation this summer? Well, God said 'Yes,' and we're going on vacation . . . **today.** *Not only that, but we're going for one day, two days, three days . . . "*

And I counted up using my fingers to 11 days and told them all the places on the west coast we were going to. And they were *incredible* places. I'll never forget their eyes and smiles getting bigger and bigger and bigger as I revealed all the details. It blessed me as a father on that special, deep level. I believe God can't wait to surprise us with the wonders of Heaven and the ages to come. He *can't wait* to experience our joy with us. So, I suspect He's saving some of the best parts as a surprise.

I don't know what your expectations of Heaven are. There have been a lot of terrible descriptions of Heaven over the years, and I can tell you with certainty you will *not* be transformed into a naked harp-playing baby for eternity!

Here's another terrible description of Heaven I've heard before: *"It'll be like a church service that never ends!"* Perhaps you're thinking, *"I've already been to several of those."* I love church services, and I love our church. But even I wouldn't want to go to a church service that never ends! I love church, but it's not Heaven. So, let's find out what Heaven is.

A NEW REALITY

We've learned that our universe will be *destroyed* at the end of the Millennial Kingdom. Jesus told His disciples:

> **Heaven and earth will pass away, but My words will by no means pass away.**
>
> —Luke 21:33

In biblical cosmology, there is a distinction between *Heaven* and the *heavenlies*—also known as *the heavens* or *the heavenly realm*. Heaven is the dwelling place of God and where His throne resides. The heavens, heavenlies, or heavenly realms refer to the supernatural dimension in which the spiritual world exists. Heaven exists in the heavenlies but is distinct from it. The heavenlies is the realm where angels and fallen angels currently wage war, and the location of the

Divine Council—the place where Yahweh meets with Satan (as depicted in **Job 1**), the gods of the nations, and mighty angels like the **"watchers"** mentioned in **Daniel 4:17**.

At the end of the Millennial Kingdom, our physical universe, the heavenlies, and even death and Hades will be destroyed. Heaven, the dwelling place of God, will *not* be destroyed. It will become part of a *new* creation.

V.1 tells us what happens next:

> ¹ **Now I saw a new heaven and a new earth, for the first heaven and the first earth had passed away.**

God will create a *brand-new* earth and heavenly realm. Why? Because our universe and the current heavenly realm have a history of *sin*. Our universe is unclean because of earth's history of sin which traces back to Adam and Eve's rebellion in Eden. The heavenly realm is tainted because it was the location of Lucifer's rebellion, and it's where he has been accusing us before God **"day and night"**[513] in the Divine Council. **Job 15:15** tells us that currently:

> **. . . the heavens are not pure in His sight . . .**

The Lord intends to give sin and death *no place* in His new creation. They shall be stricken from the record in every sense of the phrase. Things will not simply be refurbished, for **Isaiah 65:17** tells us the Lord declares:

> *. . . behold, I create new heavens and a new earth;*
> *And the former shall not be remembered or come to mind.*

---

[513] Revelation 12:10.

The word used in Isaiah for **"create"** is the Hebrew word "bara." It's the same word used in **Genesis 1:1,** and it means *"to create from nothing"* *("ex nihilo" in Latin).* Unlike us, God does not need raw materials to create. He does not require a blank canvas, paint, or a brush. He can create from absolutely nothing. God doesn't need to refurbish the heavens and the earth because He's not limited to working with what already exists. And so, once again, He will create something *brand-new.* **V.1** says:

Also there was no more sea.

What?! No beaches in the new heavens and the new earth? Not necessarily. It says, **"no more sea,"** not "no more water." We'll learn soon that there is a *river,*[514] so we know there's *water* in this new creation. All this verse means is that whatever there is instead of sea is *better.* Whatever there is does not leave sand in your cracks and crevices when you're done swimming in it. It doesn't divide people from each other. It doesn't sanitize the world's waste because there is nothing impure in eternity. It doesn't pose any type of danger. Whatever is in Heaven is *better.* Hopefully, we're all able to just trust God with stuff like this by this point. And remember, those who belong to Jesus will have *a thousand years* to enjoy the best beaches on the old earth during the Millennium.

What this sentence is really addressing is what the sea represented in the Hebrew mind. The Jews were not seafaring people. They didn't spread out across the Middle East by navigating the seas and waterways. They viewed such bodies of water as representations of *chaos* and *death*—places where dark powers exercised great power.

---

[514] Cf. Revelation 22:1–2.

The Hebrew reading **V.1** would interpret it as another way of God saying there will be no more chaos, death, or fear in His new creation.

Additionally, both the Hebrew and surrounding cultures at this time viewed the sea as a place where things are *buried* and *concealed*, and where things *disappear*. We'll see in later verses of **Chapter 21** that one of the defining traits of God's new creation is its *transparency*—literally and figuratively. There will be no secrets in it because there will be no sin and, therefore, no shame. And shame is the reason we keep secrets. In the new heavens and new earth, there will be no reason for anyone or anything to ever be hidden.

> **² Then I, John, saw the holy city, New Jerusalem, coming down out of heaven from God, prepared as a bride adorned for her husband.**

The New Jerusalem is what we refer to today as "Heaven." It's the city of God where He is currently sitting on His throne. It's the city Jesus referred to as His *"Father's house"* and the place He told His disciples He is preparing for those who love Him.[515]

The New Jerusalem is currently *isolated* from the heavens and the earth because they are tainted by sin. But in this new creation, there will be *new* heavens and a *new* earth, untainted by sin, thereby enabling the New Jerusalem, the new heavens, and the new earth to be *connected*. Heaven will *join* to the new earth because the new creation will be as pure and holy as Heaven itself. **Hebrews 12:22–24** declares to believers:

> ...you have come to Mount Zion and to the city of the living God, the heavenly Jerusalem, to an innumerable

---

[515] Cf. John 14:2.

company of angels, to the general assembly and church of the firstborn *who are* registered in heaven, to God the Judge of all, to the spirits of just men made perfect, to Jesus the Mediator of the new covenant . . .

We'll get more detail on the New Jerusalem later in this chapter but for now, just know that the New Jerusalem is where we will *live* in eternity. It'll be our forever home.

As John beholds this breathtaking city, filled with people made beautiful by the Lord, he compares what he sees to the moment a bride is revealed to the guests at a wedding. You ladies who are married are beautiful today. But you looked *unbelievably* beautiful on your wedding day. Many husbands remember, as I do, the moment the bride walked into the room at your wedding, and you thought, *"How in the world did I pull this off? How did I get **her** to marry **me**?!"* She was simply *radiant*.

The way the room *gasps* when everyone sees the bride's beauty revealed is how John describes the revealing of the New Jerusalem, full of the saints of God. Her beauty takes his breath away.

We don't know how exactly it happened, but **Hebrews 11:9–10** tells us that Abraham got a glimpse, a *revelation*, of the New Jerusalem:

By faith he dwelt in the land of promise as *in* a foreign country, dwelling in tents with Isaac and Jacob, the heirs with him of the same promise; for he waited for the city which has foundations, whose builder and maker *is* God.

Abraham lived to 175 and spent most of those years as one of the wealthiest, if not *the* wealthiest, men on earth. But because of this glimpse of the New Jerusalem, he never built a house for himself. He could have built a palace, but after seeing what God had in store for him, his attitude became, *"What's the point? Any home here is a shack compared to what the Lord has prepared for me in Heaven."*

As John beholds what Abraham had seen before him, he continues:

> **³ And I heard a loud voice from heaven saying, *"Behold, the tabernacle of God is with men, and He will dwell with them, and they shall be His people. God Himself will be with them and be their God."***

Notice that the Lord wants us to know that He will *dwell* among us. We will see Him, speak with Him, behold Him, hear Him, fellowship with Him, worship Him, and serve Him. **John 1:14** speaks of Jesus:

> **. . . the Word became flesh and dwelt among us, and we beheld His glory, the glory as of the only begotten of the Father, full of grace and truth.**

In the original language, the phrase **"dwelt among us"** means "tabernacled among us." As accessible as Jesus was to His disciples during His earthly ministry, He will be even *more* accessible to us in eternity even though He will be in His fully glorified state.

The day is coming when even *faith* will be fulfilled. What I mean by that is that the day is coming when faith won't be necessary because the Lord will be with us in such a tangible way. I don't need faith to believe that my cup of coffee exists because I'm holding it right now. That will be the nature of our relationship with God in eternity. You need faith for what you cannot yet fully see. But in eternity, we will see God face-to-face and fellowship with Him. Faith will no longer be required because it will be *fulfilled*.

OUR GOOD PASSIONS STILL INTACT

I love the phrase **"with men"** in **V.3** because it tells us that we don't turn into some kind of other species in eternity. We will still be ourselves, but we will be the *fully redeemed* version of ourselves.

I believe that in Heaven, our God-given passions are still intact because they're part of who God created us to be. I don't know anybody who has fulfilled all their God-given passions. Everybody I know, deep down, wishes they could have devoted more time and energy to their passions or fulfilled more of their potential. Maybe you feel like there's a song, a book, a machine, a building, a car, a painting, a garden—something inside you that you just can't seem to get out in this life. For nearly all of us, the limitations of *time* get in the way—work, raising children, and all the things that come with *life*.

When you're young, the word "potential" is exciting. When you're older, it stings a little because it reminds you of the things you *could've* done in your life—the things you'd *love* to do that just didn't happen, for whatever reason. Why would God put those desires in us if He knew they wouldn't be fulfilled? I believe it's because, in the ages to come, *they will be*. They are part of who we were created to be.

In the Millennium and the new creation that follows it, I believe all those unfulfilled God-given desires will be *loosed*. Time won't be an issue. Resources won't be an issue. Distractions won't be an issue. In redeemed reality, God's people will create, design, and build in an atmosphere that is stimulating and electric yet simultaneously serene and restful.

KNOWING PEOPLE IN HEAVEN

In Heaven, we will recognize our loved ones who loved the Lord. After the death of his infant son, David said, *"I shall go to him, but he shall not return to me."*[516] Not only that, but it seems we will *inherently* know who everybody is. At the Transfiguration, Peter said to Jesus:

> ... *"Lord, it is good for us to be here; if You wish, let us make here three tabernacles: one for You, one for Moses, and one for Elijah."*
>
> —Matthew 17:4

Even though Moses and Elijah weren't in their resurrected bodies yet and even though they had never met them, Peter, James, and John *recognized* them. This brings me great comfort because I am terrible with names and faces. And it is awful being a pastor who wants to make people feel loved and valued but can't remember faces and names!

> *"Great to meet you! How did you find out about the church?"*
> *"I've been coming here for three years."*
> *"And you've been a **blessing** for three years. Excuse me; I think I hear my wife calling."*

In Heaven, we will inherently know who everybody is. There won't be any awkwardness for people like me. I'll never have someone say, *"Hey Jeff!"* only for me to respond, *"Heeeeyyyyyy ... brother."*

I suggest we won't really know *anyone until* we get to Heaven. Maybe certain "challenging" Christian brothers and sisters come to

---

[516] 2 Samuel 12:23.

mind when we talk about Heaven because you immediately think, *"How am I going to avoid **them** for eternity?"* Listen, they're going to be fully redeemed. Who we truly are, who we were created by God to be, will be *unlocked* in eternity. Our full potential is going to be realized and it will be *glorious*. And when you encounter *those* people in their fully redeemed state, you're going to think, *"I love this person! They're amazing!"* And by the way, people will have the same experience when they get to know the real you and the real me!

Nobody wakes up in the morning and thinks to themselves, *"I wonder how I can alienate everyone who cares about me."* Or *"I wonder how I can drive everyone who interacts with me crazy with my annoying habits and communication style."* Or *"I wonder how I can make people dislike me by constantly complaining about everything."* The more you get to know people, the more you realize there's a reason why we are the way we are. I'm not saying there's always a *justification*; I'm saying there's always an *explanation*. Often there are negative factors that have impacted and shaped people's lives as well as positive factors that are missing from their lives.

But in eternity, all that *baggage* will be removed. All the junk is going to fall away. And when those who love the Lord are *freed* from all that, we will become the people Jesus created us to be. We will be our true selves for the first time. In Heaven, everyone will be beautiful in every sense of the word. And I promise you won't have to avoid anybody in eternity. There will be no guilt, no shame, no awkwardness, and no weirdos—just amazing people, redeemed and glorified by the grace of God. In Heaven, we'll bump into those people who used to rub us the wrong way and say, *"Wow! Look what the Lord has done! You're no longer a giant pain in the . . .* " There's no cussing in Heaven, but you get the idea.

The Apostle Paul wrote about the effect the Cross of Christ should have on how we view people here and now:

> **. . . from now on, we regard no one according to the flesh.**
>
> —2 Corinthians 5:16

That is, those who love Jesus should not view their Christian brothers and sisters based on who they are *in the flesh* presently, but rather who they are *in Christ* and who they are destined to become in eternity. I wish I were better at doing that. But I know the Holy Spirit is changing me, bit by bit and day by day, and I welcome His work in my life to make my perspective more Heavenly minded.

LOVING THE LORD MORE THAN THOSE WE'VE LOST

Look at **V.3** again:

> ***Behold, the tabernacle of God is with men, and He will dwell with them, and they shall be His people. God Himself will be with them and be their God.***

Notice that the emphasis is on God being with us and us being with God. We will recognize and know our loved ones in Heaven, but our *focus* will be on Jesus.

It's OK to long for Heaven so that you can be reunited with loved ones who loved the Lord. But it's not OK to long for that *more* than we long for Jesus. The presence of those loved ones in Heaven will be wonderful. But our joy shouldn't be based solely on the fact we will see them again. Instead, our joy should be that we will behold Jesus *together!*

I share this because I love you. If you're longing for Heaven so that you can be reunited with loved ones, just be sure that you don't allow that longing to exceed your longing to be with the Lord. Because if you do, you will have turned that loved one into an *idol*. And if they loved Jesus, that's the last thing they would want you to do with their memory. What a blessing it is that those who love Jesus will be reunited in His presence to enjoy Him *together*.

I don't know how anybody is supposed to read the next verse aloud and keep it together:

> ⁴ ***And God will wipe away every tear from their eyes; there shall be no more death, nor sorrow, nor crying. There shall be no more pain, for the former things have passed away.***

Some say this verse means there will be tears in Heaven that God needs to wipe away, and they speculate as to the *reason* for those tears—missed evangelism opportunities, regret over not living more radically for the Lord, and so forth. But that's not what this verse is saying. This verse says that *because* **"the former things have passed away,"** nothing will exist that can *cause* death, sorrow, or tears. Every source of past and potential heartache will be destroyed with the old earth and old heavens.

I read this on Twitter[517] recently:

> *All the sadness believers feel when leaving dear friends, all the nostalgia for days gone by that God blessed, all the pain that*

---

[517] @ostrachan on April 7, 2022.

rocks you when death strikes loved ones—all of it is a call from a distant land where you never part, you never mourn, and most of all, you never die.

No more sadness. No more disappointment. No more bitterness. No more depression. No more anxiety. No more fear. Our existence will be sorrow-proof. In Heaven, we won't remember our sins and our failures. Neither will we remember those who rejected the Lord—something that is both encouraging and sobering. Remember **Isaiah 65:17**. The Lord said:

> **... behold, I create new heavens and a new earth: and the former shall not be remembered, nor come into mind.**

In our earthly lives, there are seemingly *endless* sources of sorrow that could appear at any moment—issues in friendships, marriages, and families; addiction; poverty; sickness; death; and on and on the list goes. This will be news to some, but the Bible does not say that everything happens for a reason. As I've shared previously, the Bible teaches that Satan is the **"god of this age,"**[518] and Jesus has *not yet* begun to actively rule the nations. He has the authority to do so, but He has not yet *exercised* that authority. That happens in the Millennium. *This* is the promise God gives in Scripture:

> **... all things work together for good to those who love God, to those who are the called according to *His* purpose.**
> —Romans 8:28

That verse doesn't teach that everything happens for a reason,

---

[518] 2 Corinthians 4:4.

nor that only good things will happen to those who love Jesus. It says that *whatever* happens to those who love Jesus in this life, God will do something good through it. When a loved one dies unnaturally early, when sickness strikes a child, when jobs are lost, when abuse happens, and when tragedy strikes, God can and will pull something good out of all that sorrow—even when it seems hopeless. He will create a testimony. He will empower you to minister to others who have gone through the same thing. He will shake people out of complacency and make them realize the importance of eternity. He will store up treasures in Heaven for you. He will humble and shape your character to become more like Jesus. He will reveal Himself to you in a fresh way and give you greater wisdom.

God promises that our hurt and pain are never wasted. And that is a *blessing*. God ascribes meaning and significance to the trials of a believer. In contrast, the trials of the unbeliever are *meaningless*.

Romans 8:28 helps me because it reminds me that **Revelation 21:4** is talking about *Heaven*, not earth. The place where there is *"no more pain"* is *Heaven*, not earth. And this is so important because there are too many churches teaching people *lies* by leading them to believe that if you love Jesus, then everything in your earthly life will work out great. And that's not true. That's not what the Bible teaches. And it's not how our lives are going to play out. When people buy into such false teaching, they end up disillusioned with Christianity when they (inevitably) encounter trials and seasons of suffering.

Please hear me on this: *This is not Heaven.* I have walked with many people through times of tragedy, and when trouble strikes, we all naturally want to know *why*. And sometimes, we do each other a great disservice by trying to come up with baseless explanations.

A lot of the time, the reason is simply that this is a fallen world, not Heaven. And that's why we *long* for Heaven.

The bottom *will* fall out of your life one day, and it'll happen more than once. When I understand the difference between this life and Heaven, I won't get angry with God when tragedy strikes my life. I'll remember that Jesus told His Disciples, *"In the world you will have tribulation,"*[519] and we are still *"In the world."* This isn't Heaven. Don't expect it to be. Heaven is where **V.4** takes place:

> *... God will wipe away every tear from their eyes; there shall be no more death, nor sorrow, nor crying. There shall be no more pain, for the former things have passed away.*

ALL THINGS NEW

Now we come to **V.5**. A verse so great and glorious, I cannot find the words to sufficiently expound upon it:

> ⁵ **Then He who sat on the throne said,** *"Behold, I make all things new."* **And He said to me,** *"Write, for these words are true and faithful."*

John is seemingly so overwhelmed by all he's seeing that God has to snap him out of his state of shock and awe by saying, *"John! Write!"*

This verse means the world to me. And I want to tell you about the moment this verse came alive most powerfully in my life. It was early in the fall years ago on one of our family days that we try to take once a week, where we do something together as a family. We

---

[519] John 16:33.

headed down to nearby White Rock Beach. It was low tide, and we had the beach practically to ourselves because while it was clear and sunny, it was still a bit windy and cold. But, as is generally the case, children don't care.

We blinked, and they were all soaking wet from running through the shallow pools of water left behind by the tide. And they were running as only children do—for no apparent reason. Children get this surge of excitement and joy, and they just run! I was smiling and watching them play because if you're a parent, you know that your child's joy brings you joy.

When Caleb was younger, he *loved* weapons. He still likes them, but he couldn't get enough of them when he was younger. On this day, he found a stick almost as tall as him and decided that it was his lightsaber. I remember watching him play; he was utterly in his own world. He was fighting Sith lords, running, spinning around, splashing in the water, laughing, smiling—just having the time of his life.

And as I found myself alone for a minute, I was suddenly overwhelmed by *deep grief*, and a wave of profound sadness came over me. Because as I observed Caleb's unabashed joy, I realized that I didn't know how to be that kind of happy anymore. He was experiencing a level of joy that was beyond my grasp because he still possessed a measure of *innocence* that I no longer had.

Living in this fallen world has *weathered* me like a coastal rock exposed to the endless pounding of the ocean's waves. Life—just the process of *living*—wears you down and *steals* from you. Obviously, children are still fallen beings, but they're closer to Eden because, most of the time, they haven't been exposed to very many storms yet. I think that's why there's something so *magical* about children's laughter; it's a sound that comes from a place we don't know how to find anymore because life in a fallen world has robbed us of the natural optimism and joy that was once ours.

In eternity, Jesus will declare, **"Behold, I make all things new."** And His statement will include *us*. We will get back all that was lost in Eden and more. We will get back what we lost before we were even born. We will be made *new*. We've all been shaped by our life experiences in a much deeper way than we realize. What would you be like:

> If they had never made that comment?
> If that abuse had never taken place?
> If they hadn't broken your heart?
> If you had never done that one thing you constantly wish you could take back?

Now, take it even further: What if you'd never felt embarrassment . . . ever? Never been criticized? What if you'd never experienced disappointment? Who would you be? How would you live? How would you laugh? How would you sing? What would you share out loud? How would you *love?*

We will be *young* again. We will have knowledge, wisdom, and understanding, but we will be as free as children who have only known love, joy, peace, and safety. We'll bear no scars of any kind—mental, emotional, spiritual, or physical.

We'll never worry about the future. We'll never worry about *having* enough or *being* enough. We'll never worry about messing up because that won't even be possible in Heaven.

We won't be able to be self-conscious because we'll be so consumed with *Jesus* that there will be no room to be consumed with ourselves.

Heaven is the hope of all who hope in Christ, and our hope is not misplaced. Because Jesus bears the scars of the Cross forever, we will be healed from our scars forever.

CLOSING THOUGHTS

As we've dreamed about Heaven, I want to remind you that Jesus told John, *"these words are true and faithful."* The question is, do you believe Jesus? I'm not asking if you believe *in* Jesus. I'm asking if you *believe* what Jesus has told you about Heaven. Because if you do, it will be evident in how you live your life. Abraham *believed* God, and he lived his whole life in tents, wandering the Promised Land because He was convinced of the reality of the New Jerusalem. Does your life serve as evidence that you *believe* what Jesus says in His Word about Heaven? In **Matthew 24:35**, Jesus promised:

Heaven and earth will pass away, but My words will by no means pass away.

Hebrews 11:13–16 says this of the Old Testament saints:

These all died in faith, not having received the promises, but having seen them afar off were assured of them, embraced *them* and confessed that they were strangers and pilgrims on the earth. For those who say such things declare plainly that they seek a homeland. . . . they desire a better, that is, a heavenly *country*. Therefore God is not ashamed to be called their God, for He has prepared a city for them.

If you love Jesus, then He has prepared a place for you. More than that, He has prepared an *eternity* for you. And He has done so for the same reason He lived a perfect life on your behalf, the same reason He suffered and died on your behalf, and the same reason He rose from the grave in glory on your behalf—because He loves you. Because *your* joy brings *Him* joy. And He knows there is no greater joy than knowing Him and being known by Him. Therefore, He has moved Heaven and earth to make it so for you and me.

Jesus is *wonderful*. What more can we say?

REVELATION 21:6-27

THE NEW JERUSALEM

As we pick things up in **V.6**, we hear God speaking from His throne. Jesus and the Father are on the throne together, and we can reasonably assume that the Holy Spirit is with them. They speak with one voice in **VV.6–9**.[520] John writes:

> ⁶ **And He [God] said to me,** *"It is done! I am the Alpha and the Omega, the Beginning and the End.*

What a moment! On the Cross, Jesus cried out, *"It is finished!"*[521] Here God declares, *"It is done!"* The redemptive work that began with the cry of a newborn baby in the little town of Bethlehem reaches its zenith with these triumphant words. Truly, His ways are higher than ours, His plans unfathomably greater, His vision infinitely more glorious, and His wonders beyond our comprehension.

We can enjoy new *spiritual* life right now. But **V.6** is the moment

---

[520] Jesus refers to Himself as "the Alpha and the Omega" in Revelation 1:8 and 11; He uses the same title in V.6. The Father clearly speaks in V.7.

[521] John 19:30.

when God will declare that *all* things have been made new—physically, spiritually, biologically—everything! It's the moment Paul spoke of when he wrote:

> **Then *comes* the end, when He [Jesus] delivers the kingdom to God the Father, when He puts an end to all rule and all authority and power. For He must reign till He has put all enemies under His feet. The last enemy *that* will be destroyed *is* death ... Now when all things are made subject to Him, then the Son Himself will also be subject to Him** [God the Father] **who put all things under Him, that God may be all in all.**
>
> —1 Corinthians 15:24–26, 28

The words *"It is done!"* announce the end of the age of our universe and the dawn of a *new* age—a new chapter in the incredible book of the story of God. What happens in that next chapter? A new story begins. And all I can tell you about it is that it will be *wonderful.*

Have you ever been out somewhere far from the city lights, looked up, and glimpsed the universe's glory? If Jesus could create all the stars, planets, and beauty of this earth in six days, I wonder what He has prepared for us in 2,000 years?

The Apostle Paul tells us that:

> *... Eye has not seen, nor ear heard,*
> *Nor have entered into the heart of man*
> *The things which God has prepared for those who love Him.*
>
> —1 Corinthians 2:9

Jesus said in **John 14:2b:**

I go to prepare a place for you.

For you, *personally*. For me, *personally*. I don't know if we'll have rooms or houses, but I suspect there will be some type of space that is *tailored* for each of us and will reflect God's intimate knowledge of who He created us to be. I know this with certainty: we will immediately realize that we never really knew what home felt like before we arrived in Heaven.

Ladies, as incredible as it sounds, you won't want to change *anything* in your eternal home, ever! You won't want to move a sofa or change the paint color—it'll be *perfect*. And all the men will say, "Truly, the Lord has done great things."

God continues in **V.6** and tells John:

> *I will give of the fountain of the water of life freely to him who thirsts.*

"The water of life" is an idiom for the Holy Spirit given to every person who places their faith in Jesus. God is telling John that all this is for anyone who wants it—anyone who thirsts for life and, most importantly, for more of the Lord Himself. Those who experience eternal life will be those who *desire* and *long* for it. Jesus promised this in the Sermon on the Mount:

> *Blessed are those who hunger and thirst for righteousness,*
> *For they shall be filled.*
>
> —Matthew 5:6

On the last day of the Feast of Tabernacles . . .

> *. . . Jesus stood and cried out, saying, "If anyone thirsts, let him come to Me and drink. He who believes in Me, as the Scripture has said, out of his heart will flow rivers of living water."*
>
> —John 7:37–38

Jesus told the Samaritan woman at the well:

Whoever drinks of this water [earthly water] *will thirst again, but whoever drinks of the water that I shall give him will never thirst. But the water that I shall give him will become in him a fountain of water springing up into everlasting life.*
—John 4:13–14

Heaven is where these promises of Jesus are fully realized. In Heaven, we'll *always* be full of the Spirit. We'll *always* be full of His peace, joy, and life. In eternity there will be no striving; there will just be *life everywhere*.

⁷ He who overcomes shall inherit all things, and I will be his God and he shall be My son.

Eternal life is for those who desire it and those who *overcome*. How do we overcome? Let's remind ourselves once more of the words our brother John penned in his first epistle:

Who is he who overcomes the world, but he who . . .

Does enough good works? *No.*
Has a perfectly consistent devotional life? *No.*
Achieves mastery over every sin in their life? *No.*

Who is he who overcomes the world, but he who believes that Jesus is the Son of God?
—1 John 5:5

The Christian life is drinking the living water of eternal life freely offered by Jesus and then allowing it to naturally affect your life. There is a difference between a *dehydrated* person and a *hydrated* person. In the same way, there is a definite difference between the person who has drunk the living water of eternal life (receiving the Holy Spirit), and the person who has not.

How do we overcome? We believe **"that Jesus is the Son of God"** and express that belief by accepting His offer of eternal life. That's it. Salvation is the gift of God. *He* did the work so that none of us could boast[522] that we earned even the tiniest part of our salvation. The Lord did it *all*. Our job is to simply *believe it* and *receive* it. And by joining our lives to Jesus, He makes us overcomers with Him.

OUR INHERITANCE

There are multiple places in the New Testament where it refers to what awaits us in eternity as our "inheritance."[523] We've talked before about how, unbelievably, it's Jesus' desire and intent to share all He has with us in the ages to come. God tells John that all the beauty He is beholding in this new creation belongs to those who belong to Jesus.

We don't know what our *tasks* will be in this new age. We know it'll be amazing, and we also know that how we live our earthly lives will impact what we are entrusted with in eternity. We're all in training. That's why James was not blowing smoke when he wrote:

> **My brethren, count it all joy when you fall into various trials, knowing that the testing of your faith produces patience.**
>
> **—James 1:2–3**

---

[522] Cf. Ephesians 2:8–9.

[523] Cf. Acts 20:32; 26:18; Ephesians 1:11, 14, 18; Colossians 1:12; 3:24; Hebrews 9:15; 1 Peter 1:4.

Are you in a trial? Rejoice! You're in training for the ages to come! Set your heart and mind on the task of *passing* this trial. Understand that how we walk through trials has *eternal* ramifications. We're destined to rule with Jesus. We're destined to reign with Christ. We're destined to *"inherit all things."* The assignment awaiting us is significant, to say the least. Therefore, it makes sense that our preparation and training would *also* be significant.

Paul writes in **Romans 8:15–17**:

> **... you did not receive the spirit of bondage again to fear, but you received the Spirit of adoption by whom we cry out, "*Abba,*[524] *Father."* The Spirit Himself bears witness with our spirit that we are children of God, and if children, then heirs—heirs of God and joint heirs with Christ, if indeed we suffer with *Him,* that we may also be glorified together.**

This life is *preparation* for our eternal inheritance.

V.7 ends with this beautiful promise: *"I will be his God and he shall be My son."* What a fantastic thing it is that the Almighty God of Heaven and earth has adopted us as His children. Out of all the relationships He could've constructed for us, He chose the one where we call Him "Dad" for eternity. Jesus suffered and died so that we could become His brothers and sisters through adoption. If you haven't figured it out yet, God really, really loves you!

If you've been blessed with a good earthly father, you may be able to recall those few golden years when, as a child, your father's presence made you feel *completely safe*—those few years when you

---

[524] Aramaic for "Father."

didn't ever worry when your dad was around because you knew that if a gang of thugs showed up to harm you, he'd singlehandedly beat them all up and throw them in jail. We're going to feel *that* safe and secure *forever*. And not out of ignorance or naiveté, but because our Heavenly Father will have created a reality free from *anything* that could cause sorrow. We'll never look over our shoulders again.

We know and understand that God lacks nothing. He needs nothing. But that doesn't mean there's nothing that *blesses* Him. God made us to be His children for eternity because, as staggering as it sounds, God is *blessed* by His children. If you're a parent, you know your kids can bless you in an indescribable way. When you see them overcome a fear or challenge and when you see them *win*, it blesses you. We get that from being made in the image of God. Indeed, we will be *blessed* in eternity. But incredibly, we will also *bless God* in eternity. Our loving and gracious Heavenly Father will be surrounded by His children and will be *blessed* by them as He watches them create, build, oversee, overcome, and *win*.

And we don't have to wait for Heaven to be a blessing to God. Every time we choose His will over our own, we *bless* Him. Every time we decide to praise Him in difficult circumstances, we *bless* Him. Every time we soften our hearts and repent instead of hardening our hearts, we *bless* Him. And if you love the Lord, you *want* to bless Him because you're so grateful for the grace and love He has lavished upon you.

A WARNING

After revealing to John how wonderful Heaven is going to be, God takes a moment to remind the reader of the importance of taking their salvation *seriously* so that they get to spend eternity in God's blissful new creation. He doesn't want anybody to deceive themselves into thinking that all we must do is raise our hand in church and say we want to be saved to punch our ticket to Heaven. We cannot say yes to Jesus and then live the rest of our lives as our own god. Such a life proves we never actually said yes to Jesus' offer of living water. And to underscore this point, God lists a series of *behaviors* that highlight the *lack* of salvation in a person's life.

Please understand that the issue is not whether you've fallen into any of these sins after becoming a Christian. We all still sin and sometimes backslide. This list is talking about people who engage in these behaviors as a *lifestyle,* as their regular pattern of living. It's talking about people who disagree with God that these are *sins* and not *grieved* when they fall into these sins. They don't hate their sin, and they don't attempt to change. They don't confess, ask for help, or battle their sin in any way.

[8] ***But the cowardly, . . .***

Those who turn their backs on Jesus when following Him becomes inconvenient.

. . . unbelieving, . . .

Those who don't honestly believe in Jesus.

. . . abominable, . . .

Those who do evil, in general.

. . . murderers, sexually immoral, . . .

Sexual immorality refers to all sexual activity outside of God's design for sex, which is between a man and a woman in marriage.

... sorcerers, ...

Those seeking to interact with the spiritual realm outside of the instructions given in Scripture. The original Greek word is "pharmakos," which points to the use of mind-altering substances to pursue a spiritual experience.

... idolaters, ...

Those who live their lives for any god other than Yahweh.

... and all liars shall have their part in the lake which burns with fire and brimstone, which is the second death.

The phrase *"have their part"* is an intentional contrast to how God allotted each tribe of Israel their part in the Promised Land. The idea was, *"You'll each have an area that will be your own."* Terrifyingly, God says that those who reject Him will each have their own area in the eternal lake of fire.

If you ever engage in any of the sins God lists, unrepentantly and as a lifestyle, you need to question the veracity of your conversion, reflect, and ask yourself: *"Have I sincerely given my life over to Jesus? Do I want Him to be the master of my life?"*

God gives this list out of *love* because He doesn't want anyone to miss out on Heaven. If you're caught up in any of that stuff, stop. Repent. It's no small thing. Make whatever changes you need to make and make them *today*. Find a brother or sister and confess to them. Ask them to pray with you and then walk with them in honest accountability as you seek to put that sin to death.

We're talking about our *salvation*. It doesn't get more serious than this.

THE NEW JERUSALEM

> ⁹ Then one of the seven angels who had the seven bowls filled with the seven last plagues came to me and talked with me, saying, *"Come, I will show you the bride, the Lamb's wife."*

The same angel who held one of the bowls of wrath now shows John the place that Jesus has prepared for His people. This is an example of what holiness is. Holiness manifests in both *grace* and *wrath*. Holiness doesn't just deal with the good things; it brings justice to evil and wicked things. As shown in the actions of this angel, holiness loves what is good and hates what is evil.

> ¹⁰ And he carried me away in the Spirit to a great and high mountain, and showed me the great city, the holy Jerusalem, descending out of heaven from God, ¹¹ having the glory of God. Her light *was* like a most precious stone, like a jasper stone, clear as crystal.

John sees the New Jerusalem descending to the new earth and resting upon **"a great and high mountain."** It is made of something like *diamond*. It's radiant. It's emanating and refracting light in every direction, yet it's also perfectly transparent (**"clear as crystal"**).

12 GATES – 12 APOSTLES

¹² Also she had a great and high wall with twelve gates, and twelve angels at the gates, and names written on them, which are *the names* of the twelve tribes of the children of Israel: ¹³ three gates on the east, three gates on the north, three gates on the south, and three gates on the west.

New Jerusalem will be the home of not only the Church but *all* of God's people.

Paul explained[525] that the concept of God's *spiritual* children began with the patriarchs, including Abraham, Isaac, and Jacob, then continued through the prophets until the Church was created by Jesus and **"grafted in"**[526] to that lineage, like a wild branch into an already-living tree. One of the ways this spiritual lineage is commemorated in the New Jerusalem is in the form of 12 city gates that each bear the name of one of the 12 tribes of Israel. When Jesus was talking with the Samaritan woman at the well and she took a bit of a dig at the Jews, Jesus didn't say, *"Don't get me started on the Jews!"* He said, *"salvation is of the Jews."*[527] For 1,700 to 1,800 years before the advent of the Church, God was working on the earth through the patriarchs, prophets, and people of Israel. If you love the Lord, your spiritual roots trace back to them. Salvation came through Jesus, a Jew born in the line of David and spoken of by the prophets.

It's interesting that in **Numbers 2**, the Lord instructed Israel to have three tribes camp on each of the four sides of the Tabernacle,

---

[525] Cf. Romans 2:28–29; Galatians 3:27, 29.

[526] Cf. Romans 11:16–24.

[527] John 4:22.

mirroring the three gates on each side of the New Jerusalem that each bear the name of one of the 12 tribes.[528]

As another sidenote, it may surprise some to note that Peter is not checking IDs at any of these gates. The idea of St. Peter guarding the pearly gates is Catholic folklore. It's not found anywhere in the Bible.

> **[14] Now the wall of the city had twelve foundations, and on them were the names of the twelve apostles of the Lamb.**

The complete spiritual lineage we were just discussing is captured in this detail: each foundation of the city bears the name of one of the foundations of the Church,[529] the 12 apostles. These foundations may be for the city's walls, as the text says, or they may be 12 *floors* or *levels* in the New Jerusalem. In either case, the point is that the 12 tribes and the 12 apostles are commemorated in the New Jerusalem because *both* are part of the story of the children of God.[530]

> [15] And he [the angel] **who talked with me had a gold reed to measure the city, its gates, and its wall.** [16] **The city is laid out as a square; its length is as great as its breadth. And he measured the city with the reed: twelve thousand furlongs. Its length, breadth, and height are equal.**

That means John is seeing a *cube*. And its length, breadth, and height each measure 1,500 miles. That's around 2,414 kilometers, making it twice the size of the moon!

If the **"foundations"** are *floors*, you won't need to worry about

---

[528] See also Jesus' prophecy in Luke 13:29.

[529] Cf. Ephesians 2:20.

[530] Cf. Hebrews 11:10.

bumping your head because these floors have vaulted ceilings. In fact, every level would have a ceiling roughly 125 miles or 201 km high! Each floor would be 2.25 million square miles in size. That's 1,440 million acres!

If there are 3 billion people in eternity (and I think that's being generous), each person would have 5.76 acres to themselves. And if you're thinking, *"I'm a country person; I need more space than that."* Remember, there's still all of the new earth for stretching out even more.

The New Jerusalem is a *cube*. Interestingly, so was the Holy of Holies in the Tabernacle and the Temples.[531] This is our second clue connecting the New Jerusalem to the Holy of Holies—the first being the location of the city's gates mirroring the camp of Israel around the Tabernacle. The Holy of Holies was the place in the Tabernacle and Temple complexes where God's presence would dwell. It was sealed off from the people by a thick curtain because God's holiness could not tolerate being in the presence of their sin.

Do you see the picture? The New Jerusalem is the *eternal* Holy of Holies. Except God's people are not cut off from it. Instead, it is where God dwells among His people without any division. He does not *decrease* in holiness or glory, but through the work of Jesus on the Cross, He will increase *our* holiness and glory to the level where we can enjoy unrestricted fellowship with Him for eternity.

When we understand that the New Jerusalem will be the eternal Holy of Holies, **VV.2–3** are even more incredible:

Then I, John, saw the holy city, New Jerusalem, coming down out of heaven from God, prepared as a bride adorned

---

[531] Cf. 1 Kings 6:16, 20.

for her husband. And I heard a loud voice from heaven saying, *"Behold, the tabernacle of God is with men, and He will dwell with them, and they shall be His people. God Himself will be with them and be their God."*

Let's continue into **V.17**:

[17] Then he measured its wall: one hundred *and* forty-four cubits, *according* to the measure of a man, that is, of an angel.

This is a neat little note because it tells us that the angel's measurements are the same as earthly measurements. There is not some impossible heavenlies-to-metric conversion we need to do. It also makes it clear these measurements are *literal*. This measurement likely refers to the *thickness* of the city's walls and puts it at around 72 yards or 216 feet thick.

[18] The construction of its wall was *of* jasper; and the city *was* pure gold, like clear glass.

This **"jasper"** is the same material mentioned in **V.11**. It's diamond-like in its transparency but also, somehow, *gold*. This allows the glory of God to radiate and refract out from the New Jerusalem, illuminating the new heavens and new earth.

[19] The foundations of the wall of the city *were* adorned with all kinds of precious stones: the first foundation *was* jasper, the second sapphire, the third chalcedony, the fourth emerald, [20] the fifth sardonyx, the sixth sardius, the seventh chrysolite, the eighth beryl, the ninth topaz, the tenth chrysoprase, the eleventh jacinth, and the twelfth amethyst.

If your Bible gives the stones different names, don't worry about it. Precious and semi-precious stones have other names in various languages and cultures, and they've changed over the centuries. All you need to know is that these are 12 **"precious stones."** The idea is that the glory of God shines *through* these stones, casting out beams of light in every imaginable color, adding to the overwhelming beauty of the New Jerusalem John is beholding.

Many Bible scholars link these stones with the 12 stones that represented the 12 tribes of Israel on the high priest's breastplate in the Old Testament era.[532] That may well be the case, but we can't confirm that because of the issue mentioned above of stones being called different names in different cultures.

²¹ The twelve gates *were* twelve pearls: each individual gate was of one pearl.

Each of New Jerusalem's gates is made from a single, enormous *pearl*. Pearls were prized in John's day even more than they are today. Some commentators have highlighted something interesting about pearls and how they are *formed*. This could be a coincidence, or it could be intentional. I'll let you decide.

Pearls are not formed from metal or stone; they are formed when an *irritant*, usually a grain of sand, gets into an oyster. But the living organism of the oyster doesn't deal with the annoyance by *spitting it out*. Instead, it coats or *robes* the irritant in the material of *pearl*. Layer by layer, bit by bit, this insignificant grain of sand is transformed by the oyster into a beautiful and valuable pearl.

This perfectly pictures the response of God to our sin and

---

[532] Cf. Exodus 28:15–21; 39:10–14.

wickedness. Instead of spitting us out, Jesus died in our place and robed us in His righteousness, transforming us into beautified saints and treasured children of the Father. And as we pass in and out of New Jerusalem's gates, they will remind us we are only there because God did something for us that we could never do for ourselves. And we will gladly praise Him for it yet again.

And the street of the city *was* pure gold, like transparent glass.

The main street of New Jerusalem is also made of this diamond-like transparent gold. While gold is one of the most valuable materials on earth, something even more precious will be used as *concrete* in Heaven. When the Bible cautions us about devoting our lives to the pursuit of gold, it's not only spiritual advice but also practical advice. Even if you *could* take it with you, it would have no value in Heaven because something better is everywhere! If you spend your life trying to get as much gold as you can, you're going to feel pretty stupid when you get to the New Jerusalem.

The well-known concepts of "streets of gold" and Heaven's "pearly gates" come from this verse.

THE GLORY OF THE NEW JERUSALEM

[22] But I saw no temple in it, for the Lord God Almighty and the Lamb are its temple. [23] The city had no need of the sun or of the moon to shine in it, for the glory of God illuminated it. The Lamb *is* its light. [24] And the nations of those who are saved shall walk in its light, and the kings of the earth bring their glory and honor into it.

Don't you love those verses? Conceptually, there's just something about them that makes my spirit soar every time I read them. They resonate with the Spirit in me that *longs* to be with the Lord in the New Jerusalem.

Isaiah prophesied about this:

"The sun shall no longer be your light by day,
Nor for brightness shall the moon give light to you;
But the Lord will be to you an everlasting light,
And your God your glory.

—Isaiah 60:19

The term **"the nations"** is the Greek word "ethnos." In this context, it references the different *ethnicities* that will populate Heaven. We'll retain our ethnicity in eternity because it will testify to the glorious *breadth* of the saving power of the Cross. The work of Jesus saves lives and turns orphans into children of God across nations, ethnicities, languages, socio-economic classes, and every other human division. The Gospel transcends it all.

The phrase, **"the kings of the earth bring their glory and honor into it,"** speaks of the reality that all glory and fame will return to God in the New Jerusalem. As David prayed,

... Yours, O Lord, is the greatness,
The power and the glory,
The victory and the majesty;
For all that is in heaven and in earth is Yours;
Yours is the kingdom, O Lord,
And You are exalted as head over all.

—1 Chronicles 29:11

It also seems to point to there being **"kings"** on the new earth. We know they will serve and belong to Jesus and direct all glory to Him, but beyond that, all we can do is speculate as to what they will oversee in God's new creation and what it will look like:

> **²⁵ Its gates shall not be shut at all by day (there shall be no night there). ²⁶ And they shall bring the glory and the honor of the nations into it.**

The gates will never have to close because God's people will have no enemies, and there will be nothing to fear—a truth underscored by the next and final verse of the chapter:

> **²⁷ But there shall by no means enter it anything that defiles, or causes an abomination or a lie, but only those who are written in the Lamb's Book of Life.**

CLOSING THOUGHTS

D. L. Moody, the great pastor, preacher, and evangelist lost his home to the Great Chicago Fire. While Moody was surveying the ruins of his house, a friend came by and lamented, *"I hear you lost everything."* Moody replied, *"You understood wrong. I have a good deal more left than I lost."* Puzzled by this reply, the friend asked, *"What do you mean? I didn't know you were that rich."* Moody then opened his Bible and read **Revelation 21:7** (KJV) to his friend:

> **He that overcometh shall inherit all things; and I will be his God, and he shall be my son.**[533]

---

[533] Warren Wiersbe, *Be Victorious (Revelation): In Christ You Are an Overcomer—*

When the time came for Jesus to tell His disciples that He would soon be leaving them for a while, they were discouraged. This was not the path they expected His ministry to take. Things were turning very dark, very fast. But Jesus didn't tell them to think positive thoughts or *"Turn that frown upside down!"* Instead, He taught them that the antidote for discouragement is to set your mind and heart on things *above*—our eternal future. He told them:

> *Let not your heart be troubled; you believe in God, believe also in Me. In My Father's house are many mansions; if it were not so, I would have told you. I go to prepare a place for you. And if I go and prepare a place for you, I will come again and receive you to Myself; that where I am, there you may be also. And where I go you know, and the way you know.*
>
> —John 14:1–4

Think about these things. Turn your heart and hope toward Heaven, and I promise that your spirit will be lifted as your perspective is rightly readjusted.

The believers who make an impact in *this* life are the ones who understand what's coming in the *next* life. When you grasp the reality of Heaven, even a little bit, you'll be able to live free from the things the Bible calls **"the affairs of this life."**[534] Only good and fruitful things come from being Heavenly minded. In fact, it's the key to enjoying this life. Because when you're freed from placing all your hope in *this* life and released from needing everything to be

---

The BE Series Commentary, 2nd ed. (Colorado Springs, Colorado: David C. Cook, 2008), 182, Kindle Second edition.

[534] 2 Timothy 2:4.

perfect *now*, you can enjoy this life for what it is and enjoy others for who they are.

If you're playing games with the sins God listed in this chapter and you're not convicted, grieved, repentant, or desiring to change, please reflect and make sure you're genuinely saved. You cannot accept Jesus as your *Savior* without accepting Him as your *Lord*—the master of your life. If you feel no conviction over your sin, ask the Lord to touch you and give you a heart that desires to please Him. Ask the Lord to be God over your life. And then *repent*. Turn away from those sins. Confess to somebody—a pastor or a mature believer—and plan to stay in fellowship and encourage each other to walk in righteousness. Don't play games with your salvation.

I've slowed down a bit for these final chapters because they are so important. They invite us to fix our eyes on Heaven and live for eternity. And that is the perspective all believers need to live with every day.

V.7 was true for Jesus:

He who overcomes shall inherit all things . . .

And it will likewise be true for anyone who believes that Jesus has overcome sin and death on our behalf. The greatest joy in Heaven won't be finally having **"all things"**; our greatest joy will be finally fully having the *one thing* that truly satisfies—the Lord Himself.

REVELATION 22

AMEN

In the final chapter of Revelation, we're going to learn a bit more about what it's like inside the New Jerusalem, and then we'll read some closing comments from John and the Lord Jesus.

THE RIVER OF LIFE

> **¹ And he showed me a pure river of water of life, clear as crystal, proceeding from the throne of God and of the Lamb.**

John sees this beautiful river of living water flowing from the throne of the Father and Jesus. It's *literal* water, but it's also the **"water of life"**—the living water that speaks of the Spirit and salvation. It's literal but simultaneously *figurative*. In this instance, it's a picture of how abundant and free flowing the life that exists only in Jesus will be in His new creation. It'll just be *everywhere*. As we mentioned previously, there will be no striving—no focus or effort needed to abide in Christ. The presence of God will saturate the atmosphere in the new creation. If you are sitting on the banks of a perfectly clean and flowing river and find yourself thirsty, you need only scoop up some water and drink because it's right in front of you. That's the idea this scene is intended to convey regarding the *availability* of God's presence in the new creation.

> **² In the middle of its street, and on either side of the river, *was* the tree of life, . . .**

A better translation would be "in the middle of its path," referring to the river's path.

There are parallels between the new creation and Eden,[535] and this **"tree of life"** is the Heavenly counterpart to the tree of life the Lord placed in Eden.[536] When Adam and Eve sinned by eating the fruit from the tree of the knowledge of good and evil, God expelled them from the garden specifically to prevent them from eating the fruit of the tree of life. Because if they had, they would have lived forever in their sinful state, separated from God.[537] In some mystical way I don't fully understand, the tree of life could grant eternal earthly life to those who ate its fruit. The tree of life in the New Jerusalem is not what gives us eternal life. *Jesus* does that for us.

In addition to the river, John sees literal trees that also have symbolic significance. In this context, they allude to the tree of life in Eden to paint the picture that God has made a *new* "Eden" which will *never* be broken.

The things John sees, such as *trees* and a *river*, reveal that the new creation will be amazing and beyond our current comprehension

---

[535] Cf. Genesis 2:10.

[536] Cf. Genesis 2:9.

[537] Cf. Genesis 3:22–24.

but will also include elements familiar to us. When God made the earth, He looked upon His creation and declared that it was **"good."** Therefore, we should not be surprised to encounter many of those same **"good"** elements in His new creation.

V.2 continues and tells us more about the tree of life:

. . . which bore twelve fruits, each *tree* yielding its fruit every month.

Every month of the year, the tree or trees of life produce different fruit. This again is literal and figurative, and it speaks of the infinite variety of blessings and good things that will flourish in the new creation.

The mention of **"months"** causes some to wonder if there will be *time* in Heaven. I see nothing in the Bible that suggests we will exist outside of time. We know the Lord exists both outside *and* inside all of time, simultaneously. He must exist *outside* of it because time, as we currently experience it, functions in relation to properties of our universe, such as gravity and the speed of light. And the Lord had to be *outside* of our universe in order to *create* it. Simultaneously, the Lord is omnipresent in *all* of time. He sees the past and the future, and He is *in* it all and *over* it all.

I don't see any reason to believe *we* will exist outside of time, though the basis of time will change in the new creation. Any further discussion of this subject gets too deep into theoretical physics for me to swim.

Here's another fun question: Will we *eat* in Heaven? We can't know for sure, but I like to think so. I am convinced that part of the curse our sin brought on the earth is that all the best-tasting food is the worst for your health. Fried food, white breads, sugar—it's all bad for you. What's good for you? Kale. Spinach. Broccoli. There's no question in my mind that as we eat the food our doctors tell us is best for us, we should be weeping and lamenting over what our sin has wrought.

I believe the best food for you in Heaven will also be the best-tasting food. And either there won't be recommended serving sizes at all, or they will finally be reasonable. You won't pick up a package of cookies and read on the label that a serving size is two cookies. It'll read "two sleeves of cookies" instead. And you'll be able to enjoy them with a clear conscience, rather than asking the Lord to bless your poor dietary choices by miraculously holding back the calories as He did the waters of the Reed Sea for the Israelites fleeing the Egyptian Army.

I'm speculating, of course, but I am speculating in faith. We know that our resurrected bodies will be *able* to eat food because when Jesus appeared to the disciples after His resurrection, He ate some fish to prove that He had a physical body and wasn't a *ghost*.[538] Therefore, just as my Lord ate food following His resurrection, I believe I shall too.

Then we read this about the tree of life:

The leaves of the tree *were* for the healing of the nations.

The word **"healing"** in the original Greek is the word "therapeia," from which we derive the word, "therapy." A more precise translation would be "life-giving." This verse is not implying there are ailments in Heaven that this tree will remedy. Rather, it's telling us that in the new creation, there is ongoing health and life in the environment itself. There is no sickness, no loss, no entropy, no

---

[538] Cf. Luke 24:36–43; Acts 10:41; see also Jesus and two angels eating with Abraham and Sarah in Genesis 18:1–8.

decay, no deterioration—only health and blessings from everything, everywhere, for everyone, all the time.

FROM GENESIS TO REVELATION

The design of God's Word is amazing. Humanity traces its *beginnings* to a garden, and humanity will reach its *conclusion* in a garden. What I'm about to share next is profound, and I don't want you to miss it.

The ages of our earth, the millennia that have passed, and the entire story of humanity were all intended to get us to the place where we are physically with the Lord without any division or distance. The reality of **Revelation 21** and **22** was the goal before the universe was created.

God *knew* that the cost of bringing us into His family would be the life of Jesus. He knew that before our world was made. That's why Scripture calls Him **"the Lamb slain from the foundation of the world."**[539] And yet God created us so that with the life and blood of Jesus, He could love us and adopt us into His family as His children. It's *astonishing*.

The new creation is a type of *Eden redux*, but this time we will not fall into sin and sever our relationship with God because we will be remade in His image to an even greater degree than Adam and Eve were.

And the only way to arrive at this new beginning is to make the epic journey through the first Eden, the Fall, the Curse, the Patriarchs, the Law, the Prophets, the Incarnation, the Cross, the Resurrection, the Church, the Rapture, the Tribulation, the Second Coming, and the Millennial Kingdom. *All of it* is necessary to get us

---

[539] Revelation 13:8.

to a new beginning in a new creation where we will enjoy the Lord *forever*.

Everything that happens between Eden and the New Jerusalem is prerequisite to a new beginning where the sons and daughters of God enjoy, serve, and worship Him faithfully forever.

RESURRECTED BODIES

When Adam and Eve ate from the tree of the knowledge of good and evil, rebelled against God, and rejected His lordship over their lives, the result was a *sin nature*—the ability to **"*know good and evil.*"**[540] Instead of bodies that didn't desire to sin, Adam and Eve now had *fleshly* bodies that wanted to rebel against the Lord and pursue selfish sinful desires. The result of their sin was death—*physical* death and *spiritual* death. That is what we call "The Curse."

When Jesus died on the Cross in our place and rose again, He lifted the curse of *spiritual* death from us. If we receive Him as Savior and Lord, we are *delivered* from the kingdom of darkness to the kingdom of light. However, we are still currently under the curse of *physical* death. How do I know? Because we're still dying! When Adam and Eve sinned, death entered the universe on every level. Their sin ushered in the Second Law of Thermodynamics, which observes that everything in the universe is decaying and moving from order to disorder (like my teenagers' bedrooms).

Do you know that death is still largely a mystery to science? The cells in our bodies are constantly replenishing themselves, to the degree that biologists tell us that every seven years, our bodies are essentially brand-new. In other words, there is nothing in your body,

---

[540] Genesis 3:5, 22.

on a cellular level, that is older than seven years. And yet every seven years, I can't help but notice that while my body is "cellular-ly" new, I'm somehow seven years *older*. I'm being physically regenerated, but I'm still breaking down. And science doesn't really know *why*.

But we know why because the Word of God tells us. It's because the universe, including our bodies, is *broken*. We were made to live forever, then fell under the Curse. And the *evidence* of that is scientifically observable.

We're still under the curse of physical death, trapped in fleshly bodies that war against the Spirit every day. If you're a believer, your *spirit* longs to please the Lord, but your *body* longs to please itself. Have you noticed this? While the Spirit of God in us gives us a *choice* we did not have previously—the *option* to walk in the Spirit—we must deal with a body that has not yet been redeemed and still wants to do its own thing rather than submit to the will of God.

This tension is why I am so *tired* of living in this fleshly body. My spirit belongs entirely to the Lord Jesus. He's what I want more than anything. He's who I long to please more than anyone. And yet I find myself trapped in flesh that is constantly working *against* who I long to be as a follower of Jesus, and never seems to grow weary of resisting the Spirit. And that reality can be so frustrating and exhausting.

That's why **V.3** is so precious to me:

³ **And there shall be no more curse, . . .**

One day, the war I experience every day between God's Spirit and my flesh will be *over*. There won't be a voice in my head that I have to try to tune out or refute with Scripture. There won't always be something lurking in my body that desires to sin. The day is coming when my spirit will be in perfect unity with the body in which it resides. Both will have the singular desire to love and serve the Lord. Both will be *fully submitted* to Jesus.

When I think about that moment, I imagine exhaling a long breath and soaking in the fact that, for the first time in my life, there is nothing in my thoughts, emotions, or body that I must *resist*. There is no *tension*. No *willpower* will be needed. I can't imagine what that kind of *peace*, that kind of *rest* will feel like. I will finally love the Lord the way I long to—with all my heart, soul, and strength. I will finally be the kind of worshipper the Lord deserves. I can't wait.

³ And there shall be no more curse, but the throne of God and of the Lamb shall be in it, and His servants shall serve Him.

What does it mean that **"His servants shall serve Him"**? We don't know precisely. What we do know is that it implies *activity* and *purpose*. There will be things for us to *do* in eternity. Remember, the new creation is not just the *end* of our current universe; it's the *beginning* of a new age. And we are not just going to lounge around on clouds for the ages to come!

I've written previously about how we all have God-given passions that we've been unable to pursue because of challenges like time, life, work, and family. And I shared that I believe we will *fulfill* those God-given passions in eternity. I also think that eternity is where our passions and abilities will finally line up. Perhaps you love music, but you have absolutely no musical talent, and you've always thought, *"What's up with that?"* In Heaven, you'll sing out, you'll shred that guitar solo, and it will be *glorious*.

There may be some awkward moments, though. There will undoubtedly be those whom the Lord will gently place His hand upon and say with a smile, *"Beloved, now, finally, you are a gifted singer."* And that person will respond, *"What are you talking about, Lord? I've always been a gifted singer!"* And the Lord will say, *"Hey, look! The River of Life!"*

In this life, some of us have desires that don't line up with our giftings. I don't think God gave you those desires to *frustrate* you eternally; I think He gave you those desires to *fulfill* them in eternity.

We are destined to rule *with* Christ, and we are destined to *serve* Christ. We are destined to be *sovereigns* and *servants* because we'll become like Jesus, our Servant King. Incredibly, this is what Jesus told His disciples:

> ***Let your waist be girded and your lamps burning; and you yourselves be like men who wait for their master, when he will return from the wedding, that when he comes and knocks they may open to him immediately. Blessed are those servants whom the master, when he comes, will find watching. Assuredly, I say to you that he will gird himself and have them sit down to eat, and will come and serve them.***
>
> —Luke 12:35–37

This is another truth that is so scandalous that it sounds *blasphemous*. But it's in the Bible. Part of the mystery of the Trinity is that Jesus is above all things yet is also *submitted* to the Father while also being *equal* to the Father. In the Kingdom of God, things like authority and submission function in ways that are beyond our current comprehension. We glimpsed some of these mysteries in the earthly life of Jesus, and we will experience them for ourselves in eternity with Him.

How do you wrap your mind around a king who is also a servant or a master who serves His servants? When I contemplate such things, I am struck by how different the Kingdom of God is from the kingdoms of this world. When sin is out of the picture, when ego and insecurity and selfishness and greed and pride are banished, and when agape love abounds in all things, it will result in a reality so much *higher* than anything we can presently imagine.

Parenthetically, I should mention that God has built His type of leadership into His design for the family. Men, this is how we are supposed to lead our families. We are to *lead* as the *head* of our family. But that role includes girding ourselves—taking the posture of a servant—and serving our wives, children, and parents. Husband and wife are to be one as the Church and Jesus will be one in eternity. Jesus rules, but we rule with Him. We serve Jesus, but He serves us as well. And it's His joy to do so. Marriage is intended to model *that*. The problem is that we're not in our redeemed and resurrected bodies yet, so we must battle our flesh that views the word "serve" as an insult. At least we can look forward to Heaven, where behaving like Jesus will finally come *naturally* to us.

I want to suggest something else that sounds blasphemous until you read the words of Jesus in the Bible. I believe that in eternity, we will be invited into the type of love and fellowship with God that the Trinity enjoys within itself. In His great high priestly prayer, Jesus prayed these incredible words:

I do not pray for these alone, . . .

The disciples who were with Him at the time.

. . . but also for those who will believe in Me through their word; . . .

That's you and me.

> . . . that they all may be one, as You, Father, *are* in Me, and I in You; that they also may be one in Us, that the world may believe that You sent Me. And the glory which You gave Me I have given them, that they may be one just as We are one: I in them, and You in Me; that they may be made perfect in one, and that the world may know that You have sent Me, and have loved them as You have loved Me.
>
> —John 17:20–23

If you're not struck by how radical and mind-blowing those verses are, reread them until you are.

I am not saying we will become God. He will always be distinct and supreme and uncontested over all things. But I am suggesting we will be closer to Him in every way than we would dare to believe. We know God needs nothing and is fully satisfied within Himself because of the fellowship enjoyed within the Trinity. I suggest that we will be invited to take part in that fellowship. And our fellowship with God will fully satisfy us, just as God is fully satisfied within the Trinity.

If we can grasp just a little of what we're discussing, we will understand why our future with God will never be at risk and why we will never rebel or leave the Lord in the ages to come.

Is it possible that the Holy Spirit could go rogue and leave the Trinity? Is it possible that Jesus could rebel against the Father and go off and do His own thing? Of course not! But *why?* I suggest two reasons:

1. It's not in His nature. He's only righteous and pure and good.

2. There is nothing outside the Trinity to tempt Him because there is nothing better than the perfect fellowship that He enjoys within it. There is nothing that can even appear for a second to be better!

The same will be true of us in eternity. The desire to rebel will simply not be in our nature anymore. The Lord will make us wholly righteous and pure and good. And nothing outside our relationship with God will be able to tempt us because nothing will be able to compare to the fellowship we will enjoy with Him. Praise God for what He is going to do for us in eternity!

⁴ They shall see His face, . . .

You and I will see the face of God!

. . . and His name *shall be* on their foreheads.[541]

God has marked us as His property.[542]

⁵ There shall be no night there: They need no lamp nor light of the sun, for the Lord God gives them light.

We won't have to *do* anything to be full of joy and peace in eternity. Right now, we like to talk about how accessible God is, but the truth is that to experience His joy and peace, we must still *appropriate* it. We must *seek* the Lord, *dig* into His Word, *meditate* and *focus* on His promises, set aside time to pray, and so on. In Heaven, we will be *illuminated* by the glory of God. Joy, peace, and

---

[541] Cf. Revelation 3:12.

[542] Cf. Ephesians 1:13–14.

love will wash over us constantly as God's glory illuminates the new creation like the rays of the sun.

And they [the saints; you and me] **shall reign forever and ever.**

There's that mystery of the Kingdom again—we will be *servants* who *rule* and *reign*. We will follow the example of our Lord and brother (there's another Kingdom mystery), Jesus.

That concludes the description of the New Jerusalem. What a place it's going to be! The rest of the chapter is devoted to closing thoughts and comments.

THE TIME IS NEAR

⁶ **Then he . . .**

The angel introduced in **21:9**:

. . . said to me, *"These words are faithful and true."*

Jesus has twice used the phrase *"faithful and true"* as a title for Himself in the Book of Revelation.[543] The point being these words are as faithful and true as the Lord Himself.

And the Lord God of the holy prophets sent His angel to show His servants the things which must shortly take place.

John references **"the holy prophets"** to claim that the revelation he has recorded in this book should be viewed as belonging to the

---

[543] Cf. Revelation 3:14; 19:11.

same genre as Old Testament prophecy. Just as those prophets prophesied about literal events like the Babylonian Exile and the Incarnation, John claims that he is prophesying about literal events that **"must shortly take place."** John is not writing *poetry;* he's writing *prophecy.* He says so himself.

The word **"shortly"** is one of our favorite Greek phrases because it sounds like an item on Taco Bell's menu; it's "en tachos," from which we derive the word "tachometer." Your tachometer is the RPM gauge in your vehicle, and the concept of the word is *exponential* acceleration. When the angel says these **"things must shortly take place,"** he's saying that once the end-times signs described in the Book of Revelation start showing up, events will accelerate *exponentially.* They're not going to be evenly spaced apart; they will increase in frequency and intensity—like a woman's contractions in labor.

Now Jesus speaks to John and declares:

⁷ Behold, I am coming quickly!

The Greek word used there for *"quickly"* is "tachy," and it means "quickly, without delay." Jesus reiterates the angel's statement that end-times events will unfold *quickly* and *accelerate* once they begin. I pray the Lord has given you the wisdom to recognize that things are in motion and are *accelerating* before our very eyes. I pray you are *watching* and *longing* for His appearing. We are so close. We are *so close.*

Blessed is he who keeps the words of the prophecy of this book.

Here at the book's closing, Jesus repeats what He told John to write back in **Revelation 1:3**, which reads:

Blessed *is* he who reads and those who hear the words of this prophecy, and keep those things which are written in it; for the time *is* near.

Now we're at the end of the book, so we've obviously read it, which is why the Lord simply says:

Blessed is he who keeps the words of the prophecy of <u>***this book***</u>***.***

In effect, Jesus is saying to John: *"Now that you've heard it, keep it."* The original Greek word translated *"keep"*[544] means *"to guard"* and *"to observe."* In other words, live your life in light of what has been revealed in this book. Live as though you believe it!

Observe this book by rejecting the attitude that says, *"Well, I've studied that, so now I'm done with it."* Keep going back to it. Keep filtering everything going on in your world through the lens of what Jesus has shared with you in this book. Let it continually realign the priorities of your life.

You and I are not finished with the Book of Revelation. We've just had our eyes and ears and hearts *opened*. And by the grace of God, we will be affected profoundly by this book daily until we go to be with the Lord, one way or another.

Guard this book by ensuring it doesn't get played down, dismissed, discredited, relegated, undermined, or ignored in your church or among the brethren.

I want you to write a little number one next to the phrase *"this book"* because we're going to find that Jesus wants to underscore the importance of *"this book."* In fact, the Book of Revelation will be referred to seven times in its final chapter.

Note the phrase **"the prophecy"** because while we've talked about this before, it is so important. Other books of the Bible contain prophecies. Many of them, in fact. Revelation is unique because it is the only book in the Bible that is one massive, single prophecy from

---

[544] Tereo.

beginning to end. That's why it matters that you learn to not refer to the book as "Revelations" (plural) but by its actual title, "Revelation" (singular). If you don't grasp that, your understanding of this book will be distorted. We must recognize it as a single prophecy because *Jesus tells us* it is a single prophecy.

Revelation *begins* by telling you that you'll be blessed if you read it and keep it, and Revelation *ends* by telling you again that you'll be blessed if you keep it. Do you think Jesus wants us to remember what's in this book? Me too.

⁸ Now I, John, saw and heard these things. And when I heard and saw, I fell down to worship before the feet of the angel who showed me these things.

Incredibly, this is the *second* time we've seen John make the mistake of bowing to worship an angel.[545] John was so overwhelmed by the greatness of the *message* that he made the mistake of worshipping the *messenger*. It strikes me that even in his old age and spiritual maturity, a man as great as John the Apostle could still be led astray by his emotions. What a sobering warning for us and a reminder that the process of sanctification will continue until we go to be with the Lord.

But there's also encouragement here because when we find ourselves thinking, *"I really thought I'd be more spiritually mature by now,"* we can remember John. I'm sure he felt the same way after trying to worship an angel—again. But God still loved Him and didn't strip him of his title of "Apostle." On both occasions, God's response amounted to, *"Let's not do that, John."* There was no lightning from Heaven. Why? Because John was *saved*. He was covered by the

---

[545] The first was in Revelation 19:10.

blood of Jesus and was doing his best to serve the Lord. But like us, he sometimes did foolish things. And our Heavenly Father knew that.

In fact, the Lord knew every sin you would commit before you were even born—the dumb ones, the wicked ones, the intentional ones, the accidental ones, and the carefully planned ones. He knew them all. And Jesus *still* chose to die for you. So, if you struggle with sometimes thinking, *"There's no way God loves me. I've messed up way too many times."* I need to be firm here: *Stop it*. If God says He loves you, then He loves you. If He says the Cross covers all your sins, then it covers *all* your sins. And if He says you're forgiven, then you're *forgiven*. Yes, still! And the same will be true tomorrow. And next week. And next month. And next year. Until the day arrives when you're with Him face-to-face.

Now the angel *responds* to John's worship:

⁹ Then he said to me, "See that you do not do that. For I am your fellow servant, and of your brethren the prophets, and of those who keep the words of <u>this book</u>. Worship God."

As I pointed out in **19:10**, angels loyal to God never accept worship. They *always* direct people to *"Worship God."*

Note that the angel echoes John's earlier claim that he is recording Revelation as a *prophet*. Write a little number two next to *"this book."*

¹⁰ And he said to me, "Do not seal the words of the prophecy of <u>this book</u>, ... "

There's number three.

... *for the time is at hand.*

In the original language, the idea is sealing up a document, marking it "secret," and hiding it away somewhere.

How would someone in our day and age *"seal"* up the Book of Revelation? Think of the churches you've been to or the churches you grew up in. There's a 99.9% chance they did not study Revelation. And if you ever asked why that was the case, you were probably told that it wasn't important, or wasn't a good book to reach people with, or was too divisive and controversial, or too difficult to understand, or had no life application and wasn't helpful. They might say that the only thing you needed to know was that Jesus wins in the end. For one or more of those reasons, nearly all of us who grew up in the Church were in churches where Revelation was *sealed up*.

Some of my brothers and sisters in Christ have told me about the shocked reactions they've received when sharing that our church was studying through Revelation. As a pastor, I know that many well-intentioned believers look at churches like ours and think, *"Yikes. You'll never grow a church teaching verse-by-verse through books like Revelation."*

Perhaps that's why Jesus felt the need to make this the only book in the Bible with its own special blessing. Maybe that's why Jesus didn't conclude any other book with a warning to the reader to not seal it up. It's not like you get to the end of Galatians and the Lord has Paul write, *"Whatever you do, don't seal up the Letter to the Galatians."* The Lord *knew* that Satan would desperately like to seal up this book, so He explicitly *commanded* pastors and churches to study the Book of Revelation.

I'll go even further. I believe it's a *sin* for a church to fail to teach the Book of Revelation. Jesus is *clear* that He blesses those who study it and *wants* His Church to learn it.

So, thank you for taking the time to study Revelation with

me. Thank you for loving God's Word and desiring a greater understanding of this amazing book, which Jesus says is so important. Whenever I teach this book, it's not because I think it's a great way to grow a church. We study this book because we believe the Church exists to bless and honor Jesus. We believe the Church exists *for Jesus*, and her ultimate destiny is to be joined to Him forever as His bride. So, if Jesus is pleased with what we do in our churches, that's all that matters.

> **[11] *He who is unjust, let him be unjust still; he who is filthy, let him be filthy still; he who is righteous, let him be righteous still; he who is holy, let him be holy still.***

Here's what that means: When your earthly life ends, the state your soul is in will continue for eternity. If you're walking with the Lord, you'll walk with Him *forever*. If you die an enemy of God, you'll be an enemy of God *forever*. There is no purgatory. There is no "next life" where you can work out your karma. It's not possible to "graduate" from Hades and the lake of fire.

V.11 may also be a warning to the person who has reached the end of the Book of Revelation yet still refuses to believe the Gospel. That person has had the Lord pull back the curtain and reveal the true nature of reality—revealing where everything is headed, why there's pain and suffering in the world, who's pulling the strings in world politics, and so on. **V.11** seems to be saying that if a person still refuses to believe after all that revelation, then they might as well live however they want to live because they're *never* going to get it. And in His mercy, God may choose to make them *unable* to believe.

Revelation will cement your faith and spur you to a more passionate walk with Jesus, or it will cement your unbelief and rebellion against God. We saw that in the Tribulation, didn't we? We saw miracles taking place all over the earth—undeniable signs and wonders—and we saw people cursing God instead of repenting.

Revelation closes with the Bible's final call to repent and turn to Jesus.

JESUS TESTIFIES TO THE CHURCHES

Now Jesus repeats what He said back in **V.7**—almost as if He really wants us to get this:

> [12] *"And behold, I am coming quickly, and My reward is with Me, to give to every one according to his work.*

Should the world fear Jesus coming for His Church? *Absolutely.* The Tribulation is going to be horrible for them. Should the followers of Jesus fear Him coming for His Church? *Absolutely not.* Because for us, He is coming with rewards and taking us to His Father's house. He is coming with the one accolade I desire most—hearing the Lord Jesus say, *"Well done, good and faithful servant."*[546]

I want to be sure we understand that we do *not* have a works-based faith. We're not saved by anything we do; nothing we do can earn us salvation.[547] It's a *gift* from God. However, the Bible clearly teaches works-based *rewards*. What does Jesus say in the verse we just read?

> *My reward is with Me, to give to every one according to his work.*

---

[546] Matthew 25:23.

[547] Cf. Ephesians 2:8.

And not just any works, but the works our master has *asked us to do*. If a master asks his servants to paint the inside of his house while he's away, and he comes back to find that they've landscaped the garden instead, are they going to be rewarded? Of course not! In the same way, we will not be rewarded for doing whatever works *we* decide are "good." It's not a "Choose Your Own Good Works Adventure" where we can opt to do only the good works that we don't find too inconvenient. We will be rewarded for doing the things our master Jesus has *asked us to do*.

Simply put, our future rewards will be determined by our present faithfulness.

> ¹³ *I am the Alpha and the Omega, the Beginning and the End, the First and the Last.*

Jesus was *before* the universe, and Jesus will be *after* the universe. Jesus *created* the heavens and the earth, and Jesus will *destroy* the heavens and the earth . . . and then make new ones. Ages *begin* with Him, and ages *end* with Him.

> ¹⁴ **Blessed *are* those who do His commandments, that they may have the right to the tree of life, and may enter through the gates into the city. ¹⁵ But outside *are* dogs and sorcerers and sexually immoral and murderers and idolaters, and whoever loves and practices a lie.**

The Bible teaches we're not saved by any works that we do. At the same time, the Bible also teaches that the presence of the Holy Spirit in a person's life *naturally* produces good works[548] because the Spirit is continually working to *sanctify* us (i.e., make us more like

---

[548] Cf. James 2:26.

Jesus). **"Blessed *are* those who do His commandments"** because those saved will naturally desire to obey Him. And as they do, they show the *evidence* of their salvation.

The idea of **VV.14–15** is that in eternity, there are only those *inside* God's new creation and those *outside* in the lake of fire. There is no third option. *Everybody* will spend eternity in one of those two places. You want to be inside with the family of God. And the only way to do that is to give your life to Jesus. When you do that, He places His Spirit within you, giving you the **"right"** to spend eternity with Him and His family.

Some have pointed out that **V.15** seems to settle the dogs-versus-cats debate, as there is no mention of *cats* being outside the Kingdom of God. Now, *I* would never say something so divisive and controversial. I don't see how pointing that out would be helpful.

I'm just messing with you. If you're curious, at this time in history, dogs were not the beloved domestic animals they are today. They were scavengers, and calling a person a "dog" was to call them *immoral*.

> [16] *I, Jesus, have sent My angel to testify to you these things in the churches. I am the Root and the Offspring of David, the Bright and Morning Star.*[549]

Everything in the Book of Revelation is to be testified to **"in the churches."** It is a revelation and a prophecy *for the Church*.

The phrase, **"I am the Root and the Offspring of David"** means, *"David came from Me because I created him. But I also came from David because I was born on the earth in a human body in the family line that traces back to David."* It's a statement that captures the mystical dual nature of Jesus, who is fully God and yet also fully man.

---

[549] Cf. Revelation 2:28.

¹⁷ **And the Spirit and the bride say, *"Come!"* And let him who hears say, *"Come!"* And let him who thirsts come. Whoever desires, let him take the water of life freely.**

In light of everything recorded in the Book of Revelation and in light of what the Lord has planned for those who love Him, the Spirit that indwells the Church—the same Spirit that cries out *"Abba! Father!"*[550]—also cries out, *"Come, Lord Jesus!"* That has been the prayer of the Church since Jesus returned to Heaven. It is a prayer millions of believers are literally praying today. And Revelation reveals God's plan to *answer* those prayers.

Jesus called his first disciples with the words, *"Come and see."*[551] Jesus cried out to the crowd, *"If anyone thirsts, let him come to Me and drink."*[552] His Kingdom is an invitation. Not to the chosen few. Not to the best and the brightest. Not to the most righteous. But to *"Whoever desires."* The Gospel cries out to the world, *"Come and be a part of the family of God! Come! Come! Come!"* I am not the best. I am not the brightest. I am not the most righteous. But I do desire Jesus. And I'm so thankful that His response to me is, *"I can work with that."*

A FINAL WARNING

¹⁸ **For I testify to everyone who hears the words of the prophecy of <u>this book</u>: . . .**

That's number four.

---

[550] Cf. Romans 8:15; Galatians 4:6.
[551] John 1:39.
[552] John 7:37.

> **If anyone adds to these things, God will add to him the plagues that are written in <u>this book</u>;** . . .

That's number five.

> **¹⁹ and if anyone takes away from the words of <u>the book</u> of this prophecy,** ...

That's number six.

> **. . . God shall take away his part from the Book of Life, from the holy city, and *from* the things which are written in <u>this book</u>.**

That's number seven.

Did you catch the *seriousness* of what Jesus just said regarding editing the contents and message of this book? Let's look at it once more:

> **If anyone adds to these things, God will add to him the plagues that are written in this book; and if anyone takes away from the words of the book of this prophecy, God shall take away his part from the Book of Life, from the holy city, and *from* the things which are written in this book.**

Wow. The message is this: *Don't mess with this book.* Even if you find its contents disturbing or difficult or culturally offensive or too fantastic or unbelievable, *don't mess with this book.* Jesus tells us that the way it is written is how He *wanted* it written. Essentially what Jesus says is that if you mess with the contents of this book, you'll be proving that you're not saved.

Am I saying that the pastor telling his church Revelation is hard to understand is in danger of hell? No. I don't think that's what Jesus is talking about. But do I think what that pastor and church are doing is more serious than they realize? Yes, I do.

The bottom line is this: We are to take this book seriously. Because Jesus sure does. He commands His Church to read, teach, and respond to the Book of Revelation. Don't *seal up* this book. Don't *hide* this book. Don't be *ashamed* of this book. Don't lose *focus* on this book.

"I AM COMING QUICKLY"

[20] **He who testifies to these things says,** *"Surely I am coming quickly."*

Jesus mentions that He is **"coming quickly"** in **VV. 7, 12, 20**. What Jesus is trying to communicate to us is not rocket science. He wants us to know that *He is coming quickly!*

What should our *response* be to everything we've learned from this amazing book?

Amen ["so be it"]. **Even so, come, Lord Jesus!**

The Bible—the Word of God, His message to humanity—ends with these words:

[21] **The grace of our Lord Jesus Christ** *be* **with you all. Amen.**

CLOSING THOUGHTS

We're in the family of God because He called out to us and bid us come and be part of His family. And now, we are called to extend that same invitation to the world around us.

- Who are you regularly praying for? Who are you asking the Lord to save, specifically?

- Who are you investing in, relationally?

- Is there someone you have a relationship with that is ready to hear the Gospel? Maybe you need to ask them out for coffee and ask if you can have 15 minutes to share the most important thing in your life. Is there someone you need to plan that coffee with *this week?*

There are seven beatitudes in the Book of Revelation, and they serve as a good summary:

Blessed *is* he who reads and those who hear the words of this prophecy, and keep those things which are written in it; for the time *is* near.

—Revelation 1:3

...Blessed are the dead who die in the Lord from now on. "Yes," says the Spirit, *"that they may rest from their labors, and their works follow them."*

—Revelation 14:13

Behold, I am coming as a thief. Blessed is he who watches, and keeps his garments, lest he walk naked and they see his shame.

—Revelation 16:15

... Blessed are those who are called to the marriage supper of the Lamb! ...

—Revelation 19:9

Blessed and holy *is* he who has part in the first resurrection. Over such the second death has no power, but they shall be priests of God and of Christ, and shall reign with Him a thousand years.

—Revelation 20:6

... Blessed is he who keeps the words of the prophecy of this book.

—Revelation 22:7

Blessed *are* those who do His commandments, that they may have the right to the tree of life, and may enter through the gates into the city.

—Revelation 22:14

And thus concludes the Book of Revelation. I pray it leaves you in awe of Jesus.

Amen. Even so, come, Lord Jesus!
The grace of our Lord Jesus Christ *be* with you all. Amen.

APPENDIX A: END-TIMES REVIEW

To help keep the big picture and flow of Revelation in mind, here is a broad end-times overview that lays out the significant events in the order they happen:

- The first significant end-times event, the first "domino" that had to fall, was Israel's resurrection as a political nation. After teaching His disciples about the end-times, Jesus Himself prophesied that the generation that saw this take place would not die out until *all* the end-times events had unfolded.

  Against all odds, despite not existing as a political nation for around 1,900 years and almost being wiped out by the Holocaust, it happened. Israel became a nation again in 1948 and, in so doing, started the end-times "countdown clock."

  This means that the Rapture will take place before the last person (I'd suggest Jewish person) who was alive in 1948 dies.

  The next event in the timeline is the Rapture. It could happen in the next 10 seconds, or it could happen in a couple of decades. We're to be ready at any moment.

APPENDIX A

- In the aftermath of the Rapture, there will be chaos. Planes will lose their pilots in mid-flight. Cars will crash all over the place. Ships will lose their captains and run aground. Hundreds of millions of people will simply vanish from the earth instantly, likely including all children.

  The good news is that the Rapture will usher in the greatest revival in history, as millions who had heard something about it in their lifetime suddenly realize that the Christians they knew had been telling them the truth, and they'll turn to Jesus and be saved.

  The bad news is that while Satan is the god of this world, his power is presently restrained by the presence of the Church on the earth. Because the Holy Spirit lives in every believer and God has "deputized" the Church with His restraining power, the Spirit's presence limits what Satan can do on the earth. When the Church leaves the earth, Satan's power will dramatically increase. And all those people who say things like, *"Think of the society we could create if those Christians weren't slowing down our progress"* will get their wish because the restraining power of the Church will be gone. As a result, the world will fall into evil to a degree never seen before.

- The removal of the Church will enable Satan to propel the meteoric rise of a very specific man onto the world's political stage—the one infamously known as "antichrist." He will be a beloved political figure and be viewed as a savior in the years of turmoil following the Rapture.

  He'll begin his career in Europe and, through various political machinations, will emerge as the head of a revived Roman

Empire, meaning that he'll rule the countries that previously made up the Roman Empire. It'll be like a more powerful European Union, with him at the top.

He'll be able to accomplish this because he'll do things under the power of Satan that will be astonishing. We're talking about achievements like brokering peace in the Middle East between the Jews and Arabs and rebuilding the Jewish Temple on the Temple Mount in Jerusalem.

- As antichrist rises to prominence, the Bible says a seven-year period will begin. That period is most widely known as "The Tribulation." The Tribulation will see God pour out His judgment and wrath on the earth that rejected (and will continue to reject) His Son, Jesus.

- "Halfway through these seven years—after three and a half years—antichrist will be assassinated. He will be possessed by a powerful demonic spirit and rise from the dead. He will then enter the rebuilt Jewish Temple in Jerusalem, set up a throne for himself, and demand to be worshipped as God by the citizens of the world."

As a sign of allegiance, every citizen in his empire will be required to receive a "mark" on their hand or forehead, without which a person will be unable to engage in commerce (e.g., buying, selling, banking). If a person refuses to take this mark, they will be beheaded. If they choose to take this mark, they will be damned for all eternity. Each person will be choosing between God and Satan, and the Bible clarifies that everyone making that choice will understand what they're doing.

Those who have turned to Jesus post-Rapture and religiously devout Jews will refuse to take the mark. In response, antichrist will viciously persecute and execute them. Two out of every three Jews in Israel (and possibly the world) will be killed during the Great Tribulation (the last three and a half years of the seven-year period).

The Jews will finally realize that antichrist is no savior but is in fact worse even than Hitler. That's why for them this time is referred to in the Bible as *"the time of Jacob's trouble."*

- At this halfway point of the Tribulation, God's wrath turns up to "11," marking what will be the worst days of planet earth, by a mile. And while the demonstrations of God's wrath during the *first* half of the Tribulation could mostly be explained by natural causes (by those who wish to live in denial), the demonstrations of His wrath in the *second* half of the Tribulation will be undeniably supernatural (for the most part).

The last three and a half years of the Tribulation are known as "The Great Tribulation."

But amidst this backdrop of horrors, God continues His work on the earth, raising up 144,000 Jewish evangelists to preach the Gospel across the earth. He sends an angel to preach the Gospel from the skies to everyone on earth. And yet, most still refuse to repent.

Many ethnic Jews in Israel will recognize the need to flee from antichrist, and the Lord will lead them to a place of safety—likely the ancient Jordanian city of the Nabateans known as Petra. Sadly, there will also be many who will not flee and will be slaughtered.

- When it seems like the Jews are destined to die and all hope is lost, Jesus returns to the earth with all His saints. His Church left the earth as mere mortals but returns in resurrected glory, triumphantly beside their King.

    Although Jesus came the first time as the Lamb of God—the sacrifice for our sins—He will return as the Lion of Judah, the conquering King of all the earth.

    The famous Battle of Armageddon will take place, but it will be no battle. The enemies of Jesus will be annihilated. He will cast antichrist and the false prophet into the lake of fire and imprison Satan in the Abyss.

    At this time, the Jews will look upon Jesus and finally recognize Him as their Messiah. They will repent for missing Him the first time, and their relationship with Him will be restored. The whole nation of Israel will be saved.

    Jesus' return to the earth with all His saints is known as "The Second Coming."

- As Jesus sets up His throne in Jerusalem, He returns the earth to an Eden-like state. We will all experience a perfect world ruled by a perfect King. We will see what the earth was like before we broke it, and it will be this way for a thousand years in what's known as "The Millennial Kingdom" or simply "The Millennium."

- To determine who among those still alive on the earth will be permitted to enter the Millennial Kingdom, Jesus will oversee the Sheep and Goats Judgment. Those who have embraced Him as Savior and Lord will join the saints in the Millennium. Those who have no desire to be ruled by Jesus will have their wish.

Their earthly bodies will be executed, and their spirits sent to Hades to await the final judgment.

- At the end of the Millennium, Satan will be released from his prison to give a final choice to those alive on the earth in unredeemed human bodies. *Billions* of people will be born on the earth during the Millennium—sons and daughters of those who survived the Tribulation and went into the Millennium in human bodies. Those billions of people will have only experienced a perfect world ruled authoritatively by a perfect King. So, God will give them a choice. And when He does, some will side with Satan.

This will disprove the idea that man is inherently good or that we'd be good if we were only raised by the right people in the right environment. It will prove that we rebel not because we are victims of circumstance but because we love the idea of being our own god.

- At the end of the Millennium, those who choose to rebel will gather and attempt to take on Jesus and the city of Jerusalem in a final battle. But once again, the enemies of God will be destroyed in an instant, and Satan will be cast into the lake of fire.

- After this comes the Great White Throne Judgment—the final judgment of all who have rejected Jesus. Their spirits are brought up from Hades and cast into the lake of fire where they are eternally separated from God and His saints.

- The universe ends, and God creates new heavens and a new earth. We go forward, with Him, into the ages to come—ages, which are presently a mystery to us but will consist of glory and wonders far beyond our imagination.

APPENDIX B: HOW DO WE KNOW THE TRIBULATION WILL LAST SEVEN YEARS?

In **Daniel 9**, the angel Gabriel comes to Daniel, who is in exile in Babylon, and gives him a prophetic message, telling him:

> *...I have now come forth to give you skill to understand* **(V.22)**
>
> *...consider the matter, and understand the vision ...* **(V.23)**

As we read this special message given to Daniel, we encounter the word **"week"** several times. The original Hebrew word used is "sabua," meaning *"a period of seven."* In numerology, it's known as a "heptad." Most of the world uses the metric system, which is based on units of *ten*—10 mm in a centimeter, 100 cm in a meter, 1,000 meters in a kilometer, etc. The Hebrews organized their world around heptads—units of *seven*.

And in this prophetic message, we'll find that the period of seven being referred to is seven *years*—the Hebrew equivalent of a decade. So, wherever you see the word **"week"** in these next few verses, know that it's referring to a heptad of *seven years*.

In **Daniel 9:24**, Gabriel tells Daniel:

> [24] *Seventy weeks are determined*
> *For your people and for your holy city,*
> *To finish*[553] *the transgression,*
> *To make an end of*[554] *sins,*
> *To make reconciliation for iniquity,*
> *To bring in everlasting righteousness,*
> *To seal up vision and prophecy,*
> *And to anoint the Most Holy.*[555]

Let's break this down and go through the text in detail.

Seventy weeks are determined . . .

"Seventy weeks" = 70 heptads of 7 years = 490 years. To make it simple, let's rewrite the verse with that number:

> [490] *years are determined*
> *For your people and for your holy city,*

Who are Daniel's *"people"*? The Jews. What is the *"holy city"* of Daniel and the Jewish people? Jerusalem. We can rewrite the verse like this:

> [490] *years are determined*
> *For* [the Jews] *and for* [Jerusalem], . . .

---

[553] Literally "restrain."

[554] Literally "to seal up."

[555] Literally "the most holy place"; i.e., the Holy of Holies in the Temple.

Note that the subjects of this vision are the Jews and Jerusalem. While this prophecy will build our faith, it's not a message to the Church; it's a message for Israel.

> *... To finish the transgression,*
> *To make an end of sins,*
> *To make reconciliation for iniquity,*
> *To bring in everlasting righteousness,*
> *To seal up vision and prophecy,*
> *And to anoint the Most Holy.*

If we look at the world around us today, have **"sins"** come to **"an end"**? Have they been sealed up? Is the earth covered with **"everlasting righteousness"**? Is biblical prophecy finished? The answer to all these questions is no. Therefore, it should be clear that at least part of what this prophecy speaks of is yet to be fulfilled.

When *will* sin be ended, transgression restrained, righteousness reign on the earth, and all Bible prophecy be fulfilled? In the Millennial Kingdom, when Jesus returns at the Second Coming, with His Church, to rule and reign on the earth for a thousand years.

> [25] *Know therefore and understand,*
> *That from the going forth of the command*
> *To restore and build Jerusalem*
> *Until Messiah the Prince,*
> *There shall be seven weeks and sixty-two weeks;*

Speaking of Jerusalem, Gabriel says:

> *The street*[556] *shall be built again, and the wall,*
> *Even in troublesome times.*

---

[556] Or "square."

APPENDIX B

Gabriel *divides* the *"seventy weeks"* into two sections: a period of 69 weeks and a period of one week.

Why does he refer to the period of 69 weeks *("seven weeks and sixty-two weeks")* in such a strange way? It was just a way of speaking at the time, similar to how Abraham Lincoln began his Gettysburg Address with, *"Four score and seven years ago..."* Why didn't Honest Abe just say, *"87 years ago"*? It was just an antiquated style of speaking.

In **VV.25–26**, Gabriel is going to address the period of **69 weeks**. Let's look at **V.25** again:

Know therefore and understand,
That from the going forth of the command

To restore and build Jerusalem... The word *"from"* gives us our *starting point*. Incredibly, as Jerusalem lies in ruins, Gabriel tells Daniel that a day is coming when the command will be issued to *"restore and [re]build Jerusalem."* And when that command is given, the clock for the 69 weeks will start.

Fast-forward to the time that Cyrus the Great and his Medo-Persian Empire conquer the Babylonians. Soon after, Cyrus issues a decree releasing the Jews from their captivity in Babylon and commanding that the Temple in Jerusalem be rebuilt.[557] He even goes as far as offering them financial incentives to return to Israel and helps fund the Temple project.

However, less than 50,000 Jews take him up on the offer and return to Israel around 538 BC. It takes until 516 BC just for them to rebuild the Temple. And to make things even more challenging, there are hostile forces in the area constantly preventing them from

---

[557] Cf. 2 Chronicles 36:22–23; Isaiah 45:1–13.

rebuilding the walls of the city. And in those days, your city was defenseless if you didn't have walls.

Fast-forward to the year 445 BC and we find a Jewish man serving as a cupbearer and friend to the king of the earth at that time, in the fortified Persian palace of Susa. The Jewish man is Nehemiah, and the king is Artaxerxes I, King of Persia.

Nehemiah has known about the situation in Jerusalem for some time but receives a fresh report from his brothers that the city *still* has no walls and no gates. It's *still* being bullied and raided by surrounding people groups. This news devastates Nehemiah, who loves the Lord and, therefore, loves Jerusalem. So, he prays, repents on behalf of his people, and asks God to work a miracle and rebuild the city's walls.

That story is documented in the Book of Nehemiah, and in **Chapter 2 verse 1,** we read:

> **. . . it came to pass in the month of Nisan, in the twentieth year of King Artaxerxes,** *when* **wine** *was* **before him, that I took the wine and gave it to the king. Now I had never been sad in his presence before.**

Artaxerxes was apparently a believer in the power of positive thinking because if you were sad in his presence, you'd be executed. Sort of like a company that says, *"Firings will continue until morale improves."*

> **²Therefore the king said to me,** *"Why is your face sad, since you are not sick? This is nothing but sorrow of heart."*
> **So I became dreadfully afraid,** ³ **and said to the king, . . .**

Taking his life into his own hands, Nehemiah tells the truth:

> *... May the king live forever! Why should my face not be sad, when the city, the place of my fathers' tombs, lies waste, and its gates are burned with fire?*
> ⁴ **Then the king said to me,** *"What do you request?"*
> **So I prayed to the God of heaven.**

A very quick, *"God, help me!"* kind of prayer.

> ⁵ **And I said to the king,** *"If it pleases the king, and if your servant has found favor in your sight, I ask that you send me to Judah, to the city of my fathers' tombs, that I may rebuild it."*
> ⁶ **Then the king said to me (the queen also sitting beside him),** *"How long will your journey be? And when will you return?"* **So it pleased the king to send me; and I set him a time.**

Artaxerxes issues the decree to rebuild Jerusalem, including its walls and gates. That's significant because Gabriel had told Daniel, *"The street shall be built again, and the wall."*

Back in **V.1**, Nehemiah told us this took place in the month of **"Nisan,"** which is our month of March. In that same verse, Nehemiah tells us it was the **"twentieth year"** of the reign of **"King Artaxerxes."** Secular history has established that this transpired in 445 BC. Secular historians have also delved into archaeological evidence, manuscripts, and all kinds of boring details and have managed to pinpoint the exact *day* that Artaxerxes I issued that decree. It was March 14, 445 BC.

So, we know from history that the *starting point* of the 69 weeks was March 14, 445 BC. Let's keep reading in **Daniel 9:25**:

> *Until Messiah the Prince,*
> *There shall be seven weeks and sixty-two weeks;*

The word *"until"* gives us the *ending point* of the 69 weeks, when we are told that something amazing will happen: ***"Messiah the Prince"*** will appear. Messiah, the promised Savior of the world, the one talked about hundreds of times in Old Testament prophecies, the one who would take away the sins of the world—*that* Messiah, is going to be *revealed*. Daniel must have been *astounded* when he heard this.

The 69 weeks will *begin* when the decree is given to rebuild Jerusalem, including its walls. The 69 weeks will *end* with the appearance of Messiah. The precision of this prophecy is astonishing. Gabriel is telling Daniel that between those two events will be exactly 483 years (69 weeks/heptads of seven years).

If we want to turn those years into *days*, we need to remember that the Jewish calendar has exactly 30 days in every month, meaning there are 360 days in a Jewish year. So, the math looks like this:

483 (years) x 360 (days) = 173,880 days

In summary,

69 (weeks/heptads) = 483 years = 173,880 days

If we go back to our starting point—the day that Artaxerxes I issued the decree to rebuild Jerusalem on March 14, 445 BC—and count ahead in history exactly 173,880 days, we come to April 6, AD 32.

What's so significant about that date? It's considered by many to be the day Jesus rode into Jerusalem on the back of a donkey, publicly presenting Himself as the Messiah for the first time. It's the day we call "Palm Sunday."

During His earthly ministry, there were multiple times when people tried to grab Jesus and have Him lead a parade, announcing

APPENDIX B

He was the new King of the Jews. But every time that happened, Jesus would supernaturally slip away from the crowd. For example, in **John 6:15** we read:

> **. . . when Jesus perceived that they were about to come and take Him by force to make Him king, He departed again to the mountain by Himself alone.**

Why didn't Jesus let the crowd crown Him King of the Jews? He explained more than once that it was because it was *not yet His time*. It was not yet *the* time for Him to present Himself publicly as Messiah because that had to take place on a very specific date to fulfill the prophecy recorded in **Daniel 9**. And on *that* day, Jesus *chose* to ride into Jerusalem and publicly present Himself as Messiah.

The ending point of the 69-week prophecy was Palm Sunday, April 6, AD 32.[558]

And what's amazing is that this is *not*, in actuality, a very complicated prophecy. It's *clear*. The math *isn't* hard (with a calculator). And it predicts, *to the day*, the exact day Jesus would appear in public as the Messiah.

Gabriel's margin for error in this prophecy is *zero*. He told Daniel the *exact day* the Messiah would be revealed. It's a verifiable, proven, fulfilled prophecy that is so specific and impossible to fake that it proves that the Bible has a supernatural origin. There is simply no other explanation.

If you'd like to get into even greater detail on the calculations

---

[558] The exact dates of Jesus' birth and death are debated among scholars to this day. Some will disagree that Palm Sunday occurred on April 6, AD 32. Even if that's true, I suspect Daniel's prophecy would correspond with another significant event in Jesus's life (e.g., His baptism) as the date lines up with broad consensus regarding the window of history in which He ministered.

and dating involved in this prophecy, they are documented in Sir Robert Anderson's book, *The Coming Prince*.[559]

KEY PHASES OF DANIEL'S PROPHECY

To keep the big picture in view, allow me to summarize the verses we're studying in **Daniel 9**:

- **V.24** is an overview of the entire prophecy of 70 weeks concerning the destiny of Israel and the Jews.
- **V.25** covers the events marking the beginning and end of the first 69 weeks.
- **VV.26–27** will cover the events of the 70th week.

EVENTS BETWEEN THE 69TH WEEK AND THE 70TH WEEK

²⁶And after the sixty-two weeks . . .

That's a mistranslation. Gabriel is referring to the *"seven weeks and sixty-two weeks"* he referenced in **V.25**. Clearly, **V.26** should be understood to read:

And after the sixty-nine weeks . . .

After Messiah has been revealed, after the Triumphal Entry on Palm Sunday, and after the 69 weeks have been completed, some things must take place *before* the 70th week begins.

Messiah shall be cut off, but not for Himself; . . .

---

[559] Robert Anderson, *The Coming Prince*. 10th ed. (San Bernadino, California: Createspace Independent Publishing Platform, 2016).

A week after Palm Sunday—a week after the 69 weeks have been completed—Jesus was crucified and died on the Cross. The original Hebrew word used there for *"cut off"* is *"karath."* It can mean *"cut off"* or *"cut down"* or it can mean *"killed."* And when it's used as the latter, it generally refers to something being killed to establish a *covenant*.

A "covenant" is just another term for an *agreement*. In the Old Testament, one of the ways men would seal a covenant was to kill an animal, cut it in two, and then walk between the two pieces. It's strange to us, but to them it meant their covenant was as serious as blood. They would die, like the animal, rather than break the covenant they were making.

When Jesus died on the Cross, it wasn't *"for Himself"*; rather as **V.26** says, it was *for us*. It was to offer us a *blood covenant*. It was Jesus in effect saying, *"I Myself will be the sacrifice that seals this covenant."*

The covenant He offered us was this: He would live a perfect life in our place, He would *die* in our place and take the punishment for our sins, and He would conquer death on our behalf by *rising* from the grave.

Our part of the covenant is to believe in what He has done for us and lay down our lives for Him in response. Because when you truly grasp what Jesus has done for you, you can't help but give your life over to Him.

Thus, the first major event after the 69 weeks were completed was the death of Messiah.

> *And the people of the prince who is to come . . .*
> *Shall destroy the city and the sanctuary.*

"The city" is Jerusalem and *"the sanctuary"* is the Temple.

The second major event after the 69 weeks are completed was

the destruction of Jerusalem and the Temple, which famously came to pass in AD 70 when Titus Vespasian and his soldiers destroyed the Temple brick by brick and leveled the Holy City.

"The prince who is to come" is a reference to *antichrist*. And we're told that those who destroyed the Temple and Jerusalem in AD 70 were his *"people."* Who destroyed Jerusalem in AD 70? *The Romans.* As you learned in this book, antichrist's future empire will be a *revived* Roman Empire. That's what Daniel is referring to.

The end of it shall be with a flood,

In the end, Jerusalem wasn't destroyed with a *literal* flood but in a manner that was as swift and devastating as a catastrophic flood.

And till the end of the war desolations are determined.

"Desolations" just means *emptiness*. And that's exactly what happened. The Jews fled Jerusalem and Israel and scattered across the earth in the historical migration known as the Diaspora.

Note that this verse says Israel would *stay* desolate (empty) *"till the end."* Most commentators say that the point of this verse is not the mention of *"war"* but simply that Jerusalem and Israel would be empty of the Jewish people *"till the end."*

In 1948, the Jews returned to the land, and Israel became a political nation again after almost 1,900 years. This means that we're at *"the end."* Jesus taught that the generation that saw Israel become a political nation again would not die out before He returned.[560]

It's also interesting that Gabriel declared Israel would be empty of the Jews *"till the end of the war"* for this reason. What's the biggest war the world has ever seen? World War II. Israel became a

---

[560] Cf. Matthew 24:32–35.

political nation right after the *end* of WWII as a direct result of what happened to the Jews *in* WWII (the Holocaust).

> ²⁷ *Then he . . .*

The word *"Then"* tells us we're now talking about something that's going to happen at some point *after* Jerusalem and the Temple have been destroyed.

We know with certainty that *"the prince who is to come"* in **V.26** is antichrist because he is referred to in **V.27** as *"he."* Gabriel continues talking about him as the subject, and we're told that *"he"* is going to do some things that we *know* antichrist will do.

So, you might want to draw a little arrow in your Bible from the word *"he"* here in **V.27** pointing back to *"the prince who is to come"* in **V.26**.

THE 70TH WEEK

> ²⁷*Then he shall confirm a covenant*⁵⁶¹ *with many for one week; . . .*

Gabriel is now going to talk about what's going to happen during the seven years of the Tribulation, "The 70th week of Daniel," as it's often called.

We're told that what will mark the *starting point* of this 70th week will be antichrist sealing a seven-year treaty *("a covenant")* of some sort with *"many"* people, including the Jews of Israel.⁵⁶²

---

⁵⁶¹ Or "treaty."

⁵⁶² Because the subject of this prophecy is Israel and the Jews, it's logical to assume the word *"many"* includes the Jews.

Because **Revelation 6:2** introduces antichrist as riding on a white horse, we hold the view that this will be a seven-year *peace treaty* involving Israel, which means it will likely be between Israel and her current enemies. His brokering of this extraordinary deal will pave the way for antichrist's meteoric rise onto the world's political stage, while also making possible things such as the rebuilding of the Temple in Jerusalem.

The *starting point* of the 70th week will be antichrist confirming a seven-year peace treaty that will include Israel.

But in the middle of the week . . .

The middle of a seven-year "week" would be at three and a half years. After three and a half years of this peace treaty, something bad is going to happen:

He shall bring an end to sacrifice and offering.

Antichrist is going to *shut down* Jewish worship at the rebuilt Temple in Jerusalem. And we know from other places in Scripture that at this time, he will also set up an image of himself in that Temple, declare himself to be a god, and demand to be worshipped by the world.

These events will follow the *prophetic pattern* established by the actions of Antiochus IV in 167 BC, which is a story for the commentary I hope to write on the Book of Daniel.

These *specific actions* by antichrist at the halfway point of the 70th Week of Daniel will mark the beginning of the period known as the *Great* Tribulation. Simply put, the Great Tribulation is the second half, the last three and a half years of the 70th Week of Daniel.

If it's not clear, the Tribulation is a synonym for the 70th Week of Daniel. Both terms refer to the full seven-year period. "The Great

Tribulation" refers only to the *last* three and a half years of those seven years.

> *And on the wing of abominations shall be one who makes desolate, ...*

Antichrist is going to do horrific things that will leave people and the Temple *"desolate"*—empty. He will force people to choose whether to worship him or Jesus. Those who refuse to worship him will be executed. Those who choose to worship him will be damned for eternity.

These things will continue:

> *Even until the consummation, which is determined,*
> *Is poured out on the desolate.*[563]

There is a determined time of three and a half years when antichrist will be allowed to run wild. After that, both he and the false prophet will be cast into the lake of fire and Satan will be imprisoned for the thousand years of the Millennial Kingdom.

THE CHURCH AGE

We have 69 weeks and some major events that happen shortly *after* the 69 weeks are finished; this is followed by a huge gap of time before the 70th week begins. What's happening in that huge gap of time? The *Church Age*, which is where we are living right now—it's the time between the birth of the Church and the Rapture.

The Bible tells us the Church was a mystery that was *hidden*

---

[563] Or "desolator."

during the time of the Old Testament.[564] Scripture also tells us that because the Jews rejected their Messiah, they are under a partial spiritual blindness that will remain in place throughout the Church Age.

When the Church is removed in the Rapture, God's *focus* on the earth will move intensely back onto the nation of Israel, and the 70th Week of Daniel will begin shortly thereafter. As a result of that final "week," ethnic Israel will repent, turn to Jesus, recognize Him as their Messiah, and be saved. Praise God!

In Revelation, the three and a half years of the Great Tribulation (the back half of Daniel's 70th Week) is referred to as **"one thousand two hundred and sixty days,"**[565] **"forty-two months,"**[566] and **"a time and times and half a time."**[567] When we understand Daniel's prophecies, we see them confirmed in the Book of Revelation. And that is how we know that the length of the Tribulation will be *seven years*.

---

[564] Cf. Colossians 1:24–26.

[565] Revelation 11:3, 12:6.

[566] Revelation 11:2, 13:5.

[567] Revelation 12:14.

APPENDIX C: THE THEOLOGY OF SUPERSESSIONISM

Most churches that hold to reformed theology—which would include our Calvinist brothers and sisters—hold to an Amillennial or Postmillennial eschatology. Unfortunately, they have no choice. I say that because those who hold to reformed theology tend to hold to another doctrine that forces them to allegorize end-times Bible prophecies—supersessionism (sometimes referred to as Replacement or Covenant Theology).

Essentially, supersessionism is the belief that:

- The Church has replaced Israel in God's plans.

- God has no special plans for Israel outside the plans He has for all nations.

- Any unfulfilled promises made to ethnic Israel have now been passed on to the Church.

As we have seen in this study of Revelation, Israel is mentioned throughout end-times Bible prophecies. This creates an obvious problem for those who hold to any form of supersessionism: How can God be done with Israel if Israel shows up all over unfulfilled end-times prophecies? The only way to "solve" that problem is to take the position that every unfulfilled Bible prophecy that mentions Israel is actually a reference to the Church in some figurative sense.

But it gets even worse for the supersessionist because the yet-to-fulfilled prophecies about Israel mention geographical locations, Jerusalem, a rebuilt Temple, the ethnic tribes of Israel, and more. It's as if God is saying, *"I don't want anybody to be confused about who I'm referring to."* To get around this problem, the Amillennialist and Postmillennialist must paint almost all eschatological prophecies with a broad, figurative brush, leading to a tragically meaningless interpretation in which Israel isn't Israel, Jerusalem isn't Jerusalem, the Temple isn't the Temple, the 12 tribes of Israel aren't the 12 tribes of Israel, and the only thing certain is that Jesus wins in the end.

Anyone who holds to supersessionism cannot evaluate end-times Bible prophecy objectively because they are pre-committed to an overly broad figurative interpretation, whether they realize it or not.

APPENDIX D: DIFFERENCES BETWEEN GOG AND MAGOG IN EZEKIEL AND REVELATION

The satanic rebellion in **Revelation 20:7–10** takes place at the end of the thousand-year Millennial Kingdom and is sometimes confused with the prophecy regarding Gog and Magog in **Ezekiel 38–39**. Here are a few reasons why these cannot refer to the same event:

- Only a few nations, primarily from the north, attack Israel in Ezekiel.[568] In Revelation, the battle involves nations from **"the four corners of the earth . . . whose number *is* as the sand of the sea."**[569]

- Satan is not mentioned in Ezekiel but in Revelation, he is the primary character.[570]

---

[568] Cf. Ezekiel 38:6, 15; 39:2.

[569] Revelation 20:8.

[570] Cf. Revelation 20:7–8, 10.

- In Ezekiel, seven months are spent burying the dead.[571] There is no need to bury those killed in Revelation, as the battle is immediately followed by the Great White Throne Judgment,[572] the destruction of our universe, and the creation of new heavens and a new earth.[573]

- Additionally, the weapons left by dead soldiers are burned for seven *years* after the battle in Ezekiel.[574] This means the events of Ezekiel must take place either before or right at the beginning of the Tribulation. And *that* means the events of Ezekiel and Revelation are separated by at least the thousand years of the Millennial Kingdom.

- The divine purpose of the battle in Ezekiel is to bring Israel to repentance.[575] In Revelation, Israel has been faithful to God for the thousand years of the Millennial Kingdom. And those who participate in the satanic rebellion are destroyed with no remaining opportunity for repentance.

So, why are **"Gog and Magog"** mentioned in **Revelation 20:8**? It's yet another allusion to the Old Testament. In this case, it's to compare the attitudes of those who attack Israel in the battle of **Ezekiel 38–39** with those who side with Satan in his rebellion in

---

[571] Cf. Ezekiel 39:12.

[572] Cf. Revelation 20:11–15.

[573] Cf. Isaiah 65:17, 66:22; 2 Peter 3:13; Revelation 21:1.

[574] Cf. Ezekiel 39:9.

[575] Cf. Ezekiel 39:21–29.

Revelation 20. The hatred of God and His people will be shared by the attackers in both instances.

And in both instances, God will supernaturally intervene to protect Israel and crush His enemies.[576]

---

[576] Cf. Ezekiel 38:19, 21–23; Revelation 20:9–10

NOTES

Anderson, Robert. *The Coming Prince*. 10th ed. San Bernadino, California: Createspace Independent Publishing Platform, 2016.

Carey, Eustace. *Memoir of William Carey*. London, England: Jackson and Walford, 1836.

Elliot, Elisabeth, ed. *The Journals of Jim Elliot: Missionary, Martyr, Man of God*. Grand Rapids, MI: Revell, 2023.

Eusebius. *The History of the Church*. London, England: The Folio Society, 2011.

Fitzgerald, Allan D., ed. *Augustine Through the Ages: An Encyclopedia*. Grand Rapids, Michigan: William B. Eerdmans Publishing Company, 1999.

Foxe, John, and Harold J. Chadwick. *Foxe's Book of Martyrs*. Gainesville, Florida: Bridge-Logos, 2001.

Fudge, Thomas A. *Jan Hus: Religious Reform and Social Revolution in Bohemia*. London, England: I.B. Tauris, 2017. Kindle.

Gould, Jay M. *The Enemy Within: The High Cost of Living Near Nuclear Reactors*. New York: Four Walls Eight Windows, 1996.

Heiser, Michael S. *The Unseen Realm* Bellingham, WA: Lexham Press, 2015.

Hislop, Alexander. *The Two Babylons*. 7th ed. Crossreach Publications, 2017.

Hitt, Russell T. *Jungle Pilot*. Grand Rapids, Michigan: Discovery House Publishers, 1997.

Josephus, Flavius. *The Works of Josephus*. Translated by William Whiston. Peabody, Massachusetts: Hendrickson Publishers, 1985.

Kamvar, Maryam and Shumeet Baluja. "A Large Scale Study of Wireless Search Behavior: Google mobile." *Proceedings of the SIGCHI Conference on Human Factors in Computing Systems* (2006): 701–709. https://dl.acm.org/doi/10.1145/1124772.1124877.

Kittelson, James M. *Luther the Reformer: The Story of the Man and His Career*. Minneapolis, MN: Fortress Press, 2016. Kindle Edition.

Mattoon, Rod. *Treasures from Revelation*. Springfield, IL: Lincoln Land Baptist Church, 2003.

McDowell, Josh and Barna Group. *The Porn Phenomenon: The Impact of Pornography in the Digital Age*. Ventura, CA: Barna Group, 2016.

McGee, J. Vernon. "Revelation 5:7–10" (Blue Letter Bible Audio). https://www.blueletterbible.org/audio_video/popPlayer.cfm?id=9316&rel=mcgee_j_vernon/english/revhttps://.

Missler, Chuck. "The Seven Myths of Eschatology," Koinonia House, August 1, 2012. https://www.khouse.org/articles/2012/1072/.

Patton, George S. Jr. *War As I Knew It*. New York: Bantam Books, 1980. Ebook edition.

"Red China: Firecracker No. 2." *TIME Magazine*, May 21, 1965. https://content.time.com/time/subscriber/article/0,33009, 901693,00.html.

Rose, Tov, ed., *Targum Jerusalem*. Translated by J. W. Etheridge. London: Longman, Green, Longman, and Roberts, 1862. https://www.sefaria.org/Targum_Jerusalem%2C.

Seiss, Joseph A. *The Apocalypse: Lectures on the Book of Revelation*, New York: Cosimo Classics, 2007.

Shelley, Bruce L. *Church History in Plain Language*. 4th ed. Nashville, Tennessee: Thomas Nelson, 2013.

Skorecki, Karl, Sara Selig, Shraga Blazer, Robert Bradman, Neil Bradman, P. J. Waburton, Monica Ismajlowicz, and Michael Hammer. "Y Chromosomes of Jewish Priests" *Nature* 385, no. 32 (1997). https://doi.org/10.1038/385032a0.

Sproul, R. C. *The Holiness of God*, 2nd ed. Carol Stream, Illinois: Tyndale House Publishers, 1998.

Tertullian. *The Complete Works of Tertullian*: *Apologeticus pro Christianis*. Hastings East Sussex, United Kingdom: Delphi Publishing Ltd, 2016. Kindle.

Thompson, Jeff. "A Peek Behind the Curtain." Sermon preached on Luke 16:19–31 (June 5, 2016). gospelcity.ca/media/messages/a-peek-behind-the-curtain.

———. "The Days of Noah." Sermon preached on Genesis 6, (April 15, 2018), gospelcity.ca/media/messages/the-days-of-noah.

———. "World History from Daniel to Jesus," Sermon Series (2017). http://gospelcity.ca/sermon/world-history-from-daniel-to-jesus/.

Trusted News Initiative (website). British Broadcasting Corporation. https://www.bbc.co.uk/beyondfakenews/trusted-news-initiative.

Uzziel, Jonathan. *Targum Pseudo-Jonathan: The First Five Books of the Bible*, Edited by Tov Rose. Translated by J. W. Etheridge. London: Longman, Green, Longman, and Roberts, 1862–1865.

The Vatican. *Eucharisticum Mysterium—Instruction on Eucharistic Worship*, May 25, 1967. https://adoremus.org/1967/05/eucharisticum-mysterium/.

White, Ellen G. "God's Purpose for Us," *The Review and Herald*, March 9, 1905 (quoting from a sermon preached in Oakland, California on Sunday, April 12, 1903).

Wiersbe, Warren. *Be Victorious (Revelation): In Christ You Are an Overcomer—The BE Series Commentary*. 2nd ed. Colorado Springs, Colorado: David C. Cook, 2008. Kindle Second edition.

Winerman, Lea. "By the Numbers: Antidepressant Use on the Rise," *American Psychological Association*, 48, no. 10 (November 2017) https://www.apa.org/monitor/2017/11/numbers.